Urban Economics and Public Policy

Third Edition

Urban Economics and Public Policy

Third Edition

JAMES HEILBRUN
FORDHAM UNIVERSITY

with the assistance of

PATRICK A. McGUIRE
HOBART AND WILLIAM SMITH COLLEGES

ST. MARTIN'S PRESS   NEW YORK

For Carol

Library of Congress Catalog Card Number: 86-60665
Copyright © 1987 by St. Martin's Press, Inc.
All Rights Reserved.
109
fedc
For information, write St. Martin's Press, Inc.
175 Fifth Avenue, New York, NY 10010

cover design: Tom McKeveny
cover photo: Rocco Galatioto/FPG International Corporation

ISBN: 0-312-83442-X

ACKNOWLEDGMENTS

Acknowledgments and copyrights continue at the back of the book on pages 489–490, which constitute a continuation of the copyright page.

Table 3.1, "Growth of Urban and Metropolitan Population in the United States," Donald J. Bogue, *Population Growth in Standard Metropolitan Areas, 1900–1950,* Housing and Home Finance Agency, December 1953. Reprinted with permission.

Table 3.2, "Rate of Population Growth in Central Cities, Metropolitan Rings, and Nonmetropolitan Areas of the United States," Donald J. Bogue, *Population Growth in Standard Metropolitan Areas, 1900–1950,* December 1953. Reprinted with permission.

Figure 4.1, "Factors in Choosing a Minimum-Transport Cost Location," John Friedman and William Alonson, eds., *Regional Development and Planning,* M.I.T. Press, 1964. Reprinted with permission.

Table 5.1, "Characteristics of the Central Place Hierarchy in Snohomish County, Washington," Brian J. L. Berry and William Garrison, "The Functional Bases of the Central-Place Hierarchy," in *Economic Geography,* April 1958, Clark University. Reprinted with permission.

Table 5.2, "Prevalence of Selected Functions in Central Places of Snohomish County, Washington," Brian J. L. Berry and William Garrison, "The Functional Bases of the Central-Place Hierarchy," in *Economic Geography,* April 1958, Clark University. Reprinted with permission.

Table 5.4, "Changes in the Hierarchy of Trade Centers in Saskatchewan, 1941–61," Gerald Hodge, "The Prediction of Trade Center Viability in the Great Plains," *Papers* of the Regional Science Association, XV, 1965. Reprinted with permission.

Figure 6.3, "Gradient of Land Value on the West Side of Manhattan Island, 1970," from "The Empirical Investigation of a Residential Land Value Model," unpublished doctoral dissertation by Joseph E. Earley, Fordham University, 1974. Reprinted with permission.

Figure 6.6, "Effect on Land Use of Improved Transportation or Increased Popula-

Preface

In this third edition of *Urban Economics and Public Policy* I have retained the structure of the second edition while bringing the contents thoroughly up to date. Since the second edition was completed in 1981, important changes have occurred in the U.S. political and economic environment and in the urban/metropolitan system itself. First, the advent of a conservative administration in Washington, supported by and reinforcing a national mood of fiscal restraint, produced significant changes in all areas of public policy. Second, the rapid escalation of fuel prices during the 1970s—which had caused a good deal of speculation about the effect higher transportation costs might have on urban form and structure—was followed in the mid-1980s by a sharp decline. Finally, the unexpected trend toward population deconcentration in which, during the 1970s, the population of U.S. metropolitan areas for the first time grew more slowly than that of nonmetropolitan America, did not continue after 1980. I have taken care to ensure that these important changes in political, economic, and demographic trends are fully reflected in the current edition.

In order to incorporate the latest available data on population, urban structure, social and economic conditions, and public policy, I have revised almost every table in the book. Simultaneously, references to the literature on urban economic theory and policy have been systematically updated. I have also devoted more space to the discussion of quantitative studies by other economists that either measure crucial urban economic relationships or test the predictions of theory. The additional examples of empirical work will, I am sure, not only provide valuable information about the shape of the urban economy but will also illustrate, in a way that is easily accessible to students, the use of scientific method in economics.

In this volume, as in the first two editions, I have tried to bring together three elements essential to an understanding of the present economic situation of cities. The first of these is a sense of where we are now and how we got there. Thus, following the Introduction, Chapters 2 and 3 of this book provide an economic explanation of the growth of cities and metropolitan areas. They emphasize the forces of technological change that first built up great cities during the Industrial Revolution and later brought about the massive dispersion of jobs and population into the metropolitan suburbs that is still going on. In Chapter 2, I have revised the treatment of economies of agglomeration to place greater emphasis on their importance to service industries and corporate headquarters offices. Chapter 3 includes a new section on commuting patterns within metropolitan areas as well as an in-depth analysis of population change and migration since 1980.

The second essential element is an understanding of the forces that determine the location, form, and economic structure of cities. Chapters 4 through 7, which cover the fundamentals of urban economic theory, deal with these topics. Although these chapters remain largely theoretical, I have expanded the coverage of empirical studies that bear on important points of theory.

As the Introduction points out, the analysis of urban size, growth, form, and structure is vital to an understanding of urban economic problems precisely because these problems are significantly affected by the spatial organization of the city. Consequently, Chapters 2 through 7 are not only interesting in their own right but also provide the foundation for an understanding of the third part of the book, which examines four major urban problems: transportation, poverty, housing and neighborhood development, and the organization and financing of the metropolitan public sector. Two chapters are devoted to each of these subjects.

I have thoroughly revised the chapters on public policy to include the latest budgetary and economic data, to reflect changes in legislation, and to incorporate the findings of recent empirical studies. Only a few of these many changes can be mentioned here.

Chapter 9 includes new sections on user charges versus highway costs, on the causes of growing urban transit deficits, and on the distributional effects of mass transit subsidies.

Chapter 10 now covers racial segregation as well as the urbanization of poverty.

Chapter 11 has been thoroughly revised to incorporate new evaluations of employment, training, and job-creation policies and new analyses of the effects of welfare programs on migration, family structure, and work incentives.

Chapter 12 now offers a more rigorous analysis of housing abandonment and more extensive treatment of housing market discrimination.

In Chapter 13 changes in housing and community development policy initiated by the Reagan administration are analyzed.

Up-to-date figures in Chapter 14 show how fiscal restraint has affected the growth of local government spending and taxing in the 1980s. The section on property tax incidence has been revised to incorporate the results of empirical studies of the influence of assessment practice.

In Chapter 15 all measures of fiscal disparities between suburbs and central cities are brought up to date. Data on the structural problems of budget making in declining cities are carried forward into the 1980s. A new analysis examines the effect on local governmental programs of the decline in federal grants after 1978.

The approach taken in this edition, as in its predecessors, remains almost entirely nonmathematical. Consequently, the book will be easily intelligible to anyone who has had an introductory semester of economic principles. Nevertheless, the economic arguments are, I believe, rigorously developed and carefully qualified. While the book is intended primarily as a text for an introductory course in urban economics or urban economic policy, the chapters on transportation, poverty, housing, and public finance will also prove useful as supplementary reading for courses in urban sociology and politics or in urban planning.

My own experience in teaching urban economics suggests that the book contains a good deal more material than can be effectively conveyed in a single semester. Indeed, with the addition of a modest number of supplementary readings it provides enough matter for two semesters of study. Instructors limited to one semester might consider the following alternatives. If they prefer to emphasize urban economic theory, they can use Chapters 1 through 6, continue with 8 and 9, and conclude with 7. Chapters 6, 7, 8, and 9 contain enough policy analysis to bring home to students the applicability of the theory to current urban problems. On the other hand, instructors who prefer to emphasize policy can set up a sufficient theoretical foundation with Chapters 1, 2, 3, and 6 and then take up some or all of the policy issues covered in Chapters 8 through 16.

Both in the text and in the notes, the reader will find numerous references to the names and works of other urban economists. These have been expanded and brought up to date. They provide students not only with citations of the most recent books, articles, and reports but also with references to the major writers on urban economics, keyed to the topics on which I have found their work most relevant and useful. From these clues inquisitive readers will easily find their way into the literature in any part of the discipline. In order to familiarize students with major sources of information and help them to begin their own empirical work, I also provide detailed sources for most statistical data. The notes thus double as my list of "suggested further readings." I hope it may be said that they are as valuable as any other part of this book.

I am indebted to many people for their help in completing the third edition. As indicated on the title page, Professor Patrick A. McGuire of Hobart and William Smith Colleges assisted me in the preparation of this revision. He took on the job of bringing statistics up to date in the chapters on poverty, housing, and public finance. In addition, he gathered much new data and carried out extensive statistical work that made possible many new tables in those chapters. Professor McGuire also undertook preparation of the new index. His contribution to the book was an important one for which I am grateful.

The eight chapters on transportation, poverty, housing, and the metropolitan public sector, as revised for the third edition, were reviewed by Professors William G. Grigsby of the University of Pennsylvania, John F. Kain of Harvard, and Roger F. Riefler of the University of Nebraska. Their innumerable helpful comments and suggestions are gratefully acknowledged. Of course, none of them should be held responsible for the views I have expressed or for any errors of fact or logic that remain in the text.

In tracking down elusive facts and statistics, both published and unpublished, I benefited from the kindness and cooperation of many people. I wish particularly to acknowledge the help of Sheldon Danziger and the staff of the Institute for Research on Poverty at the University of Wisconsin; John Behrens, Diana DeAre, Donald C. Dahmann, Richard L. Forstall, Steven Rudolph, Donald E. Starsinic and Alan Stevens of the Census Bureau; Martin Levine of the Congressional Budget Office; Ward D. Belding, Jr., of the Bay Area Rapid Transit District; Joel Markowitz of the Bay area's Metropolitan Transportation Commission; John Neff of the American Public Transit Association; and Professors Robert J. Penella and William T. Hogan, S.J., of Fordham University. For the very able research assistance he provided at Fordham, I am grateful to Jack Connelly.

I wish to thank Peter Dougherty, Larry Swanson, and Emily Berleth of St. Martin's Press for their help in preparing this third edition, B. F. Emmer for an excellent job of copy editing, and Marie Sundberg, Margaret Heilbrun, and my wife Carolyn, who typed the revised manuscript, often under great pressure of time.

The book is again dedicated to my wife with genuine gratitude for her patience and support while I carried out the arduous and absorbing task of revision.

James Heilbrun

Contents

FOUR
The Location of Economic Activity and the Location of Cities   63

FIVE
The System of Cities and the Urban Hierarchy   81

SIX
Site Rent, Land-Use Patterns, and the Form of the City   107

FIFTEEN
Problems of the Metropolitan Public Sector: Inefficiency, Inequity, Insolvency 423

SIXTEEN
Postscript: The Future of Central Cities 481

Urban Economics and Public Policy

Third Edition

ONE

Introduction

In the second century A.D. the poet Juvenal complained about traffic jams, noise, and crime in the streets of Rome.[1] Urban problems evidently have a long history. Yet the modern era did bring a radical change, for down to the end of the eighteenth century, society everywhere had been predominantly rural. Then the Industrial Revolution caused a remarkably rapid growth of cities and metropolitan areas, altering profoundly the way most of the world's population lived.

The extraordinary pace of urbanization has been one of the most striking facts of modern history. In retrospect, the rate of change seems almost incredible. In 1790 the population of the United States was 5 percent urban and 95 percent rural; by 1980 it was 74 percent urban and only 26 percent rural. The urban proportion is now about the same in Canada and Japan and is considerably higher in many Western European countries. In the less developed nations, too, rapid urban growth is a major fact of modern life.[2]

Yet the history of cities is not simply a story of continuous growth. Old cities may decline while newer ones are still growing. In the United States some of the older, inner cities of metropolitan areas have been losing jobs and population for years. By 1980 decline at the center of the older metropolitan areas had become the rule rather than the exception and brought with it a set of problems that the earlier years of seemingly

---

1. Juvenal, *The Sixteen Satires*, Peter Green, trans. (Baltimore: Penguin Books, 1967), pp. 94–97.

2. U.S. data are from Chapter 3, Table 3.1. For the extent of urbanization elsewhere, see the United Nations' *Demographic Yearbook*, Table 6 (but note that the definition of *urban* varies from country to country). Numerous concise studies of the history of urbanization are available. See, for example, Emrys Jones, *Towns and Cities* (London: Oxford University Press, 1966), ch. 2; and Kingsley Davis, "The Urbanization of the Human Population," in *Cities* (New York: Knopf, 1965), a Scientific American Book, pp. 3–24.

endless growth had not prepared us to deal with. Clearly, the system of cities in the modern world does not stand still. In whatever country one lives today, many of the most pressing social and economic problems are associated with urban and metropolitan development.

THE SCOPE OF URBAN ECONOMICS

It is hardly surprising that in such a world students should be increasingly concerned with matters of urban public policy or that economists should have developed the special branch of their discipline that we now call urban economics. More remarkable, perhaps, is the fact that urban economics became a distinct and recognized specialty only in the last thirty years. It can be defined as a field of study in which we use the analytical tools of economics to explain the spatial and economic organization of cities and metropolitan areas and to deal with their special economic problems.

This definition has the advantage of putting first things first. Students are often impatient to go directly to the "issues." They want to investigate the problems of urban poverty, slum housing, land-use decisions, transportation, and the delivery of urban public services, and they are eager to debate the merits of the various public policies that might be used. But neither the problems nor the policies can be discussed intelligently until one understands the highly complex urban-metropolitan environment in which they occur. Hence we must deal with the spatial and economic organization of the city first, and only then with its problems.

In the definition of urban economics, the word spatial deserves particular emphasis. Traditional economic theory omits any reference to the dimensions of space by treating all economic activity as if it took place at a single point. It refers to consumers and producers, firms and industries, but not to distance or contiguity, separation or neighborhood. The fact that population and economic activity are arranged in a spatial as well as a functional order is simply ignored. In recent years the discipline known as "regional economics" has sought to restore the balance. "Regional economics," in Hugh Nourse's apt phrase, "is the study of the neglected spatial order of the economy."[3]

Regions may be areas of any size from neighborhoods to cities, river basins, farm belts, nations, or continents. Urban economics is the subcategory of regional economics that deals with the regions we call cities and metropolitan areas. It concentrates on the economic relationships and processes that contribute to the important spatial characteristics of such places, especially to their size, density of settlement, and structure or pattern of land use. And since cities and metropolitan areas undergo continuous change in all these

3. Hugh O. Nourse, *Regional Economics* (New York: McGraw-Hill, 1968), p. 1.

spatial characteristics, urban economics is also vitally concerned with the forces that attract or repel economic activity and population and thus cause growth or decline, concentration or dispersion, preservation or replacement. It seeks to understand not only the present spatial order but also the direction of change and development.

Here are a few examples of the sorts of questions about urban spatial economic organization that this book attempts to answer:

- What accounts for the enormous concentration of population and economic activity in cities and metropolitan areas?
- Is there an optimum size for cities?
- How is the size and character of any one city affected by the size, character, and location of other places in the urban system?
- Within metropolitan areas, why has there been such a marked dispersion of jobs and population from the large cities to their suburban rings in recent decades?
- Why is it principally the middle and upper classes that have been attracted to the suburbs, while low-income families continue to live in the central cities?
- Can racial segregation within cities be explained by spatial-economic factors such as the location of low-skill jobs and low-income housing, without reference to race prejudice?

Spatial Aspects of Urban Problems

The analysis of urban size, growth, form, and structure is vital to an understanding of the problems of urban transportation, poverty, housing, and public finance precisely because these problems almost always have significant spatial aspects. Transportation policy offers some obvious examples, since transportation and the spatial arrangement of land use are highly interdependent. A rail mass transit system, for example, will be feasible only if trip origins and destinations within a metropolitan area are highly concentrated, while a highway system can operate efficiently only if they are *not* concentrated. Consequently, when deciding whether to recommend the development of a rail mass transit system or the extension of a highway network, planners must look very carefully at the way a city's existing land-use pattern—the spatial distribution of jobs and homes—affects the travel behavior of its residents.

Antipoverty policy, too, has spatial aspects. In metropolitan areas, the poverty population remains heavily concentrated in the core cities, while job growth is most rapid in the suburban ring. When antipoverty policies are framed, this spatial characteristic of the poverty problem must be taken into account. It is important to know, for example, whether the separation of the poor from the areas of most rapid job growth is significantly slowing their rise out of poverty.

Or consider the connection between the housing problem and the pattern of land use. In the United States, decisions as to what will be built, and where, are taken largely in the private market for land and structures. Does this market work efficiently to give us the optimum development of each parcel and neighborhood? Or are there significant defects in the market process that justify public intervention to stimulate the redevelopment of old neighborhoods? These questions can be answered only by a careful study of the way in which the urban land market influences the spatial organization of the city.

The problems of metropolitan public finance too, have many strongly spatial characteristics. For example, the fiscal crisis of the older cities in the 1970s and their continuing fiscal stress thereafter were caused in part by the concentration of the nation's poor into the central cities just at the moment when city tax resources were being depleted by the decentralization of jobs into the suburbs. How far should the federal and state governments go in making aid available to overcome the current fiscal disadvantage of the old inner cities? This important policy issue will be examined in the specific context of the fiscal conservatism of the 1980s.

The operation of the metropolitan public sector is also strongly affected by the spatial dimensions of local governmental units. The typical metropolitan area today contains a large core city surrounded by very numerous smaller jurisdictions in the suburbs. Boundaries were generally drawn a century or more before the metropolitan area became a highly integrated economic unit. In today's circumstances, can this minutely parceled set of local governments be expected to provide the level and assortment of public services that best satisfy the desires of the metropolitan population as a whole, or do local political boundaries now interfere with the efficient and equitable operation of the public sector? If so, what changes are desirable? Urban economic analysis, as we will see, can help to answer such vital policy questions.

THE CRITERIA OF EFFICIENCY AND EQUITY

Efficiency and equity are two of the general criteria to be applied in comparing alternative economic policies. To the economist, efficiency means the most productive use of resources to satisfy competing material wants. The productive resources available in even the most affluent economy are limited. Every use that we decide to make of them has as its real cost the next best opportunity for their use that we had to forgo in choosing the one we did. ("Opportunity cost," thus defined, is the fundamental basis of real cost in economics.) If we are to achieve maximum satisfaction of material wants by the application of limited resources, it behooves us not to waste resources by using them in less than the most productive way. In the context of urban economics, this often means finding the most efficient spatial arrangements or configurations, as in the examples from land use and public finance policy cited earlier.

The term *equity* in economics usually refers to fairness in the distribution of income or wealth or, more broadly, "welfare." When we evaluate a particular public policy (such as urban renewal or subsidies for low-income housing) or a private policy (such as discrimination in housing or employment), we usually try to apply some standard of equity to the policy's outcome: Which groups does it help? On whom does it impose burdens? Are these results desirable?

The ultimate question—that of desirability—cannot be answered on strictly economic grounds. It requires an explicit ethical judgment, and economists, in their professional capacity, have no special claim to ethical authority. Nevertheless, their work is indispensable as a precondition for informed judgment of economic policies. Since we judge policies by their consequences, accurate judgment requires a clear understanding of what those consequences are. Unfortunately, causes and consequences in economics are not very easily identified. The economy is a complex network of markets that connects all persons, institutions, functions, and regions and transmits impulses among them in ways that are not always obvious. Careful analysis, however, can help us to understand how the system works so that the results of past or present policies can be deciphered, even if imperfectly, and the likely consequences of proposed future programs foreseen. By contributing to such an understanding, the economist lays a foundation upon which others can then base their own judgment about the desirability of the various alternatives.

THEME AND OUTLINE OF THE BOOK

Broadly speaking, this book moves from a historical description and economic explanation of the growth of cities in Chapters 2 and 3, through a theoretical analysis of their location, form, and economic structure in Chapters 4 through 7, to the investigation of current urban economic problems in Chapters 8 through 16. Two chapters are devoted to problems and policy issues in each of four areas: transportation, poverty, housing and land use, and the operation of the public sector.

Running through the entire book is a connecting theme: the influence of economic growth and development, as they have actually been experienced in the United States, on the spatial organization of cities and metropolitan areas and on the major economic problems they face. Growth and development result partly from technological change, so we shall be looking closely at the effect on the urban pattern of such major technical innovations as the railroad, the automobile, the airplane, and the new electronic means of high-speed information transfer. In the United States, economic development has been accompanied by rapid population increase and a high level of internal migration, so we shall examine systematically the urban consequences of those forces as well. For the individual and the family, economic develop-ment has produced a long-run rise in living standards, so we shall also look carefully at the way in which rising real income influences the urban pattern through its effect on consumer behavior.

To speak of innovation and growth is obviously to suggest that cities-change through time. Yet in a sense they are also imprisoned in their own past, for they cannot be built anew to adopt the technology and suit the needs of each new era. Although the grand designs, the structures, and the bounda-ries laid down at an earlier date are often inappropriate to the present, they can be changed only at great expense of money, effort, or disruption—and therefore only very slowly. It is precisely this tension between the needs of the present and the legacy of the past that makes the subject matter of urban economics so unusually challenging and endlessly absorbing.

TWO

The Economics of Urbanization

Economics has always been a major force determining the pattern of human settlement. Man cannot live by bread alone, but neither can he live without bread. From the earliest age, when our ancestors at the margin of historical time settled in the fertile river valleys to live by farming, to our own century, in which the rural poor migrate to the city in search of higher wages, man has moved over the surface of the earth in search, perhaps not of El Dorado but, at least, of a place where the living was easier.

Cities are themselves evidence that an economy has reached a certain stage of development. Since city dwellers do not grow food, they can survive only if someone else in the economic system produces a food surplus. As long as agriculture is relatively unproductive, most of the population is necessarily tied to the soil. In a society in which ninety farmers can produce enough food and fiber for only ninety families, all must remain farmers. If agriculture improves to the point where ninety farmers can feed and clothe one hundred families, one-tenth of the population can move off the land.

This obvious proposition enables us to characterize three major phases in the history of human settlement. The first is a society in which either agriculture is unknown and men live by hunting and fishing or agriculture is so primitive that it yields almost no surplus for the support of nonagricultural workers. In such a society, farming and fishing villages exist, but they remain very small and contain at most only a few people, such as a priestly class, who are not food producers.

The second phase is a society not yet industrialized, in which agriculture becomes productive enough to yield persistently a small surplus beyond bare subsistence. This surplus enters into trade and can support a limited urban population. True towns and cities now arise in which men specialize in nonagricultural activity. The limit to such urbanization in most areas before the Industrial Revolution appears to have been around 10 percent of the total population, although we lack anything like adequate statistics on the question. Something near that ratio probably prevailed in the Mediterranean civilization of the Roman Empire. Despite the existence of a few great cities—Rome itself may, at its zenith, have reached a population of a million or more—society remained predominantly rural.

The third phase, and the only one in which we find substantially urbanized societies, occurs with and after what we may loosely call the Industrial Revolution—loosely because a necessary condition for industrialization is a rise in output per farm worker, either in the industrializing country itself or in an area with which it trades, to support the growing industrial population. Such a rise in farm productivity in turn requires the application of scientific and mechanical techniques to farming and so may itself be treated as an aspect of industrial revolution. In the third phase we do not know what the limit to urbanization may be. Suffice it to say that the United States is today 74 percent urbanized, that most of the rural population is no longer engaged in farming, and that the nation nevertheless continues to be a net food exporter.

This chapter explains the economics of urbanization and illustrates its principles by very briefly tracing the history of cities from ancient times to our own. Chapter 3 examines in much greater detail the development of cities, suburbs, and metropolitan areas in the nineteenth and twentieth centuries.

SPECIALIZATION, TRADE, AND URBAN GROWTH BEFORE THE INDUSTRIAL REVOLUTION

Wherever cities have existed, the city dweller lives by exporting something in exchange for the produce of the countryside. Clearly, trade and its necessary correlate, the geographic division of labor, are intimately bound up with people's pattern of settlement. The great metropolis of ancient times, however, was, as Scott Greer has pointed out, engaged principally not in the export of goods but in the export of "order."[1] Cities dominated society not because they were centers of economic activity but because they were centers of government. The "order" they "exported" to the rural territory of their state consisted of defense, law, and a system of communication. In exchange for these services, the city collected taxes from the countryside, and the tax revenues in turn became the means of paying for the agricultural imports upon which the city depended for survival. Trade, except for the import of food, was limited in volume by two factors: first, the high cost of transport

1. Scott Greer, *Governing the Metropolis* (New York: Wiley, 1962), pp. 4–6.

and, second, the fact that the city could produce little that could not be produced equally well in the peasant village.

However limited the volume of trade may have been in late antiquity, it was sufficient to feed and clothe a considerable population in the urban centers of the Roman Empire. The later decline of the cities of Western Europe—say, from about the seventh to the tenth centuries—has been attributed not only to the breakup of the empire but also, in Henri Pirenne's famous thesis, to the closing of the Mediterranean to European trade by the "abrupt entry of Islam" and its "conquest of the eastern, southern and western shores of the great European lake."[2] Western Europeans were thrown back upon the self-sufficient manor, or estate, as the fundamental economic unit. The territorial division of labor, trade, and consequently urban population all declined in a self-reinforcing spiral.

Just as the decline of the cities followed the decline of trade, their revival accompanied, and in turn reinforced, the restoration of commerce that took place at about the beginning of the eleventh century, when Western Europeans, led by the energetic and thoroughly commercial Venetians, once more extended their influence across the Mediterranean. Indeed, from the eleventh century onward, the rise of the towns is one of the major themes in medieval history, with implications going far beyond the mere economics to which we are here confined.

What had been a declining spiral of city life now became a rising one. The growth of urban population led to increased demand for the commodities needed to support it. Hence trade increased further, and more and more workmen were drawn into the specialized occupations of craft and commerce, further increasing the demand for trade. Centuries later Adam Smith observed that the division of labor depends upon the extent of the market: the growing urban-rural interdependence of the late Middle Ages was, in fact, a form of territorial division of labor, within which major division the ever finer specialization by trade and craft proceeded in its turn.

Then, as now, the process was a complex one: the goods and services a town exported in order to pay for its necessary imports accounted for only a fraction of its total employment. Much urban labor has always consisted of what we now call "service employment." Every medieval clerk, every apprentice working for a tradesman, required the goods of other trades and the services of other clerks, and so the population of the towns must always have far exceeded the number of those engaged directly in trade or service to other regions.

The expansion of European influence and settlement, the growth of trade, and the rise of urban population continued down to the end of the thirteenth century. With the opening of the fourteenth century, Europe's for-

2. Henri Pirenne, *Economic and Social History of Medieval Europe* (Orlando, Fla.: Harcourt Brace Jovanovich, 1961), a Harvest Book, pp. 1–7, 39–40.

ward motion apparently ceased. A time of troubles set in. Trade and population seem to have leveled off even before the Black Death of 1347–1350 reduced Europe's population by perhaps one-third. The end of the thirteenth and the beginning of the fourteenth centuries is thus, in a sense, the high-water mark of medieval European civilization. By that date the towns had been growing for some three hundred years. How large had they grown? Not very big by today's standard. Pirenne estimates that at the beginning of the fourteenth century only a few of the largest cities had attained a population of 50,000 to 100,000. Florence in 1339 numbered perhaps 90,000 inhabitants. Venice at that period probably exceeded 100,000, while Paris may have had as many as 200,000.[3]

Europe's trade and population surged ahead once more from the mid-fifteenth century onward. The age of exploration opened up new trade routes by sea. Banking, insurance, and trading enterprises were now undertaken on a truly grand scale. The cities of Europe began to expand once again. By 1800 London, by far Europe's largest city, contained more than 950,000 people. Yet because the techniques of agricultural production had improved but little, the bulk of the European population remained tied to the soil. Kingsley Davis has pointed out that "urbanization" properly means not simply the growth of urban population but its growth relative to rural and hence to total numbers. In the three centuries before the Industrial Revolution Europe's cities grew considerably, but their margin of growth over that of the rural sector was slight indeed. Hence, as Davis points out, "on the eve of the industrial revolution Europe was still an overwhelmingly agrarian region."[4]

THE IMPACT OF THE INDUSTRIAL REVOLUTION

Why did the Industrial Revolution suddenly cause mankind to congregate in cities and towns? Why couldn't it have taken a different course, leaving workers in their rural surroundings and spreading industrial facilities thinly over the countryside? The answer emerges if we consider its effects in greater detail. Let us first note that the Industrial Revolution comprised at least three radical developments: a manufacturing revolution, a transportation revolution, and an agricultural revolution.

The last has already been described as the application of scientific and mechanical techniques to farming to bring about a sharp increase in farm output per worker. Its effect was to make possible a shift of population from agricultural to nonagricultural pursuits, but in no respect did it *require* the urbanization of those released from farming.

The transportation revolution, on the other hand, certainly encouraged urban agglomeration. Cities have, throughout history, tended to locate at eco-

3. Ibid., pp. 170–171.
4. Kingsley Davis, "The Urbanization of the Human Population," in *Cities* (New York: Knopf, 1965), a Scientific American Book, p. 8.

nomic transport points: at seaports, on navigable lakes and rivers, or at junctures of important overland trade routes. The transportation revolution of the nineteenth century consisted chiefly in the improvement in waterborne transport following the development of canals and the invention of the steamship and the even more radical change in overland transport made possible by steam railroads. These developments combined to increase enormously the transportation advantages of the points they served as compared with all other points. Both modes of transport operated not ubiquitously but along lines of movement that formed rather coarse-meshed networks. The point of service for the steamship network was the port—and the number of good ports is limited by topography. The canal and later the railroad system, on the other hand, could serve many points. Despite the topographical constraints, many possible routes existed, and the choice among them was sometimes determined by noneconomic factors. Once the system was built, however, the points it served obtained decisive cost advantages over all other places, for overland travel apart from the railroad remained in the horse-and-buggy stage throughout the nineteenth century. Thus ports and points along the railroads and canals powerfully attracted industry and often became manufacturing towns or cities.

So effectively did the railroad encourage villages to grow into towns and towns into cities that it proved to be the most powerful agglomerative invention of all time. To enjoy its benefits, one had to build directly along the right-of-way or on a short siding. Hence nineteenth-century factories huddled next to one another in the familiar railside industrial districts still visible in every manufacturing town. Moreover, the railroad was relatively more efficient for long than for short hauls. It was miraculously economical for intercity movement of both goods and people, but until the invention of the electric railway it did little to improve intraurban transport. Thus the workers in their turn lived as close as possible to the factories, and the nineteenth-century city grew up at an extraordinarily high level of density.

That it could also grow to encompass an immense population was another effect of the transportation revolution. Since long-distance haulage had become relatively cheap, it was now possible to feed huge populations concentrated at any point on the transport network by bringing food from distant agricultural zones, which, incidentally, the railroad had often helped open up. Without such a network, even if cities could have obtained sufficient food from nearby farm areas, they would have run a grave risk of famine whenever the local crop was deficient. Indeed, the wide chronological fluctuations in local death rates that occurred in, say, medieval Europe were due partly to local famines, which a better transport network could have mitigated.[5]

The manufacturing revolution consisted essentially of the development of factory methods of production incorporating power-driven machinery in

5. Carlo Cipolla, *The Economic History of World Population* (Baltimore: Penguin Books, 1962), a Pelican Book, pp. 77–80.

place of the hand-tool system of production that had prevailed for thousands of years. This encouraged urbanization in two significant ways. First, the optimum scale for a single plant, even in the early days of the Industrial Revolution, was likely to be large enough to form the economic nucleus for a small town. Second, and perhaps more important, commercial activities show a marked tendency to locate where other commercial activities already exist, and it is this process of agglomeration we now wish to examine in detail.

It is important to note that economic activity displayed agglomerative tendencies long before the Industrial Revolution. We have already pointed out that banking and financial services concentrated in the great ports and trading centers of Renaissance Europe. At the same period handicraft trades, such as the Flemish cloth-weaving complex, were geographically concentrated even though still organized as cottage industries. The economic basis of agglomeration, which we will analyze, was not much different then from now. But one of the profound effects of the Industrial Revolution was vastly to increase specialization through increased division of labor. Before the Industrial Revolution most production was carried on within the home—do it yourself was the rule in those days—and homes were mostly rural, located wherever farming was possible. The Industrial Revolution split off more and more of these domestic activities, converted them into full-time occupations within factories, and freed them to find their optimum location, no longer bound to home and farm. Thus it vastly increased the possibilities of agglomeration.

In a capitalist economy entrepreneurs will build their plants at the location where they think they can maximize profits. Precisely where on the map that will turn out to be depends on a number of discoverable factors, including the location of sources of supply and geographic differentials in transport costs, in wage rates, and in market potential. These factors are handled systematically in what is usually called the "theory of the location of industry," which will be taken up in Chapter 4. At this point, however, we will examine the matter from a different perspective, focusing on why economic activities in an industrial society generally tend to agglomerate rather than on the somewhat different question of why they tend to locate at particular points on the map, such as Buffalo, New York, or Peoria, Illinois.

Implicit in most analyses of urban growth, including perhaps the argument of this chapter, is the assumption that one must account for the fact that people move from a "natural" rural life to a somehow unnatural urban one. The argument need not proceed that way, however. R. M. Haig, in a notable tour de force, shrewdly reversed matters and suggested that "the question is changed from 'Why live in the City?' to 'Why not live in the City?'"[6] He took as his starting point the observation that the economically most effi-

6. R. M. Haig, "Some Speculations Regarding the Economic Basis of Urban Concentration," *Quarterly Journal of Economics*, February 1926, pp. 179–208; the quotation is from p. 188.

cient pattern for the production and distribution of goods would assign to metropolitan areas everyone except those needed to farm the land or extract minerals plus those needed to transport such raw materials. According to this logic, what requires explanation is not the tendency of the population to concentrate in cities but the fact that it is not *all* concentrated there.

One might also draw upon the authority of the philosophers for this point of view: man, the social animal described by Aristotle, fulfills his nature only in association with his fellows. Or in more modern terms, people want to go where the action is. Thus, one might argue, social as well as economic drives make the city the natural destination of all people. Urbanism as a way of life then requires no special justification, and no apologies.

THE AGGLOMERATION OF ECONOMIC ACTIVITY

The locational pattern of economic activity reveals a complex system of interrelationships among firms. One soon realizes that the location of any particular economic unit depends on the location of all the others. No matter where we begin the analysis we are quite likely to find the argument running in circles. But we must cut into it somewhere. Let us start, therefore, by adopting Raymond Vernon's distinction between "local-market activities, . . . which generate goods and services of the sort which are typically consumed in the area where they are produced," and "national-market activities . . . devoted to the generation of goods and services which characteristically are 'exported' over broad market areas."[7] Local market activities, as Vernon explains, "respond largely to changes which go on inside the region." Therefore, if we can explain the tendency for national market activities to concentrate at a certain place, we will also have explained the tendency of local market activities to do so: the latter expand wherever the local market expands, and the local market expands wherever the growth of national market activities stimulates local employment and income.

Within the category of national market activities, agglomeration is the result partly of a kind of inverted pyramiding. One industry—say, shipping—locates at a place that has a good natural harbor. That activity then attracts others linked to it—say, banking, insurance, inland transport. The concentration of those industries in turn attracts others linked to them—say, a stock market, a commodity exchange, a printing and publishing industry, a university. And, of course, all these build up a large demand for local market products—that is, for the services of retail traders, bakers, dentists, plumbers, police, bus drivers, schoolteachers, and all the other members of the local

7. Raymond Vernon, *Metropolis 1985* (New York: Doubleday, 1963), an Anchor Book, p. 25.

market sector, who provide services both to those in the national sector and to other local market producers.

The linkages of which we speak consist of a need for either communication or the movement of goods between firms and individuals doing business with one another. Linkage, however, need not itself imply proximity: firms have links both to their suppliers and to their customers, and proximity to both is not always possible. The locational pull exerted by such connections depends on numerous factors including the technology of communication and transport, the functions performed by the firm, and the locations of its suppliers and customers. The pull varies directly both with the need for communication and with the unit cost of accomplishing it. Since improvements in technology have reduced the relative cost of communication and transport in recent years, distance has become relatively less expensive, and some of the linkages that formerly pulled economic activity into the urban core have grown weaker. Before one can gauge correctly the effects of such changes, however, it is necessary to understand the relationship between linkages and the functions and organization of the firm.

Haig pointed out that what we call the "firm" actually comprises a "packet of functions," which may not all have the same communication and transportation needs.[8] If these functions are spatially separable, the ideal solution for the firm might be to place each at a different location. The separability of functions is in fact dependent on the state of technology. One important result of the reduced cost of communication and transportation has been to make possible increased spatial separation of functions within firms. In principle this might either increase or decrease the tendency of economic activity to agglomerate. A corporation that formerly located both its manufacturing plant and its head office in a low-wage small town might now move the head office to a large city. A firm that formerly operated a department store and warehouse in the central business district might now move the warehouse out to a lower-rent area, still within the city. A book publisher that formerly maintained its head office downtown and its storage and shipping departments in a nearby warehouse might now locate the last two in a distant suburb.

In fact, if we mean by agglomeration not just the tendency of activities to concentrate in central cities but their tendency to concentrate in metropolitan areas, the displacement of a warehousing operation from downtown to the suburbs is not deglomerating. It represents a loosening up, a spreading out of the structure of the metropolis rather than a dispersion of activity into nonmetropolitan areas. A genuine dispersion, ending at the point where urban and rural densities of activity converge and become indistinguishable, is a conceivable but still distant possibility. But this anticipates later discussion.

8. R. M. Haig, "The Assignment of Activities to Areas in Urban Regions," *Quarterly Journal of Economics*, May 1926, pp. 402–434.

Suffice it to say at this point that despite the telephone, the airplane, and the automobile, certain activities find their links to the center still strong enough to hold them. Many of these are industries that Vernon has characterized as requiring face-to-face contact with either customers or suppliers in the daily conduct of business. Such industries, he points out, generally combine two characteristics: their activities are nonroutine, and speed is crucial to their success. He calls these industries "communication oriented" in their choice of location.[9] A list of them would certainly include at least some parts of banking and finance, law, government, advertising, publishing, and broadcasting. For these activities the letter and the telephone are not adequate substitutes for face-to-face contact; their personnel, or at the very least their management personnel, must remain close to the center.

Some kinds of manufacturing certainly fall within this category, too. In a telling illustration, Vernon contrasts two cases: first, the producer of standardized goods, whose communications needs do not dictate an urban location because he can probably use the telephone to order raw materials or parts by giving the catalog number or standard specification to his supplier; second, the manufacturer of the unique or the highly styled product, such as ladies' dresses, who has to locate close to his suppliers because day in and day out he must see and compare various combinations of color, quality, and design before he can decide what materials to buy.

ECONOMIES OF AGGLOMERATION

For a fuller understanding of the causes of the geographic concentration of industry we must go beyond the concept of linkages, even the face-to-face variety, to a discussion of what have sometimes been called "economies of agglomeration." Economies of agglomeration are the savings in unit costs that may accrue to individual firms when a large enough number of them locate in one city. When such savings result from the agglomeration of firms in the same industry, they are known as "localization economies," because they depend on the local concentration of a particular activity.[10] The most important sources of savings are probably two: first, the presence of highly specialized suppliers, whose operations are feasible only because agglomeration has created a sufficient local demand, and second, the availability of a large pool of specialized, skilled labor, whose presence is similarly dependent on the high aggregate level of local demand.

The classic case of localization economies in manufacturing is provided by the concentration of the ladies' garment industry in New York City. The

9. Vernon, pp. 105–106, 139–143.

10. Edgar M. Hoover, *Location Theory and the Shoe and Leather Industries* (Cambridge, Mass.: Harvard University Press, 1937), pp. 90–91.

industry in New York is large enough to provide a profitable local market for a host of specialized suppliers. Thus, without incurring the risks and costs of carrying large inventories, the garment manufacturer who locates in New York gains ready access to a full line of the inputs needed in a trade where style requirements change rapidly and speed and flexibility are crucial. This advantage is not confined to material inputs but applies equally to the labor supply: with access to a common pool of trained labor, the firm can vary its work force without having to bear the expense of training or, alternatively, of carrying idle workers.

In the increasingly important service sector, the broadcasting industry benefits from similar effects. Production of programs for national television is concentrated in Los Angeles and New York. These two cities offer a plentiful supply of the necessary specialized inputs: writers, directors, designers, actors, musicians, dancers, technicians. Not only can the personnel be assembled as needed for individual productions, but also equipment and studios can be rented on short notice and for short periods. To appreciate the resulting cost savings, consider the opposite case: a television producer in a small town would have to import technical and artistic personnel for every production, or else keep them permanently on the payroll. Either alternative would be costly, and neither would be feasible if the small-town producer were competing for sales in the national market with firms located in Los Angeles or New York and benefiting from economies of agglomeration available there.

To measure the economic benefits of agglomeration empirically, David Segal carried out an econometric study of manufacturing in fifty-eight large metropolitan areas. He found that labor and capital were 8 percent more productive in those with a population above 2 million than in smaller metropolitan areas and took that difference to be a measure of the net benefits of agglomeration in production.[11]

Agglomeration economies can occur in selling merchandise as well as in its production. For example, by locating in New York, the garment manufacturer places a showroom in the major national market to which buyers regularly come from stores all over the country. Again, there are real unit cost savings: the expenses incurred by the buyer in canvassing the market—expenses involving real costs of time and travel, which must be recouped from customers—are minimized when markets are geographically concentrated. Similar gains accrue through geographic concentration of like stores at the microscale of the neighborhood: the consumer bent on comparative shopping saves time and money when stores are close together.

When cost savings to individual firms arise from specialization made possible not by the local concentration of a particular industry but rather by the sheer size of the local economy, they are called "economies of urbaniza-

11. David Segal, "Are There Returns to Scale in City Size?" *Review of Economics and Statistics*, July 1976, pp. 339–350.

tion." Here are a few examples among the many that might be cited: A big city has a labor market so large that it can offer not merely a large number of employment agencies but also some that specialize in finding particular kinds of personnel. It has not only many banks but banks large enough to maintain highly specialized departments for a wide variety of functions. Thus the concentration of industries, even though they be unlike industries, makes possible an efficient specialization of service firms, and these latter are the source of economies of agglomeration for the congregating firms that made them profitable.

The concentration of corporate head offices in major metropolitan areas testifies to the importance of urbanization economies. AT&T, Exxon, and General Motors have their head offices in New York not because they do business with one another but because they all want to do business with New York banks and investment houses, with Wall Street law firms, and with Madison Avenue advertising agencies. A study of the head office locations of the 500 largest industrial firms in 1975 found that 255 of them were located in metropolitan areas with a population of 2.5 million or more and another 100 in areas with a population between 1.0 and 2.5 million.[12]

The kind of linkage that gives rise to economies of agglomeration is really just a special case of what economists usually describe as complementarity between firms or industries. Bearing that in mind, we can state the necessary and sufficient conditions for economies of agglomeration to occur as follows: (1) Complementary industries or facilities exist, (2) that are not ubiquitous (that is, not found everywhere), (3) between which the cost or difficulty of cooperation increases importantly with distance. By complementary facilities we mean the button wholesaler and garment manufacturer or the advertising firm and corporate head office. Nonubiquity is essential because facilities that are found everywhere, such as the post office or the electric company, obviously cannot be the basis for attraction to any particular place. Finally, the cost or difficulty of cooperation over distance is crucial because there is no reason for complementary activities to locate in the same place if that cost is low. Complementarity would not then require proximity. As already explained, the cost of cooperating over distance has been reduced in recent years by major improvements in the technology of transportation and communication. Consequently, the locational pull exerted by economies of agglomeration has in some cases weakened, and this, as we shall see in later chapters, profoundly affects the entire "system of settlement."

We spoke earlier of the fact that the location of any one economic unit depends on the location of all the others. The complex interrelatedness of the forces that have produced spatial concentration should by now be clear:

12. John D. Stephens and Brian P. Holly, "City System Behavior and Corporate Influence: The Headquarters Location of U.S. Industrial Firms, 1955–75," *Urban Studies*, October 1981, table 7. Also see Thierry J. Noyelle and Thomas M. Stanback, Jr., *The Economic Transformation of American Cities* (Totowa, N.J.: Rowman & Allanheld, 1984), ch. 6 and app. D.

within the national market sector, one industry attracted other, related activities to its locality; this increased agglomeration produced cost savings that attracted still more firms and produced still more economies of agglomeration. As employment and income rose, local market industries also expanded, and this expansion too was potent for the creation of further economies of agglomeration and further urban growth.

To explain the growth of cities we have emphasized the advantages of large communities as places of production. The primary importance of production advantages, however, should not lead us to overlook other factors associated with community size. As Benjamin Chinitz points out, large communities also afford superior opportunities for consumption.[13] The basic necessities of food, clothing, and shelter can be purchased anywhere, but the more specialized forms of consumption goods—the "luxuries" that people turn to increasingly as their income rises—are more readily available in the larger centers. In general, the range of types of goods and services offered to the consumer increases as community size increases. Some items, such as opera performances or major league baseball games, are found only in the largest cities.

The large community also offers important advantages to the worker. Obviously, the range of job choice increases with community size. Wage levels, too, are higher in the larger centers. Within specific occupational categories there is a fairly regular pattern of rising wages as one moves from smaller to larger metropolitan areas.[14] We return to the question of income and city size in Chapter 3.

DISECONOMIES OF AGGLOMERATION

Economies of agglomeration in production and consumption make up only one side of the urban ledger. *Diseconomies* of agglomeration—the negative effects of size that cumulate as cities grow—make up the other. Indeed, the growth of cities is influenced simultaneously by both forces, the positive economies of agglomeration inducing growth while the negative diseconomies discourage it. We have concentrated on the positive effects because they have predominated in the modern period, producing rapid urban growth and cities of great size. Yet urban growth has probably always had negative effects as well. Let us examine them briefly.

Diseconomies of agglomeration occur when the concentration of population or of economic activity in one place either raises the real cost of production by requiring more inputs per unit of output or reduces the real stan-

13. Benjamin Chinitz, ed., *City and Suburb* (Englewood Cliffs, N.J.: Prentice-Hall, 1964), pp. 10–12.
14. See data in Edgar M. Hoover, *An Introduction to Regional Economics*, 2nd ed. (New York: Knopf, 1975), pp. 170–171.

dard of living by increasing the level of physical or social disamenities.[15] In many cases a single diseconomy has both effects. Air pollution and crime are good examples. Both increase with city size. The presence of air pollution raises production costs for some businesses and cleaning and health costs for households. Yet even after these costs are paid, the physical disamenity of a polluted atmosphere remains. Similarly, higher crime rates impose increased security and insurance costs on households and firms, but a residual disamenity remains, since protection is never complete. Thus pollution and crime simultaneously raise the cost and reduce the pleasure of living in cities.

Transportation requirements are the source of another diseconomy of agglomeration. Average trip length, and therefore the time spent traveling to work, increase with city size.[16] Since time is a resource to which we all attach some value, this introduces another element of cost that increases with urban scale. Traffic congestion, too, is often alleged to be a diseconomy of agglomeration, imposing increased travel time on both businesses and households as city size increases. The fact of such congestion is not in question. As Harry W. Richardson points out, however, it may reflect not a diseconomy of scale but simply a failure to expand the capacity of the local transportation system to its optimum size.[17] Optimum transportation investment will be taken up in Chapter 8. In Chapter 3 we return to the question of the advantages and disadvantages of city size and discuss their effect on individual well-being and on decisions to migrate to or from large metropolitan areas.

IS THERE AN OPTIMUM CITY SIZE?

The fact that as cities grow there are productivity gains in certain functions and losses in others has suggested to some students of urbanism the naive hope that we might be able to determine from a comparison of economies and diseconomies of urban scale exactly what the optimum size for a city is.[18] In that case, man's ancient search for utopia could at last be conducted on scientific principles. For example, according to this view, the optimum size city from the perspective of its residents would be that size at which the value of

15. Evidence of diseconomies is presented by Irving Hoch in "Income and City Size," *Urban Studies*, October 1972, pp. 299–328, and in "Variations in the Quality of Urban Life among Cities and Regions," in Lowdon Wingo and Alan Evans, eds., *Public Economics and the Quality of Life* (Baltimore: Johns Hopkins University Press, 1977), pp. 28–65; and by Harry W. Richardson in *The Economics of Urban Size* (Lexington, Mass.: Heath, Lexington Books, 1973), chs. 3 and 8.

16. See Oded Izraeli and Thomas R. McCarthy, "Variations in Travel Distances, Travel Time and Modal Choice Among SMSAs," *Journal of Transport Economics and Policy*, May 1985, table 3.

17. Richardson, pp. 25–27.

18. For a review of the theory and the evidence on optimum city size see William Alonso, "The Economics of Urban Size," *Papers of the Regional Science Association*, 26 (1971), 67–83; and Richardson. Both authors are critical of naive versions of the theory.

economies of agglomeration per capita most exceeds the value of diseconomies of agglomeration, similarly measured. Net economies of size accruing to each resident would thus be maximized.[19] From the local point of view, a welfare optimum would be achieved.

Such a formulation is naive for many reasons. To begin with, it is difficult to measure the value of economies and diseconomies of agglomeration with the precision that would be needed to determine optimum size. Next, we would expect changes in technology and income greatly to alter such values as time passed. Widespread use of automobiles, trucks, and buses, for example, added substantially to the cost of air pollution (a diseconomy of agglomeration) during the middle decades of the twentieth century. At the same time, those improvements in transportation plus others in communications probably reduced the benefits obtained by producers from proximity to suppliers and customers (an economy of agglomeration). Income changes also systematically affect the value of economies and diseconomies of agglomeration. For example, as their incomes rise, people are willing to pay more for such amenities as clean air, so that the perceived damage from air pollution—a diseconomy of agglomeration—probably rises with living standards. In the real world, changes in technology and income occur endlessly. As a result, even if we could calculate optimum city size at a moment in time, we would have to revise the goal continually and, given the slow pace at which cities adapt, would never reach it. In short, optimum city size is a static notion that has little meaning in a dynamic world.

Most important of all, the concept of optimum size is naive because it overlooks the need in every society for a variety of cities performing different functions and therefore differing systematically in size. As we shall see in Chapter 5, the cities in any nation form an interdependent network or system in which the size and character of any one place is conditioned by the size, character, and location of other places in the system. In search of the ideal, therefore, one would have to conceive not of a single optimum size applicable to all cities but of an optimum set of cities in which each city has the optimum size to perform its expected functions. No one could hope to define such a system for the dynamic society in which we now live.

Although the notion of optimum size may be a will-o'-the-wisp, cities and metropolitan areas, as we shall see in Chapter 3, do grow and decline in response to the positive and negative forces of economies and diseconomies of agglomeration. What is more, these forces are themselves constantly in flux as a result of underlying changes in the economy. Consequently, the urban system never reaches a state of equilibrium, and for better or worse, city dwellers are fated to live continually under the stress of change.

19. The existence of a point at which net economies are maximized requires, of course, that the curves representing economies and diseconomies of size have the appropriate shapes. See Richardson, pp. 11–12.

THREE

The Growth of Cities
and Metropolitan Areas

When Mark Twain informs the reader of *Huckleberry Finn* that he has painstakingly incorporated seven different dialects into the book, he excuses his explanation by saying that "without it many readers would suppose that all these characters were trying to talk alike and not succeeding." Unless a similar warning is issued here, the unwary reader may assume that *urban, metropolitan,* and *central city* are terms that sound different but have the same meaning or that *rural, suburban,* and *nonmetropolitan* are nothing more than synonyms used to ward off fatigue. In short, the time has come for some definitions. And since to define is also to understand, the labor of definition will provide a kind of spatial paradigm, a map of the essential elements of urban and metropolitan structure.

SOME DEFINITIONS

City

Let us begin with *city,* the easiest of the essential terms to define. *City* is often used loosely as a generic term for all kinds of large or dense settlements. When used with precision, however, as in classifying population data, it simply denotes the area contained within the political boundaries of a large incorporated municipality. We will make frequent use of the term *central city* in this book. A central city is the principal city (as just defined) around which some larger unit—say, a standard metropolitan statistical area—is formed.

The definition of *city* and *central city* by political boundaries has two important consequences. First, the area of a city, and hence its population, is partly the result of historical accident. If a city is originally incorporated with a large geographic area or is able to grow by annexing neighboring towns as its population expands, it will become larger than another city, equally prosperous and attractive, which either starts with a relatively small area or is unable, for political reasons, to gain much territory or population through annexation. Consider the contrast between Boston and Houston. In 1980 the population of the "Boston urbanized area" exceeded that of the "Houston urbanized area" by 266,000, yet the city of Houston contained one million more people than did the city of Boston. Houston city accounted for 66 percent of the population and covered 53 percent of the land in the Houston urbanized area. The figures for Boston were, respectively, only 21 percent and 5.5 percent.

Since cities can expand by annexation, the second consequence of the use of political boundaries to define cities is that historical comparisons of population size (or other measures) can be misleading if care is not taken to adjust for boundary changes. The place on the map defined as Indianapolis, Indiana, increased in area from 71.2 square miles in 1960 to 379.4 square miles ten years later. During the same period its population rose from 476,258 to 744,624. Without all that annexation, Indianapolis would actually have lost population over the decade: the 1970 population within the 1960 boundaries was only 437,892—8 percent less than in 1960. Which figure is the relevant one depends, of course, on the problem at hand.

Metropolitan Area

Students of urbanism have long recognized that every city is the center of a larger socioeconomic system organized around it and often extending far beyond its politically defined boundaries. The term *metropolitan area* describes the territory over which such a system extends. In order to gather data concerning metropolitan populations on a uniform and consistent basis, the government has carefully defined what is now called a "metropolitan statistical area," or MSA.

As we shall see, the metropolitan population of the United States has grown enormously in recent decades. Consequently both the number of metropolitan areas and the geographic size of the individual units have regularly increased. For the 1980 census the government recognized 318 metropolitan areas in the United States and 5 in Puerto Rico. Many of these now cover a far larger area than they did when first defined. To cite an extreme example, the Atlanta, Georgia, MSA, which included only three counties in 1950, now comprises eighteen.

Except in New England, MSAs are built up of units not smaller than whole counties. This has the practical advantage of making data collected for MSAs readily comparable with local business or government information assembled on a county basis. The MSA is fundamentally an economic unit. It defines the metropolis largely, though not entirely, by its character of being an integrated labor market. An integrated labor market might, for our purposes, be described as the smallest area that is large enough to contain the workplaces of most of the people who reside in it and the residences of most of the people who work in it. In a major metropolitan region, such as the one centered on Philadelphia, for example, the smallest area that will answer such a definition is large indeed. The Philadelphia MSA includes the city of Philadelphia plus four counties in Pennsylvania and three in New Jersey. As we shall see, the Census Bureau definition treats the web of journeys from home to workplace as primary evidence that the regional population forms an integrated social and economic system—a metropolitan system, in truth, about which it is exceedingly useful to collect statistics.

The definition of a metropolitan statistical area starts with the concept of a central city. With minor exceptions, the central city, together with its surrounding densely settled urban fringe, must have a population of at least 50,000. An MSA, then, consists of (1) the county or counties containing the central city and (2) all contiguous counties that have close economic ties to the county or counties containing the central city and are sufficiently urban in character. The labor market emphasis of this definition emerges clearly if we examine the specific standards employed with it. For example, an outlying county will be included in an MSA if at least 15 percent of the employed workers residing in that county commute to the central county or counties, provided that other criteria pertaining primarily to population density are also met.

Unhappily for the user of population statistics, Census Bureau terminology has changed over time to reflect periodic revision of the rules followed in defining metropolitan areas. The concept of a "standard metropolitan area" was introduced into the 1950 census. For the census of 1960 the definition was modified and the name changed to "standard metropolitan statistical area," or SMSA, which remained in use until after the 1980 census. The reader will find the term SMSA employed frequently in this book because it was the definition used in the three most recent census counts and in most of the empirical studies of urban economics that have been published since the mid-1960s.

In 1983 the government adopted a more complex set of definitions.[1] The basic metropolitan unit, already described, is now called the "metropolitan statistical area," or MSA. As a metropolitan area spreads out, it may flow into other nearby MSAs. Alternatively, as it grows, some of its outlying parts

1. The rules for defining SMSAs, the official list of such areas, and the precise geographic definition of each are published periodically by the federal government. Current definitions are fully explained in U.S. Bureau of the Census, *State and Metropolitan Area Data Book 1982*, pp. xv–xxiv. Also see *1980 Census of Population*, Supplementary Report, *Metropolitan Statistical Areas*, PC80-S1-S18, December 1984, which provides basic 1970 and 1980 data for metropolitan areas as they were redefined after the 1980 census.

may develop characteristics that would allow them to be defined as metropolitan areas in their own right. When such an aggregation of metropolitan areas develops, it is defined for statistical purposes as a "consolidated metropolitan statistical area," or CMSA. Its subparts are then called "primary metropolitan statistical areas," or PMSAs, to distinguish them from MSAs, a title reserved for separate or "freestanding" metropolitan areas. Thus San Jose, California, is a PMSA within the larger consolidated metropolitan statistical area known as the San Francisco–Oakland–San Jose CMSA, while metropolitan areas such as Rochester, New York, or Atlanta, Georgia, which are not part of and do not abut another metropolitan area, are MSAs. Since an MSA may be either larger or smaller than a PMSA, this classification should not be thought of as hierarchical in terms of size. It is tempting to say of this terminology, as someone remarked of Wagner's music, that "it's really much better than it sounds," but the analogy may be unfair to Wagner.

Under the new system, as of October 1984, the Census Bureau recognized in the United States 257 freestanding MSAs, 71 PMSAs, and 20 CMSAs. The CMSAs sprawl over such major metropolitan regions as the San Francisco Bay area; the area in Illinois, Indiana, and Wisconsin that centers on Chicago; and the New York–New Jersey–Connecticut metropolitan area centering on New York City. This last is the largest of all, comprising twelve PMSAs (five in New Jersey, four in Connecticut, and three in New York) and containing a population in 1984 of 17,807,000.[2] The number and size of these supermetropolises suggests that very strong agglomerative forces have been at work up to this point in determining the pattern of U.S. settlement. As we shall see, however, there are now signs that these forces are beginning to weaken.

When the Census Bureau publishes metropolitan area data, it generally subdivides them into "inside central city" and "outside central city." The latter category, which is simply the area total minus the central city total, is often referred to as "the ring," since it comprises the ring of counties that commonly surround the central city and lie within the metropolitan area. Thus the Philadelphia PMSA consists of the central city of Philadelphia and a ring of seven contiguous counties. In many cases (especially under the definitions introduced in 1983), metropolitan areas are defined as having more than one central city. These may or may not appear in the official title, but in any case the "inside central cities" category will include the total for all of them.

Urban and Rural

The terms *urban* and *rural* have proved difficult for social scientists to define. Economists offer no help here: apparently economic science has been

2. U.S. Bureau of the Census, *Current Population Reports*, series P-25, no. 976, October 1985, table 2.

able to get along without empirically meaningful definitions of these categories. Sociologists, however, to whom the concept of community is central, have given the matter a good deal of attention. The urban community, they find, displays social characteristics different from those of rural society, but they are not always in agreement as to the extent of the differences or the inferences to be drawn from them. Consequently no definition of *urban* and *rural* is universally accepted among sociologists. Moreover, it is highly improbable, as Otis Dudley Duncan has argued, that any single, scalable characteristic can provide an adequate system of classification for all purposes.[3] Hatt and Reiss, however, point out that

> a growing number of sociologists appear to share the point of view that the formal criteria of a scientific definition of urban phenomena is satisfactorily met by defining communities solely in terms of their demographic uniqueness—the variables of population and area. "Urban" usually is defined, then, as a function of absolute population size and density of settlement. Most so-called urban variables then are considered causal consequences of variation in size and density of settlements.[4]

A definition of *urban* in terms of population size and density is, in fact, what the U.S. Bureau of the Census has adopted for compiling statistics on urbanization. By common consent, however, any dichotomous definition— that is, any definition that divides all places into two mutually exclusive groups labeled "urban" and "rural"—is bound to be arbitrary. Between the polar cases of rural and urban, along whatever scale we choose, there lie many intermediate situations. There is no obvious point at which to draw the line and say "all places larger and more densely settled than this one are urban, and the rest are rural." Yet a simple, two-way classification is so convenient that it continues to predominate in statistical studies.

The Bureau of the Census adopted its present definition of *urban* for the 1950 census. Included as urban are three kinds of places:

1. All incorporated municipalities having a population of 2,500 or more
2. The densely settled urban fringe, whether or not incorporated as municipalities, around cities of 50,000 or more
3. Unincorporated places of 2,500 or more population outside any urban fringe area

All places not defined as urban in the census are counted as rural and further subdivided into rural-farm and rural-nonfarm. The neophyte should be warned not to confuse farm-nonfarm with rural-urban.

3. Otis Dudley Duncan, "Community Size and the Rural-Urban Continuum," in Paul K. Hatt and Albert J. Reiss, Jr., eds., *Cities and Society: The Revised Reader in Urban Sociology* (Glencoe, Ill.: Free Press, 1957), pp. 35–45.
4. Hatt and Reiss, p. 20.

Urbanized Areas

Since counties are often large and contain diverse kinds of settlement, parts of those included in an MSA may be thinly settled and essentially rural rather than urban. To separate out the population actually living at urban densities from the population of the usually larger MSA, which as a result of its definition in terms of whole counties may contain extensive rural portions, the Census Bureau developed the category of "urbanized areas." An urbanized area consists of one or more central cities together with their densely settled urban fringe, provided that the combined population is at least 50,000. For the 1980 census 366 urbanized areas were recognized in the United States and 7 in Puerto Rico.

The new criteria adopted in 1950 met the requirements of an up-to-date definition of *urban* and *rural* about as well as possible. One must note, however, that changes in the technology of communication and transportation during the twentieth century have made that distinction less clear and perhaps less meaningful than it had been. Down to the end of the nineteenth century, or even beyond that date, rural life, built around horse-and-buggy transport for short journeys, was still relatively isolated from the influence of cities. Today the distinction between urban and rural lifestyles is rapidly fading. For better or worse, both populations are now almost equally exposed to the powerful cultural influence of mass media. Rural life is increasingly tied to town and city by rapid communication and transport and has lost most of the characteristics attributable to its former isolation and self-sufficiency.

Central Business District

A few terms that do not have formal Census Bureau definitions remain to be mentioned. *Central business district*, commonly abbreviated as CBD, refers to the commercial center of a large city. It is characterized as "an area of very high land valuation; high concentration of retail businesses, offices, theatres, hotels and 'service' businesses; and high traffic flow."[5] However, there are no precise rules for defining a CBD according to which we could delineate comparable areas in various large cities. For each central city the Census Bureau defines the CBD in cooperation with local interests. Data are collected only for the Census of Retail Trade. Analysts concerned with "downtown" activities other than retailing and consumer services might well draw boundaries for the CBD much wider than those that are appropriate for retailing.

Suburb and Satellite City

Suburb and *satellite city* are likewise terms usually defined ad hoc. In general, these two kinds of settlement make up the ring area of an MSA.

5. U.S. Bureau of the Census, *1982 Census of Retail Trade*, Major Retail Centers in Standard Metropolitan Statistical Areas, p. iv.

Suburbs are primarily "bedroom communities" containing relatively few places of employment; they may be either urban or rural. Satellite cities are urban localities within the MSA that are places of employment and centers of commerce in their own right. As Margolis has shown in a study of the San Francisco Bay area, a set of formal definitions can be based on the ratio of local jobs to resident labor force. When the ratio was below .75, he defined the place as a "dormitory city" (i.e., suburb). When it fell between .75 and 1.25, he classified the municipality as a "balanced city" (i.e., satellite city). If the ratio exceeded 1.25, he considered the place an "industrial enclave."[6] Of course, the precise dividing lines between these categories, or others one might wish to interpose, are likely to be arbitrary. Especially since the rise of auto and truck transport, residential suburbs have increasingly sought or permitted the construction of light industry and of research and office enterprises, while satellite cities may have growing residential districts whose inhabitants commute to jobs elsewhere in the region.

THE URBANIZATION OF THE UNITED STATES

Table 3.1 summarizes the history of urban and metropolitan development in the United States. At the earliest census, in 1790, only 5 percent of the whole population lived in cities of 2,500 or more—the definition of *urban* used until the 1950 census. If we take *urbanization* to mean a rise in the proportion of population living in urban areas and *urban growth* to mean an absolute increase in urban population, the United States has been experiencing both processes almost continuously since 1790. Urbanization obviously occurs whenever urban growth exceeds rural growth, and that condition has been fulfilled in every decade of our history except 1810–1820. In the decades between 1790 and 1840, with that one exception, the urban population grew at an average rate almost twice that of the rural population. But because cities were so small at the beginning of the period—there were only twenty-four in all, of which only five exceeded the 10,000 mark—it took a long time for these high growth rates to urbanize very many people. As late as 1840 the country was still 89 percent rural and only 11 percent urban.

By the 1840s, according to most students of the subject, the Industrial Revolution was well under way in the United States, and all the economic forces making for agglomeration were unleashed. Thereafter the ratio of urban to rural growth increased markedly, and the pace of urbanization quickened. Immigration from abroad contributed to the trend, since a disproportionate number of immigrants to the United States have always stopped in the cities. The urban portion of the population reached 20 percent in 1860

6. Julius Margolis, "Municipal Fiscal Structure in a Metropolitan Region," in Ronald E. Grieson, ed., *Urban Economics: Readings and Analysis* (Boston: Little, Brown, 1973), pp. 379–395.

TABLE 3.1
Growth of Urban and Metropolitan Population in the United States

| DATE | PERCENTAGE OF TOTAL POPULATION | | PERCENTAGE OF TOTAL POPULATION | |
	Urban[a]	Rural[a]	Metropolitan[b]	Nonmetropolitan[b]
1790	5.1	94.9	—	—
1840	10.8	89.2	—	—
1900	39.6	60.4	31.7	68.3
1910	45.6	54.4	37.5	62.5
1920	51.2	48.8	43.7	56.3
1930	56.1	43.9	49.8	50.2
1940	56.5	43.5	51.1	48.9
1950	64.0	36.0	56.8	43.2
1960	69.9	30.1	63.0	37.0
1970	73.6	26.4	68.6	31.4
1980	73.7	26.3	74.8	25.2

[a]Revised definitions for 1950 and later. Using the older definitions, proportions for 1950 would have been: urban, 59.6 percent, rural, 40.4 percent.
[b]Data for 1900 through 1950 refer to the areas that would have qualified as SMAs at the given dates according to the 1950 definition, as estimated by Bogue. Data for 1960, 1970, and 1980 refer to SMSAs as defined at those census dates. "Nonmetropolitan" comprises all areas outside SMSAs
Sources: Donald J. Bogue, *Population Growth in Standard Metropolitan Areas, 1900–1950*, Housing and Home Finance Agency, December 1953; and U.S. Bureau of the Census, *Census of Population, 1960, 1970, and 1980.*

and 40 percent in 1900. Sometime between 1910 and 1920 the nation passed the historic milestone of a population half urban and half rural: by 1920, 51 percent of the population was urban. Indeed, the decade 1910–1920 was marked by an unusually high ratio of urban to rural growth. Economic mobilization for war attracted labor from the farms to the cities. The urban population grew 29 percent, while rural numbers rose only 3 percent.

Urban growth slowed drastically during the Great Depression, since there were now no job openings to attract migrants out of the countryside. However, the industrial mobilization accompanying the Second World War stimulated urbanization once again. By 1970, almost 74 percent of the U.S. population lived in urban areas. Since then, however, the urban proportion has not increased.

THE GROWTH AND DECENTRALIZATION OF METROPOLITAN AREAS

We turn next to the metropolitan areas themselves, to look both at the rise of total metropolitan population and at the profoundly important changes in spatial organization that have been taking place within metropolitan areas during the twentieth century. The history of metropolitan settlement in this century is best explained in terms of four trends: concentration and deconcentration, which refer to the ratio of metropolitan population to total U.S. population, and centralization and decentralization, which refer to the ratio of central city to ring area population *within* metropolitan areas. Let us briefly define these trends and see how they combined over time before investigating the powerful forces that lay behind them.

Concentration and Deconcentration

From the nineteenth century to the late 1960s, U.S. population was increasingly concentrated into metropolitan areas. Evidence for this is shown in Table 3.1. In 1900 areas outside SMAs contained 68 percent of our total population, while SMAs contained only 32 percent. By 1970 these figures had been almost exactly reversed: SMSAs accounted for 69 percent of the national population, nonmetropolitan areas for only 31 percent.

Increasing concentration necessarily occurs whenever the metropolitan population grows faster than the nonmetropolitan. As Table 3.2 shows, that

TABLE 3.2
Rate of Population Growth in Central Cities, Metropolitan Rings, and Nonmetropolitan Areas of the United States

DATE	NUMBER OF MSAs[a]	RATE OF GROWTH DURING PRECEDING DECADE (%)[a]			
		MSA Total	*Central Cities of MSAs*	*Ring Areas of MSAs*	*Nonmetropolitan Areas*
1910	71	32.6	35.3	27.6	15.0
1920	94	25.2	26.7	22.4	8.1
1930	115	27.0	23.3	34.2	7.1
1940	125	8.3	5.1	13.8	6.2
1950	162	21.8	13.9	34.7	6.0
1960	212	26.4	10.7	48.6	7.1
1970	243	16.6	6.4	26.8	6.8
1980	318	10.2	0.1	18.2	15.1
1984	328	4.5[b]	2.7[b]	5.9[b]	3.4[b]

[a]Data for 1910 through 1950 refer to the areas that would have qualified as SMAs at the given dates according to the 1950 definition, as estimated by Bogue. Data for 1960, 1970, and 1980 refer to SMSAs, central cities, and rings as defined at those census dates. Data for 1984 refer to MSAs and PMSAs as defined in October 1984.
[b]Percentage change 1980 to 1984.
Sources: Donald J. Bogue, *Population Growth in Standard Metropolitan Areas, 1900–1950*, Housing and Home Finance Agency, December 1953; U.S. Bureau of the Census, *Census of Population, 1960, 1970, and 1980*; and U.S. Bureau of the Census, *Current Population Reports*, series P-25, no. 976, October 1985, tables F and 8.

pattern prevailed from the earliest period for which we have estimates down to about 1970.

Quite unexpectedly, during the 1970s concentration was replaced by deconcentration: metropolitan population growth slowed considerably while growth in nonmetropolitan areas sharply increased. According to Table 3.2, the number of people living in nonmetropolitan areas actually grew faster than the metropolitan population between 1970 and 1980, which would indicate that deconcentration was taking place. Comparisons over time, however, involve problems of area definition. There are two sources of population growth for metropolitan areas between census dates. First, the population within a given set of metropolitan areas may grow over time. This is the kind of growth measured in Table 3.2. Each row in the table shows the growth during the preceding decade of the population living in metropolitan areas recognized for the census date given at the left. Thus in the decade from 1970 to 1980, the population of the 318 SMSAs enumerated in the 1980 census grew less rapidly than the population of nonmetropolitan areas as defined at the same date. This suggests deconcentration.

However, there is a second source of metropolitan growth. If the population of nonmetropolitan areas increases between two census dates, some may become sufficiently populous to be reclassified as metropolitan areas at the end of the period. Their population is then transferred in full to the metropolitan category and thus contributes to its growth. This explains why Table 3.1 shows the percentage of U.S. population living in SMSAs to have increased from 1970 to 1980, indicating continued concentration, even though Table 3.2 shows that metropolitan areas grew less rapidly than nonmetropolitan areas during that decade, which certainly suggests deconcentration. In the latter case, the number and size of SMSAs is held constant. In the former, it is not.

If we accept the proposition that areas should be held constant in measuring these trends, deconcentration did indeed occur during the 1970s. The powerful historic trend toward increased concentration, which had so long dominated our thinking about urban phenomena, apparently came to a halt.[7] But before analysts of urban events had quite recovered their bearings, the trend reversed again. After 1980, as the last line of Table 3.2 indicates, the population of metropolitan areas once more began to grow faster than the nonmetropolitan population. We will take a closer look at these trends later in this chapter.

Centralization and Decentralization

We define centralization as a rise in the proportion of metropolitan population living in central cities. It necessarily occurs whenever the population

7. See John F. Long, *Population Deconcentration in the United States*, Special Demographic Analyses CDS-81-5 (Washington, D.C.: U.S. Government Printing Office, November, 1981).

of central cities is rising faster than that of the suburban ring. Table 3.2 shows that this was, in fact, the case from the time of the earliest available data down to about 1920. In the 1920s suburban population began to grow faster than that of central cities: decentralization succeeded centralization. Table 3.2 shows that it has continued ever since.

At the opening of the century the central cities of the SMSAs were growing at a remarkable pace. Table 3.2 shows that from 1900 to 1910, their population rose 35 percent, while that of the ring areas of SMSAs grew 28 percent and the population outside SMSAs increased only 15 percent. In the next decade relatively the same pattern persisted. After 1920, however, a dramatic reversal occurred: in every decade since that date the population of ring areas has grown faster than that of the central cities, and the margin between the rates of growth has greatly increased. So far did the reversal of trend go that in the 1950s and 1960s many of the older central cities for the first time actually lost population, and in the 1970s, as Table 3.2 shows, central cities in the aggregate gained no population at all. Of the twenty-six cities that had a population of 500,000 or more in 1970, seventeen lost population in the next ten years. In some cases losses over the thirty years following 1950 reached truly staggering proportions: the population of St. Louis declined by 47 percent, that of Cleveland by 37 percent. Yet over the same period the suburban rings of those cities continued to grow rapidly.

While decentralization continued in the 1980s, the pace was decidedly slower, mainly because central-city population loss declined. For example, New York City, San Francisco, Oakland, and Boston moved from population decline in the 1970s to small or moderate gains in 1980–1984, while Atlanta and Chicago leveled off after heavy losses in the 1970s (see Table 3.3). Only ten of the twenty-six cities with population above 500,000 in 1970 continued to lose residents in 1980–1984, while four held approximately even and twelve gained.

Three Periods of Metropolitan Development

Combining the trends of concentration-deconcentration and centralization-decentralization as they overlap in time, we can divide the history of metropolitan development into three periods (dates are, of course, approximate). Period 1 (to 1920) featured increasing concentration and increasing centralization. Period 2 (1920 to 1970) saw increasing concentration and decreasing centralization. Period 3 (since 1970) is less easily characterized. Decentralization clearly continues, though its pace has slackened. As for concentration versus deconcentration, the aggregate growth rates of metropolitan and nonmetropolitan populations are now so nearly equal that the balance, at the aggregate level, can easily swing in either direction. But as we shall see, when metropolitan areas are disaggregated by age and region, several clear tendencies emerge. The current pattern of metropolitan development is complex, but it is not inexplicable.

Next let us examine the forces that lay behind the changing patterns of settlement just described.

THE IMPACT OF SUCCESSIVE REVOLUTIONS IN TRANSPORTATION TECHNOLOGY

Railroads

Behind the changing patterns of settlement revealed in Tables 3.1 and 3.2 lie the successive revolutions in transportation during the nineteenth and twentieth centuries. The Industrial Revolution began with water but soon switched to steam, and the cities of the nineteenth century grew up on a pattern influenced largely by the strengths and limitations of steam transport. As we pointed out in Chapter 2, the railroad revolutionized long-distance, intercity haulage, thus making possible great concentrations of urban population at favorable points on the rail network. These steam railroads did little to improve transportation within cities, however, since they were not efficient for short hauls that involved frequent starting and stopping of their ponderous equipment. Indeed, mass transit in the age of steam was accomplished mostly on foot, while harnessed animal power helped to move local freight. Limited to such ancient modes of intraurban transport, the "hoof-and-foot city," as Hans Blumenfeld has called it, could not extend over great distances. Factories crowded in close to the waterfront and the railroad lines, and workers' homes huddled as close as possible to the factories. Since distance within the city was costly to overcome, proximity was at a premium; close-in land was in great demand, brought high prices, and had to be used intensively. The nineteenth-century city therefore grew up at an extraordinarily high level of density.

Skyscrapers

In the second half of the century the introduction of the skyscraper made possible still greater intensity of land use. The skyscraper, in turn, was the product of two interdependent innovations, the passenger elevator and the iron-and-steel-frame method of building construction. The passenger elevator, a revolutionary means of urban transportation in the previously unexploited vertical dimension, was first perfected by Elisha Graves Otis, who personally demonstrated it at the Crystal Palace Exposition in New York in 1853. First use of the fully developed iron-and-steel frame in a tall building is credited to the architect William LeBaron Jenney in the famous ten-story "skyscraper" he completed for the Home Insurance Company of Chicago in 1885. Within a few years the steel frame largely replaced masonry construction; the race toward the modern skyscraper was under way.

Meanwhile, escape outward from the crowded center was reserved for those who could afford, if they wished, to commute to the city on steam railroads. Toward the end of the century commuters' suburbs grew up around the stations along the railroad lines leaving the principal cities. These suburbs were compact. Since local transportation was still by horse and buggy, commuters could not live far from the railroad station. Hence commuting towns were strung out like beads along the railroad lines that radiated from the city. By 1898 *Harper's Weekly* reported that more than 118,000 people arrived daily at New York City's Grand Central Terminal from Westchester and Connecticut alone.[8]

Streetcars and Subways

Between 1870 and 1900 the hoof-and-foot city was rapidly transformed into the city of the streetcar. In various ways rail transportation was adapted to serve urban needs. Horse-drawn streetcars had been in use since the middle of the nineteenth century. They were not fast enough or large enough, however, to influence urban size and form. Although the cable car was introduced in 1872, its construction was expensive, and it remained for the electric streetcar, first operated on a large scale in the late 1880s, to alter matters by radically extending the distances city dwellers could conveniently travel to their workplaces. By the first decade of the twentieth century a web of streetcar lines crisscrossed every major city and made it possible for residential neighborhoods to spread far out from the old centers. Sometimes the new neighborhoods were more spacious than the old; sometimes they repeated the old high densities. In either case, vast new areas became accessible for housing, and cities were able to grow to unprecedented size.

In the largest cities the age of the streetcar also became the age of the elevated train and the subway. New York City began to build elevated intraurban railroads in the 1870s and possessed an extensive network by 1890. Steam engines were used at first, but the lines were soon electrified. In 1900 the city began construction of its first subway, and service started in 1904. Boston had begun service on a small section of subway in the late 1890s.

The Transit-oriented Mononuclear City

Rapid transit by subway or elevated train extended the feasible journey to work or to shop and thus reinforced the effect of the streetcar in stimulating the growth of great cities. Even more than the streetcar lines, however, the rapid transit systems were laid out like the spokes of a wheel. They were intended to move people from outlying residential areas to a central business

8. Reported by John A. Kouwenhoven in *Columbia Historical Portrait of New York* (New York: Doubleday, 1953), p. 422.

and shopping district and back again to their homes. Such a system did little to improve communication between points in outlying areas. It was intended to serve a mononuclear city, and once in place it provided formidable economic support for the mononuclear structure. Only in the central business district could the large insurance companies, banks, and other office enterprises daily assemble the thousands of clerks and bookkeepers they required. Centrality was equally crucial to the large department stores. Located at the hub of the transport network, they could serve not only the downtown work force but the crowds of shoppers the system funneled toward them from all parts of the city.

During the years in which the streetcar and the subway were radically improving urban passenger transport, no similar improvement occurred in the transportation of goods. Within cities, freight was still moved by horse and wagon, often on unpaved streets. Consequently, as Alex Anas and Leon Moses point out, "the cost of moving goods inside cities . . . was high relative to the cost of moving people," and close-in locations therefore remained attractive for manufacturing.[9] By moving farther out (but still within the city) manufacturing firms could have reduced their costs of land and labor, but those savings would have been less than the increased expense of freight movement to and from outlying locations. Manufacturing, like other economic activity, therefore remained highly centralized in the early twentieth-century city.

Supported by the great transportation innovations of railroad, streetcar, subway, and elevator, central cities reached what might be called their demographic zenith in the early years of the twentieth century. Between 1900 and 1920 the population of central cities grew considerably faster than that of their ring areas and incomparably faster than the nation's nonmetropolitan population.

We have already indicated a change in the pattern when, after 1920, ring areas of SMSAs began to gain population faster than central cities. Before explaining this historic reversal from increasing centralization to increasing decentralization, we take up another important aspect of twentieth-century urban development, the rise of the new, automobile-oriented city.

CITY AGE, REGION, AND RATE OF GROWTH

The automobile came into widespread use in the United States beginning in the 1920s. Its advent had a profound effect on the form of urban development. Cities that achieved their major growth before the automobile era relied for movement on systems of mass transportation and developed to very

9. Alex Anas and Leon N. Moses, "Transportation and Land Use in the Mature Metropolis," in Charles L. Leven, ed., *The Mature Metropolis* (Lexington, Mass.: Heath, Lexington Books, 1978), pp. 150–151.

high densities: these are what we might call the "old" central cities. On the other hand, cities that grew rapidly after 1920 were laid out to be served by the automobile and truck and typically show a dispersed, low-density pattern: these we shall call the "new" cities. Since the old cities are primarily in the North and East and the new ones almost entirely in the South and West, there is a high degree of correlation between central city age and region, as well as between age and "urban structure," by which we mean the physical aspect of a city captured by such variables as population density and degree of reliance on mass transportation.

The association among these traits is illustrated in Figure 3.1. Age of central city is measured on the vertical axis and population per square mile in 1960 along the horizontal. The age of a city can be measured in a number of ways.[10] In this case we use as the age measure the percentage of its maximum population that a city had achieved by 1920. This enables us to distinguish the older cities, which enjoyed most of their growth before the era of the automobile, from the newer ones that developed primarily under the influence of rubber-tired transport. Plotted on the diagram are the age and density of the central cities of twelve SMSAs: the six largest (in 1980) in the North and East (marked by stars) and the six largest in the South and West (shown by circles). The SMSAs were selected on a regional basis in order to bring out the contrast—which we will have occasion to illustrate along many socioeconomic scales—between the older, more densely settled SMSAs of the former group and the newer, more spread out metropolitan areas of the latter.

Figure 3.1 clearly shows a high degree of association between age and density, as measured in 1960, and region. The cities of the North and East, in the upper right of the diagram, rank as far older and much denser than those of the South and West, which are clustered in the lower left corner. The only exception is San Francisco–Oakland, as old as some of the cities in the North and East and with correspondingly high density.

Age, density, and region are also associated with recent rate of population growth. Data on the present size and recent growth of population in the twelve metropolitan areas in Figure 3.1 are given in Table 3.3. From 1960 to 1970 the aggregate population of the new SMSAs of the South and West grew at more than twice the rate of the old areas of the North and East. Obviously, the new SMSAs were participating in the rapid regional growth of the Sun Belt in the South and West while the older ones were held back by the slower growth of the Frost Belt in the North and East. However, since age and region are so highly correlated, it is difficult in practice to separate their independent effects. Central cities of the six SMSAs in the South and West gained 16 percent in aggregate population between 1960 and 1970, while their counterparts in the North and East lost 2 percent. Ring areas grew rapidly in both regions, but more rapidly in the new SMSAs than the old.

---

10. See James Heilbrun, "Alternative Measures of Age of Settlement," *Northeast Regional Science Review*, vol. 5 (1975), pp. 248–260.

FIGURE 3.1

Relationship among Central City Age, Population Density, and Region[a]

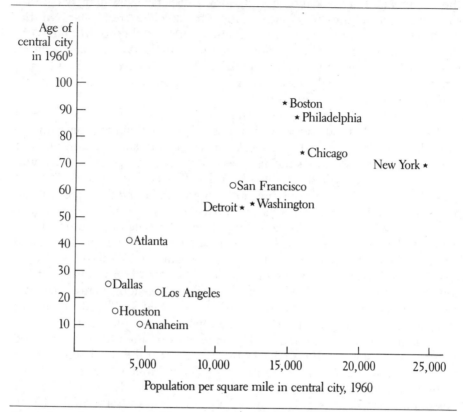

Age of central city in 1960[b]

Population per square mile in central city, 1960

[a]Data refer to the central cities of the twelve SMSAs in Table 3.3. Region is indicated as follows: ★ = Northeast and Midwest, ○ = South and West. Orange County was deducted from the Los Angeles–Long Beach SMSA data for 1960 because that county was subsequently recognized as the independent Anaheim–Santa Ana–Garden Grove SMSA.

[b]Age as of 1960 is measured as the percentage of a city's maximum population (up to 1960) that it had achieved by 1920, that is, age = $100 \times (1920$ population ÷ maximum population to 1960).

Source: U.S. Bureau of the Census, *Census of Population, 1960.*

Decentralization continued in the 1970s, accelerated by the increasing population losses of central cities. Table 3.3 shows that the six central cities in the North and East lost 12 percent of their aggregate population between 1970 and 1980. In the South and West the population of Atlanta, San Francisco, and Oakland declined and central cities of the six SMSAs in the aggregate gained only 7 percent. As the older central cities lose population, their population per square mile diminishes and they move leftward in a diagram such as Figure 3.1. As the newer central cities gain population, they move to the right. Thus the two groups are gradually converging along the density scale. It seems unlikely, however, that they will meet in the foreseeable future. The newer cities, built on the principle of automobile transportation, cannot develop to anything like the densities achieved in the older cities, with their mass transit framework. Indeed, some of the denser new cities of the South and West appear already to have reached or to be close to reaching their maximum population size.

DECENTRALIZATION: THE OVERFLOW EFFECT AND THE AUTOMOBILE EFFECT

Although many factors contributed to the decentralization of metropolitan areas that began around 1920, the most important are probably the overflow effect and the automobile effect. The overflow effect is easily described. If a central city with fixed boundaries enjoys continuous growth of numbers, vacant land will eventually be used up, and even though growth continues in the form of higher density, additional metropolitan population will tend increasingly to spill over into the suburbs. Before the outward-moving margin of continuous development reaches the central city boundaries, suburban ring development will be relatively slight, based on the growth of scattered suburbs and satellite cities. After the margin of development passes those boundaries, however, suburban population will rise at an incomparably faster pace than before and will certainly outstrip the growth rate of the central city.

The overflow effect implies that as central city density increases, the ratio of central city population growth to ring area growth will decline. But the overflow effect, by itself, cannot account for the central city population *losses* so prevalent in recent decades, nor can it explain why the ratio of ring to central city growth is so high in metropolitan areas with central city densities as low as those of Dallas–Fort Worth and Houston. Clearly, other forces have been at work as well, and the principal one is undoubtedly the automobile effect. With the automobile effect we come to the last of the revolutionary changes in transportation technology that have shaped the geographic pattern of metropolitan settlement.

Until the automobile and the truck came into widespread use, rail transport (including street railways) was the only rapid and efficient system of overland movement both for people and for goods. Rail transport, however, has important limitations. Obviously, service is restricted to points along the right-of-way. Yet the number of rights-of-way that can be operated economically is limited because high fixed costs impose a need for heavy traffic. Within cities, population density was sufficient to support a rather fine-grained network of streetcar lines, but a highly articulated network of commuter railroads, even around the largest cities, was never feasible. Instead the commuter was restricted to a few lines radiating from the central city. Suburban streetcar service, if it existed at all, was subject to the same sort of constraint at its own scale of operation. One could not profitably operate streetcar lines through thinly settled residential districts. Before the advent of the

TABLE 3.3
*Population Inside and Outside Central Cities of Major Metropolitan Areas,
1984[a]*

Six Largest Metropolitan Areas in North and East[b]	POPULATION IN 1984	CHANGE (%)		
		1980– 1984	*1970– 1980*	*1960– 1970*
New York, N.Y.–N.J.	9,221,200	1.1	− 8.6	4.6
New York City	7,164,700	1.3	− 10.4	1.5
Outside central city	2,056,500	0.4	− 1.4	18.2
Chicago, Ill.	7,215,900	1.6	1.8	12.1
Chicago city	2,992,500	− 0.4	− 10.8	− 5.1
Outside central city	4,223,400	3.0	13.7	35.0
Philadelphia, Pa–N.J.	4,768,400	1.1	− 2.2	11.1
Philadelphia city	1,646,700	− 2.5	− 13.4	− 2.6
Outside central city	3,121,700	3.1	5.4	22.8
Detroit, Mich.	4,184,800	− 3.9	− 1.8	12.3
Detroit city	1,089,000	− 9.5	− 20.5	− 9.3
Outside central city	3,095,800	− 1.7	7.8	28.1
Boston-Lowell-Brockton-Lawrence-Haverhill, Mass.	3,695,300	0.9	− 1.3	10.5
Inside central cities	872,700	1.4	− 8.2	− 4.3
Outside central cities	2,822,600	0.7	1.1	16.6
Washington, D.C.–Md.–Va.	3,219,000	5.2	5.2	37.1
Washington city (D.C.)	622,800	− 2.4	− 15.6	− 1.0
Outside central city	2,596,200	7.2	12.5	58.5
Aggregate of six SMSAs in North and East	32,304,600	0.9	− 2.5	11.2
Inside central cities	14,388,400	− 0.9	− 11.9	− 1.9
Outside central cities	17,916,200	2.1	7.0	28.3
Los Angeles–Long Beach, Calif.	7,901,200	5.7	6.2	16.6
Inside central cities	3,475,500	4.4	5.0	12.3
Outside central cities	4,425,700	6.7	7.1	20.4
San Francisco–Oakland, Calif.	3,413,300	5.0	4.6	17.4
Inside central cities	1,064,700	4.6	− 5.5	− 2.8
Outside central cities	2,348,600	5.2	9.9	31.8
Dallas–Fort Worth, Tex.	3,403,300	14.4	25.1	36.8
Inside central cities	1,388,800	7.7	4.2	19.5
Outside central cities	2,014,500	19.5	47.9	62.4
Houston, Tex.	3,350,300	15.4	45.3	39.8
Houston city	1,705,700	6.9	29.3	31.5
Outside central city	1,644,600	25.6	71.0	55.6

TABLE 3.3
(cont'd)

Six Largest Metropolitan Areas in South and West[c]	POPULATION IN 1984	CHANGE (%)		
		1980–1984	1970–1980	1960–1970
Atlanta, Ga.	2,262,100	11.5	27.2	36.5
Atlanta city	426,100	0.3	– 14.1	1.6
Outside central city	1,836,000	14.4	45.8	61.5
Anaheim–Santa Ana– Garden Grove, Calif.	2,075,800	7.4	36.0	101.9
Inside central cities	588,166	7.7	23.2	53.5
Outside central cities	1,487,634	7.3	41.8	135.6
Aggregate of six SMSAs in South and West	22,406,000	8.9	17.2	27.8
Inside central cities	8,648,966	5.4	7.1	15.8
Outside central cities	13,757,034	11.3	25.1	39.1

[a]For each metropolitan area except Boston, SMSA boundaries as defined for the 1980 census were carried forward to 1984 and backward to 1960. Thus SMSA boundaries are held constant. However, central city boundaries (and therefore outside central city boundaries) in some cases changed due to annexation. All data for Boston refer to the Boston New England County Metropolitan Area, as defined for the 1982 economic census, to maintain comparability with Table 3.4
[b]Corresponds to Northeast and Midwest census regions plus Maryland and Washington, D.C.
[c]Corresponds to South and West census regions less Maryland and Washington, D.C.
Sources: U.S. Bureau of the Census, *Census of Population, 1980* and *Current Population Reports*, series P–25, no. 976, October 1985.

automobile commuters therefore had to live near the railroad stations. Vast areas between the radiating spokes of the railroad system, if they were outside the range of the central city streetcar or subway lines, were too inaccessible for suburban settlement.

Industrial and commercial activities were similarly restricted in their choice of location. Manufacturing plants could and did locate outside the central cities along existing railroad lines. Indeed, many satellite cities thrived and grew on such an economic base during the nineteenth century. But even the lightest of industries could not move away from the railroad lines on which they depended for the movement of goods. Nor could they have assembled a daily work force at any suburban point outside the satellite towns.

Large clerical enterprises were even more restricted. Nowhere but at the hub of the central city could they find a labor supply large enough for their needs. Retailing, too, was centralized. Highly specialized stores of all sorts could find enough customers only in the central city, and often only in its central business district. Department stores grew up in satellite towns as well as in central cities, but the suburban "shopping center" in open country was not yet even an inspired land developer's dream.

Thus because rail transport could best serve a centralized metropolis, metropolitan areas grew up centralized. Indeed, centralization was a self-reinforcing process: the greater the concentration of employment in the central business district, the more it thrived as a center for specialized retail and business services; the more it developed such services, the greater its attraction as a place of business and employment. Congestion could act as an automatic brake on centralization, but, contrary to our fantasies about the ultimate traffic jam, congestion limits but does not reverse concentration at the center.

Only a radical improvement in our ability to overcome what Haig called the "friction of space" could break up this historic drive toward centralization. The automobile and the truck provided that improvement by freeing people from the need to live and work close to the fixed lines of the railroad, the subway, and the streetcar. Beginning about 1920 a vast loosening up took place within the metropolis, and as it proceeded, the self-reinforcing tide of centralization halted and was succeeded by an equally powerful process of decentralization.

What followed has sometimes been called the "suburbanization" of metropolitan America. That term may be misleading, however, if it connotes simply the rise of commuting suburbs, for the process of decentralization has involved jobs as much as residences.

DECENTRALIZATION OF JOBS

Job decentralization within metropolitan areas need not mean that firms close up shop within the central city, pack their movables into vans, and unload at new sites in the suburbs. Such moves can and do take place. But decentralization occurs also as a result of differential rates of expansion of existing firms and differential rates of formation of new establishments as between areas. In fact, these sources of decentralization cannot be disentangled except through painstaking case-by-case study of individual firms in each area.

We know, however, that the development of trucking made it possible for many firms to cut their ties to railroads and ports. Simultaneously, the widespread ownership of automobiles enabled them to break away from mass transit–oriented urban labor markets. The need for more ground space often provided the impetus either to move old plants or, when expansion was desirable, to establish new ones at suburban locations. To take advantage of assembly-line techniques and modern methods of materials handling such as the fork-lift truck, manufacturers and distributors needed extended single-story plants rather than the traditional multistory mills of the nineteenth century. Space to build such plants was far too expensive in the old urban locations but was readily available in the ring areas of the metropolis. Hence many firms, whose face-to-face contact requirements with other industries in the central city were not overriding, either moved to the suburbs or opened new plants there. They acquired space without sacrificing effective proximity to either their suppliers or their customers in the metropolitan market.[11]

In an economy built on specialization and interdependence, one new job at a particular place gives rise to others. As the manufacturers, distributors, and research laboratories moved out into the suburban rings, suburban employment in complementary service trades increased, too. The rise in job opportunities, of course, attracted population, and the increased population in turn enlarged the market for consumer services, creating still further job opportunities. In short, suburban areas were launched on a continuous round of self-reinforcing economic and demographic growth.

The decentralization of manufacturing within metropolitan areas was well under way before World War II.[12] Table 3.4 takes up the story in 1948 and charts the outward movement of manufacturing, retail, wholesale, and selected service employment that took place from that date until 1982 in the twelve major SMSAs already described. In both the older and the newer groups, every category of activity shows marked decentralization, as indicated by the rise in the ring share and the fall in the central city share of the industry total.

It is interesting to note that in all four categories the older metropolitan areas were more centralized in 1948 than were the newer areas. This is just what we would have expected, since the newer areas tended to develop during the age of the automobile, while the older areas were products of the railroad age. For the same reason, we would expect the older areas to decentralize more rapidly than the newer ones: they had, so to speak, more adapting to do under the pressure of technological change. Table 3.4 shows that this was indeed the case. From 1948 to 1967 the central city share of aggregate employment fell 17 points in the older SMSAs, while it declined only 14 points in the newer ones. Somewhat startling, however, has been the continued rapid decentralization of jobs in the older SMSAs since 1967. The central city job share fell an additional 17 points in the fifteen years after that date.

The decentralization of jobs is associated, of course, with the decentralization of population already depicted in Table 3.3, but in the older metropolitan areas the former has proceeded much faster than the latter. This can be verified by comparing the central cities' share of jobs (ninth row of each half of Table 3.4) with their share of population (eleventh row). As late as 1967 the older central cities' share of jobs exceeded their share of population by 10 points. By 1982 their share of jobs had fallen slightly below their share of population.

---

11. For a description of how this process worked itself out in New York City, see Edgar M. Hoover and Raymond Vernon, *Anatomy of a Metropolis* (Cambridge, Mass.: Harvard University Press, 1959), ch. 2.
12. Evelyn M. Kitigawa and Donald J. Bogue, *Suburbanization of Manufacturing Activity within Standard Metropolitan Areas* (Oxford, Ohio: Scripps Foundation, 1955), table II-3, p. 22.

TABLE 3.4
Decentralization of Jobs and Population in Major Metropolitan Areas

Six Largest SMSAs in North and East[a]	CHANGE IN JOBS[b] (%)		DISTRIBUTION OF JOBS BETWEEN CENTRAL CITIES AND RING AREAS (%)		
	1948–1967	1967–1982	1948	1967	1982
Manufacturing[c]					
Central city	−16.1	−44.7	72	55	41
Outside central city	73.7	−2.4	28	45	59
Retail					
Central city	−14.1	−24.2	77	55	36
Outside central city	133.3	64.0	23	45	64
Wholesale					
Central city	−5.4	−34.9	92	71	45
Outside central city	353.9	89.1	8	29	55
Selected services					
Central city	33.6	55.9	87	74	52
Outside central city	216.3	306.8	13	26	48
Total, four industries					
Central city	−8.7	−22.6	77	60	43
Outside central city	106.1	49.1	23	40	57

	CHANGE IN POPULATION (%)		DISTRIBUTION OF POPULATION (%)		
	1950–1970	1970–1984	1950	1970	1984
Population					
Central city	−5.2	−12.4	67	50	45
Outside central city	94.0	9.2	33	50	55

Six Largest SMSAs in South and West[a]	CHANGE IN JOBS[b] (%)		DISTRIBUTION OF JOBS BETWEEN CENTRAL CITIES AND RING AREAS (%)		
	1948–1967	1967–1982	1948	1967	1982
Manufacturing[c]					
Central city	67.6	13.9	61	48	45
Outside central city	179.3	27.8	39	52	55
Retail					
Central city	31.3	35.2	71	55	44
Outside central city	157.6	114.9	29	45	56
Wholesale					
Central city	31.4	28.9	87	55	46
Ouside central city	377.4	189.5	13	35	54
Selected services					
Central city	142.9	162.9	77	68	56
Outside central city	297.0	336.0	23	32	44
Total, four industries					
Central city	58.8	47.9	69	55	48
Outside central city	193.2	96.1	31	45	52

TABLE 3.4
(*cont'd*)

	CHANGE IN POPULATION (%)		DISTRIBUTION OF POPULATION (%)		
	1950–1970	*1970–1984*	*1950*	*1970*	*1984*
Population					
Central city	50.7	13.0	53	44	39
Outside central city	122.2	39.1	47	56	61

aAs defined in Table 3.3.
bSMSA boundaries are held constant as described in Table 3.3. No adjustment is made, however, for annexation of territory by central cities, which in some cases took a substantial number of jobs from ring areas between 1948 and 1982.
cManufacturing data are for 1947 rather than 1948.
Sources: U.S. Bureau of the Census, *Economic Censuses* and *Census of Population*, various dates. Population data for 1984 are from Table 3.3.

Job Losses in Older Central Cities

In the North and East, decentralization has involved an actual decline in the number of jobs in central cities. As Table 3.4 shows, only the service sector has registered an absolute increase since 1948, and that was insufficient to offset losses in the other three categories. In the suburbs of the same metropolitan areas, the number of jobs increased in all categories from 1948 to 1967 but declined slightly in manufacturing thereafter. (The weakness of manufacturing employment in metropolitan areas of the North and East is the result of two underlying structural changes in the U.S. economy: first, the relative decline in the manufacturing sector in the economy as a whole, and second, the movement of manufacturing jobs out of the Frost Belt and into the Sun Belt.)[13] In the metropolitan areas of the South and West, despite decentralization, the number of jobs in central cities rose in all categories, though least rapidly in manufacturing and most sharply in the service sector.

Generalizations about services can be misleading because the category comprises many distinct activities with correspondingly different locational tendencies. Consumer services behave like retailing and tend to follow the movement of population, while services for business respond to a more complex set of forces.[14] (See discussion in Chapters 2 and 4.) Business services are probably the industrial category now most strongly subject to economies of agglomeration. In recent years, among the older cities, those that are impor-

13. See Harry W. Richardson, "'Basic' Economic Activities in Metropolis," in Leven, *The Mature Metropolis*, pp. 254–267.
14. Even the classification into business and consumer services is too simple. For elaboration, see discussion in Harvey S. Perloff, "The Central City in the Postindustrial Age," ch. 6 in Leven, *The Mature Metropolis*, and in Thierry J. Noyelle and Thomas M. Stanback, Jr., *The Economic Transformation of American Cities* (Totowa, N.J.: Rowman & Allanheld, 1984), pp. 7–10.

tant centers for supplying business services, like New York and Boston, have fared relatively better than those that are heavily devoted to manufacturing, like Detroit, Cleveland, and St. Louis. But the tendency of business services to agglomerate in central cities is always subject to change through innovation in the technology of communication. As Table 3.4 indicates, many kinds of service activity already thrive in the suburbs. It remains an open question whether, or to what extent, central cities will continue to have a special attraction for high-level business services.[15]

As later chapters will demonstrate, job loss in the older cities of the North and East had important consequences in many areas of public policy. For example, in Chapter 11 we will show that the decline in the ratio of jobs to population in the central cities is associated with a rise in the rate of unemployment, the rate of nonparticipation in the labor force, and the rate of poverty, especially for minorities. Thus rapid job decentralization has aggravated, if it did not cause, severe social problems in the central cities. At the same time, because tax revenues fall when the number of local jobs declines, job loss weakens the power of the central cities to support policies intended to relieve those problems.

Work Trip Patterns and Changes in Urban Structure

Influenced by recollections of an earlier period, some residents of the older central cities are inclined to think of *suburbanite* and *commuter* as interchangeable terms. Table 3.4 indicates that such an interpretation has long been out of date. The last four rows in each half of the table show that jobs in the aggregate have been decentralizing even faster than population. It necessarily follows that as the suburbs have grown, the proportion of suburbanites who also work in the suburbs has steadily increased, while the proportion who commute to the central city has diminished. This conclusion is supported by the data in Table 3.5, which examines 1970 and 1980 commuting patterns in three old and three new MSAs. Without exception, the proportion of ring area residents working in the ring increased, while the proportion working in the central city fell. By 1980 those holding jobs in the suburbs outnumbered commuters to the central city by a ratio that varied between 2 to 1 and better than 4 to 1. However, since ring area population rose substantially, the *absolute* number of commuters to the central city (data not shown in table) was roughly stable during the period examined, as it had also been during the 1960s.[16]

Table 3.5 also shows that as jobs decentralized from 1970 to 1980, the proportion of central city residents working in the ring area increased. However, since central city population in most cases was falling, the *absolute* num-

15. See sources cited in Chapter 4, n. 17.
16. For commuting patterns during the 1960s see Anas and Moses, table 8.1.

TABLE 3.5
Commuting Patterns in Six Metropolitan Areas, 1970 and 1980

	LIVED IN CENTRAL CITY (%)		LIVED IN RING AREA (%)	
METROPOLITAN AREA	1970	1980	1970	1980
Chicago	100.0	100.0	100.0	100.0
Worked in central city	81.5	81.1	25.7	22.1
CBD	11.0	14.8	5.7	6.8
Other	70.5	66.3	20.0	15.3
Worked in ring area	17.0	18.3	71.6	76.0
Worked outside SMSA	1.4	0.7	2.7	1.9
Philadelphia	100.0	100.0	100.0	100.0
Worked in central city	85.2	85.2	20.6	17.0
CBD	10.3	18.6	4.1	5.4
Other	74.9	66.6	16.5	11.6
Worked in ring area	12.3	13.5	71.5	75.7
Worked outside SMSA	2.5	1.3	7.9	7.3
Cleveland	100.0	100.0	100.0	100.0
Worked in central city	74.4	70.2	41.4	33.4
CBD	10.6	15.9	8.2	10.2
Other	63.8	54.3	33.2	23.2
Worked in ring area	24.2	28.2	54.2	62.6
Worked outside SMSA	1.4	1.6	4.4	4.0
Los Angeles–Long Beach	100.0	100.0	100.0	100.0
Worked in central city	72.4	70.8	30.4	28.1
CBD	5.7	5.3	3.5	3.6
Other	66.7	65.5	26.9	24.5
Worked in ring area	25.4	26.7	65.8	66.5
Worked outside SMSA	2.2	2.4	3.9	5.4
San Francisco–Oakland	100.0	100.0	100.0	100.0
Worked in central city	84.3	82.2	28.1	25.7
CBD	24.2	25.0	8.6	8.8
Other	60.1	57.2	19.5	16.9
Worked in ring area	13.8	15.8	66.4	66.9
Worked outside SMSA	1.9	2.0	5.6	7.4
Phoenix	100.0	100.0	100.0	100.0
Worked in central city	83.9	82.5	34.0	33.1
CBD	7.6	12.7	2.9	5.3
Other	76.3	69.8	31.1	27.8
Worked in ring area	14.6	16.5	63.5	65.0
Worked outside SMSA	1.5	1.0	2.4	1.9

Note: Percentages may not add to 100 due to rounding.
Sources: U.S. Bureau of the Census, *Census of Population*, 1970 and 1980.

ber of these "reverse commuters" sometimes decreased. Finally, the table allows us to measure the changing importance of the central business district relative to the rest of the central city. It shows that in every case except Los Angeles–Long Beach the proportion of workers holding jobs in the CBD rose while the proportion employed in the remainder of the central city fell. Undoubtedly, this reflects the relative rise of service employment, which is strongly oriented to the CBD, and the declining importance of manufacturing jobs, usually located farther out in the central city.

We see, then, that as jobs and residences have dispersed in the pattern we have called decentralization, the web of work trips has become increasingly complex and certainly less and less focused on the inner city. We shall explore the implications of decentralization for urban transportation policy in Chapter 9.

DECENTRALIZATION OF POPULATION

We have yet to examine in detail the forces that led to the decentralization of metropolitan population in the twentieth century. Obviously, this movement has depended on some of the same technological forces—especially the automobile effect—that led to the decentralization of jobs. Nevertheless, the change in residential patterns also depended on other factors and is important enough to warrant separate analysis.

For the resident of the metropolis, the automobile made possible a home in the previously inaccessible areas between the spokes of the railroad lines radiating from the central city. The commuting towns, which had once appeared as compact beads strung out along the railroad lines, began to spread out. Wholly new residential settlements were built in what had been rural areas, miles from the nearest railroad station. By the 1980s open space in the suburban rings around major cities had all but disappeared.

Evidence of the Automobile Effect

Population statistics dramatically illustrate the abrupt change in pattern that occurred in the age of the automobile. In every decade up to 1930, urban places in the ring—the satellite cities and the compact, rail-oriented commuter towns—had gained population far faster than had the rural ring areas. Even during the 1920s, when automobiles were coming into widespread use, the rates of growth were 48 percent for urban ring places and only 19 percent for rural ring areas. But with the decade of the 1930s the relationship suddenly reversed. Thereafter, rural parts of the ring gained residents far faster than urban ring places. It is important to note that the change in pattern from faster ring-urban to faster ring-rural growth took place at the same date in all size classes of metropolitan area (except the very smallest).[17] This coincidence in time reinforces the belief that the change relates to the nationwide impact of the automobile on patterns of settlement rather than to factors associated with the size or stage of development of individual metropolitan areas.

Influence of Rising Living Standards and Changes in Consumer Preferences

The advent of the automobile and the truck was a necessary condition for the rise of suburbia in its present low-density pattern. Even in conjunction with the overflow effect, however, it was not a sufficient force to produce the degree of suburbanization we find in metropolitan America today. Rising living standards are another factor that deserves mention. In the technical language of economics, living space is a "superior good"—that is to say, a good people want more of as their incomes rise. To be sure, they can obtain more space by moving into larger quarters in the city. But there is reason to believe that many who lived in the city while they were poor will choose more space in the suburbs rather than more space in the city as they grow wealthier. That reason lies in the peculiarly fixed nature of commuting costs. A poor family might just possibly find inexpensive housing in the suburbs. But for any given location, commuting costs are fixed: it will cost a poor person as much to ride a train from Tarrytown to New York City as it costs any of the Rockefellers. A low-income family will find that cost simply prohibitive. As income rises, however, the barrier of fixed commuting costs looms less and less large, and eventually the family surmounts it. Thus many who chose the city when they were poor will be found to choose the suburbs as their income rises, just as many who drove used cars when they were poor will buy new cars when their fortunes improve. It is their income, not their taste, that changes. The steady rise of living standards generates a flow of migration from city to suburb quite independently of any change in consumer tastes or in the cost of satisfying them. (The effect of higher income on locational choice is a complex matter that is dealt with at greater length in Chapter 6. See Figure 6.6 and the related text.)

Yet consumer preferences, or tastes, do change as well. Images of the good life are difficult (before the age of the sociological questionnaire one might have said impossible) to measure and quantify. It does seem likely, however, that the suburban lifestyle—informal, fecund, child-centered—exercised a more powerful appeal after the end of the Second World War than it had before the war, even for those who could then have afforded it. If this change in the underlying preferences of the population did indeed occur,

17. Donald J. Bogue, *Population Growth in Standard Metropolitan Areas, 1900–1950,* Housing and Home Finance Agency, December 1953, tables 1 and 16.

it simply worked to reinforce a process of suburbanization that would have occurred in any case without it.

Quite clearly, the pendulum has now swung in the other direction. The sharp drop in the birth rate, the increase in the number of two-worker households, the rise of the new feminism, the increasing questioning of the desirability of the traditional nuclear family, all suggest that at least some Americans are now moving away from the values that have hitherto been the foundation of suburban life. A rapidly growing segment of the population is a new class of young adults, including a fast-increasing number of working women, who are either unmarried or, if married, do not intend to raise large families. These men and women are more likely to be attracted to the inner city than were the generation that produced the postwar baby boom, and when they share two incomes they can often afford to live in convenient downtown neighborhoods. It is not clear that they will be numerous enough to halt the recent population declines of our older central cities, but they are already having an impact on inner city housing markets.[18] We will take a closer look at this new wave of urban settlers in Chapter 16.

Influence of Public Policy

The growth of the suburbs has, in the main, been a natural consequence of changes in technology and rising living standards. However, we should not overlook the fact that public policy has been an indirect influence. It has stimulated suburban as opposed to central city development by favoring home ownership, typical of suburban living, over home rental, which is largely a city phenonmenon. This bias is manifold and coincides in time with the impact of the automobile.

First of all, the federal income tax, which was introduced in 1913 and reached the mass of Americans beginning with the Second World War, treats homeowners more favorably than home renters. Suppose that a woman, now living in a rented house, inherits some capital. On the one hand, she can invest the inheritance in stocks and continue to live in a rented house. In that case the investment earns dividends on which she must pay income tax. On the other hand, if she invests the inheritance in a house and occupies it herself, she pays no rent, and the investment yields no taxable income under U.S. law. An economically neutral tax system would add to the income of the owner-occupant an estimate of the gross rental value of the house and allow her to deduct interest, property taxes, maintenance, and depreciation as expenses of earning that income. The difference between these amounts is the imputed net income the owner could have earned had she leased the house

18. For a wide-ranging examination of the probable effects of the declining birth rate and changing household arrangements on urban phenomena, see William Alonso, "The Population Factor and Urban Structure," in Arthur P. Solomon, ed., *The Prospective City* (Cambridge, Mass.: M.I.T. Press, 1980), pp. 32–51.

to someone else at the going market price instead of occupying it herself. U.S. tax law favors homeowners twice over. It does not tax them on the imputed net rental value of their homes, yet it does allow them to deduct the interest and property-tax costs of producing that income. Because taxable income is being understated, the tax saving is greater the higher the homeowner's marginal tax bracket.[19] Consequently, U.S. tax law not only favors home ownership, it stimulates home ownership by the rich more than by the poor and therefore encourages the segregation of the rich in the suburbs and the poor in the central cities.

The notion that the imputed rental value of housing ought to be counted as income is not, incidentally, as farfetched as it may appear to the reader whose concept of income is based on conventional rather than logically consistent reasoning: the Department of Commerce, in measuring national income and gross national product, has always included an estimate of imputed annual home rental in the grand aggregate.

A second source of bias in public policy is the long-standing federal policy of intervening in the mortgage market to encourage home ownership. Since the Great Depression this intervention has taken many forms, of which the most important was and is the Federal Housing Administration's program of home mortgage insurance. The FHA has been startlingly successful in achieving its purpose of reducing both the down payments and the monthly carrying costs on new owner-occupied housing, and that is all to the good. But for many years its program was administered so as to favor ownership in new suburban areas, and it failed to develop equally powerful institutional supports for the construction of new urban rental housing. By and large the FHA, from the inception of its mortgage insurance program, underwrote the advertising copywriter's version of the good American life as requiring a Cape Cod cottage, surrounded by a hedge and a well-cropped lawn and filled with new home appliances. Since the Second World War, policies to aid urban as well as suburban housing have gradually gained momentum. But for about twenty-five years—say, from the early 1930s until the late 1950s—the net effect of federal intervention was surely to hasten the flight to the suburbs.

To summarize briefly, we have now cited five forces that contributed to the rapid growth of suburban relative to central city population during the twentieth century: the overflow effect, the effects of technological innovations, the rise in living standards, a probable change in consumer preferences among lifestyles, and the effects of biases in public policy. Each of these can be thought of as a separate force that would have acted even in the absence of the others. Acting together, they provided a remarkably powerful stimulus for change. (In Chapter 6 we will reexamine the first three in the tighter theoretical framework of an urban land-use model.)

19. For detailed estimates, see Henry J. Aaron, *Shelter and Subsidies* (Washington, D.C.: Brookings Institution, 1972), ch. 4. Aaron also examines depreciation provisions under the income tax that favor rental rather than owner-occupied housing.

MIGRATION AND METROPOLITAN GROWTH

Where did the people come from who filled the cities and suburbs of twentieth-century America? There are only two possible sources of local population growth: natural increase, which occurs when local births exceed local deaths, and migration from other places. Until recently, the rate of natural increase was probably higher outside than inside metropolitan areas. Hence, in the absence of migration, nonmetropolitan population would have grown faster. Since, on the contrary, metropolitan population increased more rapidly than nonmetropolitan, we know that migration from nonmetropolitan areas and/or from overseas into SMSAs has long been taking place. (This abstracts from the relatively minor complication that nonmetropolitan places, after sufficient growth, are reclassified as metropolitan for statistical purposes.)

Published data on migration usually refer to the "net" flow, that is, to the difference between the number of people who moved into an area and the number who moved out during a given period. *Rates* of net migration are calculated as the flow during a given period divided by the population of the area at the period's starting date.

As we pointed out earlier, foreign immigrants into the United States have always moved disproportionately to urban destinations. Immigration from abroad was therefore a major source of urban growth down to the mid-1920s. Then restrictive quotas, and later the Great Depression, sharply reduced the inflow. Since 1950 it has gained in significance once again. More important, however, in explaining urban and metropolitan development is the internal migration that has probably been going on at least since the early nineteenth century. According to Fred Shannon, farmers' sons who moved to the city outnumbered those who became owners of new farms by ten to one.[20] Although aggregate earlier data are unavailable, figures for 1920 through 1954 show that during those thirty-five years the *net* migration from farms to urban areas totaled 24 million. For the sake of comparison, the *net* migration of aliens into the United States during the twenty-four years 1907 through 1930, while immigration was still at a relatively high level, amounted to only 8.4 million.[21]

The farm sector in the United States is now so small that it can no longer be a significant source of population for the rest of the country. The reader should bear in mind that the nonmetropolitan population today is not principally a farm population. Rather, it consists of people living in small cit-

20. Fred A. Shannon, "A Post-mortem on the Labor-Safety-Valve Theory," *Agricultural History*, vol. 19 (1945), pp. 31–37, cited in Conrad Taeuber and Irene B. Taeuber, *The Changing Population of the United States* (New York: Wiley, for the Social Science Research Council and the U.S. Bureau of the Census, 1958), p. 106.
21. Taeuber and Taeuber, pp. 54 and 107.

ies and towns outside the boundaries of metropolitan areas or in rural districts accessible to nonfarm employment in such towns and cities.

Net migration into metropolitan areas held at a very high level during the 1940s and 1950s. It reached a peak of 8.1 million during the latter decade, when there was a net inflow of 5.5 million migrants from nonmetropolitan areas and almost 3 million from abroad. In-migration to metropolitan areas slowed considerably during the 1960s, but the decline received relatively little attention at the time, which made the transition to deconcentration in the 1970s seem more abrupt than it actually was.

Patterns of Migration by Race

Nonwhites accounted for a substantial portion of the net movement to metropolitan areas between 1940 and 1970. This flow consisted principally of blacks leaving the nonmetropolitan South as mechanization displaced labor in southern agriculture. Most of the black migration into MSAs until 1970 was destined for central cities. This inflow was offset or more than offset by heavy out-migration of whites from central cities to suburbs. The suburbs also received substantial white in-migration from nonmetropolitan areas. Largely as a result of these flows, the black proportion of central city population increased rapidly, while the suburbs remained very nearly all white. Since blacks moving into central cities often had lower incomes, whereas whites moving to the suburbs were mostly from the middle class, racial change had substantial economic consequences for central cities. (Race, migration, and urban poverty will be discussed in greater detail in Chapter 10.)

Deconcentration in the 1970s, Reconcentration in the 1980s

Students of urbanism had become so accustomed to the long-established trend of concentration into metropolitan areas that it came as something of a shock when, in the early 1970s, annual population estimates by the Census Bureau indicated a change of direction: the nonmetropolitan areas of the United States began growing faster than the MSAs. Final figures for the 1970s (shown in Table 3.2) revealed that the nonmetropolitan population rose 15.1 percent, well above the 10.2 percent gain for metropolitan areas.

There were some dramatic changes. Until 1970 it was almost unheard of for a major metropolitan area to lose population. Only one of the twenty-four SMSAs whose population exceeded one million in 1960 failed to grow in the following decade, and that one—the Pittsburgh SMSA—lost only trivial numbers. On the other hand, ten of the thirty-four metropolitan areas whose population exceeded one million in 1970 registered losses by 1980, certainly a dramatic increase.

Equally surprising was a reversal in the direction of net migratory flow. Except perhaps during periods of severe depression, the direction of flow had always been from rural and nonmetropolitan America to the cities and metropolitan areas. Yet this historic trend reversed after 1970. As Table 3.6 shows, from 1970 to 1980 the net movement was strongly in the other direction.[22] For the first time on record, U.S. metropolitan areas had become a source of population growth for the rest of the country. (Daniel R. Vining and Thomas Kontuly have shown that in many of the more developed countries, internal migration into the principal or "core" metropolitan area either fell sharply or reversed from positive to negative in the late 1960s and early 1970s. Their study does not suggest, however, that migration to metropolitan areas in the aggregate had turned negative.)[23]

Did changes in individual locational choices made by households in the United States during the 1970s indicate that Americans were beginning to turn away from the metropolitan way of life? Were we witnessing, if not a back-to-the-soil movement, at least a new preference for small towns and cities? Some observers thought so, but even as economists, sociologists, and demographers searched for answers, the situation changed once more. Table 3.2 tells the story of these reversals in the simplest possible terms. From 1920 to 1970 population growth in nonmetropolitan areas had been remarkably stable at 6 to 7 percent per decade, well below the level for metropolitan areas. Suddenly in the 1970s it doubled to 15 percent, which put it moderately above the metropolitan area growth rate: the balance thus shifted from concentration to deconcentration. In the early 1980s metropolitan areas continued to grow at about the same pace registered in the previous decade, but population increase in nonmetropolitan America slowed down, though not quite to its pre-1970 rate: hence the balance shifted back from deconcentration to concentration. The shift is confirmed in Table 3.6, which shows that after 1980 the net flow of internal migration was again from nonmetropolitan to metropolitan areas.

A full economic explanation of these puzzling reversals has yet to be worked out. Most analysts, however, include the following factors while also recognizing that by themselves these do not provide a complete account of what has been going on.

1. *Dispersion of manufacturing away from large centers.* Beginning in the 1960s and continuing into the 1970s, manufacturing industry grew faster in nonmetropolitan than in metropolitan areas. Firms were typically choosing sites in small nonmetropolitan cities where wages were lower and union pressures less intense than in large MSAs. The completion of the federal inter-

---

22. The data in Table 3.6 are based on questions in the *Current Population Survey* in which respondents are asked where they live now and where they lived at an earlier date.

23. Daniel R. Vining, Jr., and Thomas Kontuly, "Population Dispersal from Major Metropolitan Regions: An International Comparison," *International Regional Science Review*, Fall 1978, pp. 49–73.

TABLE 3.6
Net Migration for Metropolitan Areas, Central Cities, and Suburbs[a]

	METROPOLITAN AREAS	CENTRAL CITIES	SUBURBS
1970–1975	– 1,594,000	– 7,018,000	5,423,000
1975–1980	– 1,344,000	– 6,346,000	5,001,000
1980–1981	– 194,000[b]	– 2,236,000	2,042,000
1981–1982	– 149,000[b]	– 2,509,000	2,360,000
1982–1983	22,000[b]	– 2,231,000	2,254,000
1983–1984	351,000	– 1,749,000	2,100,000

[a]Minus sign indicates net out-migration.
[b]Not statistically different from zero.
Source: U.S. Bureau of the Census, Current Population Reports, series P-20, Geographic Mobility, various years.

state highway system duing those years facilitated this dispersion by greatly improving the accessibility of countless nonmetropolitan locations. At the same time metropolitan areas, especially those in the Northeast and Midwest where the oldest plants were usually located, went through what Daniel H. Garnick has called "an industrial shakeout" involving a major loss of manufacturing jobs (see Table 3.4). This shakeout precipitated substantial out-migration of population to both the metropolitan and nonmetropolitan areas of the South and West.[24]

During the 1980s, as Garnick points out, the constellation of forces changed. Metropolitan centers of heavy manufacturing, largely in the Midwest, continued to lose jobs as imports, aided by a strong dollar, put domestic producers under great pressure. Elsewhere, however, large MSAs were gaining jobs as a result of the rapid growth of business and financial services (with an associated boom in office construction) and of defense and high-technology manufacturing. Consequently, in the early 1980s, metropolitan areas as a whole enjoyed greater real economic growth than they had in the 1970s.

2. Regional effects of raw materials price trends. The two oil crises of the 1970s drove international fuel and raw materials prices to new heights and greatly stimulated the U.S. mining and extractive industries. Exploration and the development of new sources of supply brought job growth to many nonmetropolitan counties, especially in the West. Jobs increased not only in the extractive industries themselves but also in the retail and service activities needed by the new workers and their families. This growth slackened in the

24. Daniel H. Garnick, "Patterns of Growth in Metropolitan and Nonmetropolitan Areas: An Update," Survey of Current Business, May 1985, p. 36. Also see Larry Long and Diana DeAre, Metropolitan-Nonmetropolitan Industrial Changes and Population Redistribution, paper presented at the annual meeting of the American Association for the Advancement of Science, Detroit, May 30, 1983.

early 1980s as fuel and raw materials prices declined. Falling farm prices had a further depressing effect on income and job growth in nonmetropolitan areas.

3. *Growth of recreation and retirement communities.* The growth in the 1970s of recreation and retirement communities provided the base for an expansion of population in many nonmetropolitan counties that offered the appropriate combinations of physical amenities.[25] High interest rates in the late 1970s and early 1980s probably slowed growth in this sector, which is highly sensitive to the cost of funds for new construction.

4. *Weakening of agglomerative forces.* The deconcentration that took place during the 1970s involved the dispersion of jobs and population from larger to smaller centers.[26] This process may have been facilitated by a weakening of agglomerative forces in the U.S. economy. Earlier in this chapter we argued that the decentralization of metropolitan areas, dating from early in this century, depended importantly on radical improvements in transportation and communication and especially on the introduction of the truck and the automobile. We have already suggested that the dispersion of manufacturing jobs in the 1960s and 1970s was encouraged by major highway improvements. It can plausibly be argued that deconcentration in all its aspects has been stimulated by analogous improvements in other types of transportation and in communications. Today men and women who wish to enjoy the advantages of living in nonmetropolitan areas can do so while still remaining in relatively close touch with large urban centers. Those who want to combine a rural lifestyle with a metropolitan area job can settle in an adjacent county and commute to the MSA to work. Others may choose both to live and to work in more remote areas. They can nevertheless keep in touch with any metropolitan center by telephone or reach it quickly by air. Cheaper and faster transportation and communication have allowed many people to indulge preferences for locations that they would once have found too costly in terms either of money spent for those two functions or of urban opportunities forgone.

The Question of Metropolitan "Spillover"

Whatever rule one chooses for drawing the boundaries of a metropolitan area, there will always be places just beyond the line that are in some degree functionally related to the metropolis by means of high-speed transportation and communications but not sufficiently so to be included within its boundaries. When deconcentration occurred in the 1970s, analysts wondered

25. See Calvin L. Beale, "The Recent Shift of United States Population to Nonmetropolitan Areas, 1970–75," and Kevin F. McCarthy and Peter A. Morrison, "The Changing Demographic and Economic Structure of Nonmetropolitan Areas in the United States," *International Regional Science Review*, Winter 1977, pp. 113–122, 123–142.

26. Long and DeAre, "Metropolitan-Nonmetropolitan Industrial Changes," table 2.

TABLE 3.7
Population Growth in Metropolitan and Nonmetropolitan Areas, by Region, Size, and Percentage Commuting, 1970–1984

	CHANGE IN POPULATION (%)	
	1980–1984	*1970–1980*
All MSAs	4.5	10.6
Northeast	1.1	− 1.0
Midwest	0.4	2.7
South	8.1	21.8
West	8.2	22.7
Over 5 million	3.4	3.4
2.5 to 5 million	4.5	10.9
1 to 2.5 million	4.9	11.9
500,000 to 1 million	5.3	14.2
250,000 to 500,000	4.8	15.6
Less than 250,000	5.3	17.7
All nonmetropolitan counties	3.4	14.3
15% or more commuting	4.6	18.3
10% to 14% commuting	3.3	15.4
5% to 9% commuting	3.4	14.9
Less than 5% commuting	3.2	13.3

Source: U.S. Bureau of the Census, *Current Population Reports*, series P-25, no. 976, October 1985, table 8.

how much of it could be explained as the expansion of settlement into such adjacent areas. Perhaps the "functional field" of the MSA had simply been expanding faster than its officially recognized boundaries.[27]

Evidence on this point is presented in Table 3.7. In the lower panel, nonmetropolitan counties are grouped according to the extent of their attachment to an MSA as measured by the percentage of their resident workers who commute to jobs in a metropolitan area. As the figures in the second column show, the rate of population growth in nonmetropolitan counties during the 1970s was higher the more closely they were integrated with a metropolitan labor market. Thus adjacency does affect growth. But it is also true that during the 1970s even the most remote counties, in which commuting was below 5 percent (last row of the table), were growing faster than the aggregate of metropolitan areas (top row). When growth slowed in the early 1980s, no group of nonmetropolitan counties was found to grow faster than

27. See discussion in William Alonso, "The Current Halt in the Metropolitan Phenomenon," in Leven, *The Mature Metropolis*, pp. 30–31, and in Hans Blumenfeld, "Metropolis Extended: Secular Changes in Settlement Patterns," *Journal of the American Planning Association*, Summer 1986, pp. 346–348.

MSAs in the aggregate, but counties with the strongest commuting ties did grow as fast. So adjacency continued to matter.[28]

Table 3.7 also highlights significant differences in metropolitan area growth rates among regions and across size classes. These are examined next.

Region, Migration, Size of MSA, and Rate of Growth

For many years prior to 1960 the pattern of interregional movement in the United States had been one of net migration out of the South, then by far the nation's poorest region, and into the Northeast, the Midwest, and the West. This changed gradually in the 1960s as the South, enjoying rapid indus-trialization, began to attract a small net inflow of migrants. During the 1970s the trickle to the South became a flood. The Northeast and Midwest regions now lost substantial numbers through out-migration, while the South and West were large gainers in a pattern that has been widely described as "Sun Belt versus Frost Belt." These strong regional movements must be thought of as underlying the recent pattern of population change among metropolitan areas.[29]

Table 3.7 shows that since 1970 there has been a striking regional differ-ential in the growth rates of metropolitan areas. MSAs in the Northeast and Midwest have registered little, if any, population increase, while those of the South and West have gained at the brisk rate of about 20 percent per decade. All of the large MSAs in which population declined during the 1970s were lo-cated in the Northeast and Midwest. Table 3.3 shows that the six largest all lost numbers. In every case there was a sharp drop in central city population; in five out of six cases (New York being the exception) suburban population increased during the 1970s, but not enough to offset central city losses. On the other hand, in the South and West, the six largest MSAs continued to grow during the 1970s, though usually at a slower pace than before.

Table 3.7 also shows that in the 1970s there was a marked association between growth and MSA size. The population growth rate was lowest in the largest MSAs and CMSAs and highest in the smallest size class. The size ef-fect was also related to region, since more of the large metropolitan areas were located in the Northeast and Midwest and more of the small ones in the South and West. Unfortunately, the correlation between the two explanatory variables of region and size makes it difficult to separate their independent ef-fects on growth.

In the 1980s the inverse relationship between MSA size and rate of pop-ulation increase was much weaker. (See the first column of Table 3.7, but bear in mind that growth rates for 1980–1984 must be multiplied by 2.5 to be

28. For further details, see *Current Population Reports*, series P-25, no. 976, October 1985, pp. 1–11.

29. For a concise summary of regional growth patterns, see Benjamin Chinitz, "The Re-gional Transformation of the American Economy," *American Economic Review*, May 1986, pp. 300–303.

comparable with those for 1970–1980.) In particular, population increase accelerated in the largest size class. This can be explained in part by the fact that the largest central cities, which had previously suffered massive population decline, stopped losing population or even registered small gains from 1980 to 1984 (see Table 3.3).

The current pattern of population change and migration for the largest U.S. metropolitan areas can be summarized as follows. The largest MSAs in the South and West continue to receive substantial net in-migration, supporting a fairly high rate of population increase. By contrast, the largest in the Northeast and Midwest, although now gaining population at a modest rate, continue to be sources of substantial net out-migration.

MIGRATION AND ECONOMIC OPPORTUNITY

The classic explanation of migration has always been that people move in search of economic opportunity. We expect them to leave places where incomes are low or job opportunities are scarce and to move to places where incomes are higher or jobs more plentiful. Just as one would expect migration to flow in the direction of higher income, so one would also expect the result of migration to be a gradual decline in the geographic income differentials that initially gave rise to it. This follows from the influence of migration on the local labor supply. In areas experiencing out-migration the labor supply is reduced, which tends to raise wages. On the other hand, areas to which migrants move enjoy an increase in the labor supply, which tends to hold wages down. The combined effect should be to reduce interarea differentials.

Moreover, we would expect capital to migrate in the opposite direction from labor and to contribute further to the reduction of interarea wage and income differentials. This expectation is based on marginal productivity analysis. Low per capita regional income usually results from (among other things) a scarcity of capital relative to labor. Because the ratio of capital to labor is low, the average worker has relatively little capital to work with, the marginal product of labor is low, and wages, which depend on marginal productivity, are also low. But it is a corollary proposition that when capital is scarce relative to labor, so that the marginal product of labor is *low*, the marginal product of capital, and therefore the return to capital, will be *high*. Thus we would expect that capital, searching out areas of low wages and high returns, would migrate in just the opposite direction from labor. This would tend to reduce interarea wage differentials because the inflow of capital stimulates the demand for labor in the low-income area by creating additional jobs. As the demand for labor rises relative to its supply, wages, and hence incomes, will tend to rise, and interarea differentials will be further diminished.

Until 1970 experience in the United States broadly conformed to these expectations. We have already seen that net migration was then flowing from nonmetropolitan areas to MSAs. Table 3.8 shows that this was in the direc-

TABLE 3.8
Median Family Income by Place of Residence and Race

	MEDIAN FAMILY INCOME (1983 DOLLARS)[a]		INCOME RATIO, METROPOLITAN TO NONMETROPOLITAN
	Metropolitan Areas	*Nonmetropolitan Areas*	
1959			
All races	21,404	15,337	1.40
White	22,268	16,232	1.37
Black	12,952	5,845	2.22
1969			
All races	28,083	20,880	1.35
White	29,022	21,710	1.34
Black	18,036	10,771	1.67
1983			
All races	26,488	20,938	1.27
White	27,948	21,761	1.28
Black	15,304	11,964	1.28

[a]Income in 1959, 1969, and 1983 for families by place of residence in 1960, 1970, and 1984.
Sources: Data for 1959: U.S. Bureau of the Census, *Current Population Reports*, series P-23, no. 37, June 24, 1971, table 7. Data for 1969: *Current Population Reports*, series P-23, no. 75, November 1978, table 17. Data for 1983: *Current Population Reports*, series P-60, no. 146, April 1985, table 21.

tion of higher income. In 1959, for all races, median family income was 40 percent higher in MSAs than in nonmetropolitan areas. For blacks it was more than twice as high. No wonder, then, that blacks made up such a substantial portion of net migration to metropolitan areas. If this emphasis on money income differences as determinants of the flow of migration seems unduly materialistic, one can readily broaden the concept of income to take account of the value of the greater degree of choice offered by the metropolis—greater choice among jobs, among social groups, among the specialized forms of material goods themselves.

Until recently the pattern of interregional movement also conformed to expectations. Incomes were substantially lower in the South than elsewhere, and as we have already noted, the predominant flow of net migration was from the South to other regions. Regional, metropolitan, and racial patterns of migration were, of course, interrelated. Rural blacks in the South earned incomes even lower than the southern average. The movement of blacks out of the nonmetropolitan South into the central cities of the Northeast and North Central regions made up a substantial part of national migratory flow before 1970.

As expected, too, these flows were accompanied by a reduction of income differentials between areas. Table 3.8 shows that the metropolitan-nonmetropolitan differential declined from 1959 to 1969. In fact, convergence can be demonstrated from as far back as we have data. Commerce Department figures indicate that per capita income in SMSA counties was 131 percent higher than in non-SMSA counties in 1929. By 1950 the margin had been cut by more than half, to only 60 percent.[30] Interregional differences have diminished, too, as per capita income in the South rose toward the level in other sections of the United States. As expected, capital flowing from the North helped finance the very rapid industrialization of the South, multiplying the number of jobs there and pushing wages and incomes up.

It is clear that migratory flows in the United States until about 1970 are easily explained by conventional economic analysis. It is much more difficult to account for the change in those flows since 1970.[31] The South is now a major recipient of migration, even though the average income there is still well below the level in the other three regions. During the 1970s (though not the 1980s) there was a substantial flow of net migration from metropolitan to nonmetropolitan areas, despite the fact that the income advantage of the former over the latter remained substantial (see Table 3.8). Within the metropolitan sector, the rate of in-migration was highest in the smallest MSAs and lowest or even negative in the largest ones. Yet per capita income is generally higher, the larger the metropolitan area.[32] Finally, studies of migration to nonmetropolitan counties found that in the 1970s the expected positive relationship between per capita county income and level of immigration had weakened or even reversed.[33]

Economists found these facts puzzling. Just as they do not expect water to flow uphill, so they were surprised when people were found to migrate from areas of higher income and wider job choice to places that appear to rank lower on both scales. They were reluctant to conclude that economic motives no longer matter but did begin to suspect that money income might be an unreliable measure of local well-being.

Income, Well-being, and City Size

One obvious problem in using money income as a measure is the fact that living costs vary with city size. Making use of what little cost-of-living data are available for individual cities, Irving Hoch found that living costs in-

30. "Metropolitan Area Income in 1967," *Survey of Current Business*, May 1969, table 2, p. 26.

31. For an assessment of motives for migration in the 1970s, see Larry H. Long and Diana DeAre, *Migration to Nonmetropolitan Areas: Appraising the Trend and Reasons for Moving*, Special Demographic Analyses CDS-80-2 (Washington, D.C.: U.S. Government Printing Office, November 1982).

32. See Victor R. Fuchs, *Differentials in Hourly Earnings by Region and City Size, 1959*, occasional paper 101 (New York: National Bureau of Economic Research, 1967). For 1983 data, see U.S. Bureau of the Census, *Current Population Reports*, series P-60, no. 146, April 1985, table 21.

33. Beale, table 1 and p. 116; McCarthy and Morrison, p. 138.

crease significantly as size of place increases. (The principal cause is probably that land rent and transportation costs are higher in large cities, as we shall see in Chapter 6.) Hoch was then able to adjust data on local income for differences in living costs, to produce an index showing the variation of *deflated* income by size of place. He found that in every U.S. region this adjusted measure of income rises with city size (although only about half as fast as the unadjusted measure does).[34]

As we have already argued, economists expect migration to reduce intercity differences in income, producing an equilibrium when workers of equal skill earn equal cost-of-living-adjusted incomes in all cities. Instead we find that in the United States such differences still exist, yet net migration to many of the larger, higher-income MSAs has in fact already ceased. What can account for the persistence of these disparities in adjusted income? Hoch suggests an interesting explanation. He hypothesizes that the *nonpecuniary* returns to urban living are, on balance, negative and that these net costs also increase with city size. If that is so, income differences by city size that remain after adjustment for differences in the cost of living can be interpreted as "compensatory payments" to city workers needed to offset the net, nonpecuniary disadvantages of urban living, which increase with city size.[35]

How can producers in large cities afford to pay the higher wages needed to cover both higher living costs and (if they exist) compensatory payments? The answer is that the economies of scale and agglomeration discussed in Chapter 2 add enough to factor productivity as city size increases to finance such payments.[36] (That does not mean, however, that labor appropriates the whole gain from economies of agglomeration. As we shall see in Chapter 6, a major portion probably goes to landowners in the form of rent.)

When it comes to naming nonpecuniary disadvantages of urban living, each of us will have his or her own list. Certain disadvantages, however, are widely perceived as important. Some of these have already been pointed out in the discussion of diseconomies of agglomeration in Chapter 2. There is strong evidence that environmental degradation, as measured, for example, by air and noise pollution, increases with city size; crime rates, too, are higher in larger cities.[37] On the other hand, larger city size also confers nonpecuniary advantages, principally wider choice among jobs and a wider variety of consumer goods and of cultural activities. It must be emphasized that in the

34. Irving Hoch, "Income and City Size," *Urban Studies*, October 1972, tables 2, 3, and 4, pp. 310–311. Also see Hoch, "Variations in the Quality of Urban Life among Cities and Regions," in Lowdon Wingo and Alan Evans, eds., *Public Economics and the Quality of Life* (Baltimore: Johns Hopkins University Press, 1977), pp. 50–53.

35. Hoch, "Income and City Size," p. 302, and "Variations in the Quality of Urban Life," p. 28.

36. A theoretical demonstration can be found in Michael S. Fogarty and Gasper Garofalo, "Urban Size and the Amenity Structure of Cities," *Journal of Urban Economics*, November 1980, pp. 356–360.

37. See Hoch, "Income and City Size," pp. 318–324.

present state of our knowledge we cannot demonstrate by direct measurement that the nonpecuniary "bads" of living in large cities outweigh these nonpecuniary "goods." Rather, that conclusion is inferred by Hoch from the persistence of income differentials for which he finds no other plausible explanation.

Expansion of the Metropolitan System

It would be unfortunate if the foregoing discussions of deconcentration, of migration out of the older metropolitan areas, and of the dramatic slowdown in their population growth were to obscure the fundamental fact that the U.S. metropolitan system as a whole continues to expand. Whether the balance favors slightly faster nonmetropolitan growth, as it did in the 1970s, or slightly faster metropolitan growth, as in the 1980s, the number of MSAs and their aggregate population and land area continue to increase decade by decade. This growth is reinforced by the fact that when nonmetropolitan areas attract sufficient population, they are automatically reclassified as metropolitan. Larry Long and Diana DeAre point out that as this process unfolds, the United States is becoming a nation where eventually almost everyone will live either in a metropolitan area or in a county adjacent to one.[38] Evidently we are witnessing what William Alonso has described as "the dispersion of urban areas over the countryside."[39]

38. Long and DeAre, *Metropolitan-Nonmetropolitan Industrial Changes*, p. 19.
39. Alonso, p. 39.

FOUR

The Location of Economic Activity and the Location of Cities

The rise of cities at particular places in an industrialized society depends largely on the forces that determine the location of economic activity. In Chapter 2 we explained that economic activity tends to concentrate geographically because external economies of agglomeration have the effect of reducing costs or increasing sales for many types of industry. A description of the external economies of agglomeration, however, is by no means a complete account of the forces affecting the location of firms or of people. In particular, it tells us nothing about *where* agglomeration is likely to occur. We must now look into the matter more systematically.

Traditional Anglo-American economic theory has been called "spaceless." As Walter Isard puts it:

> Transport costs and other costs involved in movement within a "market" are assumed to be zero. In this sense the factor of space is repudiated, everything within the economy is in effect compressed to a point, and all spatial resistance disappears.[1]

Even international trade theories have sometimes abstracted entirely from the elements of space and distance. Students of urban phenomena, however, have generally sought to incorporate in their theories as many regularities in spatial relationships as they could discover or accommodate. This and the following chapter deal with the interurban aspects of space. In this chapter we start with the individual location decisions of firms, explaining why firms locate in one place rather than another, and consequently account for the fact that cities of a particular

1. Walter Isard, *Location and Space-Economy* (New York: Wiley and M.I.T. Press, 1956), p. 26.

kind and size are where they are instead of someplace else. Chapter 5, adopting a somewhat different but complementary point of view, looks at the spatial relationships between cities and explains why it makes sense to speak of a "system of cities" or of an "urban hierarchy." In Chapter 6 we will take up the problem of intraurban location: why firms and people locate in one part of the city rather than another and why cities consequently display a certain regularity of form.

EFFECTS OF TRANSPORT COSTS ON CHOICE OF LOCATION

Isard has suggested that the forces affecting a given business firm's choice of location can be classified conveniently into three groups: (1) transport costs, the distinguishing feature of which is that they vary systematically with distance; (2) other input costs, which, if they vary at all from place to place, do so in what is from the spatial point of view a haphazard manner; and (3) economies and diseconomies of agglomeration, which are a function not of geographic position but of the magnitude of activity gathered in one place, wherever it may be.[2]

It is convenient to begin by examining the influence on the location of a single firm of transport costs considered in isolation. To do so we must postulate a radically simplified world. It will suffice to assume the following:

1. The firm in question is so small in relation to the relevant markets that its activities have no perceptible effect on the prices of the goods it buys or sells and no effect on the location of other economic units.
2. The prices of land, labor, and capital are everywhere equal. Raw materials that are not ubiquitous are priced at the source, net of transportation.
3. There are no economies or diseconomies of scale or of agglomeration.
4. The market for the product of the firm is concentrated at a point rather than geographically extensive. (This assumption is not necessary to isolate the effect of transport costs, but it helps to simplify the argument.)

The profit-maximizing firm will obviously seek out the profit-maximizing location. Under the conditions we have postulated, production costs are everywhere equal. The location at which profits are maximized will therefore be the one at which transport costs per unit of output are minimized.

2. Ibid., pp. 138–139.

The transport costs in question are the costs of transporting raw materials from their point of origin to the manufacturing plant and the costs of transporting finished goods from the plant to the customer. Using Alonso's terminology, we may call the former "assembly costs" and the latter "distribution costs."[3]

If the customer instead of the manufacturer were to bear the cost of transport from the plant it would make no difference; under our assumptions, the price of the final good is already established at the market. If a firm required customers to pay for transportation, they would refuse to buy unless price at the plant were below the established market price by the amount of the required transport costs. Hence it is in the interest of the producer to minimize total transport costs per unit of output, including cost of delivery to the market, no matter who actually pays the carrier.

If the firm used only ubiquitous raw materials, like air, it is obvious that production at the market would minimize transport costs and maximize profits. It is only because indispensable raw materials are not ubiquitous that a manufacturing firm in our radically simplified world might find it desirable to locate close to materials sources rather than the market.

To begin with the simplest case, consider a firm that requires only a single raw material: a sawmill manufacturing finished lumber. Suppose that logs are available from a forest at point M and the firm wishes to manufacture lumber to be sold in a market at C. Points M and C are connected by a railroad. The railroad charges the same rate per ton-mile to haul logs or to haul finished lumber. Should the lumber mill locate at M, at C, or at some point in between?

The answer can be seen at once. If the raw materials that have to be assembled at the plant weigh more than the finished product they yield, it pays to locate the plant at the source of the materials and pay transport charges only on the lighter product. On the other hand, if the finished product weighs more than the raw materials that must be assembled, it pays to locate the plant at the market and pay transport charges only on the lighter raw materials.

The former case is called a "weight-losing" process, the latter a "weight-gaining" one. Clearly lumber milling is a weight-losing process: the finished boards weigh less than the logs. Consequently, the firm would build at M, where the logs originate, rather than at C.

Materials Orientation versus Market Orientation

Since, other things being equal, weight-losing processes tend to locate near their source of raw materials, they are often called "materials-oriented."

---

3. William Alonso, "Location Theory," in John Friedmann and William Alonso, eds., *Regional Development and Planning: A Reader* (Cambridge, Mass.: M.I.T. Press, 1964), p. 83.

Prominent examples, in addition to sawmilling, are steelmaking, smelting of other ores, and raw materials processing in general.

Weight-gaining processes, on the other hand, since they tend to locate near their markets, have been called "market-oriented." One may well wonder, given the principle of the conservation of matter, how any process could be "weight-gaining." The answer found in the traditional literature on location theory is that some processes use ubiquitous materials, such as air and water, whose weight has thus far been left out of account. Soda bottling, for example, results in a large weight gain if one does not count the water on the input side. The argument has traditionally been that since water is available everywhere, it doesn't have to be transported and so may be left out of transport cost calculations. For the soda bottling industry this may be a supportable oversimplification. Water does, in fact, have to be transported, but the cost of moving it is so low in relation to the value of the soda produced that the bottler can afford to ignore geographic differentials in the cost of "assembling water." As a general rule, however, it is no longer safe to treat water as a ubiquity in the United States. Increasingly, it is becoming a scarce resource, exerting a locational pull of its own.

An effect similar to weight gain occurs when a finished good, though not heavier than the materials that go into it, nevertheless gains in bulk, fragility, or perishability and so takes a higher transport rate per ton-mile than do its constituent materials. Such a rise in transport rate has the same locational effect as a gain in weight, pulling the plant toward its market and away from its source of (nonubiquitous) materials. The automobile industry provides a good example of this sort of thing. The assembled car weighs no more than the parts that go into it. Nevertheless, the large multiplant firms build their assembly plans near important markets because it is cheaper to ship the constituent parts to an assembly plant than to ship the bulky, and in its own way fragile, finished vehicle to the market.

Broadly speaking, the early stages in a production process are likely to be materials-oriented, since they frequently result in great weight loss in the refining of raw materials. The later stages, however, are often market-oriented, since as a product approaches the final form in which it is to be consumed it is likely to gain in fragility or perishability.

The Mathematics of Rates, Weights, and Distances

It is worthwhile recasting what has been said so far in a simple mathematical statement.[4] We will employ the following symbols:

w_m = tons of material m needed to make one unit of final product

w_c = weight of one unit of final product in tons

4. Adapted from ibid., pp. 83–84 and 99.

r_m = rate per ton-mile to transport material m

r_c = rate per ton-mile to transport final product c

t = rail distance in miles between points M and C

K = transport cost per unit of output

Then transport cost per unit of output for location at M can be expressed as the cost of delivering the finished good to market, or

$$K_m = w_c \cdot r_c \cdot t$$

and for location at C as the cost of assembling the raw materials at the market, or

$$K_c = w_m \cdot r_m \cdot t$$

It follows that if

$$w_m \cdot r_m > w_c \cdot r_c$$

the firm will prefer location at M to location at C, and if

$$w_m \cdot r_m < w_c \cdot r_c$$

the firm will prefer location at C to location at M.

The product of rate times weight is what Alfred Weber, in his seminal book on location theory, called the "ideal weight" of the material or product in question.[5] In the one-material, one-market case we are dealing with, the firm will locate at the material's source if the ideal weight of the material is greater and at the market if the ideal weight of the product is greater. The reader can see by reference to these ideal weights the locational choice that is optimal in case of weight gain, weight loss, differences in transport rate on account of bulk, perishability, and the like, or some combination of these.

So far, however, we have dealt only with end-point locations. How do we know that transport costs will not be minimized at some intermediate point along the railroad line? The answer can be deduced as follows. For each mile that the firm shifts its location from M toward C, it adds $w_m r_m$ to its assembly costs and subtracts $w_c r_c$ from its distribution costs. The net change in total unit transport costs is therefore $w_m r_m - w_c r_c$ for each mile the firm moves from M toward C. If this difference is positive, transport costs rise continually as the firm moves from M toward C; hence no intermediate point can be as desirable as M. The firm is materials-oriented. If the difference is negative, transport costs fall continuously as the firm moves from M to C, and no intermediate point can be as desirable as C. The firm is market-oriented. Only if

---

5. Written in German and published in 1909, the book was translated into English by Carl J. Friedrich under the title *Alfred Weber's Theory of the Location of Industries* (Chicago: University of Chicago Press, 1929).

the ideal weights of material and product are equal could an intermediate location be as attractive as an end point.

Effect of Terminal Costs and Declining Rates

The likelihood of an end-point is increased by two characteristics of the structure of transport costs that we have so far neglected. These are, first, the fact that the movement of goods involves terminal costs as well as ton-mile carrying charges and, second, the fact that ton-mile carrying charges themselves generally decline as distance increases.

Terminal costs arise if the shipper has to bring goods to the loading point of the carrier at one end of the journey and take them away from the unloading point at the other end. For example, if shipment is by rail or water, it will be necessary to haul the goods by truck to and from the freight terminal or pier. In addition, the shipper will bear administrative expenses in the form of supervision and paperwork.

We may speak of loading and unloading expenses as constituting one set of terminal costs. Terminal costs vary according to the mode of carriage. They are generally lower for truck than for rail and for rail than for water shipment. Since terminal costs do not vary with the length of the haul, they have the effect of making long hauls cheaper per ton-mile than short hauls, even if the carrier charges ton-mile rates that are constant for all distances.

In practice, however, carriers do *not* charge constant ton-mile rates. In general, the rate per ton-mile declines as distance increases because the carrier can spread fixed expenses per shipment over a larger number of miles. Thus the charge for a single shipment of 1,000 miles will generally be far less than for five similar shipments of 200 miles.[6]

How do terminal costs and rates that decline with distance reinforce the likelihood of an end-point location? Consider the consequences if the lumber-milling firm should choose to build at some point, call it L, along the railroad line between M and C. The firm would now have to pay two sets of terminal costs: one set for loading at M and unloading at L and a second set for loading at L and unloading at C. If located at M or at C, however, the firm would have to pay only one set, clearly an advantage. Furthermore, the rate structure would generally penalize location at L: the two short hauls, M to L and L to C, would cost more per ton-mile than a single long haul from M to C.

Figure 4.1, adapted from Alonso, summarizes the problem of choosing a minimum-transport-cost location exactly as we have discussed it so far. The diagram is drawn with one corner at M, another at C. The horizontal axis measures, in one direction, distance from M and, in the other direction, distance from C. The vertical axis measures transport costs.

---

6. For further discussion of the "structure of transfer costs," see Edgar M. Hoover, *An Introduction to Regional Economics*, 2nd ed. (New York: Knopf, 1975), pp. 37–59.

FIGURE 4.1
Factors in Choosing a Minimum-Transport-Cost Location

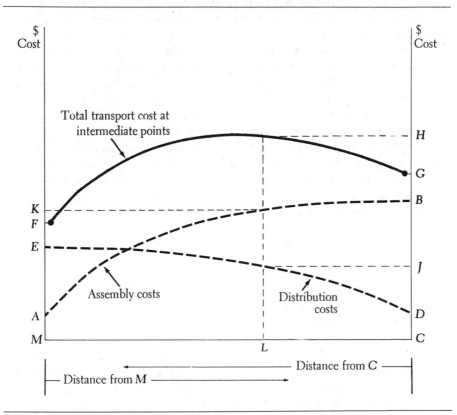

Source: Adapted from William Alonso, "Location Theory," in John Friedmann and William Alonso, eds., *Regional Development and Planning* (Cambridge, Mass.: M.I.T. Press, 1964), fig. 6, p. 86.

The curve *MAB* shows how the cost of transporting a unit of raw material weighing w_m increases as plant location moves away from *M* toward *C*. Terminal costs of loading and unloading the material are indicated by the segment *MA*. If transport rates per ton-mile charged by the carrier were invariant with distance, the segment *AB* would be an inclined straight line, its constant slope indicating the constant marginal rate. As drawn here, the curve flattens out. Its diminishing slope indicates a diminishing marginal transport rate as distance increases. If the plant locates at *C*, assembly costs rise to *CB* per unit of material, while distribution costs are zero.

If the plant locates at *M*, assembly costs are zero, but now the firm must pay distribution costs of carrying the product all the way to *C*. These costs are indicated by the curve *CDE*, where *CD* is the terminal cost and the curve *DE* indicates how cost of carriage to *C* rises as the plant moves away from *C* toward *M*. If the plant locates at *M*, distribution costs total *ME* per unit of product. Since *ME* < *CB*, it is clear that in this case location at *M* is preferable to location at *C*.

The curve *FG* shows transport costs for all intermediate points. *FG* is nothing but the vertical sum of the curves of assembly cost and distribution cost. At an intermediate point, such as *L*, the firm would pay assembly costs of *MK* for a unit of raw materials coming from *M* and distribution costs of *CJ* for a unit of product sent to *C*. The sum of these costs is *CH*, indicated by the height of the curve of total transport costs at *L*.

For any intermediate location, the extra set of terminal costs incurred is shown by segment *EF* or *BG*. The disadvantage of making two short hauls instead of one long one is indicated by the fact that *FG* is higher in the middle than at either end. The diagram shows how these effects combine to reinforce the attractiveness of end-point locations.

Transport Advantages and Urban Growth

We can now begin to see how the transportation advantages of certain locations explain why they become great centers of economic activity. Let us start with a very simple case: raw materials deposits attract materials-oriented industry, industry creates markets for intermediate goods used in production and for consumer goods for its employees, and these markets in turn attract market-oriented industry. Thus great urban industrial complexes grow up in regions that are rich in raw materials: one thinks immediately of the Pittsburgh region in Pennsylvania or the Ruhr Valley in Germany, in both of which proximity to coal deposits (plus accessibility to other complementary materials) explains the subsequent growth of industry.

Yet we know that proximity to raw materials is only a small part of the story. New York, Chicago, Buffalo, and many other important manufacturing centers are not cheek-by-jowl with great raw materials deposits. These cities do, indeed, owe their unusual growth to transport factors, but of a sort different from those we have considered so far. Let us extend the analysis.

Returning to our original scheme of materials at *M*, market at *C*, and an intermediate point at *L*, we can imagine that *M* and *L* are on opposite shores of a body of water. (Figure 4.1 no longer applies.) Transportation is therefore by ship from *M* to *L* and by rail from *L* to *C*. Point *L* may now be a feasible location for industry. A manufacturer or processor who set up at *L* would no longer pay the penalty of extra terminal costs and higher transport rates. Terminal costs are incurred at *L* in any case, since the mode of transport changes there. For the same reason, two short hauls rather than a single long one are required whether one locates at L, M, or C. In this fashion, any point at which a break in the transport network requires transshipment of goods gains important advantages. Of course, an end-point location might still be preferable if there were a significant difference between the ideal weight of the materials $(w_m r_m)$ and the ideal weight of the finished product $(w_c r_c)$, but it would no longer be virtually dictated by the structure of transport charges.

The choice of a minimum-transport-cost location becomes more complicated when firms have multiple materials sources or markets. In some cases location at one market or at the source of one material will still be preferable—as, for example, when the ideal weight of one material or market is greater than the sum of all the others. When such a "dominant weight," to use Weber's term, is not present, the minimum-transport-cost location, taking account of terminal costs, may turn out to be at a materials source, at a market, or at an intermediate route junction.

Probably the most often cited case of a city that has attracted industry because it is a transshipment point is Buffalo. An enormous flour-milling industry developed there because grain could be carried inexpensively across the Great Lakes from the grain belt of the North Central states, unloaded at Buffalo, the easternmost port on Lake Erie, there milled into flour, and then shipped by rail to the large East Coast markets. But there are many other examples. Crude oil produced overseas comes into Gulf Coast ports where it is refined before shipment to domestic markets. West Coast ports perform the same function for Alaskan crude oil. New York and Boston both refine sugar received by the shipload in crude form from overseas and then distribute it to regional markets by rail or truck.

In most cases port cities, in addition to being transshipment points, gain the further advantage of nodality. To return to our hypothetical example, the port L would be likely to develop shipping connections with other materials sources or markets in addition to M and would become a railhead for lines radiating to other points besides C. If a manufacturer required bulky materials from several sources or wished to be in close contact with several markets, a junction point such as a port, though not itself either a market or a materials source, might well be the best location. Of course, a junction has this advantage even when it does not connect unlike modes of transport but joins only different routes on a rail or road network.

In addition, as Edgar M. Hoover has pointed out, ports and other modal interchange points are apt to offer the advantage of economies of scale in terminal operations and will generally "be better provided than most other points with specialized facilities for goods handling and storage."[7] In short,

7. Ibid., p. 57.

economies of scale and of agglomeration in freight handling give major transportation centers an advantage that helps explain why they attract industrial activity.

Moreover, as new modes develop in competition with old ones, the transportation advantages of major centers tend to be self-perpetuating. For example, with the growth of air transportation in the United States, New York and Chicago, which had been, respectively, the nation's leading port and railroad center, became principal nodes in its air traffic network, a position that undoubtedly helps to sustain their economic importance.

LOCATIONAL EFFECTS OF PRODUCTION-COST DIFFERENTIALS

Up to this point we have restricted the analysis to cases of pure transport orientation by assuming (1) that the prices of land, labor, and capital are everywhere equal and (2) that there are no economies or diseconomies of scale or agglomeration other than those associated with transportation. These two assumptions ensure that production costs will be everywhere equal and consequently that the firm will choose its location by reference to transport costs alone. Let us now relax these assumptions and see what effects geographic product-cost differentials might have.

Returning to our hypothetical example, suppose that we are dealing with a weight-losing process for which M is the minimum-transport-cost location. Suppose also that production costs are everywhere equal except that at L the prevailing wage rate for the same quality of labor is lower than elsewhere. A firm would locate at L instead of at M if the saving on production costs per unit of output at L exceeded the loss due to higher transport costs per unit as compared with M. The same sort of calculus applies in the case of any geographic difference in input prices.

Note that L's advantage is measured in terms of reduced *production* costs per unit of output rather than reduced labor costs per unit of output. This is necessary because a firm producing at L would tend to use a more labor-intensive technique than a firm located elsewhere—it would substitute labor for other factors of production. Only by comparing all production costs per unit of output at L and M can we take account of the fact that as a result of substitution, the producer at L uses a different mixture of inputs than the producer at M.

Indeed, substitution is pervasive in economic processes. Isard has shown that location theory itself can be handled within the substitution framework of the traditional theory of production.[8] For example, we have assumed that transport costs per unit of output are higher at L than at M, while

8. Isard, passim.

wages, and therefore production costs, are lower at L. Thus in moving from M to L a firm would, in Isard's terminology, substitute dollar outlays on transport for dollar outlays on production, while at the same time substituting physical inputs of one factor of production, labor, for physical inputs of the others.

Production-Cost and Transport-Cost Orientations Compared

Industries for which geographic differentials in production cost are more important than geographic differentials in transport cost are said to be "production-cost-oriented" rather than "transport-cost-oriented." No precise classification is possible, however, since an industry may be significantly affected by both factors. In general—and again this is no more than a rough rule—an industry will be transport-cost-oriented if the ratio of bulk to value in its manufacturing process is high and production-cost-oriented if the ratio of bulk to value is low.

The iron and steel industry illustrates the first case. At the input end of the process, between 3 and 3.5 tons of raw material are required to produce one ton of crude steel, a ratio that ensures that the transportation cost of obtaining materials will account for a significant fraction of total cost. At the output end, finished steel products sell in the range of $300 to $400 a ton, or 15 to 20 cents a pound. The low value of finished steel in relation to its bulk means that the cost of transporting it to market is bound to be high relative to its price. Thus transportation costs are important at both ends of the process, and the iron and steel industry is highly transport-cost-oriented.[9]

Steel mills tend to locate where the combined transportation cost of assembling the materials and delivering the product to market is minimized. Since the two principal materials, coal and iron ore, can be obtained from a number of sources, but not usually side by side, many locations for mills are feasible in the United States. For example, mills at Pittsburgh enjoy very low transportation costs for coal, which is mined nearby, but pay relatively high charges to obtain ore from the Lake Superior region and Canada. Mills at the Great Lakes ports, on the other hand, can bring in ore relatively economically by water from around Lake Superior but pay higher transportation costs per ton of coal. Mills along the Atlantic coast in Maryland and Pennsylvania pay relatively low shipping costs to bring in ore by sea from eastern Canada, Brazil, and Venezuela but bear higher costs than do Pittsburgh mills to obtain coal. All of these locations are relatively close to major market areas.[10]

9. Current figures are estimated by Professor William T. Hogan, S.J., Fordham University. On changes in the technology, materials sources, and locational pattern of the industry, see his *Economic History of the Iron and Steel Industry in the United States* (Lexington, Mass.: Heath, 1971).
10. See data in Walter Isard, *Methods of Regional Analysis* (New York: Wiley and M.I.T. Press, 1960), table 4, p. 351.

Over the years the tonnage of material required to produce steel has been gradually reduced. Today's figure of 3 to 3.5 tons of material per ton of crude steel can be compared with a range of 4.5 to 5 tons in the late 1930s.[11] The reduction of input requirements has gradually made the industry less materials-oriented and more market-oriented. It bears repeating, however, that both of these are types of transport-cost orientation.

The cotton textile industry offers a good example of production-cost orientation. Originally concentrated in New England, the industry moved south beginning in the late nineteenth century, in order to take advantage of the lower wage level there. Cotton textiles illustrate the general rule that an industry will tend to be production-cost-oriented if the ratio of bulk to value in its processes is low. At the input end, weight loss in the production process is negligible—a 480-pound bale of cotton lint will yield enough yarn to weave about 450 pounds of cotton print cloth. This is not quite comparable to the weight-loss figure cited for steel since it ignores fuel consumption, but it suffices to show that textile production is not a heavily weight-losing process. Neither is it a fragility- or perishability-gaining process. Hence it is not materials oriented. At the output end, a cotton print cloth in its gray or unfinished state sells for about 72 cents a yard and runs about 4 yards to the pound, indicating a value of about $2.88 per pound.[12] This high value in relation to bulk means that the cost of transportation to market is a relatively small part of total cost, and the industry therefore feels little pressure to locate close to its markets. We see at once why the steel industry is far more sensitive to inter-site transport-cost differentials than the textile industry: transport costs are an important part of the whole in the case of steel but only a very small part in the case of textiles.

Types of Production-Cost Orientation

Production-cost orientation is sometimes further subdivided according to the sort of input involved. One can distinguish "labor orientation" (e.g., textiles), "power orientation" (e.g., aluminum refining), "amenity orientation" (e.g., research and development laboratories), or "agglomeration orientation" (e.g., corporate head offices).

Amenity orientation is increasingly important in the United States. It means simply locating the plant in a place where the firm's most specialized, highly paid employees would particularly like to live. Research scientists and engineers, for example, seem to have a strong preference for areas with good

11. Edgar M. Hoover, *The Location of Economic Activity*, paperback ed. (New York: McGraw-Hill, 1963), table 3.1, p. 43.
12. Data on cotton supplied by courtesy of L. B. Gatewood, Economic and Market Research Service, National Cotton Council of America, Memphis, Tenn.

schools for their children and interesting recreation for their leisure time. Consequently, research laboratories are attracted to areas such as southern California or the suburbs of New York or Boston, where, apparently, good schools and good living are found together.

Logically, amenity orientation is really a subclass of labor orientation: there must be some salary differential that would induce scientists to leave Santa Monica by the thousands and take up research employment on the plains of North Dakota. But as long as Santa Monica offers free sunshine and ocean sports there is no reason why the laboratory should not take advantage of them and acquire for itself a contented scientific staff at no premium in salary. Amenity orientation should not be dismissed as a mere curiosity. As the workweek shrinks, leisure time grows; as living standards rise, people can afford increasingly complex and expensive forms of recreation and will increasingly wish to live where these are available. The income elasticity of demand for yachts is high. In the long run it is bound to influence the location of economic activity.

The concentration of research and development in specific places cannot, however, be accounted for solely by amenities of the physical and social environment. Economies of agglomeration probably play an important part as well.[13] These economies were defined in Chapter 2 as savings in unit costs that may accrue to individual firms when a large enough number of them locate in one city. A distinction was drawn between "economies of localization" that result from the local concentration of firms in the same industry and "economies of urbanization" that result from the concentration of unlike firms—in other words, from the sheer size of the local economy. In either case the relevant effect of agglomeration is to bring into existence a variety of specialized suppliers. Firms that are attracted to the area by their presence are said to be agglomeration-oriented. Since cost reduction is usually the motive, agglomeration orientation can be regarded as a type of production-cost orientation.[14]

Occasionally in the literature on the economics of location one encounters the term *footloose* or *foot-free*. Sometimes this is used as a catchall for industries that locate without reference to any identifiable influence. As Alonso has pointed out, however, this usage might suggest erroneously "that one place is as good as any other," which is surely not the case.[15] It is better to describe as footloose those industries for which transport costs are relatively unimportant and which are therefore free to use some other criterion in choosing a location.

13. For a discussion of agglomerative forces in high-technology industries, see Peter Hall and Ann Markusen, eds., *Silicon Landscapes* (Boston: Allen & Unwin, 1985).
14. "Usually" because in some cases the motive is greater sales rather than lower costs.
15. Alonso, p. 101.

SUMMARY OF LOCATIONAL ORIENTATION

Table 4.1 summarizes our analysis of the locational orientation of the firm. Necessarily, it omits much detail and many qualifications. The table, and indeed the analysis up to this point, may be misleading if it suggests that every firm can be classified according to a single factor that dominates its choice of location. Quite probably the optimum location will be determined by a combination of factors. For example, it may be one that offers neither the lowest transport costs nor the lowest production costs but the lowest combination of these. In short, the table simplifies a complex world.

CHANGES IN THE DETERMINANTS OF LOCATION

As the U.S. economy developed, technological change and rising living standards gradually modified the economic forces that determine the location of industry. Technological progress appeared to be bringing about a persistent decline in the importance of transport-cost orientation. Alonso offered three cogent reasons for believing that it was declining.[16] Foremost was the long-run tendency for transportation to become cheaper, quicker, and more efficient. Second, one of the fruits of technical progress is a gradual reduction in the quantity of raw material used to produce a unit of a given product. (This has already been described in the case of steel smelting.) Third, products have been gradually improved through ever more complex fabrication, so that value per unit of weight increases. (As the advertising copywriter might put it, "There's a lot more car in today's car.") Each of these tendencies reduced the ratio of transport outlays to total costs and therefore also reduced the likelihood that geographic differences in transport costs would dominate location decisions of manufacturers.

Some observers now speculate that technological progress will have an analogous effect on location decisions in the service industry. High-level business and financial services (and corporate head offices) are agglomeration-oriented because of their dependence on face-to-face communication. It is possible that improvements in the technology of communication will eventually weaken that dependence, allowing service firms the freedom to disperse from large metropolitan areas.[17]

16. Ibid.
17. See George Roniger, "Economic Development in a Footloose World," *New York Affairs*, 7, no. 4 (1983), 20–29; Norman Macrae, "Tomorrow's Agglomeration Economics," in Charles L. Leven, ed., *The Mature Metropolis* (Lexington, Mass.: Heath, Lexington Books, 1978), ch. 7; and Benjamin Chinitz, "The Influence of Communications and Data Processing Technology on Urban Form," in Robert B. Ebel, ed., *Research in Urban Economics*, vol. 4 (Greenwich, Conn.: JAI Press, 1984), pp. 67–77.

TABLE 4.1
Types of Locational Orientation of Industry

ORIENTATION	DECISIVE CHARACTERISTIC	OPTIMUM LOCATION	EXAMPLES
Transport-cost-oriented	High bulk-to-value ratio, hence transport inputs relatively important.		
Materials-oriented	Weight- or perishability-losing process	Close to materials sources	Ore refining, steel, fruit and vegetable canning.
Market-oriented	Weight-, perishability-, or fragility-gaining process	Close to market	Brewing, baking, automobile assembly
Production-cost-oriented	Low bulk-to-value ratio, hence transport inputs relatively unimportant		
Labor-oriented	Labor-intensive process	Low-wage area[a]	Textiles
Power-oriented	Power-intensive process	Cheap-power area	Aluminum refining
Amenity-oriented	Employs high proportion of specialized, highly paid personnel	Attractive physical and social environment	Research and development
Agglomeration-oriented			
Economies of localization	Need for specialized ancillary services and labor	City of specialized character	Apparel manufacturing, broadcasting
Economies of urbanization	Need for face-to-face communication with customers or suppliers	City of sufficient size	Corporate head offices, advertising, law, investment banking

[a]For labor of the required skill level.

Improvements in transportation and communication have also facilitated interregional migration in the United States, and migration of labor and capital have gradually reduced differences in wage levels among regions and between metropolitan and nonmetropolitan areas. In the long run this must be expected to weaken the locational pull of geographic labor-cost differentials. In the short run, however, improvements in transportation and communication also make it easier for firms to respond to whatever geographic differentials remain. Thus the dispersion of manufacturing toward small cities and nonmetropolitan areas that occurred during the 1960s and 1970s and was widely attributed to the search for lower wages and less unionization is not inconsistent with the argument that geographic wage differentials are gradually diminishing.

Finally, as explained in the preceding section, rising living standards have increased the average citizen's interest in local amenities, thus strengthening the pull of geographic differences in amenities. These changes, combined with the decline in the relative importance of transport costs, have brought about what might be called a "gradual revolution" in the location of population and industry: people and social institutions are increasingly free to move away from the old transport-determined points of production and start over again in an environment of their own choosing. George Roniger argues that the older cities must now adapt their municipal policies to this new reality. Instead of depending on their natural advantages or their advantages in transportation and communications to attract or hold jobs and businesses, they will have to pay more attention to the things that make a city "a good place in which to live."[18]

The Question of Energy Costs

The energy crisis of the 1970s focused new attention on the relationship between energy costs and locational choice. The location decisions of firms are directly affected by energy costs in two ways. First, energy prices *do* vary geographically. They tend to be lower in producing areas like Texas, Louisiana, and Oklahoma (oil), West Virginia (coal), and Washington (hydroelectric power) and higher in areas like New England, New Jersey, and New York that have to import all their fossil fuels and lack substantial hydroelectric power.[19] If the production process used by a firm is energy-intensive, other things being equal, the firm will favor a location where energy prices are low. Second, energy is an input for all modes of transportation. We have already shown that transportation costs importantly affect locational choice in some indus-

18. Roniger, p. 29.
19. See Roger W. Schmenner, "Energy and Location," in Anthony Downs and Katharine L. Bradbury, eds., *Energy Costs, Urban Development and Housing* (Washington, D.C.: Brookings Institution, 1984), tables 4–7; and Irving Hoch, *Energy Use in the United States by State and Region*, research paper R-9 (Washington, D.C.: Resources for the Future, 1978), p. 27.

tries. By increasing the cost of transportation relative to other inputs, higher energy prices would tend to increase the weight given to transport considerations in choosing sites.

Studying the problem in the early 1980s, however, economists concluded that the higher fuel prices of the 1970s had not substantially affected industrial locations and were not likely to do so at their then current level. Roger Schmenner suggested a number of explanations. First, when fuel prices rose sharply in 1973–1974, U.S. industry quickly adopted more energy-efficient processes, which greatly reduced the impact of higher prices. Second, firms that were now sensitive to energy price differentials had probably always been so, so their existing locations were already likely to be energy efficient. The same point can be made with respect to transport costs: if a firm was transport-cost-oriented, it would already have chosen its location on that basis; a subsequent increase in transport costs would not be likely to cause much locational change.[20] Third, geographic differentials in energy costs across the United States have been greatly reduced in recent years and continued to decline even after the onset of the energy crisis.[21] Finally, differences in energy costs between regions are not among the half dozen factors that firms usually consider most important when choosing a location.[22]

LIMITATIONS OF THE ANALYSIS

Throughout this chapter we have used the method of partial equilibrium analysis, or, as it has sometimes been called, "one thing at a time" analysis. The method proceeds by asking, in effect, if all other things except the location of one firm are held constant, where will that one firm locate? We set the scene for this sort of analysis when we explicitly assumed that the firm in question is so small in relation to the relevant markets that its activities have no perceptible effect on the prices of the goods it buys or sells and no effect on the location of other economic units. We thus assumed away the possibility that our one firm's decisions would in fact alter the prices, costs, and other magnitudes we had specified as given. We could then find the equilibrium location for a single firm in a world of given markets, prices, and costs.

Suppose, however, that we are dealing with a firm so large in relation to its economic environment that it must in fact have an impact on local markets, prices, and costs. In that case the method of partial equilibrium analysis breaks down. For example, our analysis of transport orientation takes as given a market of a certain size and production costs of a certain level at C. But if a large firm decides to locate at C instead of M, won't that perhaps increase em-

---

20. Schmenner, pp. 216–217.
21. Ibid., tables 4–7.
22. Ibid., pp. 204–206; and see his longer study, *Making Business Location Decisions* (Englewood Cliffs, N.J.: Prentice-Hall, 1982), pp. 31–39.

ployment, wage rates, production costs, incomes, and market size at *C*, thus altering all the determinants of location not only for this firm but for others both at *C* and elsewhere? Clearly, there are limits to the valid use of the partial equilibrium method.

In contrast to this approach, the method of general equilibrium attempts to reveal simultaneously the equilibrium locations for all firms. To do this it must, of course, also simultaneously yield equilibrium prices and quantities for goods and services in all markets. Needless to say, such an analysis is complex and difficult to carry through, but for certain problems, such as planning a new city that will maximize some specified value or calculating the impact of a proposed new urban transit facility on citywide real estate values, it would appear to be indispensable.

THE CONTRIBUTION OF LOCATION THEORY
TO AN UNDERSTANDING OF URBAN GROWTH

In this chapter, we have attempted to explain why economic activities locate in particular places—for example, why a large flour-milling industry developed at Buffalo rather than Albany or why textile mills are concentrated in North Carolina rather than northern New Jersey. The explanation has turned out to depend almost entirely on the existence of irregularities in space, including variations in the physical configuration of the land, discontinuities in the means of transportation, and the facts that resources are localized rather than ubiquitous and climate is not spatially uniform. Because of these irregularities and discontinuities, the business firm's costs of production or transportation are potentially lower at some places than at others. Places offering lower costs attract economic activity, become centers of production, and therefore increase in market size and attract market-oriented activity, which contributes to further growth. As they grow, they offer increasingly important economies of agglomeration, which then reinforce their initial locational advantage. By these processes the railroad junction or the little river port of 1850 becomes the large city of 1900 and the great metropolitan area of 1980. An entire urban-metropolitan economy grows from the small seed of initial locational advantage.

The next chapter continues the discussion of location theory. However, the focus shifts: instead of examining the question of why cities grow up at particular places, we will be investigating the spatial relationships *between* cities. The theories offered in the two chapters are entirely complementary. A full account of urban reality must recognize that there are not just individual urban places whose character, development, and location can be studied. Rather, there is a "system of cities," and this system is marked by important spatial-economic regularities.

FIVE

The System of Cities
and the Urban Hierarchy

It is meaningful to speak of a "system of cities" because the size and character of any one urban place—or, in dynamic terms, its power to attract activity—is conditioned by the size, character, and location of other, related places. The nature of this system is dealt with in a branch of urban study known as "central place theory," which began with work done by Walter Christaller in the 1930s and was subsequently extended and systematized by August Lösch.[1] Central place theory is, in fact, an integral part of the theory of the location of economic activity. The link between the two is provided by market area analysis, as will emerge shortly.

CENTRAL PLACE THEORY

The analysis in the preceding chapter realistically assumed a world of differentiated topography, discontinuous transportation facilities, and nonubiquitous resources. Central place theory, on the other hand, is best expounded by assuming just the opposite sort of world. Instead of explaining the location of activity in terms of the unique features of

---

1. Christaller's work was published in German. For an English translation see Carlisle W. Baskin, *Central Places in Southern Germany* (Englewood Cliffs, N.J.: Prentice-Hall, 1966). An early, concise description of it is Edward Ullman's well-known article "A Theory of Location for Cities," reprinted in William H. Leahy, David L. McKee, and Robert D. Dean, eds., *Urban Economics* (New York: Free Press, 1970), pp. 105–115.

Lösch's major work, published in German in 1941, appeared in an English translation by W. H. Woglom and W. F. Stolper as *The Economics of Location* (New Haven, Conn.: Yale University Press, 1954).

particular places, it begins by assuming away all unique features. It postulates a perfectly uniform physical world, consisting of a featureless plane on which transportation is equally efficient in any direction and resources are evenly distributed.

J. H. von Thünen had first postulated a uniform land surface as early as 1826, in his explanation of the formation of concentric agricultural belts around a market city (see Chapter 6, note 1). Central place theory shows us how, in a similar environment, a regular network of urban places would be expected to form to provide various services to an evenly distributed, homogeneous rural population.

Economic Basis for a Central Place

In explaining the development of central places, Lösch begins by assuming that self-sufficient farms are the only producing units on the uniform transport surface. He then asks whether, if one of the farmers decides to produce a surplus of some commodity and offer it for sale, he will be able to do so. The answer, fundamental to all analysis of market areas, is that "he will be helped by the economies of large scale production, and handicapped by costs of transportation."[2]

In a much simplified version of Lösch's argument, let us assume that farmer F has decided to produce a surplus of bread to sell to his neighbors. They will be willing to buy it from him if he can deliver it to their farms at a price below what it would cost them to make it themselves. Farmer F will be able to deliver at such a price only if the cost he saves by baking in larger quantities outweighs the expense of delivery. Otherwise the potential customers would be better off continuing to bake at home.

The situation is illustrated in Figure 5.1. Farmer F is located at point O. Distances from O are measured along the horizontal scale and unit costs along the vertical. The average unit cost of producing bread at home is OA. Farmer F, however, produces on a larger scale and therefore at lower cost. Suppose that he finds he can maximize profits by setting an f.o.b. price of OB.[3] His customers must also bear the cost of transportation, which rises with distance from O as indicated by the line BC. The delivered price at any given distance is shown by the height of BC above the horizontal at that distance from O. Thus a customer at point D would pay a delivered price of OG per unit, of which BG is the cost of transportation and OB the price at the source. Under the monopolistic conditions assumed, farmer F would serve a circular market with a radius of OE miles. Beyond that distance his delivered price

2. August Lösch "The Nature of Economic Regions," in John Friedmann and William Alonso, eds., *Regional Development and Planning: A Reader* (Cambridge, Mass.: M.I.T. Press, 1964), p. 108.

3. *F.o.b.* stands for "free on board." The "f.o.b. price" is the charge at the source for goods that the seller places on board a carrier provided by the purchaser.

FIGURE 5.1
Factors Determining Market Area for a Single Seller

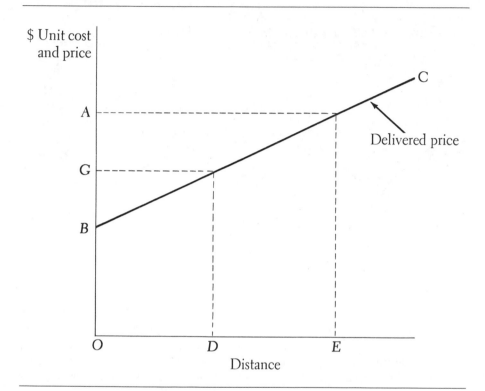

would exceed the cost to potential customers of producing at home; sales would be zero. (Throughout the following analysis matters are greatly simplified if we continue to assume that the producer sells to all customers at a uniform f.o.b. mill price. Buyers pay all delivery costs. The seller engages in neither price discrimination nor freight absorption.)

A more extended analysis of farmer *F*'s situation would show explicitly the relationship of price, market area, quantity sold, cost of production, and total profit. Such a detailed picture, however, is not necessary for our purposes. It suffices, as in the general case for monopolists, to say that the price, *OB*, at which he maximizes profits must be the price at which the marginal revenue from sales just equals the marginal cost of production. The spatial-monopoly situation analyzed here differs from the standard textbook monopoly case only in this respect; in the spatial setting it can be shown explicitly that a reduction in price results in a greater quantity being sold both because existing customers buy more and because a lower price extends the boundary of the market outward to take in additional customers.

FIGURE 5.2
Network of Circular Markets Leaves Some Areas Unserved

Market radius = OE miles   Shading indicates unserved areas

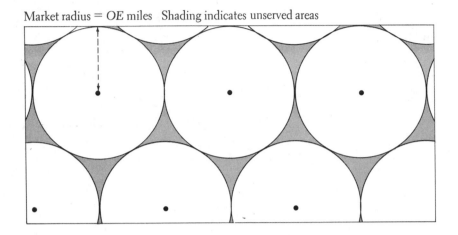

A Network of Central Places for a Single Service

Let us now assume that other farmers can set up bakeries under the same cost conditions enjoyed by farmer *F*. To maximize profits each would locate away from other producers in order to sell as a monopolist to a circular market of optimum size (i.e., the same size as farmer *F*'s). If the whole region were to be filled up by such sellers, a map of their markets would show a series of tangent circular areas, each having a radius of *OE* miles, as in Figure 5.2. Since each bakery would be earning monopoly profits, however, there is no reason to assume that this situation would persist. On the contrary, one would expect additional firms to be attracted by the high profits. The new-comers would locate between the existing producers and by their competition reduce the market areas of the former monopolists.

The situation would now take on the characteristics of monopolistic competition as defined by E.H. Chamberlin.[4] We assume that bread is an un-differentiated product, so each customer buys from the nearest supplier. Producers are differentiated in the eyes of their customers not by differences in their product but by differences in their location. The effect is the same, however; instead of facing the horizontal demand curve of perfect competition, each firm faces a negatively sloped demand curve: as it reduces the f.o.b. price, sales to existing customers increase, and also the radius of the market is extended to take in new customers at the geographic margin. The competi-

4. E. H. Chamberlin, *The Theory of Monopolistic Competition*, 8th ed. (Cambridge, Mass.: Harvard University Press, 1965), ch. 5.

FIGURE 5.3
Network of Hexagonal Markets Serves All Areas

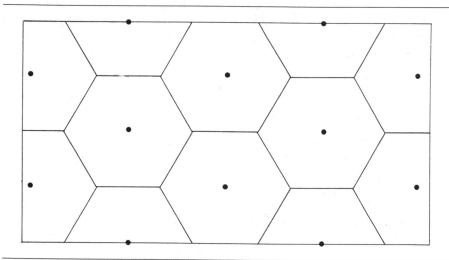

tion of new firms pressing in to fill the terrain, however, ensures that no producer can take advantage of a spatial monopoly (with its negatively sloped demand curve) to earn monopoly profits. When competition is fully effective, each firm will find that its market area has been so compressed by the entry of other firms that the most profitable nondiscriminatory price level it can establish will yield only the normal rate of return (that is, its demand curve will be tangent to the average cost curve at that price level; it is assumed that average cost includes an allowance for "normal profit").

Since we assume that all firms produce under similar cost conditions and that population and effective demand are spread uniformly over the region, it follows that f.o.b. prices will be the same in all markets and that all markets will be the same size. As Lösch points out, this size will also be the minimum threshold size for a firm producing the given service.

The geometrical shape to be expected theoretically for such markets in a system that has reached equilibrium has been a matter of debate. The early central place theorists realized that if markets were circular, as in Figure 5.2, unserved areas would remain between the points of tangency of the circles. They argued that this could not be an equilibrium scheme and concluded that the most efficient arrangement that would leave no place unserved would be a network of regular hexagons, with a central place at the center of each, as shown in Figure 5.3. A more recent analysis, however, has shown that other outcomes are possible.[5]

5. Edwin S. Mills and Michael R. Lav, "A Model of Market Areas with Free Entry," *Journal of Political Economy*, June 1964, pp. 278–288.

The hypothetical scheme of monopolistic competition in space outlined here for a single good can readily be extended to take in any number of products or services. Let us call the goods so distributed "central services." Each such service would develop market areas of a characteristic size. The economy would thus contain not a single net of markets but a system of nets overlaid upon each other, each net delineating markets for a different good or service.

Determinants of Characteristic Market Size

The forces that determine the characteristic market size for each central service are a matter of great interest, since, as we will see, they also determine the dimensions of the entire central place system. For each service, then, market size depends on three factors:

1. *The extent of economies of scale in production of the service.* Market areas will tend to be larger when economies of scale are attainable, since large-scale firms will then be able to produce at lower unit cost than smaller firms and will be able to drive the latter out of business. The survivors will necessarily have markets large enough to support large-scale output.

2. *The density of demand for the service.* The greater the demand for a service per unit of land area, the smaller the area needed to support a producing firm of optimum size. Demand per unit of land area is a function not only of price but also of population density and income level of the population. Therefore, the greater the population density and/or the average income level in a region, the smaller the characteristic market areas for given services in that region will be.

3. *The cost of transporting the good or service.* At first glance it would appear that the lower the cost of transportation, the larger the typical market area would be. In Figure 5.1 the cost of transport per unit of output per mile is shown by the slope of the gradient *BC*. If transport were cheaper and this slope consequently were flatter, it would appear that farmer *F*'s market could extend farther before his delivered price rose to the level of the home-production cost, *OA*. As we will see, however, the case is more complicated than that. Although transportation costs certainly affect market size, one cannot assume a priori that lower rates will always make for larger markets.

A HIERARCHY OF CENTRAL PLACES

The fact of wide variation in the characteristic market size for different central services implies the existence of a hierarchy of central places or, as it is sometimes called, an "urban hierarchy." In an economy of fixed extent, the number of individual markets necessary to handle the distribution of a given

good, such as haircuts, over the entire economy would be inversely proportional to the characteristic area of a haircut market. Some goods, including
haircuts, would in fact be distributed through many small markets; others, say
finished lumber or television broadcasts, through a smaller number of larger
markets. To take advantage of economies of agglomeration in both production and marketing, firms selling these various services will tend to cluster in
villages, towns, and cities instead of seeking isolated locations. But if there are
fewer television stations than lumberyards and fewer lumberyards than barber shops, it is apparent that many towns will have only barber shops, while a
smaller number will have barber shops and lumberyards, and still fewer will
offer all three central services. Thus we could describe a central place hierarchy by classifying places according to the number and types of central services they offer. We would find that size of city increased and number of cities decreased as we moved up the scale from first-order places (those offering
the fewest services) to the highest-order place (which offers the most services).

It is worth noting that higher-order places offer not only more services
but services of an entirely different sort than lower-order places. A major center, for example, not only contains more kinds of retail stores than does a
small town but also provides services like wholesaling and transshipment that
are entirely absent in the smaller place.

Indeed, as Allen Philbrick has shown, one can define a hierarchy of
places in terms of the level or nature of the functions performed rather than
by their sheer number. Using economic functions only, he suggests a seven-
fold hierarchy in which the seven levels of function from lowest to highest order are consumption (the household function), retail, wholesale, transshipment, exchange, control, and leadership.[6]

Philbrick's scheme emphasizes the fact that a developed economy is
highly specialized by function, that specialization requires exchange of goods
and of information by means of flows along well-defined paths, that cities are
focal places in the organization of such flows, and that their rank in the hierarchy is defined by the stage in the process of production and distribution for
which they serve as a focal place. Thus a town with a retail store is a focal
place for the activities of a group of household consumption units, a city containing a wholesale establishment is a focal place for the activities of a group
of towns containing retail stores, and so forth up the table of organization to
the highest-order place, which provides leadership to the economy as a whole.

Such an organization is not unlike the plan of a telephone network.
Each subscriber cannot have a direct line to every other; instead, each is connected to a local exchange, which is in turn connected to other focal points
through a long-distance network. As Philbrick has pointed out, this sort of

6. Allen K. Philbrick, "Areal Functional Organization in Regional Geography," *Papers of
the Regional Science Association,* 3, (1957), pp. 87–98.

FIGURE 5.4
Schematic Diagram of an Urban Hierarchy

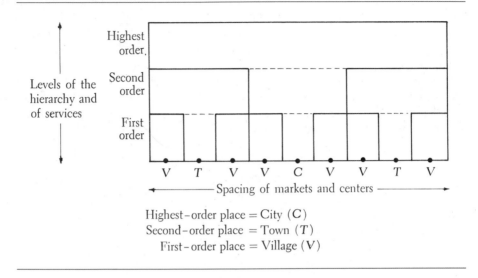

Highest-order place = City (C)
Second-order place = Town (T)
First-order place = Village (V)

scheme can be used to describe the hierarchy of political and social as well as economic functions.

As the discussion to this point indicates, theoretical models of central place systems display a high degree of internal regularity. For example, at each level of the hierarchy all the towns serve market areas of the same size and shape. Each town is at the center of its market area, and the markets do not overlap. Consequently, towns of each hierarchical order are uniformly spaced. The number of towns decreases as we move up the hierarchy, and, necessarily, the average distance between them increases at successively higher levels. At each level we could map out a perfectly regular set of mutually exclusive market areas that would exhaust the space of the economy. Each would contain a town of appropriate size at its center. Each city of a higher order would provide services to the same number of towns of the next lower order. In addition, each would provide for itself all the services performed for themselves by all places lower in the hierarchy. Figure 5.4 is a diagram of such a system containing three levels. The number of market areas decreases by a factor of 3 as we move up from level to level of this hypothetical system.[7]

7. There are many possible internally consistent "geometries" for central place systems. For a review see Brian J.L. Berry, *Geography of Market Centers and Retail Distribution* (Englewood Cliffs, N.J.: Prentice-Hall, 1967), chs. 3 and 4; and Leslie J. King, *Central Place Theory* (Beverly Hills, Calif.: Sage Publications, 1984), pp. 32–46.

Systematic Exceptions to the Hierarchical Order

No central place theorist would expect to find in the real world a hierarchy of places as perfectly ordered as the one depicted in Figure 5.4. First of all, resources and population are not spread evenly over the earth as central place models usually assume. Extractive industries necessarily concentrate where the resources are and attract population to such regions. Topographical irregularities, too, obviously interfere with the uniform spacing of economic activity, both directly and through their influence on the transport network. Thus ports and navigable rivers attract concentrations of activity and population. Climate and other natural amenities also strongly influence the location of people and of industry. And if population and industry are unevenly distributed over the map, central places will obviously also be unevenly distributed; their size and spacing will not display the regularity to be found in theoretical models of central place systems.

So far as manufacturing is concerned, the scheme applies, even roughly, only to industries, such as baking, that are locationally consumer-market-oriented. Manufacturing industries that are materials-oriented locate near materials sources, and if the sources are not evenly distributed, they, like the extractive industries, will concentrate in a few favored areas from which they serve the entire economy. The geographic concentration of the coal, iron, and steel industries is a good example. In similar fashion, manufacturing firms that are production-cost-oriented frequently breach the scheme by competing for the entire national market from a single plant, perhaps in some relatively small town that otherwise performs only the lowest-order functions. For these and other reasons (including the economies of localization analyzed in earlier chapters), cities may become specialized in the production of particular goods and, in effect, earn a living by exporting them to other cities across the economy. Yet as Noyelle and Stanback point out, classical central place theory unrealistically "makes no provision for any commerce among cities of the same size category."[8]

Large cities, too, may develop disproportionately in the sense that they perform one higher-order function without performing others to the expected degree. Thus Pittsburgh, clearly not a highest-order metropolis, nevertheless ranked fourth in the United States in nonlocal banking activity in 1960, ahead of Philadelphia, Boston, Los Angeles, and Cleveland, all larger cities and in many respects more "metropolitan."[9]

Central place theory best applies in two cases: consumer-market-oriented manufacturing and the general run of service industries. Even for

8. Thierry J. Noyelle and Thomas M. Stanback, Jr., *The Economic Transformation of American Cities* (Totowa, N.J.: Rowman & Allanheld, 1984), p. 38. See chs. 3 and 4 of their study and the sources cited therein for a description of the U.S. system of cities more realistic than that provided by classical central place theory.

9. Otis Dudley Duncan et al., *Metropolis and Region* (Baltimore: Johns Hopkins University Press, 1960), pp. 116–117.

these, however, there is an important qualification to the deductive model: the market areas of individual suppliers are rarely mutually exclusive. Since most products and services are differentiated either by brand names, like loaves of bread, or by the personal qualities of the supplier, like automotive repair services, consumers do *not* always purchase from the nearest source. This alone would make for interpenetration of markets. In addition, however, many producers employ pricing practices such as freight absorption in a deliberate effort to foster sales to distant customers. Though usually mentioned in connection with industries serving national markets, freight absorption is equally important locally. Retail distributors of home heating oil or bottled gas, for example, do not charge for delivery. In such cases nearby customers are, in effect, subsidizing distant ones. The customer has no incentive to seek out the closest supplier. We must allow for a great deal of cross-hauling, both of goods going to customers and of customers shopping for goods.

THE PROBLEM OF EMPIRICAL VERIFICATION

A large number of empirical studies have sought evidence in the real world of economic geography for the regularities that central place theory predicts will exist. Most of these have examined relatively thinly settled agricultural regions, such as the Farm Belt of the American Midwest and Canada, where central place theory's assumption of an even distribution of population and resources is approximately realized. In such areas (and in many parts of the world) the central place system has, indeed, been found to display a high degree of regularity.[10]

At this point the alert reader may detect a problem in scientific methodology: is there really an urban hierarchy containing classes of cities with demonstrably different characteristics, or is there merely a continuum of cities from small to large on which we have arbitrarily imposed the character of hierarchy? For if we take the cities and towns of a given region and array them by size we will, of course, find that there are more small than large towns and more large towns than cities. Average market area size and average distance between places will therefore necessarily increase as we go up the scale from small to large places. We will also certainly find that the number of establishments performing central services and the number of different services performed typically increases as population size of centers increases. A town of 200 might have only four establishments providing two or three different services, while a town of 1,000 in the same region has thirty establishments covering twenty-four functions, and a town of 3,000 has one hundred establishments in forty service categories. Yet the plain fact is that we could use an

---

10. Much of the empirical work is reviewed in Berry, *Geography of Market Centers*, chs. 1, 2, and 6, and in Peter E. Lloyd and Peter Dicken, *Location in Space: A Theoretical Approach to Economic Geography*, 2nd ed. (New York: Harper & Row, 1977), ch. 3.

arbitrary rule to partition an array of towns into a number of size classes, and no matter where we drew the lines, we would certainly find those kinds of regularity. Consequently, such a finding would not demonstrate the existence of a hierarchy. In Berry and Garrison's phrase, the analyst would merely have "used an arbitrary division and then proved what he had in fact assumed."[11]

Two Case Studies: Washington and Saskatchewan

Berry and Garrison set out to test the hypothesis that the central places in Snohomish County, Washington, form an observable hierarchy rather than merely a continuum from small to large. They concluded that a hierarchy was indeed observable. Their procedure need not be described here in detail. In summary, they found that the towns in their study area could be "arranged into three types . . . defined on the basis of the presence of urban functions . . . in varying degrees." They then demonstrated that "these center types differ more one type from another than they differ within types."[12] By using appropriate statistical tests they were able to show that their classification of types was not arbitrary but, instead, led to statistically significant groupings. Moreover, the three groups, or types, of central places differed significantly from one another not only in number of functions performed but in types of function.

Table 5.1 summarizes the dimensions of the hierarchy revealed in Berry and Garrison's study. Obviously, the mean population size of central places increases as we move up the scale from hamlets to villages to towns. So also does the average number of establishments per place and the average number of different functions performed. Since the former increases faster than the latter, the number of establishments per function also increases as we move up the hierarchy. The individual hamlets rarely have more than one or two establishments of a single type. A town, on the other hand, might easily have six or more establishments in categories such as food stores, restaurants, churches, or filling stations.

A different perspective on the system is presented in Table 5.2, which measures the prevalence of selected functions in the three classes of central place. The functions are ranked down the table from most common (filling stations) to least common (public accountants) on the basis of Berry and Garrison's estimates of minimum threshold population size for each. Almost without exception, all four towns in the study area had at least one establish-

11. Brian J. L. Berry and William L. Garrison, "The Functional Bases of the Central-Place Hierarchy," *Economic Geography*, April 1958, pp. 145–154.

For a later test that verifies the existence of an observable central place hierarchy over a much larger region of the Pacific Northwest, see Richard E. Preston, "The Structure of Central Place Systems," reprinted in L. S. Bourne and J. W. Simmons, eds., *Systems of Cities* (New York: Oxford University Press, 1978), pp. 185–206.

12. Berry and Garrison, p. 147.

TABLE 5.1
Characteristics of the Central Place Hierarchy in Snohomish County,
Washington

	CLASSES OF CENTRAL PLACES		
	Hamlets	*Villages*	*Towns*
Number of places in class	20	9	4
Average population per place	417	948	2,433
Total number of establishments in class of places	138	490	596
Average number of establishments per place	6.9	54.4	149.0
Total number of functions in class of places	118	289	239
Average number of functions per place	5.9	32.1	59.8
Average number of establishments per function	1.2	1.7	2.5

Source: Brian J. L. Berry and William Garrison, "The Functional Bases of the Central-Place Hierarchy," *Economic Geography*, April 1958, table 2, p. 150.

ment in every functional class. The nine villages without exception offered all of the more common functions, but halfway down the table they showed a pronounced falling off. Fewer than half of the villages are represented in the selected functions with the largest threshold sizes. As for the hamlets, they drop out almost completely when we reach central services with a population threefold larger than an elementary school. It is interesting to note this inference from Table 5.2: with very few exceptions, the central place hierarchy of Snohomish County possesses the characteristic (predicted by the theory) that places of a higher order provide for themselves all services that are found in places lower in the hierarchy.

A hierarchy is by definition a systematic arrangement of the classes of an object. Central place theory emphasizes especially the systematic nature of the spatial arrangement of centers. The best analogy is to a planetary system in which the units are held in place by the gravitational forces between them. Thus central place theory purports to show that each particular urban settlement is, so to speak, held in place within a system of cities; it suggests that the development of each is affected in a predictable way by its position within the system.

Gerald Hodge's study of central places in Saskatchewan verifies this characteristic of the system.[13] Hodge distinguished seven classes of trade centers in Saskatchewan and studied changes in the relative importance of each

13. Gerald Hodge, "The Prediction of Trade Center Viability in the Great Plains," *Papers of the Regional Science Association*, 15 (1965), pp. 87–115.

TABLE 5.2
Prevalence of Selected Functions in Central Places of Snohomish County,
Washington

	NUMBERS OF PLACES IN CLASS HAVING AT LEAST ONE ESTABLISHMENT		
TYPE OF FUNCTION[a]	*Hamlets (20)*	*Villages (9)*	*Towns (4)*
Filling stations	17	9	4
Food stores	7	9	4
Churches	8	9	4
Restaurants	6	9	4
Elementary schools	13	9	4
Physicians	0	6	4
Appliance stores	0	8	4
Barber shops	5	9	4
Insurance agencies	0	5	3
Drugstores	2	9	4
Lawyers	0	5	4
Apparel stores	0	6	4
Banks	2	7	4
Dry cleaners	1	4	4
Jewelry stores	0	4	4
Department stores	1	3	4
Hospitals and clinics	0	1	3
Public accountants	0	1	3

[a]Functions are ranked from smallest to largest by estimated minimum threshold population size.
Source: Brian J. L. Berry and William L. Garrison, "The Functional Bases of the Central-Place Hierarchy," *Economic Geography,* April 1958, table 2, P. 150.

of these classes in the system as a whole between 1941 and 1961. A given trade center was said to have "declined" during the period if it either shifted downward one or more classes in the hierarchy or disappeared altogether as a center. Central place theory would predict that, other things being equal, at any given level in the hierarchy, towns that are nearer than the average to centers of like character will be more likely to decline than the average in their class, for they will be too near their competitors. Hodge's study showed just such a result. He found: "Of hamlets thus situated [i.e., closer than average to other hamlets], 66 percent declined from 1941–61 compared to 46 percent for all hamlets in the same period. Similar differentials of decline were found for the other types of centers studied."[14] Here is direct evidence that central places behave not as independent entities but as parts of a coherent "system of cities."

14. Ibid., p. 101.

HOW THE SYSTEM OF CITIES DEVELOPS
AND CHANGES OVER TIME

Probably the most interesting contribution of central place theory is the help it provides in understanding the historical trend of changes within the system of cities. Under the impact of technological innovation and economic development, profound alterations occur in the pattern of urban settlement, the size distribution of cities, and the division of functions among cities at various levels of the hierarchy. Central place theory helps to illuminate these complex changes.

We have already shown that the various dimensions of the central place system (number, size, and spacing of cities; number and location of functions and of establishments; etc.) depend largely on the size of the characteristic market areas for central services. Therefore, the obvious point of entry for an analysis of change in those dimensions is to consider what might cause the typical market area to alter in size.[15] It was pointed out earlier that market area size for any central service depends on three factors: the extent of economies of scale in its production, the level of demand for the service per unit of area, and the cost of transporting it. We must now examine the effects of technological change and economic growth on these three factors. Five types of change will be analyzed:

1. Growth of population
2. Rise in living standards (i.e., increased per capita income)
3. Innovation leading to the development of greater economies of scale in production
4. Innovation leading to a reduction in transport costs
5. Rise in fuel prices leading to increased transport costs

To keep the discussion within bounds we will use retail trade as the illustrative case and derive conclusions from it that are applicable to central services in general. Figure 5.5 depicts three spatially separated competing retail outlets, *A*, *B*, and *C*. As before, we measure distance along the horizontal scale, average unit cost of production and unit delivery cost along the vertical.

Assume initially that the outlets are old-fashioned general stores, selling a variety of goods such as groceries, housewares, and the like. The unit cost of this merchandise, measured on the vertical axis, is the cost of a composite of items that a typical consumer might buy and carry home on a single shopping trip. Since the buyer carries the goods home, delivery cost is to be interpreted as the cost of making a round trip from home to store and back. This consists of two elements: first, the money cost of the trip and, second, a nonmonetary

---

15. For a more complex analysis that relates arithmetically the number and population size of centers at each level of the hierarchy to the population of the market areas they serve, see Hugh O. Nourse, *Regional Economics* (New York: McGraw-Hill, 1968), pp. 40–44 and 209–218.

FIGURE 5.5
Economies of Scale, Transportation Costs and the Market Areas of Competing Central Places

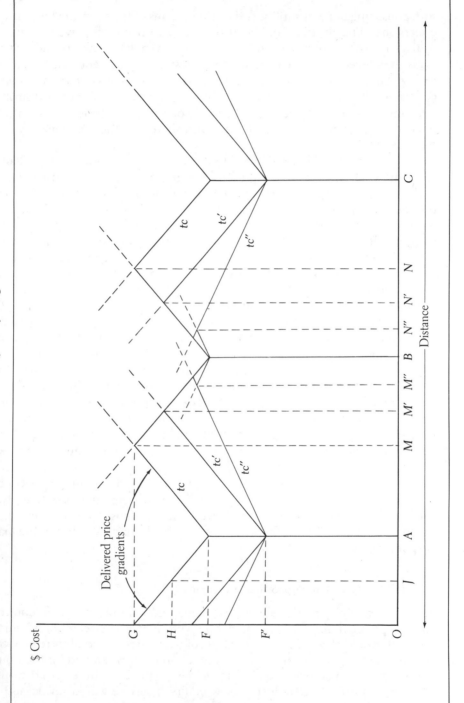

cost, consisting of the disutility of the trip in terms of time lost and discomfort undergone. The disutility of the trip can, in principle, be given a money equivalent: the amount the shopper would pay not to have to undergo it. Thus the two costs can be combined into a single money equivalent, which, for a given route and mode of transport, can be expressed as a cost of so many cents per mile. Now in the ordinary case in which the nonmonetary disutility of a journey is positive, the faster the mode of transport, the less the disutility of covering a given distance and the lower, therefore, the nonmonetary cost per mile.

In Figure 5.5, then, we start with three general stores located at villages A, B, and C along a line that represents geographic space. The villages are of equal size. Rural population is spread uniformly in the space between them at residential locations that are assumed to remain fixed. We also assume that more such stores are located at regular intervals to the left and right of the segment we are looking at. Initially these spatial competitors are in equilibrium. Each has a store of optimum size and can just manage to earn a normal return by supplying a unit of goods at an f.o.b. price of OF. The absence of monopolistic profits indicates that stores have been "packed in" as closely as is consistent with long-run equilibrium.

Shoppers who do not live in a village travel to market by automobile. Their round-trip travel costs, a combination of monetary and nonmonetary elements, are a linear function of their distance from the store. Each buys in that store for which the sum of f.o.b. price plus travel costs is least. This sum, which we may call the "delivered price," is shown for any point of residence by the height above the horizontal at that point of the delivered price gradient from the supplier. The slope of the gradient equals round-trip travel cost per unit of distance. Initially, the relevant gradients are those labeled tc. Thus a customer living at J would pay OF for a unit of merchandise and incur travel costs of FH in going from home at J to the store at A and returning. For this customer, total cost per unit is therefore OH. The market boundary between stores A and B is at point M, where the delivered price gradients of these two suppliers intersect. A customer at M would incur a cost OG per unit when buying from either A or B. Similarly, N marks the boundary between the markets of B and C.

Effect of a Rise in Population or Income

We examine first the effect of a geographically uniform increase in the region's population. A rise in population, with income per capita remaining constant, would clearly increase the level of demand for general store services per unit of area. Store owners at A, B, and C would find demand for their output rising and would begin to earn above-normal profits. These profits would attract new firms to the industry. New points of service would spring up between previously existing centers, and the markets of store owners at A, B, and C would be compressed by this competition. At the higher level of demand density, a store of optimum size could earn normal returns with a smaller market area. The end result would be an increase in the number of firms and in the number of central places and a decrease in the characteristic size of market areas for general stores. The distance between centers would decrease.

Let us assume that these general stores and the villages at which they are located make up the lowest order of the central place hierarchy. We can see that the changes taking place at this level would have their counterparts at higher levels, too. The number of higher-order firms and centers would also increase (for example, more wholesalers would be needed to service the larger number of general stores), their market areas would grow smaller, and the distance between higher-order centers would also diminish.

Berry has amply documented these and other effects of varying population density by comparing the central place systems in Iowa with those in much more thinly populated South Dakota.[16] To be sure, this approach is cross-sectional rather than longitudinal: it examines areas having unequal densities at a single point in time instead of observing a single area as its population density changes through the years. Such a cross-sectional method, however, has the great advantage that it holds constant other crucial variables, such as the technology of transportation, which could not be held constant in a study running over time. With "other things remaining the same" one can isolate more successfully the effect of the single factor of population density.

The general effect of a rise in per capita income with population held constant would be much the same as the effect of a rise in population with per capita income held constant, since in both cases the areal density of demand increases. Consequently, we need not repeat the argument for the case in which income rises.

Effect of Increased Economies of Scale

To examine the effect of a technological innovation leading to increased economies of scale in production, let us assume that the owner of store A "invents" the principle of the self-service supermarket. This innovation allows average unit cost to be reduced, provided that the scale of operation can be sufficiently enlarged. The owner of store A calculates that by creating a supermarket she can achieve economies of scale such that she will maximize profits by reducing the f.o.b. price from OF to OF'. With this lower price, owner A can expect to increase sales for two reasons: first, if the demand of individual consumers is elastic, she will sell more to her present customers; second, if her competitors do not also build supermarkets, she will

16. Berry, *Geography of Market Centers*, ch. 2.

capture their outlying customers. For example, when A lowers her price to OF', the delivered price gradient shifts to tc' (parallel to tc, since transportation cost is unchanged). If B does not respond in kind, A's market boundary now moves out to point M'.

If owner C also builds a supermarket, B's market area will be squeezed from both sides, contracting from MN to M'N'. Initially, B was earning a normal return. Now his return will fall, and he may decide to close up, leaving his customers to be divided between supermarkets A and C. This, of course, is precisely what has happened since the advent of the supermarket: many small stores have disappeared. But suppose B had also attempted to open a supermarket. In that case none of the firms could have expanded its market area. Unless demand were so elastic that lower prices permitted considerably enlarged sales within fixed market boundaries, not all the supermarkets could survive. Some suppliers would be forced out until those remaining could earn normal returns by enlarging their market areas. This seems the most likely outcome provided that population, income, and transportation costs remain constant.

Granted that increased economies of scale will probably lead to a reduction in the number of establishments providing the given service, what effect will that have on the number and spacing of central places? The answer depends on the situation from which one starts. In Figure 5.5 we assume that general store retailing is the only service provided by villages, which are the lowest-order places in the hierarchy, and that there is only one store per village. In that case a reduction in the number of firms necessarily means a reduction in the number of villages and an increase in their spacing.

Of course, other possibilities abound. Initially, for example, villages A, B, and C might have provided several central services in addition to general store goods. In that case, B could continue supplying other central services even though supermarkets at A and C had eliminated its general store. Economies of scale would then have reduced the number of central service establishments in the system as a whole but not the number of centers, although some centers would have been weakened relative to others.

If we assume, however, that economies of scale increase substantially in the production of many types of central services rather than in only one, it seems highly probable that some of the smallest centers will be eliminated entirely as services are gradually concentrated into larger towns. Within the category of retail services, such consolidation is also affected by the importance of economies of agglomeration in shopping. Other things being equal, the retail customer will prefer to shop at the center where more needs can be satisfied on a single trip. If villages A and B provided the same services, the customer midway between them would be indifferent as to where he or she shopped. But if A provided more services than B, it would probably be preferred even for those goods also available at B. Thus the existence of agglomeration economies in shopping accelerates a process of consolidation that may begin with the development of scale economies in a particular service: each function lost at a small center weakens those that remain.

Effect of a Change in Transportation Costs

We come next to the question of transportation costs. How would a change in transport costs per mile affect the central place system? This is both the most interesting and the most complex question we can ask about the response of the system to the forces of economic change. Let us assume that a technological innovation significantly reduces transportation costs. The historical reality we here attempt to capture in simplified form is the impact of the automobile, and the improved highways that were built for it, on the twentieth-century central place system.

Consider a situation such as the one described initially in Figure 5.5. Producers at competing centers operate under identical cost conditions. Their market areas are identical in extent and just large enough to afford each a normal rate of return from a plant of optimum size. Analyzing this case, Edgar M. Hoover has argued that a reduction in transport costs has two distinguishable effects: an output effect (or, as he calls it, an "income effect") and a substitution effect.[17] Since the output effect of reduced transportation costs makes market areas smaller, while the substitution effect makes them larger, one cannot say, without knowing the details of each case, what the net effect will be.

This situation is a familiar one in the economic theory of production. For example, if a firm uses two production inputs, labor and machinery, and the relative price of machinery falls, the firm will tend to substitute machinery for labor in its production process. Clearly, the substitution effect will be to use more machinery and less labor to produce a given quantity of goods. But there will also be an output effect: since the cost of one of the firm's inputs has fallen, it will be able to sell at lower prices and therefore in larger quantities. Output will rise above its previous level, and the output effect will cause the firm to purchase more of both labor and machinery. Purchases of machinery will certainly rise, since both effects make for that result. But purchases of labor may either rise or fall, since the substitution effect reduces labor inputs while the output effect increases them.

Using Isard's method of treating transport as an input to the production process that is substitutable for other inputs, Hoover shows how the output and substitution effects operate in the case of declining transportation costs. The output effect works as follows. When transport costs per mile are reduced, the delivered price of each supplier of a central service falls for all customers not located at the very center of the market. Consequently, at what-

17. Edgar M. Hoover, "Transport Costs and the Spacing of Central Places," *Papers of the Regional Science Association*, 25 (1970), pp. 255–274.

ever f.o.b. price he chooses, each supplier can now sell more than he previously did to customers within his existing market area. His profits therefore rise above the normal rate of return he had previously been earning. This is the output effect of the fall in transport rates. It makes for smaller market areas because new firms are attracted to the production of the central service by the existence of above-normal profits. They press in upon the previously existing firms. Market areas are compressed, the number of centers increases, and the distance between them falls.

The substitution effect, Hoover argues, works in the opposite direction. As transport becomes relatively cheaper, profit-maximizing producers increase the use of transport inputs relative to other inputs by delivering the service to greater distances. Market areas become larger, centers fewer and farther apart. Since the substitution and output effects work in opposite directions, the net effect of reduced transport costs is theoretically uncertain.

It is most important, however, to note the stringent initial asumption of this analysis: that all firms operate with identical production costs. The outcome is quite different where production costs are *not* assumed to be equal for all suppliers. Moreover, the latter case is probably much the more significant in explaining the impact of economic change on the central place system. To illustrate it, let us return to the situation depicted in Figure 5.5.

Suppose that owners A and C have installed supermarkets but owner B had decided to continue running his general store, even though his market has been cut down to size M'N'. (This can be made more plausible if we recognize that in reality points A, B, and C may initially have had not one but two or three stores each and that the construction of supermarkets at A and C would then result in a reduction in the number of stores at all points. In that case a lone survivor at B could well continue to earn normal returns.) Now suppose that with the passage of time a technological improvement, in the form of better roads, speeds up travel, thus reducing transport costs. On the diagram this appears as a flattening of the delivered price gradients from tc' to tc''. Even though B's gradients flatten out as much as the others, his market boundaries move inward from M' and N' to M'' and N''. Thus A and C once again expand their territory at his expense. Indeed, B may well be forced out of business.

Why does B lose market ground to A and C when transportation costs drop uniformly in all three markets and the f.o.b. price differential between them does not change? The answer is that the lower transport costs per mile drop, the more miles a consumer will travel to save a price differential of given magnitude. For example, if A's f.o.b. price is $4.00 less than B's, and transport cost to market is 50 cents a mile, the customer would be willing to travel up to 8 miles farther to deal with A than with B, since $4.00 \div .50 = 8$. If transport costs fall to 25 cents a mile, the extra distance a customer would travel to save the same $4.00 rises to 16 miles. Consequently, A's market area expands at the expense of B's. An analogous principle was shown to be at work in connection with problems of industrial location: if, as a result of technological improvements, transport costs drop relative to other costs, industries tend to become less transport-cost-oriented and more production-cost-oriented.

We have already argued that an increase in economies of scale in production interacts with economies of agglomeration in shopping to strengthen larger retail centers at the expense of smaller ones. Precisely the same interaction occurs when a reduction in transport costs eliminates high-cost suppliers while extending the markets of low-cost firms. To the extent that economies of agglomeration exist, either in shopping or in production, the centers at which low-cost suppliers are concentrated will find themselves gaining cumulative advantages over the smaller centers at which functions are being eliminated. The smaller centers will suffer progressive loss through what might be called the "diseconomies of deglomeration."

Transportation Costs and the Scale of Social Organization

The general principle that for any given industry a reduction in transport costs benefits low-cost and large-scale producers at the expense of high-cost and small-scale producers is of the greatest importance in spatial economics. It helps to explain why the scale of organization throughout society is steadily increasing. It lies at the root of Hoover's observation: "Other things being equal, high transport costs mean scattered local production, and cheap transport means localized (i.e., concentrated) production."[18]

With a little imagination the reader can change the terms employed in our example and see that it is a paradigm for a large number of cases. For instance, in the public rather than the private sector, it explains why the "scale" of local schools and their districts increased and the number of schools diminished when a faster form of transportation, the school bus, replaced a slower one, shank's mare. The change in organizational scale of the school system is easily verified from national data. Between 1930 and 1983, the number of public elementary and secondary schools in the United States diminished from 262,000 to 84,700, while enrollments increased from 25.7 million to 39.3 million.[19] Average enrollment per school—a good measure of scale—consequently soared from 98 to 464. If we substitute cost and ease of communication for cost and ease of transportation, we can understand how technological improvements have enabled all kinds of economic and social

18. Edgar M. Hoover, *Location Theory and the Shoe and Leather Industries* (Cambridge, Mass.: Harvard University Press, 1937), p. 20. More recently Hoover has added a caveat, however. He notes that some interlocal variation in production costs may itself be related to transport costs insofar as the latter affect the cost of transported inputs or cause factor immobilities. "Consequently," he concludes, "cheaper transport might well be expected to narrow such cost differentials . . . and thus run against the tendency for the cheaper locations to eliminate the more expensive ones" ("Transport Costs and the Spacing of Central Places," p. 271). However, this reservation does not apply to cost differentials based on economies of scale.

19. *Statistical Abstract of the United States, 1972,* tables 152 and 154, and *1986,* tables 205 and 209.

institutions to expand from a local to a regional scale of operation or from a regional to a national or international scale.

Fuel Prices and the Central Place System

Because fuel prices influence the cost of transportation, their volatility since the early 1970s raises the question of how changes in energy costs would be expected to affect the dimensions of the central place system. In principle, the effect of higher fuel prices would simply be the reverse of that attributed in the preceding pages to a decline in transportation costs. Thus if transportation cost per mile *rises*, the distance consumers will travel to obtain a given f.o.b. price differential *declines*. Higher-cost local suppliers begin to gain customers at the expense of lower-cost, more distant ones. The further consequences of this should by now be clear: smaller centers gain strength at the expense of larger ones and may become more numerous, the distance between centers declines, and so on.

In the case of personal transportation, however, the impact of a change in fuel prices on trip cost is less dramatic than the casual observer might expect. The marginal cost of a trip for an automobile user is the sum of operating costs, parking charges, the cost of time in transit, and the cost of any other disutility of travel. As we explain in Chapter 8, the equivalent money cost of travel time typically equals or outweighs operating cost in the commuter's calculus, and fuel cost is only a fraction of operating outlays. Consequently, doubling the cost of gasoline increases marginal trip cost only about 25 percent. This contrasts with the case of the transportation innovation analyzed earlier. The effect of introducing the automobile was precisely to speed up travel, thus reducing time cost, and simultaneously to increase comfort, which reduced other elements of disutility as well. Energy costs would have to rise very high indeed to have as dramatic an effect in raising the cost of personal transportation as the introduction of the automobile had in lowering it. (See the last section of Chapter 9 for further detail.)

Moreover, the general increase in the scale of social organization, as it is reflected in the central place system, owes as much to improvements in communication as it does to those in transportation, and such improvements are not adversely affected by higher fuel costs. Indeed, a substantial increase in transportation costs, should it occur, would be expected to encourage the development and use of even more sophisticated communication techniques, since communication can often serve as a substitute for personal transportation.

Economic Development and the Impact of "Latent" Central Services

A complicating factor, largely ignored in the literature of central place theory, remains to be mentioned. The analysis to this point assumed implicitly that despite the impact of economic change and growth, the number of central services to be performed in the region remained constant. But this helpful simplification is wholly unrealistic. There are at all times and in any region "latent" central services that might be brought to the threshold of feasiblity by either an increase in demand density or a decrease in transportation cost. For example, a given population with a given average level of income might have a desire to see motion pictures, but because local transportation is so costly it is impossible to collect enough customers at any one point to make even the smallest sort of establishment pay. Suppose that the nearest motion picture theater is fifty miles away. When transportation becomes cheaper, the probable result is not that local residents now make a hundred-mile round trip to the movies, thus extending the market area of the distant producer. Rather, a local theater now becomes feasible because the cost of reaching it has fallen. A central service new to the region comes into existence. A like effect, of course, occurs when rising population or per capita income lifts demand for some latent central service to the threshold at which it becomes commercially feasible to produce it.

It is clear, then, that economic growth and declining transportation costs increase the number of central functions actually provided. The impact of such an increase on the central place system, however, cannot be determined a priori. It might seem probable, for example, that an increase in the number of functions would reinforce the tendency of rising population and income to increase the number of centers and reduce their spacing. Such an outcome, however, cannot be taken for granted. If the new services are subject to significant economies of scale in production (as bowling alleys or movie theaters are, for example) they will tend to locate in the larger centers and, by adding to agglomeration economies at those points, further erode the position of smaller centers. Each new service, however, will have its own characteristics. There appears to be no general principle upon which to predict the impact of new services on the system as a whole.

EVIDENCE FOR THE EFFECTS
OF GROWTH AND DEVELOPMENT

We have now analyzed the impact on the central place system of five factors associated with economic growth and development. Four of these factors—increased population, increased real income, economies of scale in production, and reduced transportation cost—have operated simultaneously and powerfully throughout this century. The fifth—higher fuel costs—has yet to make its influence clear and so can hardly be subjected to empirical test. What evidence can be found to test the effects of the other four? These effects can be summarized as follows. Either rising population or increased income per capita would lead to smaller market areas and a larger number and closer spacing of centers. On the other hand, increased economies of scale in the output of central services would, under the most probable circumstances, reduce the number of very small centers and strengthen the larger ones. The impact of reduced transport costs is uncertain when all suppliers have identical costs of production but favors large, low cost-suppliers when there are interfirm cost differentials. This almost certainly leads to a cumulative strengthening of large at the expense of small centers—and probably to the elimination of some of the latter. Thus the four factors associated with economic growth prior to the onset of the energy crisis must have had offsetting effects on the development of the central place system.

Although we analyzed these factors one by one, they were in fact operating on the central place system simultaneously, which makes it difficult to verify their individual impact. We can, however, observe the net effect on the central place system of all of them operating together. Among the lower-order places in the United States and Canada during the twentieth century the pattern of change is quite clear: towns and small cities have been growing in number relative to villages and hamlets. In recent years the very smallest places have declined not only in relative importance but also in absolute number.

Two sets of data indicate this tendency. Table 5.3 shows how the number of places in the United States, classified by population size, has changed

TABLE 5.3
Changes in the Number of Places by Size in the United States, 1900–1980

SIZE AND TYPE OF PLACE	NUMBER OF PLACES			INCREASE (%)
	1980	*1930*	*1900*	*1930–1980*
Total, all places, urban and rural	22,529	16,643	10,673	35
Urban, total	8,765	3,179	1,740	176
25,000–50,000	675	185	83	265
10,000–25,000	1,765	607	281	191
5,000–10,000	2,181	853	465	156
2,500–5,000	2,665	1,342	833	99
Less than 2,500[a]	1,016	—	—	—
Rural, total	13,764	13,464	8,933	2
1,000–2,500	4,434	3,107	2,130	43
Less than 1,000	9,330	10,357	6,803	−10
Urban and rural, less than 2,500	14,780	13,464	8,933	10

[a]Definition of *urban* changed in 1950. Previous to that date, all places with population under 2,500 were classified as rural.
Source: U.S. Bureau of the Census, *Census of Population, 1980,* U.S. Summary, PC80-1-A1, table 5.

during the twentieth century. The table reveals that the rate of growth in the number of places per size class increases steadily as size class increases for all classes from the smallest up to 50,000 population. Thus the number of places with population under 2,500 increased only 10 percent between 1930 and 1980, while the number of places with a population of 10,000 to 25,000 increased 191 percent, and the number in the 25,000 to 50,000 class rose 265 percent. Places with a population of less than 2,500 made up 81 percent of all places in 1930 but only 66 percent in 1980.

Precisely because they cover the whole United States, however, it may be objected that the data in Table 5.3 are too highly aggregated to be really satisfactory. In each size class, places located in growing regions and declining regions, in metropolitan areas and nonmetropolitan areas, are lumped together. In addition, the census definition of *place* changes over the interval covered and, in any case, does not correspond with the definition of *central place* employed in central place theory.

These objections, however, cannot be raised against the data in Table 5.4, which are drawn from Hodge's study of the central place system in the southern part of Saskatchewan. Hodge identified seven orders of central place in the study area, which is a relatively homogeneous farming region. The total number of such places declined from 906 in 1941 to 892 in 1951 and 779 in 1961. The number of places in the four highest orders increased from 90 in 1941 to 125 in 1961, while the number in the three lowest orders fell from 816 to 654. The three lowest orders made up 90 percent of all places in

TABLE 5.4
Changes in the Hierarchy of Trade Centers in Saskatchewan, 1941–1961

	1941		1951		1961	
CLASS OF TRADE CENTER	*Num-ber*	*Per-centage*	*Num-ber*	*Per-centage*	*Num-ber*	*Per-centage*
Primary wholesale-retail	2	0.2	2	0.2	2	0.2
Secondary wholesale-retail	5	0.6	8	0.9	9	1.2
Complete shopping	26	2.9	23	2.6	29	3.7
Partial shopping	57	6.3	66	7.4	85	10.9
Full convenience	171	18.9	169	18.9	100	12.7
Minimum convenience	287	31.8	191	21.4	150	19.4
Hamlet	358	39.3	433	48.6	404	51.8
All trade centers	906	100.0	892	100.0	779	100.0
Four highest orders	90	9.9	99	11.1	125	16.1
Three lowest orders	816	90.1	793	88.9	654	83.9

Source: Gerald Hodge, "The Prediction of Trade Center Viability in the Great Plains," *Papers of the Regional Science Association*, 15 (1965), table 2, p. 95.

1941 but only 84 percent in 1961.[20] Studies by Berry and others of central place systems in farming areas of the American Midwest reveal similar tendencies there.[21] These patterns of development are quite similar to the one suggested by the aggregate data for the United States in Table 5.3: under the impact of economic change and growth, central service functions have been gradually concentrating into fewer and larger places.

INTRAMETROPOLITAN PATTERNS: NOT EXPLAINED BY CENTRAL PLACE THEORY

It is no accident that this discussion of central place theory has focused on villages, towns, and small cities rather than on the great urban centers or metropolitan areas of the nation. True, we can observe hierarchical differences among large cities as well as among smaller places. Major cities and metropolitan areas can be differentiated into hierarchical classes by the order of services they provide and the regions for which they are the dominant provider. Thus they, as well as the smallest towns, are a part of the "system of cities," and our insight into urban phenomena is greatly enhanced by understanding that. Yet within metropolitan areas themselves the pattern of market areas and centers for the distribution of goods and services that is described in classical central place theory tends to break down. While it is still possible to distinguish levels in the retail hierarchy (convenience stores, neighborhood shopping, regional shopping centers, etc.), the population is so dense and travel relatively so easy that shoppers habitually visit many suppliers, and the market areas of suppliers cease to be even approximately exclusive. Under these conditions, as Berry has pointed out, the locational pattern of central service firms becomes a complex of "ribbons" and "specialized areas" as well as of "centers."[22]

In the face of this complexity, economists have, after the manner of their kind, looked for some underlying, simplifying principle that would explain the essence of the whole intrametropolitan pattern of location. They have employed as their point of departure a model that does not break the metropolis up into a hierarchically related system of submarkets but assumes instead that it is a single market area, organized into specialized districts around a single, unchallenged center. It is to this model that we turn in the next chapter.

20. Hodge, table 2, p. 95.
21. See Berry, *Geography of Market Centers*, pp. 114–117, and references cited therein.
22. Ibid, pp. 44–58 and 117–124.

SIX

Site Rent, Land-Use Patterns, and the Form of the City

Just as transport costs influence the location of producers and therefore of cities, so, too, they systematically affect locational patterns within the city itself. We are all conscious of the general form of the city: concentrated activity and development at the center; a gradual decline of intensity as one moves out toward the edge. This characteristic form is constantly impressed on us by the clusters of tall buildings and the dense crowds of people and vehicles we see at the center, so dramatically different from the lower skyline and the smaller crowds we find at the periphery.

It is not difficult to construct economic models that will generate this easily observed pattern as a function of transport cost and the need for accessibility. Although these relatively simple models do not account for the full complexity of land-use arrangements that are found in the city, they do explain successfully the general pattern of land use, land value, and density of development. In addition, they are vitally important because they illuminate the process by which the real estate market sorts out potential occupants of land, allowing those who can make the most productive use of central sites to obtain them and pushing those less dependent on centrality out toward the edge. From an understanding of this process much can be gained. The city planner learns the strengths and weaknesses of a free market in land as a rational allocator of scarce central sites. Students of housing and urban renewal gain insight into the economics of "land-use succession," the process by which "renewal" occurs (or fails to occur) in a freely functioning market. The transportation analyst learns the interdependence of land values, land use, and the transportation network.

In all such models of land use, the price of urban land at various sites plays a crucial role. This price can be expressed either as the capital value of a site or as its annual rental value. Although land is more commonly sold than rented in the United States, it is usually more convenient for purposes of analysis to use annual rent rather than capital value as the measure of price. The relationship between the two concepts is, in any case, simple enough: the capital or market value of a site is the present value of the stream of net returns it is expected to yield in the future. Since land in uses other than agriculture does not "wear out," its expected future life is infinitely long. If, then, its yield is expected to be constant per year, the expression for its present capital value reduces to the formula for evaluating the worth of a perpetual income: capital value equals the expected perpetual annual net return divided by the interest rate appropriate for capitalizing an income of that degree of risk.

A SIMPLE MODEL: RESIDENTIAL LAND USE

Let us start with a drastically simplified model based on the following assumptions: (1) a city has sprung up on a flat plain, or transport surface, of the sort assumed in the explanation of central place theory in Chapter 5; (2) all production and distribution activity in this city takes place at a single point at its center; (3) the populace consists of families of uniform size, taste, and income who must live in rented single-family homes of uniform house and lot dimensions ranged around the central production and distribution point; (4) the cost of building and maintaining houses (site rent excluded) is constant throughout the city[1]. Since housing costs other than site rent are spatially invariant, differences in total rent paid by tenants at two different sites clearly represent differences in the site rent component of the total. Site rent itself we define as the rent paid for a site less the rent it could command in an agricultural use.

Under these assumptions it can be shown that site rent for residential lots will be highest adjacent to the business center, will decline along any radial from that point, and will fall to zero at the periphery. Beyond the periphery land will command agricultural rent only.

In Figure 6.1 we place the center of the city at O and measure distance from the center along the horizontal axis to the right. The vertical axis measures costs per family unit on an annual basis. Let us assume that for a given

---

1. The land-use model that we apply here to the city had its origin in J. H. von Thünen's work *Der isolierte Staat*, published in 1826. Von Thünen made use of the featureless plain and the need for access to a market center to explain the pattern of agricultural land uses that typically formed around a market town. In the twentieth century urban economists have relied almost exclusively on a similar model to explain the pattern of urban land use. For a summary of twentieth-century theories of the economics of urban land use to 1960, see William Alonso, *Location and Land Use* (Cambridge, Mass.: Harvard University Press, 1964), ch. 1. The heart of Alonso's book is a model, far more elaborate than the one attempted here, that comprehends residential, business, and agricultural land uses within the now familiar von Thünen framework.

FIGURE 6.1
Site Rent and Transportation Cost: A Simplified Model

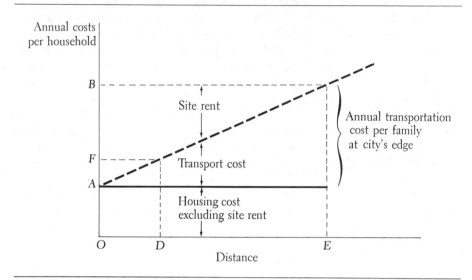

population and lot size and with no vacancies, the area needed to accommodate all families is provided when the city extends as far out as point E on the horizontal axis.

The vertical distance OA on the cost axis represents the annual cost of housing per unit, exclusive of site rent. This cost is equal for all locations, as indicated by the horizontal line at height OA. Since jobs and all consumer services are concentrated at the center, each household must bear an annual transportation bill for trips to the center and back. The annual cost of these trips increases with the household's distance from O and is shown by the rising transportation cost curve. Transport costs per family rise from zero at the city center to a maximum of AB for households located at the city's edge.

We can now show how site rent would arise as a payment for the saving in transport cost that could be obtained by living at any particular site. Consider, for example, a site adjacent to the city center. The owner of such a parcel could ask an occupant to pay as much as AB in site rent. If all houses are occupied, a householder would be willing to pay that much site rent to locate at the center, since the alternative would be to move just beyond the present edge of the city, where site rent would be zero but it would be necessary to bear transportation costs equal to AB.

Under the usual assumptions about competition of occupants for houses and of landowners for maximum rent, the same argument can be extended to all sites: at any point within the city, occupants would be willing to pay as site rent the difference between transportation costs at that site and the higher transportation costs that would be incurred if they moved to the city's edge. Under these conditions the combined cost of housing plus transportation plus site rent is the same at all sites and equals *OB* in Figure 6.1.

In Figure 6.2 site rent itself is plotted against distance from the center. (We have simply inverted the site-rent triangle of Figure 6.1 while retaining its dimensions and labels.) Rent declines from *BA* at the center to zero at the edge. Thus our simple model approximates observed reality, in which land values are highest downtown and fall off with some consistency as one moves out to the metropolitan periphery.

The declining line in Figure 6.2 is usually described as a "bid rent curve," since it shows the maximum site rent that households would willingly bid at each location. Since by assumption in this model no other land users compete with households for urban sites, the bid rent curve of households becomes in fact the "rent gradient" for the city. Later, when introducing other land uses, we will show that the actual rent gradient in a city is produced from competition among uses and can be depicted by graphically combining their several bid rent curves.

Economic Character of Site Rent

The very simplicity of the model employed so far is a virtue, since it enables us to see clearly many of the important characteristics of rent in general and of site rent in particular. *Economic rent* is defined by economists as a payment to a factor of production in excess of its opportunity cost (for which reason it is also called an "economic surplus"). The opportunity cost of a factor in a given use is the payment it could command in its next best employment. The next best employment for urban sites is as agricultural land. Since site rent is a payment in excess of this opportunity cost for urban sites, it clearly conforms with the general definition of economic rent.

Factors of production command an economic rent only to the extent that they are "scarce," and they are scarce in the long run only to the extent that they are nonreproducible. Again urban sites illustrate the general case. While land on which to build is plentiful, land with accessibility to economic centers is scarce; it is the scarce attribute of accessibility that gives rise to site rent. In our simplified model sites can be added indefinitely by extending the edges of the city, but each incremental ring of sites has less accessibility than the adjacent ring closer to the center and commands correspondingly less rent. Accessibility to a given center cannot be reproduced, though it can be altered by changes in the technology of transportation.

Although rent is a payment in excess of opportunity cost and can therefore be described as an economic surplus, it is nevertheless a payment equal in value to the marginal product of the factor to which it accrues. Site rent payments are therefore consistent in every respect with the marginal productivity theory of distribution and, as we will see, perform an essential function in bringing about an efficient allocation of land among competing uses. That

FIGURE 6.2
Rent Gradient: Simplified Model

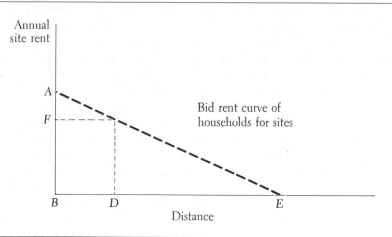

site rent equals the marginal product of the site can easily be seen from Figure 6.1. Compare, for example, site *D* with site *E*. The rent at *E* is zero; at *D* rent equals *FB*. Suppose the site at *D* were vacant and a family moved there from *E*. At *E* the family would have borne transportation costs equal to *AB*, as compared with transportation costs of *AF* at *D*. The reduction in transportation costs brought about by the move is given by *AB − AF = FB*. This reduction is a saving in real resource costs, and this saving is precisely the marginal product of the occupied site at *D*. It is also precisely the competitive site rent payable at *D*. Hence under competitive conditions rent equals marginal product.

Limitations of the Simple Model

The model we have developed yields results that are unrealistic in several respects. First of all, numerous studies have been made in recent years of actual urban site rent gradients. Most of these have concluded that the gradients are not linear—that is, they do not have a constant slope as in Figure 6.2. Instead they tend to be steepest at the center and to flatten out toward the edge, a shape that is generally best approximated by a negative exponential curve.[2] Such a curve has the characteristic of declining at a constant *relative* rate, instead of at the constant *absolute* rate of a linear gradient. Along a nega-

---

2. See Edwin S. Mills, "The Value of Urban Land," in Harvey S. Perloff, ed., *The Quality of the Urban Environment* (Washington, D.C.: Resources for the Future, 1969). In addition to reporting his own findings (which are discussed at length later in this chapter), Mills summarizes the work of several other investigators.

tive exponential curve, site rent would decline by the same percentage for each mile of movement away from the center. It should be added that the rate of decline of the rent gradient appears to vary widely from city to city.

Our initial site rent model is unrealistic in a second respect. We know from casual observation that density of urban settlement is not spatially uniform, as the model requires, but instead is much greater at the center. Again, statistical studies have verified the pattern. Like the gradient of site rent, the gradient of population density in modern cities has usually been best approximated by a negative exponential curve. Although the heights and slopes of such gradients do vary widely among cities, the negative exponential form has been found to hold with remarkable consistency not only in cities of the United States, Canada, Australia, New Zealand, and Western Europe but also in those of less developed countries.[3]

Finally, the site rent model in Figure 6.1 is also unrealistic in its treatment of building density. Greater population density at the center is associated with greater density of improvements—that is, with more cubic feet of building per acre. The visible evidence of this is, of course, the higher skyline we observe at the center, not just for office buildings but for apartment structures as well.

Figure 6.3 shows the gradient of land value per square foot on the west side of Manhattan. The curve traces values along a ray extending from the edge of the central business district at Sixty-second Street to the northern tip of the island. It displays the diminishing slope with movement away from the center that is typical of large modern cities. In the next section we show how such a gradient can be generated by our residential model if we relax some of its initial simplifying assumptions.

A MODEL THAT GENERATES SYSTEMATIC VARIATION IN DENSITY OF DEVELOPMENT

In constructing a more realistic model, we retain the assumption of a mononuclear city built on a transport surface with all commercial activity concentrated at a point in the center. Under these conditions, the transport-cost gradient remains as in Figure 6.1—a linear function, rising as distance from the center increases. We continue to assume that families are uniform in size, taste, and income and that they occupy units of standard size. However, the requirement of uniform density of housing per acre is abandoned. Instead, we allow developers to pile units up on a given lot by building verti-

3. See, for example, Colin Clark, *Population Growth and Land Use* (New York: St. Martin's Press, 1969), ch. 9; Brian J. L. Berry and Frank E. Horton, *Geographic Perspectives on Urban Systems* (Englewood Cliffs, N.J.; Prentice-Hall, 1970), ch. 9; Barry Edmonston, Michael A. Goldberg, and John Mercer, "Urban Form in Canada and the United States: An Examination of Urban Density Gradients," *Urban Studies*, June 1985, pp. 209–217; and Edwin S. Mills and Jee Peng Tan, "A Comparison of Urban Population Density Functions in Developed and Developing Countries," *Urban Studies*, October 1980, pp. 313–321.

FIGURE 6.3
Gradient of Land Value on the West Side of Manhattan Island, 1970[a]

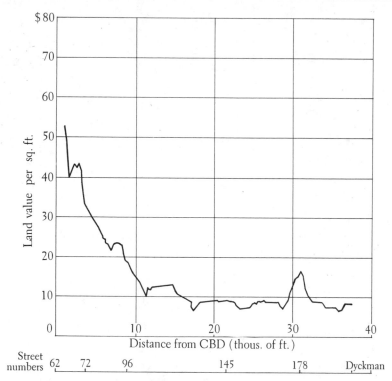

^a Five-block moving average of land value per square foot

Source: Joseph E. Earley, *The Empirical Investigation of a Residential Land Value Model*, unpublished PhD dissertation, Fordham University, 1974.

cally. It is assumed that building developers do not own the sites on which they build but lease them from site owners. Tenants, in turn, rent space in buildings from the developers. Thus the market has three tiers: site owners, buildings owners, tenants. This institutional arrangement is used only occasionally in the United States, but it is quite common in England. It is assumed here only as a convenience and does not affect the outcome of the analysis.

The new model is depicted in Figure 6.4. The right-hand panel shows transport costs and housing rent per family at various distances from the city center at O. The left-hand panel shows annualized costs to developers of building and operating standard-size apartment units in multiple dwellings of varying heights.

Let us first examine the right-hand panel. Rent per apartment and transport cost per family are measured on the vertical scale between the two

FIGURE 6.4
Site Rent with Variable Density of Development

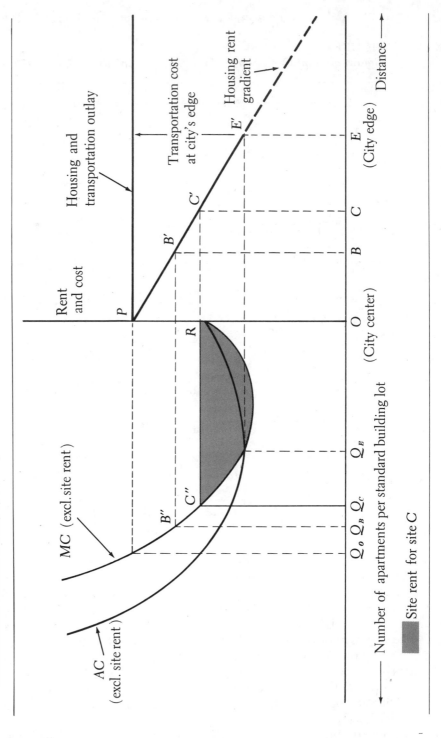

panels. To simplify the argument, we assume that all families arrange their budgets so as to pay a constant sum (equal for all families) for the combination of housing plus transportation. This outlay equals OP along the vertical scale, and the horizontal line through P indicates that the outlay is constant for all families regardless of location. At the center, transportation cost per family is zero, so OP is available as rent per apartment. Since transportation costs per family increase with mileage from the center, the sum available for rent decreases with distance and is shown by the housing rent gradient, which declines from P at the center to E' at the city's edge. Transportation costs at any site away from the center are shown by the vertical distance between the horizontal line through P and the declining housing rent gradient.

The left-hand panel is a mirror image of the conventional diagram of the long-run cost curves of a business firm, in which AC represents average cost and MC, marginal cost. In this instance the curves measure annual long-run average and marginal cost, per apartment, of building and operating apartment structures of varying heights on lots of standard size. Cost includes normal profit but, unlike the conventional case, excludes site rent. The horizontal scale shows number of apartments per structure, increasing in the leftward direction. Moving leftward from the vertical axis at the center, there is an initial stage of declining average cost (i.e., *increasing* returns) as structure size increases from zero. This decline reflects the fact that construction and operating cost per square foot diminishes as floor area size increases, if height is held constant.[4] Thus a very small building on the standard lot would probably cost more per unit than a building that made maximum permissible use of the ground area. However, as more stories are added, the increasing cost of building higher eventually offsets this initial gain. Diminishing returns to the use of land set in for buildings larger than Q_E. Marginal and average costs per apartment rise, beyond a certain structure height, because the construction cost per apartment of adding additional stories begins to rise as the building grows taller. The rise in cost has two sources: first, the need for heavier foundations and structural elements and, second, the shrinkage of rentable interior space per story as height rises, on account of required building setbacks and the need for additional space-using elevator shafts.[5]

Taken together, the two panels of Figure 6.4 show the intensity of development that will occur and the site rent that will be generated at any distance out from the center. For example, at site C, tenants will be willing to pay CC' in housing rent. We assume that builder-operators behave as perfect competitors, treating the going rent level at any distance from the center as if it were independent of their own decision to build. Builders at distance OC from the center will be guided by rent level CC' in determining how inten-

4. See John J. Costonis, *Space Adrift* (Urbana, Ill.: University of Illinois Press, 1974), pp. 95 and 101–02.

5. Concerning these increasing costs, see Ralph Turvey, *The Economics of Real Property* (London: Allen & Unwin, 1957), pp. 15–16; and Costonis, pp. 95–97 and 101–102.

sively to develop their sites. They will build structures to the height at which the last story adds apartments whose marginal cost just equals the rent offer CC'. In other words, they follow the conventional rule for the perfect competitor, which is to extend output to the point at which marginal cost just equals price. Price at site C is shown by the horizontal line extending left from C'. This intersects the marginal cost curve at C''. The builder at C therefore puts up a structure containing Q_C apartments.

What about site rent, which is not included in the cost curves depicted in Figure 6.4? The maximum annual site rent that a builder could pay at any site is the difference between total annual housing rent and total annual cost (excluding site rent) for an optimum-size structure at that distance from the center. Total housing rent that could be realized in a building at site C containing Q_C apartments equals the product of the rent per unit times the number of units, which is shown by the area of the rectangle $OQ_CC''R$. Total cost (excluding site rent) equals the sum of all marginal costs and is shown, for site C, by the area under the marginal cost curve up to the quantity Q_C. Maximum site rent is the difference between these two areas, shown by the saucer-shaped shaded area on the left-hand panel. Since builders are competing to obtain scarce sites, actual site rent will in the long run tend to equal the indicated maximum.

Our example illustrates the fact that site rent arises as a residual in the pricing process. Out of the proceeds from the sale of output (in this instance, housing services) producers must pay the going market price for whatever reproducible inputs they employ, including capital. The owners of nonreproducible scarce factors, such as urban sites, can then command as the price for the use of such factors whatever residual remains when all other inputs have been paid for by producers. The size of this residual depends on the price producers can obtain for their products and, therefore, on the level of demand. It is for this reason that rent is usually said to be "price-determined" rather than "price-determining."

We can now use Figure 6.4 to demonstrate two points. First, as we move toward the city center, say from site C to site B, the intensity of development increases. Builders at B can obtain higher rents per unit than builders at C. They therefore carry development on the site farther before reaching the point at which MC = rent: Q_B is to the left of Q_C, indicating that buildings at B are taller than those at C.

Second, it is easily seen that site rent is higher at B than at C, since the saucer-shaped site rent area grows larger as rent per apartment rises to BB' and the number of apartments increases from Q_C to Q_B. But we can say more: the increase in site rent per mile of movement toward the center is greater for each successive mile. This means that the bid rent curve for housing sites that could be derived from the left-hand panel of Figure 6.4 does not have the constant slope displayed by the simpler model in Figure 6.1. Rather, the increased intensity of development as we move toward the center generates increasingly large increments to site rent, so the bid rent curve for sites grows steadily steeper as it nears the center. This result can easily be deduced from the shape of the site rent area. Each mile of movement toward the center in the right-hand panel generates a constant increase in housing rent per apartment equal to the transportation cost saved by locating one mile nearer the center; apartment rent rises along a gradient of constant slope. But these successive, equal-per-mile increments to apartment rent, which could be measured along the vertical center scale, generate *increasing* increments to site rent, as demonstrated by the fact that the layers added to the saucer-shaped site rent area are successively longer as they pile up in the vertical direction. These layers are longer only because intensity of development increases as we move toward the city center.[6]

Intensity of development at the city's edge equals Q_E apartments per building lot. At that location, housing rent just covers average unit cost at the lowest level at which a developer could break even. Nothing is available for site rent, which is therefore zero. Tenants need not pay site rent to live in housing at the city's edge, since they have the alternative of building on adjacent vacant land for which site rent is zero. At the city's center, development reaches a density of Q_O apartments per building lot, and site rent (the saucer-shaped area above the marginal cost curve) is at a maximum.

We have shown that the model in Figure 6.4 generates a skyline that rises higher and a bid rent curve for housing sites that grows steeper as we approach the center of the city. Since the model assumes housing to be the only land use, the bid rent curve for housing sites is by assumption also the site rent gradient for the city. It displays the characteristic shape found in empirical studies of land value in major cities.

EFFECT OF COMPETING
LAND USES ON URBAN FORM

Our analysis can now be modified to cope with something closer to the full complexity of land uses in a typical city. Although in principle the argument could be extended to any number of uses, let us for convenience combine city functions into three major groups and see how competition among them for sites will establish a land-use pattern and site rent gradient for the city. The first group, which we will call "central office functions," includes

6. Edgar M. Hoover used a price line and a rising marginal cost function to derive a site rent gradient of increasing slope for agricultural land uses in *Location Theory and the Shoe and Leather Industries* (Cambridge, Mass.: Harvard University Press, 1937), pp. 24–26. The model in Figure 6.4 applies his argument to the urban case. It is interesting to note, however, that the entire argument of this section (and the following one on competing land uses) could equally well have been derived from the work of Alfred Marshall. See his *Principles of Economics*, 8th ed. (London: Macmillan, 1930), pp. 447–450.

For a somewhat different derivation of an increasingly sloped urban site rent gradient, see Harold Brodsky, "Residential Land and Improvement Values in a Central City," *Land Economics*, August 1970, pp. 229–247.

such activities as corporate headquarters, banks and other financial institutions, and law and accounting firms, all of which are complementary in providing high-level business services that require frequent daily contact between firms. The second group, which we will call "ancillary services," includes such categories as office equipment, parts and supply houses, printing shops, maintenance and repair firms, and telephone exchanges, whose function is to provide routine rather than high-level services to the central office sector. The third category is housing.

We assume that each of the business sectors operates under conditions of perfect competition. We continue to posit a city on a flat transport surface so that movement is equally costly per mile in any direction. Within this city, central office functions and ancillary services, since they require frequent contact between firms, will exert a mutual attraction and will therefore locate close together rather than occupying scattered sites. It follows that the city will have a well-defined business district and that the center of this district will be the point offering greatest accessibility to other firms. The question to be answered is, How will the three kinds of land use locate in relation to this central point? The answer turns out to be that when various uses are competing for sites, the one that can pay the highest site rent at each particular location will come into possession there. Consequently, the first point to investigate is, What determines the spatial pattern of demand for sites by each use?

To simplify the argument we make these additional assumptions: First, as in the housing case analyzed earlier, buildings are constructed and operated by developers who rent sites from landowners and in turn lease shelter space to tenants. Second, all structural types have similar cost characteristics. More specifically, all display identically increasing marginal and average cost per unit of floor space per year for building and operating structures of increasing height on lots of standard size. Thus the left-hand panel of Figure 6.5 shows cost curves resembling those of Figure 6.4. However, the horizontal scale to the left now measures quantity in square feet of floor space per structure rather than in number of apartments. As before, increased quantity (i.e., increased output per site) is obtained by building higher.

In the right-hand panel of Figure 6.4 we drew a bid rent curve of households for apartments, showing the maximum price that would be paid at each location as a decreasing function of distance from the center. The curve represented utility-indifferent positions for individual households. In the same fashion, bid rent curves can be drawn for floor space to be occupied by each of the other types of activity, and each of these will show the maximum rent that can be paid consistent with earning a normal competitive return. This rent will decrease with distance from the city center.

First consider central office functions. Each firm in this group is heavily dependent on daily face-to-face contact between its own executives and their counterparts in firms with which it deals. The closer each firm can come to location at the center of the business district, the less costly to it in time and

FIGURE 6.5
Urban Form with Competing Land Uses

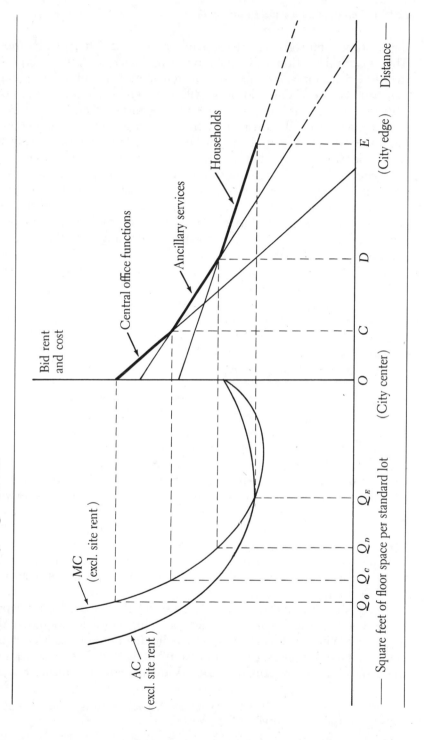

transportation outlay will be the task of maintaining contact with other firms. Thus a central location will reduce the firm's own costs (other than rent). For the same reason it will reduce the cost to others of maintaining contact with that firm. Hence a central location will also increase the firm's sales volume. Thus the rent per unit of floor space that a central office firm can pay while still earning a normal return will increase with proximity to the center both because transportation and communication costs will be decreasing and because sales will be increasing as distance from the center diminishes.

Much the same argument applies to the group of ancillary services. Firms in this group are in business to supply services to the central office firms (and to one another). They, too, will find costs (except rent) decreasing and sales increasing as distance from the center diminishes. Thus the rent they can pay per unit of floor space while still earning normal returns will also rise with proximity to the center.

Would the bid rent curve for floor space be steeper for central office functions or for ancillary services? What determines its steepness in either case? Three factors can be distinguished. First, its steepness is greater, the greater the cost per unit of output of maintaining contact with the center. Second, its steepness is greater, the larger the number of units of output the firm produces per square foot of floor space occupied. Third, it is steeper, the less readily other inputs can be substituted for floor space in the production process as the price of floor space rises.[7]

It seems probable that central office functions would have a steeper bid rent curve than ancillary services. First, since they are less routine and less standardized than ancillary services, they are likely to require more frequent personal contact between firms. In addition, since contact by central office firms frequently involves highest-echelon executives, whereas contact for ancillary service is more apt to be carried out by lower-salaried personnel such as salesmen, truck drivers, or repairmen, it is probable that travel time would be valued far more highly for the former group than for the latter. Second, the quantity of output per unit of floor space is likely to be larger for a central office function than for an ancillary service. Comparable units of "output" are difficult to conceive of in this instance, but the point is that central office functions are in some sense able to make more intensive use of space than are ancillary services.

We show the bid rent curve for households as the least steep of the three. The household typically has less need for central location than do business firms. Whereas the firm wishes to facilitate numerous daily contacts with customers and suppliers, the household need make only one daily journey to the center for each working member. (We have not introduced shopping ac-

---

7. For a more extended discussion of these factors, see Hugh O. Nourse, *Regional Economics* (New York: McGraw-Hill, 1968), pp. 96–110.

tivity into the model.) To shorten these daily trips, households are willing to pay higher rent, as shown by a bid rent curve that rises toward the center, but they are not willing to pay as much for centrality as do business firms. Thus the household curve lies below the inner (more central) portions of the other two.

The spatial distribution of the three land uses within the city is determined by the relationships among their bid rent curves. At each location building owners, in order to maximize net income, rent space to the highest bidder. Hence the use with the highest bid-rent curve takes over occupancy at each point. In Figure 6.5, central office functions occupy the segment from *O* to *C*, ancillary services are located between *C* and *D*, and households occupy the segment from *D* to the edge of the city at *E*. Thus the highest portions of the three bid rent curves (as indicated by the heavier line) become the rent gradient for the city. In this instance the gradient refers to rent per square foot of shelter space, but, as we have argued before, a unique land-rent gradient is, under the assumed conditions, associated with it. Both gradients become steeper as they approach the center. If we rotate either one about the city center we generate a corresponding rent surface. Looking down at such a surface from above, we would see that the city is circular, that central office functions occupy the center, and that the other land uses are ranged thereabout in concentric rings.

The Doctrine of "Highest and Best Use"

In the system depicted in Figure 6.5, the several economic activities of the city compete for the privilege of occupying sites. As the following argument suggests, the resulting land-use pattern is demonstrably an efficient one. The slope of a bid rent curve measures the benefit that accessibility confers on a given activity: the greater their need for accessibility in terms of reduced cost or increased sales, the more firms of a particular type are willing to pay in higher rent to move one mile closer to the center. The more they are willing to pay per mile, the steeper their bid rent curves. The slope of the bid rent curve of a particular activity therefore measures the benefit that accessibility confers on it. Industries that can benefit the most from accessibility have the steepest curves and occupy the center. Hence the model behaves efficiently in the economic sense: it allocates the scarce resource of accessibility to those who can make the most productive use of it.

Consistent with the foregoing argument, it is often said that a competitive real estate market allocates urban sites to their "highest and best use." Competition puts sites in the hands of the highest bidder. The highest bidder is the one who can make the most economically productive use of the site. The market operates so as to maximize rent from each site. We have already shown that site rent equals the marginal product of land. Hence the market also maximizes the contribution (i.e., marginal product) that each site adds to total output. It is in that sense that "highest" is also "best" from the viewpoint of society as a whole.

As we will see in Chapter 13, however, the process by which one use *succeeds* another on a given site is far more complicated. If a cleared site is thrown on the market, it will obviously be sold to the highest bidder, who will then construct a building on it that represents the highest and best use of the site. If, however, a site has an old building on it that is still capable of rendering service, that old use may be sufficiently profitable to persist on the site even though it is not the kind of building that anyone would now construct if the site were already cleared. Frequently observed examples of this sort are the old four-story commercial buildings that stand cheek-by-jowl with skyscrapers in the CBD or the small, walk-up apartment houses scattered among tall, modern elevator structures in a residential district. These cases are not exceptions to the doctrine of highest and best use. Properly interpreted, the doctrine comprehends them. However, the matter will not be taken up in detail until we analyze the economics of land-use succession in Chapter 13.

EXTERNALITIES AND LAND-USE ZONING

A major qualification to the argument that competitive land markets operate efficiently in the assignment of sites must now be introduced. We have treated land uses as though they were independent of one another except for connections made through market transactions. Thus we have ignored external, or neighborhood, effects. These arise when activity at one site confers benefits or imposes costs on the occupant of another site for which no fee can be charged or no recompense collected. For example, a beautiful garden in front of one house produces a free aesthetic benefit for neighbors and passersby, while the noise and fumes from a boiler factory impose unrequited damages on the occupants of nearby sites. Such effects are especially likely to occur in densely built-up urban areas.

If the owners of the boiler factory could somehow be made to bear its external costs, they would either contrive to reduce the output of noise and fumes or else move to a more remote location where such emissions would cause less offense. Land-use zoning arose as an attempt to meet this problem, not by inducing occupants of sites to internalize the costs they impose on others, but by direct regulation of land use. Although some forms of land-use regulation appeared earlier, comprehensive zoning in the United States is usually dated from the adoption of a zoning resolution by New York City in 1916.[8] Zoning was intended to minimize what we now call "externalities" in

8. See John Delafons, *Land Use Controls in the United States* (Cambridge, Mass.: M.I.T. Press, 1969), pp. 16–31.

two ways. First, incompatible uses were to be kept from impinging on one another. Second, regulation was to prevent overintensive development of one site from imposing burdens on its neighbors. Incompatible uses could be kept apart by zoning certain areas for residential development to the exclusion of all industry and others for residential, commercial, and light industrial uses, while confining truly "noxious" activities, such as boiler factories or stockyards, to peripheral locations. The same zoning ordinance could prevent individual improvements from blocking the light and air of their neighbors or imposing other burdens on them by regulating the height and bulk of buildings or requiring open space along lot boundaries.

Land-use zoning was quickly accepted in the United States after the Supreme Court in 1926 upheld its constitutionality in the *Euclid* case. Zoning ordinances are adopted and administered by local government, under authority granted to them by state law. The preparation and periodic review of such ordinances is often one of the principal functions of a city planning commission.[9] Exceptions (known as "variances") to the specific requirements of an ordinance are usually provided for preexisting uses that do not conform, and additional variances can generally be granted by a board of standards and appeals.

In recent years many economists have begun to question whether zoning, as it is practiced in the United States, is either an efficient or an equitable way of regulating land use. Examining the issue of effficiency, Edwin Mills points out that land-use zoning purports to control nuisances such as noise pollution when in fact it merely moves them about. While not opposing some degree of use separation through zoning, Mills argues that antipollution policies aimed directly at externalities would often be more effective and would render some traditional zoning controls redundant. Appropriate policies would include greater reliance on such devices as effluent fees or other charges that encourage economically efficient marginal adjustments in the behavior of firms and individuals, in place of the all-or-nothing system of toleration or prohibition through zoning.[10]

The all-or-nothing structure of zoning not only prevents efficient marginal adjustments but also contributes to the politicization of the zoning pro-

9. For a description of zoning from the viewpoint of the city planner, see Anthony J. Catanese and James C. Snyder, eds., *Introduction to Urban Planning* (New York: McGraw-Hill, 1979), ch. 10; and Richard F. Babcock, "Zoning," in Frank S. So et al., eds., *The Practice of Local Government Planning* (Washington, D.C.: International City Managers' Association, 1979), pp. 416–443.

10. Edwin S. Mills, "Economic Analysis of Urban Land-Use Controls," in Peter Mieszkowski and Mahlon Straszheim, eds., *Current Issues in Urban Economics* (Baltimore: Johns Hopkins University Press, 1979), pp. 511–541. The article includes a useful bibliography. For a more extended economic analysis, see David E. Ervin et al., *Land Use Control: Evaluating Economic and Political Effects* (Cambridge, Mass.: Ballinger, 1977). A set of papers highly critical of zoning can be found in M. Bruce Johnson, ed., *Resolving the Housing Crisis* (San Francisco: Pacific Institute for Public Policy Research, 1982).

cess. Whenever a particular use for which there is strong market demand has been forbidden by zoning—say, the construction of apartment houses in a neighborhood zoned exclusively for single family homes—a powerful incentive is created for an aggressive developer to profit by obtaining a zoning variance that breaks the restriction. Political forces are brought into play. Zoning then becomes a game in which the prize is the potential private gain from changing the initial rules.

The most frequently voiced objection to zoning on grounds of equity, however, is not that the zoning process itself is highly political but rather that it can be used by one class of citizens to the disadvantage of another. For example, by manipulating zoning regulations, well-to-do suburban towns can effectively prevent families of low or moderate income from moving in. This sort of "exclusionary zoning" will be examined in detail in connection with housing policy in Chapter 13.

EFFECTS OF CHANGE AND GROWTH

The land-use model depicted in Figure 6.5 is wholly static. Ignoring time and change, it shows us what the equilibrium pattern would be if a city were suddenly to be built *de novo* under given conditions. It does not tell us how land-use patterns evolve as cities age or as the things assumed constant in the model—especially population, income level, and technology—change over time. It leaves out of account all the dynamic forces of urban evolution that for better or worse prevent the achievement of any final equilibrium. Because structures and, to an even greater extent, the underlying framework of streets and utilities are long-lived, the pattern of land uses that exists at any given time is never the same as the optimal pattern that could be produced by a wholly fresh start at that moment. The aging of structures and the process of land-use succession on given sites will be examined in detail in Chapter 13. At this point we wish to analyze the general, or macrolocational, effects on land use of changes in transportation cost, population, and income.

The consequences of such changes have been worked out very clearly by William Alonso, and the following discussion is based largely on his work.[11] Although Alonso's study covers business and agricultural as well as residential patterns, he simplifies the formal analysis of the effect of changes in technology and the like by restricting it to the latter sector. (The results are fundamentally the same for urban business uses as well.) Alonso's model, like the highly simplified one we use, assumes a transport surface and a mononuclear city. It is far more complex, however. Among other things, it explicitly rejects the assumption of constant residential lot size. Rather, lot size is one

11. Alonso, pp. 105–116.

of the variables to be solved for. What follows is not the Alonso model itself but one of its applications.

Effect of an Improvement in Transportation Technology

Figure 6.6 shows the bid rent curve of households for land (or, as Alonso calls it, the price structure for residential land) in a metropolis with its business and employment center at O. The land units in terms of which price is expressed may be square feet, acres, or what have you. Initially, the price structure is given by line *AB*. *OA* equals rent at the center, and point *B* marks the edge of urban settlement. Now suppose that an improvement in technology takes place that reduces the time and/or money cost of transportation from the outlying areas to the center. Rent at the center is based on the saving in transportation cost obtained by locating there instead of at the city's edge. Accordingly, rent at the center will be reduced by the technological im-

FIGURE 6.6
Effect on Land Use of Improved Transportation or Increased Population

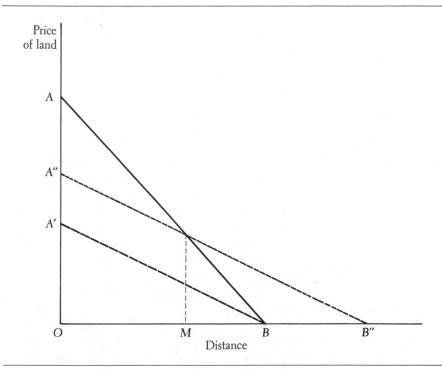

Source: Adapted from William Alonso, *Location and Land Use* (Cambridge, Mass.: Harvard University Press, 1964), fig. 32, p. 112.

provment, other things remaining the same. More specifically, if lot size were held constant, the outer edge of settlement would remain at B and the bid rent curve would fall to $A'B$. But with the price of land reduced, lot size will *not* remain constant. Alonso's model incorporates the important fact that to the householder space is a consumer good as well as an impediment to access. Other things being equal, if the price of land drops, householders will increase their consumption of it: lot size will increase. That in turn means that the area needed to house a given population will also increase. The margin of settlement will move out—say, to B''. Instead of falling to $A'B$, the bid-rent curve will shift to a position such as $A''B''$.

We know that A'' must be above A'—in other words, that rent at the center falls less than it would have if lot size had remained constant—because when the city's edge moves from B out to B'', the transportation cost saved at a central location increases, and therefore so does rent at the center. It is interesting to note that although the new bid rent curve $A''B''$ shows rents lower than before at the center, it also shows them to have increased beyond some point, M. Why should households beyond M be paying higher rents after the improvement in transportation than they paid before? The answer is that people living farther out than M could pay more rent than before and still be better off than they were because the technological change has allowed them to gain utility through reduction in the time and/or money cost of transportation.

Effect of an Increase in Population

The effects of population change also are easily deduced from Alonso's model. An increase in population will increase the demand for residential sites. To accommodate the new households, the margin of the city will move outward. As it does, the cost of transportation from the edge to the center will increase, and the bid rent curve will shift upward and to the right. For example, an increase in population, while transportation technology and income remain unchanged, will cause the bid rent curve to rise from a position such as $A'B$ in Figure 6.6 to something like $A''B''$. The result will be higher land costs for all households and a tendency to reduce lot size. Hence the city's area will increase less than in proportion to the increase in population. Thus, as Alonso points out, a rise in population, other things being equal, will cause an increase in both land prices and density of settlement as well as in the physical extent of the urban area.

Figure 6.6 also enables us to compare expected land costs in cities that differ in population size. The diagram predicts that land prices, and therefore housing costs, will generally be higher in large than in small cities, and that is indeed the case. As we pointed out in Chapter 3, these higher costs in turn help to explain why the cost of living rises with city size. (See "Income, Well-being, and City Size" in Chapter 3.)

Effect of an Increase in Income

We next examine the impact of changes in average household income. Alonso deals with the effect of differences in income among households rather than with the effect of a change in its average level. Once the former effect is established, however, we can easily transform the argument to describe the latter.

The facts are not in doubt. In U.S. cities wealthier families tend to settle near the periphery, while poorer households remain close to the center. Thus the gradient of income rises with distance from the center. This is crudely verified, later, in Tables 10.5 and 11.7. Within SMSAs, median family income is lower in the central city than in the suburbs. (It is equally clear that the U.S. pattern is not a universal norm. In many cities of Latin America, for example, the well-to-do live near the center, while the poor occupy peripheral sites.)[12]

As we shall see, there are two alternative explanations of the U.S. pattern. Both are plausible, but they have very different implications for housing and renewal policy in the central city. Both will be examined in detail.

Alonso argues that higher income, in and of itself, can lead families to choose suburban rather than central city locations. By close theoretical reasoning he shows that wealthy families will tend to have bid rent curves less steep than those of poor families and therefore settle on large lots of relatively cheap land toward the city's edge, while the poor tend to occupy very small portions of higher-priced land near the center. The argument is complex. An important factor in it, however, is the cost of commuting. Assume to begin with that the cost of commuting increases directly with distance but does not vary with income. (We will reconsider this assumption in a moment.) On the other hand, the cost of housing per square foot declines with distance because the land component becomes cheaper with movement away from the center. Households therefore face the following choice: at locations close to the center, commuting costs are low but the unit costs of land and housing are high; at locations farther out, commuting costs are high, but the unit costs of land and housing are low. For the poor family, the increase in commuting costs as distance increases will diminish rapidly the small fund of income available for housing. Consequently, the poor cannot bid much for locations where commuting is expensive. On the other hand, since commuting costs are invariant with income or quantity of land occupied, the rich, who desire ample housing space and are prepared to spend large sums on housing, find the barrier of commuting costs rather inconsequential and can bid higher prices than the poor for land at distant locations. In choosing such locations, the rich gain more by consuming larger quantities of cheaper housing than they lose by paying additional transportation costs. (Of course, Alonso recog-

---

12. See Leo F. Schnore, "On the Spatial Structure of Cities in the Two Americas," in Philip M. Hauser and Leo F. Schnore, eds., *The Study of Urbanization* (New York: Wiley, 1965), pp. 347–398.

nizes that individual tastes are not uniform. Some wealthy families with a strong aversion to commuting and a weak preference for added space will always continue to live in luxury housing near the center.)

Figure 6.7 may help the reader to visualize the outcome just described. Consistent with the above explanation and with the earlier treatment of housing and transportation outlays in Figure 6.4, it illustrates the way in which income influences household locational choices.[13] In this interpretation, households regard commuting outlays as part of the cost of occupying housing. At all levels of income they are assumed to budget 20 percent of income for housing and commuting costs combined. This implies that the income elasticity of demand for housing is 1.0, since housing expenditures always rise in proportion with rising income. Each household seeks the location at which it can obtain the largest quantity of housing space for the outlay budgeted. Thus households do not have preferences among locations as such but choose solely on the basis of housing cost per unit of space.

In Figure 6.7 quantity of housing consumed per household is measured in square feet along the horizontal axis. The vertical axis measures annual dollar outlays for housing and commuting. Cost curves relating outlay to square feet consumed are shown for three locations. The commuting cost at each location is given by the intercept of the cost curve on the vertical axis. Thus annual commuting cost to the center of the city from location A is OA, and the curve AA' relates housing outlay to square feet occupied at A. Likewise, OB is the cost of commuting at location B, which is farther out than A, and the slope of BB' measures the cost of housing at B. The slope of OO' indicates housing cost at the center, where commuting costs are zero. Since commuting costs are directly proportional to distance, intercepts on the vertical axis can be read to indicate relative distance of each location from the center. As indicated by the diminished slopes of successive curves, cost per unit of housing space declines as distance increases because land costs fall with distance. (Housing quality is assumed constant in this analysis.)

Figure 6.7 illustrates locational choices for households at three income levels. The outcome for each household is read on the diagram by following that household's horizontal income line to the right and finding its intersection with the housing cost curve that lies farthest out along the quantity scale. Household J, with an income of $5,000, budgets $1,000 a year for housing and commuting. At that level of spending, the largest number of square feet is obtained by living at the center of the city, where commuting costs are zero. Household K, with a budget of $2,000 for housing and commuting, finds that location A offers the most space, while household L, spending $4,000 a year, settles still farther out at B. If housing cost curves for all locations within commuting range of the center were plotted, the successive portions that lie far-

13. Figure 6.7 is an interpretation of the income-distance effect that does not appear in Alonso.

FIGURE 6.7
Income, Commuting Cost, Housing Consumption, and Locational Choice

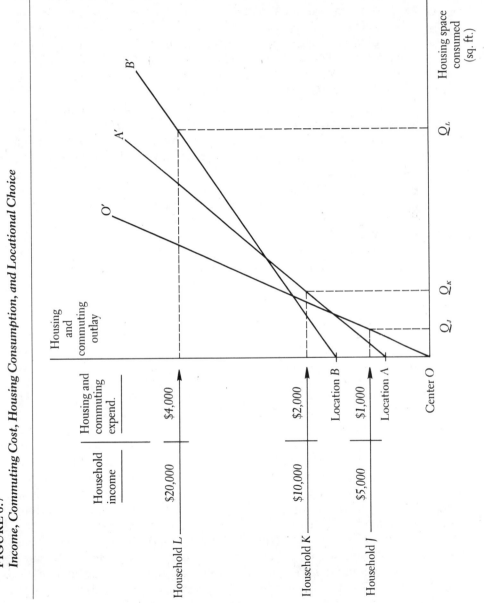

thest to the right would generate something approaching a smooth curve from which one could read the location that would be optimal for households at every income level. Under the conditions assumed here, household choices would yield an income gradient rising continuously with distance from the center. The forces producing that result can be observed in Figure 6.7. Housing outlays double as we move up the income scale from J to K and from K to L. Likewise, distance doubles from A to B. But for each doubling of income or distance, the market offers more than twice the quantity of housing space: Q_K is more than double Q_J, and Q_L more than double Q_K.

This interpretation of Alonso's argument can readily be extended to cover the effect of an increase in the average level of income as well as the effect of income differences among households. As the income of American households increases over time, they move gradually up the vertical scale of Figure 6.7. Consequently, the proportion of the population that chooses to take up suburban living increases. This means that even if population, tastes, and the technology of transportation were constant, rising living standards alone would suffice to increase the suburban population and diminish that of the inner cities. This process would also produce the trend in geographic income differentials that we do in fact observe and will discuss at length in later chapters: average family income is rising far faster in the suburbs than in the central cities.

Income and Travel Cost

The results obtained from Figure 6.7 are unambiguous because it was assumed explicitly that commuting cost is a function of distance but not of income. This was a convenient simplifying assumption that must now be given up. As already explained in Chapter 5, travel cost in general consists of two parts: first, the money cost of making a trip and, second, the nonmonetary cost comprising the value of time lost and of discomfort undergone. It is reasonable to assume that the money cost is proportional to distance—that is, so many cents per mile—and that it does not vary with income. The time cost of travel, however, is a different matter. As we shall explain in Chapter 8, empirical studies indicate that individuals value travel time at some fraction of their wage rate. The perceived time cost of covering a given distance will therefore rise with income, although not necessarily in proportion to it.

In models of the Alonso type, the effect of income on the locational choices of households depends on whether the demand for space or the marginal cost of travel increases faster with income. If the income elasticity of demand for space is greater than the income elasticity of the marginal cost of travel, the rich will tend to locate farther out than the poor. This is the case depicted in Figure 6.7, where the former elasticity is assumed to be fairly high while the latter is assumed to be zero. If, however, the latter elasticity were to exceed the former, the burden of distance would increase faster with income than would its advantages. The income-distance pattern would then be re-versed, with the rich living at the center and the poor toward the edge.

Alonso, Muth, and others who argue that higher income per se explains the peripheral location of the well-to-do in U.S. cities do so from a belief that in the United States the income elasticity of demand for space exceeds the income elasticity of the marginal cost of travel. This belief gains plausibility from the fact that the total cost of travel for any individual will always be less responsive to income than the time cost, because the total includes a money cost component that depends only on distance.[14]

William C. Wheaton, however, questions whether the Alonso-Muth spatial income effect is really an important determinant of residential location. Using data for a sample of households in the San Francisco Bay area, he estimated the effect of income on locational choice. He concluded that it was relatively weak because the estimated income elasticities of land consumption and of travel cost proved to be very similar in magnitude. On the other hand, in a recent study of the Montreal urban area, Minh Chau To, Alain La Pointe, and Lawrence Kryzanowski obtained results consistent with the Alonso-Muth model.[15] Further empirical work is obviously required to resolve the issue.

If the income effect per se should turn out to be as weak as Wheaton's findings suggest, the suburbanization of middle- and upper-income families in the United States must, of course, have had other causes. Which causes in fact produced the present pattern is an important question, since the answer has implications for policies intended to stimulate central city revival.

An Alternative Explanation of the Spatial Income Pattern

The principal alternative to the Alonso-Muth explanation is the view that the outward movement of the middle and upper classes is the result of the growth, development, and aging of the central city over time. Based on observations in Chicago, this theory was first put forward by the sociologist Ernest W. Burgess in the 1920s and has been highly influential.[16] It holds that the wealthier classes, who originally lived in fashionable districts near the city center, moved outward for two reasons. First, the expansion of the CBD as the city grew encroached on their close-in residential zone, destroying its

14. Richard F. Muth, *Cities and Housing* (Chicago: University of Chicago Press, 1969), p. 31.

15. William C. Wheaton, "Income and Urban Residence: An Analysis of Consumer Demand for Location," *American Economic Review*, September 1977, pp. 620–631; and Minh Chau To, Alain La Pointe, and Lawrence Kryzanowski, "Externalities, Preferences, and Urban Residential Location: Some Empirical Evidence," *Journal of Urban Economics*, November 1983, pp. 338–354.

16. Ernest W. Burgess, "The Growth of the City," in Robert E. Park, Ernest W. Burgess, and Roderick D. McKenzie, *The City* (Chicago: University of Chicago Press, 1925).

amenities. Second, since the close-in housing was the oldest, it was also the first to become obsolete. Because it is easier to build new on vacant land than in built-up districts, the wealthy tended to move to the periphery to construct another round of up-to-date housing. Older housing was abandoned to poorer classes, and the oldest of all (adjacent to the CBD) to the immigrants whose arrival fed the city's growth.

This theory of city form has come to be known as the "concentric zone theory," because Burgess described four distinct types of housing, which he believed were grouped in concentric rings around the CBD. He identified the zones and their residents as follows (moving from the center outward):

1. The central business district (in Chicago, "The Loop")
2. The zone in transition: as the CBD grows, business and light manufacturing encroach on old slums and rooming houses, making this the least desirable residential area
3. The zone of workingmen's homes: inhabited by laborers who have escaped from the deterioration of zone 2 but wish to live close to their central workplaces
4. The residential zone: a restricted or exclusive district consisting of high-class apartments and single-family homes for the middle and upper classes
5. The commuters' zone: suburban areas and satellite cities, outside the city limits but within commuting distance of the CBD

In the late twentieth century the central business districts of U.S. cities are no longer expanding, so that part of Burgess's explanation of the spatial arrangement of urban social classes no longer obtains. The remainder of his theory, however, can easily be brought up to date in a way that preserves its emphasis on aging and deterioration at the center as the basic cause of middle- and upper-class movement to the suburbs. Poor ethnic minorities now replace European immigrants as the occupants of slum housing at the city's core. Racial tensions grow. Poverty brings not only crime but also municipal fiscal distress and rising tax rates. The white middle class seeks relief from these burdens in suburban communities segregated by income class as well as by race. A considerable number of empirical studies support the conclusion that such inner city problems have indeed contributed significantly to the suburbanization of middle- and upper-income families in U.S. metropolitan areas.[17] (The effect of fiscal incentives on household location decisions will be carefully examined in Chapter 15.)

---

17. See W. Norton Grubb, "The Flight to the Suburbs of Population and Employment," *Journal of Urban Economics*, May 1982, pp. 348–367; Barbara S. Burnell, "Metropolitan Fiscal Disparities and the Geographic Distribution of Income," *Urban Studies*, August 1984, pp. 285–293; and Michael J. Wasylenko, "Disamenities, Local Taxation, and the Intrametropolitan Location of Households and Firms," in Robert B. Ebel, ed., *Research in Urban Economics*, vol. 4 (Greenwich, Conn.: JAI Press, 1984), pp. 97–116.

Policy Implications of Alternative Theories

Alternative explanations of the suburbanization of the middle and upper classes clearly have different policy implications. For example, if housing obsolescence at the core is an original cause of the exodus, policies that stimulate inner city housing renewal might stem and eventually reverse the outflow and thus encourage general central city revival. This argument was used to support federal subsidies for urban renewal projects, including the construction of new luxury housing at the center, in the 1950s and 1960s (see Chapter 13). The situation is entirely different if rising income by itself is a sufficient explanation for the outward movement of the wealthy. In that case, urban renewal in the older central cities will be relatively ineffective in stemming their outward migration or attracting a return flow.

There is no reason to assume, however, that the Alonso-Muth income effect and the central city deterioration argument are mutually exclusive. As long as deterioration per se has a significant effect, policies to overcome structural obsolesence, mitigate social problems, and improve fiscal performance may also help to attract the middle and upper classes back to the city. Such policies are, of course, likely to be desirable for other reasons as well.

Recapitulation: The "Automobile Effect," the "Overflow Effect," and the "Income Effect"

It is worth noting that with regard to the causes of dispersion within metropolitan areas, the inferences drawn from Alonso's formal land-rent model coincide with those cited in the essentially descriptive-historical analysis of the same process presented in Chapter 3. Referring to Figure 6.6, assume for convenience that *M* marks the fixed boundary between a central city and its suburbs. Formal theoretical analysis then supports the following conclusions:

1. An improvement in transportation, other things remaining the same, allows the margin of urban settlement to move out. If total population remains constant, this causes population to rise in the suburbs and fall in the central city. This is the "automobile effect" of Chapter 3.

2. An increase in total metropolitan population, other things remaining the same, also pushes the margin of settlement out. It leads, by way of reduced lot size, to greater density and therefore to a larger population in the central city as well as in the suburbs. However, since the suburbs start with a smaller population base, the percentage increase recorded there will be greater than in the central city. This is the essence of the "overflow effect" cited in Chapter 3.

3. An increase in the average standard of living, other things constant, reduces the demand for central sites and increases the demand for more distant ones. Average lot size increases, and again the margin of settlement

moves out. With no change in total numbers, this means a smaller population in the central city and a larger one in the suburbs. This is the "income effect" of Chapter 3.

We see then that each of the three effects, taken separately, leads to increased suburban population, while two reduce and one—the population effect—increases central city numbers. Since early in the twentieth century all three have operated simultaneously. What were the consequences for the pattern of settlement? As we showed in Table 3.2, the growth rate of central city population was at its height in the first decade of the century. It slowed down more or less steadily thereafter and turned negative for some of the older central cities in the 1950s and 1960s. It thus appears that for a long time the strength of the population effect was sufficient to maintain some central city growth despite the strong impetus to dispersal from improved transportation and rising living standards. As metropolitan population growth slowed, however, it was less and less able to offset the other two effects, which continued to make for dispersion. After 1970 central cities as a whole showed little further population growth.

TOWARD GREATER REALISM:
TRANSPORTATION CORRIDORS, INTERPENETRATION
OF USES, AND THE DECLINE OF MONONUCLEARITY

The model illustrated in Figure 6.6 is unrealistic in a number of respects. We have employed it because its basic implications are valid and important, but we must now recognize some real-world complications.

It must be admitted, first of all, that cities are not built on featureless transport surfaces. Topographical irregularities abound. Differences in elevation, view, wind direction, or proximity to natural features such as lakes, beaches, or mountains have an effect on locational choice. Equally important, transportation itself is not ubiquitous but is always channeled into corridors. These corridors themselves are often distorted by topographical irregularities, and the modes of transport vary according to corridor and purpose. Since major corridors offer superior accessibility along their own length, they generally command higher rents than minor streets or roads. Corridors, in effect, become centers.

Second, land uses are not arranged by the market into mutually exclusive districts, whether of concentric rings or any other shape. Not only are types of business intermixed within the CBD, but business and residential uses interpenetrate in both the central city and the suburbs. Retailing, for example, is found in all parts of the metropolis. This, however, is only the most obvious exception; other types of business, too, survive and prosper at a wide variety of locations.

Third, and most important of all, the dispersion of business activity has made metropolitan areas increasingly multinuclear. As we stressed in Chapter 3, urban evolution, driven by the force of changes in the technology of transportation, has moved steadily away from the nineteenth-century pattern of business activity concentrated at the center toward a much more decentralized arrangement. It was shown in this chapter that an improvement in transportation causes the city's residential zone to spread out, its population dispersing into a pattern of lower-density settlement. The results are similar for business firms. Cheaper transport allows them both to obtain from suppliers and to offer to customers as much accessibility as before in terms of time and money cost at a greater distance out from the center, where they can afford larger sites because land costs are lower. Some firms, at least, will be induced by this change to move outward. The greater the possibility of substituting space for other inputs in the production process, the more likely they are to move. For that reason automotive assembly plants or wholesale food distributors are more likely to disperse than are corporation law offices or advertising firms. There is also an indirect effect of lower suburban land costs: the suburbs offer somewhat lower wage levels, since suburban employers do not have to compensate workers, who can live nearby, for the higher cost of central city housing. (See discussion in latter part of Chapter 11.)

It should be emphasized that the business dispersion described here is not the spreading out of a discrete central business district at the heart of the city. Rather it is the dispersion of activity from that center toward the periphery—in other words, the suburbanization of industry. In the process new subcenters are created in the ring area. (To be sure, "satellite cities" already existed there.) These new centers often arise at intersections on the transport grid. Each exerts its own attraction for certain functions and emerges as a lesser peak on the urban rent surface.

Table 3.4 showed the extent of employment decentralization in twelve major MSAs after 1948. The analysis in Chapter 3 and the population data in Table 3.4 also made it clear that the outward movement of jobs encourages, and is in turn encouraged by, the outward movement of population.[18] Since jobs are moving together with people, it follows that the suburbanization of population does not imply an increase in commuting. (See Chapter 3, "Work Trip Patterns and Changes in Urban Structure.")

EMPIRICAL EVIDENCE OF LAND-VALUE CHANGES OVER TIME

Empirical studies of changes in urban land-value gradients over time show that they have changed in the way our model would suggest under the impact of urban growth and decentralization. Mills estimated land-value gra-

---

18. Whether decentralization of jobs causes decentralization of population or vice versa is investigated in Donald N. Steinnes, "Do 'People Follow Jobs' or Do 'Jobs Follow People'? A Causality Issue in Urban Economics," *Urban Studies*, May 1982, pp. 187–192. Also see articles by Grubb and Wasylenko cited in n. 17.

dients for Chicago from data gathered by Homer Hoyt for 1836, 1857, 1873, 1910, and 1928.[19] Mills's technique was to regress land value on distance from the CBD. He tested three forms of relationship at each date: linear in both variables, which fit poorly at all dates; log of land value against arithmetic distance—the equation for a gradient of the negative exponential type; and log of land value against log of distance. Since the negative exponential form fitted as well as any, we use it as the basis for this discussion.

Mills found that between 1836 and 1857 the slope of the land-value gradient increased moderately. The coefficient of determination, R^2, of the line of regression also increased, indicating that the negative exponential curve provided an increasingly good fit to the data. From 1857 to 1928, however, both the slope of the gradient and the value of R^2 gradually diminished. The flattening of the gradient is just what theory would have led us to expect as a result of successive improvements in the technology of intrametropolitan transportation. Moreover, Berry and Horton, building on Mills's analysis, have shown that the decline in the slope of Chicago's land-value gradient over that period is paralleled by a decline in the slope of the population-density gradient—again, just the combination that theory would predict.[20]

Mills's analysis also shows that while the slope of the land-value gradient was diminishing, its height at the center was steadily rising, so the whole gradient at each later date lay above its position at each earlier time. This rise in the level of the gradient is precisely what the mononuclear model would predict as a result of the vast increase in population during the period.

The decline in the value of the coefficient of determination, R^2, for the fitted gradients between 1857 and 1928 suggests, as Mills himself points out, that the mononuclear model has become less valid with the passage of time. As a result of the dispersion of business activity and the growth of other centers, distance from the CBD is gradually losing its once commanding power to explain intrametropolitan variation in site value. Economists are now developing more sophisticated approaches to the problem of intrametropolitan location, primarily through the use of computerized urban simulation models. The need for these complex techniques, however, does not render the simpler mononuclear theories useless as explanatory devices. Even in more advanced models the fundamental logic of business location decisions depicted in this chapter remains essentially intact: firms locate where they expect to maximize profits and are strongly influenced in so doing by the trade-off between accessibility to customers and suppliers on the one hand and the site rent they must pay to obtain that accessibility on the other. Despite the complexities of real-world location patterns, each class of urban activity does display a characteristic, measurable locational tendency. In fact, the observed

19. Mills, "The Value of Urban Land."
20. Berry and Horton, p. 302 and fig 9.18. Chapter 9 of their volume reviews the extensive empirical work that has been done on population-density gradients and their change over time.

complexity is simply evidence that for most functions there remains a sufficiently wide range of feasible locations at going rent levels to produce considerable overlapping in spatial distribution.

THE ROLE OF SITE RENT
UNDER DYNAMIC CONDITIONS

Whatever their differences in either structure or complexity, theories of intraurban location do not disagree on the crucial role of site rent as the free market's allocator of land among alternative uses. We opened this chapter with the analysis of rent as an allocator under static conditions. It is appropriate now to examine the role of rent under the impact of change and development.

Consider the situation in a city with a rapidly growing population. Land value per acre in such a city will generally be rising, just as theory suggests. The rise in value and the growth of population stem from a single source: the economic advantages that the city offers in terms of individual income and business profit as compared with other places. To the extent that a given site confers valuable access to these gains, its owner can appropriate a share of the city's net advantages in the form of urban site rent. These net advantages, as was explained in Chapter 2, consist of the difference between the economies and the diseconomies of agglomeration. Assuming perfect competition in factor markets and full geographic mobility of all nonland factors of production, landowners as a group would, in the long run, be able to appropriate the entire value of the city's net locational advantages. This would equal the difference between the aggregate returns that the nonland factors of production can earn when used in the city (net of any payments to compensate them for bearing the diseconomies of agglomeration) and the returns they could obtain if employed at a place where urban site rent was zero. The aggregate of site rent in a city is thus one measure of the net economics of location and agglomeration that the city offers.[21]

To the individual business that must rent space, high site costs per se are, of course, a disadvantage. As the city grows, some firms that found it profitable to locate there when rents were low may find it unprofitable to remain as they rise and will choose to move away. But the fact that site rents are rising (relative to the general level of prices) is in itself sufficient evidence that the city's net advantages to land users as a whole have increased. Were it otherwise, bidders would not be pushing site rents up. Thus, from the point of

---

21. For an empirical study of the relation between aggregate land value (assumed to measure net economies of agglomeration) and city population size, see Matthew Edel, "Land Values and the Costs of Urban Congestion: Measurement and Distribution," *Social Science Information*, December 1971, pp. 7–36.

view of society as a whole, high site rents should not be regarded as one of the diseconomies of agglomeration. On the contrary, they measure the extent of the positive economies of agglomeration and location to be found there.

In practice the spatial redistribution of activity that occurs under the pressure of rising site rents may take forms other than the movement of whole firms. Haig long ago pointed out that business firms actually comprise many distinct functions that need not all be carried on at the same place.[22] As site rents in the CBD rise, firms often separate functions that do not require centrality—manufacturing, warehousing, and record keeping, for example—and move them to less costly areas on the periphery or even to points outside the metropolis. In the end perhaps only the head office will remain in the CBD. A prominent recent example of this has been the tendency of book publishers, who are still heavily concentrated in New York, to move their distribution, storage, and billing operations to localities on the outskirts of the metropolitan area, where rent is lower, while retaining head office, editorial, and sales functions in New York City.

TRANSPORTATION PLANNING AND LAND USE

The argument of his chapter has focused exclusively on the way the private land market determines patterns of urban land use. No mention has been made of public planning or intervention, apart from zoning. This was deliberate but also unrealistic, for the land-use pattern in any city results from a combination of private and public decisions. In choosing where to locate, households and firms (the private sector) have to trade off the value of greater accessibility against the cost of obtaining it. In the real world, however, as opposed to the world of the "transport surface" assumed at the beginning of this chapter, the accessibility of any point is determined not only by its distance from the city center but also by its relationship to an existing transport network, and transport networks, including streets, highways, and the mass transit system (if any), are planned and paid for by the public sector. The actual urban land-use pattern thus results from interaction between the private sector, in which individual location decisions are made, and the public sector, which plans and develops a transport network that inevitably influences subsequent private decisions. In this chapter we have dealt only with the private side. In Chapters 8 and 9, which deal specifically with the economics of transportation, we will tell the other half of the story when we examine the impact of public policy on transportation and, through transportation, on urban form.

22. R. M. Haig, "The Assignment of Activities to Areas in Urban Regions," *Quarterly Journal of Economics*, May 1926, pp. 402–434.

SEVEN

The Urban Economic Base and Economic Policy

The economics of location have dominated the first six chapters of this book. We have examined, both historically and theoretically, the forces that draw industry and population together to form cities and metropolitan areas and, within those places, distribute them into orderly patterns of settlement. We have examined linkages among industries and between industries and population in a spatial context, emphasizing the way the technology of transportation and communications establishes physical connections between activities and determines the distance at which they can best locate with respect to one another. This chapter brings a change of perspective. We will look at the urban community as a functioning economic unit, examining the employment- and income-creating relationships between activities instead of their spatial relationships, which can now be taken for granted.

The employment- and income-generating activities of the city have often been called the "urban economic base." We now wish to examine the structure and behavior of that base and to see especially how its internal characteristics interact with external forces to determine the level, stability, and growth of local income and output. When those relationships have been made clear, we will move on to the problem of local economic policy, explaining the methods by which local authorities try to influence the level of income and output and examining the implications of these methods for both local and national welfare.

It is well to start with the distinctions between internal structure and external relationships. At any moment in time the city possesses a stock of useful resources in the form of labor skills, land, capital, and entrepreneurship. These are the available factors of production. When they are fully and efficiently employed, the city is producing as much as it can. These factors of production and the relationships among them make up the internal economic structure.

It is obvious, however, that a city is very much an "open economy." It does not produce everything it consumes; nor does it consume everything it produces. Even if a great city could turn out all the manufactured goods its residents wanted, it could never be the source of all the necessary food and raw materials. These goods, at least, must be imported, and to pay for them the city must send exports to the rest of the world. Trade is not merely incidental to the city's life; it is absolutely indispensable. Thus even if there were no migration of the factors of production between areas, trade would suffice to open up the city to the influence of exogenous forces—that is to say, forces arising outside its boundaries.

The two principal methods that have been devised to analyze the urban economic base recognize the fundamental openness of the urban economy and therefore stress the importance of its relationships with the outside world. They differ, however, in the extent to which they simplify the complex reality of the city's internal structure and therefore of its external relationships. The simpler (and less reliable) of the two is the basic-nonbasic approach. A more complex but ultimately more satisfactory method is input-output analysis. We shall take up both approaches in considerable detail. The purpose is not so much to elucidate the methods themselves—although that is important—as to provide an understanding of how the urban economy functions; the simplifications these methods impose on reality, both when they are tenable and when they are not, are the best means we have to that understanding. Indeed, the weaknesses of these theories are often as instructive as their strengths, and we will show that despite some very important differences, they share a common logical structure and therefore common weaknesses and limitations.

THE BASIC–NONBASIC THEORY

The basic-nonbasic theory derives its odd name from the causal significance it attaches to exports as compared with other local activity. (Strictly speaking, it is a "theory" rather than a "method" precisely because it does postulate a particular causal relationship between the variables it deals with.) According to this theory, a city's export industries are its economic foundation, its source of growth, and are therefore rightly called "basic." Other industries are said to live by servicing these basic industries (and one another) and are therefore called "nonbasic." If there is a change in the level of employment, or of activity measured in some other way, in the basic (i.e., export) sector, it will lead automatically to a change in the same direction in the nonbasic (i.e., service) sector. The theory holds that the ratio of nonbasic to basic

TABLE 7.1
Employment Forecast for a Hypothetical City

	ACTUAL EMPLOYMENT, 1985	PREDICTED EMPLOYMENT, 1995
Basic employment (exports)	20,000	30,000
Nonbasic employment (service)	40,000	60,000
Total employment	60,000	90,000
Ratio of nonbasic to basic	2	2
Ratio of total to basic (the "multiplier")	3	3

employment (or activity) can be measured and is sufficiently stable so that future changes in total employment can be derived from forecasts of basic employment. And from future total employment it is but one step further to a prediction of future population.

The basic-nonbasic theory was first worked out in full by Homer Hoyt in the 1930s.[1] As an economist with the Federal Housing Administration in Washington, he needed a simple model of urban economic performance in order to assess the economic prospects of a multitude of cities. Thus from the very beginning, simplicity has been an intended feature of the basic-nonbasic theory. And despite subsequent refinements, when the theory is compared with other methods, simplicity remains its leading virtue today.

Table 7.1 illustrates an application of the theory using hypothetical data. Suppose that in 1985 total employment in a certain city was 60,000, of which 20,000 was basic employment and 40,000 was nonbasic. The ratio of total to basic employment was therefore 3:1 in 1985. The analyst is asked to predict total employment in 1995. The basic-nonbasic theory (at least in its simplest form) holds that the total-to-basic ratio will remain constant over time. Therefore if the analyst can predict employment in the basic sector, the problem is solved. Total employment in 1995 will simply be three times basic employment. In the hypothetical case the analyst predicts that basic employ-

---

1.For an account of the origin of the basic-nonbasic theory, see Richard B. Andrews, "Mechanics of the Urban Economic Base: Historical Development of the Base Concept," reprinted in R. W. Pfouts, ed., *The Techniques of Urban Economic Analysis* (West Trenton, N.J.: Chandler-Davis Publishing, 1960), pp. 5–17. Andrews points out reference to an export-versus-service dichotomy in the pathbreaking *Regional Survey of New York and Its Environs*, I (1928), directed by Robert M. Haig for the Regional Plan Association.

Subsequently, Max R. Bloom came upon an anonymous article in *The Monthly Magazine*, an English journal dated February 1, 1811, that now stands as the earliest statement of the basic-nonbasic relationship. See "Economic Base and City Size: An 1811 Commentary on London," reprinted in L. S. Bourne and J. W. Simmons, eds., *Systems of Cities* (New York: Oxford University Press, 1978), pp. 441–444.

ment will rise to 30,000. It follows that nonbasic will increase to 60,000 and total to 90,000. As this example makes clear, the total-to-basic ratio is, in effect, an employment "multiplier." The change in basic employment times the multiplier yields the change in total employment.

The multiplier in the table is stated in terms of an average relationship, and the example shows that this average relationship is expected to be maintained over time. As a city grows, however, the ratio of total to basic employment typically increases (for reasons we will explain). If this is the case, the ratio of total to basic employment for changes at the margin must be greater than the average ratio. When there is reason to believe that the marginal ratio differs from the average, the analyst will prefer to use the marginal multiplier, which equals the ratio of change in total employment to change in basic employment. Stated that way, the relationship takes on a strong resemblance to some forms of the Keynesian multiplier. It is interesting to note, however, that the basic-nonbasic multiplier effect was worked out quite independently of the Keynesian analysis.

The operational simplicity of the basic-nonbasic method derives from several factors. First of all, instead of having to predict changes in each industry, the analyst need be concerned only with the export trades. In any city these are a minor fraction of the whole. In addition, they often have the added virtue of being characterized by large firms. The time and effort needed to make predictions are thus minimized. Second, the method makes use of the most easily available local data, those on employment. True, the basic-nonbasic theory could be stated instead in terms of total payrolls or value added. Indeed, value added might be theoretically the soundest unit of account. But employment is an acceptable proxy for value added, and the data are easier to come by.

Lack of data on economic activity in cities is an acute problem and frequently dictates the form that a study of the urban economic base must take. In particular, although measurement of the relationship between the local economy and the nation as a whole is important in any such study, no data are regularly published by any statistical agency on the flow of goods or capital funds into or out of even the largest cities.[2] Unless the analyst can pay the cost of a sample survey to measure the size of such flows, it will be necessary to fall back on some form of approximation. Here again, the basic-nonbasic method has the advantage of simplicity. It requires information only about the volume of local and export activity. Imports and capital flows are ignored. In the absence of direct data, the technique of approximation most frequently used to estimate export activity is the location quotient method.

2. See discussion in Andrew M. Isserman, "Estimating Export Activity in a Regional Economy: A Theoretical and Empirical Analysis of Alternative Methods," *International Regional Science Review*, Winter 1980, pp. 179–180.

Location Quotients as Export Allocators

The "location quotient" is a statistical device that measures, usually in terms of employment, the degree to which a given industry is concentrated in a given place. Quite apart from its role in estimating the level of exports, it is an extremely useful descriptive measure in urban studies. It is defined as the percentage of local employment accounted for by a given industry divided by the percentage of national employment in that industry. Suppose that in our hypothetical city, shoe production makes up 2.5 percent of all employment, while in the United States as a whole it accounts for 2.0 percent. The location quotient for shoe production in the hypothetical city is $.025 \div .020 = 1.25$. When the value of the quotient is exactly unity, the industry in question is present at the given place to just the same extent as in the whole nation. When it is above unity, the industry is relatively concentrated at that place; when below unity, it is relatively scarce.

Now let us see how this device can be used to estimate the level of export activity. It will be convenient to use the following terms:

e_i = local employment in the ith industry
e = total local employment
E_i = national employment in the ith industry
E = total national employment

Then the location quotient for the ith industry is

$$\frac{e_i/e}{E_i/E}$$

To use this coefficient as the basis for estimating export activity, we must make the three following assumptions: (1) patterns of consumption do not vary geographically; (2) labor productivity does not vary geographically; and (3) each industry produces a single, perfectly homogeneous good. Suppose that we are dealing with the shoe industry in our hypothetical city. Given the assumed uniformity of consumption patterns, local residents will wish to buy the same quantity of shoes per capita as does the nation as a whole. Barring international trade, the nation as a whole obtains the desired quantity of shoes when E_i/E percent of the national labor force is devoted to shoe production. Given the assumption of uniform labor productivity, it follows that the local demand for shoes can be satisfied from local production when $e_i/e = E_i/E$, which occurs when the location quotient for shoe production equals one. In short, when the location quotient for a particular industry is unity, local consumption can just be satisfied by local production. There will be neither exports nor imports. It follows that when the quotient exceeds unity, the city will be exporting, and when it falls short of unity, importing. The amount of employment in each industry that can be assumed to serve the export sector is precisely the amount that, so to speak, pushes the location quotient above one. This may be written algebraically as follows: let

$$X_i = \text{export employment in the } i\text{th industry}$$

Using terms previously defined,

$\dfrac{E_i}{E}$ = the percentage of local employment that would have to be devoted to production of the ith good to supply local demand

$\dfrac{e_i}{e}$ = the actual percentage of local employment devoted to such production

Then

$$X_i = \left(\frac{e_i}{e} - \frac{E_i}{E}\right) \cdot e$$

If the two terms inside the parentheses are equal, the location quotient equals one, and export employment in the ith industry is zero.

In our hypothetical city, total local employment in 1985 was 60,000. For shoe production we gave the following: $e_i/e = .025$, $E_i/E = .020$. In that case we can calculate export employment in the shoe industry as follows:

$$X_i = (.025 - .020) \cdot 60{,}000 = 300$$

If we make a similar calculation for every local industry for which the location quotient exceeds one and sum the results, we obtain an estimate of total basic employment in the city. All other employment can then be classified as non-basic. Thus the location quotient method allows us to estimate the size of the basic (or export) sector even though we have no direct observations of goods flows.

Unfortunately, such an estimate is open to question because the three assumptions on which the analysis rests are in varying degrees doubtful. The assumption of geographically uniform consumption patterns is not strictly valid. Climate in particular causes variation in the consumption of such things as clothing and heating fuels and equipment. Nor is the assumption of uniform productivity entirely accurate. These are minor shortcomings, however. The real difficulty lies in the third assumption: that each industry, taken over the whole nation, produces a single homogeneous good. Unless this is true, there is simply no warrant for assuming that when the location quotient equals one, local production will be entirely absorbed by local consumption, leaving nothing for export.

The Need for Disaggregation

To see why this is so we must consider the problem of defining the "industries" for which location quotients are to be calculated. Data on industrial production and employment in the United States are published in categories established by the Office of Management and Budget's Standard Industrial Classification system. Here's an illustration of how the SIC system works. Under the heading of "Manufacturing" we find:

Code No.
20	FOOD AND KINDRED PRODUCTS
202	*Dairy products*
2021	Creamery butter
2022	Cheese, natural and processed
2023	Condensed and evaporated milk
2024	Ice cream and frozen desserts
(etc.)	

Suppose that an analyst estimating exports by means of the location quotient method uses data classified at the "two-digit" level. In that case, "Food and Kindred Products" (SIC 20) is treated as an "industry." Now assume that in the hypothetical city of West Greenbush the location quotient for employment in SIC 20 turns out to be exactly equal to one. The analyst concludes that West Greenbush consumes all of its locally manufactured food products and exports none. But suppose that the only food manufacturing plant in the town actually makes nothing but ice cream and frozen desserts (SIC 2024). The analysis requires us to believe that West Greenbush consumes all of that ice cream and ships none of it to other localities. This is obviously wrong and shows that estimates of basic (or export) employment arrived at by the location quotient method are systematically biased downward. And if exports are underestimated, the multiplier, which equals total employment divided by basic employment, is necessarily overestimated.

The most detailed classification in the SIC system is the "four-digit" level, and if location quotients are calculated at that level, the downward bias in export estimation is greatly reduced. For example, given that West Greenbush has an ice cream factory, its location quotient for SIC 2024 is likely to be far above one, since not every town has such a plant. Consequently, if calculations are made at the four-digit level, West Greenbush will be found to have a good deal of export employment in its food industry (the result of ice cream exports). Andrew Isserman found that using data disaggregated to the four-digit level rather than the two-digit level increased the estimated export share by an average of 45 percent.[3] Unfortunately, as a practical matter, govern-

3. Ibid., table 1.

TABLE 7.2
Estimates of Export Percentages Based on Surveys and on Location Quotients, 1955–1956

	DECATUR		INDIANAPOLIS	
MANUFACTURING INDUSTRIES	Survey	Location Quotient	Survey	Location Quotient
Food	87	71	63	24
Chemicals	98	44	100	50
Printing	—	—	51	24
Primary metals	97	20	99	0
Fabricated metals	—	—	98	11
Nonelectrical machinery	97	74	98	38
Electrical machinery	—	—	100	67
Transportation equipment	100	45	100	68

Source: Charles M. Tiebout, *The Community Economic Base Study* (New York: Committee for Economic Development, December 1962), Supplementary Paper 16, table 10, p. 49.

ment rules against disclosing data in categories where there are very few firms make it unlikely that much data at the four-digit level will be available for manufacturing, except in fairly large cities. Moreover, even where they are available, data at that level of detail do not fully overcome the problem of heterogeneous goods. Within most four-digit industries there is a great deal of geographic cross-hauling of products. Almost certainly, West Greenbush will both export its own brand of ice cream and import other brands from other cities.

A questionnaire survey is probably the most accurate method of estimating exports, although, depending on the size of the city, it may be fairly expensive. Charles M. Tiebout, who wrote extensively on economic base studies, compared export percentages estimated by survey techniques with those arrived at by the location quotient method.[4] His figures for Indianapolis and Decatur are reproduced in Table 7.2. Clearly, the downward bias imparted by the location quotient method is not trivial, and since it varies from city to city and from industry to industry, there is no practical way to adjust for it.

Measuring Indirect Exports

Tiebout concluded that despite its shortcomings, the location quotient method should not be rejected out of hand, since it does cope, even if imper-

4. Charles M. Tiebout, *The Community Economic Base Study* (New York: Committee for Economic Development, December 1962), Supplementary Paper 16.

fectly, with the tricky question of indirect exports.[5] This problem deserves careful attention. Suppose that in order to measure the export sector of a city the analyst surveyed all local firms to find out how many workers they employed and what percentage of their sales were made to purchasers outside the city. It would then be possible to divide each firm's labor force between export and local employment by using the export percentage revealed in the survey. Summing for all industries would yield a figure for total export employment. But this would be a measure of "direct exports" only. In leaving out "indirect exports," it would understate the true size of the local export sector.

Indirect exports occur whenever one local firm sells to another that in turn ships its products outside the city. Any local firm that supplies a local exporter is thus producing indirect exports. Its dependence on the export market is just as real as that of the direct exporter and must be appropriately taken into account. Does the location quotient method do so? To some extent, yes. For example, if the printing industry has a high location quotient in a given city, activities that specialize in direct service to that industry are likely to have high location quotients, too, and will therefore also appear as exporters. As we will see, however, this is not the best way of taking the indirect effects of exports into account. Only the input-output method comes close to representing the true interrelatedness of industries in the local economy.

A Critique of the Basic-Nonbasic Method

Because its data requirements were so easy to meet, the basic-nonbasic method was frequently used for empirical studies in the 1940s and 1950s. Unfortunately, the method suffers from so many serious defects, both in theory and practice, that few economists today would endorse its use.[6] It will suffice here to mention just a few of these difficulties.

Excessive Aggregation

First of all, the model loses a great deal in being so highly aggregated. The division of activity into only two classes is too gross to capture the complex interindustry relations of an urban economy. This is not merely a matter of theoretical nicety. It also reduces the accuracy with which the model does its job of prediction. The basic-nonbasic multiplier represents the average response of the whole nonbasic sector to a change in the level of all exports. If only one industry's exports were to increase, there is no reason to assume that

5. Ibid., pp. 48–49.
6. See Harry W. Richardson, "Input-Output and Economic Base Multipliers: Looking Backward and Forward," *Journal of Regional Science*, November 1985, p. 646.

nonbasic activity would respond in this average way. For example, an export industry that relies heavily on imported components and materials will certainly transmit weaker impulses to the nonbasic sector than will an export industry that buys heavily from local suppliers. Hence predictions made by the model about the level of total activity are likely to be wrong unless all exports are expected to change simultaneously by the same percentage.

This problem can be looked at in another way. One of the purposes of economic bases analysis is to predict the impact on the local economy of expected changes in the export sector. For example, a city with a large defense plant wants to know what will happen if a policy of disarmament closes that plant down. Not only will the basic-nonbasic model probably predict the wrong overall impact for the reasons just given, but also it will be unable to say which parts of the nonbasic sector will suffer more and which less. Such details would be far more useful than a simple statement about the average impact, even if it were correct. As we will see, the difficulties that result from excessive aggregation can be overcome by using the more complex input-output method.

Instability of the Multiplier in the Short Run

A second series of difficulties centers around the time dimensions of the basic-nonbasic model. The analysis may be thought of as dealing either with the short run or the long run. A typical short-run problem would be a defense-industry impact study of the sort just described or a prediction of the consequences for the local community of an expected swing in the national business cycle. The method assumes that impulses from the export sector have a multiplied effect on the local economy as a whole, that the size of the multiplier can be calculated, and that its value will be sufficiently stable over the short run to warrant using it to predict the extent of the local economy's response to exogenous change. Unhappily, the multiplier has not proved to be stable in the short run and is consequently unreliable as a tool for short-run prediction.[7]

The instability of the multiplier in the short run can probably be ascribed to lagged adjustment. Let us grant that for a city with a given population, economic structure, and location, at a given time in economic history, there is a "true" or equilibrium ratio of service to basic activity. If the level of basic activity changes, the response of service activity will not occur instantly and may well be drawn out over many years. Indeed, if its export sales are continually in flux, a city may be always moving toward its "true" ratio without ever reaching it. Under these circumstances the difficulty of determining

---

7. See evidence cited in Walter Isard, *Methods of Regional Analysis* (New York: Wiley and M.I.T. Press, 1960), p. 201. The book offers a detailed analysis of the basic-nonbasic method on pp. 189–205.

the "true" ratio or of deciding what other ratio to use and how to allow for time lags in making short-run forecasts is obviously enormous. Given the other weakness of the basic-nonbasic method, this sort of refinement has not seemed worth undertaking.

Changes in the Multiplier over the Long Run

Even if the basic-nonbasic analysis is ineffective for short-run prediction, might it still be reliable for long-run forecasts? Here the objective would be to predict the long-run growth of employment and population in a metropolitan area on the basis of the long-run prospects for its exports. Will the method perhaps work better in the long run when fluctuations in the multiplier can somehow be averaged out to determine its true value and the usual adjustment lags will no longer matter? The answer is clearly no, for in the long run all the variables of taste, technology, population size, and economic structure that must be held constant in order even to conceive of a "true" or equilibrium ratio are free to vary. If there is a true ratio, it will almost certainly change as time passes. Once again, the effort that would be required to overcome the difficulty—for example, by estimating long-run changes in the multiplier for a particular city—is simply not justified, given the other limitations of the basic-nonbasic method.

One source of long-run change in the ratio of basic to nonbasic activity is the growth of a city's population. Central place analysis, presented in Chapter 5, tells us that the larger the market in a community, the more services that community will provide for itself and the fewer it will have to import from other centers, for as a city grows in population it will pass successive "threshold" levels at which local provision of additional services becomes profitable. Translated into basic-nonbasic terminology, this means that the ratio of nonbasic to basic activity will rise as a city grows and that the multiplier, which equals the ratio of total to basic activity, will also rise.

Empirical studies do confirm the tendency of the nonbasic sector to grow relative to the basic as a city's population rises through time. For example, Britton Harris calculated values of the basic-nonbasic multiplier for sixty-seven SMAs in 1940 and 1950.[8] Population increased in each of these metropolitan areas over that interval. The nonbasic-to-basic ratio—which necessarily equals the multiplier minus one—rose in fifty-seven of the sixty-seven cases. Its failure to increase in the remaining ten cases might well be evidence of the lagged adjustment process.

The same tendency can be observed if we compare the nonbasic-to-basic ratios of large and small cities at a given moment in time. Table 7.3, de-

---

8. Britton Harris, "Comment on Pfouts' Test of the Base Theory," *Journal of the American Institute of Planners*, November 1958, p. 236. Harris's calculations are based on data from the *Census of Population*.

TABLE 7.3
Ratios of Nonbasic to Basic Activity in Large and Small Metropolitan Areas, 1972

SMSA	POPULATION (THOUSANDS)	BASIC EMPLOYMENT AS A PERCENTAGE OF THE TOTAL	NONBASIC EMPLOYMENT ÷ BASIC EMPLOYMENT
Six Largest SMSAs			
New York	11,565	39.7	1.52
Chicago	7,054	28.0	2.57
Los Angeles–Long Beach	6,972	25.4	2.93
Philadelphia	4,843	27.1	2.69
Detroit	4,212	32.1	2.12
Boston	3,773	28.3	2.53
Mean of largest areas	—	—	2.39
Six Small SMSAs			
Canton, O.	372	39.9	1.51
Erie, Pa.	271	35.9	1.79
Battle Creek, Mich.	141	48.7	1.05
Muncie, Ind.	133	40.0	1.50
Kenosha, Wis.	120	41.0	1.44
Danville, Ill.	97	42.6	1.35
Mean of small areas	—	—	1.44

Source: Andrew M. Isserman, "Estimating Export Activity in a Regional Economy: A Theoretical and Empirical Analysis of Alternative Methods," *International Regional Science Review*, Winter 1980, tables 2 and 3.

rived from data developed by Isserman, compares the ratios in 1972 for the nation's then six largest SMSAs and for six very small ones. The nonbasic-to-basic ratio averaged 2.39 in the largest areas but only 1.44 in the smallest. New York is exceptional among the six large centers in having a relatively high percentage of employment devoted to exports, a result which apparently reflects its specialization in "high-level" trade and service activities. This should serve to remind the reader that a city's nonbasic-to-basic ratio depends on the idiosyncrasies of local economic structure as well as on size.[9]

Undoubtedly, as central place analysis would suggest, the location of a given city in relation to competing centers also affects the relative size of its nonbasic sector. We would expect a small city that is close to a large metropolis to have fewer local service activities than a city of equal size that is geographically isolated. Harris's data illustrate the point. They show that in 1950 South Bend, which is less than a hundred miles from Chicago, had a nonbasic-to-basic ratio of only 1.84, while El Paso, a metropolitan area then

9. See discussion in Isserman, pp. 174–176.

about the same size as South Bend that is many hundreds of miles from any large center, had a ratio of 3.42.

The inability of simple two-sector models to depict urban economic structure adequately has been amply demonstrated. In recent years most students of the urban economic base have therefore favored the multisector approach known as input-output analysis. This method, as we will see, enables one to lay bare both the internal and the external relationships of an urban economy in great detail. In this respect it overcomes many of the defects of the simpler methods, especially for purposes of short-run analysis. So far as long-run applications are concerned, however, input-output analysis does not in itself offer a solution to the problem of predicting growth and change. We will return to this problem later.

INPUT–OUTPUT ANALYSIS

Input-output analysis was developed by Wassily W. Leontief at Harvard, beginning in the 1930s. Inspired by Walras's theory of general equilibrium, which depicted the interrelationship of each economic sector with every other, Leontief sought a scheme in which those interrelationships could be quantified to yield an actual working model of the economy. The result was input-output analysis, a method specifically designed to portray in great detail the actual interindustry relationships of a real economy. The method was first applied to the national economy of the United States. In the 1950s economists began to adapt it for regional and urban use.[10]

Although input-output analysis can become highly complex, its analytical framework is based on a simple accounting identity that can be stated as follows: for each sector or industry the sum of all outputs (sold to other sectors or industries) must equal the sum of all inputs (purchased from other sectors or industries), provided we take care not to omit any transactions. This is equivalent to the accounting identity for an individual firm, which states that total receipts must equal total costs plus profit. If such an identity holds for each industry and sector separately, it must also be true in the aggregate: total inputs to the economy equal its total output.

The full array of input-output relationships for an economy can be shown conveniently in a two-way table or matrix such as Table 7.4. Down the left-hand side are listed the sectors or industries producing outputs. Across the top the same sectors or industries are listed as purchasers of inputs from the sectors at the left.

---

10. For a more detailed account of input-output analysis in a regional setting that is nevertheless comprehensible to the beginning student, see Isard, ch. 8. William H. Miernyk's *Elements of Input-Output Analysis* (New York: Random House, 1965) also provides an excellent introduction to the subject.

TABLE 7.4
*Input-Output Table for a Hypothetical City*a

SECTOR PURCHASING	PROCESSING SECTOR			FINAL DEMAND SECTOR	ROW TOTALS
	1	2	3	4	
SECTOR PRODUCING	Manufac- turing	Services	House- holds	Exports	(Output)
1. Manufacturing $(\dot{X}_m)$	—	10	40	50	100
2. Services (X_s)	30	—	60	10	100
3. Households (X_h)	30	70	—	—	100
4. Imports	40	20	—	—	60
Column totals (inputs)	100	100	100	60	360

aFlows are expressed in millions of dollars.

A crucial assumption is introduced in order to simplify the relationships between the sectors: the assumption that all production processes have fixed technical coefficients. This means that no matter what the level of production in a given industry, it is assumed that inputs are required in fixed proportions to output. For example, the same number of tons of coal will be required to produce a ton of steel whether steel output is high or low, and the same number of yards of cloth and hours of labor will be needed to make a suit of clothes whether clothing production is up or down.

As a further simplification, the input-output method states the input coefficients not in physical units but in cents worth of input per dollar of output. Thus the input of electric power needed to produce aluminum would be stated not as kilowatts per ton but as cents worth of electricity per dollar's worth of aluminum output. An input-output model is generally employed to analyze change through time rather than simply to describe a perfectly static situation. In that case the use of constant input coefficients expressed in monetary units implies an assumption that as the level or composition of output changes over time, the relative prices of all goods will remain as they were in the base year.

Table 7.4 shows a highly compressed version of an input-output table for a hypothetical city. The unit of measurement is millions of dollars per year. To simplify matters it is assumed that labor and management are the only factors of production. Since capital is not employed, all transactions are on current account, and it is unnecessary to have a heading for capital transactions. The government, if there is one, exists without levying taxes or spending money, so no government sector appears in the table.

Of course, this example contains nothing like the detail that would be incorporated in an actual input-output study. In addition to including separate sectors for government and capital transactions, such studies attempt to divide industry into relatively fine classes. The degree of detail achieved depends on the time and money available for the study. Generally it varies from twenty or thirty sectors to the nearly six hundred used in the Philadelphia Region Input-Output Study directed by Walter Isard.[11]

In this highly compressed version, industry is divided into only two types—manufacturing and service. In addition, the table shows a household sector and a foreign trade sector. Moving across each row one reads the sales by the industry or sector named at the left to the industries and sectors named across the top. For simplicity it is assumed that there are no sales within sectors (an assumption that is not made in actual studies). Thus the first column in the first row is blank. Reading to the right across the first row shows that manufacturers sell $10 million of output per year to the service sector and $40 million to households and that they ship $50 million of exports to purchasers outside the area. The sum of these sales is total manufacturing output of $100 million shown in the right-hand column. Output and sales by the service industry are shown in row 2.

Household "output," recorded in row 3, consists of labor and management compensated by wages and salaries. The table indicates that each year households sell $30 million worth of labor and management to manufacturing and $70 million worth to service industries. The total value of this output— $100 million, as shown in the last column—is also total household income.

Just as each row shows sales by the sector listed at the left, so each column shows purchases by the sector named at the top. The entry at the bottom of each column is the sum of that sector's purchases. Because inputs equal outputs for each sector, the figure for total purchases at the bottom of each sector's column equals the figure for total sales at the end of that sector's row. Since the table shows the sales of each local sector to every other as well as the transactions of each with the outside world, it offers a complete and logically consistent picture of economic activity in the area under study.

This highly simplified model, unrealistic though it may be, is convenient for showing how input-output analysis works. The logical starting point for such an explanation, however, is not Table 7.4 but Table 7.5. The latter shows the same industries and sectors as the former, but instead of presenting sales and purchases it records the value of the various input coefficients for industries in our hypothetical city. For example, column 1 indicates that the manufacturing industry requires 30 cents worth of service inputs, 30 cents worth of household inputs (i.e., labor and management), and 40 cents worth of imports for each dollar of output. A somewhat different set of coefficients appears in the service industry column: the service industry uses more labor and less imports per dollar of output than does manufacturing. The input co-

11. Walter Isard, E. Romanoff, and T. W. Langford, Jr., *Working Papers: Philadelphia Region Input-Output Study* (Philadelphia: Regional Science Research Institute, 1967).

TABLE 7.5
Input Coefficients of Industries in a Hypothetical City

INPUTS PURCHASED FROM:	DOLLARS' WORTH OF INPUTS PER DOLLAR OF OUTPUT IN:		
	1 Manufacturing	*2 Services*	*3 Households*
1. Manufacturing	—	.10	.40
2. Services	.30	—	.60
3. Households	.30	.70	—
4. Imports	.40	.20	—
Sum of coefficients	1.00	1.00	1.00

efficients for households, while analogous to those for industry, might better be thought of as representing the division of household purchases between locally produced manufactures (40 percent) and locally produced services (60 percent). Households import nothing directly. The input coefficients in every column add up to unity.

The Relationship between the Structural Matrix and the Final Demand Sector

In any application of the input-output method, industries or sectors must be divided into two groups, one called collectively the "final demand sector," the other collectively the "processing sector" or "structural matrix." The division will vary according to the scope and purpose of the analysis. It is intended to reflect in each case a distinction between "outside" (exogenous) sectors in which the level of activity is autonomously determined and "inside" (endogenous) sectors in which the level of activity can be explained by the model. The former group make up the final demand sector, the latter group the processing sector. The entire analysis rests on the premise that the autonomous "outside" forces to which the processing sector responds are those issuing from the final demand sector. The level and composition of final demand thus determine the level and composition of activity inside the structural matrix. The relationship can be expressed another way. The industries within the structural matrix are regarded as a set of "processors" whose output goes to satisfy the requirements of the final demand sector. Once the dollar value of those final demand requirements is specified, the value of all the inputs and outputs necessary to supply it is automatically determined.

The manner in which industries within the structural matrix respond to demands put upon them from the outside is controlled entirely by the input coefficients that establish relationships within the matrix. The logic of input-output analysis therefore reduces to this: calculate input coefficients to delineate the processing sector, confront that sector with a set of final demands, and it follows that the output of every industry, its transactions with every other industry, and the output of the system as a whole will be fully determined.

In the hypothetical urban economy shown in Tables 7.4 and 7.5, the final demand sector consists only of exports. Manufacturing, services, and households are placed within the structural matrix. Thus the model posits that the level of activity in the two local industries and the income of households, which depends on that level, are determined entirely by the demand of the outside world for the city's exports. In a more complex and realistic analysis the final demand group would also include the government and capital-formation sectors omitted here. These sectors would be placed in the category of final demand because the levels of activity within them cannot reasonably be explained by means of fixed coefficients relating their output to the level of activity in the industries within the structural matrix. Instead, the dollar value of government activity and of capital formation is assumed to be autonomously determined.

Simple Mathematics of Input-Output Analysis

The relationship between the parts of an input-output table can best be understood by means of some simple mathematics. Each row of the table of input coefficients can be read as part of an equation for the total output of the industry named at the left end of that row. Let us employ the following terms:

$$X_m = \text{total manufacturing output}$$
$$X_s = \text{total service output}$$
$$X_h = \text{total household output}$$

Using the input coefficients given in Table 7.5, we can show that the equations for these outputs are

$$X_m = .1X_s + .4X_h + \text{exports}$$
$$X_s = .3X_m + .6X_h + \text{exports}$$
$$X_h = .3X_m + .7X_s + \text{exports}$$

The first equation states that total manufacturing output must be sufficient to supply the required manufacturing exports (i.e., final demand) and to supply in addition the other two processing sectors with the manufacturing inputs that *they* need. What the other sectors require is given to us by the table of input coefficients. We know that the service industry needs 10 cents worth of manufacturing inputs for every dollar of its output. Its output will be X_s. Therefore the service industry will require $.1X_s$ of manufacturing inputs. This is the first term in the equation for required manufacturing output. Similarly, the table of input coefficients tells us that households will require 40 cents' worth of manufacturing inputs for every dollar of their output. There-fore the second term in the equation for manufacturing output is $.4X_h$. The equations for service output and household output are similarly constructed.

We have written three equations, which appear to contain six un-knowns: X_m, X_s, X_h, and the level of exports for each of the three sectors. Ex-ports, however, are not an unknown to be solved for in the analysis. Rather they are the "final demands" that the local economy responds to. Their value is determined outside the system. Let us assume that the manufacturing sec-tor must produce $50 million of exports, the service sector $10 million, and the household sector none. The three equations thus become

$$X_m = .1X_s + .4X_h + 50$$
$$X_s = .3X_m + .6X_h + 10$$
$$X_h = .3X_m + .7X_s + 0$$

Since the three equations now contain only three unknowns, a solution must exist, and anyone who recalls high school algebra can find it by the usual method for solving simultaneous equations. (In actual practice input-output tables contain far too many sectors and therefore too many simultaneous equations to permit solution by simple hand methods. The job can be done, however, by using matrix algebra and a computer.) In this instance the solu-tion has already been given in Table 7.4. Total output of each of the process-ing sectors will be $100 million, which, as the input-output table shows, will enable each sector to supply the required exports plus the inputs simulta-neously needed by each of the other sectors. Since total inputs equal total output for each sector, imports into each can be calculated by subtracting all other inputs from total output. The total income generated by the local econ-omy is the sum of all returns to local factors of production. Since the factors of production—in this case labor and management—are provided by house-holds, locally generated income equals household receipts of $100 million.

Advantages of a Disaggregated Model

Input-output analysis is flexible enough to serve many purposes. The simplest of these is straightforward description. A detailed input-output table is a unique map of an economy as it functions in a particular year, showing the flows of goods and services among all the local sectors and between each of them and the outside world. More interesting, however, is the way in which the method can be used to answer questions about the effects of pre-dicted changes. Because it is so much more highly disaggregated than the basic-nonbasic model, it answers questions not only in greater detail but, in all likelihood, with far greater accuracy.

Suppose, for example, that we wish to know what the effect on the local economy will be of a predicted change in the level of exports. The basic-nonbasic method uses an aggregate multiplier that is averaged over all the export sectors. Therefore the predicted effect of, say, a $10 million increase in exports will be the same no matter which exporting industry enjoys the increase. Not so with input-output analysis, as the following example will demonstrate.

Let us assume that the situation in the base year is represented in Table 7.4. Exports total $60 million, of which $50 million is from the manufacturing and $10 million from the service sector. Local income equals $100 million per year. Now compare the effects of a $10 million increase in exports alternatively of the manufacturing sector and of the service sector. The results are shown in Table 7.6, which contains two entries in each cell of the input-output table. The upper entry in each cell shows the outcome when manufacturing exports rise from $50 to $60 million while service exports remain at $10 million. The lower entry shows the results when service exports rise from $10 to $20 million while manufacturing exports are held constant at $50 million.

TABLE 7.6
Results of Export Expansion in a Hypothetical City: Two Cases[a,b]

SECTOR PRODUCING		PROCESSING SECTOR 1 Manufac- turing	2 Services	3 House- holds	FINAL DEMAND SECTOR 4 Exports	ROW TOTALS (Output)
1. Manufacturing	1st case	—	11.5	46.2	60.0	117.7
	2nd case	—	12.7	48.9	50.0	111.6
2. Services	1st case	35.3	—	69.4	10.0	114.7
	2nd case	33.5	—	73.4	20.0	126.9
3. Households	1st case	35.3	80.3	—	—	115.6
	2nd case	33.5	88.8	—	—	122.3
4. Imports	1st case	47.1	22.9	—	—	70.0
	2nd case	44.6	25.4	—	—	70.0
Column totals (inputs)	1st case	117.7	114.7	115.6	70.0	418.0
	2nd case	111.6	126.9	122.3	70.0	430.9

[a]Flows are expressed in millions of dollars.
[b]The two cases are as follows:

  1st case: manufacturing exports = $60 million, service exports = $10 million
  2nd case: manufacturing exports = $50 million, service exports = $20 million

The outcome is entirely different in the two cases. Most notably, household income rises to $122.3 million when service exports increase by $10 million but reaches only $115.6 million when manufacturing exports rise by that amount. Why should service exports have so much stronger an effect, dollar for dollar, on local income? The answer can be deduced from an examination of the input coefficients in Table 7.5. The manufacturing sector uses 40 cents' worth of imports per dollar of production, while the service sector uses only 20 cents' worth. Consequently, a dollar increase in service exports involves much less leakage of spending outside the economy in the form of increased imports than does a dollar increase in exports of the manufacturing sector. Less leakage means a larger increase in the demand for local output and hence a greater ultimate expansion of local output and income.

The expansion process can be viewed as a round-by-round series of increments. When manufacturing exports rise by $10 million, the input coefficients in column 1 of Table 7.5 show that the direct requirements to produce that output are $3 million of service inputs, $3 million of household inputs, and $4 million of imported goods. But that is only the first round of requirements, since those inputs themselves must be produced, giving rise to a second round of expansion. Specifically, in order to produce that $3 million of output sold to the manufacturing sector, the sevice sector requires $2.1 million of hosehold inputs, $.3 million of manufacturing inputs, and $.6 million of imported goods. Likewise, the household sector receiving $3 million of additional income from sales to the manufacturing sector will buy (as, so to speak, its additional inputs) $1.2 million of manufactured goods and $1.8 million of services. These requirements comprise the second round of the expansion. Since they, too, must be produced there is a third round, and so on in diminishing series. The final expansion, as shown in Table 7.6, is the sum of this infinite series of rounds. We can now see that a $10 million increase in service exports leads to a greater expansion of local income than a similar increase in manufacturing exports primarily because on the first round of service industry expansion $8 million of spending remains within the community, whereas for an equal increase in manufacturing exports only $6 million of first-round spending would do so. And if the first round is smaller, subsequent rounds based on it will be reduced, too.

This illustration suggests another of the many uses for input-output analysis: it can show precisely what the total direct and indirect input requirements would be for an expected increase in output for final demand by a particular sector. Information of that kind might be crucial to city planners—for example, in anticipating the requirements for indirect services such as housing and transportation that would accompany a projected expansion of a major local industry. Or if the trend is reversed and cutbacks are expected in a major local industry—say, a defense plant—the analysis will tell not just the aggregate output reduction to be expected as the sum of direct plus indirect effects but also precisely which sectors will suffer how much of a decline in activity.

Input-Output Multipliers

The expansion or contraction of a local economy in response to a change in final demand as explained by input-output analysis is as much a multiplier process as was the expansion previously described by means of the basic-nonbasic method. This is one ground for stating, as we did earlier, that the two models are fundamentally similar in structure. A second ground is the division of the economy in both cases into an outside, or exogenously oriented, sector in which the level of activity is autonomously determined and an inside, or endogenous, sector that responds passively to the stimulus transmitted from the other. A third is the mathematically similar character of the multiplier relationships. In both models the multiplier is based on one or more system coefficients that are assumed to be fixed, at least in the short run: the basic-nonbasic ratio in one case, the set of technical input coefficients in the other.

As we have shown, however, the value of the multiplier under input-output analysis varies according to which sector receives the initial impulse. Conceptually a variety of multipliers can be distinguished in an input-output model.[12] We have been discussing one that can be defined as the change in income divided by the change in exports. For our hypothetical city, the different values this multiplier takes—depending on the composition of the change in exports—are shown in Table 7.7. The first two rows have already been explained. The third represents the special case of a uniform expansion of exports: each sector's exports increase by the same ratio, in this case one-sixth. The resulting rise in income is $16.7 million. Initial income was $100 million, and $16.7 \div 100 = \frac{1}{6}$. Thus income has increased by the same proportion that exports increased. The case illustrates a basic property of the input-output model: if every element in the final demand sector increases by a given percentage, the entire transactions matrix expands by the same percentage. In short, it "blows up" uniformly. This characteristic results from the assumption that input coefficients remain constant as the economy expands. In the particular case of a uniform export expansion, the input-output model therefore produces the same result as the basic-nonbasic method: an increase of k percent in exports leads to an increase of k percent in output and income.

The theoretical superiority of input-output analysis to other methods of analyzing the urban economic base is abundantly clear. Unfortunately, there are severe data problems. It is difficult enough to gather the numbers required for an input-output table for the United States as a whole. It is even more difficult for smaller regions, since in general the smaller the area, the less statistical detail is available in published sources. Basically there are two alternatives: conduct an independent interview and questionnaire survey of the local area, or use the technical coefficients already calculated by the Department of Commerce for national input-output tables. The second alterna-

---

12. See Miernyk, pp. 42–55.

TABLE 7.7
Variation in Multiplier Effect Depending on Which Sector Expands Exports

	CHANGE IN EXPORTS	CHANGE IN INCOME (MILLIONS OF DOLLARS)	MULTIPLIER
	(ΔE)	(ΔY)	$\Delta Y/\Delta E$
1st case: manufacturing exports rise by $10 million	10	15.6	1.56
2nd case: service exports rise by $10 million	10	22.3	2.23
3rd case: each export category rises by ⅙ (manufacturing rises $8.33 million; service rises $1.67 million)	10	16.7	1.67

Note: In each case the total increase in exports equals $10 million. All changes are measured from initial equilibrium shown in Table 7.4. Full results for the first two cases, but not the third, are shown in Table 7.6.

tive, though widely adopted, runs the risk of throwing away precisely the special features of the local economy that may have suggested the need for a study in the first place and that in any event it is risky to suppress. Therefore the first is preferable.[13]

Limitations of a Static Model

The input-output model discussed up to this point is essentially a static one. Fundamentally, it is a highly detailed map of the interindustry relationships in an economy *at a moment in time.* Such a model is highly effective for analyzing short-run problems such as the impact of an anticipated change in final demand on the level and composition of local activity and income. A static model, however, cannot cope with the long-run problems of urban change and growth. Economic development and urbanization are processes in which crucial relationships are continually changing. They cannot even be approximated by the linear expansion of a system whose internal relationships are fixed. The assumption of fixed input coefficients is not tenable over the long run.

As numerous students of input-output analysis have pointed out, fixed coefficients of production and fixed relative prices are unlikely to prevail in the long run for a variety of reasons. Most basic of these is the pervasive influence of technological innovation, which consists precisely either of changes

13. The task of surveying a moderate-size local economy is not prohibitively difficult. See, for example, Patrick McGuire, *A Simulation Model of the Rochester, New York, Region*, unpublished doctoral dissertation, Fordham University, 1973.

in the way inputs are combined to produce given outputs or in the development of entire ranges of new products that render old goods and the methods of producing them obsolete. The revolutionary effect of the automobile and truck suggests how profound these influences can be over a period of a few decades. They not only made other modes of transportation obsolete for certain purposes but also rendered obsolete the physical layout of the older central cities themselves.

Technological change affects relative input prices directly. Quite apart from that, however, differential price changes among inputs or, for a given input, among regions may occur either because resource supplies are limited or because the demand for various resources changes differentially over time. And we know that as relative input prices change, producers will substitute those that are becoming relatively cheaper for those that are not. In recent years, for example, homeowners and builders have been using more insulation and less heating oil to produce housing services because the price of oil has risen relative to the cost of insulation. In the face of such changes, input coefficients will not remain fixed.

In the long run, local growth itself is bound to affect local input coefficients. First of all, growth fosters economies of agglomeration. These, by their very definition, are increases in the technical efficiency of certain inputs as city size increases. Second, there are the central place effects of growth operating through market size. As an urban market grows, it becomes profitable to produce locally services that were formerly imported. Thus increasing urban size inevitably means change in urban economic structure.

Changes in local population characteristics, especially as a result of migration, are also likely to have important effects over the long run. Population change might affect both supply conditions, via changes in labor productivity, and demand conditions, through shifts in the pattern of consumption.

There is no need to extend the list. Most of what we see currently as major urban problems have been caused by the long-run, dynamic forces of technological change, economic growth, and population movement. Can input-output analysis be made to handle these dynamic forces? The best answer, perhaps, is that its proponents believe it can, and they are trying. Fundamental technological innovations are unpredictable, but the rate at which existing technical improvements will be adopted by industry can be estimated. Long-run trends in relative prices can be measured. One can also estimate the effects of local market growth in bringing about the substitution of local production for imports. As Miernyk has shown, the probable results of these changes can be incorporated in a new set of local input coefficients to be used when making long-run projections based on input-output analysis.[14] The application of these dynamic adjustments, depending heavily as it does on the

14. Miernyk, ch. 6. Also see Richardson, pp. 641–642, for a review of recent work along these lines.

judgment of the analyst, is still far from an exact science. Nevertheless, it appears to offer the only real hope we presently have for obtaining useful long-run projections of local economic activity.

URBAN AND REGIONAL SIMULATION MODELS

In recent years economists and city planners, spurred by the capacity of computers to operate with large systems of equations, have used computer simulation techniques in an attempt to create dynamic models of the urban economy that are even more comprehensive than an input-output analysis. What these models "simulate" is the movement of a city's or a region's economic system through time. Prescott and Mullendore, for example, constructed a simulation model for the eight-county region centered on Des Moines, Iowa.[15] The model contains five subsectors: demographic, employment, output, final demand, and capital. The last three actually constitute an input-output model made dynamic by the inclusion of a sector linking net capital formation with the expansion of output. Thus the system as a whole is actually a dynamic input-output model with two additional sectors included to explain the growth of employment and population in a way that is consistent with the growth of output.

The following simplified explanation suggests how the parts of such a model are put together. The rate of growth of local output depends on the growth of exogenous demand and also on population growth determined in the demographic sector of the model and investment demand determined in its capital sector. Employment growth depends on the growth of output, moderated by an assumed trend in labor productivity. Employment provides a link between the output sector of the model and the demographic sector. To convey the sense of how simulation models work, let us examine the latter in somewhat more detail. The size and age distribution of the population and the local birth, death, and labor-force participation rates are found or estimated for the base period. From these data the natural annual increase in the labor force is calculated. Migration is then made to depend on the difference between job growth and natural increase in the labor force. When the model runs over time, immigration occurs if job growth exceeds natural labor force growth, out-migration if vice versa. Migration plus natural increase yields change in total population. The effects of population change are continuously fed back into the input-output sector of the model via changes in household demand and in outlays by the state, local, and federal governments, which are assumed to rest on a per capita basis.

The accuracy of such a model can be tested by seeing how closely it reproduces actual changes over some observed past period. If it fits the facts

15. James R. Prescott and Walter Mullendore, "A Simulation Model for Multi-County Planning," *Proceedings of the American Real Estate and Urban Economics Association*, 4 (1969), 183–207.

reasonably well, it can be used to predict the future course of the economy, given various assumptions about future changes in demand, productivity, fertility, and so on. That it fits the past data from which its parameters were estimated does not, of course, ensure that it will accurately predict future trends. Because simulation models are so recent a development, their predictive accuracy can scarcely be said to have been established. If they prove successful, however, they will become an indispensable tool for urban and regional planning.[16]

The sort of simulation model just described is a nonspatial one. Although it generates a level of business activity, employment, and population for a region, it makes no attempt to specify the location of these activities within the study area. Spatial concerns are simply omitted. We have used that particular sort of model as an illustration both because it is relatively simple and because its aims are similar to those of the other methods of economic base analysis dealt with in this chapter. In principle, however, simulation models can be developed to reproduce the movement of any social or physical system through time. Urban economists have now developed models that simulate the spatial form and land-use pattern of an actual metropolis. These models attempt to reproduce spatial reality by assigning population and business activity to specific sites within the metropolitan area. They deal, at a high level of sophistication, with the whole range of topics in intraurban location that were introduced in Chapter 6, as well as with aspects of housing market economics to be taken up in Chapter 12. Like other simulation models, they are intended to be used as tools for policy planning and evaluation.[17]

STUDYING THE "SUPPLY SIDE" OF THE LOCAL ECONOMY

Traditional methods of studying the urban economic base have long been criticized for overemphasizing the role of demand in determining the level and rate of growth of local economic activity. In a widely cited article

16. There is also a class of economic models of urban areas that do *not* employ the input-output framework. See Barry M. Rubin, "Econometric Models for Metropolitan Planning," *Journal of the American Planning Association*, October 1981, pp. 408–420; and Roger Bolton, "Regional Econometric Models," *Journal of Regional Science*, November 1985, pp. 495–520.

17. The development of models that assign activities to locations is summarized in Britton Harris, "Urban Simulation Models in Regional Science," *Journal of Regional Science*, November 1985, pp. 545–567. Also see David L. Birch et al., *The Community Analysis Model*, HUD-PDR-363-2 (Washington, D.C.: U.S. Department of Housing and Urban Development, January 1979); John F. Kain and William C. Apgar, Jr., "Simulation of Housing Market Dynamics," *Journal of the American Real Estate and Urban Economics Association*, Winter 1979, pp. 505–538; and Gregory K. Ingram, John F. Kain, and J. Royce Ginn, *The Detroit Prototype of the NBER Urban Simulation Model* (New York: National Bureau of Economic Research, 1972). An earlier influential intraurban location model was developed by Ira S. Lowry. See his *Model of Metropolis* (Santa Monica, Calif.: Rand Corp., 1964).

Benjamin Chinitz wrote that "our efforts so far have been almost exclusively devoted to the demand dimensions of interdependence. The supply side has been virtually ignored."[18]

This comment applies with as much force to input-output and simulation methods as it does to the simpler basic-nonbasic model. The fact that the input-output and simulation methods depict the flows of goods and services betwen the sectors of local industry in great detail is all to the good but does not bear on this point. Chinitz argues that we must look not only at the flows between local industries but at the way in which the structure of local industry affects factor supply prices, production costs, and entrepreneurial behavior within the local economy. He suggests, for example, that the supply of entrepreneurship and risk capital for launching new ventures may be significantly greater in a city where the industrial structure is largely competitive than in one that is dominated by a few very large firms. Thus the organizational structure of local industry may in the long run affect the way the local economy responds to opportunities for growth and diversification.

As Tiebout put it, a study of the supply side "deals with the nature of the local economy as an economic environment."[19] An examination of the supply side would attempt to uncover the strengths and weaknesses of the community as a place in which to live and to conduct business. Once these were known, local policymakers could set about using its strengths and ameliorating its weaknesses in order to increase the area's productivity and attractiveness and help to ensure the long-run growth of its output and living standards.

It is a limitation, if not a defect, of the methods of economic base analysis that (with some modification in the case of simulation models) they ascribe changes in the level of local activity entirely to changes in the level of an exogenously determined final demand. As John F. Kain has pointed out in another context, this way of looking at the local economy inevitably focuses attention on matters over which local authorities have no control—the exogenously determined components of final demand—while distracting attention from the very thing they *can* influence—the nature and attractiveness of the local economic environment.[20] It is well to recognize that in the short run, local activity will fluctuate in response to shifts in outside demand, but that is no reason to neglect the importance of internal supply factors in determining the course of events over the long run.

Precisely what can be done to take the supply side into account? First of all, location or feasibility studies can be made to discover what industries can

18. Benjamin Chinitz, "Contrasts in Agglomeration: New York and Pittsburgh," reprinted in Ronald E. Grieson, ed., *Urban Economics: Readings and Analysis* (Boston: Little, Brown, 1973), pp. 26–37.

19. Tiebout, p. 18.

20. See Kain's review of Wilbur R. Thompson's *Preface to Urban Economics* in *Journal of the American Institute of Planners*, May 1966, pp. 186–188.

best make use of the area's physical location and economic advantages. Second, the city can examine its local supply of labor, land, capital, and entrepreneurship to see whether these can be marshaled more effectively for economic growth. Third, the city can survey its public "infrastructure" of transportation facilities, schools, public services, and recreation areas— indeed, its whole "physical and social plan"—to see whether they are attractive, well balanced, and efficient or inadequate, uncoordinated, and stultifying.

Policies to improve the local environment as a place to live and conduct business, and which thereby attract business and population, are in their very nature policies that increase both material productivity and population well-being. However, the suggestion that population and activity might be attracted from another place raises an issue that is often overlooked in discussing local economic policy: What happens in the other place? Any statement about the welfare effects of a policy requires a definition of the relevant population. Since local economic policy often affects people living outside the specific jurisdiction, it is necessary to investigate the connection between local policy and national welfare.

LOCAL ECONOMIC POLICY AND NATIONAL WELFARE

Suppose that a city adopts a policy of stimulating economic growth but that the resulting growth occurs mainly in very low wage industries and attracts an influx of low-skilled population. In such a case the growth of the local economy might reduce rather than increase the average level of local family income. Has welfare increased or decreased? The answer depends on whose welfare one takes into account. The preexisting local population may be worse off after the low-income population increases if the newcomers cost the locality more via increased public expenditure than they contribute in additional tax revenue.[21] On the other hand, the low-skilled in-migrants are presumably better off in the town to which they moved than in the place from which they came; they would not otherwise have migrated (barring ignorance and uncertainty). If we somehow aggregate the well-being of both groups, welfare may be found to increase as a result of in-migration. If we count only the welfare of the preexisting population, it may decrease. A full account of the welfare effects of a local policy would have to go even further and look not only at changes in the welfare of the preexisting local population and of the potential in-migrants but at effects on the rest of the nation. If we fail to examine this last element, we run the danger of advocating policies that bene-

21. This should not be taken to imply that the tax-expenditure calculus gives an adequate account of changes in individual welfare. On this point see Julius Margolis, "On Municipal Land Policy for Fiscal Gains," *National Tax Journal*, September 1956, pp. 247–257.

fit a local area while harming the nation as a whole. In short, the relevant welfare universe for discussing the effects of local economic policy is not the local population, either before or after the policy takes effect, but the entire nation. Where does this lead us?

To simplify matters, let us assume that localities will not knowingly pursue policies harmful to themselves and that all policies that are beneficial locally will either be neutral toward other areas in the nation or else impose some loss on them. In that case we can say that for any local policy, the net effect on national welfare must be equal to the local gain less the losses (if any) elsewhere. For the nation as a whole it would be desirable (if it were possible) to insist that localities act not to maximize local gain but to maximize national welfare. This is not quite the same thing as saying "maximize local gain subject to the condition that local gains exceed outside losses." For under the latter rule localities might adopt policies that would lead to large local gain at the expense of large outside loss when from the national point of view it would have been better for them to choose alternative policies that entail moderate local gain at the cost of much smaller losses elsewhere.

We see, then, that consideration of the nation's welfare requires not that localities avoid policies that hurt other localities but only that losses elsewhere be properly taken into account. Of course, this proposition is, in the present state of economic knowledge, quite impossible to put into effect. It requires some way of quantifying welfare for various populations so that gains and losses can be compared along a common scale. Economists are not hopeful of discovering the "social welfare function" (or formula) that would make such comparisons possible. Even if we were to retreat from welfare to income as the relevant unit of account, the rule is presently impracticable because the effects of alternative policies on local income and, even more so, on outside income are extraordinarily difficult to measure.

Subsidizing Industrial Relocation

Despite the absence of reliable ways of measuring welfare, the foregoing argument does help in judging some real policy questions. Consider, for example, local subsidies intended to influence the location of industry. Many cities that want to promote economic growth or stem decline try to attract new industry (and the jobs that go with it) by offering subsidies in the form of low-cost leases, industrial development loans, tax abatements, and the like.[22] Consistent with the conclusions of the basic-nonbasic theory, new industries that can export to the rest of the nation are seen as a way of strengthening the city's "economic base."

22. See Michael J. Wolkoff, "The Nature of Property Tax Abatement Awards," *Journal of the American Planning Association*, Winter 1983, pp. 77–84.

Careful analysis, however, demonstrates that a policy of attracting new industry by means of subsidies violates the welfare rule proposed in the preceding section. Let gains and losses be measured simply in terms of net changes in local income. Now suppose that the town of West Greenbush, suffering from unemployment, attracts a textile mill from some other location by means of a subsidy sufficient to overcome the higher transportation costs from West Greenbush to the market. The mill's output and exports, we may assume, are the same in West Greenbush as they were at the previous location. The factor incomes added by the mill at its new location will therefore just equal the incomes lost by its leaving the other place. In effect, West Greenbush exports its unemployment. From a welfare point of view, however, the situation is not a standoff, because the net income gain to West Greenbush equals the rise in factor income *less* the locally financed subsidy needed to attract the mill from its preferred location. Hence the net gains at West Greenbush must be less than the losses at the old location by the amount of the annual subsidy.

Since we do not assume *general* unemployment, the added transportation costs cannot be counted as net increases in factor incomes. They measure only the opportunity cost of factors transferred from some other employment into transportation. The added transportation cost—or its equivalent, the reduced output in other industries from which factors were shifted into transportation—equals the net annual loss to society as a whole from this method of attracting export industry. (To this must be added the one-time loss equal to the cost of moving the firm.)

Repelling Low-Income Migrants

The important issue of low-income population movement is another question on which the proposed welfare rule casts much light. High-income suburbs all over the United States quite correctly see that their own self-interest is served by keeping low-income populations out. Even our great central cities that have always contained large numbers of the poor now wonder if they should make themselves less open to new arrivals. It should be obvious, however, that local policies to exclude the poverty-stricken do not diminish the total number of the poor in the nation. Indeed, by denying full mobility and therefore maximum choice of occupation and environment to the poor, such policies probably interfere with progress toward reducing poverty. At the very least this is an area where policies that maximize local welfare are unlikely to be in the national interest. Yet we know that local voters and local politicians will always be tempted to serve local self-interest. If the national interest is to prevail, it will have to be asserted via state and national policies that limit local discretion to control the variables of housing, zoning, and welfare benefits through which localities currently influence the movement of the poor.

These conclusions may seem painfully obvious. Unfortunately, they are easily lost sight of when attention is focused on solving intense local problems. A stunning example of this occurs in Jay Forrester's influential study *Urban Dynamics*.[23] Forrester wished to examine the effects of alternative public policies in combating the stagnation and decay of the older central cities. To do this he devised a simulation model, calibrated it with hypothetical data, and ran it through centuries of time. He deliberately set his hypothetical city in what he described as a "limitless environment." The connections between the city and the environment he put in the form of "attractiveness for migration multipliers," the size of which depended on the values of key variables within the city. For example, the attractiveness-for-migration multiplier that affected the influx of low-income workers was made to depend in part on the vacancy rate in the city's low-rent housing. The multiplier would rise as the vacancy rate increased. As the model ran through time it showed that a rise in the city's low-income population either caused or exacerbated a great many problems and was a principal factor in the city's stagnation and decay.

Forrester tested the effects of various public policies on the city's economic health by building them into the model and running it through time. One of these policies was a subsidy for low-income housing. He found that even if the subsidy cost were paid entirely from sources outside the city, a policy of building low-income subsidized housing would have deleterious effects on the city's economic health because it would attract a larger number of the poor. The reader was left to draw the conclusion that subsidies to low-income housing must be avoided if we wish to rescue our older cities from decay.[24] Surely one must ask whether that is the right way to view the problem.

The issue is not whether low-income populations create problems for cities; quite obviously they do. The point is, rather, that Forrester's framework is wholly inappropriate for judging the welfare consequences of alternative policies. In his model, everything outside the city is part of the "limitless environment." It could better be described as a limitless void, since we do not know what goes on out there. Given this void, the model can tell us nothing about the national welfare effects of either local or national urban policies. It is capable of registering nothing but the local gains or losses from local policies. Forrester concludes that a policy of low-income housing subsidies is bad because it attracts low-income families. This overlooks two crucial points: first, if low-income housing were equally subsidized everywhere, the subsidy would have *no* effect on migration. Consequently, if the heavy concentration of low-income populations in large cities is undesirable, the solution is not necessarily to do away with housing subsidies but rather to use state or national policy to achieve a more desirable spatial distribution of the poor. Second, the low-income population may be better off in Forrester's central city

23. Jay W. Forrester, *Urban Dynamics* (Cambridge, Mass.: M.I.T. Press, 1969).
24. Ibid., pp. 65–70.

than in the place from which it came. A model that considers only one city is simply incapable of addressing this important welfare question.[25]

Local "Growth Control"

The arguments used in judging the welfare effects of a policy of repelling low-income migrants can also be applied to a local policy of "growth control." In recent years many towns, especially in the exurban fringe of metropolitan areas, have sought to limit population growth by means of exclusionary zoning, limitations on the annual number of building permits issued, or other forms of control over development. (These policies are examined in greater detail in Chapter 13.) Such policies may, in fact, promote the welfare of the people already living in the town. But they are clearly against the interests of those who would move in if not thus prevented. As Alonso has pointed out, from a national perspective these are not growth control policies at all, since they do nothing to influence the size of the national population. Rather, they are "distribution" policies, affecting "not whether these people and their children shall exist, but where and how."[26]

Like a policy of repelling low-income migrants, these so-called growth controls operate on the principle of "beggar thy neighbor." Since the population in question must go somewhere, whatever gain accrues in localities where population is held down is presumably offset by losses in towns where it finally settles. There remains a net loss to the nation as a whole because freedom of movement is curtailed. Individuals are deprived of the freedom to choose a residential location that an unrestricted market would provide. The resulting land-use pattern may be wasteful of resources (including gasoline!) since those whose locational choices are restricted probably cannot make the optimal adjustment of residence to workplace and are therefore likely to travel farther to work than they otherwise would.

---

25. Forrester does attempt, in a two-paragraph afterthought, to meet the criticism that his model overlooks effects on the outside world. He writes (ibid., p. 116):

> The policies for controlling population balance that the city must establish are not antisocial. No purpose is served by operating a city so that it is a drain on the economy of the country and a disappointment and frustration to its occupants. An urban area that maintains effective internal balance can absorb poor people from other areas at a faster rate than can one that is operating in deep stagnation.

Indeed, this may be so. But the Forrester model is certainly incapable of demonstrating it. The inadequacy of Forrester's single-city model as a basis for testing national policies is developed at greater length by Leo P. Kadanoff in "From Simulation Model to Public Policy," *American Scientist,* January–February 1972, pp. 74–79. Also see the penetrating critique by Gregory K. Ingram in his review of *Urban Dynamics* in *Journal of the American Institute of Planners,* May 1970, pp. 206–208.

26. William Alonso, "Urban Zero Population Growth," in Mancur Olson and Hans H. Landsberg, eds., *The No-Growth Society* (New York: Norton, 1973), pp. 191–206. Also see Richard F. Babcock, "The Spatial Impact of Land-Use and Environmental Controls," in Arthur P. Solomon, ed., *The Prospective City* (Cambridge, Mass.: M.I.T. Press, 1980), pp. 267–270.

Pollution Control

Pollution control is another area in which self-interested local policy may conflict with national welfare objectives. Here again the motive may be a desire to offer location inducements to industry. An industrial town may fear that if it raises its antipollution standards, it will drive industry away. Taking account only of their own welfare, the local citizens may correctly prefer to suffer the consequences of pollution rather than lose their jobs. In so deciding, however, they overlook the pollution costs thrown off by local industry onto neighboring towns whose interests they have not consulted. This is the familiar problem of external costs. Local industry is, in effect, being subsidized to stay put, and the subsidy is paid partly by those living outside the benefiting jurisdiction, who bear some of the pollution costs. The solution here, as in the somewhat different case of low-income housing policy, is to raise the decision-making power to a higher level of government: a pollution-control jurisdiction must be found or created that is large enough to capture most of the externalities. Efficient pollution control requires a combination of regional and national standards.

Policies to Improve the Local Economic Environment

There are, of course, many ways in which localities can attract or hold industry that do not violate a national welfare rule. We have already described them in the discussion of taking the supply side into account. By and large, these are policies that would improve the local economy as an economic environment. As the environment becomes more productive for industry and more desirable for residents it will attract additional industry on its own merits, and growth will be achieved without special subsidies. While competition among cities to attract industry by means of subsidy is, as we have shown, necessarily harmful from the point of view of the nation as a whole, competition that takes the form of creating more attractive environments can hardly fail to be generally beneficial. True, not all places would prosper under such a regime, but it would not be difficult to show that the national welfare would be enhanced. Of course, the question of subsidy is not so easily put aside as the foregoing statement may seem to suggest. We have already pointed out that location subsidies may take an indirect form, as in the case of low pollution-control standards. "Fair competition" would likewise rule out attracting industry by reducing business taxes to the point where firms receive local services at less than cost.

In a classic article criticizing the basic-nonbasic theory for its irrational export bias, Hans Blumenfeld performed the tour de force of turning the theory upside down. He pointed out that the great metropolitan areas of modern times are centers of production that have shown remarkable persistence in the face of economic change and concluded with this passage:

> The bases of this amazing stability are the business and consumer services and other industries supplying the local market. They are the permanent and constant element, while the "export" industries are variable, subject to incessant change and replacement. While the existence of a sufficient number of such industries is indispensable for the continued existence of the metropolis, each individual "export" industry is expendable and replaceable.
>
> In any commonsense use of the term, it is the "service" industries of the metropolis that are "basic" and "primary" while the "export" industries are "secondary" and "ancillary." The economic base of the metropolis consists in the activities by which its inhabitants supply each other.[27]

In this sense the service sector is essentially the "economic environment" of the city, and the appropriate aim of local economic policy is to render that environment efficient and attractive by means that are consistent with the objectives of national policy.

27. Hans Blumenfeld, "The Economic Base of the Metropolis," reprinted in Pfouts, pp. 229–277.

EIGHT

The Economics of
Urban Transportation

Cities exist to facilitate human interaction. If transportation were instantaneous and costless we would not need cities; we could have as much interaction as we wished while living at the four corners of the globe. However, what Haig called "the friction of space" cannot be overcome costlessly. We invest substantial time and quantities of resources in moving people and products from place to place. The relationship between transportation costs and the spatial and economic organization of cities has been analyzed in detail in earlier chapters. The history and impact of successive innovations in the technology of urban transportation were reviewed in Chapter 3. We saw in Chapter 4 that cities grow up at locations possessing transportation advantages and in Chapter 5 that transportation costs are an important determinant of the dimensions of the urban hierarchy. The land-use model developed in Chapter 6 showed that within cities, higher rent is paid for the privilege of occupying more accessible sites because at such locations the need for transportation outlays is reduced. Throughout those chapters we emphasized the way in which changes in transportation technology, by altering the cost of accessibility, profoundly affect both the system of cities and the form of the metropolis.

INTERDEPENDENCE OF TRANSPORTATION
AND LAND USE

Chapter 6 explained how a competitive land market determines the pattern of urban land use through a process in which individual land users adapt to a given system of transportation. In this and the following chapter we shall see that government decisions concerning transportation also profoundly affect land-use patterns because they establish the frame of reference within which individual location decisions are made.

The relationship between transportation systems and land use is a reciprocal one. The land-use pattern depends on the character of the transportation network, while the viability of the transportation network depends on the land-use pattern. To some extent new transportation links, whether urban expressways or additional transit lines, are built in response to visible traffic demand generated by private locational decisions. But causality runs the other way, too. A major traffic facility, once in place, exerts a powerful influence on subsequent private market development. This is easily demonstrated at the microlocational scale. For example, commercial development inevitably springs up around subway stations, highway interchanges, and airports.

More important, however, are the macrolocational effects of transport systems as a whole. The transportation framework a city adopts at the time of its major growth profoundly influences its later development, and that choice is obviously constrained by the technological alternatives then available. It was pointed out in Chapter 3 that cities like New York and Chicago that achieved their major growth before the era of the automobile and truck relied for movement on systems of mass transportation and rail freight that then represented the most advanced technology available. Because such systems were focused on the central business district, those cities became highly centralized and densely developed. On the other hand, cities that grew up largely after the widespread introduction of the auto and truck tended to rely primarily on highway transportation as they developed and consequently became decentralized, low-density metropolitan areas like Los Angeles and Houston. In Figure 3.1 we showed how greatly highway-oriented cities differ from transit-oriented cities in population per square mile.

Although these relationships emerge very clearly when we examine the past, recent studies indicate a much weaker connection in the present: improvements in urban transportation of the sort that are now feasible are not having the radical effect on land use that occurred, say, with the introduction of the electric streetcar in the late nineteenth century or the first urban express highways in the mid-twentieth. John R. Meyer and José A. Gómez-Ibáñez suggest why this may be so.[1] First, in the earlier period, the new modes of transportation penetrated into low-density areas where urban settlement patterns had not yet been established. Consequently, the basic land-use patterns were readily influenced by the new transportation system. By contrast, today's improvements are usually introduced into already developed areas where the inertia of the built environment greatly retards adjustment to changes in transportation cost. Second, since the level of transportation service available in most metropolitan areas today is already so high, further improvements do not have the radical impact that was possible in earlier times.

1. John R. Meyer and José A. Gómez-Ibáñez. *Autos, Transit and Cities* (Cambridge, Mass.: Harvard University Press, 1981), pp. 104–106.

The inertia of the existing pattern of land use is an important constraint on plans for introducing new transportation systems. Once an urban expressway network has been built, the decentralized, low-density land-use pattern that develops cannot be served economically by mass transit, since the latter requires concentrated origins and destinations to operate efficiently. Likewise, once a highly centralized city has developed around a mass transit system, it becomes impossible to replace mass transit with highway transportation, because the latter operates efficiently only when destinations are *not* concentrated.

OUTLINE OF CHAPTERS 8 AND 9

A great many public policy issues arise in connection with urban transportation. Before addressing them, however, it is necessary to understand the economic character of the transportation system itself. Consequently, we divide the discussion into two parts. The economics of urban transportation—how the system works—is explained in this chapter, while public policy issues, with a few exceptions, are reserved for Chapter 9.

We begin with a brief description of the modes of transportation available in metropolitan areas and then analyze the way consumers choose among those modes—providing, in effect, an analysis of consumer demand for urban trips. The second half of this chapter deals with the supply (or cost) side of urban transportation. Applying the standard concepts of microeconomics, we look at the nature of transportation costs in both the short and the long run. The point of view is normative, in that the analysis of cost is used to develop rules for the most efficient operation of the system. The normative question in the short run is, Given the nature of short-run costs, what prices should be charged for the use of an existing transportation system if it is to operate with maximum efficiency? In the long run the existing system can be altered by investment. The normative question then becomes, Given the nature of long-run costs, what is the optimum transportation investment policy? The chapter closes with a review of some empirical cost studies that put statistical flesh on these bare bones of theory.

Local government is inevitably involved both in planning and developing an urban transportation network and in regulating its use by the public. The federal government is heavily involved in financing these local efforts. Chapter 9 will focus on urban transportation policy at both levels of government.

THE URBAN TRANSPORTATION SYSTEM

The argument in Chapter 6 was greatly simplified by assuming that the city had sprung up on a "transport surface," a featureless plain on which transportation required no improved right-of-way and was equally efficient in any direction. Transportation was thus reduced to a technologically determined transport cost per mile, uniform throughout the city. We had eliminated by assumption all the complicating features of any real transportation system, among them the following:

1. *Channels and networks.* Far from being equally easy in any direction, transportation moves along rights-of-way that form channels into which traffic is concentrated. A transportation system is a network of channels. Sites along such channels, and especially at nodes in the network, have greater accessibility than sites not so located.

2. *Alternative modes.* The transportation system serving a metropolitan area usually consists of several modes of transportation differing from one another in cost, speed, comfort, and convenience. For some journeys the modes are complementary; in many cases they are competitive.

3. *Segmentation.* Commuting trips from the suburbs to the CBD must accomplish three functions, which have been described as residential collection, line-haul (along a corridor to the center), and downtown distribution.[2] In some cases the three functions are accomplished door to door in a single vehicle. Often they are segmented among different modes or involve transferring from vehicle to vehicle on a single mode. There may be a walking segment at either end or between modes.

If we leave aside bicycle and shoe leather, then automobile, bus, trolley, streetcar, subway, and elevated train make up the list of alternative modes of urban passenger transportation. The important distinction between "private" and "public" modes places autos in the private category and all the others in the public. It is worth noting that the classification is based not on ownership but on the general public's right of access. For example, although the buses in a transit system may be owned and operated by a private firm, they provide "public" transportation because any member of the public may use them. Likewise, automobiles are classified as "private" not because they are privately owned—after all, the streets and highways they require are *publicly* owned—but because, except for taxis, they are not individually open to public use.

The proportions in which public and private modes are used varies greatly from place to place, but the variation is highly systematic. In Table 8.1 the transportation mix in metropolitan areas is measured by looking at data on the type of transportation workers choose to reach their jobs. Obviously, public transportation is used much more frequently in central cities than in suburbs. In urbanized areas as a whole in 1980, residents of central cities employed public modes for 14 percent of their journeys to work, compared with only 5 percent for suburban residents. Use of public transportation also in-

2. J. R. Meyer, J. F. Kain, and M. Wohl, *The Urban Transportation Problem* (Cambridge, Mass.: Harvard University Press, 1965), p. 171.

TABLE 8.1

Mode of Transportation in Metropolitan Areas, 1980

| | | JOURNEYS TO WORK (%)[a] | | | |
| | | *Auto or Truck* | | *Public Transportation* | |
	SMSA 1980 POPULATION (MILLIONS)	*Central City Residents*	*Suburb Residents*	*Central City Residents*	*Suburb Residents*
Six Largest SMSAs in North and East					
New York, N.Y.–N.J.	9.1	29.9	78.2	55.8	14.4
Chicago, Ill.	7.1	58.1	84.1	32.4	9.3
Philadelphia, Pa.–N.J.	4.7	57.1	85.6	30.1	6.8
Detroit, Mich.	4.4	82.7	94.6	11.8	1.4
Washington, D.C.– Md.–Va.	3.1	47.5	83.4	38.0	10.3
Boston, Mass.	2.8	47.3	79.1	33.7	11.3
Six Largest SMSAs in South and West					
Los Angeles–Long Beach, Calif.	7.5	81.3	88.9	10.3	4.3
San Francisco– Oakland, Calif.	3.3	53.0	82.7	33.6	9.0
Dallas–Fort Worth, Tex.	3.0	88.3	94.4	7.0	0.7
Houston, Tex.	2.9	89.7	94.9	4.7	0.8
Atlanta, Ga.	2.0	69.5	92.4	24.5	3.9
Anaheim–Santa Ana– Garden Grove, Calif.	1.9	90.8	91.0	2.5	1.9
U.S. total[b]	—	75.7	88.0	14.4	5.2

[a]Not shown are the following categories, which bring totals to 100 percent: bicycle, motorcycle, walked only, worked at home, other means.
[b]U.S. total is for urbanized areas rather than SMSAs.
Sources: U.S. Bureau of the Census, *1980 Census of Population*, "General Social and Economic Characteristics: U.S. Summary," table 101; and state vols., table 118.

creases with SMSA size and city age. Public transportation accounts for 56 percent of work trips by New York City residents, by far the highest proportion for any city, just as New York is by far the largest city and SMSA. In small metropolitan areas (not shown in the table) public transportation is almost nonexistent.

When size is held constant, public transportation is far more important in old central cities than in new ones. This follows from the fact, already emphasized in Chapter 3, that the older cities of the North and East were built to exploit the advantages of mass transit, while the newer ones of the South and West were laid out to accommodate widespread use of the automobile and truck. The effect can be seen in Table 8.1 by looking at old and new SMSAs of equal population size. For example, compare the use of public modes in the relatively old central city of Chicago (32 percent) and in much newer Los Angeles–Long Beach (10 percent) or in very old Boston (34 percent) and much newer Houston (5 percent).

Reversing the procedure, if age is held constant, the importance of public transportation increases with SMSA population size, as one can see by comparing transit use in equally old Philadelphia and New York. This occurs because among SMSAs of the same age, those that have larger populations also have higher population densities (as the theory developed in Chapter 6 would predict), which renders automobile operation less advantageous.

It has been estimated that in 1970 the automobile accounted for 94 percent of all passenger miles traveled in urban areas.[3] One can infer from Table 8.1 that public transportation today has an important share of the market *only* in very large and relatively old cities. Table 8.2, however, shows that it was not always so.

Mass Transit versus the Automobile

Public transportation has become less important over time, in part because the automobile predominates in the suburbs and in the newer central cities, where population growth has been fastest, but also because even in the old, transit-oriented core cities transit use has fallen precipitously as residents have switched to automobiles. Ridership by type of transit since 1950 is displayed in Table 8.2, which also shows vehicle miles traveled by passenger cars in urban areas during the same period.

Transit ridership reached its peak just after World War II. It then declined steadily until 1972. Since that date it has recovered moderately, helped along by massive federal subsidies that encouraged the extension of service and, during the 1970s, by rising gasoline prices and intermittent fuel shortages. Nevertheless, in 1984 transit ridership remained 53 percent below its 1950 level. Urban auto use more than quadrupled in the same interval. It must be borne in mind that the numbers in Table 8.2 are not adjusted to a per capita basis. If they were, transit use would be seen to decline even more sharply, because urban population has increased markedly since 1950, while the number of passengers was declining.

As this chapter and the next will make clear, the rivalry between mass transit and the automobile has been an important component in a wide range

3. U.S. Department of Transportation, *1972 National Transportation Report*, July 1972, table VI–1, p. 189.

TABLE 8.2
Trends in Urban Transportation Use

	PASSENGER CARS: VEHICLE MILES IN URBAN AREAS (BILLIONS)	TRANSIT: TOTAL PASSENGER RIDES (MILLIONS)				
		All Modes	*Subway and El*	*Street-car*	*Trolley Coach*	*Motor Bus*
1950	182.5	17,246	2,264	3,904	1,658	9,420
1960	284.8	9,395	1,850	463	657	6,425
1972	567.2	6,567	1,731	211	130	4,495
1984	773.6	8,030[a]	2,361	137[b]	160[b]	5,422[b]
PERCENTAGE CHANGE						
1950–1984	+ 324	− 53	+ 4	− 96[c]	− 90[c]	− 42[c]
1972–1984	+ 36	+ 22	+ 36	− 35[c]	+ 23[c]	+ 21[c]

[a]Details do not add to total because streetcar, trolley, and motor bus data are for 1983.
[b]Data are for 1983.
[c]Percentage change to 1983.
Sources: Federal Highway Administration, *Highway Statistics*, various years; American Public Transit Association, *Transit Fact Book*, 1985, and unpublished APTA data.

of urban public policy debates. Given the great difference in their effects on both urban form and the urban environment, it could hardly be otherwise. At stake is something fundamental: the physical nature of the city itself as a place to live and work. On this matter city planners especially are likely to have strongly held convictions, which give the debates over transportation policy at times an almost ideological intensity.

The data in Table 8.2 tell us that when offered a choice, on the terms that prevail almost everywhere, users have been choosing the automobile rather than public modes of transportation with a high degree of regularity. Before analyzing urban transportation policies, many of which call for altering urban travel behavior, we had better understand how such choices are made. The analysis of modal choice is thus an essential prerequisite to the investigation of urban transportation policy.

ANALYSIS OF MODAL CHOICE

Faced with alternative modes of transportation, the consumer selects among them on the basis of money cost, time cost, comfort, carrying capacity, reliability, and convenience. To simplify the analysis, we assume only two modes, the automobile and public transportation. First, consider their money cost. In the case of public transportation, money cost is simply the fare. Most commonly it does not vary with distance, provided the rider stays on the same vehicle. Transferring to a vehicle on an intersecting route may entail paying all or part of another full fare. The money cost of automobile travel is far more complex. It includes both operating costs, such as gasoline, repairs, parking, and tolls, and ownership costs, such as depreciation, garaging, and insurance. An estimate of these costs over the normal life of an automobile, divided by the number of miles expected to be driven, produces a figure for average cost per mile. Table 8.3 shows that cost per mile over the life of an automobile was estimated at about 28 cents in 1984. Operating costs account for a bit less than half of the total.

The quality we call "comfort" when analyzing competing modes needs no explanation in theory, though it is difficult to quantify in practice. "Convenience" refers to scheduling and proximity. The automobile has the great advantage of allowing self-scheduling by the user; on public transportation, the user must either adhere to a known schedule or allow for waiting time between vehicles. Moreover, journeys by public transit often require one or more transfers, each of which potentially adds waiting time or complicated scheduling. Proximity often favors the auto, too. At the home end of the journey, at least in low-density neighborhoods, the car owner has service right at the door, whatever the situation may be at the other end of the trip. For shopping the automobile also has the advantage of far greater package-carrying capacity. On the other hand, the automobile may incur parking charges. On trips into the CBD such charges can easily outweigh other money costs.

Time as a Cost of Travel

Transportation analysts recognize that time cost as well as money cost enters into modal choice.[4] Consumers often select a high-speed, high-cost mode in preference to a low-speed, low-cost one. The obvious explanation of this behavior (leaving aside possible differences in comfort and convenience) is that savings in time cost outweigh the higher money cost of the more expensive mode.

As we shall see in Chapter 9, the time cost of travel also enters importantly into transportation investment analysis. Reduced travel time is usually one of the expected benefits of an improvement in the transportation system. Such time savings, however, must be given a dollar value before they can be entered into the investment calculus. The question How much is an hour of travel time worth? has not been easy to answer. For example, there is evidence that commuters place a higher value on waiting time and walking time than they do on in-vehicle travel time.[5] In what follows, we shall ignore this complication and treat travel time as homogeneous.

---

4. See, for example, Donald Dewees, "Travel Cost, Transit, and Urban Motoring," *Public Policy*, Winter 1976, pp. 59–79 and references cited in his note 2, p. 61.
5. Ibid., p. 61.

TABLE 8.3
Estimated Cost of Owning and Operating an Automobile, 1984

	TWELVE-YEAR AVERAGE CENTS PER MILE[a]
Depreciation	8.60
Gas and oil, including taxes	6.74
Insurance	5.58
Repairs and maintenance	4.52
Parking and tolls	.94
Other	1.46
Total	27.84
Ownership costs	15.97
Operating costs	11.87

[a]Assumes intermediate-size sedan, twelve-year life span, 120,000 miles driven.
Source: Federal Highway Administration, *Cost of Owning and Operating Automobiles and Vans*, 1984, table 3.

Opportunity cost is the basis of all real cost in economics. If time spent traveling is thought of as time that might have been devoted to working, the opportunity cost of travel time is the individual's wage rate net of marginal income taxes. Although the results of statistical studies vary, it appears that in practice individuals value travel time at not more than half their wage rate.[6] Most people are not, after all, free to set their own work schedules so that they can work a little longer if they travel a little less. Even allowing for wide variation in the statistical estimates, however, it is clear that the value of time is a very important component of urban travel cost. Moreover, as long as the value individuals attach to it is positively related to income, we would expect the well-to-do to value time more highly than the poor, and that is what statistical studies have found.

Income, Value of Time, and Modal Choice

These relationships are illustrated in Table 8.4, which compares the journey-to-work decisions of two hypothetical individuals: White, a middle-class commuter who values travel time at $6.00 an hour, and Green, a working-class commuter who values it at $3.00 an hour. Both work in the business district of the central city and must decide whether to commute by car or public transportation. To simplify matters we assume that considerations of comfort and convenience cancel out for the two modes—the conve-

6. See M. E. Beesley, *Urban Transport: Studies in Economic Policy* (London: Butterworths, 1973), pp. 160, 179.

TABLE 8.4
Modal Choice for the Journey to Work

	WHITE: MIDDLE-CLASS COMMUTER		GREEN: WORKING-CLASS COMMUTER			
			Inbound		Outbound	
	Auto	Transit	Auto	Transit	Auto	Transit
One-Way Trip Length						
Miles	10	10	5	5	10	10
Minutes	25	50	20	30	25	50
Cost, Round Trip						
Operating						
@ 12¢/mile	2.40	—	1.20	—	2.40	—
Transit fare						
@ 75¢ per segment	—	3.00	—	1.50	—	3.00
Parking	3.00	—	3.00	—	—	—
Time cost						
@ $6/hour	5.00	10.00	—	—	—	—
$3/hour	—	—	2.00	3.00	2.50	5.00
Total cost ($)	10.40	13.00	6.20	4.50	4.90	8.00

nience of self-scheduling enjoyed in using a car is offset by the greater effort of driving as compared with riding in a public conveyance.

How the money cost of driving a car should be measured depends on the assumed circumstances. If neither White nor Green owns a car and would consider buying one only to commute, the full cost per mile, including both operating and ownership costs, would be the relevant figure. If both already own cars, the decision whether to use it would logically seem to depend only on operating cost per mile, which is a little less than half the full cost. There is a third possibility. It is sometimes argued that in making trip choices, owners perceive only "out of pocket" costs such as gasoline, tolls, and parking, while ignoring all other operating costs. Out-of-pocket costs would be slightly more than half of operating costs or about a quarter of full costs per mile. In Table 8.4 we assume that both parties already own cars and that they base their commuting decisions on operating rather than out-of-pocket costs. As suggested by the data in Table 8.3, these are calculated at 12 cents per mile.

White lives in a suburb ten miles out. Commuter rail service is not available. She can reach her job either by driving at a cost of 12 cents a mile and parking at a daily cost of $3.00 or by taking a bus and then the subway at 75 cents apiece for a total fare cost of $1.50 each way. The trip, including walking and waiting time, takes 25 minutes by auto or 50 by public transportation. Travel time therefore costs $2.50 each way by auto or $5.00 each way by public transportation. The total round-trip cost by auto, including parking, is

$10.40. Since a round trip by public transportation would cost $13.00, White uses her car. (However, she would not do so if the decision to drive to work entailed buying a second car and taking into account its full cost of 28 cents per mile.)

Green, whose income is much lower than White's, lives in a working-class neighborhood five miles from the center of the city and a short walk from the subway. He can be at his job in 30 minutes by public transportation at a fare of 75 cents and a time cost of $1.50, or he can drive to work in 20 minutes, incurring $1.00 in time costs, 60 cents in operating expense, and $3.00 in parking fees. The round trip via transit costs $4.50 as compared with $6.20 when driving. Green will therefore prefer to ride the subway, even though he owns a car. His evaluation of time cost would have to rise to $8.10 an hour before driving would appear as attractive as riding public transportation.

If White lived at Green's location she would not drive to work despite her higher valuation of travel time. Her choice would be influenced, among other things, by the fact that in our hypothetical example (as in the real world) the relative speed advantage of the automobile as compared with public transportation is less at the close-in location. For the suburban commuter the automobile cuts travel time in half. For the resident at Green's location it reduces it only 33 percent.

It is interesting to note that if Green lived in the central city and worked in the suburbs, he would probably drive to work, even though his workplace could be reached by public transportation. The right-hand panel of Table 8.4 shows hypothetical data for a "reverse commuter" at Green's income level who faces transportation choices in commuting outward that are essentially the same as those facing White for the inward journey to work. Since suburban employers usually provide free parking, automobile cost does not include parking charges, and the round trip amounts to only $4.90, far less than the $8.00 cost via public transportation. Car-pooling is common among reverse commuters, so even if Green did *not* own his own car he might very well make the reverse commuting trip via automobile. This probability is reinforced by the fact that routes and schedules of public transportation systems are generally arranged to accommodate the inbound rather than the outbound commuter. (See the discussion in Chapter 9.) It is unlikely that, as we have assumed in Table 8.4, Green would have outbound public transportation choices as favorable as those available to White for the inbound journey.

An advantage similar to car-pooling occurs when a family owns a car. If they use public transportation, each member pays a fare. When they ride together in a car, cost per person drops as the number of passengers rises. Coupled with the fact that operating costs are far lower than full costs per mile (and *perceived* costs may be lower still), this effect heavily favors the use of the automobile, once it is owned, even where good public transportation is available. For example, members of the Green family may use public transportation to reach downtown jobs. But since the family owns a car they are very likely to use it as well for evening recreation or for shopping within the metropolitan area. Instead of riding on public transportation to shop or go to the movies "downtown," they may now drive out to nearby suburban shopping or entertainment centers.

This example helps to explain why the sharpest drop in mass transit ridership has occurred in the off-peak rather than the rush hours. It also illustrates the interdependence of land use and transportation. The introduction of the automobile does not mean simply that people make the same trips in automobiles that they formerly made via public transportation. Often it means that they substitute new destinations for old, thereby encouraging or reinforcing change in metropolitan land-use patterns.

Income, Automobile Ownership, and Modal Choice

We have seen that income influences modal choice indirectly through its effect on time value. Even though Green owns a car he is more likely than White to choose transit for the journey to work because his income is lower and he therefore places a lower value on time savings. However, income also affects modal choice through its influence on automobile ownership: family car ownership rises sharply with income, and the proportion of individuals driving to work increases systematically with family car ownership.[7] In short, the poor are less likely than the rich to own a car and therefore are less likely to drive to work.

Income also affects modal choice *indirectly* through its influence on residential location. We have shown in Chapter 6 that residential location depends in part on income: as their incomes rise, families tend to move out to the suburbs to indulge their appetite for living space. But public transportation is generally less available and convenient in the suburbs than in the central city. Hence the higher its income, the less likely a family is to live where public transportation is an attractive alternative to the private car.

For a variety of reasons, then, consumers buy less public transportation as their incomes rise.[8] No doubt this helps to explain the long-run decline in transit ridership shown in Table 8.2. It also necessarily has a chilling effect on plans for expansion of the nation's mass transportation system. We generally take it for granted that living standards will continue to rise in the future. But unless other conditions change in offsetting fashion, rising incomes could mean that in the long run, demand for rides on public transit will continue to shift down, jeopardizing new and old facilities alike.

7. See John F. Kain and Gary R. Fauth, *The Effects of Urban Structure on Household Auto Ownership Decisions and Journey to Work Mode Choices*, Research paper R 76–1 (Cambridge, Mass.: Harvard University, Department of City and Regional Planning, May 1976), tables 3–2, 3–3, 3–4, 3–7.

8. For additional evidence, see 1972 *National Transportation Report*, p. 191 and table VI–4, p. 254.

Elasticity of Demand for Transportation

The responsiveness of travel behavior to changes in one or more components of travel cost depends on the elasticity of demand for transportation
services. Elasticity in this case can be defined as the ratio of the percentage
change in the number of trips taken to the percentage change in trip cost that
brings it about. Since travel demand depends on both time and money cost,
which can be manipulated independently by policymakers, it is generally useful to measure elasticity of demand separately for each of these costs.

It should be recalled that price elasticities carry a negative sign because
the quantity purchased always changes in the opposite direction to the price.
A value between 0 and − 1 indicates an *inelastic* demand relationship, one in
which price changes bring about *less* than proportional changes in quantity
demanded. If a price change induces a *more* than proportional change in
quantity taken, price elasticity exceeds − 1 and the demand relationship is an
elastic one.

Statistical studies indicate that commuting behavior is not very responsive to changes in money price, whether these occur via alteration of transit
fares or of automobile operating costs. A word of caution may be warranted,
however. The studies cited in the following discussion refer to short-run price
elasticity. In the longer run, when they have had time to adapt, consumers
may be more responsive to price changes than these figures suggest. Consequently, there is some risk involved in using short-run elasticities to guide
long-run policies.

Michael Kemp summarizes the available evidence by pointing out that
estimates of the fare elasticity of transit demand in the developed countries of
Europe and North America fall in the range of − .1 to − .7. He adds that in
very large cities and at peak hours, when the alternatives to transit are more
costly, elasticities usually fall in the lower end of that range.[9] Indeed, it has become a kind of rule of thumb among transit operators, when they adjust fares,
to expect a percentage change in ridership about one-third the size of any
percentage change in fares, which implies an expected price elasticity of
− .33.

Table 8.5 presents a set of travel demand elasticities estimated by
Thomas Domencich, Gerald Kraft, and J. P. Valette for the Boston metropolitan area. It includes estimates for auto as well as transit demand, for time cost
as well as fare cost, and it separates journey-to-work trips from shopping trips.
Transit money and time costs are divided into a line-haul and an access component. The latter covers all costs except those incurred on the principal
travel mode, which is the "line-haul." Auto money costs are divided into a
"line-haul" component, which covers operating but not ownership costs per
trip, and an out-of-pocket component, which covers tolls and parking charges.

9. Michael A. Kemp, "Some Evidence of Transit Demand Elasticities," *Transportation*, 2
(1973), p. 25.

TABLE 8.5
Elasticity of Demand for Urban Transportation

	AUTO TRIPS	
	Line-Haul Cost[a]	*Toll and Parking Cost*
Money Cost Elasticity		
Work trips	−.494	−.071
Shopping trips	−.878	−1.65
	In-Vehicle Time	*Out-of-Vehicle Time*
Time Cost Elasticity		
Work trips	−.82	−1.437
Shopping trips	−1.02	−1.440
	TRANSIT TRIPS	
	Line-Haul Cost[b]	*Access (Feeder-Line) Cost*[c]
Money Cost Elasticity		
Work trips	−.09	−.10
Shopping trips	−.323[d]	
	Line-Haul Time	*Access Time*
Time Cost Elasticity		
Work trips	−.39	−.709
Shopping trips	−.593[d]	

[a]Includes operating cost from origin to destination. Ownership costs are excluded.
[b]Includes fare paid on principal transit mode. Fares on feeder lines at either end of of line-haul are excluded.
[c]Includes cost of access from origin to principal mode, plus cost of travel from that mode to destination.
[d]Transit shopping sample too small to permit disaggregation of components.
Source: Thomas A. Domencich, Gerald Kraft, and J. P. Valette, "Estimation of Urban Passenger Travel Behavior: An Economic Demand Model," in M. Edel and J. Rothenberg, eds., *Readings in Urban Economics* (New York: Macmillan, 1972), pp. 464–465.

Auto time costs per trip are divided into in-vehicle and out-of-vehicle components.

The results in Table 8.5 conform closely with a priori expectations. Transit fare elasticity is very low, though slightly higher for shopping than for work trips. Auto money cost elasticity is also low for journey-to-work trips, though not as low as transit elasticity.

For both modes elasticity is considerably higher with respect to time cost than money cost. This is consistent with the fact, illustrated in Table 8.4, that the time cost of travel often outweighs its money cost. Consequently, a reduction of x percent in time cost will have a greater impact on total trip cost than a reduction of the same proportion in money cost.

Within the time category, elasticity is much higher for access time than for line-haul time of transit trips and for out-of-vehicle than for in-vehicle time of auto trips. This would seem to confirm that travelers find walking and waiting time more onerous than time spent riding or driving.

Policy Implications of Inelastic Transit Demand

A policy of "free transit" has often been advocated as a dramatic step to improve the economic health of the older central cities. It has been argued that free transit would help to revive fading central business districts, reduce the diseconomies of highway congestion and air pollution, and improve job access for ghetto-bound minorities. Kraft and Domencich used the data summarized in Table 8.5 to evaluate these claims. The low elasticities shown there mean that free transit would produce only very modest increases in ridership and therefore at best would have slight effect in reaching the intended objectives. The authors concluded that other policies were available to do the job far more effectively and without entirely discarding the rationalizing influence of market prices (to which we will return).[10]

While it is true that low transit fare elasticities make it difficult to increase ridership by *reducing* transit charges, the other side of the coin (or, in some cities, token) is that low elasticities also mean ridership will decline very little if fares are *increased*. Hence higher fares will generally produce higher revenues, a lesson well known to both public and private transit operators.

Since the time elasticities in Table 8.5 are much higher than the fare elasticities, Kraft and Domencich inferred from the data that faster and more frequently service would do more than lower fares to encourage transit ridership. Moreover, time elasticities are higher for access time than for line-haul, from which they inferred that service improvements in the residential collection and downtown distribution systems would be more effective in attracting riders than would attempts to speed up the main-line service.

Perhaps because the fare level is such a politically potent symbol of concern with urban problems, transit pricing policies often run directly counter to these inferences. When the object is to promote ridership, operating authorities usually reduce the fare instead of improving service. Or, if they are under pressure to cut financial losses without raising fares, they economize by reducing the frequency of service, thus losing customers (and revenues) by increasing the time cost of using the system.

Is it possible that service improvements would be so attractive as to be self-financing? That would occur only if the incremental revenue they bring in equals or exceeds the incremental cost of providing them. The incremental revenue depends on the service elasticity of demand. If service elasticity were unitary, ridership, and therefore revenue, would rise in proportion to the in-

---

10. Gerald Kraft and Thomas A. Domencich, "Free Transit," in Matthew Edel and Jerome Rothenberg, eds., *Readings in Urban Economics* (New York: Macmillan, 1972), pp. 459–480.

crease in service. The incremental cost depends on production conditions in the industry. If additional units of service can be produced at the same unit cost as existing service (that is, if the industry produces at constant unit cost), then with unitary elasticity of demand, service improvements would be just self-financing. On the other hand, if the industry produces at *decreasing* unit cost (evidence on this point is discussed at the end of the chapter), improvements could be self-financing even if the service elasticity of demand were less than one. A recent survey by Lago, Mayworm, and McEnroe of studies drawn from several countries found that service elasticities were almost always less than unity.[11] From similar evidence Kemp concludes that "service improvements . . . can significantly improve ridership, but rarely to the extent of recovering the full incremental cost of the improvements."[12] If it were otherwise, of course, an "urban transportation problem" would not exist: we could have mass transit systems in our large cities that offered high-quality service and were also self-financing. Transit operators, though much criticized, cannot be so incompetent as to have missed that sort of opportunity.

The difficulty that policymakers face in trying to influence urban travel patterns can also be illustrated by referring to modal choice data for hypothetical commuters Green and White. Suppose, for example, that the government wished to discourage commuting by automobile in order to reduce air pollution or encourage fuel saving. What would the transit fare have to be to lure well-to-do commuter White out of her private car? Table 8.4 shows that fares would have to be reduced to 10 cents a ride to make transit as attractive as driving. This outcome reflects the fact that time costs "dominate" White's decision: radical changes in other costs would therefore have to occur before she would alter her behavior.

In Green's case it is only the considerable cost of parking—obviously reflecting high land values in the CBD—that would discourage him from driving to work if his job were located centrally. Were he to become a reverse commuter with a job in the suburbs, we have already seen that he would drive to work. Even free transit would not suffice to divert him from the highway. He would require a cash bonus of 10 cents per round trip in addition.

These results are not entirely fanciful. Leon Moses and Harold Williamson, Jr., in a well-known 1963 study based on a survey of Chicago automobile commuters, estimated the transit fares that would be required to divert commuters from autombiles to their "best alternative" mode. They found, for example, that of those auto users who listed "el or subway" as the best alternative, only 18 percent would be diverted to that mode even if it were free. It would have required an additional bonus (or "negative price") of 40 to 50 cents per one-way ride to induce as many as half of such commuters to use

11. Armando M. Lago, Patrick Mayworm, and J. Matthew McEnroe, "Transit Service Elasticities," *Journal of Transport Economics and Policy*, May 1981, pp. 99–119.
12. Kemp, p. 38.

the el-subway system. The authors concluded, "If our results are at all reasonable, the possibility of significantly reducing auto congestion by reasonable reductions in the price of public transportation appears slight."[13]

Substitute *air pollution* for *congestion* and the statement is equally relevant to that problem. Metropolitan air pollution and automobile use are directly related. Pollution could be reduced if commuters were diverted from private automobiles to mass transportation, provided—and this is an important qualification—that the level of demand is high enough so that transit vehicles are reasonably well filled. The Moses and Williamson study shows that even in a transit-oriented city such as Chicago it would be impossible to achieve much diversion by manipulating transit fares unless the price were pushed well below zero. Moreover, it should be emphasized that the technically correct way to handle the pollution problem is to raise the cost of automobile operation to include its air pollution costs rather than to reduce auto use by subsidizing competing modes. (See discussion in Chapter 9.)

Fuel Prices and Modal Choice

The hypothetical data in Table 8.4 also help to explain why the very sharp rise in fuel prices during the 1970s produced so little diversion of auto users to mass transit. The effect of fuel prices on travel behavior is moderated by the fact that time costs—and, in the case of journeys to the CBD, parking charges—make up so much of the full cost of a trip. In the hypothetical world of Table 8.4, the cost of oil and gas, including taxes, comes to about 7 cents a mile. At that level it accounts for only 13 percent of White's commuting costs and about 29 percent of Green's (as a reverse commuter). The cost of gasoline would have to rise above 22 cents a mile to divert the outward-bound Green to public transportation and above 20 cents a mile to divert White. In other words, the price of gas would probably have to triple to pull these two commuters out of their automobiles.

The effect of higher fuel prices on modal choice following the energy crises of the 1970s was also moderated by the fact that auto users tended to purchase smaller, more fuel-efficient cars as fuel prices rose. Consequently, cost per mile for the average driver did not increase as fast as cost per gallon. Though modal choice for commuting may respond little to higher fuel prices, other aspects of travel behavior are much more likely to be affected. We would expect consumers to make more multipurpose trips and to rely less on the automobile for long-distance travel. Whether in the longer run choice of residential or job locations might also be affected is a question to which we return at the end of Chapter 9.

Up to this point we have concentrated on the demand side of the mar-

---

13. Leon N. Moses and Harold F. Williamson, Jr., "Value of Time, Choice of Mode, and the Subsidy Issue in Urban Transportation," *Journal of Political Economy*, June 1963, p. 262.

ket for urban transportation. We turn next to the supply side, examining highway costs in the short run in order to develop rational pricing rules for operating an existing transportation network.

OPTIMUM TRANSPORTATION PRICING IN THE SHORT RUN

It is an important objective in any society to make efficient use of productive resources. The student of economics learns in the elementary course that an optimum, or "efficient," allocation of resources could be achieved if all goods were produced and sold under conditions of perfect competition and no externalities occurred in production or consumption. Under perfect competition, the price of every good sold would equal the marginal private cost of producing it. In the absence of externalities, marginal social cost could not exceed marginal private cost. Thus the price charged in the marketplace would cover the full cost to society of producing the marginal unit of every commodity. No one could consume any commodity for which he or she was not willing to repay the full social cost. At the same time, competition among producers would guarantee that the sales price of a commodity could never *exceed* its marginal cost. Consumers would be assured of receiving all goods for which they were willing to pay at least the full social cost. "Marginal cost pricing" would thus lead automatically to optimum resource use in the short run.

Unhappily, no such automatic optimization can be expected in the urban transportation sector, which departs from the ideal in several crucial respects.

1. Instead of perfect competition, with its many sellers, we find competition among a few modes, each of which is typically operated by a public or private monopolist. Consequently, regulated prices are the rule rather than the exception.
2. In many cases the "decreasing cost" nature of production makes the usual "marginal cost equal to price" solution peculiarly difficult to attain.
3. Finally, externalities in the form of congestion, air pollution, noise, and other disamenities abound in the urban transportation sector, so that the private cost of a mile of urban travel is often significantly less than its full social cost.

Transportation is a multidimensional service. The number of trips per hour over a given route is usually taken as the measure of output, but, ideally, the output measure should also reflect both degree of comfort and reliability of service. So far as urban mass transit is concerned, the cost of producing a unit of output depends very much on how the service is organized. How frequent is it? How many scheduled stops are made per mile? How fast are the vehicles? These and many more factors affect cost and output. Herbert Mohring's economic model of an urban bus route contains no fewer than thirteen variables.[14]

Transportation analysts usually begin by examining the highway case, since it is somewhat simpler than urban mass transit and serves to illustrate the main issues in optimum pricing policy. Once these have been clarified, application of the analysis to urban mass transit systems is quite straightforward. We begin with the analysis of highway pricing in the short run, when the set of facilities can be taken as fixed. Optimum short-run pricing is essential if society is to use existing facilities efficiently.[15] It also provides a crucial link to optimum long-run investment policy, which will be taken up subsequently.

Pricing Highway Services in the Short Run

Let us assume that a network of roads exists by virtue of past public investment. The existing roads are owned and operated by a public authority. On what terms should that authority make them available to individual users? In the short run, efficient pricing requires that road users make payments for each trip equal to the cost of all the resources used up as a result of that trip.[16] These resource costs can be classified as follows:

1. Highway maintenance costs dependent on use, borne by the highway authority
2. Automobile operating and time costs, borne by the trip maker
3. External costs, borne by neither the trip maker nor the highway authority
   a. Congestion costs, borne by other highway users
   b. Environmental costs (air pollution, noise, etc.), borne by the adjacent population

If the auto trip maker can be made to bear all of the costs listed, he or she will undertake only trips whose utility is at least equal to their full incremental cost. As long as the trip maker is not charged *more* than the sum of these costs, he or she will make *all* trips that yield utility greater than cost. Society will be making optimum use of the existing highway network.

14. Herbert Mohring, *Transportation Economics* (Cambridge, Mass.: Ballinger, 1976), pp. 149–150.

15. One of the earliest advocates of marginal cost pricing for urban transportation facilities was William S. Vickrey. See his 1963 article, "Pricing in Urban and Suburban Transport," reprinted in Ronald E. Grieson, ed., *Urban Economics: Readings and Analysis* (Boston: Little, Brown, 1973), pp. 106–118, which contains many illustrative applications.

16. The following analysis draws heavily on A. A. Walters, *The Economics of Road User Charges* (Baltimore: Johns Hopkins University Press, 1968), chs. 2 and 3.

FIGURE 8.1
Optimal Pricing on a Congested Highway

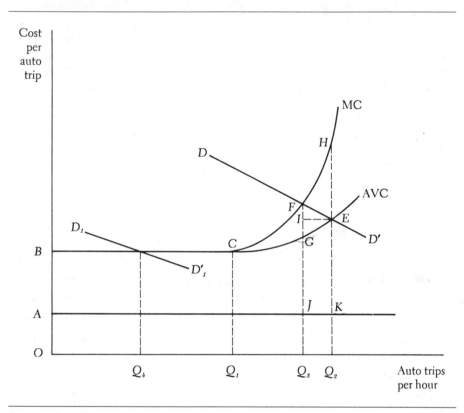

Source: Adapted from A. A. Walters, *The Economics of Road User Charges* (Baltimore: Johns Hopkins University Press, 1968), fig. 2, p. 24.

Pricing on Congested Roads

Since the cost of travel, especially in urban areas, is often affected by congestion, we begin with the problem of optimal pricing when congestion is present. Figure 8.1 will help to clarify the relationship between trip cost and the level of highway use. It depicts the components of cost for journeys along a given stretch of highway. The horizontal axis measures number of auto trips per hour along the highway segment. The traffic flow increases as we move to the right. The vertical axis measures cost per trip, including components 1, 2, and 3a of the above list. (To simplify the argument we assume, at this point, that environmental pollution costs are zero.)

A part of highway maintenance cost depends on weather and the passage of time, but part also depends on the number of vehicles using the highway. Walters calls the latter "variable maintenance costs," since they vary directly with the number of vehicles using the road. In Figure 8.1 the amount of these costs per vehicle is OA. The variable maintenance cost curve, AJK, is a horizontal line because the amount OA per vehicle remains constant over a wide range of traffic volumes.[17]

The distance AB measures automobile operating and time costs per trip when traffic on the highway segment is light. These costs remain constant up to traffic volume Q_1. At that point congestion sets in: the traffic flow becomes heavy enough so that cars begin to get in one another's way and average speed drops. Because trips now take longer, their time cost increases. The curve BCGE begins to rise. Its height above B at any point to the right of Q_1 shows the extent to which an individual driver bears the cost of congestion as a private cost at that level of traffic. Its height above the horizontal axis measures the average variable cost of a trip—including road maintenance, vehicle operation, and driver time costs—at each level of traffic. Hence it is labeled AVC.

Congestion is a social as well as a private problem. Suppose traffic is at level Q_1 per hour. If an additional driver—call him Smith—then enters the flow, congestion begins. Not only Smith but every other traveler then on the road finds the going slower. Smith bears the cost of congestion only insofar as it increases his own travel time. But by entering the traffic stream he has imposed a like cost on every other traveler. Thus congestion costs are a form of externality: the action of one individual imposes costs on others in addition to those he bears himself. The external costs of congestion are shown by the curve CFH, which rises above BCGE once congestion sets in. The external cost that a single additional vehicle entering the stream at any given level of traffic flow will impose on all other drivers is measured by the vertical distance between the two curves. For example, if the traffic flow equals Q_2, an additional driver entering the stream imposes congestion costs of HE on the aggregate of other drivers already on the road. CFH shows the increment to total social cost occasioned by one additional trip at any level of traffic greater than Q_1. Since it measures the increment to total cost, it is a marginal cost curve in the usual meaning of that term and is labeled MC.

The demand for the use of the road segment analyzed in Figure 8.1 is shown by DD'. Demand is depicted as fairly elastic because there are presumably other routes that drivers could choose between the points served by this segment.

Let us assume that the highway authority charges each driver a toll equal to OA, thus covering the maintenance expenditures attributable to use of the road. Then the curve BCGE represents the cost to each driver of using the highway segment. BCGE becomes, in effect, a supply curve, showing the price at which journeys can be obtained, for any level of traffic flow. The demand curve DD' shows how many trips drivers will wish to make at any given

17. Ibid., p. 23.

price. The traffic flow will actually settle at level Q_2, determined by the inter- section of the supply and demand curves at point E. At that level each driver will pay a maintenance toll of OA and, in addition, bear private costs of KE per journey.

Q_2, however, is not the optimal traffic level because the pricing system thus far assumed ignores the external costs of congestion. The full cost of the Q_2th journey is not $OA + KE$, as paid by the marginal road user, but $OA + KE + EH$, where EH measures the increment to aggregate congestion costs attributable to the marginal journey. To achieve optimum road use the highway authority, in addition to charging maintenance toll OA, must levy a congestion toll equal to the external cost of congestion. That cost varies with the level of traffic and equals the vertical distance between curves BGE and CFH. If such a congestion toll were charged, the supply curve of journeys would effectively be shifted to $BCFH$. Intersection with the demand curve would then occur at point F, and the flow of traffic would be reduced from Q_2 per hour to Q_3.

It can easily be shown that Q_3 is the optimum flow. At traffic level Q_3 the marginal traveler places a dollar value of $OA + JF$ on a journey, as shown by the height of the demand curve at F. This just offsets the full social cost of the trip, shown by the height of the full-cost curve CFH at F. To the right of Q_3 the demand curve drops below the full-cost curve. The marginal traveler would be consuming journeys that were valued at less than their full cost. To the left of Q_3 the demand curve lies above the full-cost curve. Travelers would be foregoing journeys that were worth more to them than their full social cost. In either case, resource use would be less than optimal.

Note that the optimum solution at Q_3 does not eliminate all congestion. As much congestion remains as travelers are willing to pay for. Of course, it must be borne in mind that we are dealing here only with the short run, in which, by definition, the stock of highways is fixed. As we shall see, a suffi- ciently high level of congestion tolls would be taken as a signal that more highways should be built. Even in the long run, however, when society has obtained an optimum network of roads, there would continue to be conges- tion at many points. We shall return to this question. In the meantime, it must be added that no variable congestion tolls yet exist in the United States. The theoretical, practical, and political objections to them will be taken up subsequently.

Pricing on Uncongested Roads

Suppose that in Figure 8.1 the demand for trips were shown by D_1D_1' instead of DD'. With less demand for trips, the road would be uncongested, since the intersection of D_1D_1' with the supply curve $BCGE$ occurs to the left of point C, where congestion begins. In that case the appropriate toll would be only OA, a charge sufficient to cover variable maintenance costs. In addi- tion, drivers would bear their own operating and time costs, AB.

Pricing on Roads Subject to "Peaking"

It cannot have escaped the reader's attention that in urban areas the journey to work and back often generates morning and evening traffic jams. Radial highways connecting large-city CBDs with the suburban ring are particularly subject to such congestion. This sort of "peak loading" greatly complicates the problem of urban transportation, including, in the short run, the achievement of optimal pricing.

Referring again to Figure 8.1, imagine that DD' represents demand during the peak morning and evening hours while D_1D_1' shows demand at other times. In that case the theory of road pricing suggests that a congestion toll should be charged only during the "rush hours," since the road is not otherwise congested. Thus, the highway authority would be called upon to vary its charges according to time of day and direction of flow. During rush hours, highway space becomes a relatively scarce commodity. By charging a price for its use, the highway authority allocates it to those who value that use most highly. During nonrush hours, if the road is not congested, highway space is not scarce and need not be rationed. Users are then charged only the cost of the wear and tear they impose on the facility, a toll of OA. An empirical estimate of optimum peak and off-peak congestion tolls for the San Francisco Bay area is presented in Table 8.6.

Pricing on Urban Mass Transit Systems

If we are willing to accept a certain degree of abstraction from the complexity of actual bus or subway operations, Figure 8.1 can also be taken to represent short-run costs in urban mass transit. The quantity on the horizontal axis becomes hourly flow of passengers past a given point on the particular line in question. Fixed costs are not shown. The curve $BCGE$ represents average variable costs. As Martin Wohl has suggested, such a curve begins to rise beyond a certain flow level for reasons analogous to those that explain rising costs in the highway case.[18] First, increased passenger crowding on vehicles eventually leads to discomfort (for example, lack of seating), which adds to the perceived cost of a trip. Second, congestion eventually reduces average vehicle speed, thus increasing the time cost of a trip (for example, when the number of riders increases, buses and trains take longer at each stop to discharge and board them). The segment CGE shows how these congestion costs are borne by the individual user. As in the case of highways, when the external costs each additional user imposes on all others are added to individual costs, we obtain the curve CFH. The height of CFH above CGE measures these externalities at each level of traffic.

Using rational pricing principles, an urban transit authority would

18. Martin Wohl, "Congestion Toll Pricing for Public Transport Facilities," in Selma Mushkin, ed., *Public Prices for Public Products*, (Washington, D.C.: Urban Institute, 1972), pp. 245–246.

charge the following prices: during nonrush hours, a toll just sufficient to cover the marginal cost to the authority of an incremental passenger; during rush hours, the marginal cost to the authority *plus* the congestion cost that the marginal passenger imposes on the riding public at the rush-hour traffic level.

OPTIMAL LONG-RUN ADJUSTMENT
OF TRANSPORTATION SYSTEMS

Congestion tolls provide the link between the optimum short-run operation and the optimum long-run adjustment of a transportation network. If congestion tolls on a given highway segment appear sufficient to cover the cost of an increase in capacity, it seems intuitively correct to argue that capacity should be expanded. (Indeed, one of the strongest arguments for charging congestion tolls is that they would provide valuable information about when and where to invest in expansion.)

The logical connection between tolls and expansion can be shown most readily if we adopt a useful simplifying assumption suggested by A. A. Walters. Let us suppose for the moment that roads are made of "pure putty."[19] In that case, Walters points out, roads could be expanded quickly and by very small fractions: one would simply add to, stretch, or squeeze the putty. Awkward discontinuities such as the jump from two lanes to three or from unlimited to limited access would be eliminated because pure-putty roads would be infinitely malleable. Let us further assume that under these conditions expansion could be carried out at a constant cost per additional unit of capacity. We can show that it would then be desirable to expand each road as long as the congestion tolls collected from the users exceeded the cost of expanding capacity sufficiently to accommodate one more vehicle at a given level of congestion. (This analysis of optimum long-run adjustment differs from the benefit-cost analysis of transportation projects to be presented in Chapter 9 because that calculus takes external benefits and costs systematically into account, while this one ignores them.)

The case of constant cost is illustrated in Figure 8.2. This diagram is similar to Figure 8.1, but in addition to the relationships shown there, it displays short-run average total cost (SATC), long-run average total cost (LATC), and long-run marginal cost (LMC). As in Figure 8.1, average variable cost (AVC) includes road maintenance, vehicle-operating, and driver time costs, while short-run marginal cost (SMC) shows the increment to total cost, including the cost of congestion, occasioned by one additional trip.

Figure 8.2 shows a road at two different capacity levels, A and B. The peak-load problem is eliminated by assumption: we assume that traffic flow is the same at all times of day. The horizontal axis therefore measures daily ve-

19. Walters, pp. 31–32.

FIGURE 8.2
Optimal Adjustment of Highway Capacity: The Case of Constant Long-run Cost

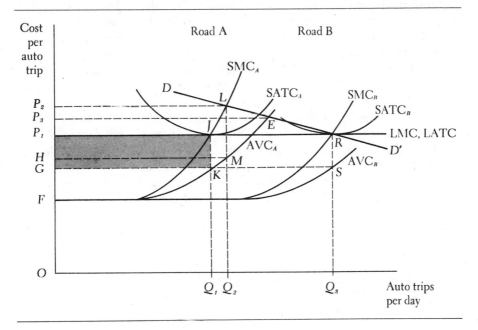

hicle trips. Because the road can be expanded at constant cost per unit of additional capacity, the long-run average total cost curve is a horizontal line. Moreover, it is an elementary proposition in microeconomic theory that if long-run average total cost is constant, long-run marginal cost is also constant and equal to it. Hence on the diagram LMC corresponds to LATC.

By definition, average fixed cost equals average total cost minus average variable cost. In Figure 8.2, when Q_1 vehicles per day use highway A, average fixed cost per day is given by JK, which also equals P_1G. This means that a toll of P_1G collected daily from Q_1 users will provide sufficient revenue over the life of the highway to finance the construction of highway A. This daily revenue of $Q_1 \times P_1G$ is shown by the area of the shaded rectangle P_1JKG. To expand this constant cost highway by a single unit of capacity it would be sufficient to collect the toll of P_1G from a single additional trip maker each day. Another way of putting it is that P_1G equals the daily cost of borrowing the capital needed to expand the capacity of the highway by one unit. If the same toll P_1G were collected daily from Q_3 users, the additional revenue $P_1G \times (Q_3 - Q_1)$ would pay for the expansion of capacity from Q_1 to Q_3. Thus the constant cost of expansion per unit of capacity is P_1G per day, collected over the life of the highway.

Highway A is the optimum-size road to carry a daily flow of Q_1 vehicles, because the short-run average total cost of highway A (SATC$_A$) reaches its minimum point at flow Q_1. However, it is *not* the optimum-size road in the situation depicted in Figure 8.2. The demand for trips is shown by DD'. If highway A is the existing road and the highway authority employs optimum short-run pricing, it will limit traffic to the flow Q_2 indicated by the intersection of the short-run marginal social cost curve (SMC_A) and the demand curve, doing so by charging a congestion toll of LM. That highway A is not the optimum size for traffic flows greater than Q_1 is demonstrated by the fact that $SATC_A$ rises above LATC to the right of Q_1. For larger flows, a larger road would be desirable. Moreover, the revenue generated by congestion toll LM collected from Q_2 users (the area of rectangle P_2LMH) exceeds the revenue needed to finance the fixed costs of A (the area of rectangle P_1JKG). We can be certain of that because both dimensions of the former rectangle are larger than those of the latter. Since we assume there are no discontinuities in highway construction, expansion of A is clearly warranted.

Given the demand for trips indicated by DD', the highway should be expanded from scale A to scale B. Figure 8.2 shows that the latter is the optimum-size road to cope with existing demand. To the left of Q_3 the demand curve lies above the long-run marginal cost curve, which means that users are willing to pay more for additional trips than the full incremental cost to society of producing them (including increments to fixed as well as variable cost). Too little highway capacity is being supplied. To the right of Q_3, the situation reverses. DD' falls below LMC, indicating that users are not willing to pay the full cost of trips beyond level Q_3. Highway capacity is being oversupplied.

However, when highway B is in place we find that users are just willing to pay a price (OP_1) that equals both long- and short-run marginal cost. That means that in constructing B, the highway authority reaches both a long- and short-run optimum: long-run because they are supplying that amount of capacity for which users are just willing to pay the full cost, short-run because they are allowing to use the road every consumer who is willing to pay the full marginal cost (including the congestion cost) of an additional trip.

It is important to note that the expansion in scale from A to B is self-financing. The increment to fixed cost per day necessary to pay for expansion is the area of the rectangle KJRS. But this is also precisely the amount added to daily toll revenue when journeys increase from Q_1 to Q_3 per day.

The theory of highway pricing, then, leads to a clear set of rules for operation. These have been summarized by Mohring as follows:

> Given constant returns to scale . . . (1) Establish short-run marginal cost prices for the use of each link. Doing so would require levying tolls equal to the difference between the short-run marginal and average variable costs of trips. And (2) alter the size of each link to the point where the toll revenues generated by it equal the costs to the authority of providing that link.[20]

20. Mohring, p. 21.

Following these simple rules, we would have the best of all possible road systems: a self-financing highway network of optimum size, with every link operating at the optimum level of traffic flow. Moreover, if urban mass transit systems displayed constant returns to scale, the same rules would apply to them, with the same happy consequences.

If matters were truly that simple, of course, there would be no transportation problem, urban or otherwise. Much of the next chapter will be devoted to reintroducing "real-world" complications into the analysis.

Why Aren't All Roads Congested

The theory of road pricing just expounded leads to the curious conclusion that if we have an optimum road network operating under conditions of long-run equilibrium, every part of it would be congested: witness optimum-size road B of Figure 8.2, on which congestion tolls of RS are collected from each user. According to the theory, any road segment with zero congestion (for example, road B if traffic flow were only Q_2) is too large for the level of traffic it serves. The reader, recalling that by far the greater part of the United States' road system is *not* congested, may wonder whether it is the theory or the road system that is at fault.

The answer would appear to be that there are economies of scale in the construction use of highways at the small end of the size spectrum such that it is uneconomical to build and operate very small roads. For example, one-lane roads require extremely low operating speeds and cause great difficulty in passing, both features that add enormously to the time cost of a trip. Consequently, it pays to build two-lane roads, even though in rural areas most of these will never be congested.[21] The theory of road pricing can accommodate these aspects of reality. Let us abandon the assumption of long-run constant cost that is incorporated in Figure 8.2 and introduce economies and diseconomies of scale.

Pricing with Economies and Diseconomies of Scale

If a large highway can be constructed or operated at a lower average cost per vehicle trip than a small highway, we say that highways are subject to economies of scale or, what is the same thing, that highway services display decreasing long-run cost. The optimum pricing policy under these conditions is the same as before. In the short run the highway authority should charge tolls that equate the price to users with the short-run marginal cost (including congestion cost) of a trip. In the long run, facilities should be expanded (or contracted) until the price, equal to short-run marginal cost, also equals the long-run marginal cost of providing journeys.

21. See Walters, pp. 36–41, 83–84.

Although the "pricing rule" is the same as before, the result differs in one important respect: when marginal cost pricing is employed under conditions of long-run decreasing cost, revenues from optimum-size facilities necessarily fall short of covering full costs. Highways will no longer be self-financing. This outcome is explained as follows. In the case of a decreasing-cost facility, the long-run marginal cost curve (LMC) lies below the long-run average total cost curve (LATC). Now suppose the highway authority, employing the pricing and investment rules explained above, expands the facility up to the point where the demand curve intersects LMC. This point necessarily lies below LATC. Consequently, charging tolls based on marginal cost results in a deficit equal to the excess of average over marginal cost per journey.

A simplified version of the decreasing-cost case is shown in Chapter 9, Figure 9.1. Referring to that diagram (and reinterpreting it to represent a highway rather than mass transit), the reader will see that the optimum-size facility is indicated by the intersection of DD and LMC at point A. On a facility of that size, if the highway authority employs marginal cost pricing and the level of traffic is Q_A per day, a daily deficit will occur equal to the area $P_A P_B BA$.

It is a standard proposition in microeconomic theory that decreasing cost firms employing marginal cost pricing will run deficits. In the presence of decreasing costs, marginal cost pricing can be adopted only if firms are subsidized or if an additional special charge is levied. Whether marginal cost pricing continues to be desirable under those circumstances and how subsidies or special charges should be arranged are subjects to which we return in Chapter 9.

Suppose roads are subject not to decreasing but to increasing long-run costs. In that case marginal cost pricing on the optimum-size road results not in a deficit but in a surplus. In the case of increasing costs, the long-run marginal cost curve lies *above* the long-run average total cost curve. When marginal cost pricing is employed on an optimum-size facility, the intersection of the demand curve with LMC will therefore occur at a level *above* rather than below LATC. Surplus revenues will be generated equal to the excess of marginal cost over average total cost per journey.[22]

To summarize the economic theory of transportation in the long run, we can clearly define three cases that apply to mass transit as well as to highway systems:

1. *Constant cost.* If facilities can be expanded at constant cost, marginal cost pricing on optimum-size facilities will yield revenues that just equal full costs. Transportation will be self-financing.
2. *Decreasing cost.* If cost decreases as facilities are expanded, marginal

---

22. The case is depicted in Wohl, fig. 10.7, p. 259.

cost pricing will fail to cover the full cost of optimum-size facilities. Transportation will operate at a deficit.

3. *Increasing cost.* If expansion entails increased unit cost, marginal cost pricing on optimum-size facilities will yield revenues in excess of costs. Transportation will yield a surplus.

EVIDENCE ON TRANSPORTATION COST

We have reviewed the theory of optimum transportation pricing in the long run and found that the outcome depends importantly on the behavior of costs. What, in fact, do empirical studies tell us about transportation costs in the long run?

Highway Costs

Whether highway services are produced under conditions of constant, increasing, or decreasing long-run cost is not an easy matter to sort out. The answer depends not only on how construction cost per lane-mile varies as the number of lanes increases but also on how much traffic flow each additional lane adds to the carrying capacity of a highway. Moreover (and this is especially the case when the subject is urban highways), these costs should be measured not along isolated strips of roadway but in the context of a network of intersecting, interconnected roads.

It has already been pointed out that economies of scale exist at the low end of the road-size spectrum. Consequently, we build two-lane rather than one-lane roads in rural areas except where the traffic level is extraordinarily low. These economies of scale result from the fact that a two-lane road allows much higher operating speeds than a one-lane road. Engineering studies of the U.S. Bureau of Public Roads indicate that vehicle capacity per lane continues to increase up through the fourth lane (when there are two lanes in each direction) to a maximum sustainable flow of about 2,000 passenger vehicles per lane per hour. Capacity per lane levels off thereafter. A four-lane highway has a total capacity of about 8,000 vehicles per hour, while a two-lane highway (one in each direction) has a total capacity of only about 2,000 per hour.[23]

The behavior of construction cost as highway width increases has been a matter of some debate. Analysis is complicated by the fact that costs per mile depend not only on the scale of a highway but also on the extent of urbanization in the area through which it runs. Urbanization increases highway

23. Highway Research Board, *Special Report 87: Highway Capacity Manual* (Washington, D.C.: Highway Research Board of the National Academy of Sciences—National Research Council, 1965), pp. 75–76.

costs, because both the price of land and the number of interchanges, over-passes, and other connections that must be provided increase with population density. These matters are scarcely in doubt. Since, however, highway width and degree of urbanization tend to be associated, the effect of urbanization becomes confounded with that of width.

In a study of highway costs and service levels in the San Francisco Bay area, Theodore E. Keeler and his associates assembled information on fifty-seven road segments in nine counties for the purpose of making cost compari-sons on the evidence of consistent data. Based on an analysis in which they controlled statistically for the effects of urbanization, they concluded that the evidence is "consistent with the hypothesis of constant returns" in the con-struction of highways.[24] In other words, there are neither economies nor dis-economies of scale in construction; costs per lane-mile do not vary as the number of lanes increases. More recently Marvin Kraus concluded that there may be very slight economies of scale in urban highway networks, a result he characterized as "not that different . . . from Keeler and Small."[25]

An Estimate of Optimum Congestion Tolls

With constant returns to scale, an optimal system of congestion and maintenance tolls will just cover the full cost of each segment of a highway. However, since cost per segment rises sharply with degree of urbanization, optimal tolls and congestion levels will be much higher in central cities than in rural or suburban areas. Where there is a peaking problem, as in most met-ropolitan highway systems, tolls will also be much higher in peak than in off-peak periods. Keeler and his associates calculated optimal peak and off-peak tolls based on their data for the San Francisco Bay area and using alternative assumptions concerning the rate of interest and the average value of travel time. It should be noted that these are optimum *long-run* tolls in which the cost of long-run expansion as well as short-run congestion is taken into ac-count (as in Figure 8.2). A summary of Keeler's results is shown in Table 8.6. All calculations are in terms of 1972 dollars.

At an assumed interest rate of 6 percent, optimal peak-period tolls were estimated to rise from about 3 cents per vehicle mile in outlying areas to 15 cents per vehicle mile in Oakland and San Francisco. Daytime, off-peak tolls were less than one cent in all areas. When interest rates are assumed to be 12 percent, the range of peak-period tolls approximately doubles. Off-peak tolls are far less sensitive to the interest rate. The connection between interest rates and tolls is straightforward. A higher rate of interest implies a higher

24. Theodore E. Keeler and Kenneth A. Small, "Optimal Peak-Load Pricing, Investment and Service Levels on Urban Expressways," *Journal of Political Economy*, February 1977, p. 7.
25. Marvin Kraus, "Scale Economies Analysis for Urban Highway Networks," *Journal of Urban Economics*, January 1981, p. 20. Also see Meyer, Kain, and Wohl, pp. 199–208; Mohring, pp. 140–45; Walters, pp. 183–184.

TABLE 8.6
Optimal Congestion Tolls, San Francisco Bay Area, 1972 (in cents per vehicle mile)

HIGHWAY LOCATION	PEAK		DAYTIME OFF-PEAK	
	$i = 6\%$	$i = 12\%$	$i = 6\%$	$i = 12\%$
Rural-Suburban				
V = 4.50	2.7	5.3	.6	.8
V = 2.25	3.1	6.9	.4	.4
Urban, Outside Central City				
V = 4.50	3.3	7.0	.7	.8
V = 2.25	4.2	9.1	.4	.5
Central City				
V = 4.50	14.5	31.0	.9	.9
V = 2.25	17.4	34.3	.5	.5

i = assumed interest rate.
V = assumed time value in dollars per hour.
Source: Theodore E. Keeler and Kenneth A. Small, "Optimal Peak-Load Pricing, Investment and Service Levels on Urban Expressways," *Journal of Political Economy*, February 1977, table 5, p. 18.

cost of borrowing the capital that is embodied in the highway and therefore higher total costs to be covered by tolls.

The relationship of time value to tolls in more complex. Calculations were carried out for alternative values of $4.50 and $2.25 an hour. Since the cost of congestion is principally a time cost, one would expect, as Keeler points out, that "a lower value of time would lead to lower toll." That turns out to be true in the off-peak but not in the peak hours. An optimal road segment will have fewer lanes if time values are lower. Such a road might then become more congested during peak hours than the wider road that would be built if time values were higher.[26] However, Table 8.6 shows that optimal congestion tolls, especially at the peak period, are not very sensitive to variation in the assumed average value of time.

Mass Transit Costs

Cost studies of rail and bus transit systems are less numerous than those of highways. Mohring has studied urban bus transit. Meyer, Kain, and Wohl undertook a pathbreaking comparison of costs on all three modes in their volume *The Urban Transportation Problem*. Boyd, Asher, and Wetzler later compared rail and bus costs in the urban commuter market. Keeler and his associ-

26. Keeler and Small, p. 17.

ates also examined rail and bus transit, together with highways, in their San Francisco Bay area study.[27]

Unlike later investigators, Meyer, Kain, and Wohl did not include the value of time as a cost in trip making. Despite this and other differences in method, the results of the three intermodal cost comparisons are strikingly similar. Keeler's findings are summarized in Figure 8.3, which shows the full cost of a trip from a residential suburb to the CBD on each mode as a function of the peak hourly traffic in a single corridor. Since peak traffic volume, plotted on the horizontal axis, is a measure of output quantity, the relationships depicted in Figure 8.3 are, in effect, long-run average cost curves.

Following Meyer, Kain, and Wohl, Keeler defines the complete work trip as consisting of three segments: residential collection, line-haul, and downtown distribution. If the trip is by auto, the commuter completes the three segments in a single vehicle and parks it downtown. For the bus trip, too, the commuter is assumed to use a single vehicle, which collects passengers on a trip through a residential neighborhood, then runs as an express along a freeway to reach the CBD, where it enters city streets to accomplish downtown distribution. The rail transit trip is assumed to be a combination of feeder bus for residential collection, followed by line-haul and downtown distribution on San Francisco's BART system. For each type of trip the authors calculate the combination of inputs that would minimize total costs, including time costs of users. Calculations are for peak-hour traffic levels varying from 1,000 to 30,000 passengers per corridor in the major direction. Dividing total cost by traffic volume yields the estimates of average cost shown in Figure 8.3. Because the optimum factor combination has been chosen to produce each level of output, these are the minimum long-run average costs for each level of traffic.

Long-run average cost declines for both bus and rail mass transit as systems are expanded to accommodate larger volumes of traffic. We have previously shown that if transportation is produced under conditions of decreasing cost, marginal cost pricing will fail to cover the long-run cost of optimum-size facilities. Thus bus or rail transit systems employing marginal cost pricing and expanded to their optimum size would not in all likelihood be self-financing. (We will return to intermodal cost comparisons in Chapter 9).

The definition of costs employed in Figure 8.3 is a broad one. It covers both the costs incurred by the user (including the value of time spent traveling) and the costs borne by the agency that builds and operates the facility. In

27. See Mohring's *Transportation Economics*, pp. 147–157, and "Optimization and Scale Economies in Urban Bus Transportation," *American Economic Review*, September 1972, pp. 591–604; Meyer, Kain, and Wohl, chs. 8–11; J. Hayden Boyd, Norman J. Asher, and Elliot S. Wetzler, *Evaluation of Rail Rapid Transit and Express Bus Service in the Urban Commuter Market*, prepared for the U.S. Department of Transportation (Washington, D.C.: U.S. Government Printing Office, October 1973); Theodore E. Keeler, et al., *The Full Costs of Urban Transport*, part 3, monograph 21 (Berkeley, Calif.: Institute of Urban and Regional Development, University of California, July 1975).

FIGURE 8.3

Intermodal Comparison of Trip Costs as a Function of Traffic Volume

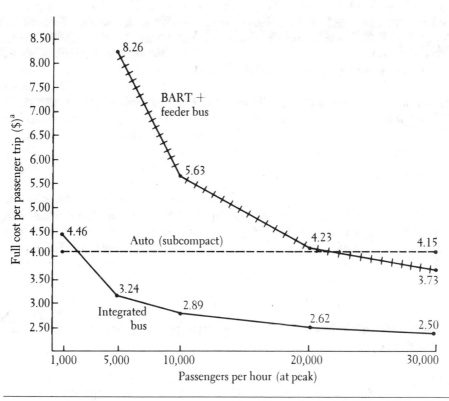

[a]Cost in 1972 dollars of a six-mile line-haul trip plus residential collection and downtown distribution.

Source: Adapted from Theodore E. Keeler et al., *The Full Costs of Urban Transport,* part 3, monograph 21 (Berkeley, Calif.: Institute of Urban and Regional Development, University of California, July 1975), fig. 4, p. 128.

the case of mass transit, economies of scale apparently occur with respect to both kinds of cost. Mohring studied urban bus transportation, using data from the Twin Cities, Minneapolis and St. Paul, to calibrate a model of a city bus route. His results indicate that with optimum long-run adjustment, both average agency cost and average user time cost decline as the number of users rises. Marginal cost is therefore below average cost. If marginal cost pricing were used, riders would pay fares in the neighborhood of 17 cents for a three-mile trip at peak hours and between 9 and 12 cents at the off-peak. These charges are far below the level of agency costs, requiring the payment of subsidies that vary from about 31 cents per ride at low levels of patronage to about 5 cents at very high levels.[28]

The decline in average agency costs as ridership increases can be explained by the fact that it costs little more to run a full bus than an empty one. User time cost declines because as ridership increases, service is more frequent and average waiting time is reduced. The same factors operate for rail mass transit. In the rail case, however, the decline in average cost is greater and extends over a wider range of traffic. This reflects the additional influence of indivisible fixed costs for the contstruction of rail trackage: a two-track line is both the minimum and the maximum needed for most traffic densities.[29] Heavy fixed trackage costs make the average cost of a trip very high at low traffic levels, but since these expenses do not rise with traffic density, average cost falls markedly as patronage increases.

Walters has objected that Mohring's results for an urban bus system depend heavily on his "implicit assumptions of a monopoly supplier of bus services and a fixed size of [large] bus."[30] He argues that if bus size were allowed to vary and competition were permitted to replace franchised monopoly, the nature of bus service would change radically: much smaller buses would be employed on many routes and would operate at greater frequencies. As a result, the economies of scale found by Mohring would be greatly reduced or even eliminated, since they are heavily dependent on the high operating cost and great capacity of large buses. In that case, as we have explained in this chapter, economic theory tells us that there might be no justification for subsidy: at the optimum scale of operation, urban bus service would be self-financing.

Walters cites numerous examples of the successful use of "minibuses" under unsubsidized, unregulated, competitive conditions in cities like Buenos Aires, Istanbul, and Manila. It remains an open question whether that mode of operation would also work in highly developed European and North American economies.[31] However, as we shall point out in the next chapter, most economists would agree that the publicly owned bus systems operating in large U.S. metropolitan areas are far too rigid and unresponsive and that urban transportation service would benefit from less regulation, more competition, and more innovation.

28. Mohring, *Transportation Economics*, tables 12-2 and 12-3, pp. 153–54.

29. Keeler et al., p. 126.

30. A. A. Walters, "Externalities in Urban Buses," *Journal of Urban Economics*, January 1982, p. 60.

31. See Mohring's response to Walters: "Minibuses in Urban Transportation," *Journal of Urban Economics*, November 1983, pp. 293–317; and Stephen Glaister, "Competition on an Urban Bus Route," *Journal of Transport Economics and Policy*, January 1985, pp. 65–81.

NINE

Urban
Transportation Policy

Transportation systems are largely planned, built, financed, and operated by governments. In this chapter we analyze urban transportation policy: what government does, or could do, to develop transportation systems that operate both efficiently and equitably. Short-run questions are covered first. Under what pricing policies are existing systems actually operated? What financial problems do they face, and how have these been dealt with? What effects do transportation subsidies have on the distribution of income?

The second part of the chapter, "Choosing among Transportation Systems," deals with problems of the longer run. What are the costs and benefits of alternative transportation systems? How can cities make rational decisions to invest in new facilities?

A third major section covers government policy and transportation choices. The chapter closes with a discussion of the connection among energy prices, transportation behavior, residential location, and urban form.

TRANSPORTATION PRICING IN PRACTICE

The gap between theory and practice in transportation pricing is considerable. Historically both highway and transit charges have been based on average cost calculations rather than on the marginal cost principles explained in Chapter 8. Although serious transit deficits have developed, they certainly cannot be blamed on marginal cost pricing, since that system has rarely been used in transit operations.

In the case of highways, tolls are charged only on major bridges, tunnels, and a few heavily traveled turnpikes. Even in those cases the

TABLE 9.1
Highway Expenditures and Receipts from Users, 1975 (Pay-as-You-Go Basis)

	TOTAL (MILLIONS OF DOLLARS)		PER VEHICLE MILE (CENTS)	
	Expenditures	*Receipts from Users*	*Expenditures*	*Receipts from Users*
All roads	26,176	21,194	2.00	1.62
Urban roads	10,327	11,672	1.48	1.68
Rural roads	15,849	9,522	2.59	1.56

Source: Calculated from data in John R. Meyer and José A. Gómez-Ibáñez, *Autos, Transit and Cities* (Cambridge, Mass.: Harvard University Press, 1981), tables 11.4–11.7. Meyer's figures were computed from data in Kiran Bhatt, Michael Beesley, and Kevin Neels, *An Analysis of Road Expenditures and Payments by Vehicle Class (1956–1975)* (Washington, D.C.: Urban Institute, March 1977).

tolls are almost always flat rates that do not vary, as a marginal cost–based toll would, according to the degree of congestion. The major charges paid by highway users are state and federal gasoline taxes; federal excise taxes on trucks and buses, tires, parts, and accessories; and state registration and license fees. These are indeed "user charges" in that they are paid more or less in proportion to highway use. Whether these payments equal or fall short of the aggregate annual cost of building, maintaining, and servicing highways in the United States depends on how capital outlays are treated. Table 9.1, based on a study by Meyer and Gómez-Ibáñez, shows that when costs are calculated on a pay-as-you-go basis, user payments covered only 81 percent of expenditure in 1975. Moreover, the table does not include indirect or external costs, such as accidents or pollution. Until 1965, highway-related revenues approximately equaled expenditures, but since most gasoline taxes are fixed in terms of cents per gallon, tax revenues failed to increase as costs rose with inflation after that date.

Regardless of whether roads in the aggregate are paying their own way, large intersectoral subsidies undoubtedly occur *within* the highway system, which is therefore not efficiently priced at the microlevel. As indicated in Table 9.1, urban roads as a whole generated revenues in excess of costs in 1975, while rural roads ran a very large deficit. Within each sector there are also substantial inequalities. Meyer and Gómez-Ibáñez estimate that the cost of providing extra lanes to accommodate rush-hour traffic on urban expressways in the center of large cities may run as high as 30 cents per vehicle mile (in 1973 dollars).[1] Thus the rush-hour driver would have to pay a toll of about 30 cents a mile to cover the marginal cost (not including externalities) of accommodat-

1. John R. Meyer and José A. Gómez-Ibáñez, *Autos, Transit and Cities* (Cambridge, Mass.: Harvard University Press, 1981), pp. 198–199, 205.

ing a trip to the CBD of a large city. That is twenty times the urban average shown in Table 9.1, and about in line with the peak-period congestion tolls that Keeler calculated for San Francisco in 1972 (see Table 8.6).

Opposition to Congestion Tolls

Raising tolls to the levels indicated in these studies would surely arouse opposition among highway users. Reservations about the desirability of congestion tolls, however, have also been voiced by a respectable number of transportation economists. One objection is based on short-run welfare considerations. The theory of short-run congestion tolls was illustrated in Figure 8.1. Examining such a case, Wohl points out that in the short run all users of the road segment are made worse off by the imposition of congestion tolls.[2] The reduction in trips from Q_2 to Q_3 results from the fact that those drivers who decline to pay the new charges are "tolled off" the road. They must be worse off than before because they have given up trips (at least by this route) that formerly were desirable. The drivers who continue to use the road after imposition of a toll are also worse off. Congestion is reduced, so each driver's private costs fall from KE to JG. The saving in private cost amounts to GI. But to save GI in congestion cost, each driver pays a toll of GF and therefore suffers a net loss of $GF - GI = IF$. We reach the seemingly paradoxical conclusion that an optimal short-run pricing policy leaves all users of the road worse off.

But there is no paradox. Before imposition of higher tolls, users may have been paying less than the full cost of the road. They are receiving an unjustified subsidy, which is now taken away—no harm in that. If the higher tolls lead to a surplus of revenue above full cost, then (assuming constant long-run cost) the road should be expanded until tolls just cover average long-run costs. Users will then benefit by the provision of a highway developed to optimal capacity.

Indeed, it can be shown that users paying an optimal congestion toll on the expanded road will be better off than they were on the smaller facility *before* congestion tolls were imposed. Referring to Figure 8.2, suppose that road A were operated without congestion tolls. Equilibrium would occur at E, where the driver's average variable cost curve, AVC_A intersects the demand Curve DD'. Cost per trip would be OP_3, with no congestion toll being paid. (This corresponds to the solution at point E on Figure 8.1.) If, now, congestion tolls are imposed and the highway is expanded to its optimum size (road B), equilibrium occurs at R. Cost per trip falls to OP_1, which is less than OP_3, even though OP_1 includes a congestion toll and OP_3 does not. Each driver

---

2. Martin Wohl, "Congestion Toll Pricing for Public Transport Facilities," in Selma Mushkin, ed., *Public Prices for Public Products* (Washington, D.C.: Urban Institute, 1972), pp. 245–247.

benefits because the saving in congestion costs to each vehicle (GP_3) exceeds the required congestion toll on the expanded road (RS).

A second objection to congestion tolls is based on the cost of implementing a highly articulated toll system in which charges could vary by direction, time of day, and position on an entire road network. Not only are there costs of collection, but also, if toll booths are used, drivers will bear time costs, since toll collection reduces average trip speed. This problem has spawned some interesting proposals that would use sophisticated technology in place of the toll booth. For use in city streets, Vickrey has described a computerized electronic tracking system that could plot the course of every vehicle passing through congested areas, compute appropriate tolls, and render monthly bills to vehicle owners. Much less complex and less precise in their impact are proposed licensing systems that would simply require those driving into designated congestion-prone areas to display a special license for which they would pay an appropriate fee.[3]

A third objection concerns differential effects by income class. Since individual evaluations of time vary directly with wages, the poor tend to have lower time values. It has sometimes been argued that congestion tolls based on "average" evaluations of time will therefore be a bargain for the rich and a burden for the poor. Given the paucity of data about the incomes of those who drive through congested areas in peak hours, the question has been a difficult one to resolve.[4] A standard reply to this objection is that congestion tolls are part of a general price system necessary to achieve efficient resource use and should not be manipulated with an eye to their effects on income distribution. Moreover, the poor, as heavy users of urban bus systems (see Figure 9.2), stand to gain from improvements in bus service that would occur when tolls reduced passenger car congestion on urban streets and highways.

No doubt there is strong political opposition to the introduction of highway congestion tolls. Users are opposed because, as a group, they will be made worse off, at least in the short run. The poor believe that they will be disadvantaged as compared to the rich. In addition, there is the force of habit: drivers do not object to paying tolls on bridges or roads that were built as toll facilities, but they are outraged at proposals to institute tolls on previously free facilities. And there may be a deeper force at work as well. Perhaps people (especially Americans) feel, although they do not articulate it, that they have a fundamental, almost constitutional right to movement, which the gov-

---

3. See William S. Vickrey, "Pricing in Urban and Suburban Transport," reprinted in Ronald E. Grieson, ed., *Urban Economics: Readings and Analysis* (Boston: Little, Brown, 1973), pp. 111–113; and the discussions in Michael A. Kemp and Melvyn D. Cheslow, "Transportation," in William Gorham and Nathan Glazer, eds., *The Urban Predicament* (Washington, D.C.: Urban Institute, 1976), pp. 321–324, in Meyer and Gómez-Ibáñez, pp. 222–225, and in José A. Gómez-Ibáñez and Gary R. Fauth, "Downtown Auto Restraint Policies: The Costs and Benefits for Boston," *Journal of Transport Economics and Policy*, May 1980, pp. 133–153.

4. One of the most elaborate studies is Damian J. Kulash, *Income Distributional Consequences of Roadway Pricing* (Washington, D.C.: The Urban Institute, 1974).

FIGURE 9.1
Marginal Cost Pricing with Declining Long-run Costs

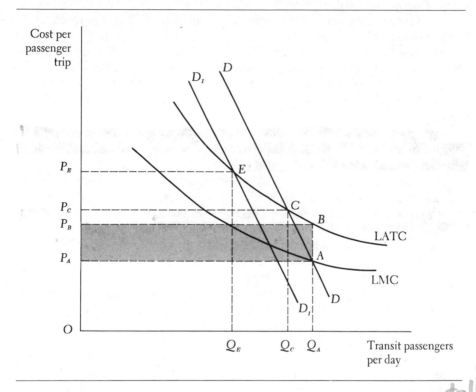

ernment ought not to infringe by anything that looks like a tax on mobility. Keeler and Small recognize that "there may be political obstacles to such tolls" but conclude that "the more general understanding there is of the benefits . . . the more feasible they will be."[5]

The Problem of Deficits under Marginal Cost Pricing

We explained in Chapter 8 that under declining-cost conditions, marginal cost pricing will generate deficits. Figure 9.1 displays declining long-run average and marginal costs such as might obtain in mass transit. To focus on financial deficits, user time costs are now ignored. The curves show agency costs only, and, to avoid clutter, short-run cost curves are omitted. When demand is given by *DD*, equilibrium under marginal cost pricing is at *A*, where the marginal cost curve intersects the demand curve. The transit authority

5. Theodore E. Keeler and Kenneth A. Small, "Optimal Peak-Load Pricing, Investment and Service Levels on Urban Expressways," *Journal of Political Economy*, February 1977, p. 24.

charges a fare of P_A, and traffic flow is Q_A trips per day. However, the average cost of a trip is P_B, well in excess of P_A. The transit authority runs a daily deficit shown by the shaded rectangle $P_A P_B BA$.

Average cost pricing would lead to equilibrium at C, where price, given by the demand curve, just covers agency cost as indicated by the average cost curve. There would be no deficit. However, the average cost solution is economically inefficient because $Q_A - Q_C$ customers are denied the use of the system even though they would be willing to pay prices (indicated by the demand curve between points C and A) in excess of the marginal costs they impose.

Economists have long debated the question of how deficits generated by marginal cost pricing should be covered. One solution would call for subsidies to be paid out of tax revenue. But taxes levied for that purpose might have harmful effects elsewhere that would offset the efficiency advantages of marginal cost as compared with average cost pricing.

Another proposal is the so-called two-part tariff. Users would be charged the marginal cost price for each unit of service taken. In addition, in order to qualify as a user, each consumer would have to pay a flat annual fee. These fees, equivalent to membership dues, would be used to cover the deficit from marginal cost pricing. Though not perfect, such an arrangement would probably cause less inefficiency in resource use than the alternative of average cost pricing.[6] It also has the advantage of ensuring that users themselves defray the full cost of the facilities that serve them instead of relying on the general taxpayer to share their burden.

Musgrave and Musgrave point out that where the facility in question produces a local service, a general local tax to cover the deficit "may be viewed as the flat-charge component of the two-part tariff, since participation in the service hinges on local residence."[7] Thus economic theory provides an argument for the use of local tax revenues to subsidize local transit deficits. In practice, however, urban transit operators may be giving us the worst of both worlds by running deficits *without* simultaneously offering the advantage of marginal cost pricing.

FINANCIAL STRESS IN THE TRANSIT INDUSTRY

The U.S. transit industry as a whole has been running at a deficit since 1963. By 1983 the aggregate annual operating loss amounted to $5.5 billion. Operating revenues covered only 37 percent of expenses. These and other industry statistics are summarized in Table 9.2. Two periods can be distinguished: the years of ridership decline, ending in 1972, and the period of mod-

6. This point is more fully developed in Richard A. Musgrave and Peggy B. Musgrave, *Public Finance in Theory and Practice*, 4th ed. (New York: McGraw-Hill, 1984), pp. 736–737.
   7. Ibid., p. 737, n. 3.

TABLE 9.2
Transit Industry Revenues and Costs[a]

	1950	1965	1972	1983	PERCENT CHANGE, 1972–1983
Output					
Total passenger rides[b] (millions)	17,246	8,253	6,567	7,889	20.1
Vehicle miles operated (millions)	3,008	2,008	1,756	2,117	20.6
Operating results					
Operating revenues (millions of dollars)	1,452	1,444	1,729	3,231	86.9
Operating expenses (millions of dollars)	1,386	1,454	2,242	8,736	289.7
Operating surplus (or deficit) (millions of dollars)	66	(10)	(513)	(5,505)	973.1
Average fare (cents)	10.0	19.7	31.4	54.9[c]	—
Financial assistance					
Total operating assistance (millions of dollars)	NA	NA	NA	5,022	—
Local and state	NA	NA	NA	4,195	—
Federal	NA	NA	NA	827	—
Federal capital grant approval (millions of dollars)	—	50.7	508.6	3,162	521.7
Labor costs					
Average annual earnings per employee ($)	3,479	6,645	10,515	20,114	91.3
Number of employees	240,000	145,000	138,420	194,960	40.8
Vehicle miles per employee	12,533	13,848	12,686	10,858	−14.4
Total passenger rides per employee	71,858	56,917	47,443	40,465	−14.7

[a]Includes rail transit, trolley coach, and motor bus.
[b]The sum of rides by initial-board revenue passengers, plus rides by transfer passengers and by those entitled to free service.
[c]Average fare for 1983 not strictly comparable with earlier years, hence percentage change omitted.
Source: American Public Transit Association, *Transit Fact Book, 1981 and 1985.*

est recovery since that date. The number of passenger rides fell 62 percent from 1950 to the low point reached in 1972. Ridership recovered slightly thereafter but by 1983 was still 54 percent below its 1950 level. We have seen that transit service benefits from economies of scale as demand increases. Unfortunately that means it suffers from diseconomies if demand moves the other way: cost per trip rises as demand falls.

As illustrated in Figure 9.1, an urban transit operator might traditionally have charged an average cost fare and broken even at point C. However, with the rise of automobile ownership and the decline of central city population, the demand for trips shifts steadily to the left and average cost rises. Nevertheless, as long as the demand curve continues to intersect the average cost curve at all, the point of intersection indicates a fare at which the operating authority could meet its costs out of fare revenues. Conceivably, demand could shift so far to the left that no intersection occurs and deficits become unavoidable. Kemp and Cheslow, however, find little evidence that such a disjunction has actually occurred.[8]

In the period from 1950 to 1972, as Table 9.2 shows, the average fare rose 214 percent. That was far in excess of the 74 percent increase in the cost of living but was not sufficient to keep up with operating costs per trip, which rose not only because of the decline in ridership but also as a result of rapidly escalating labor costs. Transit fares are a highly visible charge. With the rise of public transit ownership they have also become a major political issue. Elected officials frequently run on a "save the fare" plank. They try to avoid fare increases until every alternative has been exhausted. One alternative is to reduce service frequency, which has less political impact. Unfortunately, since ridership is more sensitive to service levels than to fare levels, it contributes strongly to the further decline of patronage.

That transit deficits should have developed during the years when ridership was declining is scarcely to be wondered at. That the deficits should have increased even more sharply after 1972, when ridership began a gradual recovery, has been both surprising and disturbing.

Subsidies for Mass Transit

Public subsidy is, of course, the only possible source of funds to cover transit deficits. Since most mass transit systems are now owned by local public authorities, deficits are the responsibility primarily of local governments. In some cases states bear some of the burden, and since 1974 the federal government has also contributed operating subsidies through the Urban Mass Transportation Administration (UMTA; see data in Table 9.2).

In 1983 federal government subsidies amounted to $827 million and covered about 15 percent of operating deficits. Federal funds are distributed

8. Kemp and Cheslow, p. 333.

by a formula heavily weighted by population. Since large cities have a much higher proportion of transit users than small cities, they receive a systematically smaller subsidy per user. This strikes many observers as perverse. Mahlon Straszheim points out that such a formula is intended "to avoid the disincentives associated with basing assistance on the size of the operating deficit."[9] It probably also reflects a need to spread aid widely among congressional districts if it is to muster enough political support for passage.

Explaining Growth of the Transit Deficit

A study completed for UMTA in 1983 helps to explain how the transit industry got so deeply into the red. The study accounts for the growth in operating deficits between 1970 and 1980 as follows.[10]

1. *Reduction in fares and expansion of service*. The failure of fares to rise as rapidly as the general price level accounted for an estimated 28 percent of the deficit's growth. (Table 9.2 shows that the average fare less than doubled from 1972 to 1983, while the cost of living went up 138 percent.) Increases in vehicle miles operated, which raised costs, accounted for another 16 percent of the increase. (Table 9.2 shows a 21 percent increase in vehicle miles operated between 1972 and 1983.)

This portion of the findings must be interpreted with care. On the one hand, the availability of operating subsidies undoubtedly made it easier for transit authorities to run deficits and so encouraged deficits to grow. On the other hand, it was the clear intention of the government that subsidies be used to hold down fares and extend service by introducing new routes in the hope of increasing ridership and thereby reducing air pollution and energy consumption. Consequently, one cannot fault transit operators for doing those things, even though they produced larger deficits.

2. *Increase in cost per vehicle mile*. Rising operating expense per vehicle mile accounted for 55 percent of the growth in the deficit. Of this, 25 percent was the result of increased compensation per labor hour. (Real hourly compensation in transit rose almost one-third during the decade, far in excess of the gain among private-sector workers.)[11] Another 18 percent of deficit growth resulted from falling labor productivity. (Table 9.2 shows the decline in vehicle miles per employee.) Higher fuel, power, and miscellaneous costs accounted for the remaining 12 percent.

9. Mahlon R. Straszheim, "Assessing the Social Costs of Urban Transportation Technologies," in Peter Mieszkowski and Mahlon Straszheim, eds., *Current Issues in Urban Economics* (Baltimore: Johns Hopkins University Press, 1979), p. 227.

10. Don H. Pickrell, *The Causes of Rising Transit Operating Deficits* (Washington, D.C.: U.S. Department of Transportation, Urban Mass Transportation Administration, July 1983), table 2.2. Also see John Pucher et al., "Impacts of Subsidies on the Costs of Urban Public Transport," *Journal of Transport Economics and Policy*, May 1983, pp. 155–176.

11. Pickrell, p. 32.

Apparently, the availability of operating subsidies encouraged transit authorities to grant generous wage increases during the 1970s while at the same time weakening their incentive to use labor productively. These outcomes, which account for more than 40 percent of the growth in the deficit, were certainly *not* intended by policymakers and make up one of the principal arguments against the use of transit operating subsidies.

It must be added, however, that operating cost per vehicle mile has also been pushed upward by a cause over which transit operators have relatively little control: the increased concentration of trips into the morning and evening peak hours. It was pointed out in Chapter 8 that the automobile has great advantages for off-peak shopping and recreation trips. Transit operators must continue to bear the great expense of providing adequate peak hour capacity but have fewer and fewer off-peak riders over whom to spread the resulting costs.[12]

In addition, the transit industry provides a classic example of the "productivity lag" problem that afflicts many local government services (see Chapter 14). Even if wage settlements were not excessive, transit wages would have to rise at more or less the same rate as private industrial wages. But labor productivity in the transit industry not only lags behind the increases registered in the private sector, but is actually falling. Unit labor cost equals wages per worker divided by output per worker. With wages rising and output per worker falling, unit labor cost in the transit industry has increased sharply in recent years. If transit wages in the new era of austerity do no more than keep up with the cost of living, "productivity lag" nevertheless makes the outlook for transit finances decidedly grim.

Grimmest of all is the outlook in declining older cities that have rail mass transit systems. Since rail mass transit displays marked economies of scale, it also suffers pronounced diseconomies when population and therefore patronage fall off. Once such an interconnected system is built, one cannot economize by abandoning portions of it. There is no way to cut the cost of operating and maintaining the system except by reducing service frequency, and that, as we have already argued, is likely to lower patronage even further and certainly imposes severe waiting costs on remaining users.

Income Effects of Mass Transit Subsidies

What effect do mass transit subsidies have on the distribution of income? Who gains and who loses from this policy? The answer is not self-evident and can only be worked out through a complex series of estimates that assign benefits and tax burdens to each income class and then calculate the gain or loss to each as the net difference. After carrying out such a study using 1979 data for both operating and capital subsidies, John Pucher con-

12. Ibid., p. 25; and Meyer and Gómez-Ibáñez, p. 55.

FIGURE 9.2
Percentage of Users in Each Income Class for Each Mode of
Transportation, U.S. Metropolitan Areas, 1977–1978

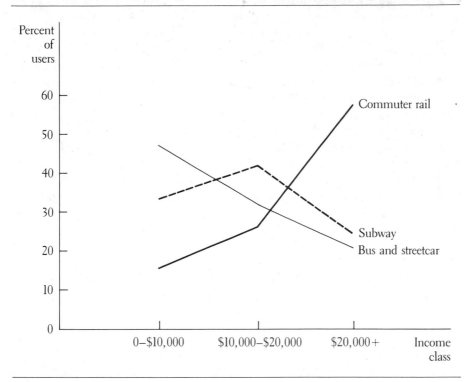

Source: Calculated from John Pucher, "Equity in Transit Finance," *Journal of the American Planning Association*, October 1981, table 1, p. 389.

cluded that for the nation as a whole, the poor *do* make net gains, albeit rather small ones, from the transit subsidy program.[13]

On the revenue side, Pucher made the standard assumptions about tax incidence, leading to the conclusion that federal taxes supporting transit subsidies are quite progressive with respect to income, while state and local taxes in the aggregate are mildly regressive. In 1978 the weight of the federal contribution was sufficient to make the combined tax effort slightly progressive. Pucher assumed that subsidy benefits were distributed to each income class in proportion to the use that class made of each subsidized mode, as calculated from a national survey (see Figure 9.2). Transit comprises three modes: subway, bus and streetcar, and commuter rail. Use of the first two is heavily

13. John Pucher, "Equity in Transit Finance: Distribution of Transit Subsidy Benefits and Costs among Income Classes," *Journal of the American Planning Association*, October 1981, pp. 387–407.

concentrated in the lower and middle income ranges, while use of commuter rail is largely by those in the highest income class. When use of the three modes is combined, per capita subsidy benefits are found to be higher for the relatively poor than the relatively rich.[14] Subtracting estimated taxes from estimated benefits for each income class, Pucher found that lower-income groups are net gainers and upper-income groups are net losers on account of transit subsidies.

These results were estimated from aggregate national data. For particular localities the outcome might be different, depending on what kinds of transit are subsidized and what taxes are levied to pay the cost. For example, some of the new rail transit systems, such as San Francisco's BART, have not been designed to serve the central city (as the old subway systems were) but rather to bring suburban commuters into the CBD. We know that the gradient of income in U.S. metropolitan areas rises with distance from the central city. Hence BART's riders, like those using commuter rail in Figure 9.2, are predominantly from the high end of the income scale. If somewhat regressive local taxes are used to subsidize that kind of system, the result may be a perverse redistribution of income from the relatively poor to the relatively rich. Such, at least, was one researcher's conclusion regarding BART.[15] On the other hand, in a study of five individual metropolitan areas having a typical mix of transit modes (none of them new rail systems) Pucher found the distribution of benefits (measured in terms of reduced fares) to be sufficiently pro-poor so that even if transit subsidies were financed only by regressive state and local taxes, the poor would still be net gainers.[16]

In theory, however, distributional effects should not be given much weight in establishing a policy for transit subsidies and fares. Economists usually argue that it is best, where possible, to let the pricing system do its work of allocating resources efficiently and then, if income adjustments are desirable, to make them by direct transfers that interfere as little as possible with efficient pricing. In that spirit, Kemp and Cheslow suggest that if we wish to help the "transportation disadvantaged" through subsidies, we might develop programs that would specifically select them to ride at lower cost while "setting fares to the rest of the population . . . solely on the basis of making the urban transportation system work most efficiently."[17]

CHOOSING AMONG TRANSPORTATION SYSTEMS

Because the choice of a transportation system influences a city's land-use pattern and therefore its very lifestyle, decisions about transportation in-

14. Ibid., table 4.

15. E. Gareth Hoachlander, "Bay Area Rapid Transit: Who Pays and Who Benefits?" Working Paper no. 267 (Berkeley, Calif.: Institute of Urban and Regional Development, University of California, July 1976).

16. John Pucher and Ira Hirschman, "Distribution of the Transit Tax Burden in Five U.S. Metropolitan Areas," *Transportation*, March 1982, pp. 23–25.

17. Kemp and Cheslow, p. 342.

vestment are recognized by the public, by city planners, and by politicians as having paramount importance. True, the existence of structures inherited from the past makes it a rare occasion when a city can choose to develop a whole new system. But decisions must frequently be made to expand or contract, to maintain or to abandon what already exits. Localities must make choices about how to use not only their own monies but also funds of the state and federal governments. To make rational transportation investment decisions, one must know both the costs and the benefits of alternative modes. Let us look first at costs.

Intermodal Cost Comparisons

The results of Keeler's intermodal cost comparison for a suburb-to-CBD commuter trip were presented in Figure 8.3. Costs comprise both agency outlays and the value of user inputs, including time. Although the results of intermodal cost comparisons depend on particular assumptions as to interest rates, time values, and trip lengths, Keeler's findings are broadly consistent with those of earlier studies.[18] For the suburb-to-CBD trip, integrated bus is by far the least costly mode, except at very low traffic densities. Even at the highest assumed volume of 30,000 peak-hour passengers in the major direction in a single corridor, the full cost (not just the fare) of a one-way, six-mile BART plus feeder bus trip is $3.73, almost 50 percent more than a trip by integrated bus. As traffic volume drops below 30,000, the cost advantage of bus over rail increases markedly. In terms of cost, auto is competitive with bus at low traffic volumes. More surprising, it is significantly cheaper than BART until a volume of 20,000 per corridor per hour is reached.

Since the average cost of public transit depends heavily on traffic volume, it is important to know what the actual range of volumes is. For years around 1960, Meyer, Kain, and Wohl have reported the approximate volume of peak-hour traffic per corridor leaving the CBD in selected U.S. cities. New York was far ahead of any other city, with a volume averaging above 60,000 persons. Chicago was next, with 30,000 to 40,000. Philadelphia, Boston, and Washington averaged between 20,000 and 30,000, Los Angeles and San Francisco between 13,000 and 20,000. Cleveland, Detroit, Atlanta, and Baltimore ranged between 9,000 and 13,000.[19]

No other U.S. city is likely ever to approach the peak-hour traffic volume generated in New York City. Keeler's study and other intermodal comparisons indicate that at the maximum traffic densities existing elsewhere, and under today's construction and operating cost conditions, integrated express bus offers a far cheaper ride than rail mass transit. Indeed, the figures suggest that at the traffic levels generated in most cities, even the private automobile is cheaper than rail.

18. See studies cited in ch. 8, n. 27.
19. J. R. Meyer, J. F. Kain, and M. Wohl, *The Urban Transportation Problem* (Cambridge, Mass.: Harvard University Press, 1965), table 25.

Five of the older large cities—New York, Chicago, Philadelphia, Boston, and Cleveland—have had rail mass transit for many years. In those cities the cost of construction has long been properly treated as a sunk cost, not relevant for any current decisions, which should be based only on the cost of continuing to operate existing systems as compared with the cost of providing alternatives. In such comparisons rail undoubtedly continues to be the least costly alternative. Other cities—including San Francisco, Washington, Atlanta, Miami, Baltimore, and Buffalo—have recently completed rail transit systems. For these cities, too, construction is now a sunk cost. Except in the case of San Francisco, however, the cost disadvantage of rail as compared with bus was already under discussion at the time they began building, as a result of Meyer, Kain, and Wohl's work. The later studies cited here merely confirmed it. Why new systems were built despite their cost disadvantage is a matter to which we shall return.

It is important to remember, however, that cost minimization is not an objective in economics except when it can be said that all other things are equal. That is certainly not the case with respect to urban trip making. Even apart from differences in time and money cost, few riders will judge trips by auto, bus, and rail to be perfectly equivalent in other respects. The average rider appears to regard the automobile as superior in both comfort and convenience to either of the public modes.

The high cost of the new rail systems is attributable in part to the desire to provide a ride that can compete with the automobile in speed and comfort, in the hope of luring drivers out of their cars and reducing traffic congestion, air pollution, and fuel consumption. Buses are often thought to be less comfortable and attractive than modern rail transit, but there is increasing evidence to the contrary. In a number of large cities private firms now operate high-quality bus service from the suburbs to the CBD that apparently competes on comfort and price with the auto and rail alternatives and is profitable, even though completely unsubsidized.[20]

In comparing modes, flexibility must also be taken into account. Rail mass transit is extraordinarily inflexible. Once the lines have been built, they cannot be moved. If they turn out to have been built in the wrong place, a great deal of capital will have been wasted. Bus systems, on the other hand, are highly flexible. Capital costs account for only a small part of the cost per ride, if we make the reasonable assumption that buses do not have to bear the cost of highway construction. Old bus routes can be contracted or abandoned and new routes developed using the same equipment. The only construction costs involved (and risked) would be for reserved entry and exit ramps or special traffic controls used in developing express bus service. Failure to predict

20. See Ronald J. Fisher, "'Megatrends' in Urban Transport," *Transportation Quarterly*, January 1984, pp. 92–93; and Edward K. Morlok and Philip A. Viton, "Recent Experience with Successful Private Transit in Large U.S. Cities," in Charles A. Lave, ed., *Urban Transit* (San Francisco: Pacific Institute for Public Policy Research, 1985), pp. 121–149.

traffic demand accurately in a changing world thus involves much less risk in the case of buses than that of a fixed rail system.

Pollution and Other External Costs

The full social cost of transportation includes not only the costs borne by the individual user and by the operating agency but also external costs caused by transportation but thrown off onto third parties. It must be emphasized at the outset that these external costs are extraordinarily difficult to measure. Data are generally inadequate, and results are highly sensitive to assumptions made by the analyst. The art of measuring "full social costs" is still in its infancy.

We have already analyzed congestion costs as a form of externality. This and several other externalities are included, though not shown separately, in Keeler's estimates of the full costs of urban trips in Figure 8.3. However, since the cost of pollution and other externalities, especially those due to the automobile, is a public issue in its own right, it merits separate attention. A list of external costs (other than congestion) attributable to the automobile would include the following.

1. *Air pollution.* Automobile emissions are acknowledged to be an important source of air pollution. However, the damage costs that an automobile produces per vehicle mile vary greatly according to the age of the car, which determines what sort of emission controls it has, and the location in which it is driven, which determines how likely emissions are to accumulate locally. Natural air movement provides every locality with some capacity to disperse pollutants—a capacity that varies with local topography. However, the number of automobiles and other sources of pollution rises as population per square mile increases. Therefore, the larger the metropolitan area, the less able are natural air movements to disperse the resulting pollutants. Consequently damage cost per vehicle mile rises with population size and density.

Given the difficulties of measurement and the extent of local variability, economists recognize that their estimates of automobile air pollution costs are highly tentative. Keeler placed the cost at about .5 cents per vehicle mile in the Bay area in 1972.[21] Straszheim, using a different approach, estimated a value of about 1.3 cents per vehicle mile for urban areas as of 1975.[22] Meyer and Gómez-Ibáñez estimated the cost per vehicle mile at about .8 cents averaged over all urban areas in the early 1970s.[23]

21. See Theodore E. Keeler et al., *The Full Costs of Urban Transport*, part 3, monograph 21 (Berkeley, Calif.: Institute of Urban and Regional Development, University of California, July 1975), pp. 51–54, for estimates of this and other automobile externality costs.

22. Straszheim, table 7.5, p. 214. This is the sum of pollution abatement costs (.77 cent) and residual (unabated) pollution damage (.50 cents). Straszheim's estimates of other automobile costs appear in the same table.

23. Meyer and Gómez-Ibáñez, pp. 206–207.

2. *Noise, smell, aesthetic loss.* It is generally agreed that major highways create undesirable noise and smell and diminish aesthetic values for adjacent properties. Keeler evaluated Bay area noise pollution at .1 cent per vehicle mile. Straszheim, using noise as a proxy for all such proximity effects, estimated the cost at .6 cents along urban freeways. He then added another .3 cents for property losses in the form of inadequate compensation to owners whose property is acquired for a highway right-of-way after the foreknowledge of construction has already reduced its value.

Elevated urban expressways can cause particularly grave aesthetic damage. Probably the most awful example is downtown Boston's Fitzgerald Expressway. Based on an estimate of lost property value, Meyer and Gómez-Ibáñez place the resulting aesthetic damage cost at the astounding figure of $.66 to $1.16 per vehicle mile of utilization, in 1979 dollars.[24] Given aesthetic costs of those dimensions, it is no wonder the citizens of San Francisco halted construction of the Embarcadero Freeway along the Bay and those of New Orleans blocked a highway that would have passed in front of the old French Quarter.

3. *Disruption of communities.* In addition to the losses highways impose on nearby property owners, they may cause wider damage to entire communities. A limited-access highway built through a city may permanently obstruct access between the neighborhoods on either side, adding to the communication costs of individuals and weakening or destroying social organizations that depend on a community base. This form of externality, however, has not been measured.

4. *Government service costs.* The operation of a highway system entails public sector costs for planning, administration, traffic control, and police service that are not included in conventional calculations of highway costs, nor are they reimbursed out of highway-related revenues. These are, in a broad sense, external costs thrown off by highway beneficiaries onto the public sector. Keeler estimates their value at .5 cent per vehicle mile. Straszheim does not count them.

The costs tallied by Keeler come to 1.1 cents per vehicle mile. Figure 8.3 shows that he estimated the full cost of a six-mile auto trip (including the value of time and the cost of parking) at $4.15. Pollution costs apparently account for only 7 cents out of that total—not enough to affect intermodal cost comparison significantly.

According to Straszheim's estimate, externalities other than congestion amounted to 2.2 cents per vehicle mile for urban areas in 1975. Exclusive of externalities (and excluding the value of time and the cost of parking), he calculated the private cost of operating an automobile plus the public cost of providing roadways at 14.5 cents per vehicle mile in the same year. Including

24. Ibid., pp. 176–177, citing a study by David Segal. Also see Jon P. Nelson, "Highway Noise and Property Values," *Journal of Transport Economics and Policy,* May 1982, pp. 117–138.

externalities would add 15 percent to that narrower cost figure. Seen in that light, the external costs of automobile pollution are far from trivial.

Benefit-Cost Analysis of Transportation Projects

In principle, transportation investment decisions ought to be made on the basis of a benefit-cost analysis of alternatives.[25] For each alternative, a complete accounting should be made in money terms of all benefits and costs, both direct and external, estimated over the useful life of the project. Next, both the benefit stream and the cost stream should be discounted to obtain present values.[26] The aggregate present value of benefits should then be compared with that of costs and the excess of benefits over costs calculated for each alternative. This excess, or net benefit, measures the net gain to society as a whole from undertaking a given project.

The appropriate decision rule to follow when using benefit-cost analysis depends on such circumstances as whether or not the projects under consideration are mutually exclusive and whether or not budgetary constraints exist. In the case of transportation projects, the alternatives usually *are* mutually exclusive—one builds either a large bridge or a small one, but not both. In such cases the public authority should choose the alternative that yields the largest excess of benefits over costs within the budget constraint, if there is one.

There is a strong formal similarity between the benefit-cost calculus prescribed for investment decisions in the public sector and the profit-maximizing calculus of the ordinary private investor. Net benefit in the former is the excess of benefits over costs, including the cost of capital. Economic profit in the latter is the excess of revenues over costs, including the cost of capital. The appropriate decision-making rules are the same in both sectors if the circumstances are similar.

In one respect, however, the benefit-cost calculus is superior to its private-sector counterpart. At least in principle, benefit-cost analysis takes external costs and benefits systematically into account, whereas the private sector almost always ignores them.[27] Admittedly, the measurement of external-

---

25. For an introduction to the theory and practice of cost-benefit analysis that contains numerous citations to its use in connection with transportation investment, see A. R. Prest and R. Turvey, "Cost-Benefit Analysis: A Survey" in International Economic Association, *Surveys of Economic Theory*, vol. 3 (New York: St. Martin's Press, 1966), pp. 155–207.

26. For an explanation of the meaning of present value and of its importance in comparing cost and benefit streams, see Musgrave and Musgrave, pp. 178–179, or some other standard text on public finance.

27. Since the publication of R. H. Coase's classic article on "The Problem of Social Cost" (*Journal of Law and Economics*, October 1960, pp. 1–44), it has generally been agreed that if the private-sector parties concerned are few enough in number, we should expect them to arrive through bargaining at a solution in which externalities are fully (and optimally) taken into account. In practice, however, the parties are usually too numerous to permit such a "market solution" to the problem of externalities.

ities is fraught with difficulty, but it is not impossible, as the preceding section demonstrated.

Unfortunately, the benefit-cost approach to evaluating investment alternatives cannot readily be applied to whole transportation systems. Its analytical method assumes a given economic context, or state of the world, in which the benefits and costs of alternatives can be measured. Entire alternative systems, however, are likely to produce environments so different as to render quantitative comparison between them virtually impossible. On the other hand, benefit-cost analysis has proved useful in dealing with increments to existing networks. As we shall see in the next section, however, the impact of a new facility on an existing transportation system can be very complicated to measure. Quantitative results must be regarded as approximate at best.

Transportation Benefits

In their well-known benefit-cost study of the Victoria Line, a proposed addition to the London underground, C. D. Foster and M. E. Beesley traced out systemwide benefits according to the scheme outlined here.[28] Although developed for the analysis of a mass transportation project, these benefit categories apply equally well to improvements in an urban highway system.

1. *Benefits to diverted traffic.* A new link added to a transit system will attract some riders who previously made the trip by a different mode or route. These passengers are diverted to the new line because it offers a superior alternative to the means used previously. Their net benefits may take the form of time savings, greater comfort due to reduced crowding, or, if they had previously used an automobile, savings in vehicle operating costs.

2. *Benefits to undiverted traffic.* The diversion of traffic to a new link reduces congestion or discomfort on other transit routes or on city streets, thereby spreading benefits systemwide. People who continue to use other routes or modes make gains in the form of improved comfort, greater speed, or both. In addition, there may be cost savings to the transit authority in operating fewer vehicles on the preexisting network. Foster and Beesley estimated that net benefits to undiverted traffic would account for 52 percent of total net benefits of the Victoria Line. The size of this component underscores the importance of looking at systemwide effects when evaluating transportation improvements.

3. *Benefits to generated traffic.* A new facility, by improving the accessibility of certain destinations, will induce people to make additional trips. The value to be attributed to these generated trips is probably the most uncertain

28. "Estimating the Social Benefit of Constructing an Underground Railway in London," reprinted in M. E. Beesley, *Urban Transport: Studies in Economic Policy* (London: Butterworths, 1973), ch. 1. Foster and Beesley's study was originally published in 1962; the Victoria Line was built subsequently and completed in 1969.

calculation of all. As a first approximation, it can be measured by the fares that riders willingly pay for them.

Foster and Beesley estimated the value of the expected benefits of the Victoria Line under each of the three headings. The aggregate present value of benefits over the life of the project far exceeded expected costs. Consequently, the study showed that building the Victoria Line would produce a substantial net gain for society. The authors did not estimate the external costs or benefits of the line because the necessary information was not available at the time. They were convinced, however, that the omitted externalities would have provided additional net benefits.

The expected rate of return provides another perspective on the desirability of an investment project. Foster and Beesley estimated that the internal rate of return on the Victoria Line project would be about 10.5 percent. This number is calculated as the rate of discount that will make the present value of all expected benefits equal to the present value of all expected costs. When the internal rate of return is higher than the opportunity cost of capital, a project is held to be worth undertaking. The private market rate of interest is one possible measure of the opportunity cost of capital, but whether it is the most appropriate measure has been a matter for extended debate among economists.[29] In any case, a return of 10.5 percent in 1962 was well in excess of any then current measure of the opportunity cost of capital. Hence the Victoria Line looked like a socially profitable undertaking. However, since benefit-cost studies were not conducted simultaneously for alternative projects, one could not be certain that it was the most desirable of all possible ways to improve London's transportation.

External Benefits of Mass Transit

Since the automobile is a major source of air pollution and other environmental damage, it can be argued that substitution of mass transit for the automobile, when traffic levels are sufficiently high, will tend to reduce environmental damage. Such reduction can legitimately be counted as an external benefit of mass transportation. However, since we have already treated these environmental effects as external *costs* of automobile transportation, it is not necessary to repeat the discussion, and it would in fact be double-counting were we also to reckon their removal as an external *benefit* of mass transit in an intermodal benefit-cost comparison.

Distribution of Transportation Benefits

The direct benefits of a passenger transportation system are those that accrue to its users. The characteristics of users, and hence the distribution of

29. See Musgrave and Musgrave, pp. 179–182.

benefits, vary systematically by mode. A highway-passenger automobile system, for example, cannot be used by the young, the old, the infirm, or those too poor to own a car. These groups, sometimes referred to as the transportation-disadvantaged, are more dependent than the rest of the population on the use of public transportation. As our earlier discussion of transit pricing and subsidies suggests, the question of how the benefits of new projects or policies will be distributed among social and economic classes has received increased attention in recent years. We return to it below in connection with "paratransit."

GOVERNMENT POLICY AND TRANSPORTATION CHOICES

The consumer is the ultimate judge of transportation systems. The rise of the automobile and the decline of public transportation no doubt reflect fundamental shifts in demand as consumers' incomes increase and as technological change offers them new choices. Yet transportation choices are also influenced by decisions of government. Urban transportation is not supplied under conditions of competition in which one might assume a sort of automatic, incremental response of supply to the dictates of demand. On the contrary, investment is "lumpy" rather than incremental, service is usually in the hands of a monopolist, and the hands are frequently those of government. Consequently, public policy does matter. Federal policy is particularly important, not only because of the federal government's superior financial capability but also because it can and does use its financial strength to influence state and local policy by attaching conditions to its grants. In keeping with the developmental perspective employed throughout this book, it is appropriate to describe the broad trends in federal transportation policy as they have affected the development of urban and metropolitan areas.

Focus on Highways: 1916 to 1964

Federal aid to the states for highway construction began in 1916 and increased almost yearly thereafter. In 1956 the Highway Trust Fund was established to finance the new federal interstate highway system out of receipts from federal excise taxes on vehicles, gasoline, and tires. By 1965 federal aid to state and local governments for highway programs (including Trust Fund payments) had reached $4 billion per annum. Yet that was the first year in which mass transit received substantial federal support.

Furthermore, federal money for the interstate system was available on a 90–10 matching basis: local officials could obtain 90 cents of outside funds by putting up 10 cents from their own taxpayers. That is an offer difficult to refuse, especially when one considers that new roads bring not only transportation benefits but also the local economic stimulus and political leverage that come from expensive construction projects. There can be little doubt that the 90–10 highway formula distorted local choices away from alternative transportation investments and led to the construction of some roads that local users would never have agreed to pay for on their own.

For fifty years, then, federal policy facilitated the financing of highways, and consequently the suburbanization of metropolitan America, while ignoring the problems of public transportation. It is true that for much of the period highways were not being subsidized, since user-based taxes approximately covered costs. Nevertheless, it was important that an institutional arrangement had been developed to finance highways, while no such financial mechanism was devised for public modes.

Capital Grants for Mass Transit, 1964 to the Present

In the early 1960s there began a revival of interest in rail mass transit, in cities that previously lacked it, as an alternative to continued expansion of urban highway systems. Many influences converged to bring this about, among them the rising concern with air pollution, to which automobiles are a major contributor; dissatisfaction with the traffic congestion associated with urban growth; and, perhaps most important of all, the increasingly effective opposition to the destructive effects of major highways on the aesthetic character and daily life of urban neighborhoods.[30] (Somewhat later the energy crisis, with its suggestion that we may come to regret an exclusive commitment to the fuel-hungry automobile, added an additional argument for reconsidering mass transit.)

With these forces operating, a second period in the development of federal policy began. Instead of emphasizing highway construction as the solution to all urban transportation problems, the federal government now sought to encourage the development of "balanced" transportation systems in metropolitan areas.[31] "Balance" meant support for public modes as well as for highways. The Urban Mass Transportation Act of 1964 authorized the first substantial federal grants to support urban public transit. In 1966 the U.S. Department of Transportation was established, and in 1968 the Urban Mass Transportation Administration was created within the department to coordinate its urban efforts.

During its first ten years, the federal assistance program emphasized grants for capital improvements and for demonstration projects. The rationale for the new approach was spelled out in an influential study by Lyle Fitch and William S. Vickrey. They argued that it was important "to put com-

30. See Kemp and Cheslow, pp. 299–308, for an extended discussion of "discontent with the automobile."
31. Meyer and Gómez-Ibáñez, pp. 9–11.

peting forms of urban transportation—private automobile and public transportation—on an equal footing" with regard to public support. They favored federal capital grants to public transportation systems to be used either for modernization of old facilities or for construction of new ones, and they held out the hope that many transit systems could "be given a new lease on life with the application of modern, low-operating-cost, efficient technology."[32]

This line of reasoning led the federal government to an early emphasis on capital grants for rail mass transit. Existing systems were extended in the old cities of the North and East, and new systems were built or planned in Washington, Atlanta, Baltimore, Miami, and Buffalo. The matching ratio was 2:1 until 1973, when it was increased to 4:1. Supporters of these new systems believed that modernized, comfortable, high-speed rail transit would prove able to compete effectively with the automobile. Political pressures also supported rail transit as opposed to such alternatives as modernized express bus systems. What mayor would not prefer to run for reelection as builder of an elaborate new subway line rather than as sponsor of a possibly more efficient but certainly less visible express bus system?

Politics also influenced the configuration of the new rail systems. In order to marshal financial support from well-to-do suburbs, sponsors tended to choose route layouts that maximized the suburban catchment area while slighting intra–central city service.[33] Indeed, the new rail systems were consciously designed to take on the automobile in head-to-head competition for the suburb–to–central city work trip. We turn next to an evaluation of the first of these new systems to be completed.

San Francisco's BART

Although the Bay Area Rapid Transit system eventually met about 18 percent of its capital cost with federal grants, it was begun before federal aid was contemplated, with funds raised through a local bond issue. Because it was the first of the post–World War II systems in the United States to have been completed—partial service began in 1972 and full service in 1974—BART offers the longest record on which to judge performance. Consequently, evaluating the Bay area system is the best way to illustrate the difficulties new U.S. rail transit facilities have faced or are likely to encounter.[34]

BART was built with the intention of reducing the Bay area's dependence on the automobile by offering commuters a rail route from relatively distant suburbs to the central business districts of Oakland and San Fran-

32. Lyle Fitch et al., *Urban Transportation and Public Policy* (San Francisco: Chandler, 1964), pp. 209, 210.
33. See the discussion in Kemp and Cheslow, pp. 309–311.
34. This discussion draws heavily on Melvin M. Webber's comprehensive article, "The BART Experience: What Have We Learned?" *The Public Interest,* Fall 1976, pp. 79–108.

cisco. This orientation is indicated by the fact that only thirteen of the system's thirty-four stations are within those two cities.[35] One might ask, however, why a system that connects the central city with the suburbs cannot carry city workers to suburban jobs as readily at it transports suburban commuters to jobs in town. The answer can be deduced from what we know about the pattern of metropolitan job locations. The job destinations of the inbound commuter are typically concentrated in the CBD (as a result of nineteenth-century centralization). Those of the reverse commuter are typically scattered throughout the suburbs (as a result of twentieth-century decentralization). Thus for inbound journeys the system connects scattered suburban residential points with concentrated downtown job locations, while for outbound journeys it must connect scattered central city residential points with even more scattered suburban job locations. This asymmetry strongly affects user convenience.

The inbound commuter, using a system such as BART, either drives a car or takes a feeder bus to the transit line, then rides the train to a CBD station that is within a short walk of his or her place of work. Disregarding the final walk, there are only two segments to the journey. The outbound commuter, by contrast, usually must take a bus to an inner city transit station (which in the case of new systems like BART that have few stops inside the city is not likely to be within walking distance of home) and then rides the train to the suburbs. That makes two legs already, but the worst is yet to come. The job is not likely to be close to a suburban rail station, since radial transit lines diverge to wide spacing in the suburbs and jobs are not concentrated near them. The reverse commuter, however, has no car waiting at the suburban station but must rely on bus service. If such a connection exists, it makes a third leg to the journey. (Often it does not exist, and reverse commutation can be accomplished only by auto.) For the sake of parity, we disregard a possible final walk from bus to job. Even so, the outbound commuter's journey, if indeed it can be accomplished using public transportation, requires one leg more than that of the inbound commuter, with all that implies for extra waiting time and additional scheduling problems.

Disappointment and Recovery

BART's record in its first twelve years of operation was one of severe early disappointment followed by partial recovery. When the system was planned, its advocates provided what can now be seen as much too optimistic projections of the ridership it would attract, the reduction it would thereby cause in Bay area highway congestion, and the fare-box revenues it would

35. Regarding BART's strong orientation toward serving the suburb-to-CBD commuter, see Andrew Marshall Hamer, *The Selling of Rail Rapid Transit* (Lexington, Mass.: Heath, Lexington Books, 1976), pp. 61–67, 75–77.

TABLE 9.3
BART's Ridership, Revenues and Costs (fiscal years)

	1975	1981	1986
Average weekday patronage (June)	121,337	173,792	204,244
Revenues and Costs (thousands of dollars)			
Net operating revenue	16,157	52,822	82,071
Net passenger revenue	15,695	46,207	73,052
Total operating expense	49,822	103,257	160,894
Operating surplus or (deficit)	(33,665)	(50,435)	(78,823)
Fare-box ratio[a]	.32	.45	.45

[a]Fare-box ratio is the proportion of total operating expense (line 4) covered by net revenue collected from passengers (line 3).
Source: Bay Area Rapid Transit District, *Budget Performance Report* and BART *Patronage Report*, June 1975, 1981, 1986.

generate. Furthermore, when the system finally went into operation in 1974 (much behind schedule), it was plagued by mechanical failures that held down ridership for several years. However, when these problems were corrected, the system became highly reliable and ridership improved steadily. Thus, how one evaluates BART depends on the standard adopted: measured against the claims originally made by its advocates, it has not been a success; judged by what it actually does, it looks a good deal better, though one may still have reservations.

By fiscal year 1985 the Bay area system was attracting about 212,000 riders on the average weekday, almost double the number it carried in 1975, but still somewhat below the 258,000 originally projected at full operation.[36] In 1986 the growth trend was interrupted: weekday ridership declined to an average of 204,000, in part because fares were increased 30 percent on January 1st. Table 9.3 summarizes BART'S performance history.

The Bay Bridge, which connects San Francisco on the western side of the Bay with Oakland on the east and carries commuters from East Bay suburbs into downtown San Francisco, is the most critical bottleneck in the regional transportation system. BART's transbay tube parallels the bridge and was intended to increase capacity and relieve congestion in that corridor. BART's sponsors predicted that 61 percent of its projected riders would be diverted from automobiles. A 1976 survey, however, found that only about 35 percent had been so diverted. Unexpectedly, half of the system's transbay passengers turned out to have been former bus patrons.[37] Traffic congestion

36. Service on the transbay tube, connecting Oakland and the East Bay counties with San Francisco, began in September 1974.
37. Webber, pp. 85–86.

on routes that closely parallel its tracks was temporarily reduced when full BART sevice began in 1975, but normal traffic growth soon resumed, so the gains were short-lived. Yet the fact that demand for highway travel had continued to increase in the Bay area, regenerating the congestion that BART at first relieved, should not be counted as a failure of the new rail system. In a prosperous and growing region, highway traffic will naturally tend to expand until restrained by congestion or by congestion tolls or relieved by the construction of more capacity.

BART's greatest contribution to regional transportation may be the added capacity it provides for Bay crossings. Population around the Bay area has continued to increase since BART opened (see Table 3.3). San Francisco is a "world class" city with a CBD that provides a rapidly increasing concentration of employment. The number of people crossing into San Francisco each morning in the Bay Bridge corridor has increased from between 50,000 and 55,000 just before BART's transbay service began in 1974 to 75,000 in 1984, by which date its trains carried about 28,000 inbound morning passengers. Suppose BART had not been built. Since congestion-related tolls were not tried we do not know whether, on the one hand, they would have reduced road traffic sufficiently to make another crossing unnecessary or, on the other, would have indicated a level of demand sufficient to justify another bridge. Additional buses on the Bay Bridge could have accommodated some of the traffic carried by BART, but Joel Markowitz concludes that "without BART, it seems unlikely that the bridge could support the current level of peak trip making in the corridor."[38]

BART's Revenues and Costs

In 1962 BART's sponsors predicted that when fully operational, the system would generate a substantial operating surplus to help defray capital costs. Instead, as Table 9.3 shows, BART has always run a deficit. In the early years, when ridership was particularly low, fare revenue covered less than 40 percent of operating cost. As ridership picked up in the 1980s the ratio rose to about 45 percent, which is in line with the highest ratios reported for older, less automated rail transit systems in the Northeast.

These figures do not include BART's capital costs. Webber estimated their annualized amount at $82.4 million in 1975–1976.[39] Using the same figure for 1986 and dividing by the 58.9 million passengers carried produces a capital cost per trip of $1.40. Operating cost per trip similarly calculated came to $2.73 in 1986, bringing average total cost to $4.13. Since the mean fare was only $1.24, the average user was being subsidized by about $2.89 per ride, a figure that would have to be doubled for a round-trip commuter.

38. Joel Markowitz, *BART Impact Update*, paper prepared for the 64th annual meeting of the Transportation Research Board, January 1985, p. 8.
39. Webber, table 4.

So far we have discussed *money* costs only, rather than full costs including the value of time and of externalities, as shown in Figure 8.3. That figure (based on 1972 prices) can be used to estimate the full cost of a trip on BART and the bus and automobile alternatives, provided we know the peak-hour volume in the corridor in question. In 1984 the peak one-way volume on BART's transbay tube was about 15,300 passengers per hour.[40] That is well above the 8,000-per-hour figure reported by Webber for 1976 but still below the 20,000 at which BART would become competitive with a subcompact car. At a volume of only 15,000, Figure 8.3 indicates that the full cost of a BART trip is about double the cost by express bus and about 20 percent more than the cost of using a private car.

Comparisons such as these have led many analysts to criticize BART as too costly for the benefits it has delivered. Cost by itself is, of course, not a valid criterion. If a trip on BART were so far superior to the alternatives that riders were willing to pay for its high cost, there would be no ground for objection. But of course, riders have *not* been paying its high cost. They ride at a better than two-to-one subsidy, when capital as well as operating costs are counted.

BART's capital costs can be looked at from several perspectives. Great as they appeared at the time of construction, they look like bargain prices compared with the cost of systems built during and after the rapid inflation of the 1970s. The Bay area system cost $23 million per mile to construct, whereas Washington's Metro, built almost a decade later, is expected to cost at least $67 million per mile. On the other hand, if one looks at capital cost per rider rather than per mile of track, the Bay area system comes out less well because it generates so much less ridership per mile.[41] An important reason for this is that Metro has a relatively dense network of lines serving Washington's CBD, while BART has only a single line through San Francisco's. It is too early, however, to make a systematic comparison of performance between BART and rail systems built subsequently, since the latter are either still under construction or were only recently finished.

As already suggested, the Bay area system's relatively low ridership per mile is a direct result of its design. Webber explains that its promoters believed that "high speed, high comfort, high style and downtown delivery were the attributes that matter most to motorists; and BART was then designed to outdo the car on those four counts."[42] BART's management delivered a system that has exactly the qualities its designers sought. Why haven't auto users flocked to it? The answer is that to achieve those attributes BART's designers gave up others that are even more important to motorists. For example, to

40. Data supplied by Joel Markowitz, Metropolitan Transportation Commission, Oakland, Calif.

41. Robert E. Skinner, Jr., and Thomas B. Deen, "Second Generation U.S. Rail Transit Systems: Prospects and Perils," *Transportation*, March 1980, table 4.

42. Webber, p. 99.

maximize line-haul speed from suburb to central city they chose rail, with wide spacing between stations. The high capacity and high cost of a rail corridor in turn dictated that there be only a few lines radiating into the suburbs. The combination of wide station spacing and few lines inevitably meant that most commuters would live far from the nearest BART station. Consequently, much time and effort would be required just getting to and from the rail line. Here came the unkindest cut of all. Studies of travel behavior (unfortunately carried out *after* BART was conceived) repeatedly show that trip makers find time spent walking or waiting to make connections about three times as onerous as in-vehicle time. Thus BART's design minimized time spent on the pleasantest part of the journey—and riding on a BART train is indeed very pleasant—while making the unpleasant part as time-consuming as possible. Webber concludes that this "fundamental mistake" in design explains BART's inability to divert motorists.

In a recent summary Webber concludes that BART should provide a lesson to other metropolitan areas in the western United States. If a rail transit system is not economically efficient in the Bay area, where topography provides many impediments to easy access by automobile, it will certainly not be so in Houston or Los Angeles, which are built on wide plains. He advises those cities to experiment with other kinds of transit systems, especially "paratransit" (discussed in the next section), if they want to find alternatives to the private automobile that are efficient in such a low-density environment.[43]

Future Policy Directions

Many transportation analysts believe that the best hope for raising the general level of urban transportation service now lies in opening up the market to more competition both between modes and among firms.[44] This can be (indeed, in some cities, has been) accomplished by selective deregulation. The basic argument is that the public would be better served if there were more suppliers. In most cities, public transportation is provided almost exclusively by large municipally owned agencies that are highly inflexible and, in many instances, inefficient. Despite the vast locational shifts that have occurred in this century in both place of work and place of residence, many city buses continue to follow routes identical to those of the streetcar franchises that they replaced fifty or sixty years ago. Monopolistic conditions typically contribute to this inflexibility, for no matter how unresponsive the operating agency, there are no competitors to take business away. In addition, residents acquire a vested interest in the continued operation of ancient lines that

43. Melvin M. Webber, "BART: The Lesson," *WestPlan*, California Chapter of the American Planning Association, Fall 1983, p. 13.
44. See the papers collected in Lave, ed., *Urban Transit*.

makes it politically hazardous for an operating authority to abandon old routes in order to reallocate resources to new ones.

We have created an artificial situation, it is asserted, in which the urban transportation market is dominated by two modes that lie at opposite ends of a spectrum. The public mode (usually bus) operates as a tradition-bound, unresponsive monopoly. The principal alternative, opposite in every respect to the public mode, is the highly flexible, rather expensive, and completely private automobile. Between these two extremes, so the argument runs, there is not only room but in fact real need for an intermediate type, combining some features of each. The generic name *paratransit* has been coined for this intermediate mode.[45]

Paratransit comprises forms of transportation that combine some of the convenience and flexibility of the private car with some of the economy inherent in public transportation. Included are such traditional modes as taxicabs, rental cars, and car pools, as well as such innovative arrangements as dial-a-ride, subscription bus, and organized van pool. These modes provide personalized service, usually picking up the customer at a prearranged time at the point of origin. Yet given the quality of the service, they are relatively economical as compared with the private car because their cost is shared among many users. Like the automobile, car pools and van pools have the advantage that no paid labor is required, an advantage that increases as transit wages rise relative to the national average.

Advocates of paratransit believe that it can produce high-quality, economical service on routes or in neighborhoods where demand is not sufficiently dense to support regular public transportation. It may also be the most humane and effective way to provide mobility for the elderly and the handicapped, who are severely disadvantaged by the decline or disappearance of public transportation, which, in any case, does not serve them very comfortably.

If taxis are a form of paratransit, however, why do we need any others? Obviously, taxis have long provided a service blending the virtues of public and private transportation. They provide it, moreover, on a surprisingly large scale: Wohl reports that *fleet* taxicabs alone "now handle almost 40 percent *more* passengers than do all U.S. rapid transit systems combined, and carry about 60 percent as many passengers as all bus transit systems."[46] Nor are taxis merely the playthings of the rich: the distribution of taxi riders by income class is almost as propoor as that of bus riders. (For the latter, see Figure 9.2.) Unfortunately, however, the taxi industry is almost everywhere heavily and irrationally regulated. Such regulation usually prevents operators from offering the variety of services that the mode is inherently capable of. For ex-

45. See Ronald F. Kirby et al., *Para-transit: Neglected Options for Urban Mobility* (Washington, D.C.: Urban Institute, 1975).

46. Martin Wohl, "The Taxi's Role in Urban America: Today and Tomorrow," *Transportation*, June 1975, p. 150.

ample, casual cab sharing is generally outlawed, and taxis cannot legally operate as car pools, although both services would be very useful to consumers.
Regulation also frequently involves severe restrictions on entry to the industry. A form of monopoly is thus created artificially, the supply of cabs is reduced, fares are higher, and vehicles are less readily available than they would
otherwise be. It is time we took seriously the taxi's potential contribution to
urban mobility, instead of making it into a petty monopoly ineptly regulated
to the detriment of the public interest.

Meyer and Gómez-Ibáñez point out that no single "solution" has solved
(or is likely to solve) the urban transportation problem in post–World War II
America. Most transportation economists would probably agree that there are
no simple fixes and that the best hope for improving the system is to aim for
small advances on many fronts, including economically more efficient management of the automobile and of public transportation, selective deregulation, and more imaginative use of those in-between modes, the many forms of
paratransit.[47]

ENERGY COSTS, TRANSPORTATION CHOICES,
AND URBAN FORM

Since the oil crises of 1973–1974 and 1979, transportation policy in the
United States has been shaped in part by national concern with the energy
problem. Each short-run crisis interrupted established patterns of travel behavior and stimulated discussion of less fuel-intensive lifestyles than those we
had become accustomed to. Although consumption in the United States was
sharply reduced following the price increases of the 1970s and fuel prices subsequently declined, the prospect of their continued volatility means that energy considerations are still relevant to urban economic analysis and policy. In
this section we discuss the connections among energy prices, transportation
behavior, residential location, and urban form.

Fuel Costs, Travel Behavior, and Urban Form

The sharp rise in fuel prices during the 1970s was accompanied by a
good deal of speculation about possible effects on travel behavior and urban
form. In Chapter 8 we pointed out several reasons why higher fuel costs
might not have much effect on the modal choices made by commuters. First,
the effect of higher fuel prices is moderated by the importance of time costs
in the total cost of a journey. Second, auto users can reduce fuel consumption

---

47. Meyer and Gómez-Ibáñez, pp. 4, 13–14, and ch. 14. Also see Anthony M. Pagano,
"Private Sector Alternatives for Public Transportation," *Transportation Quarterly*, July 1984, pp.
433–447.

by making more multipurpose trips, thus reducing total miles driven. Third, they can buy smaller, more fuel-efficient cars as the price of gasoline rises.

In fact, the energy crises of 1973–1974 and 1979 did bring about short-run reductions in driving and temporary increases in transit patronage. Average miles driven per automobile fell from 10,046 in 1978 to 9,002 in 1981, then gradually recovered to 9,809 in 1984.[48] The long-established year-to-year decline in transit ridership reached bottom in 1972. Over the next twelve years, patronage increased 22 percent (see Table 8.2). It is far from certain however, that this change in trend, if it can be called that, was primarily a consequence of the energy crisis. Transit patronage may have been leveling off anyway, after its prolonged decline, and large public subsidies were beginning to stimulate the extension and improvement of service. Based on experience since 1973, those who were skeptical that higher fuel prices would greatly alter travel behavior have been proved right.

What about possible effects on urban form? Since the steep decline in transportation costs during the nineteenth and twentieth centuries was a powerful force in producing metropolitan decentralization, it seemed possible that the sharply higher fuel prices of the 1970s, by raising the cost of transportation, might moderate, or even reverse, that long-established trend. Such, at least, was the hope of many a central city mayor and downtown property owner.

There is no easy way of directly observing the effect of higher fuel costs on location patterns, since locational choices are affected by so many forces simultaneously. What economists can do, however, is to measure the actual increase in commuting cost attributable to higher energy prices and then compare its magnitude with other elements that affect residential location choice, such as housing cost. Muth did so and found that higher gasoline prices during the 1970s caused the average annual cost of commuting per mile to rise from $44.50 to $47.81 (in 1973 dollars). In comparison with average annual housing costs of $1,800 per family, an increase of only $3.31 per mile is so small that he concluded it "could have only a negligible effect upon the choice of residence in the central city over the suburbs."[49]

Increased Multinucleation

Even if energy prices at some future date were to rise sufficiently to have perceptible effects on residential location, it seems unlikely that they would lead to a recentralization of population into the old central cities. History is not like a home movie in which one can reverse the projector motor and watch the children leap out of the swimming pool and back onto the div-

48. Federal Highway Administration, *Highway Statistics*, various years, table VM-1.
49. Richard F. Muth, "Energy Prices and Urban Decentralization," in Anthony Downs and Katharine L. Bradbury, eds., *Energy Costs, Urban Development and Housing* (Washington, D.C.: Brookings Institution, 1984), p. 104.

ing board. Central cities will not again experience population growth unless job growth also occurs there, and higher energy prices do not seem likely to bring that about. If they were to have any effect on location, it would probably be to increase what Anas and Moses call "multinucleation," defined as "the formation of distinct and quite dense suburban and exurban centers."[50] Instead of recentralization into the old CBD, we would see increased centralization of activity at a number of ring-area locations. Multifamily housing would increase around these suburban nuclei, and as population density rose, better public bus transportation would be provided.

The attractive power of that pattern lies in the fact that it would allow for a systematic shortening of the journey to work, while not forcing households to abandon the automobile. Shopping trips, too, might be expected to grow shorter if, as seems likely, increased residential density were to support the growth of neighborhood stores at the expense of more remote regional shopping malls. As already indicated, one would expect bus transportation to improve as increased density made more frequent service feasible. It should be noted, however, that multinucleation would certainly not create origin-destination densities high enough to support new rail transit facilities for intrasuburban movement.

---

50. Alex Anas and Leon N. Moses, "Transportation and Land Use in the Mature Metropolis," in C. L. Leven, ed., *The Mature Metropolis* (Lexington, Mass.: Heath, Lexington Books, 1978), p. 161.

TEN

Urban Poverty and Segregation

Ever since America rediscovered its poor in the early 1960s, the words *poverty* and *city* have been almost automatically linked in our public vocabulary. It was not always so. To an earlier generation, poverty appeared to be mainly a rural phenomenon. As late as 1959 considerably more poor people were living outside metropolitan areas than in them. Since then the proportions have changed dramatically. Today more than three-fifths of the poor live in metropolitan areas.

In this chapter we briefly examine definitions of poverty, then investigate recent changes in its geography and explain some of the causes and consequences of those changes. In the chapter that follows we will analyze the great variety of policies that have been either tried or proposed to combat poverty in our cities.

DEFINITIONS AND TRENDS

Definitions of poverty may be either relative or absolute. An absolute definition specifies some level of purchasing power per person or per family that is deemed sufficient to buy a minimum of life's necessities. Households with incomes below that level are classified as living in poverty. A relative definition, on the other hand, classifies households as living in poverty if their income falls below some fraction of the national median or mean. For example, a family with an income of less than half the national median might be defined as living in poverty.

"Official" poverty statistics for the United States go back only to 1959. In compiling them, the federal government employs an absolute definition of a poverty-line income that varies according to family size

TABLE 10.1
Absolute and Relative Poverty

	1959	1974	1985
Incidence of Poverty among Persons (%)			
U.S. total	22.0	11.2	14.0
White	18.1	8.6	11.4
Black	55.1	30.3	31.3
Spanish origin	—	23.0	29.0
Distribution of Aggregate Income among Families (%)			
Lowest fifth	4.9	5.5	4.6
Second fifth	12.3	12.0	10.9
Third fifth	17.9	17.5	16.9
Fourth fifth	23.8	24.0	24.2
Top fifth	41.1	41.0	43.5

Sources: U.S. Bureau of the Census, *Current Population Reports*, series P-60, no. 154, August 1986, Table B; no. 151, April 1986, table 12; and no. 152, June 1986, table 1.

and composition and is adjusted annually for inflation. The poverty-line income in 1985 for a family of four was $10,986.[1]

When an absolute definition of poverty is retained for a number of years while the average living standard in the nation gradually increases, the incidence of poverty (as defined) is almost certain to diminish. Only if the distribution of income became more unequal as income per capita rose could a reduction in absolute poverty fail to occur. The situation is quite different when a relative definition is used. The extent of poverty then depends entirely on the distribution of income and not at all on its level. A reduction in poverty can occur only if the distribution of income among families is changed in an appropriate fashion; a uniform percentage increase in living standards for all income classes has no effect.

Indeed, it may well be argued that progress registered under an absolute definition of poverty is in part illusory. Historical experience demonstrates that in a dynamic economy the absolute standard of income sufficiency accepted by the social consensus at one period will no longer seem appropriate at a later date. Thus absolute standards tend periodically to be revised upward by common consent, which washes out some, though not all, of the reduction in poverty that seems to accrue during the intervals in which the standards remain fixed. In effect, we do think of poverty as partly a relative matter.

Table 10.1 summarizes the recent history of poverty in the United States. The overall incidence or rate of poverty as measured by the official,

1. U.S. Bureau of the Census, *Current Population Reports*, series P-60, no. 154, August 1986, table A-1. For a detailed explanation of the federal definition, see series P-60, no. 133, July 1982, pp. 2–7.

absolute standard (top line of table) fell sharply from 22.0 percent in 1959 to 11.2 percent in 1974. (The incidence of poverty for any population group is simply the proportion of that group living below the poverty line.) Those were years of rapid real economic growth and a rising average standard of living. But in addition, the distribution of income was becoming more equal. As shown in the lower part of the table, the proportion of income going to the lowest fifth of families rose from 4.9 percent to 1959 to 5.5 percent in 1974. The poor were getting a larger share (albeit still very small) of a larger pie. After 1974 these favorable trends were reversed. Real economic growth slowed, the average standard of living stopped rising, and the distribution of income became steadily more unequal. By 1983 the overall rate of poverty had risen to 15.2 percent, its highest level since 1965. Although the poverty rate fell to 14.0 percent by 1985, the relative share going to the poorest fifth of families was a mere 4.6 percent, the lowest it had been since 1961. The connection between these trends and public policy to combat poverty will be discussed in Chapter 11. We next look at changes in the geographic distribution of the nation's poor.

THE CHANGING GEOGRAPHY OF POVERTY

The top part of Table 10.2 shows the percentage distribution of the U.S. poverty population by place of residence in 1959, 1974, and 1985. It clearly documents the increasing concentration of poverty in metropolitan areas. In 1959 the poor living outside metropolitan areas outnumbered those living inside them by a ratio of 5 to 4. During the 1960s and 1970s, however, poverty declined much more sharply outside SMSAs, so that by 1985 more than 70 percent of the nation's poor were metropolitan residents. The causes of this historic shift will be discussed below.

The lower part of Table 10.2 shows the rate or incidence of poverty by area and race. In 1959 the rate of poverty was twice as high outside as inside metropolitan areas. It fell in both areas during the 1960s and early 1970s, but much more rapidly in metropolitan areas. By 1985 the incidence of poverty had turned upward in both areas but the rise was relatively greater inside SMSAs. Thus the metropolitan and nonmetropolitan rates have been converging.

If we look at the metropolis itself, two facts stand out. (1) Within metropolitan areas the incidence of poverty is far higher in the central cities than in the suburban rings, and the gap between rates in the two areas has widened dramatically since 1959. (2) After having declined in the 1960s, the rate of poverty in central cities began to rise once more in the 1970s and early 1980s. In 1985 it was higher than it had been in 1959. These points are shown clearly

TABLE 10.2
Geographic Distribution and Incidence of Poverty

	1959	1974	1985
Distribution of Persons in Poverty (%)			
United States	100.0	100.0	100.0
Metropolitan areas	43.9	59.3	70.4
Central cities	26.9	35.8	42.9
Outside central cities	17.0	23.4	27.5
Nonmetropolitan areas	56.1	40.7	29.6
Incidence of Poverty among Persons, by Area and Race (%)			
All Races			
United States	22.0	11.2	14.0
Metropolitan areas	15.3	9.7	12.7
Central cities	18.3	13.7	19.0
Outside central cities	12.2	6.7	8.4
Nonmetropolitan areas	33.2	14.2	18.3
White			
United States	18.1	8.6	11.4
Metropolitan areas	12.0	7.2	10.1
Central cities	13.8	9.4	14.9
Outside central cities	10.4	5.9	7.4
Nonmetropolitan areas	28.2	11.5	15.6
Black			
United States	55.1	30.3	31.3
Metropolitan areas	42.8	26.7	29.1
Central cities	40.5	28.3	32.1
Outside central cities	50.9	21.3	21.7
Nonmetropolitan areas	77.7	41.1	42.6

Sources: U.S. Bureau of the Census, *Current Population Reports*, series P-60, no. 124, July 1980, table 4; and no. 154, August 1986, table 18.

in the lower part of Table 10.2. For all races combined, the incidence of poverty in the central cities was 18.3 percent in 1959, 13.7 percent in 1974, and 19.0 percent in 1985. In the suburban rings the comparable rates were 12.2, 6.7, and 8.4 percent.

The rate of poverty is generally higher in central cities of large than of small SMSAs. For example, in 1983 when the poverty rate in central cities as a whole stood at 19.8 percent, the rate was 23.4 in New York City, 21.4 in Los Angeles–Long Beach, 27.2 in Chicago, 24.8 in Philadelphia, and an astonishing 36.4 in Detroit.[2] This reverses the pattern that obtained in 1959, when

2. U.S. Bureau of the Census, *Current Population Reports*, series P-60, no. 147, February 1985, table 10.

poverty rates were higher in central cities of smaller SMSAs. As we shall see, this outcome is at least partly the result of past patterns of migration.

RACE AND POVERTY

Thus far we have not considered racial differences in either the level or the rate of poverty. Although whites make up two-thirds of the nation's poor, Table 10.1 shows that the rate of poverty is almost three times as high among blacks. In both population groups the table shows that the incidence of poverty fell rapidly in the 1960s and early 1970s but has increased considerably since then. (We shall have more to say about this in the next chapter.) Over the whole period 1959 to 1985 the rate of poverty for blacks declined from 55.1 percent to 31.3 percent, while the rate for whites fell from 18.1 percent to 11.4 percent.

If we look at blacks by place of residence (in Table 10.2), an important distinction appears: from 1974 to 1985 the incidence of poverty among blacks rose much faster in central cities than elsewhere. It is clear that the situation of urban blacks is peculiarly difficult and deserves special attention.

The systematic collection of poverty data for persons of Spanish origin began only in the 1970s. Hence this ethnic group is not shown separately in Table 10.2. However, Table 10.1 shows that the national rate of poverty in the population of Spanish origin stood at 23.0 percent in 1974, substantially above the rate for whites but below that for blacks. Thereafter it rose somewhat faster than the rate for blacks, reaching 29.0 percent in 1985. In central cities (not shown in table), it stood at 33.6 percent in 1985.

By comparing median family incomes of ethnic minorities with those of whites, we gain another perspective on the connection between race and income. Table 10.3 shows that blacks made substantial gains relative to whites during the 1960s and early 1970s. The ratio of median black income to median white income rose from .52 in 1959 to a peak of .62 in 1975. Since then it has gradually fallen back to the range of .55 to .58, only a few points above its 1959 to 1964 level. The income ratio is somewhat higher for Spanish-origin families than for blacks but has moved in a similar pattern. In 1972 (the earliest available year) it stood at .71. By 1985 it had declined to .65.[3]

The Problem of Female-headed Families

In studying movements in black income it may be misleading to concentrate on average measures like those in Table 10.3, since there is evidence of

3. For a detailed analysis of the trend in black/white male earnings differentials, see James P. Smith and Finis R. Welch, *Closing the Gap: Forty Years of Economic Progress for Blacks*, doc. no. R-3330-DOL (Santa Monica, Calif.: Rand Corp., February 1986).

TABLE 10.3
Ratios of Black and Spanish to White Income

| | MEDIAN FAMILY INCOME RATIOS | | |
	Black and Other Races to White	Black to White	Spanish Origin to White
1950	.54	—	—
1959	.54	.52	—
1964	.56	.54	—
1969	.63	.61	—
1972	.62	.59	.71
1975	.65	.62	.67
1980	.63	.58	.67
1982	.62	.55	.66
1985	.64	.58	.65

Sources: U.S. Bureau of the Census, *Current Population Reports*, series P-23, no. 80, 1979, table 14, and series P-60, no. 154, August 1986, table 2.

increasing socioeconomic divergence within the black population. Black husband-wife families as a group have made progress toward equality with whites, while black families headed by women with no husband present have remained far behind. The growing size of this latter group accounts for the increased rate of poverty among urban blacks in the 1970s and 1980s.

Income divergence within the black population is shown in Table 10.4. Between 1970 and 1985 the median income of black husband-wife families (in dollars of constant purchasing power) rose 14 percent, while the median for female-headed households, no husband present, fell 6 percent. For the same types of white families, the change was respectively up 6 percent and down 1 percent. As a result, between 1970 and 1985, the black-to-white income ratio for husband-wife families rose from .73 to .78, while the ratio for female-headed households fell from .62 to .59.

In recent years the number of families living in female-headed households has increased rapidly among all ethnic groups. Because a large proportion of women heading such families are either not in the labor force or if they work, typically earn far less than a man would, female-headed families have a much higher probability of being poor. The rate of poverty in 1985 was 29.8 percent among white and 53.2 percent among black female-headed families. These figures are between three and four times the rate among persons in all other types of families. The problem is particularly acute for the black population. Families headed by women made up 41.5 percent of the black total in 1985, as compared with about 28 percent in 1970. In 1978 fully 82 per-

TABLE 10.4
Median Income by Type of Family and Race

TYPE OF FAMILY	1970	1985	PERCENT CHANGE, 1970–1985
White			
Husband-wife families			
Number (thousands)	41,092	45,924	11.8
Median income (1985 dollars)	29,690	31,602	6.4
Female householder, no husband present			
Number (thousands)	4,386	7,111	62.1
Median income (1985 dollars)	15,932	15,825	−.7
Black			
Husband-wife families			
Number (thousands)	3,235	3,680	13.8
Median income (1985 dollars)	21,640	24,570	13.5
Female householder, no husband present			
Number (thousands)	1,506	2,874	90.8
Median income (1985 dollars)	9,900	9,305	−6.0
Ratios: Black to White Median Income			
Husband-wife families	.73	.78	—
Female householder, no husband present	.62	.59	—

Sources: U.S. Bureau of the Census, *Current Population Reports*, series P-20, no. 350, May 1980, table 24; and series P-60, no. 154, August 1986, table 1.

cent of all poor black families in central cities had female heads.[4] As we shall see in the next chapter, the increasing concentration of urban poverty in female-headed households has serious implications for antipoverty policy.[5]

WHY POVERTY IS CONCENTRATING IN THE CITIES

The urbanization of poverty in the United States is not difficult to account for. It is the local outcome of the changing pattern of settlement that has already been described in earlier chapters. The mechanization of agriculture in the twentieth century caused a massive migration of displaced labor from rural areas and small towns to metropolitan areas. Superimposed on

4. U.S. Bureau of the Census, *Current Population Reports*, series P-60, no. 154, August 1986; and series P-60, no. 124, July 1980.
5. For further discussion of the implications of socioeconomic divergence within the black population, see Thomas F. Pettigrew, "Racial Change and the Intrametropolitan Distribution of Black Americans," in Arthur P. Solomon, ed., *The Prospective City* (Cambridge, Mass.: M.I.T. Press, 1980), pp. 54, 66–67, 73.

this, so to speak, was a flow of migration from relatively poor regions, such as Appalachia, the South, and Puerto Rico, to relatively prosperous regions, such as the Middle Atlantic, Great Lakes, and Pacific states. Both the poor and the nonpoor migrated. The simple statistical consequence of this massive movement of population was, first, to shift the principal locus of poverty from the countryside to the cities and, second, to slow the reduction in the incidence of poverty in the cities below the rate that otherwise would have obtained.

A recent study of interregional migration, which includes information on the incomes of migrants, confirms the widely accepted view that the South was long a net source of low-income migrants to the rest of the nation. It also shows, however, that when U.S. patterns of migration shifted in the late 1960s and early 1970s (see discussion in Chapter 3) the direction of low-income migration also changed. After 1971 the South became a net recipient of low-income migrants, while the Northeast and North Central regions became net sources.[6] Whatever their direction, however, current migratory flows are unlikely to have much immediate effect on the average rate of urban poverty. In earlier decades interregional migration contributed to the urbanization of poverty because it included a substantial flow of the poor from rural and nonmetropolitan areas to the urban North and West. Current interregional movements of the poor are more likely to be from city to city than from city to suburb or city to nonmetropolitan area, leaving the average rate of urban poverty more or less unchanged.

Distribution of Poverty within Metropolitan Areas

Within metropolitan areas the concentration of poverty in the central cities and its lower incidence in the suburban rings can be explained largely as the result of three sets of forces: the process of metropolitan growth and development, the impact of public policy, and the pressure of racial prejudice. The process of metropolian development tends to hold the poor close to the center both because the center is the place with the largest concentration of old, and therefore cheap, housing and because it is the area that provides easiest access to a large number of jobs—especially the types of casual employment that the unskilled are often forced to rely on. Easier job access at the center, in turn, has two aspects. First, the center contains more jobs than does any single place in the ring. Second, it is usually served by a public transportation network that efficiently connects close-in residential neighborhoods with central city places of employment.

We have described previously the process by which the development of highway transportation, the rise in family incomes, and the force of public

---

6. See Larry H. Long, *Interregional Migration of the Poor: Some Recent Changes*, U.S. Bureau of the Census, November 1978, tables 1 and 2.

policy in home finance and income taxation induced the middle and upper classes to move to the suburbs. These inducements scarcely affected low-income families, who could not afford either new suburban housing or the relatively high cost of suburban self-transportation. However, the exodus of the middle class from the central city reinforced its attraction for the poor and the blacks by releasing large quantities of housing in the older neighborhoods that they could afford or that could readily be adapted to their low rent-paying capacity. Here was an example of the "filtering" process in the housing market operating on a huge scale. (Filtering will be examined in detail in Chapter 12.) The process of racial and income-class change became a circular, or self-reinforcing, one because racial tensions rose as the black population of central cities increased and provided the white middle and upper classes with an additional impetus to move to the largely white suburbs.

If the "natural" process of metropolitan spatial-economic development and the indirect effects of public policy were the only operative forces, we would expect to find poor whites as heavily concentrated in the central cities, and hence as underrepresented in the suburbs, as poor blacks. Since we do not find an equal concentration of poor whites in the cities, it is difficult to avoid the conclusion that racial factors are also at work. Persuasive evidence on this point is provided by Kain. He predicted the number of blacks who would have been expected to live in the suburbs of U.S. SMSAs in 1980 if metropolitan blacks had been distributed geographically by income level, household type, and age in the same pattern as all households. He found the actual number to be only half the predicted level, confirming the hypothesis that racial discrimination is an additional factor limiting black movement to the suburbs.[7] The point is reinforced by a less complex calculation: in 1983 some 54 percent of metropolitan white families with incomes below $10,000 lived in the suburban ring, while only 23 percent of such black families did so.[8] To a significant extent, then, the concentration of poverty in the central cities appears to be reinforced by the essentially noneconomic forces of prejudice that restrain the low-income black population from dispersing into the suburbs.

Shift in Relative Income Level: Central Cities versus Suburbs

As might be expected, the dispersion of the middle and upper classes to the suburbs and the influx of a substantial low-income population to the central cities has brought about a historic shift in the relative income levels of the two areas. Scattered evidence from earlier periods indicates that prior to 1950

7. John F. Kain, "Black Suburbanization in the Eighties: A New Beginning or a False Hope?" in John M. Quigley and Daniel L. Rubinfeld, eds., *American Domestic Priorities* (Berkeley: University of California Press, 1985), p. 264.

8. U.S. Bureau of the Census, *Current Population Reports*, series P-60, no. 146, April 1985, table 21.

TABLE 10.5
Income Differentials between Central Cities and Their Metropolitan Areas

	MEDIAN FAMILY INCOME: RATIO OF CENTRAL CITY MEDIAN TO SMSA MEDIAN			
	1949	1959	1969	1979
Six Largest SMSAs in North and East				
New York, N.Y.–N.J.	.95	.93	.89	.87
Chicago, Ill.	.97	.92	.86	.77
Philadelphia, Pa.–N.J.	.96	.90	.85	.77
Detroit, Mich.	.99	.89	.83	.69
Washington, D.C.–Md.–Va.	.89	.79	.74	.69
Boston, Mass.	.92	.86	.80	.70
Average of six SMSAs in North and East	.95	.88	.83	.75
Six Largest SMSAs in South and West				
Los Angeles–Long Beach, Calif.[a]	.98	.98	.96	.92
San Francisco–Oakland, Calif.[a]	1.00	.95	.89	.85
Dallas–Fort Worth, Tex.[a]	1.03	1.01	.96	.90
Houston, Tex.	1.02	.98	.97	.90
Atlanta, Ga.	.91	.87	.79	.64
Anaheim–Santa Ana–Garden Grove, Calif.[a]	—	—	.96	.89
Average of six SMSAs in South and West	.99	.96	.92	.85

[a]Ratio is for first-named central city only.
Sources: U.S. Bureau of the Census, *Census of Population, 1950, 1960, 1970, 1980.*

the level of per capita income was higher in central cities than in the surrounding ring areas. More recently the advantage has lain with the ring areas and has been steadily widening.

For example, in their study of the New York metropolitan region, Hoover and Vernon estimated that per capita personal income in the "core" counties fell from 108 percent of the regional average in 1939 to 105 percent in 1947 and 98 percent in 1956, while per capita income in the "inner ring" of suburban counties rose from 88 percent of the regional average in 1939 to 97 percent in 1947 and 111 percent in 1956.[9] Thus the mean income in the suburbs rose from 19 percent below the core county average in 1939 to 13 percent above it in 1956.

Table 10.5 shows a like pattern developing from 1949 through 1979 in the twelve large SMSAs that were examined in detail in Chapter 3. (The same pattern can, of course, be found in U.S. metropolitan areas as a whole; see Ta-

9. Edgar M. Hoover and Raymond Vernon, *Anatomy of a Metropolis* (Cambridge, Mass.: Harvard University Press, 1959), p. 226.

ble 11.7.) Since separate income data are not available for ring areas in all cases, Table 10.5 measures intrametropolitan disparities by taking the ratio of median family income in the central city to median family income in the SMSA as a whole. A ratio below unity means that family income must be lower in the central city than in the rest of the metropolitan area.

City Age and Intrametropolitan Income Differentials

It is interesting to note that the income disadvantage of central cities is larger in the six metropolitan areas of the North and East than in the six of the South and West. This regional pattern is strongly associated with differences in the "age" of the central cities in the four regions.[10] As explained in Chapter 3, the older central cities of the Northeast and North Central regions enjoyed most of their population growth before the age of the automobile. They were built as "mass transit" cities and therefore developed high density levels. It was these older cities that suffered the earliest loss of jobs and of middle- and upper-income population to the suburbs when the truck and the automobile, coupled with rising living standards, made possible a more dispersed pattern of settlement. As middle-class families, in search of low-density neighborhoods, moved to new homes in the suburbs, old housing became available at low rents in the inner city to accommodate an influx of low-income population. Thus the income and wealth status of the older central cities fell below that of their suburbs as early as the 1950s.

On the other hand, the newer cities of the South and West were built largely after the age of rubber-tired transport had begun. To accommodate the automobile, they were laid out at much lower levels of density than the older cities. They are therefore more nearly suburban in physical character. Thus they are less affected by decentralizing forces than are the older central cities. In addition, they often have the advantage of very extensive boundaries and easy annexation of suburban territory. When dispersion does occur, it is therefore more likely to remain within the city limits or be recaptured by annexation. Consequently, their income status relative to suburban areas, although declining, is still fairly high. Moreover, since the structural distinction between central city and suburbs is less marked in the newer metropolitan areas of the South and West, it cannot be assumed that they will ever display central city–suburban income and wealth disparities as great as those of the older eastern and midwestern SMSAs.

The sharp relative decline in income in the older cities of the North and East shown in Table 10.5 has implications for metropolitan public finance that will be examined in Chapter 15.

10. In a careful statistical study, Leo F. Schnore has shown that age of an urbanized area is a significant predictor of city-suburban income differentials. See his *Urban Scene* (New York: Free Press, 1965), pp. 206–209. Schnore measured age by the census year in which a central city first reached a population of 50,000. In Chapter 3 we applied a somewhat different age measure.

Income Differences within Central Cities

In recent years growth of the urban poverty population combined with out-migration of the middle- and upper-income classes has not only held down the average level of income in the central city but has also led to an increasingly unequal distribution of income. The extent of the inequality can be measured by taking the proportion of families with incomes above 150 percent of the median to represent the well-to-do and the proportion below 50 percent of the median to represent the poor. In the central cities of SMSAs of one million or more, the former proportion increased from 23.5 percent in 1969 to 29.0 percent in 1983, while the latter rose from 20.0 percent to 24.9 percent. Consequently, the proportion of families whose incomes lie between 50 percent above and 50 percent below the median—comprising what might be described as the middle and lower middle classes—declined from 56.5 percent to 46.1 percent in just fourteen years.[11] The income distribution is moving in the same direction in the central cities of smaller SMSAs, but according to the measure used here, it is not yet as unequal. Thus central cities, especially the larger ones, are rapidly becoming the home of the poor and the well-to-do, while their middle class dwindles.

GROWTH AND SEGREGATION OF THE URBAN BLACK POPULATION

The same internal migration pattern that brought about the urbanization of poverty has, of course, also produced the urbanization of American blacks. Philip Hauser points out that

> in 1910, before large migratory streams of Negroes left the South, 73 per cent of the Negroes in the nation, as compared with 52 per cent of the Whites, lived in rural areas. . . . By 1960, the distribution of Negroes by urban-rural residence had become completely reversed, with 73 per cent of the Negro population residing in urban areas. . . . In fact, in 1960, Negroes were more highly urbanized than Whites.[12]

By 1980 fully 85 percent of the black population was living in places classified by the Census Bureau as urban.

Blacks moving out of the South before 1970 tended to settle in large rather than medium-sized or small metropolitan areas in other parts of the country.[13] Consequently, the black proportion of central city population increases markedly with SMSA size. Given the link between race and poverty,

11. Estimated from data in U.S. Bureau of the Census, *Current Population Reports*, various years.

12. Philip M. Hauser, "Demographic Factors in the Integration of the Negro," in Talcott Parsons and Kenneth B. Clark, eds., *The Negro American* (Boston: Beacon Press, 1967), p. 75.

13. John F. Kain and Joseph J. Persky, "The North's Stake in Southern Rural Poverty," in *Rural Poverty in the United States: A Report by the President's National Advisory Commission on Rural Poverty*, 1968, pp. 291–292.

TABLE 10.6
Racial Composition of Population in Central Cities and Suburbs

	COMPOSITION OF SMSA POPULATION[a] (%)			
	Central Cities		*Outside Central Cities*	
	1970	1982	1970	1982
White	77.8	72.9	94.4	91.3
Black	20.5	23.6	4.6	6.2
Spanish origin[b]	7.4	11.1	3.7	5.5

[a]Refers to the 243 SMSAs defined for the 1970 census. Hence areas are held constant.
[b]Persons of Spanish origin may be of any race.
Source: U.S. Bureau of the Census, *Current Population Reports*, series P-23, no. 130, December 1983, table 6.

the rapid growth and large size of the black population in central cities of large SMSAs helps to explain why the average poverty rate is so high in the central cities of large metropolitan areas.

Measuring the Extent of Racial Segregation

Table 10.6 shows that within metropolitan areas the blacks, like the poor, are highly concentrated in the central cities. Racial segregation on a heroic scale is indicated by the fact that in 1982 blacks made up almost 24 percent of total central city population as compared with less than 7 percent of population in the suburban ring. And, of course, there is a high degree of racial segregation *within* central cities as well.

Several indices have been developed to show the extent of racial segregation in cities and metropolitan areas. The most commonly used is one that measures the dissimilarity between two distributions. When applied to the spatial distributions of, say, the black and white populations in a given city, it shows the extent to which they are different, that is, segregated, from each other.

To illustrate, suppose that a city is divided into twenty districts of equal population size. If blacks and whites are distributed uniformly, each district will contain one-twentieth of the city's blacks and one-twentieth of its whites; there is no segregation. But if one tract contains three-quarters of the city's blacks and each of the others contains only 1 or 2 percent, there is clearly racial segregation. The index of dissimilarity, D, measures it as follows: Let b_i and w_i equal, respectively, the proportions of the city's blacks and whites that reside in the ith neighborhood. Then

$$D = \frac{1}{2} \sum_{i=1}^{n} \left| b_i - w_i \right| \times 100$$

TABLE 10.7
Segregation Indices for Selected U.S. Cities[a]

	POPULATION 1980 (THOUSANDS)	SEGREGATION INDEX		
		1960	*1970*	*1980*
National average of 28 central cities	—	88	87	81
Selected Cities, by Region[b]				
Northeast				
New York	7,071	79	77	75
Philadelphia	1,688	87	84	88
Baltimore	787	90	89	86
Washington	638	80	79	79
Midwest				
Chicago	3,005	93	93	92
Detroit	1,203	85	82	73
Indianapolis	701	92	90	83
Milwaukee	636	88	88	80
South				
Houston	1,594	94	93	81
Dallas	904	95	96	83
Memphis	646	92	92	85
New Orleans	557	86	84	76
West				
Los Angeles	2,967	82	90	81
Oakland	339	73	70	59

[a]For 1960, indices refer to black-white segregation; for 1970 and 1980, to black-nonblack segregation. All indices are calculated from block statistics.
[b]Of the 28 cities in the 1980 source, the four largest central cities in each region are shown. Only two are available in the West.
Sources: For 1960, Karl E. Taeuber and Alma F. Taeuber, *Negroes in Cities* (Chicago: Aldine, 1965) table 4; for 1970 and 1980, Karl E. Taeuber, *Racial Residential Segregation, 28 Cities, 1970–1980*, Working Paper 83–12 (Madison: University of Wisconsin, Center for Demography and Ecology, 1983), table 1.

When there is no segregation, $b_i = w_i$ for every district: the absolute-value term and consequently the index itself have a value of zero. At the other extreme, if blacks are concentrated into districts that are 100 percent black (in which case the same must be true for whites), the index will have a value of 100, indicating complete segregation of the races. For values of less than 100, the index indicates the proportion of either race that would have to be moved to eliminate any difference in the spatial distributions.[14]

Table 10.7 presents residential segregation indices for a number of U.S. cities in 1960, 1970, and 1980. Obviously, the level of segregation is high, but

14. See Karl E. Taeuber and Alma F. Taeuber, *Negroes in Cities* (Chicago: Aldine, 1965), pp. 29–31, 235–238.

in most cases it is also gradually diminishing. (The connection between racial segregation and discrimination in housing will be taken up in Chapters 12 and 13.)

The black proportion of central city population has increased in recent decades as a result of three factors: in-migration of blacks, out-migration of whites, and a higher rate of natural increase among blacks than whites.[15] Black in-migration, however, is no longer a factor. From 1970 to 1980 blacks moving out of central cities outnumbered those moving in by a substantial margin.[16] The second and third factors, however, continue to operate. Although fertility rates have been falling for both races, the black rate of natural increase still exceeds the white, and net migration of whites out of central cities continues on a massive scale. Unless black out-migration from central cities to suburbs rises very substantially, we must therefore expect the black proportion of central city population to go on increasing for some time to come.

Because many Americans are disturbed by the prospect of a society made up of increasingly black central cities surrounded by rings of largely white suburbs, a number of policies have been proposed, and some carried out, to encourage the suburbanization of blacks. These will be discussed in relation to antipoverty policy in Chapter 11 and housing policy in Chapter 13.

15. For a statistical study of the relative importance of each of these factors from 1950 to 1970, see Larry H. Long, "How the Racial Composition of Cities Changes," *Land Economics*, August 1975, pp. 258–267.

16. U.S. Bureau of the Census, *Current Population Reports*, series P-20, no. 368, December 1981, table F.

ELEVEN

Antipoverty Policies

Broadly speaking, there are three ways of relieving poverty. The first is to give money income to the poor; the second is to provide the poor with goods and services either free or below market price; the third is to help people acquire the skills and find the jobs with which they can earn adequate incomes by their own effort. The first method can be accurately described as "income-support policy." It includes both the existing forms of public aid (or "welfare"), which had their origin in the Social Security Act of 1935, and numerous proposals to supplement or replace those programs with a guaranteed minimum income or some other comprehensive system of direct income transfers. The second category, sometimes described as "benefits in kind," includes such programs as medical assistance (Medicaid), food stamps, and housing subsidies. The third category covers a variety of strategies that is difficult to describe with a single phrase; for want of a better term these are usually called "employment policies."

A fourth group, which does not fit easily into this system of classification, comprises policies directed toward specific, geographically identifiable areas. Because these policies (when applied in the urban context) are concerned explicitly with the question of where the poor live within metropolitan areas and what effect location has on their welfare, they are of particular interest to students of urban economics. Included in this category are programs such as enterprise zones that are intended to stimulate economic activity inside urban poverty areas, as well as policies to encourage the dispersion of the poor—out of their central city neighborhoods and into the suburbs, where employment opportunities are presumed to be greater.

We will look first at employment policies, then at income-support and benefit-in-kind programs, and finally at policies that are area-oriented. Benefit-in-kind programs will be discussed simultaneously with income-support schemes, since eligibility for them is always linked to the income level of the claimant, and the two types of program are often jointly administered. Housing subsidies for the poor will be treated at length in Chapter 13.

It must be emphasized at the outset that employment policies and income-support policies are complementary rather than alternative ways of dealing with the problem of poverty. Obviously, employment policies can help only the employable poor. Those who cannot work, including children, the disabled, and others who are for some reason unemployable; those whom society decides ought not to be forced to work, including the elderly and the single head of household with young children; and those whose earning capacity even after reasonable training leaves them still impoverished will always require some form of income support to raise them out of poverty. Nor can the time dimension be ignored: some, though not all, employment policies operate slowly, whereas income support, once established, can be effective immediately.

THREE TYPES OF EMPLOYMENT POLICY

Employment policies have been heavily emphasized in federal legislation since the early 1960s. The War on Poverty may be said to have begun with the passage of the Economic Opportunity Act in 1964. The very title of that act revealed its commitment to employment: the "opportunity" it sought to open up to the poor was the chance to rise out of poverty by improving their skills and finding decently paid jobs.

Employment policies can be divided into three types according to the point at which they have impact on the labor market. The three types are policies affecting the supply side, policies affecting the demand side, and policies intended to match supply and demand more effectively.[1] We will first describe these three types and then attempt to evaluate them.

Training, Education, and Human Capital

Policies "on the supply side" are those that try to improve the training and education of the poor. Their purpose is to raise individual productivity so that the poor become better qualified to fill existing vacancies or to advance out of low-end jobs that leave them still impoverished. These policies operate on the supply side of the labor market because their effect is to increase the supply of productive skill. (Hence they are sometimes called "skill creation"

1. Sar A. Levitan, *Programs in Aid of the Poor for the 1970s* (Baltimore: Johns Hopkins University Press, 1969), p. 49.

policies.) By themselves, however, they do not increase the demand for labor in the sense of shifting the employer's demand curve upward.

The provision of training and education can be regarded as a form of investment—investment in human resources or, as it is now called, "human capital." Human capital is the store of productive knowledge and skill that the individual possesses. Lester Thurow explains the link between human capital and income as follows:

> Human capital . . . is one of the key determinants of the distribution of income. Individuals with little education, training, and skills have low marginal productivities and earn low incomes. With very little human capital they earn poverty incomes. . . . What might be called the productivity approach to the elimination of poverty and low Negro income is thus aimed at improving the quantity and distribution of human capital.[2]

Job Creation

At the other end of the spectrum of employment policies are those that operate on the demand side of the market. These strategies attempt to help the poor by stimulating the demand for labor. In effect, they operate by shifting the demand curve for labor upward and to the right so that the total number of jobs available at existing wage rates increases. (Hence they are often called "job creation" policies.) They include such programs as providing special jobs in the public sector for unemployed or disadvantaged workers or subsidizing private employment for the long-term unemployed. Demand-side and supply-side policies can be coordinated, as when workers who take subsidized jobs are simultaneously provided with on-the-job training and counseling or, in the opposite sequence, if workers are first trained and then offered subsidized employment.

Job creation also includes the macroeconomic policy of operating the economy at high pressure in order to hold overall unemployment to a bare minimum. According to the "queuing" theory of the labor market, employers rank the corps of job seekers available to them at any particular moment along a continuum from most to least desirable. This continuum is the "queue" from which employers always hire as near to the front end as possible. The low-skilled, the disadvantaged, the minorities are concentrated at the rear end of the queue. The theory consequently predicts that they will be "last hired, first fired." If nationwide unemployment rises, their rate of unemployment will rise faster than the average; if nationwide unemployment falls, their rate will fall faster than the average. If these propositions are true, then the relative economic position of poor minority groups and the disadvantaged can be improved substantially by macroeconomic policies that maintain tight labor markets.

2. Lester C. Thurow, *Poverty and Discrimination* (Washington, D.C.: Brookings Institution, 1969), p. 66

A final entry under the broad heading of job creation is the prescription that strong economic growth would automatically produce enough jobs to allow most of the poor to work their way out of poverty. In the version endorsed by conservatives in the 1980s this policy requires not that the government take positive action to stimulate growth but rather that it simply "get out of the way" of the private sector by cutting taxes and reducing regulation. This prescription reverses the assumptions under which the War on Poverty began. In 1964 the President's Council of Economic Advisers provided the justification for a positive antipoverty policy by arguing just the opposite case: "In the future economic growth alone will provide relatively few escapes from poverty. Policy will have to be more sharply focused on the handicaps that deny the poor fair access to the expanding incomes of a growing economy."[3]

Overcoming Discrimination

Between the policies that increase supply and those that rely on demand lies a third group, which attempts to help the poor by overcoming "imperfections" in the labor market itself. Among imperfections that have serious effects on the poor, the foremost is probably employment discrimination against blacks and other minorities. The problem of discrimination in employment has been attacked by all levels of government through various forms of fair employment practices legislation.

The effects of employment discrimination have been demonstrated repeatedly in studies comparing the returns to education earned by whites with those earned by blacks. Using the human capital approach and nationwide data for 1960, Thurow studied the returns to education and to work experience. He estimated that with twenty years of experience and eight years of education, white males earned $1,367 more per year than blacks similarly situated. Holding experience constant but increasing education to twelve years raised the white advantage to $1,750. With sixteen years of education completed (a college degree), the gap widened to $3,556.[4] As Thurow stresses, not all of this difference can be attributed to employment discrimination against blacks. Many other factors are at work. But a part of the difference is undoubtedly caused by discrimination in the sense of lower pay for equal work, restricted access to better-paying jobs, and less opportunity for promotion.

Education, occupation, sex, and age (the last as a proxy for experience) are among the principal determinants of individual earnings. When these factors are controlled for, data from the 1980 census show that substantial differences still remain between the mean earnings of employed blacks and employed whites. For example, Table 11.1 shows that in 1979 black males aged

3. Quoted in Peter Gottschalk and Sheldon Danziger, "Macroeconomic Conditions, Income Transfers, and the Trend in Poverty," in D. Lee Bawden, ed., *The Social Contract Revisited* (Washington, D.C.: Urban Institute Press, 1984), p. 185
4. Thurow, table 5-2, p. 79.

TABLE 11.1
Earnings Disparities between Black and White Males with Four Years of College Education: 1979 and 1969

	RATIO OF MEAN BLACK TO MEAN WHITE EARNINGS BY AGE GROUP[a]		
	25–34	35–44	45–54
Earnings in 1979			
Executive, administrative, and managerial occupations	.80	.67	.61
All occupations	.83	.70	.61
Earnings in 1969			
Managers and administrators, except farm	.75	.56	
All occupations	.77	.60	

[a]For males who worked year-round, full-time.
Sources: U.S. Bureau of the Census, *1980 Census of Population*, PC 80-2-8B, April 1984, tables 3 and 4; *1970 Census of Population*, PC (2)-8B, January 1973, tables 1 and 2.

35 to 44 with four years of college education, in the occupational category of executive administrators and managers, earned 33 percent less than their white counterparts. Some of this disparity probably results from differences in the distribution of blacks and whites among the subcategories of this large occupational group and among regions of the United States in which incomes vary, but part of the difference also reflects the effects of employment discrimination. It is interesting to note that the racial income disparity in the same occupational group for men aged 25 to 34 was only 20 percent in 1979. This can be interpreted optimistically as indicating that blacks who entered the labor force recently faced less discrimination than did their predecessors. On the other hand, there is a less cheerful aspect to the data. The 1970 census indicates that in a comparable (though not identical) occupational group, black males *then* aged 25–34 *then* earned 25 percent less than whites. This is the cohort that was aged 35–44 ten years later, by which time the disparity had increased to 33 percent. It thus appears that the disparities blacks face when they enter the labor force as managers and administrators subsequently grow larger because blacks fail to obtain pay increases or promotions on a par with whites. Data for all occupations taken together show a strikingly similar pattern (see Table 11.1). Evidently, the force of discrimination is not abating as fast as the gains made by the youngest cohort of black workers would suggest.[5]

5. For a longer view and a more optimistic interpretation, see James P. Smith and Finis R. Welch, *Closing the Gap: Forty Years of Economic Progress for Blacks*, doc. no. R-3330-DOL (Santa Monica, Calif.: Rand Corp., February 1986), pp. 4–20.

Lack of job and career information is another form of market imperfection that is thought seriously to restrict the earnings of the poor and especially of those living in poverty areas where they are out of the economic mainstream. Counseling and information services have therefore been made an important component of many antipoverty programs.

THE GROWTH AND DECLINE OF EMPLOYMENT
AND TRAINING PROGRAMS

Federally assisted employment and training programs expanded rapidly after the mid-1960s. In 1964, when the War on Poverty began, federal outlays on employment services, training programs, and miscellaneous manpower aids came to $389 million. By 1970 the total had increased to $1.6 billion and by 1978 to a peak of $9.7 billion before declining to about $4 billion in 1986 (see Table 11.2). During that interval a diverse array of employment programs was put into operation or at least tested. No attempt will be made here to list them all. Instead, we will try to convey a sense of the whole by outlining the development of antipoverty policy and analyzing some representative programs.

In the 1960s supply-side policies predominated. The strategy of the War on Poverty was based on a belief that, as Robert Haveman put it, "the poor . . . could earn their way out of poverty if given additional education and skills."[6] Most antipoverty programs therefore contained a large training component, together with emphasis on counseling, job information, and placement. Few of the programs of the 1960s operated on the demand side in the sense of subsidizing specific new positions for the poor or the unemployed. It was widely recognized that training and counseling would be fruitless unless jobs were available at the end of the road. However, the government relied on general macroeconomic stimulation rather than direct job creation through antipoverty initiatives to ensure the necessary demand for labor and keep the job market "tight."

The early 1970s brought a change in emphasis. The policy of maintaining tight labor markets in order to fight poverty ran into trouble. Advocates of that policy always recognized that it would cause some price inflation, perhaps even a higher rate of inflation than most people had previously thought tolerable, but they believed that given the trade-off between price stability and full employment, it was desirable to accept some price inflation for the sake of greater success in fighting poverty. After 1970, however, the rate of inflation seemed to be getting out of hand. The federal government shifted toward increasingly restrictive monetary policies in the hope of restraining in-

6. Robert H. Haveman, "Direct Job Creation," in Eli Ginzberg, ed., *Employing the Unemployed* (New York: Basic Books, 1980), p. 146.

TABLE 11.2
Federal Expenditures on Employment and Training (fiscal years, millions of dollars)

	1978	1981	1984	1986 (EST.)
Grants to states and localities for training and work experience programs	2,378	3,117	1,886	1,883
Job Corps	280	540	600	614
Summer Youth Employment	670	769	825	775
Public Service Employment	5,764	2,387	0	0
Other programs[a]	608	787	651	965
Total	9,700	7,600	3,962	4,237

[a]Includes programs for dislocated workers, the Work Incentive Program (WIN), programs for older workers, and other national programs.
Sources: Vee Burke, *Cash and Non-cash Benefits for Persons with Limited Income* (Washington, D.C.: Congressional Research Service, various years); *Budget of the United States Government, Fiscal Years 1986, 1987.*

flation, even at the price of higher rates of unemployment. Inevitably, the price was paid. The average rate of unemployment for all workers rose from 4.8 percent in the 1960s to 6.2 percent in the 1970s. For whites it rose from 4.3 percent to 5.6 percent, for blacks and other races from 9.0 percent to 11.0 percent. (It is a standard observation that black unemployment rates are twice those of whites.)

In this context, with the economy suffering simultaneously from inflation and unemployment, antipoverty policy moved increasingly to the demand side, and it did so by putting much greater emphasis on direct job creation. Subsidized jobs, made available directly to the poor and the long-term unemployed could, so it was argued, reduce unemployment and meet the objectives of antipoverty policy without generating much inflationary pressure. In 1971 Congress adopted the Public Employment Program (PEP), the first large-scale job-creation initiative since those of the Great Depression. PEP provided a federal subsidy of up to 90 percent of the cost of approved new public employment programs in state and local governments.

The Comprehensive Employment and Training Act

In 1973 Congress passed the Comprehensive Employment and Training Act (CETA), establishing the legal framework under which most employment and training programs were to operate for the next ten years.[7] The ob-

7. See John L. Palmer, "Employment and Training Assistance," in J. A. Pechman, ed., *Setting National Priorities: The 1978 Budget* (Washington, D.C.: Brookings Institution, 1977) p. 150–151.

jective was to simplify and decentralize administration of a vast array of programs by giving state and local governments control over many of the federally funded plans operating within their boundaries. Included under the CETA umbrella were the following:

- A nationwide program of comprehensive training, employment, counseling, and placement programs, to be administered locally
- A set of nationally administered programs for categorically defined groups in which the federal government took a specific interest, including youth, migrant workers, and Native Americans
- The Job Corps, a program initiated by the Office of Economic Opportunity in 1964 to serve disadvantaged youth, and the only federal undertaking that provides training and counseling in a residential/ institutional setting
- Two public service employment schemes, one a permanent program as successor to PEP, the other an emergency program to combat cyclic unemployment by financing jobs in state and local government

Declining Expenditures during the 1980s

Table 11.2 shows federal outlays for the principal categories of employment and training activity. The peak level reached in the late 1970s is accounted for by the public service employment programs adopted by the Carter administration to stimulate economic recovery from the mid-1970s recession. These programs were phased out in 1980 and 1981.

In 1982 under the Reagan administration, CETA was replaced by JTPA, the Job Training Partnership Act. State and local control over training programs was extended, and new, local "private industry councils" were set up as overseers. In keeping with conservative economic principles, the new act made no provision for using public service employment programs in aid of the poor. In addition, outlays for training and work experience programs, by far the largest remaining category, were cut back sharply under President Reagan. As the top line of Table 11.2 shows, they fell almost 40 percent between 1981 and 1986. Indeed, no other major category of domestic spending was reduced as sharply.[8]

The decline in outlays for training and employment came about not only because the Reagan administration was determined to reduce domestic spending but also because doubts about their effectiveness had arisen among liberals as well as conservatives. What can we say about the success of such programs in reducing poverty? Which kinds have worked? How much improvement have they produced? We look first at training policies.

8. See Marc Bendick, Jr., "Employment Training and Economic Development," in John L. Palmer and Isabel V. Sawhill, eds., *The Reagan Experiment* (Washington, D.C.: Urban Institute Press, 1982), ch. 8.

Evaluation of Training Programs

Programs intended to raise the skill level and employability of the disadvantaged have consisted of classroom training, on-the-job training, work experience, or some combination of the three. (Work experience programs attempt to increase employability by instilling acceptable work habits rather than concentrating on particular skills.) All three of these are relatively amenable to benefit-cost analysis. Consequently, there is a large body of literature on the evaluation of poverty-oriented training programs.[9] As we shall see, however, there remains considerable disagreement about the validity of particular evaluations.

In a benefit-cost analysis of a training scheme, benefits arc usually defined as the gain in earnings of trainees as compared either with their pre-enrollment level or with the earnings of a control group of nontrainees. If the study is conducted within a year or two after the program ends, the analyst must supply an estimate of how far into the future the gain in earnings is expected to persist. Many studies stop at this point. Instead of carrying out a full benefit-cost analysis, they focus on the important underlying question of how large an earnings gain (if any) the program produces. If costs are to be examined as well, the categories that must be included are the costs of instruction and administration and the earnings forgone by trainees while enrolled in the program. The expected benefit stream and the computed costs are then both discounted to obtain present values, and the end result is a comparison between the present value of benefits and that of costs. As long as the former exceeds the latter, undertaking the program will produce a net gain for society. In principle, if budget funds are limited, public authorities should choose the combination of programs that will produce the largest total net gain within the budget constraint.[10]

Like much else in economics, that is easier said than done. Difficult problems arise in carrying out the analysis. Perhaps the most difficult is to establish a "control group" of nontrainees with whom graduates of the training program can be compared in order to estimate the effects of training on earnings. The only scientifically correct procedure is one that randomly assigns individuals from the initial pool into two groups, one to receive training, the other not. The latter then serves as the control group. But random assign-

9. For surveys of this literature see Michael E. Borus, "Assessing the Impact of Training Programs," in Eli Ginzberg, ed., *Employing the Unemployed* (New York: Basic Books, 1980), ch. 2; Henry M. Levin, "A Decade of Policy Developments in Improving Education and Training for Low Income Populations," in Robert H. Haveman, ed., *A Decade of Federal Antipoverty Programs* (New York: Academic Press, 1977), ch. 4; and Congressional Joint Economic Committee, *The Effectiveness of Manpower Training Programs: A Review of Research on the Impact on the Poor,* (Washington, D.C.: U.S. Government Printing Office, November 1972).

10. A. R. Prest and R. Turvey, "Cost-Benefit Analysis: A Survey," in International Economic Association, *Survey of Economic Theory,* vol. 3 (New York: St. Martin's Press, 1966), pp. 105–207, provides an excellent introduciton to the theory and practice of cost-benefit analysis. It discusses applications to general education but refers only briefly to manpower training.

ment can occur only if the program is originally set up as an "experiment" rather than as a training program, and that has rarely been the case. For the most part, analysts have had to create comparison groups by statistical means, that is, by finding nontrainees whose observable socioeconomic characteristics closely match those of the trainees. But this procedure can never eliminate all doubts about the estimated effects of training. For example, it may be that those who voluntarily enrolled in the training program were more strongly motivated to seek economic gains than were the otherwise similar nonenrollees in the comparison group. In that case, the gains made by trainees might be the result of their stronger motivation rather than their training.[11]

Second, if training does increase worker productivity and we observe this in the first year after training, how far into the future can we expect the gain to persist, given the rapid obsolescence of specific skills? Until recently, follow-up studies rarely extended beyond the first year, so the probable duration of benefits remained an unresolved question. The analyst had to settle it by assumption, and the assumption was likely to be crucial to the outcome: an assumed ten-year benefit stream almost always produced a favorable benefit-cost verdict; an assumed five-year stream sometimes did not.[12] In some cases it is possible to resolve this problem by studying "longitudinal" data—that is to say, data that follow the wage history of particular workers through time. Making use of such information, which is now available from Social Security records, Orley Ashenfelter analyzed the incomes earned through a five-year posttraining period by workers who completed a government-sponsored training course in 1964.[13] Trainee earnings were compared over time with those of a randomly selected control group that had not received training. Ashenfelter estimated that the courses produced an increase in the earnings of all trainee groups in the period immediately following course completion. The increase for both white and black women was on the order of $300 to $600 per year and did not decline over time. The increase for men was smaller and declined by about half over the five-year period. Ashenfelter did not carry out a benefit-cost analysis, but his rough estimate was that the programs in question probably yielded a very high rate of return over cost for women and an acceptable rate of return over cost for men.[14]

11. See Laurie J. Bassi and Orley Ashenfelter, "The Effect of Direct Job Creation and Training Programs on Low-skilled Workers," in Sheldon H. Danziger and Daniel H. Weinberg, eds., *Fighting Poverty: What Works and What Doesn't* (Cambridge: Harvard University Press, 1986), pp. 138–140, 150–151.

12. Congressional Joint Economic Committee, p. 30.

13. Orley Ashenfelter, "Estimating the Effect of Training Programs on Earnings," *The Review of Economics and Statistics*, February 1978, pp. 47–57. Needless to say, the Social Security data used in studies of this type are made available in a way that does not reveal worker identity.

14. Ibid., p. 56. For a more favorable estimate of the outcome using the same data, see Howard S. Bloom, "Estimating the Effect of Job-training Programs Using Longitudinal Data: Ashenfelter's Findings Reconsidered," *Journal of Human Resources*, August 1984, pp. 544–556.

A third source of uncertainty in the evaluation of training programs is the possible existence of indirect benefits. Economists generally recognize that training programs may have socially beneficial indirect effects associated with the increased incomes they produce, such as a reduction in crime and civil disorder or an improvement in family stability or health. These indirect benefits are usually omitted from benefit-cost calculations because it is so difficult to estimate their monetary value. Leaving them out, however, may impart a significant downward bias to measured benefit-cost ratios.

A final problem is the question of job creation versus job displacement. If a formerly unemployed youth receives subsidized training and then finds a job, we cannot be sure whether that job represents an addition to total employment that would not have taken place without the training program (i.e., job creation occurs) or whether it is simply a job that would have existed anyway and would otherwise have gone to a nontrainee (i.e., there is job displacement). If job creation occurs, the economic gains made by the trainee are also gains to society as a whole, and a benefit-cost analysis from the social point of view is likely to be favorable. But if job displacement occurs, there is no net gain to society. Employment and income have simply been redistributed from losers to gainers. Thus a training program may be successful in producing enhanced earnings for its graduates without necessarily producing direct benefits for society.[15] (There might, of course, be indirect benefits, as already discussed.)

So much for the caveats. What have the many evaluations of antipoverty training programs purportedly shown? It would be impossible to summarize the literature in a few sentences, but it is fair to say that a consensus has emerged on some major points:

1. Training has often substantially increased the earnings of women participants but has usually been ineffective for men.
2. Trainees with the least amount of labor market experience tend to benefit the most.
3. Consistent with points 1 and 2, economically disadvantaged minority women are among those who register the largest gains.
4. Gains attributable to training result mainly from more hours worked per year rather than from higher wages earned per hour.
5. Classroom training, on-the-job training, and work experience have all been effective in raising earnings, although the last has sometimes ranked below the other two.

These conclusions can be illustrated with results from some specific studies. In an evaluation prepared for the Congressional Budget Office and

15. See the discussion of displacement effects in G. G. Somers and W. D. Wood, eds., *Cost-Benefit Analysis of Manpower Policies: Proceedings of a North American Conference* (Kingston, Ontario: Industrial Relations Centre, Queen's University, 1969), passim, and in Bassi and Ashenfelter, p. 33.

the National Commission for Employment Policy, Howard S. Bloom and Maureen A. McLaughlin estimated that CETA training programs raised women's annual earnings by $800 to $1,300 per year in 1980 dollars.[16] These gains did not diminish during the two or three years after training. Changes in men's earnings were statistically insignificant. Approximately four-fifths of the gains for women resulted from increased labor time, reflecting increased labor force participation, a higher frequency of employment, and more hours worked per week when employed. Only one-fifth was due to higher posttraining wage rates.[17] The average cost per participant in the programs under review was $2,400.[18] The report made no benefit-cost calculations, but it pointed out that for persons with limited previous employment experience (a group that would include many minority women) "the discounted value of the participants' increased earnings during the next several years approximately equaled the federal costs of training."[19] That strongly suggests that a benefit-cost analysis of programs aimed at disadvantaged women would produce a favorable judgment.

The results obtained from the National Supported Work Demonstration are consistent with the findings just cited for training programs under CETA. Initiated in 1975 with a planned life of five years, Supported Work was an experimental program with a built-in research component that was undertaken to find out whether a carefully developed work experience program could help people with severe employment handicaps to join (or rejoin) the labor force. Four groups were eligible to enroll: women who had long been on AFDC (Aid to Families with Dependent Children—in common parlance, "welfare"), former drug addicts, unemployed ex-offenders, and young school dropouts. Participants were employed at sites staffed by the project, where they were supervised and gradually prepared for real-world jobs. Thus the program combined three elements: training, employment, and counseling. The fact that participants were randomly divided between the training and control groups should increase our confidence in the findings from this experiment.[20]

The effects of the Supported Work Demonstration were highly favorable for the AFDC group, reasonably good for ex-addicts, and weak for the two other groups. Stanley Masters reports that when they had completed the program, earnings of AFDC participants averaged $59.23 a month (or about $710 a year) more than earnings of the control group. In relative terms, partic-

16. Howard S. Bloom and Maureen. A. McLaughlin, *CETA Training Programs: Do They Work for Adults?* (Washington, D.C.: Congressional Budget Office, July 1982), summary table 2.

17. Ibid., p. 21.

18. Ibid., table 4.

19. Ibid., p. xxi.

20. See Gary Burtless and Robert Haveman, *Policy Lessons from Three Labor Market Experiments*, discussion paper no. 746-84, University of Wisconsin, Institute for Research on Poverty, March 1984, pp. 10–15.

ipation appears to have raised earnings about 28 percent.[21] The benefit-cost ratio was estimated to be 2.17 for the AFDC group and 1.83 for the ex-addicts, indicating that from society's point of view the intensive guidance and training supplied to these highly disadvantaged groups did indeed pay off. On the other hand, the ratio was only .71 for the youth group and was ambiguous for ex-offenders.[22]

What general conclusions can we reach on the basis of these very numerous program evaluations? On the one hand, since female-headed families are the most rapidly growing segment of the poverty population, it is good news to find that remediation programs are efficient in helping impoverished women, including even the most disadvantaged, to increase their earnings. On the other hand, the absolute size of the income gain is usually quite small. In a survey of more than two dozen studies, Michael Borus found that it is typically well under $1,000 a year and therefore "will not substantially reduce the number of persons in poverty."[23] We are left with the paradox of having discovered worthwhile programs that nevertheless do not make much difference.

Evaluation of Demand-Side Policies: Tight Labor Markets

We turn next to the evaluation of demand-side antipoverty policies. One of these is the policy of maintaining tight labor markets by using the tools of monetary and fiscal policy to keep aggregate demand in the economy at an appropriately high level.

We have already pointed out that job-creation programs and skill-creation programs are complementary. If the demand for labor is weak, graduates of training programs will have difficulty in obtaining jobs. Their training may go to waste. Furthermore, the power of training programs to attract and hold trainees depends on their record of success in leading to employment. trainees *do* find jobs while unemployment is widespread, it may be reasonable to assume that they have taken positions that otherwise would have been filled by qualified nontrainees: job displacement occurs, and there is no net gain to society as a whole. By reducing the probability of displacement, tight labor markets promote the efficient operation of training programs.

In addition to the fact that it complements training programs, a policy of maintaining tight labor markets also has a direct, positive effect on the relative income status of the disadvantaged. Let us see why. We have already pointed out that the unemployment rate of blacks is generally twice the rate

---

21. Stanley Masters, "The Effects of Supported Work on the Earnings and Transfer Payments of Its Target Group," *Journal of Human Resources*, Fall 1981, table 4.
22. Manpower Demonstration Research Corp., *Summary and Findings of the National Supported Work Demonstration* (Cambridge, Mass.: Ballinger, 1980), tables 8-1 through 8-4.
23. Borus, p. 38.

for whites. To simplify the argument, suppose that this ratio is constant over the course of the business cycle. In that case, as the economy moves toward full employment, for every decline of 1.0 in the white unemployment rate, the black unemployment rate will fall by 2.0. Relative to the size of their respective labor forces, twice as many blacks as whites will be moving from unemployment into jobs. We would therefore expect black income to rise much faster than white. In a recession, the situation would be reversed. Black unemployment would increase twice as fast as white, and black income would therefore fall much faster.

A study by Edward M. Gramlich and Deborah S. Laren verifies the existence of such a pattern. They analyzed longitudinal data for more than 3,000 families over the period 1967 to 1980 and found that a one percentage point rise in the national unemployment rate led on average to a 2.0 percent decline in the earnings of nonwhite males but only a 1.2 percent decline for white males. Differential effects by income class were even stronger than those by race. A given rise in the unemployment rate caused a percentage drop in earnings for low-income families two to four times as large as that suffered by those with high incomes.[24]

Evaluating Direct Job Creation

Despite its capacity to raise the relative income status of the poor and of minorities, the policy of maintaining tight labor markets was abandoned in the 1970s because it was contributing to the acceleration of inflation. In place of macroeconomic measures, the federal government turned increasingly to direct job creation as the preferred policy to boost the demand for labor.

Direct job creation operates by subsidizing new positions specifically for the poor and the unemployed. Proponents of this approach argue that it can produce additional employment with much less inflation than would occur under a policy of general economic stimulation. As Robert Solow explains it, one version of this argument is based on "the premise that the general wage level is really determined in an industrial and occupational core of the economy. This core comprises large firms in major industries . . . employing many highly skilled workers in regular jobs, paying high wages, which have often been determined by collective bargaining." An expansionary policy of tax cuts or increases in government expenditure would immediately stimulate activity in this "core," thereby driving wages up in all sectors and accelerating inflation. In contrast to this, direct job creation can take place in peripheral areas of the economy, "exercising little influence on the general wage level."[25] In addition, job creation can be focused on areas or population

24. Edward M. Gramlich and Deborah S. Laren, "How Widespread Are Income Losses in a Recession?" in Bawden, table 3, p. 165.
25. Robert M. Solow, "Employment Policy in Inflationary Times," in Ginzberg, pp. 136–137.

groups that have a particularly high rate of unemployment. For these reasons it would be expected to generate more jobs and less inflationary pressure per dollar of expenditure than would general macroeconomic stimulation.

Direct job creation, however, brings its own set of problems, often involving conflicts between individually laudable objectives. We look first at three problems of job creation in the public sector.

1. *Displacement effects.* Job creation policies fulfill their purpose only if they cause a net expansion of employment. If the subsidized job simply takes the place of a previously existing unsubsidized one, there is displacement rather than expansion—no job creation has taken place. When CETA funds became available to subsidize local government jobs in the mid-1970s, a substantial amount of displacement occurred. However, after eligibility rules for CETA jobs were tightened up in 1978, displacement was sharply reduced.[26]

2. *Value of the job and of its output.* Unless a subsidized job produces useful output, it is a delusion to weigh it in the same scales as ordinary employment. As Baily and Tobin put it, "Shifting a person from recorded unemployment to employment in a job empty of product and training is useless or worse."[27] Yet the desire that subsidized jobs produce useful output clearly conflicts with the need to avoid displacement. The most useful, or at least the most "doable," things are presumably already being done, even by local governments not noted for their efficiency. The jobs that can be done without displacement are therefore unlikely to have highly valued outputs.

3. *Incentives for public-sector managers.* If the local managers of subsidized workers are expected to produce useful output, they will try to hire the most skilled and experienced workers among those who are eligible for subsidy, rather than the most disadvantaged (a practice known as "creaming"). In that case there is a fair probability that the workers they hire would otherwise have found an *un*subsidized job. A form of displacement will have occurred. On the other hand, if the managers are told that the objective is just to provide "jobs" for some low-skill workers, they are not likely to make the effort needed to organize useful work. Without belaboring the point, it should be obvious that organizing useful, subsidized employment in the public sector is a very difficult task.

Federal outlays for public service employment reached a very high level in the late 1970s (see Table 11.2) because the Carter administration used that program as a way of combining antipoverty policy with macroeconomic stimulation. "At its peak in March 1978," according to Marc Bendick, "the program enrolled more than 750,000 persons, about 10 percent of all those unem-

26. Charles F. Adams, Jr., et al., "A Pooled Time-Series Analysis of the Job Creation Impact of Public Service Employment Grants to Large Cities," *Journal of Human Resources,* Spring 1983, pp. 283–294.

27. Martin Neil Baily and James Tobin, "Inflation-Unemployment Consequences of Job Creation Policies," in John L. Palmer, ed., *Creating Jobs: Public Employment Programs and Wage Subsidies* (Washington, D.C.: Brookings Institution, 1978), p. 73.

ployed at that time."[28] Outlays declined after 1978, and the program was ultimately halted in 1981 for a combination of reasons. First, the economy had recovered from the recession of the mid-1970s, so economic stimulation was no longer needed. Second, the program had been criticized, apparently with some justification, for waste and mismanagement. Third, amendments adopted in 1978 restricted eligibility to the economically disadvantaged. Bendick argues that this made the program less attractive to local governments, which had previously "been free to hire less disadvantaged employees" and therefore "political support for the program waned."[29] Finally, the Reagan administration, though going through another recession in 1982–1983, was opposed on principle to using public service jobs either to counteract unemployment or to provide opportunities to the poor.

The job-creation initiatives of the 1970s had included a private-sector as well as a public-sector component. The New Jobs Tax Credit was instituted in 1977 but was replaced by the Targeted Jobs Tax Credit, effective in 1979. TJTC was continued by the Reagan administration since its private-sector orientation was consistent with the administration's philosophy. It is a program to subsidize jobs in the private sector for special categories of workers, including disadvantaged youth, the disabled, and welfare recipients. Employers receive a tax credit equal to 50 percent of the first $6,000 of wages paid to qualifying workers during the first year of their employment and 25 percent during the second year. Unfortunately, very little use has been made of this program.[30]

Job Creation through Economic Growth

Last among job-creation policies is the plan of relying on economic growth to generate the jobs that will raise the poor out of their poverty. How effective is that policy likely to be? We know that economic growth, by virtue of its definition, raises the average standard of living. It was explained at the beginning of Chapter 10 that if an absolute standard of poverty is employed and the distribution of income does not become more unequal over time, a rise in the average standard of living will reduce the rate of poverty. There is abundant evidence that growth has had that effect in the past. By today's standards most Americans in the 1920s were living in poverty. Looking at more recent history, Peter Gottschalk and Sheldon Danziger estimate that increases in the average standard of living (due to economic growth) and increases in the average level of transfer payments were of roughly equal importance in reducing the official rate of poverty from 14.2 percent in 1967 to 11.7 percent in 1979. The rate then *rose* to 15.0 percent by 1982 because the aver-

28. Bendick, p. 256.
29. Ibid., p. 258.
30. Dave M. O'Neill, "Employment Tax Credit Programs: The Effects of Socioeconomic Targeting Provisions," *Journal of Human Resources*, Summer 1982, p. 453.

age standard of living now *fell* (i.e., real growth was negative), the distribution of income became more unequal, and the rise in transfer payments was insufficient to offset those forces.[31]

No one doubts that as economic growth resumes in the United States it will again help to reduce poverty. The debatable question is, How strong will that effect be? Pessimists point out that the poverty population is increasingly concentrated in households headed by women (49 percent in 1984, compared with only 26 percent in 1959) and that because many of these women are not in the labor force, a large segment of the poverty population is not in a position to benefit much from economic growth.[32] In other words, demographic changes are making the distribution of income more unequal, which tends to offset the poverty-reducing effect of growth.

Other analysts who are a little less pessimistic point out that economic growth, by raising prospective earnings, will induce more female heads of families to work, thus raising at least some of them out of poverty. Furthermore, it can be argued that with sustained growth men will have better economic prospects, which will encourage stable marriages, stem the increase in female-headed households, and thus contribute indirectly to a reduction in the rate of poverty.[33] But few of those endorsing the virtues of economic growth would claim that its effects are powerful enough to solve the problem of poverty for the nation's minorities without the help of some forms of special assistance.

In the next section we analyze income-support programs as antipoverty policy. In recent years income transfers have substantially reduced poverty in the United States. No one questions that, but as we shall see, there is a good deal of debate about the form that income support should take and how far it should be carried.

THE ROLE OF INCOME SUPPORT

No matter how successful employment policies may prove to be, income support in the form of transfer payments from the government is undoubtedly necessary to combat poverty. In any society there is a large number of families whose adult members are outside the labor force either because they have retired or are disabled or because society believes they should not work. If these families have inadequate pensions or other sources of income, they can be raised out of poverty only by some form of transfer payment. Another large group consists of families with heads whose earning power is so

31. Gottschalk and Danziger, pp. 199–200.
32. Ibid., p. 207, and see Danziger and Gottschalk, "Do Rising Tides Lift All Boats? The Impact of Secular and Cyclical Changes on Poverty," *American Economic Review*, May 1986, p. 410.
33. See June A. O'Neill, "Comments," in Bawden, pp. 218–219.

low that even when they are employed full-time, their families remain below the poverty line. Although some of these "working poor" may raise themselves out of poverty by acquiring higher skills or better-paying jobs, others will remain impoverished unless they are relieved by direct cash payments.

In the last quarter century the composition of the poverty population has changed radically. The proportion of poor families with no wage earner rose from 24 percent in 1959 to 40 percent in 1984. These are the families who necessarily rely on income support. At the same time, the proportion with a family head who worked year-round at a full-time job (the working poor) fell from 32 percent to 17 percent. Both changes result from the same cause: the rising trend of labor productivity. As Thurow points out:

> Those who are able to take advantage of better job opportunities or of government programs to increase individual productivity are gradually drawn out of the poverty pool. Those who cannot benefit are left at the bottom of the income distribution and consequently represent an increasing fraction of the poor. . . . The bottom of the income distribution will be increasingly made up of those not in the labor force.[34]

Thus as time passes and the number of families living in poverty declines, we must expect the proportion (through not necessarily the number) who need income support to increase markedly.

Scope of Current Programs

The dimensions of existing income-support and benefit-in-kind programs are indicated in Table 11.3. Only those with an income-based eligibility test are included. Social Security and other forms of social insurance are not shown because although they do provide income support to many beneficiaries who would otherwise be poor, individual payments are not related to current income.

During the 1960s and 1970s means-tested benefit programs were one of the fastest-growing categories in the combined budgets of federal, state, and local governments. In 1968 they amounted to only 1.9 percent of gross national product. Ten years later their share had more than doubled to 4.0 percent. Measured in constant 1982 dollars, program outlays reached a peak of $127.8 billion in 1981, the last year of the Carter administration. Since that date they have declined slightly. The lower priority given to these programs under the Reagan administration is indicated by the fact that their share in the federal budget fell from a peak of 14.1 percent in the late 1970s to 11.8 percent in 1984.

Means-tested programs are supported by a bewildering variety of financial arrangements. Several of the largest federally authorized programs are financed jointly with the states under arrangements that had their origins as far

34. Thurow, pp. 140–141.

TABLE 11.3
Expenditure on Need-Tested Benefit Programs

	TOTAL FEDERAL, STATE, AND LOCAL SPENDING (FISCAL YEARS, MILLIONS OF DOLLARS)			FEDERAL SPENDING AS A PERCENTAGE OF TOTAL
	1968	1978	1984	1984
Medicaid	3,686	18,949	37,631	53.4
Other medical benefits	1,116	4,781	8,661	74.2
Aid to Families with Dependent Children	5,234	11,839	16,069	53.4
Supplemental Security Income	0	7,194	11,151	81.5
Other cash benefits	2,293	5,675	9,729	67.4
Food stamps	187	5,885	13,332	93.8
Other food benefits	652	3,463	6,292	97.3
Housing benefits	783	6,992	12,724	100.0
Jobs and training	752	9,763	4,047	97.9
Other	1,359	8,135	14,644	98.4
Total in current dollars	16,062	82,675	134,276	74.8
As a percentage of GNP	1.93	3.95	3.75	—
As a percentage of federal budget	6.4	14.1	11.8	—
Total in constant (1982) dollars	48,821	118,530	122,851	—

Sources: Vee Burke, *Cash and Non-cash Benefits for Persons with Limited Income* (Washington, D.C.: Congressional Research Service, June 8, 1982, and September 30, 1985); and Congressional Joint Economic Committee, *Income Security for Americans: Recommendations of the Public Welfare Study*, December 5, 1974, tables 3 and 4.

back as the Social Security Act of 1935. Matching formulas vary from program to program. Since the states are given considerable freedom of action within limits set by federal law, benefit levels and the details of eligibility rules vary widely among the states. So, too, does the financial contribution required by the states of their local governments.

Table 11.3 shows that in 1984 the federal government paid 75 percent of the total cost of means-tested programs. However, the proportions differ widely by program (see last column of table). Except for the cost of administration, food stamps are paid for entirely by the federal government. Aid to Families with Dependent Children, Medicaid, and Supplemental Security Income are paid for jointly. In 1984 state and local governments paid 47 percent of Medicaid costs and the same proportion of AFDC. These two categories account for most of their "welfare burden." In a majority of cases this burden is borne entirely by the state, but some states do require substantial local contributions. One estimate placed the local share of all welfare costs in 1975 at about 18 percent of the combined state-local amount.[35]

The principal aid programs can be very briefly described as follows. Supplemental Security Income (SSI) was established in 1974 to provide cash assistance, depending on need, to the aged, the blind, and the disabled. It consolidated three programs that had been established for the same purposes under the Social Security Act in 1935. The federal government pays for benefits at a basic level, but states may voluntarily supplement that, so benefit levels vary geographically.

Medicaid, the largest and one of the fastest-growing categories of public assistance, was written into the Social Security law in 1965. It pays medical expenses for persons who are on the rolls of AFDC and, in most states, SSI. A majority of states make other categories of the poor eligible as well, but some restrict Medicaid to those two groups. In that case a considerable part of the poor population—for example, poor, childless couples or single persons under 65, will not be eligible for medical assistance.

Aid to Families with Dependent Children (AFDC), authorized by the Social Security Act in 1935, is the program commonly referred to as "welfare." Until 1961 families were eligible for AFDC only if one parent was absent or had died. The law was amended in 1961 to permit states also to assist families in which the father was present but unemployed, but only a little over half the states have adopted this policy. Benefits paid under AFDC vary greatly from state to state. In January 1985 the maximum monthly benefit for a four-person family in the continental United States ranged from a low of $120 in Mississippi to a high of $660 in California. The median level was $379.[36] Moreover, the range from highest to lowest actually increased (in real terms) from 1970 to 1985.

35. George E. Peterson, "Finance," in W. Gorham and N. Glazer, eds., *The Urban Predicament* (Washington, D.C.: Urban Institute, 1976), table 17.
36. Congressional Budget Office, *Reducing Poverty among Children*, May 1985, table III-4.

The food stamp program was initiated in 1964 and has grown very rapidly. Benefit levels are tied to income. Eligibility rules were tightened in 1977 to eliminate persons whose net income exceeded the poverty line and were further tightened in 1981. Food stamps are unique among the major public aid programs in providing benefits that are uniform in the continental United States and available to *all* low-income persons rather than only to selected categories of the poor.

Impact on the Rate of Poverty

The cash transfers and benefits-in-kind shown in Table 11.3 have had a considerable effect in reducing the incidence of poverty. Because of the way the Census Bureau defines income, however, the full effect does not show up in the official poverty statistics, such as those cited in Chapter 10. In calculating the official figures, the Census Bureau counts as family income both social insurance benefits, such as receipts from Social Security, and cash transfers received under public aid programs, such as AFDC. *Not* counted as part of a family's income, however, is the value it receives from benefits in kind, such as food stamps, Medicaid, and housing assistance. If these values were added to family income, fewer families would be found to have incomes below the poverty line. Benefit-in-kind payments have increased much faster than cash transfers since the 1960s (see Table 11.3). Consequently, the official figures increasingly understate the impact of the nation's antipoverty program.

To measure the effect of noncash benefits on the rate of poverty, the Census Bureau now publishes a selection of data adjusted to include their value in the recipient's income. Table 11.4 shows some of the results for 1984. The aggregate national rate of poverty in that year according to the "official" definition was 14.4 percent. Adjusted for benefits in kind (at their market value), it fell to 9.7 percent, almost one-third lower. The impact of benefits in kind was greater for blacks, reducing their poverty rate by 39 percent.

Table 11.4 further emphasizes the geographic disparities in our highly fragmented welfare system. In the Northeast, where benefit levels tend to be highest, the inclusion of benefits in kind reduces the rate of poverty by 42 percent, lowering it from 13.2 percent to 7.6 percent. In the South, where the rate of poverty is highest and benefit levels are relatively low, benefits in kind reduce the rate of poverty from 16.2 percent to 11.3 percent, a reduction of only 30 percent.

In measuring the impact of a benefit program, the concept of a national "poverty gap" is helpful. This gap is defined as the aggregate sum of money that would have to be transferred to the poor to raise every poor person just to the poverty line. The bottom line of Table 11.4 shows that using the official definition of poverty, the gap stood at $45.2 billion in 1984. That is the income deficit that remained *after* cash payments to the poor, including AFDC and SSI. The poverty gap in the absence of such payments would

TABLE 11.4
Effect of Benefits in Kind on Poverty Rate, 1984

| | RATE OF POVERTY AMONG PERSONS IN 1984 (%) | | |
| | 1 | 2 | 3 |
	Official Poverty Definition	*Adjusted for Benefits in Kind*[a]	*Percentage Difference (Col. 2 − Col. 1) ÷ Col. 1*
All persons	14.4	9.7	− 32.6
White	11.5	8.0	− 30.4
Black	33.8	20.5	− 39.3
Spanish origin	28.4	19.9	− 29.9
Northeast	13.2	7.6	− 42.4
Midwest	14.1	9.2	− 34.8
South	16.2	11.3	− 30.2
West	13.1	9.6	− 26.7
Poverty gap, 1984 (billions of dollars)	45.2	26.8	− 40.7

[a]Benefits in kind calculated as the market value of food, housing, and all medical care.
Sources: Rates of poverty, official definition: U.S. Bureau of the Census, *Current Population Reports,* series P-60, no. 152, June 1986; poverty gap and adjusted rates of poverty: U.S. Bureau of the Census, *Estimates of Poverty Including the Value of Noncash Benefits, 1984,* Technical Paper 55, August 1985.

have been about $63 billion in 1984, and the poverty rate would have been 15.3 percent instead of 14.4 percent.[37] If benefits in kind are also counted as income, the 1984 gap is reduced to $26.8 billion. To put that number in perspective, consider that there were 22.6 million people in poverty under the latter definition of income in 1984. Therefore, the gap averaged $1,186 per individual.

Dissatisfaction with the Welfare System

No aspect of American social policy has been more widely criticized in recent years than its "welfare," or public assistance, programs. The multitude of objections refer essentially to three points. The first is that the nation's welfare system is not, in fact, a "system." Over the years we have accumulated a set of programs designed to alleviate certain carefully defined categories of hardship, not to attack poverty across the board. As a result, large areas of need are left untouched. Many of the poor—including the working poor,

37. Data on the poverty gap and poverty rate *before* welfare payments are from Christine Ross, "The Trend in Poverty, 1965–1984," University of Wisconsin, Institute for Research on Poverty, September 1985, tables 1 and 6.

childless couples, and able-bodied single persons under the age of 65, whether or not they are working—are not covered by any mandatory, nationwide program except food stamps, which provided average monthly benefits of only $42.76 per participant in 1984.[38]

A second major criticism is that U.S. welfare programs lack geographic uniformity. Although poverty in a society open to easy internal migration is essentially a national problem, our public aid programs allow enormous interstate variation in benefit levels and coverage. In addition to the data on AFDC benefits already cited, consider the following. A study of the combined impact of Medicaid, AFDC, SSI, food stamps, and general assistance found that in 1976 the aggregate outlay per poor resident varied from a low of $419 a year in Arizona (the only state without Medicaid) to a high of $2,924 a year in Massachusetts. In the Northeast the average level was $2,428, in the South, only $784.[39]

Large interstate differences in welfare benefits raise serious questions of equity not only in the treatment of beneficiaries but also as among taxpayers. States that undertake seriously to relieve poverty through public assistance must tax themselves heavily to do so. If localities within the state are required by state law to contribute to local public assistance programs (as is sometimes the case), a heavy burden is placed on taxpayers in localities having a high proportion of citizens in need of aid.

Interstate differences may also be economically inefficient. From the point of view of society as a whole, it is desirable for the poor to move to areas of better economic opportunity, where they can earn higher incomes on the basis of higher real productivity, but it is certainly *not* desirable that their decision to move be influenced by interarea differences in the level of transfer payments, since these are not connected with differences in productivity.

Whether poor migrants are, in fact, attracted to states with high benefit levels has been much debated among both economists and state legislators. Studies showing that very few of those "on welfare" in the high-benefit states are recent arrivals were at one time thought to refute the view that benefit levels affect migration. Recent research, however, indicates that there is a connection. Using data for a sample of 66,577 AFDC families, Lawrence Southwick confirmed a double effect of differences in benefit payments: higher benefit levels induce in-migration of welfare recipients and also retard their out-migration.[40] The second effect may help to explain why so few of those on welfare are recent arrivals. Instead of leaving when they run into adversity, the poor tend to stay put in places where benefit levels are high. In such places welfare recipients gradually "pile up," and recent in-migrants therefore make up only a small proportion of the whole.

38. *Statistical Abstract of the United States, 1986,* table 201.
39. *Statistical Abstract of the United States, 1979,* table 572.
40. Lawrence Southwick, Jr., "Public Welfare Programs and Recipient Migration," *Growth and Change,* October 1981, pp. 22–32. It should be noted that his data are for 1967.

Gramlich and Laren, using data for 1974 to 1981, also found a positive and statistically significant relation between state benefit levels and in-migration. They describe the migration process as very sluggish but quite important in the long run. In addition, they found that in-migration causes the receiving states gradually to reduce the real level of benefits offered.[41] This confirms the hypothesis that competition among states to avoid attracting migratory welfare cases keeps benefits below the level that voters would otherwise consider optimal and constitutes a strong argument for adopting a nationally uniform benefit standard. (See the discussion of tax competition in Chapter 15.)

Finally, U.S. welfare programs are criticized on the ground that they have socially undesirable effects on the behavior of beneficiaries. It has often been argued that AFDC eligibility rules contribute to the breakup of families. Until 1961 benefits were available to a mother and children only if no father was present. This was alleged to encourage real or feigned desertion. In that year the law was amended to permit states also to assist families in which the father was present but unemployed, and half the states adopted that provision. The new rule, however, did not eliminate the incentive to desert on the part of the *employed* father: society will assist his family if he leaves but not if he stays.

It is also frequently alleged that our welfare system interferes with work incentives.

Work Incentives in the Current Welfare System

Welfare benefits can affect work incentives in two ways. First, if income earned by those on welfare is taxed at too high a rate, they will be discouraged from working. AFDC provisions have been criticized in this regard. Until 1967 beneficiaries who worked gave up a dollar of benefits for each dollar earned. In effect they were placed in a 100 percent income tax bracket for their initial earnings, thus facing the ultimate disincentive to work. A 1967 amendment permitted beneficiaries to retain $30 a month plus one-third of earnings. But that was still nearly a 67 percent marginal tax rate on earnings— hardly a powerful incentive to work. In 1981 as part of the Reagan administration's drive to reduce welfare costs and concentrate benefits on those most in need, the law was changed again. After four consecutive months of employment, recipients were no longer allowed to "disregard" one-third of their earned income, and after twelve months they also lost the $30 monthly exclusion. Thus the 100 percent marginal tax rate on earnings was restored. The effect of this change on the actual work effort of welfare recipients is a matter of current debate.[42]

41. Edward M. Gramlich and Deborah S. Laren, "Migration and Income Redistribution Responsibilities," *Journal of Human Resources*, August 1984, pp. 489–511.

42. See discussion in Robert Moffitt, "Work Incentives in the AFDC System: An Analysis of the 1981 Reforms," *American Economic Review*, May 1986, pp. 219–223.

The availability of multiple benefits aggravates the problem of marginal tax rates. If a family on AFDC also receives food stamps or lives in subsidized housing, the benefits obtained under those income-conditioned programs will also diminish as earned income rises, pushing the aggregate marginal tax rate well above the level implicit in the AFDC rule.

Work incentives under welfare programs depend on the level of benefits as well as on the marginal tax rate on earnings. Other things being equal, the higher the benefit level, the less need the beneficiary will feel to work for additional income. Again, the availability of multiple benefit programs must be taken into account. A study based on a large sample of 1974 AFDC cases in New York City found that in-kind transfers such as Medicaid, food stamps, and day-care services contributed $2,235 in annual value on top of an average cash grant of $3,393 per year. Among four-person, female-headed AFDC cases, 83 percent received aggregate benefits that placed them above the poverty line, and 95 percent received benefits in excess of what a single worker could have earned, if employed year-round at the minimum wage rate (then $2.00 an hour).[43] Clearly, such high benefit levels, coupled with the stiff tax rate on earnings that is implicit in multiple-benefit welfare programs, would leave an unskilled welfare recipient with little incentive to work.

As we shall see, a good deal of insight into the effects of welfare on the behavior of beneficiaries was obtained from experimental tests of a guaranteed income plan. We take up that subject next.

A Guaranteed Income Plan

In the late 1960s and early 1970s many people favored adopting a universal guaranteed income scheme to replace existing welfare programs. They believed that such a plan would, in and of itself, overcome the many objections to the fragmented, "categorical" system outlined in the preceding discussion. By its universality an income guarantee would eliminate gaps in coverage and provide uniform national benefit standards. By its simplicity it would do away with administrative confusion and waste. Finally, it would provide an opportunity to deal systematically with the problem of work incentives.

We use *guaranteed income* as a general term to cover proposals known variously as the negative income tax, the credit income tax, or the family assistance plan. Versions of these schemes were proposed to the Congress by President Nixon (the Family Assistance Plan) and President Carter (the Program for Better Jobs and Income). Neither was adopted, and opposition to the idea has probably increased with time. Nevertheless, they merit discussion because by examining them we can better understand the structural problems inherent in cash transfer plans and throw considerable light on the issues in welfare reform.

43. David W. Lyon et al., *Multiple Welfare Benefits in New York City* (Santa Monica, Calif.: Rand Corp., August 1976), table 4.6 and fig. 5.1.

All rational guaranteed income proposals call for 100 percent financing by the federal government. Whatever benefits they provide would be paid for entirely out of national tax revenues, with no contribution by state or local governments. The objective is to create a uniform national standard for the relief of poverty, without categorical restrictions of any kind. It would be impossible to accomplish this without federal financing, since the poorer states could never afford to pay benefits at the level deemed appropriate by the nation as a whole.

The technical structure, shared by all income-maintenance proposals, consists of three elements. First, a guaranteed minimum income per person or per family, which the government will provide when the beneficiary has no other income. Second, a "take-back rate" at which the government reduces cash payments if the beneficiary does earn any income. Third, a "break-even level" at which earned income is high enough so that benefit payments under the plan cease.

A simple illustration, worked out in Table 11.5, shows how these elements fit together. Suppose that the income guarantee is set at $1,750 per person. A family of four would then receive $7,000 per year if it had no other income. Next assume that benefits are reduced by $50 for every $100 of income the family earns. The take-back rate, in other words, is 50 percent. For example, if the family earns $2,000 during the year, benefit payments will be reduced by $.5 \times \$2,000 = \$1,000$. The family will receive net benefits of $\$7,000 - \$1,000 = \$6,000$. Its total income will be $\$2,000 + \$6,000 = \$8,000$. (See the second line of the table.)

If the family's earned income rises, its benefits under the plan decrease. When earned income reaches $14,000 a year, net benefits fall to zero, since

TABLE 11.5
Hypothetical Guaranteed Income Plan for a Family of Four[a]

1	2	3
	NET BENEFIT PAID TO FOUR-	TOTAL INCOME BEFORE INCOME
EARNED INCOME	PERSON FAMILY ($7,000 − .50 × COL. 1)	TAX (COL. 1 + COL. 2)
0	$7,000	$7,000
2,000	6,000	8,000
4,000	5,000	9,000
6,000	4,000	10,000
8,000	3,000	11,000
10,000	2,000	12,000
12,000	1,000	13,000
14,000	0	14,000

[a]Income guarantee $(Y_g) = \$1,750$ per person
Take-back tax rate $(t_e) = .50$

the take-back rate applied to earned income yields a sum just equal to the initial income guarantee (.5 × $14,000 = $7,000). Thus $14,000 is the break-even level of earned income at which the net benefit payments under the plan cease for a four-person family.

The three structural elements of an income-maintenance plan are related by a simple mathematical formula.[44] Let

Y_g = income guarantee per person when earned income is zero
Y_e = earned income
t_e = take-back tax rate on earned income
R = break-even level of earned income

Then the relationship between the three structural elements is given mathematically by

$$R = \frac{Y_g}{t_e}$$

This equation can be explained as follows: By definition, R is that level of Y_e such that

$$Y_g - t_e Y_e = 0$$

which can be rewritten as

$$Y_e = \frac{Y_g}{t_e}$$

Substituting R for Y_e, we obtain

$$R = \frac{Y_g}{t_e}$$

Putting data from Table 11.5 into the equation, we observe that

$$\$14,000 = \frac{\$7,000}{.50}$$

It is apparent that once the values of any two of the three structural elements are specified, the value of the third is mathematically determined. In other words, we can freely choose values for any two of them but not for all three. This is obviously an important constraint on the design of guaranteed income schemes.

44. Christopher Green, *Negative Taxes and the Poverty Problem* (Washington, D.C.: Brookings Institution, 1967), p. 63. In practice, guaranteed income plans have to mesh with the income tax system so that the beneficiary moves smoothly from the former to the latter as earned income rises. The problem is not treated here, but see the discussion in Congressional Budget Office, *Welfare Reform: Issues, Objectives and Approaches*, July 1977, pp. 24–25.

Formulas and Policy Objectives

Each of the three structural elements just described above is related directly to one or more of the major objectives of antipoverty policy. Consider first the objective of eliminating poverty by transferring income: the adequacy of an income-maintenance plan to relieve poverty depends directly on the level chosen for Y_g. Unless Y_g provides those who have no other resources with sufficient income to raise them out of poverty, the plan will not entirely close the poverty gap (which stood at $63 billion, before cash benefits to the poor, in 1984). In the plan described, Y_g is clearly too low to close the poverty gap completely. Poverty-line income for a four-person family was calculated to be about $10,600 in 1984, but the proposed income guarantee to that family is only $7,000. That still leaves a considerable "gap."

Closing the aggregate national poverty gap by means of income allowances requires large-scale transfers, not only because the gap itself is wide but also because there is no way of closing it, consistent with the other objectives of antipoverty policy, that does not involve a good deal of "excess redistribution." Part of this "excess" goes to raise people from below the poverty line to some point above it (for example, the family in Table 11.5 with $8,000 of earned income). Another part goes to supplement the incomes of those who were above the poverty line even before receiving benefits (for example, the family with $12,000 of earned income in Table 11.5). The result is an aggregate redistribution that far exceeds the size of the poverty gap itself.

A second objective of antipoverty policy is to encourage (or at least not to discourage) work effort by the poor. As explained in the last section, one would expect work effort under a welfare plan to vary inversely with both the size of the basic guarantee and the rate at which benefits are reduced as earnings increase. This means that both Y_g and t_e affect work incentives. The plan described in Table 11.5 has relatively low levels for both factors. Hence it would be expected to have relatively favorable effects on work effort.

Finally, there is the objective of designing a plan that is affordable. The budgetary cost of a guaranteed income plan is strongly influenced by the value of R, the break-even level of earned income. Everyone with earned income less than R receives net cash benefits under a guaranteed income plan. Hence the higher the level of R, the greater the number of persons receiving benefits and, for any given value of Y_g, the greater the total cost of benefits paid. Consequently, the level of R is a key factor in cost comparisons among alternative proposals. In 1984 the median income of four-person families in the United States was $31,097. About 16 percent of them had incomes below $14,000, the break-even level for the plan illustrated in Table 11.5.[45] That plan would therefore have paid net benefits to one-sixth of all four-person families.

The unavoidable trade-off among the essential characteristics of any income guarantee plan proved frustrating to policy designers: a high guarantee

45. U.S. Bureau of the Census, *Current Population Reports*, series P-60, no. 151, April 1986, table 18.

level (Y_g) would produce a high break-even level (R) and consequently a very costly program unless the tax rate (t_e) was also high. But a high tax rate was thought likely to undermine work incentives. On the other hand, a low guarantee rate, while holding down program cost and facilitating use of a lower tax rate, could not possibly meet the objective of raising out of poverty those who could not be expected to work. In framing his Family Assistance Plan, President Nixon was unable to put together a winning combination of these variables. Twice passed by the House of Representatives, the plan was never approved in the Senate. Some thought it provided inadequate support, while others opposed it as overly generous; some thought it undermined work incentives and others that its incentive structure was too strong.

Measuring the Effects of an Income Guarantee

Even as President Nixon's proposal was being debated in Congress, the government was engaged in a set of large-scale experiments intended to measure scientifically what effect a guaranteed income plan would have on work effort. The last and largest of these, and probably the most reliable, was the Seattle-Denver Income Maintenance Experiment carried out during the 1970s. SIME/DIME, as it was known, tested a variety of plans over a period in excess of five years on approximately 5,000 families. In order to achieve the most reliable possible results, the test and control groups were created by random assignment from a pool of the eligible poor. The plans consisted of combinations of three alternative guarantee levels, corresponding to 95, 120, and 140 percent of officially defined poverty-line income, and four tax rates on earned income, varying upward from 50 percent. The guarantee levels were decidedly generous in comparison with most actual proposals for a guaranteed income or with actual AFDC benefits in most states. Families in the control group were free to accept AFDC or other welfare benefits for which they were eligible. Hence the experiment tested the effects of an income guarantee as compared with the existing "policy environment." It did *not* test the effects of an income guarantee (or of AFDC) as compared with a "no-welfare environment."

The experiment measured labor supply effects of an income guarantee separately for husbands, wives, female family heads, and youths. In all cases work effort was found to decline. The drop in hours of work supplied by husbands averaged about 9 percent and appeared to increase the longer they stayed in the program, indicating that long-run effects would be greater than those averaged over the short run.[46] As theory would predict, the more generous the income guarantee, the stronger the negative effect on labor supply turned out to be. On the other hand, higher tax rates, expected in theory to reduce work effort, appeared to make no consistent difference.

---

46. U.S. Department of Health and Human Services, Office of Income Security Policy, *Overview of the Seattle-Denver Income Maintenance Experiment Final Report*, May 1983, table 4.

The percentage decline in work effort was notably greater for participants other than husbands. It averaged about 20 percent for wives, 14 percent for female heads of families, and 24 percent for youths. In all cases long-run effects appeared to be even stronger, and in most cases, as for husbands, the more generous the guarantee, the greater the decline in hours worked.[47]

Although designed primarily to test labor supply response, SIME/DIME also produced evidence concerning effects on family stability. The conventional view, it should be recalled, was that AFDC was contributing to marital dissolution through its failure to provide benefits to intact needy families. A universal income guarantee, its proponents believed, would eliminate that problem since all families would be eligible for benefits on the basis of need and regardless of structure. Contrary to expectations, however, white and black participants in SIME/DIME showed rates of marital dissolution much higher than the control group. Only Chicanos showed no statistically significant effects. For a variety of reasons, however, these results are regarded as less reliable than those for work effort.[48] (We will return to the question of poverty and family structure.)

How are we to judge these results? The experiment did show unambiguously that a guaranteed income scheme reduces the work effort of participants. Whether the reduction is viewed as "large" or "small" is now probably irrelevant. Proponents had hoped and expected the experiment to show that work effort for at least some groups would increase or else at worst that declines would be inconsequential. Instead, as Henry J. Aaron has written, the change in work patterns was "enough to matter."[49] Support among economists melted away. The opposition had always believed that such a plan would undermine the American work ethic. The results of the experiment (so they thought) confirmed that fear.[50] Guaranteed annual income is no longer on the national agenda.

Back to Categorical Assistance

With the demise of proposals for a universal guaranteed income, economists are now casting a fresh eye on categorical assistance (both cash and noncash) and finding it relatively more attractive than they did ten or fifteen years ago. AFDC, the principal form of categorical cash assistance, is now thought to have more virtue (or at any rate fewer defects) than they had at one time believed. Here are a few examples. Although the last word has surely not been said on the subject, several recent studies suggest that AFDC is not

47. Ibid., tables 5 and 6 and p. 17.
48. Ibid., table 10 and pp. 21–25.
49. Henry J. Aaron, "Six Welfare Questions Still Searching for Answers," *Brookings Review*, Fall 1984, p. 13.
50. See Charles Murray, *Losing Ground* (New York: Basic Books, 1984), pp. 145–153; and Martin Anderson, *Welfare: The Political Economy of Welfare Reform in the United States* (Stanford, Calif.: Hoover Institution Press, 1978), ch. 5.

a major factor in causing family breakup and the admittedly alarming rise of the female-headed welfare family. Instead the finger is now pointed at joblessness, which drastically reduces the "marriageable pool" of men among ethnic minorities.[51] Or consider the problem of youth employment: the income-maintenance experiments found that among all the groups studied, 16- to 21-year-olds showed the greatest percentage reduction in work effort under an income guarantee, nor "was the decrease in hours worked accompanied by an increase in time spent in school."[52] Since bringing minority youths into the labor force is a prime objective of antipoverty policy, it is a serious defect of a universal guaranteed income scheme to discourage that process. A categorical assistance plan like AFDC avoids that difficulty by not offering anything to youths unless they have children.

As for *noncash* categorical aid, its principal attraction is the practical fact that the public is willing to support it. Voters and legislators who were deeply troubled by the notion of a universal income guarantee and are also suspicious of categorical cash assistance such as AFDC have proved far more willing to endorse assistance in the form of benefits in kind. One reason for this is that payments in kind are provided through the distribution of particular goods, such as food, housing, or health care, that the public believes to be especially beneficial for the poor. (See the discussion of merit goods in Chapter 12.) Another is political: as Aaron has observed, "Support for aid to the poor increases if the aid appears to create jobs for the nonpoor—in the construction trades, for example, or on farms."[53] Economic theory can easily prove that consumers never find benefits in kind preferable to cash and sometimes find them inferior. Yet the political lesson is clear: to provide substantial aid to the poor, you had better be willing to make transfers in the form of goods and services. During the 1970s food stamps, Medicaid, and housing assistance multiplied many times over while the level of AFDC benefits, adjusted for inflation, steadily declined. In the median state, the maximum AFDC payment to a four-person family dropped 33 percent in real terms between 1970 and 1985.[54]

Despite its declining relative importance, AFDC continues to be the object of many proposals for reform. A perennial suggestion is that the federal government establish national minimum benefit levels. By raising payments per family in states where they are now very low, such a plan would increase horizontal equity within the welfare system and reduce the influence of inter-

51. See the following papers in Danziger and Weinberg, eds., *Fighting Poverty*: William Julius Wilson and Kathryn M. Neckerman, "Poverty and Family Structure"; Mary Jo Bane, "Household Composition and Poverty"; David T. Ellwood and Lawrence H. Summers, "Poverty in America: Is Welfare the Answer or the Problem?" and Frank S. Levy and Richard C. Michel, "Work for Welfare: How Much Good Will It Do?" *American Economic Review*, May 1986, pp. 402–403.

52. *Overview*, p. 17.

53. Aaron, p. 16.

54. Congressional Budget Office, *Reducing Poverty*, table III-4.

state benefit differentials on family choice of location. Full equalization is probably out of the question at this time, not only because it would be very costly but also because wage levels in unskilled occupations are generally much lower in the low-benefit states, and those states would quite understandably resist adopting payment schedules that were competitive with market wages.[55] Less ambitious proposals, however, remain under discussion. It has been estimated that in fiscal 1986, if a minimum standard were adopted under which the combined value of AFDC payments and food stamps came to at least 65 percent of poverty-line income, benefit levels would rise in forty-one states. AFDC outlays would increase by $3.4 billion, or about 20 percent. Under present burden-sharing formulas, the federal government would pay $2.1 billion of that total and the states $1.3 billion.[56]

AFDC is primarily a program for supporting children in poor, single-parent households, usually those in which no father is present. The failure of absent fathers to help support their own children, whether born in or out of wedlock, is a notorious problem, very costly to the welfare system and demeaning to the mothers it forces into welfare dependency. Since 1975 the federal government has increasingly sought to help the states enforce conventional court-ordered child-support awards. It is uphill work, to say the least. Now Irwin Garfinkel has proposed a radical new system in which "all parents who live apart from their children would be liable for a child-support tax . . . [and] all children with a living absent parent would be entitled to benefits equal either to the child-support tax paid by the absent parent, or a minimum benefit, whichever is higher."[57] Some aspects of the plan are being tested in Wisconsin. Such a system, if successful (which is surely not to be taken for granted), would simultaneously raise many mothers and their children out of poverty, remove some from the welfare rolls, reduce the public cost of child support, and return responsibility for it to its rightful bearers.

Though many economists now defend AFDC as preferable to a universal income guarantee, they also recognize that the need for the program on such a large scale symbolizes a major failure of U.S. antipoverty policy: the growth of an underclass of the dependent poor. Their fear is that the underclass will become self-perpetuating and therefore permanent; their hope is that wise policy can still prevent that from happening, that categorical programs to shift child-support responsibility to absent fathers and to draw "welfare mothers" back into the labor force will, in combination with increased economic growth and lowered population pressure, gradually reduce the ranks of dependency.[58]

55. See discussion in Morton Paglin's *Comment* (on Ellwood and Summers's "Poverty in America"), conference paper, University of Wisconsin, Institute for Research on Poverty, March 1985, p. 8.

56. Congressional Budget Office, *Reducing Poverty*, table III-1.

57. Irwin Garfinkel and Elizabeth Uhr, "A New Approach to Child Support," *Public Interest*, Spring 1984, p. 116.

58. See, for example, Eugene Smolensky, "Is a Golden Age in Poverty Policy Right around the Corner?" *Focus*, Spring 1985, pp. 9–11, 18.

URBAN POVERTY AND RACIAL SEGREGATION

We come last to antipoverty strategies that are oriented toward particular geographic areas. In the urban context these are policies that take specific account of the connections among race, segregation into ghettos, and preponderant poverty. The urban riots of the 1960s, coinciding with the rapid increase in the black population of central cities, inevitably drew the nation's attention to the problems of the ghetto. What would be the most effective public policy to deal with them? Although discussion has tended to concentrate on black poverty, the analysis itself is usually applicable to the situation of other poor urban minorities as well—the Mexican-Americans of the South and West or the Puerto Ricans and other Spanish-origin groups in the North and East. We take up three kinds of specifically urban antipoverty policy that are distinguished by differences in the way they approach the fact of racial segregation.[59] The first has sometimes been called "ghetto economic development." This policy would attempt to relieve poverty by taking advantage of possibilities for direct action within the racial ghetto itself. The second policy, a sort of polar opposite to the first, would attempt to relieve ghetto poverty by helping and encouraging the population of central city ghettos to disperse into the largely white metropolitan suburbs. The third policy, standing logically between the other two, would use the conventional tools of antipoverty policy to integrate urban racial minorities into the central city's economy. Supporters of this policy may not approve of segregation, but they do not usually believe that the ghetto itself is a crucial factor that must be dealt with in antipoverty policy.

This third, or intermediate, policy relies on the conventional tools of manpower training, job information, and placement services focused intensively on residents of poverty areas. Since we have already examined these programs, nothing more need be said here. However, we will now examine the other two policies—ghetto development and ghetto dispersal—in greater detail.

Ghetto Economic Development

The "black capitalist" approach. Policies to stimulate the economic development of poverty areas may take numerous forms. One approach is to try to stimulate the growth of minority-owned private business enterprise. The

59. See Anthony Downs, "Alternative Futures for the American Ghetto," *Daedalus*, Fall 1968, pp. 1331–1378; John F. Kain and Joseph J. Persky, "Alternatives to the Gilded Ghetto," *Public Interest*, Winter 1969, pp. 74–87; Matthew Edel, "Development vs. Dispersal: Approaches to Ghetto Poverty," in Matthew Edel and Jerome Rothenberg, eds. *Readings in Urban Economics* (New York: Macmillan, 1972), pp. 307–325; the papers in part 1 of George M. von Furstenberg, Bennett Harrison, and Ann R. Horowitz, eds., *Patterns of Racial Discrimination*, vol. 1: *Housing* (Lexington, Mass: Heath, Lexington Books, 1974), pp. 3–101; and Bennett Harrison, "Ghetto Economic Development," *Journal of Economic Literature*, March 1974, pp. 1–37.

failure of American blacks to develop the strong business tradition found among many other ethnic minority groups in America has long been recognized.[60] The most recent figures show that in 1977, when blacks made up almost 12 percent of the population, they owned only 2.6 percent of all non-farm sole proprietorships, .9 percent of nonfarm partnerships, and .2 percent of nonfarm corporations; further, because black-owned firms were typically far below the average size, their share of total business receipts was smaller still.[61]

The weakness of the black business tradition can readily be explained as the result of a long history of slavery, followed by oppressive economic discrimination. Unfortunately, it deprives the black community of effective economic power and a chance to enjoy what is now often referred to as "a piece of the action." The "action" includes not only current profits but an ownership stake in expected economic growth. The policy of fostering "black capitalism" is intended to make good these deficiencies. It will contribute to ghetto economic development if it helps to bring new businesses into existence or to expand old ones within the poverty area.[62] The problem is to discover what kinds of business can thrive in the ghetto. Opportunities for expansion in the retail and service sector are severely constrained by the near-poverty level of average local income. Thus significant expansion of the ghetto economy can come only with the establishment of firms that sell to a wider market than the ghetto—for example, to an entire metropolitan area or to the nation as a whole.[63] Finding such business opportunities is a slow process, however, and usually requires the skills of an experienced entrepreneur.

The rapid expansion of the black business sector is hampered by two shortages—of experienced black entrepreneurs and of venture capital. Unfortunately, experience has shown that a policy of forcing the pace of expansion in the minority-owned sector by means of government-subsidized loans leads to a sharp increase in the new-business failure rate and therefore entails high financial cost.[64]

Community development corporations. A second approach to ghetto economic development calls for the use of "community development corporations." These corporations (known as CDCs) vary considerably in structure

60. See, for example, Gunnar Myrdal, *An American Dilemma* (New York: Harper & Row: 1944), pp. 304–318.

61. Calculated from U.S. Bureau of the Census, 1977 *Survey of Minority-owned Business Enterprises*, December 1979, table 8, and Internal Revenue Service, 1977 *Statistics of Income*, Corporation and Business Returns series.

62. See James Heilbrun and Stanislaw Wellisz, "An Economic Program for the Ghetto," *Urban Riots: Violence and Social Change*, Proceedings of the Academy of Political Science, July 1968, pp. 72–85.

63. For evidence of the constraining effect of low neighborhood income, see James Heilbrun, "Jobs in Harlem: A Statistical Analysis," *Papers of the Regional Science Association*, 25 (1970), 181–201.

64. Timothy Bates and William Bradford, *Financing Black Economic Development* (New York: Academic Press, 1979), ch. 9.

and intent.[65] Some of them are "strictly business" and operate through the conventional institutions of private enterprise. They devote themselves to assisting new minority-owned firms by providing management counseling and direct loans and by arranging access to banks and other sources of financial assistance and to markets for their products. They aim at nothing more complex than the creation of independent, black-owned business firms—in other words, "black capitalism" in the most traditional sense.

Frequently, however, CDCs set themselves more amibitious goals. They substitute a degree of community initiative for reliance on private enterprise by taking an active role in planning, financing, developing, and operating large-scale undertakings such as shopping centers and housing projects. They make housing rehabilitation loans, run training and employment programs, and provide a variety of other nonprofit community services.

It has generally been the expectation of community groups founding CDCs that profits from their business and financial operations would be available to support their nonprofit services. The goal was to make the community truly self-sufficient. However, creating new businesses in the highly competitive American economy is a risky and difficult undertaking—certainly riskier and more difficult in the ghetto than elsewhere. CDC business operations have thus far not proved very profitable. Community services have therefore been carried on with the help of outside funding. After a careful evaluation of three of the largest CDCs—the Bedford Stuyvesant Restoration Corporation in Brooklyn, the Woodlawn Organization in Chicago, and the Zion Non-profit Charitable Trust in Philadelphia—analysts at the Urban Institute reached this conclusion: "Each of the CDC's will require subsidy, over at least the next five to ten years, if even current programs . . . are to be sustained. Relatively few of the potential profit centers within the CDC's are currently profitable."[66] Realistically, the goal of self-sufficiency may never be realized. Nevertheless, CDCs will probably endure, since they perform many useful functions within their communities. As the Urban Institute report concluded, it is not clear that in solving difficult problems within poverty areas either the government or the unaided private market would do a better job.

Urban enterprise zones. In the early days of the War on Poverty a number of attempts were made to bring jobs into racially segregated neighborhoods by inducing large employers (primarily major white-owned corporations) to open branches there. Some racial ghettos, such as the Watts district in Los Angeles, are relatively isolated from major centers of employment.

---

65. See Sar A. Levitan, Garth L. Mangum, and Robert Taggart III,. *Economic Opportunity in the Ghetto: The Partnership of Government and Business* (Baltimore: Johns Hopkins University Press, 1970), pp. 75–79; and Martin Skala, "Inner-City Enterprise: Current Experience," in William F. Haddad and G. Douglas Pugh, eds., *Black Economic Development* (Englewood Cliffs, N.J.: Prentice-Hall, 1969), pp. 162–170.

66. Harvey A. Garn, Nancy L. Tevis, and Carl E. Snead, *Evaluating Community Development Corporations: A Summary Report* (Washington, D.C.: Urban Institute, 1976), p. 148.

Thus the rationale of this approach was to improve the ghetto residents' access to jobs, both physically and in terms of informal job information flows. More recently, "enterprise zones" have been proposed as a systematic way of stimulating business activity in urban poverty areas. The concept of the enterprise zone was first developed in Great Britain. Extrapolating from the economic success of such free-enterprise enclaves as Hong Kong and Singapore, it was argued that if all planning controls and regulations were suspended and taxes reduced within specified zones, entrepreneurs would seize the opportunity to create new businesses, thus generating jobs and income.

In the United States a number of states have already authorized the creation of enterprise zones, and federal legislation has been proposed since as far back as the Kemp-Garcia Bill of 1980. The notion appealed to the philosophically conservative Reagan administration, which indeed made a proposal for federally authorized enterprise zones the cornerstone of its urban assistance program. The proposal has yet to be enacted, however. Since the United States has far fewer planning controls than Britain, it is not surprising that the American proposals stress tax relief more and relief from regulation and planning less than do the British.[67]

Although the benefits conferred on investors in enterprise zones are bound to stimulate local activity, it should be obvious that some (perhaps a large part) of the local gain will come from the diversion of activity that would otherwise have occurred elsewhere. That is not necessarily bad: a public choice might be made to foster the redevelopment of certain depressed areas. What sorts of areas, however? There is a conflict of aims at the heart of this scheme. Is it intended to stimulate the economy of the whole city or only to help specific distressed populations and neighborhoods? If the object is to stimulate the employment of minorities living within the designated zones, benefits to firms must be conditional on their hiring previously unemployed neighborhood residents. But such conditions are likely to inhibit investment. It is no simple matter to find large-scale business operations that can be carried on profitably from a ghetto location under a commitment to hire the hard-core unemployed and to pay them competitive wages. On the other hand, if benefits are *not* conditional on employment practice but simply go to any new activity located within the zone (and not previously located elsewhere in the city), there will be a greater stimulus to investment and thus to the whole urban economy but relatively little impact on the neighborhood poor.

67. For the general argument, see Stuart M. Bulter, "Free Zones in the Inner City," in Richard D. Bingham and John P. Blair, eds., *Urban Economic Development*, vol. 27, Urban Affairs Annual Reviews (Beverly Hills, Calif.: Sage Publications, 1984), ch. 7. For analysis of the Reagan proposal, see Susan E. Clarke, "Enterprise Zones: Seeking the Neighborhood Nexus," *Urban Affairs Quarterly*, September 1982, pp. 53–71.

Demonstration Effects

In general, policies that encourage local economic development are likely to have favorable social and psychological effects. In communities where deprivation has produced apathy and hopelessness, demonstrations of success either in business or in jobholding will encourage others to emulate the pattern of success. Furthermore, local development opens up opportunities for talented and ambitious residents and encourages them to remain in the poverty area instead of taking their exceptional energies and abilities elsewhere. Thus it helps to prevent poverty areas from being deprived of some of their best human resources. Advocates of local development policy believe that success will attract the talent and create the self-confidence out of which greater success can flow.

Yet we must conclude by recognizing the limitations on poverty-area development policy as a means of increasing local incomes. Most residents of minority ghettos work in the larger, outside economy and must continue to do so, for ghetto neighborhoods are essentially residential in character. For example, a study of Harlem, one of the more highly developed black ghettos, estimated that in 1966 the neighborhood contained approximately 19,500 jobs. The number of employed Harlem residents was about five times as large. Thus even if Harlem residents held every local job (which was certainly not the case), no more than one-fifth of them could have worked inside their own community.[68] While many poverty areas could accommodate more workplaces than they do now, it would be virtually impossible and very probably undesirable to make them over into major centers of employment.

Moreover, as whites have moved to the suburbs and inner city population has declined, the black population has spread far from its sites of earlier concentration, which now often contain large areas of abandoned housing. In the face of so much mobility, the case for focusing economic development on particular inner city neighborhoods loses much of its cogency. Or, to look at the same facts from an opposite perspective, as blacks and the Spanish-origin population come to make up a larger and larger proportion of the inner city total, policies that promote the general prosperity of the inner city economy and that strive simultaneously to integrate minorities into its mainstream become increasingly relevant. To support that integration we must continue to make available the conventional tools of education, training, job information, and placement discussed at the beginning of this chapter.

As pointed out earlier, "ghetto dispersal" policies would stress integration in a different locale, by encouraging and even subsidizing the movement of minorities to the suburbs. We examine next the rationale for such a policy.

68. Heilbrun, pp. 185–186.

Urban Poverty and Metropolitan Decentralization

It is one of the ironies of our times that the nation's poor minorities migrated to the cities at the very moment when job opportunities there were threatened by the forces of decentralization. In recent decades jobs have been dispersing within metropolitan areas. (On this point, see Table 3.4.) Many of the older central cities have actually suffered a loss in total jobs since the late 1940s, while their suburbs have enjoyed enormous job growth. Unfortunately, while metropolitan-area jobs have been moving farther and farther away, the poor—especially the minority poor—have remained highly concentrated in the inner cities, for they face segregation not only at the microscale of the neighborhood but also at the macroscale of central city versus suburb. Table 10.6 showed the extent of such macrosegregation. In 1982 blacks made up only 6.2 percent of suburban population as compared with almost 24 percent of population in central cities. To be sure, the black proportion in the suburbs has increased moderately since 1970, but that "dispersion" is offset to some degree by the simultaneous growth of the black proportion in central cities. As a result, the proportion of metropolitan-area blacks living in the suburbs rose only from 26.6 percent to 27.9 percent.

Within metropolitan areas, job dispersion is most marked among blue-collar jobs in manufacturing, wholesaling, and distribution, least pronounced in white-collar jobs and in service industries. The poor are usually better qualified for blue-collar than for white-collar employment. Hence the inner portions of the central cities, where the poor typically live, are an increasingly disadvantageous base from which to look for work. The problem is particularly acute in the largest metropolitan areas. Not only are blue-collar jobs moving steadily away from inner city poverty areas; they are moving to places that are scarcely accessible by public transportation (see discussion in Chapter 9). To the inner city worker with no automobile, the cost in time and money of reaching a suburban job by commuter railroad and/or multiple bus connections is often prohibitive when compared with his or her low earning capacity. Moreover, the casual, informal sort of employment information on which many job seekers rely also thins out with distance. In short, the inner city resident, especially when isolated in a racial ghetto, is increasingly out of touch with the labor market. There is a clear policy implication: if job dispersion is depriving poor minorities in the central cities of large metropolitan areas of opportunities to earn a better living, then to help relieve poverty we must encourage the dispersion of blacks and other minorities into the suburbs.

Measuring the Black Disadvantage in Central Cities

The economic deprivation suffered by blacks because of central city residence is multidimensional, but three of its principal components are higher

TABLE 11.6
Unemployment Rates and Nonparticipation Rates inside and outside Central Cities of SMSAs

	INSIDE CENTRAL CITIES		OUTSIDE CENTRAL CITIES	
	1970	1980	1970	1980
Unemployment Rate				
All races, both sexes[a]	4.7	7.3	3.9	5.7
White, both sexes	4.1	5.7	3.7	5.4
Male	3.8	5.9	3.2	5.3
Female	4.4	5.4	4.5	5.4
Black, both sexes	6.9	12.8	6.4	9.6
Male	6.7	13.9	5.8	9.7
Female	7.3	11.7	7.2	9.4
Rate of Nonparticipation in Labor Force, Workers Aged 25–64[b]				
All races, both sexes[a]	30.0	26.6	30.8	25.6
White, both sexes	29.6	25.6	30.8	25.7
Male	8.6	11.6	6.0	8.9
Female	49.0	39.0	54.5	41.9
Black, both sexes	30.0	28.9	29.4	23.6
Male	14.3	20.2	15.7	16.3
Female	42.9	35.7	41.8	30.2

[a]"All races" includes white, black, and others not shown separately.
[b]Rate of nonparticipation equals the number of persons not in the labor force divided by the total population for the designated age group.
Sources: U.S. Bureau of the Census, *Census of Population: General Social and Economic Characteristics, 1970,* tables 107, 112, 124, and 126; *1980,* table 144.

rates of unemployment, lower rates of labor force participation, and lower earnings when employed.

Table 11.6 shows that in 1970 the unemployment rate for both races was slightly higher in central cities than in the rings of metropolitan areas. Unemployment rates rose in both areas from 1970 to 1980 as the nation adopted anti-inflationary macroeconomic policies. When unemployment rates by area and race are examined, it is clear that the most rapid increase occurred for blacks living in central cities. Black central city males registered the sharpest increase of all: their rate of unemployment doubled in ten years. In the suburbs the rate of increase in unemployment was about the same for both races.

As John Kasarda argues, however, "Rising central city unemployment rates for minorities illustrate only a portion of the problem" because a significant number of blacks living in central cities have become so discouraged that

TABLE 11.7

Median Family Income by Race inside and outside Central Cities of SMSAs

	MEDIAN FAMILY INCOME[a] (1985 DOLLARS)			
	1959	*1969*	*1979*	*1985*
Central Cities				
All races[b]	21,752	27,515	26,801	25,337
White	23,112	29,472	29,560	28,001
Black	14,193	19,245	17,183	16,187
Outside Central Cities				
All races[b]	24,490	32,417	33,992	32,724
White	24,886	32,895	34,556	33,285
Black	12,853	20,298	22,294	22,452

[a]Income in the year shown for families by place of residence in the following year.
[b]Includes other races not shown separately.
Sources: U.S. Bureau of the Census, *Current Population Reports*, series P-23, no. 37, June 24, 1971, table 7; series P-23, no. 75, November 1978, table 17; and unpublished Census Bureau tabulations from the Current Population Survey.

they have dropped out of the labor force entirely.[69] Since they have given up the search for employment, they are no longer counted as being unemployed, a classification that requires that one be actively seeking work. The lower part of Table 11.6 shows the rate of *non*participation in the labor force by race, sex, and place of residence. Between 1970 and 1980 the rate of nonparticipation increased far more rapidly for central city black males than for any other group.

Finally, there is the question of earnings. Table 11.7 shows that median family income in constant dollars is now 39 percent higher for black families living in the suburbs than for those in central cities and that the gap has been widening steadily. In 1969 black income in the suburbs had been only 5 percent higher. This would seem to confirm a growing suburban advantage for blacks. The figures can be misleading, however, if used to compare the virtues of the suburban and central city labor markets. First, some of the people residing in each place, to whom the data refer, actually work at jobs in the labor market of the other area. Second, the populations living in the two areas are not identical in their personal characteristics. Blacks living in the suburbs and blacks living in the central city are not random samples of a single black population. Rather they are self-selected groups and may differ significantly in relevant ways. This is, of course, equally true of the white population of the two areas.

Several attempts have been made to deal with the second difficulty by making comparisons between earnings of central city and suburban residents

69. John D. Kasarda, "Urban Change and Minority Opportunities," in Paul E. Peterson, ed., *The New Urban Reality* (Washington, D.C.: Brookings Institution, 1985), p. 58.

that control for differences in race, education, work experience, sex, occupation, and other factors that could be expected to influence individual earnings. The objective is to divide the earnings disadvantage of central city blacks into a discrimination component (blacks versus whites), a location component (central city versus ring area), and a component explained by the education, occupation, and experience characteristics of blacks. Richard Price and Edwin Mills, using 1978 data, estimated that earnings of the average central city black male would be increased 9.4 percent if he were residing in the suburbs and received the same compensation for occupation, experience, and so on, as does a black suburban male.[70] This estimate of the "location penalty" suffered by blacks because they live in the central city is probably smaller than most analysts would have anticipated. Considerably larger is the penalty imposed, even in the suburbs, by racial discrimination. According to Price and Mills, the earnings of the average central city black male might rise as much as an additional 35 percent if he were compensated for his personal characteristics in the same way as are white suburban males.[71] Given the difficulties inherent in such comparisons, however, these estimates should certainly not be regarded as the final word.[72]

The Losses Imposed by Segregation

Instead of comparing economic opportunity in central cities and suburbs in an attempt to decide where blacks are most likely to prosper, John F. Kain devised another way of analyzing the connection among racial segregation, job decentralization, and minority-group poverty. Kain concentrated on the effects of housing segregation on job opportunities for minorities and on other indicators of minority-group welfare. In a widely discussed empirical study, he tested the following three interrelated hypotheses: that "racial segregation in the housing markets (1) affects the distribution of Negro employment and (2) reduces Negro job opportunities, and that (3) postwar suburbanization of employment has seriously aggravated the problem."[73] Among the important reasons for expecting housing segregation to affect black employ-

70. Richard Price and Edwin Mills, "Race and Residence in Earnings Determination," *Journal of Urban Economics*, January 1985, p. 12.
71. Ibid., pp. 12–13.
72. Quite different estimates were obtained by John Vrooman and Stuart Greenfield in "Are Blacks Making It in the Suburbs? Some New Evidence on Intrametropolitan Spatial Segmentation," *Journal of Urban Economics*, March 1980, pp. 155–167. Their results were later corrected by Clifford Reid in "Are Blacks Making It in the Suburbs? A Correction," *Journal of Urban Economics*, November 1984, pp. 357–359.
73. John F. Kain, "Housing Segregation, Negro Employment and Metropolitan Decentralization," *Quarterly Journal of Economics*, May 1968, p. 176. Kain's study has been criticized on a number of grounds. See Joseph D. Mooney, "Housing Segregation, Negro Employment: An Alternative Perspective," *Quarterly Journal of Economics*, May 1969, pp. 299–311; Paul Offner and Daniel H. Saks, "A Note on Kain's 'Housing Segregation, Negro Employment,'" *Quarterly Journal of Economics*, February 1971, pp. 147–160; and Kain's reply in von Furstenberg, Harrison, and Horowitz, vol. 1, pp. 5–18.

ment is the fact that segregation limits workers' freedom to move close to job locations and therefore imposes high travel costs that may discourage them from taking otherwise desirable jobs.

To test his three hypotheses, Kain used data for the metropolitan areas of Chicago and Detroit. He started with two sets of facts for each area: a given segregated pattern of black residence and a given spatial distribution of all jobs in the central city and the suburbs. Using statistical techniques, he then examined the effect of the segregated housing pattern on the proportion of blacks in the work force at each job location. Next he compared the actual level of black employment at each location with an estimate of what its level would be if the black population were distributed evenly over all residential areas instead of being confined to a few ghettos. He found that housing segregation imposed job losses on blacks in both cities. The estimated loss was 22,000 to 24,000 in Chicago and 4,000 to 9,000 in Detroit.

It is but one step from these findings to the argument that the continuing decentralization of jobs within metropolitan areas is likely to reduce black job opportunities still further. Trapped in the inner city, the great majority of blacks find themselves living at an increasing average distance from the aggregate of job locations. (That job decentralization has indeed continued since Kain's study was published in 1968 has already been shown in Chapter 3.)

In order to test Kain's hypothesis that housing discrimination affects black employment opportunities, Mahlon Straszheim reformulated the theoretical argument as follows. White workers are free to live where they choose, and housing prices (as we have argued in Chapter 6) decline with distance from the metropolitan center. This implies that wages for whites will also decline with distance from the center, since employers at suburban sites will not have to compensate white workers (who can live nearby) for the higher cost of housing at the center. The situation is different for blacks, especially those with little education and low skills. Because they face formidable suburban housing barriers, they are largely confined to living in the central city. Wages earned by blacks working in the ring area must be *higher* than those earned in or near inner city ghettos in order to induce them to commute outward to distant (and inaccessible) suburban jobs. Simultaneously, black wages in the inner city are held down by the large supply of locally resident black workers. In short, the wage gradient for low-skilled blacks is expected to slope *up* with distance from the center, while white wage gradients should slope down.[74]

Straszheim tested these expectations, using household survey data for the San Francisco Bay area in 1965. He divided both the black and the white samples into three groups, using educational attainment as a proxy for skill level, and estimated wage gradients for each by means of multiple regression. Results conformed closely to expectations. The wage gradient for low-skilled

74. Mahlon R. Straszheim, "Discrimination and the Spatial Characteristics of the Urban Labor Market for Black Workers," *Journal of Urban Economics*, January 1980, pp. 134–135.

blacks sloped upward toward the suburbs, with the lowest incomes earned at jobs located in central city ghettos and the highest in the most distant suburbs. The gradients for all white groups sloped downward toward the suburbs. Gradients for blacks with intermediate and higher levels of education fell somewhere between those of whites and those of low-skilled blacks. Finally, for less educated workers, income differentials between blacks and whites were greatest at the city center, just as the theory would predict. Straszheim concluded that "the empirical evidence indicating a reverse wage gradient for low income black workers is persuasive evidence in support of Kain's view."[75]

As Kain has argued elsewhere, the reduction in well-being suffered by blacks as a result of housing segregation goes beyond job losses of the sort just estimated. In addition, those blacks who *do* find employment at outlying job locations are likely to spend more on transportation to work than would be necessary if their housing choices were unrestricted. Moreover, the restriction of housing choice imposes a welfare loss on blacks by limiting and distorting their consumption of housing itself.[76] The conclusion is inescapable that by limiting freedom of choice, segregation cannot help and very probably hurts the segregated minority population. The policy prescription that follows from the analysis is obviously to encourage desegregation, and the appropriate area over which to accomplish desegregation is not just the central city but the entire metropolitan region.

Other Arguments for Dispersion

The case for encouraging voluntary dispersion of minorities gains strength from other considerations as well. In the first place, minorities certainly ought to enjoy equal access to suburban residence as a matter of right. As we will see in Chapter 13, they are presently denied that right by restrictive zoning and other discriminatory practices. Their outward movement would be encouraged by a program that simply guaranteed them the equal access to which they are justly entitled.

Equally important, the national commitment to the goal of integration requires that we take positive action to stem the development of a society in which most blacks live in central cities and most whites in the suburbs. Even though net black in-migration to central cities has ended, the absolute size of the black central city population continues to rise as a result of natural increase. In the near future it is unlikely that dispersion can operate fast enough to prevent substantial further growth of the minority population within central cities. That is one reason why dispersion should be thought of

---

75. Ibid., p. 139.
76. See J. R. Meyer, J. F. Kain, and M. Wohl, *The Urban Transportation Problem* (Cambridge Mass.: Harvard University Press, 1965), ch. 7; and John F. Kain and John M. Quigley, "Housing Market Discrimination, Homeownership and Savings Behavior," *American Economic Review*, June 1972, pp. 263–277.

not as an alternative to other policies aimed at the relief of urban poverty but as complementary to them.

The present pattern of macrosegregation by race and income not only defeats the hope of achieving an integrated society but also weakens the nation's antipoverty program. As we shall see in Chapter 15, local governments help to finance a considerable fraction of all public services, including some that are poverty-related. The concentration of poverty within their borders adds to their financial burden while simultaneously weakening the tax base that must bear it. As a result central city residents, including the poor, either receive less in the way of public services or pay higher tax rates to receive the same level than do their counterparts in the suburbs. No one would argue that this outcome is either equitable or consistent with an all-out attack on poverty.

A variety of policies have been suggested to encourage the voluntary dispersion of ethnic minorities into the suburbs. Most of them focus on the need to end racial discrimination in housing and to open up the suburbs to low-income and lower-middle-income families. These will be taken up in detail in Chapter 13. Also potentially important are the proposals, outlined in Chapter 15, that call for state assumption of all public education costs and federal assumption of all costs of welfare. These changes would help to reduce the opposition of wealthy suburban communities to low-income migrants, who, under present fiscal arrangements, are thought to add more to local expenditure needs than they produce in local tax revenues.

In an often quoted passage, the National Advisory Commission on Civil Disorders in 1968 expressed the view that "our nation is moving toward two societies, one black, one white—separate and unequal." Since that date, to be sure, we have managed a modest reduction in the incidence of poverty. But as the nation has grown richer and the remaining poverty has become increasingly concentrated in specific segments of the black and Spanish-origin communities, the prosperous white majority has gradually lost interest in the problem. The geographic projection of the two societies—the separation into poor, heavily black cities and affluent, large white suburbs—is still clearly etched on the map of metropolitan America. We cannot fail to recognize the threat that this geographic pattern poses to the institutions of a democratic society; yet to this moment we have hardly begun to deal with the problem.

TWELVE

The Problem of Urban Housing

In the United States housing and neighborhood conditions persist that seem to most observers to be wholly unacceptable in a highly affluent society. A walk through any of our older cities will reveal that despite decades of economic progress and countless housing reforms, the slums are still very much with us.

The Housing Act of 1949 contained a famous statement of intent: "The Congress hereby declares that the general welfare and security of the Nation and the health and living standards of its people require . . . the realization as soon as feasible of the goal of a decent home and suitable living environment for every American family." Thereafter, as housing acts followed one another with bewildering frequency, the goal proclaimed in 1949 was sought by means of a continuously changing array of federal programs. Although there was substantial improvement in the condition of the nation's housing, it was not always clear that public policy had helped very much to achieve it. The frequency with which one widely heralded federal program supplemented or replaced another gave rise finally to the suspicion that it was not merely the mechanics but perhaps indeed the very premises of public policy that were mistaken.

We will deal with public policy in Chapter 13. This chapter provides the necessary background. It begins with a discussion of the problem of measuring housing and neighborhood quality. That is followed by a description of the urban housing market, intended to explain why the market might fail to produce "a decent home and suitable living environment for every American family." Both good and bad housing in the United States are largely the products of our system of free enterprise and competitive markets. It is only against the background of private market action that we can sensibly evaluate public policy toward housing.

MEASURING THE QUALITY OF HOUSING AND OF NEIGHBORHOODS

Urban housing policy has long been concerned with the quality of the units that city dwellers occupy. How can such quality be reliably measured? What we wish to isolate is the level of service rendered by a given structure. This has proved exceedingly difficult to measure. Ideally, the following dimensions of housing service ought to be taken into account:

1. Physical condition of the building. Is it structurally sound and well maintained?
2. Number and quality of utilities and equipment. For example, are heat, electricity, and complete plumbing provided?
3. Adequacy of the design. For example, does the unit have sufficient light, air, and separation of functions?
4. Intensity of occupancy. How many rooms or how many square feet of floor space does the unit contain per person?

In each decennial census of housing, a series that began in 1940, the Census Bureau has gathered systematic data on the condition of the nation's housing stock. Of the four dimensions of quality listed, only the third— adequacy of design—has totally eluded the statisticians. To measure overall physical condition, the Census Bureau, from 1950 through 1970, made use of a variety of categories such as "sound," "deteriorating," and "dilapidated." Census enumerators were asked to judge the condition of each structure they visited. However, postcensus evaluations revealed these judgments to be so unreliable that the questions on physical condition were not included in the 1980 census.[1]

To measure adequacy of equipment, the census records the presence or absence of a long list of items such as water supply, bathing facilities, toilet facilities, type of heating equipment, and type of cooking fuel. For the principal plumbing facilities a further distinction is made between those shared and those for exclusive use of one dwelling unit. Plumbing facilities have been singled out as the equipment most relevant to an overall evaluation of housing conditions. By combining information on the extent of plumbing with information on structural condition, U.S. housing agencies arrived at a final set of categories to describe the physical aspect of housing conditions: through 1970, "standard" housing was defined as housing that was not dilapidated and that contained all enumerated plumbing facilities; "substandard" housing comprised all units that were either dilapidated or lacking one or more of

---

1. See the discussion in John C. Weicher, "Substandard Housing: The Trend and Current Situation," in *Housing Delivery System* (Columbus, Ohio: Center for Real Estate Education and Research, Ohio State University, 1980), pp. 61–62; and U.S. Bureau of the Census, *Measuring the Quality of Housing*, working paper no. 25, 1967.

the enumerated plumbing facilities. Since 1970, because data on "condition" have not been collected, "standard" and "substandard" refer only to the presence or absence of complete plumbing.

To measure crowding, the Census Bureau records the number of persons and the number of rooms in each dwelling unit and then calculates a persons-per-room ratio. Admittedly, this measure leaves out of account differences in the size of rooms among various units at any one date and changes in the average size of rooms over time. However, it does indicate the extent to which a home provides privacy and separation of functions, which a floor-space measure would not do. A ratio of 1.01 or more persons per room is taken to indicate "overcrowding" according to standards now widely accepted in the United States. (By world standards, 1.01 persons per room would be regarded as normal or, in many places, luxurious. A United Nations survey found that in the 1960s the average persons-per-room ratio was 2.5 in the less developed nations and 1.1 in Europe and Japan.)[2]

A new set of data on housing conditions has been available since 1973. Each year the Annual Housing Survey (AHS) conducted by the Census Bureau and the Department of Housing and Urban Development collects a vast array of information on a nationwide sample of housing units.[3] In addition to data on crowding and on the extent of plumbing, utilities, and equipment comparable to that in the decennial census, the AHS contains questions on equipment breakdowns and on objective evidence of physical condition such as leaky roofs, holes in floors, and broken plaster. It also elicits subjective data such as the occupant's rating of structure condition on a scale from poor to excellent and the occupant's desire to move. However, no summary measure of structural condition comparable to "dilapidated" is included, so substandard housing, as it was traditionally estimated through 1970, cannot be directly measured with AHS data.

Neighborhood Quality

To this point we have discussed measures of housing quality that are intended to isolate the quality of service rendered in particular structures. A broader definition would attempt to incorporate neighborhood characteristics as well. When people choose housing they take into account not only the quality of service associated with the particular dwelling unit but the attractiveness of the neighborhood as a place to live. Desirable neighborhood characteristics include such features as adequate park and recreation facilities,

2. See Leland S. Burns and Leo Grebler, *The Housing of Nations* (New York: Wiley, 1977), table 1.4.

3. Results for the nationwide sample are published each year in six parts. See U.S. Bureau of the Census, *Current Housing Reports*, series H-150, parts A–F. In addition, sixty individual SMSAs are surveyed in rotation, currently fifteen each year. See *Current Housing Reports*, series H-170, for separate volumes on each SMSA.

good schools, clean streets, and, of particular concern in recent years, freedom from crime.

Observation of housing markets indicates that consumers are willing to pay for the attributes of housing and neighborhood quality that appeal to them. Moreover, what they are willing to pay is one measure of the economic value of such attributes. Kain and Quigley studied a large sample of rental and owner-occupied housing in St. Louis for which they had very detailed information on both housing and neighborhood quality characteristics. They estimated multiple-regression equations to explain the variation in monthly rent (for rental units) or house value (for owner-occupied dwellings). According to these estimates, the quality characteristics of a dwelling unit and its immediate physical environment had approximately as much effect on price as did such standard quantitative measures as number of rooms, number of bathrooms, and lot size. Clearly, housing and neighborhood quality do matter.[4]

Until the early 1960s housing analysts, following a tradition that went back to the reforms of the late nineteenth century, concentrated their attention on housing conditions, narrowly defined, and devoted relatively little attention to the characteristics of neighborhoods. However, the urban riots of the 1960s, the subsequent rise of neighborhood activism, and more recently the problem of massive housing abandonment focused attention on the importance of neighborhood to social well-being. Reflecting this growing interest, the Annual Housing Survey collects data on a wide range of neighborhood conditions. It would be virtually impossible in a nationwide survey to assemble objective data such as local crime rate or extent of street litter for neighborhoods. Consequently, the information collected by the AHS is subjective in nature. Occupants are asked to indicate whether they are dissatisfied with conditions such as street noise and crime or with services such as schools, recreation facilities, and police protection. In short, the survey indicates how residents feel about their neighborhoods.

Before examining the evidence on housing and neighborhood conditions in American cities, we turn to a description of the urban housing market, since an understanding of that market is essential to the analysis of those conditions.

4. John F. Kain and John M. Quigley, "Measuring the Value of Housing Quality," *Journal of the American Statistical Association*, June 1970, pp. 532–548. Numerous other studies have estimated the influence of individual housing and neighborhood attributes on rent and price. See, for example, Robert F. Gillingham, *Place-to-Place Rent Comparisons Using Hedonic Quality Adjustment Techniques*, BLS staff paper no. 8, U.S. Bureau of Labor Statistics, 1975; Mingche M. Li and H. James Brown, "Micro-neighborhood Externalities and Hedonic Housing Prices," *Land Economics*, May 1980, pp. 125–141; and the review of the literature by A. Myrick Freeman III, "The Hedonic Price Approach to Measuring Demand for Neighborhood Characteristics," in David Segal, ed., *The Economics of Neighborhood* (Orlando, Fla.: Academic Press, 1979), pp. 191–217.

AN "ADAPTIVE" MODEL OF THE HOUSING MARKET

How does the housing market function to produce the mixture of good and bad housing that is found in every U.S. city? For the sake of simplicity, the following discussion assumes that the market is entirely a rental one. Although only 41 percent of urban housing units are renter-occupied, focusing on rental housing is justified by the fact that it contains a majority of the overcrowded and substandard urban units. Introducing an ownership sector would add greatly to the complexity of the analysis while not substantially changing its conclusions.

Rapkin, Winnick, and Blank have pointed out that if we use terms from conventional economic theory, the rental housing market in a large city is probably best thought of as an instance of monopolistic competition among a large number of sellers.[5] Competition cannot be described as "pure," since the units supplied are clearly differentiated by size, quality, and location. On the other hand, the very large number of sellers and the small size of the largest in relation to the whole market ensure that effective competition takes place. There is no possibility of monopoly, no collusion among sellers, no tendency for suppliers to become involved in oligopolistic strategies: each building owner behaves as if the market situation were "given" and assumes that his or her own decisions have no effect on it. (To be sure, there are some important imperfections in the urban housing market—most notably the prevalence of racial discrimination, to which we will return later in this chapter.)

Because buildings are expensive, durable, and immovable, the housing market differs in important respects from most other consumer goods markets. From the high cost and durability of shelter it follows that in any one year almost the entire supply of housing services is provided by the standing stock. New construction on the average adds only 2 or 3 percent per year to the housing supply of the nation as a whole, and a part of that goes to offset the annual toll of demolitions and losses from other causes. If the adjustment of supply to changes in demand could take place only through new construction, the process would be even more cumbersome, slow, and expensive than in fact it is. Fortunately, adjustments on the supply side take place not only through new construction but also through a series of complex changes by which the quality of existing units, and therefore their rent level, is "adapted" to the pattern of demand expressed in the market for housing services. For example, if a given class of occupants gradually moves out of a neighborhood, the housing they leave behind is usually too valuable to be demolished, since

5. Chester Rapkin, Louis Winnick, and David M. Blank, *Housing Market Analysis* (Washington, D.C.: Housing and Home Finance Agency, 1953), p. 22. The widely accepted view that rental housing markets are competitive has recently been challenged. See Francis J. Cronin, "Market Structure and the Price of Housing Services," *Urban Studies*, August 1983, pp. 365–375.

it is still capable of rendering service. Hence it will generally be adapted by alteration of its quality to meet the needs of another class. Thus the character of the housing stock in a particular place changes under the influence of market forces in ways that neither city planners nor housing policy administrators can readily control. Probably the greatest weakness in U.S. housing policy has been its failure to acknowledge the power (and therefore to anticipate the consequences) of the adaptive process in the urban housing market. We will therefore return to a detailed examination of that process.

In analyzing any housing market it is well to keep in mind one seemingly obvious but frequently neglected fact: every person has to live somewhere (though not necessarily in a separate dwelling unit). Hence the function of the market is, broadly speaking, to match up the population of families with the existing stock of housing. Since family income is the principal determinant of housing demand, this function reduces essentially to matching up a distribution of families by amount of income with a distribution of housing units by rent level. The market operates like a game of musical chairs—except that almost everyone ordinarily ends up with a chair. Unless the number of separately residing households or the stock of housing changes, each move that fills one vacancy creates another somewhere else. When the stock increases relative to the number of households, each new unit that attracts a tenant creates a vacancy elsewhere; likewise, each demolition that removes a unit fills up a vacancy in some other part of the stock, unless the number of households is diminishing. Obviously, partial equilibrium analysis restricted to one sector of a city's housing market can be very misleading. It is usually necessary to trace out the consequences of any change for the entire stock within a given market.

If we continue to abstract from the problem of racial discrimination, it seems reasonable, despite the difference between rich family and poor and between luxury housing and the slums, to treat the central city rental housing market as a continuum, for there is a distribution of housing over all rent classes and a distribution of families over all income levels. The market thus provides a series of small steps by which a household can move up or down the scale of housing quality. The possibility of families making these small substitutions binds the entire range of housing into one market, since there are no well-defined gaps at which one can draw logical dividing lines.

In housing market analysis it is important to take into account the changing propensity of adults to form separate households. This propensity increased significantly from 1960 to 1980 as a result of numerous factors, including a rise in the divorce rate, postponement of marriage, increased availability of housing subsidies, and a rise in the average level of income. Average size of household dropped during this period from 3.33 to 2.76 persons. Because household size has fallen, the number of households in a given city may continue to increase even while its total population is declining. In cities where population has fallen sharply, the decline in the number of households is invariably more moderate.

Varying the Supply of Housing "Quality"

Looked at from the supply side, the urban housing market is bound together by the adaptability of structures. Just as tenants can move from one rent class into the next, so owners can "move" their buildings from one rent class to another by remodeling, dividing, or combining units or by changing the level of outlays for operation and maintenance.[6] It is useful to think of the owner not just as an "investor" in real estate but as an entrepreneur who is in the business of operating rental housing. The owner's objective is to maintain and operate a building at the level of quality that will maximize profits. Higher levels of quality of housing service will command higher rents but will also cost more to produce. The owner's task is to find the most profitable combination.

Given the basic structure and layout of a particular building, the quality of housing service produced in it depends on two factors. The first is the annual level of operating outlays incurred by the owner. For example, higher outlays might take the form of increased expenditures for cleaning and painting or for heating fuel, minor repairs, or security against crime. The owner will expand these outlays as long as each dollar of additional expense generates more than a dollar of additional gross income from rents. The most profitable combination occurs at the level of operating expense at which one more dollar of outlay would just return one more dollar of rent. In the conventional terminology of price theory, the owner pushes service output to the point at which marginal revenue equals marginal cost.

The second factor that affects quality in a given structure is the frequency with which deteriorating structural parts or equipment are replaced. In general, major elements of structure or equipment do not suddenly and completely cease to function. Rather they deteriorate gradually, as a plumbing system does, providing less satisfactory service as they grow older. It follows that the shorter the average period over which such elements are re-

6. For further elaboration of this point and for references to earlier literature on the housing market, see James Heilbrun, *Real Estate Taxes and Urban Housing* (New York: Columbia University Press, 1966), chs. 2 and 4. Adaptive models of the housing market have also been formulated by Richard F. Muth in *Cities and Housing* (Chicago: University of Chicago Press, 1969), ch. 6; and Edgar O. Olsen, "A Competitive Theory of the Housing Market," *American Economic Review*, September 1969, pp. 612–622. John F. Kain and William C. Apgar, Jr., describe a simulation model of an urban housing market containing an adaptive mechanism in "Simulation of Housing Market Dynamics," *Journal of the American Real Estate and Urban Economics Association*, Winter 1979, pp. 505–538. A review of economic analyses of urban housing markets and an extensive bibliography are provided in John M. Quigley, "What Have We Learned about Urban Housing Markets?" in P. Mieszkowski and M. Straszheim, eds., *Current Issues in Urban Economics* (Baltimore: Johns Hopkins University Press, 1979), pp. 391–429.

placed, the higher the level of service rendered in the building. But also, the shorter the period of replacement, the higher the annual amount of depreciation that the owner must charge as a cost. Those who wish to enjoy high-quality housing service must be willing to pay a high enough rent premium for new as compared with old equipment to make frequent replacement investment profitable to the owner.

Finally, structures themselves can be altered by investment in remodeling. This is the most obvious way of "moving" a building within the rent distribution to meet changed conditions of demand. Apartments can be divided into smaller units or combined into larger ones, or they can be remodeled to overcome design obsolescence and/or to introduce more up-to-date equipment. The owner will invest in remodeling if the expected return on the required funds exceeds the opportunity cost of capital.

Demand for Housing Space and Quality

Housing units differ from one another in three important respects: location within the city, size, and quality. In general the rent or value per square foot will be higher the more central the location, the larger the number of rooms, and the higher the quality of the dwelling. For a given outlay a family can obtain a smaller apartment of higher quality or a larger unit of lower quality. Each family will presumably choose the combination of space and quality that best suits its needs, income, and tastes.

Since quality and space compete for the consumer's housing dollar, it is apparent that given the level of consumer incomes, attempts to raise the quality of housing may, if they require a rise in rents, tend to *increase* the degree of overcrowding. Conversely, overcrowding could be reduced by increasing the supply of *low*-quality, low-price housing. Thus the two major objectives of public policy toward housing—to increase quality and to reduce overcrowding—are potentially in conflict, given the constraint of a fixed level of consumer income and rent-paying capacity.

Effect of Income on Demand for Housing

The principal factors shaping a family's demand for housing are income and family size. The higher its income, the more it will spend on housing. The response of housing expenditures to change in the level of income is measured by the income elasticity of demand, which is defined as percentage change in expenditure divided by percentage change in income.

The income elasticity of demand for housing has been studied repeatedly and with varying results. In his important theoretical and empirical analysis of urban housing, Muth estimated the income elasticity of demand in

1950 separately for each of six cities. His results tended "to cluster around a value just slightly greater than + 1."[7] Margaret Reid, in an earlier comprehensive analysis, had estimated that the income elasticity of consumption of rooms per person was only about one-third as high as the income elasticity of housing consumption.[8] This means that although consumption of space rises as family income goes up, the amount spent on increased space can account for only a minor share of the increase in family housing expenditure that occurs as income rises. The major share must therefore be accounted for by a rise in the quality of the space consumed—that is, by a rise in rent paid per room. In short, these figures imply that the income elasticity of demand for housing *quality* is quite high. Muth's study directly confirmed the effects of income on housing quality. He found a very strong inverse relationship between family income and both substandard housing and overcrowding, and he attributed much of the improvement in housing conditions in the United States during the 1950s to the substantial rise in the real level of income.[9]

Recent estimates of the income elasticity of demand that employ data for individual households rather than averages for households grouped by census tract find values well below the level estimated by Muth and Reid. Stephen K. Mayo, in a review of more than two dozen studies, concludes that the technically most reliable estimates of income elasticity fall in the range of .3 to .5 for renters and .5 to .7 for owner-occupants.[10] Mayo goes on to question the common (but basically unwarranted) assumption that a single income elasticity applies at all levels of income. In fact, there is considerable evidence that the income elasticity of demand for housing rises with the level of household income. Keith R. Ihlanfeldt, for example, estimated income elasticities in the range of .72 to 1.1 for homeowners with incomes above $22,000, compared with .14 to .62 for those with incomes below $12,000.[11]

As we shall see, the incidence of substandard and overcrowded housing has declined rapidly in the United States since 1950. Although rising living standards undoubtedly account for much of the improvement, the strong relationship between housing quality and income also suggests that substandard conditions are likely to persist where poverty persists.

7. Muth, p. 199.

8. Margaret G. Reid, *Housing and Income* (Chicago: University of Chicago Press, 1962), pp. 376, 378.

9. Muth, pp. 199–200, 278–280.

10. Stephen K. Mayo, "Theory and Estimation in the Economics of Housing Demand," *Journal of Urban Economics*, July 1981, p. 103. For a review of the earlier studies, see Frank de Leeuw, "The Demand for Housing: A Review of Cross-section Evidence," *Review of Economics and Statistics*, February 1971, pp. 1–10.

11. Keith R. Ihlanfeldt, "Property Tax Incidence on Owner-occupied Housing: Evidence from the Annual Housing Survey," *National Tax Journal*, March 1982, table 2. A similar income effect is reported in J. Sa-Aadu, "Another Look at the Economics of Demand-Side versus Supply-Side Strategies in Low-Income Housing," *Journal of the American Real Estate and Urban Economics Association*, Winter 1984, table 4.

The High Cost of New Construction

For many years one of the major sources of dissatisfaction with the whole enterprise of housing has been the high cost of new construction. Over the years economic progress has greatly reduced the "real cost" of most consumer goods in the United States: historically, per capita income has been rising much faster than the prices of the things people buy, so decade by decade the average family finds its real income, or level of purchasing power, rising. Housing is something of an exception, however. Through most of this century the cost of new residential construction has been rising faster than the general price level.

Figure 12.1 displays construction cost, price and income trends since 1960. (An earlier starting point would show much the same thing.) From 1960 to 1985 per capita disposable income rose 476 percent. Consumer prices on the average rose 259 percent over the same period. Real disposable income per capita (disposable income measured in constant dollars) increased by 74 percent.[12] This last figure means that consumers could, on the average, buy 74 percent more goods and services with their 1985 incomes than they had been able to purchase with their smaller incomes in 1960. Residential construction costs, however, rose 345 percent from 1960 to 1985, far above the rate of increase for consumer prices as a whole. Consequently, for the average consumer, the capacity to purchase new housing has increased far less rapidly than the ability to purchase most other goods. (Admittedly, indices of construction cost must be used cautiously in analyzing housing problems. First of all, comparisons between widely separated points in time are subject to a degree of error on account of changes in quality and in the mix of physical elements that constitute "housing." Second, the capital cost of housing is only one item among the many that contribute to the annual cost of occupancy; others include maintenance and operating costs, taxes, interest rates on mortgage loans, and insurance.)[13]

Our concern at this point, however, is not with the problem of the high cost of housing but rather with the way high construction costs affect the functioning of the housing market: in recent years the construction of dwellings that meet minimum standards in our large cities has been so expensive that only relatively well-to-do families can afford to live in new unsubsidized housing. For example, at a conservative estimate, the market rent for a newly constructed two-bedroom apartment in a large city in the mid-1980s was in the range of $700 to $800 a month, or $8,400 to $9,600 a year. To live in such an apartment at a rent-income ratio of .25 (about average for the United States) a family would need to earn between $33,600 and $38,400 a year. Yet

12. It should be noted that the consumer price index is *not* the deflator used by the Commerce Department in calculating real per capita income.
13. See U.S. Department of Housing and Urban Development, "The Cost of Housing," in *Housing in the Seventies* (Washington, D.C.: U.S. Government Printing Office, 1974), ch. 8.

FIGURE 12.1
Comparison of Trends in Construction Cost, Income and the Price Level

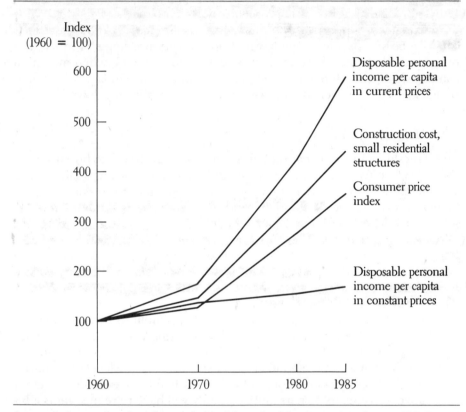

Sources: Index numbers have been calculated from the following statistical series: U.S. Department of Commerce series on per capita disposable personal income in current prices and in 1982 prices; E. H. Boeckh and Associates, index of construction costs for small residential structures; Bureau of Labor Statistics, consumer price index.

in 1983 only 26 percent of families in the central cities of large SMSAs earned as much as $35,000, and the median level was only $21,858.[14]

For the majority of families, new, commercially financed housing in large cities is now clearly out of reach. Apart from the possibility of living in new units subsidized in some way by the government, they are consigned to the secondhand market in housing. Of course, this is not necessarily to be deplored. Most people live in secondhand housing—as William Grigsby has remarked, even Queen Elizabeth does. The point is, rather, that the inability of

14. U.S. Bureau of the Census, *Current Population Reports*, series P-60, no. 146, April 1985, table 21.

most families to afford new housing does clearly shape the process by which new construction is absorbed into the standing stock: new housing, unless subsidized by the government, enters near the upper end of the rent distribution and triggers a series of adjustments by which older housing then shifts down into lower rent classes. This hand-me-down process is known as "filtering." To be sure, some of the low-rent, low-quality housing still in use was built for the low end of the market to begin with, at a date when minimum standards, and therefore costs, were lower than they are today. A large portion of it, however, reached the low-rent category by "filtering down."

The Filtering Process

Grigsby points out that the term *filtering* seems to cause no misunderstanding when used in casual discussion but that when housing analysts have attempted more precise definitions, they find agreement difficult.[15] This is hardly surprising, since the single term *filtering* must bear the burden of describing a large part of the complex process by which adjustments take place in the match-up between the stock of housing units and the resident population. For our purposes it will suffice to use one of the conventional general definitions and say that filtering takes place when housing once occupied by a higher-income group is released by them and becomes available at a lower cost to households with lower incomes.

The filtering process gets under way when families in the middle and upper classes move into new housing. The housing thus vacated becomes available to others, to whom it appears better than the dwellings they had. Let us assume no change in the number of households or in the level of family incomes while this process goes on. In that case, when the well-to-do move out of their old housing, its owners quite certainly will have to reduce rents a bit to attract tenants from the next lower income class. The tenants so attracted will vacate other units whose owners will in turn reduce rents to attract a still lower income class. Thus a whole chain of moves will take place, made possible by a series of rent reductions. At the end of the chain the poorest families will, presumably, leave the worst housing for something slightly better, and the worst housing will stand vacant or be demolished.

This is a highly schematic explanation, blessedly simplified by the assumption of static population and income. But let us stick to our simplifications a little longer. Why under these circumstances would the upper-income classes wish to move into new housing? Numerous motives exist, provided we do not insist on a completely static world. Improvements in transportation open up new areas for development, new neighborhoods become fashionable, old buildings become unfashionable or do not offer the latest equipment

15. William Grigsby, *Housing Markets and Public Policy* (Philadelphia: University of Pennsylvania Press, 1963), pp. 85–86.

and conveniences, new modes of housekeeping lead to changes in interior design, architectural styles change, and so on.

It is sometimes suggested that age per se leads to physical deterioration of housing and that the well-to-do move out to avoid this. But housing need not deteriorate with age if it is well maintained. In most cases, therefore, physical deterioration should be regarded not as an independent causal factor but as the result of a change in the demand for particular units, which in turn leads to a reduced level of maintenance. As we argued earlier, reducing outlays for maintenance (and for operation as well) is one of the ways in which owners "move" buildings from one segment of the market to another in response to changes in demand. This view of the matter is supported by the obvious fact that old buildings are often moved up rather than down when an old neighborhood becomes newly fashionable. The inner city housing renovation process known as "gentrification" (further discussed in Chapter 16) is just such an upward movement of old housing.

Filtering is sometimes defended as the principal way in which we can hope to raise the housing standards of the poor—and is often attacked for having failed to do just that. This conflict is correctly resolved by granting that each contention is true in a specifically definable way. In earlier discussion of the housing market it was pointed out that the quality of housing service provided in a given building depends partly on its fixed physical features and equipment and partly on the level of maintenance and operating expenditures applied to them as, so to speak, "variable inputs" by the owner. Filtering *can* raise housing standards insofar as these are concerned with the more or less permanent physical characteristics of buildings; it *cannot* do so insofar as they depend on the owner's inputs of maintenance and operating expense that vary directly with the rent level he or she is attempting to establish. There are undoubtedly some families now living in standard, filtered-down housing for whom it respresents an improvement over what they could have paid for out of the same real income in decades past. The improvement, however, is likely to be not in the level of maintenance or operating services but in the physical features of design and equipment: more light and air, more plumbing, fireproof construction, and so on.

On the debit side, it must be admitted that some of the substandard housing now in use has reached its present disreputable state precisely by the process of filtering down. This is hardly surprising, since low-income tenants usually require low-rent housing, and low-rent housing is often substandard. When the supply of low-rent units is insufficient to meet demand, the market is capable of creating more of them either by breaking up large units or by economizing on maintenance and operating outlays. In the process, additions may be made to the substandard stock. Or, if one thinks in terms of occupancy rather than physical standards, units that filter down may well move into the "overcrowded" category, since lower-income tenants economize on rent by using space more intensively. In short, filtering is one of the mechanisms by which the adaptive market we have been describing adjusts the services supplied by the housing stock to the demands of the resident population.

Against this background we can now examine recent trends in U.S. housing conditions.

TRENDS IN U.S. HOUSING CONDITIONS

According to all the standard measures, housing conditions in the United States have improved markedly in the past forty years. Table 12.1 shows separately the incidence of overcrowding (more than 1.0 persons per room) and of substandard housing (units that lack complete plumbing or are dilapidated), as recorded by the census in 1950, 1960, and 1970 and by the Annual Housing Survey in 1977 and 1983. Whether one looks at urban or rural areas or at white- or black-occupied units, the trend is the same: there has been a remarkable decline in both overcrowding and substandard conditions.

It comes as no surprise to see in Table 12.1 that the housing condition of blacks is inferior to that of whites in urban as well as rural areas. However, the table also reveals that urban (but not rural) housing conditions have improved noticeably faster for blacks, so that their disadvantage relative to whites has been substantially reduced.

We have argued that income is an important determinant of housing quality. Is it possible that the inferior housing condition of blacks can be explained entirely by their lower incomes or other differences in family characteristics? A study by Bianchi, Farley, and Spain found that in 1977 such factors as income, age of head, family size, and residential location could explain only one-third of the black-white difference in overcrowding and 45 percent of the difference in structural inadequacy.[16] The authors concluded that despite marked improvement in their housing condition over the period studied, blacks in 1977 still suffered a measurable "net penalty" on account of race.

Since the mid-1970s, the Annual Housing Surveys have made available a wide range of new information on both housing and neighborhood conditions. Table 12.2 shows some of its results for rental housing when respondents are classified by race, income, and place of residence. Three indicators are presented. Two show the percentage of tenants whose overall rating of their building or neighborhood is "poor"; a third indicates the percentage of tenants who wish to move because of bothersome neighborhood conditions. Each number in the table can therefore be read as an index of "substantial

16. Suzanne M. Bianchi, Reynolds Farley, and Daphne Spain, "Racial Inequalities in Housing: An Examination of Recent Trends," *Demography*, February 1982, pp. 47–48 (and see editorial correction in May 1982 issue).

TABLE 12.1
Trends in the Condition of Urban and Rural Housing by Race of Occupant, 1950–1983[a]

	ALL RACES		WHITE[b]		BLACK[c]	
	Urban	*Rural*	*Urban*	*Rural*	*Urban*	*Rural*
Overcrowded Housing (percentage of units occupied by 1.01 or more persons per room)						
1950	13.3	20.6	—	—	—	—
1960	10.2	15.1	8.5	12.9	24.7	40.8
1970	7.6	10.1	6.3	8.8	18.1	30.1
1977	4.4	5.0	3.8	4.3	9.6	16.4
1983	3.5	3.5	2.9	3.1	7.0	10.2
Substandard Housing (percentage of units dilapidated or lacking complete plumbing facilities)						
1950	21.9	62.4	18.2	59.1	61.2	96.3
1960	9.6	32.6	7.0	28.0	31.8	85.5
1970	5.5	16.0	4.3	13.7	15.2	65.4
1977[d]	1.3	5.0	1.0	3.6	3.6	27.8
1983[d]	1.0	3.9	0.9	3.0	2.1	19.0

[a]Data refer to combined totals for owner-occupants and renters.
[b]In 1950 and 1960 includes only whites; in later years includes whites and other races except black.
[c]In 1950 and 1960 includes all nonwhites; in later years includes only blacks.
[d]Since data on dilapidation were not collected, figures refer to plumbing condition only.
Sources: U.S. Bureau of the Census, *Census of Population and Housing*, 1950, 1960, 1970; *Annual Housing Survey, 1977* and *1983*, part E; and Housing and Home Finance Agency, *Our Nonwhite Population and Its Housing*, 1963.

TABLE 12.2
Opinions of Structure and Neighborhood by Race, Location, and Income for Metropolitan Area Rental Housing, 1983

	PERCENTAGE OF HOUSEHOLDS REPORTING EACH OPINION BY INCOME CLASS				
	Less than $10,000	$10,000 to $20,000	$20,000 to $35,000	Over $35,000	All
Whites and Other Nonblacks					
Central cities					
Opinion of structures: poor	7.0	4.0	2.6	1.3	4.7
Opinion of neighborhood: poor	6.4	5.0	3.2	1.7	4.9
Bothersome neighborhood conditions, want to move	19.6	18.1	15.0	17.5	18.0
Outside central cities					
Opinion of structures: poor	5.8	2.9	1.4	2.1	3.3
Opinion of neighborhood: poor	4.3	2.7	1.6	0.6	2.6
Bothersome neighborhood conditions, want to move	13.0	11.6	9.9	14.2	11.8
Blacks					
Central cities					
Opinion of structure: poor	10.8	9.0	9.3	3.7	9.8
Opinion of neighborhood: poor	9.0	6.9	7.3	7.5	8.1
Bothersome neighborhood conditions, want to move	23.3	23.1	20.8	26.8	23.0
Outside central cities					
Opinion of structure: poor	10.0	6.3	6.2	5.0	7.5
Opinion of neighborhood: poor	7.5	5.2	3.3	0.0	5.5
Bothersome neighborhood conditions, want to move	18.6	17.1	14.8	26.7	18.1

Source: U.S. Bureau of the Census, *Annual Housing Survey*, 1983, part B, July 1985, tables A-2, A-3, A-14 and A-15.

dissatisfaction." Three conclusions stand out. First, both inside and outside central cities, the rate of dissatisfaction with housing and neighborhood conditions is substantially higher for blacks than for nonblacks.[17] Second, for both racial groups, dissatisfaction is more frequent in central cities than in suburbs, but the difference is not as great as might have been expected. Third, as anticipated, there is an inverse relationship between tenant income and opinion of structure and neighborhood. However, the relationship between the desire to move because of unsatisfactory neighborhood conditions and income appears to be quite irregular.

That the poor are less satisfied with their housing condition than the well-to-do reflects the fact that their housing conditions are demonstrably inferior. Using AHS data for 1977, the Congressional Budget Office defined a housing unit as "in need of rehabilitation" if it suffered from one or more of a list of major deficiencies. They found that among renters the incidence of such housing declined from 19.8 percent for very poor households to 8.2 percent for those of middle and upper income.[18]

How are these evaluations affected by size of metropolitan area? Donald Dahmann, using data from the 1979 AHS, found, first, that the pattern of greater dissatisfaction with neighborhoods in central cities than in suburbs was independent of SMSA size and, second, that the overall level of dissatisfaction was uniform across size classes up to 3 million population but distinctly higher in the 3 million-plus category.[19]

Migration, Filtering, and Housing Conditions

Table 12.1 shows that despite great improvement, housing conditions remain far worse for rural than for urban blacks. The surprisingly large percentage of rural black housing that still ranks as substandard is undoubtedly a tribute to the persistence of the rural outhouse. For the black population as a whole, however, the high incidence of substandard and overcrowded housing in rural areas is mitigated by the very rapid decline in the absolute size of the rural black population. That decline came about as a result of the massive mi-

---

17. It might be questioned whether racial differences in opinion of housing and neighborhood arise from true disparities in circumstance or merely from differences in racial attitudes. A recent study found that more than half the difference in opinion can be accounted for by objectively measurable differences in housing conditions and socioeconomic status. See Stephen C. Casey, "The Effect of Race on Opinions of Housing and Neighborhood Quality," in George Sternlieb et al., *America's Housing: Prospects and Problems* (New Brunswick, N.J.: Center for Urban Policy Research, Rutgers University, 1980), pp. 485–542.

18. Congressional Budget Office, *Federal Housing Assistance: Alternative Approaches*, May 1982, tables 1 and 2.

19. Donald C. Dahmann, "Assessments of Neighborhood Quality in Metropolitan America," *Urban Affairs Quarterly*, June 1985, pp. 518, 524

gration of blacks from rural to urban areas, and migration in turn accounts for much of the improvement in black housing conditions since 1950.

First of all, in migrating, blacks moved from rural areas where housing codes were almost unknown and standards were low to urban areas with relatively stringent housing codes: occupancy of housing without full plumbing facilities is now illegal for families in most large cities. Second, black migration into cities was linked to white out-migration through the filtering process. Blacks were able to move into housing that filtered down to them as whites moved out to the suburbs. Much of that housing had been built to middle-class standards of an earlier era and was equipped with full plumbing (and other physical features) to meet the demands of its original higher-income occupants. By and large, these physical features remained intact as the units filtered down to lower-income occupants. Finally, the rapid decline in overcrowded conditions among urban blacks is also associated with the out-migration of the white population. As whites have moved out, the number of households in many central cities has declined sharply, leaving room within the housing stock for the black population to spread out, thus reducing the extent of overcrowding.

Average black family income has, of course, increased substantially in the past forty years and undoubtedly played a part in the long-run improvement of black housing conditions. It would be a mistake, however, to overlook the importance of the gross population movements described. For example, the real income of black families in central cities actually declined during the 1970s (see Table 11.7). Hence the reduction in overcrowding after 1970 cannot be an effect of higher income; it may well have been an effect of population decline.

Is There Still an Urban Housing Problem?

The persistent and impressive decline in the incidence of substandard and overcrowded urban housing traced in Table 12.1 has brought us to the point where it is legitimate to ask, Is there still a housing problem? Let us try to summarize the present situation.

Despite the general improvement in urban housing conditions, most studies concur in citing these remaining problems:

1. The high cost of housing, and especially its burden on low-income households
2. Concentrations of bad housing in the poverty areas of inner cities
3. The rise of seemingly intractable neighborhood problems in poverty areas
4. Continuing discrimination in housing markets

The question of discrimination in housing will be taken up later in this chapter. Within the housing markets of inner cities the other three problems are interconnected, and it is to them that we now turn.

In the United States the proportion of renter households paying one quarter or more of their income for housing rose steadily from 31 percent in 1950 to 55 percent in 1983. Among renter households with very low incomes (defined as less than half the area median income), 63 percent had rent-income ratios above .30 in 1977. Some 29 percent paid more than half their income in rent.[20]

We have shown that the median level of real family income in central cities has fallen since 1969, substantially so for black families (see Table 11.7). Many of the urban poor lack the rent-paying capacity needed to sustain minimum standard housing in the face of rapidly inflating costs. Frank Kristof has concluded that in cities with large poverty populations "the household budgets of one-quarter to one-third of their households do not permit these households to pay the full cost of proper maintenance of older existing housing."[21] Under these circumstances one would expect landlords in low-income neighborhoods to reduce the level of maintenance and operating outlays, bringing about a gradual deterioration in the condition of housing. In fact, that is just what is going on. Much of the housing in low-income neighborhoods is not being maintained at a stable, if low, level of quality. Instead, it is being used up, its physical structure literally being consumed rather than maintained. A process of disinvestment is under way, one that frequently ends in abandonment. In this process measurable housing conditions in the aggregate of occupied buildings may not be found to deteriorate because population decline enables the poor to move on when buildings become uninhabitable. As we shall see, however, the process itself is dangerous and painful and destroys not only buildings but whole neighborhoods as well.

The Problem of Abandonment

The phenomenon known as housing abandonment first came to public attention in the late 1960s. In city after city, owners of rental housing in low-income neighborhoods simply "walked away" from their properties. Evidently they had found that their buildings could no longer be operated profitably and could not be sold, since other investors were also trying to withdraw from the low-income rental sector. Under the circumstances owners attempted to retrieve some capital by "milking" their properties—continuing

20. Congressional Budget Office, *Federal Housing Policy: Current Problems and Recurring Issues,* June 1978, table 3; U.S. Bureau of the Census, *Annual Housing Survey,* 1983, part C, table A–3; and Congressional Budget Office, *Federal Housing Assistance,* table 3.

21. Frank S. Kristof, "Federal Housing Policies: Subsidized Production, Filtration and Objectives: Part II," *Land Economics,* May 1973, p. 171.

to collect rent while withholding maintenance and operating services and failing to pay taxes and mortgage charges. When the building finally became uninhabitable, they abandoned it.[22]

In analyzing abandonment it is useful to distinguish between macro- and microcauses. Macrocauses are the changes in the supply and demand for housing in a particular city that determine the total number of units of the older housing stock to be removed from use during a given period. Microcauses are the forces operating on particular buildings and neighborhoods that determine how and where removal will occur.

The macrocauses can be summed up in an accounting identity that shows the components of change in the size of the housing stock over the course of any one year.
Let

H = change in the number of households
    in the city
U = number of housing units newly
    added to the stock
N = number of old units removed from
    the stock

To simplify the argument, we assume no change in the number of vacant units that are available for use.[23] In that case it is necessarily true that

$$N \equiv U - H$$

For example, if in one year 20,000 new units are added to the stock through new construction, conversion from other uses, and the splitting up of larger units, while the number of local households rises by only 5,000, there is an excess supply of 15,000 units (20,000 − 5,000) that must somehow be eliminated.

In this era of declining central cities it is quite possible for the number of households to *decline* rather than increase. Other things being the same, the excess supply of housing would then be even larger: if 20,000 new units were added while the number of households fell by 5,000, it would be neces-

22. For further detail see George Sternlieb and Robert W. Burchell, *Residential Abandonment: The Tenement Landlord Revisited* (New Brunswick, N.J.: Center for Urban Policy Research, Rutgers University, 1973); William Grigsby, Morton Baratz, and Duncan Maclennan, *The Dynamics of Neighborhood Change and Decline*, Research Report no. 4 (Philadelphia: University of Pennsylvania, Department of City and Regional Planning, January 1984), esp. pp. 64–71; U.S. Department of Housing and Urban Development, *The Dynamics of Neighborhood Change*, HUD-PDR-108, 1975; Peter D. Salins, *The Ecology of Housing Destruction* (New York: New York University Press, for the International Center for Economic Policy Studies, 1980); and Michael A. Stegman, *Housing Investment in the Inner City: The Dynamics of Decline* (Cambridge, Mass.: M.I.T. Press, 1972).

23. For a version in which vacancies are allowed to vary, see Brian J. L. Berry, "Islands of Renewal in Seas of Decay," in Paul E. Peterson, ed., *The New Urban Reality* (Washington, D.C.: Brookings Institution, 1985) p. 86, n. 61.

sary to remove 25,000 older units (20,000 + 5,000) from the stock. In many of the cities that have reported high rates of abandonment—St. Louis, Cleveland, and Detroit, for example—the number of households declined substantially during the 1960s and 1970s as a result of the exodus of middle- and upper-income families.[24] Of course, other combinations are possible as well. Although New York City's population fell 10.4 percent during the 1970s, the number of households declined only 1.7 percent. Nevertheless, there was enough new construction and conversion of commercial lofts into housing to produce a substantial decline in the number of older units remaining in use.

Normal "Removal" versus Abandonment

When the housing market is operating "normally," the elimination of excess units from the stock occurs as the last step in the filtering process. After a series of moves by tenants, the worst low-rent housing is vacated and withdrawn from the active stock. But in a normal market removal would not occur as abandonment. Owners would not walk away from their properties. Instead, they would either demolish them to make way for a more profitable use or would board them up and wait for an increase in housing demand.[25]

If we wish to understand why owners might abandon rental properties, we must look at the microcauses of abandonment. These do not influence the total number of units to be withdrawn but do determine which units are removed and how. Microcauses include the following interrelated factors:

- Low tenant income, which reduces rent-paying capacity below the minimum needed to maintain stable building quality
- Rent-skipping behavior, which reduces actual rents below their contract level
- Vacancies, which directly reduce owner income and in high-crime neighborhoods also invite vandalism
- Vandalism, which greatly increases owner's costs, renders the structure uninhabitable, or both

In neighborhoods where the combination of these four factors makes rental housing investment unusually risky, financial institutions are likely to withdraw mortgage support, making the owner's situation even more difficult. If the outlook for profitable reuse of the site is poor or very distant, owners in such neighborhoods are likely to choose "milking" and, ultimately, abandonment as (from their point of view) the best way out. On the other

---

24. See U.S. General Accounting Office, *Housing Abandonment: A National Problem Needing New Approaches*, doc. no. CED-78-126, August 10, 1978, p. 1. The report contains detailed studies of abandonment in Philadelphia, St. Louis, and Detroit.

25. For a description of the boarding-up process on Manhattan's Lower East Side during the Great Depression, see Leo Grebler, *Housing Market Behavior in a Declining Area* (New York: Columbia University Press, 1952) pp. 39–43 and app. D.

hand, if a currently run-down neighborhood is so situated that the outlook for future reuse is good, owners are likely to keep operating if they can or, if not, board up or demolish the building while retaining ownership (or selling it) for future redevelopment.

In the end, the general character of the neighborhood, measured in terms of the factors just listed, determines the fate of individual units. A bad building in a good neighborhood will not be abandoned. On the other hand, a good building in a bad neighborhood may well suffer that fate, since it frequently cannot resist the rising tide of negative externalities as more and more nearby buildings are deserted by their owners. For example, Kristof reported that 64 percent of the housing lost through demolition or abandonment in New York City between 1960 and 1970 was recorded as up to standard (full plumbing and not dilapidated) in 1960.[26]

The Problem of Neighborhood Quality

Clearly, the problem of deteriorating inner city neighborhoods is closely bound up with that of abandonment. When housing units go under, neighborhoods are left with seemingly bombed-out blocks, strewn with rubbish and litter. Gradually the social as well as the physical structure of neighborhood life crumbles. Because population declines, stores go out of business, and shopping choices are reduced; professional services are withdrawn; churches and other community-based organizations wither for lack of membership. As yet no policies have been developed that would guide depopulation in order to minimize these destructive consequences.[27] And of course, neighborhood problems are not limited to places suffering from abandonment. Crime, vandalism, and litter now seem to be endemic in the inner cities.

We have seen that dissatisfaction with neighborhood conditions in metropolitan areas is now greater than dissatisfaction with housing itself. Since almost everyone living in cities now has full plumbing, and since overcrowding has been drastically reduced, the housing problem, as measured by traditional standards has, indeed, almost disappeared. As Sternlieb puts it, "The old era of absolute housing want has largely come to an end."[28] What remains elusive, especially in the older central cities, is the other goal declared to be a part of the national purpose by the Housing Act of 1949: the provision of a "suitable living environment for every American family."

26. Frank S. Kristof, "Housing and People in New York City," *City Almanac* (New York: Center for New York City Affairs of the New School for Social Research, February 1976), p. 6.
27. See James Heilbrun, "On the Theory and Policy of Neighborhood Consolidation," *Journal of the American Planning Association*, October 1979, pp. 417–427.
28. George Sternlieb, "Epilogue: A Note on Federal Housing Policy," in Sternlieb et al., p. 546.

SEGREGATION AND DISCRIMINATION IN HOUSING

Although almost two decades have passed since the Civil Rights Act of 1968 conferred equal rights for minorities in the housing market, housing segregation remains a major social problem in the United States, and the existence of racial discrimination is one of the principal "imperfections" in U.S. housing markets. Racial separation in many large cities declined slightly between 1970 and 1980, but we have already shown that it remains at a very high level in most places (see Table 10.7). As the black population increases within large cities, old black neighborhoods expand outward and new enclaves of black settlement grow until they, too, are large, and largely all-black, communities. Few neighborhoods achieve and retain racial balance. As we pointed out in Chapter 11, segregation imposes losses on blacks both because it reduces their employment opportunities and because it limits and distorts their housing choices. In addition, it surely makes school integration difficult, if not impossible, to achieve.

Is the fact of racial separation sufficient to prove the existence of discrimination in housing markets? Or might the observed degree of racial segregation be explained entirely by economic factors, such as the location of low-skill jobs and of old, inexpensive housing, which would cause low-income blacks to concentrate in particular neighborhoods? The answer is that economic forces alone cannot explain what we see. Anthony Pascal tested the hypothesis that economic factors could account for racial segregation by estimating multiple-regression equations to predict black residential location in Chicago and Detroit. He found that economic variables could "explain" only one-third to one-half of the observed degree of segregation.[29]

Sean-Shong Hwang and his colleagues arrived at a similar conclusion by a different route: in a study of more than two dozen Texas central cities in 1970 and 1980 they found that socioeconomic differences between blacks and whites were not significantly related to changes in the level of segregation.[30]

But is it possible that blacks are so highly segregated because they choose voluntarily to live in predominantly black neighborhoods? After all, other urban ethnic minorities have tended to cluster out of preference for their own culture and kinfolk. Pascal tested this possibility, too. Using data for Chicago, he compared the observed degree of segregation for Italian-Americans—who are reputed to have a strong tendency toward self-segregation—with that of middle- to upper-income nonwhites. The segrega-

---

29. Anthony H. Pascal, "The Analysis of Residential Segregation," in John P. Crecine, ed., *Financing the Metropolis* (Beverly Hills, Calif.: Sage Publications, 1970), p. 407.

30. Sean-Shong Hwang et al., "The Effects of Race and Socioeconomic Status on Residential Segregation in Texas, 1970–80," *Social Forces*, March 1985, pp. 737, 741.

tion index for nonwhites was more than five times that for Italian-Americans. Such a difference could hardly be attributed to voluntary self-segregation alone.[31] In any case, the stated preference of most blacks in Pascal's study was for integrated housing. In addition, as Kain points out, the self-segregation argument cannot explain why black segregation has remained at high levels for something like seventy years, while the segregation of ethnic minorities has steadily declined.[32]

Although the existence of discrimination can be inferred from the extent of housing segregation, it is difficult to prove its existence by direct observation, especially since the Civil Rights Act of 1968 specifically forbids discrimination in the sale or rental of housing. That discrimination nevertheless continues has often been reported on the basis of anecdotal evidence. It has now also been demonstrated by means of a carefully designed survey of market practices carried out by HUD. In 1977 black and white auditors were sent out in matched pairs to shop for housing that had been advertised in newspapers in a large sample of metropolitan areas. Systematic data were collected on the treatment accorded these prospective customers. Analysis revealed a clear pattern of discrimination. To cite just a few examples, agents were more likely to tell blacks than whites that what they wanted was not available and less likely to volunteer information to blacks about waiting lists. When all forms of discriminatory practice regarding rental housing availability were combined, it was estimated that blacks encountered discrimination in 27 percent of their visits to agents. In the market for owner-occupied housing the like figure was 15 percent. Surveys of the same type conducted by other agencies in Dallas (1979) and Boston (1981) produced evidence of even higher levels of racial discrimination.[33]

Do segregation and discrimination impose higher housing costs on blacks relative to whites? This important question has been studied frequently in recent years. While results vary, most studies based on data through 1970 found that blacks were paying prices on the order of 10 to 15 percent higher for housing inside the ghetto than whites were paying for similar units in all-white neighborhoods. Some studies found that blacks also paid more than whites for housing within the same submarkets, including the suburbs.[34] It is, of course, possible that as population declines and blacks spread

31. Pascal, pp. 409–410.

32. John F. Kain, "Black Suburbanization in the Eighties: A New Beginning or a False Hope?" in John M. Quigley and Daniel L. Rubinfeld, eds., *American Domestic Priorities* (Berkeley: University of California Press, 1985), p. 263.

33. U.S. Department of Housing and Urban Development, *Measuring Racial Discrimination in American Housing Markets*, April 1979, and *Recent Evidence on Discrimination*, April 1984.

34. See the excellent summary of research, including his own, in John Yinger, "Prejudice and Discrimination in the Urban Housing Market," in Mieszkowski and Straszheim, pp. 430–468. Studies of price differentials are discussed on pp. 450–457. For a study of racial price differentials that examines suburban as well as central city markets, see Robert Schafer, "Discrimination in the Boston Housing Market," *Journal of Urban Economics*, April 1979, pp. 176–196.

out within the older cities the adverse inner city price differentials will disappear. However, we would expect that blacks moving into suburban neighborhoods where discrimination exists and housing is not in excess supply would continue to pay differentials.

Antidiscrimination and antisegregation policies are examined from a different perspective in the next chapter, when we deal with proposals to "open up" the suburbs to low- and moderate-income families and to racial minorities.

THE RATIONALE FOR SUBSIDIZING HOUSING

Urban housing policy comprises a great many actual or proposed forms of public intervention in the markets for land and housing. Some are regulatory in nature, such as antidiscrimination laws and zoning ordinances, and are intended to overcome particular imperfections in the housing and land markets. Other forms of intervention, however, are subsidy programs, such as public housing, below-market-interest-rate loans, or rental assistance payments, whose essential purpose is to increase the supply of housing and/or directly reduce its price to consumers. The funds from which these subsidies are paid have alternate uses in either the public or the private sector. What justifies the particular use to which we put them? Why do we subsidize the output or consumption of housing instead of allowing the market to follow its own course, as in many other instances?

Over the years, a number of justifications for housing subsidies have been suggested; four predominate.

1. Housing is a "merit want," or "merit good," in the sense first defined by Musgrave.[35] A merit good is something that is better for people than they realize. Consequently, individual consumers, if left to themselves, are likely to consume less of such goods than the amount that would maximize their welfare within the constraints of their income. The concept is easily understood in the reverse case of "demerit goods": we control the use of narcotics on the ground that otherwise many people would use them in ignorance of the harm they cause. In the same fashion, it may be argued that we must subsidize the distribution of, say, education, medical services, or housing because otherwise, largely through ignorance, people would consume less of them than they ought to. Who is to determine the "correct" level of consumption of such merit goods? In a democratic society, that is presumably the function of the well-informed, who must then persuade the majority to adopt the appropriate policies.

35. Richard A. Musgrave, *The Theory of Public Finance* (New York: McGraw-Hill, 1959), ch. 1, and "Policies for Housing Support: Rationale and Instruments," in U.S. Department of Housing and Urban Development, *Housing in the Seventies: Working Papers*, vol. 1 (1976) esp. 218–222.

2. Poverty, or the unequal distribution of income, prevents some families from obtaining housing that meets a socially desirable minimum standard. In order to bring the poor up to the defined minimum standard, the government provides them with more housing than they can or would pay for out of their low incomes. This argument is actually a variant of the first, for it implies that housing is a merit good. If it were not a merit good, it would be unnecessary to provide housing benefits in kind. One could simply grant cash subsidies to the poor—along the lines of the income-maintenance plans discussed in Chapter 11—and rely on them to spend a sufficient portion of the extra cash on housing. Since we do not do that, the argument clearly implies that people do not spend as much of their income on housing as we think they "ought" to—in other words that housing is a merit good. The only difference between the poverty argument and the merit good argument, then, is that the former suggests, and the latter does not, that above some level of family income we can assume that everyone will voluntarily obtain enough housing.

3. Better housing reduces the cost of providing social services by lowering the incidence of fire, communicable disease, crime, and other social disorders. This is the "external social benefits" argument. If better housing does have these desirable social effects, individual consumption decisions will result systematically in too little housing being consumed. From the principle of diminishing marginal utility we conclude that the marginal private benefit to the consumer declines as his or her annual consumption of housing increases. Each individual reaches an optimum by consuming up to the point where the (declining) marginal private benefit received from an additional unit of consumption just equals the marginal cost paid for that unit. But this is short of the socially optimal quantity of consumption because the individual ignores the external marginal social benefits generated by his or her act of consumption. Society would be justified in subsidizing housing so that individual consumption of it is carried to the point where the sum of marginal private benefits plus marginal social benefits equals marginal cost. Since marginal social benefit is positive, this equality will occur at a higher level of housing consumption than the individual would choose to pay for in an unsubsidized market. (A graphic version of the argument for subsidy when there are external benefits is presented in Figure 15.1.)

4. Housing subsidies are an expedient way of redistributing income to the poor. Thus one might favor such subsidies while remaining skeptical about the merit good or external benefits arguments. Economists have generally agreed that income redistribution is most efficiently accomplished not by making transfers in kind but by making cash transfers, which leave the recipient free to choose whatever additional goods he or she most desires. Yet the "realist" who wishes to redistribute income may believe that it is politically easier to legislate adequate transfers in kind than in cash and that

this consideration outweighs the contrary argument based on economic efficiency.[36]

Let us examine some of these contentions in greater detail. We have already shown how the merit good argument serves to justify subsidies. Less obvious is the point that it also justifies the use of housing codes intended to keep housing up to a minimum standard of quality. To be sure, housing codes (other than occupancy standards) may be regarded simply as an effort-saving convenience. Instead of letting each tenant see to it that the landlord maintains decent standards in a building, we set up a specialized government agency to do the job for us. A good many regulatory activities of government can be so justified. In addition, tenants are generally unable to recognize such technical problems as unsafe elevators or deficient wiring. But there is probably more to it than that. The fact that we adopt housing codes also suggests a belief that some tenants will not insist on high enough standards. Given their low incomes, they prefer substandard or overcrowded housing at low prices to standard or less crowded housing at higher prices. Thus one justification for codes is the merit good argument that at least some consumers fail to realize how important adequate housing is to their own welfare.

Does Housing Confer Indirect Benefits?

What reason can there be for believing that housing is, in fact, better for people than they realize? The answer must lie in the existence of some sort of indirect benefit of which the consumer is not aware, for surely consumers can judge for themselves the direct satisfaction obtained from housing qua housing. The indirect benefits to the consuming family would have to be such things as better physical and mental health, higher educational achievement, and less likelihood of family members turning to narcotics, crime, or juvenile delinquency. These same indirect effects—disease, crime, and delinquency—are an important source of the external costs allegedly thrown off onto society at large by bad housing, and therefore they are also a source of the external social benefits attributable to housing improvement. Thus the merit good argument and the external benefit argument turn out to be rooted in the same phenomenon: indirect effects of housing quality on physical well-being and/or behavior.

What evidence do we have that such effects actually exist? A virtual utopia of indirect benefits has been alleged. In the 1930s, when slum clearance and public housing first became objectives of national policy, claims for the beneficent effects of good housing were widely accepted. A good deal of "evi-

---

36. See discussion in Henry J. Aaron, "Policy Implications: A Progress Report," in Katharine L. Bradbury and Anthony Downs, eds., *Do Housing Allowances Work?* (Washington, D.C.: Brookings Institution, 1981), pp. 93–96.

dence" was amassed to support the extravagant claims of housing reformers. It might easily be shown, for example, that rates of crime, delinquency, illegitimacy, disease, and death were lower in public housing projects than in the surrounding slum areas from which the tenants were selected. At first it was overlooked that the very process of tenant selection accounted for much of the gain. The old, the criminal, the socially disorganized were systematically excluded in favor of stable working-class families with children. In short, public housing tenants were not a random sample of the slum population.

Valid conclusions about the effects of the dwelling environment can be reached only if the sample of public housing tenants is carefully matched on a variety of socioeconomic characteristics with a selected control group of those remaining in the surrounding slums. A well-known study of the impact of housing on family life conducted in Baltimore in the 1950s employed just that test design.[37] It revealed that public housing is associated with statistically significant improvements in some, but by no means all, of the indices of health, psychological adjustment, and school performance for which tests were made. The effects of better housing were usually in the expected direction, but the magnitudes of the effects were not very impressive.

More recently the International Housing Productivity Study carried out careful tests of the effects of massive housing improvements on health, worker productivity, education, and social deviance at selected sites in developing countries and in less developed regions of the United States. Statistically significant benefits of housing were found on health at two out of seven sites, on worker productivity at two out of four sites, on education at one of four sites, and on social deviance at the one site where that effect was tested. These results, not unlike those of the Baltimore study, are quite ambiguous. In summarizing the study, Leland Burns and Leo Grebler concluded that "the results of the work reported here do not provide any strong, consistent support for the hypothesis that housing investment yields substantial unperceived internal benefits and externalities . . . The evidence is mixed."[38]

Studies such as these are sometimes criticized on the ground that they do not extend over a long enough period to capture all the possible benefits of housing improvement. Even a finding of statistically significant benefits, however, would not provide sufficient grounds for endorsing a subsidy program. In addition, one would have to attach monetary values to the measured

37. Daniel M. Wilner et al., *The Housing Environment and Family Life: A Longitudinal Study of the Effects of Housing on Morbidity and Mental Health* (Baltimore: Johns Hopkins University Press, 1962). The volume also contains a useful review of other studies of the effects of housing quality.

38. Burns and Grebler, p. 168. See their ch. 7 for a full analysis of the results and their ch. 6 for a review of the literature on housing externalities. Also see Claude S. Fischer et al., "Crowding Studies and Urban Life: A Critical Review," *Journal of the American Institute of Planners,* November 1975, pp. 406–418, for a survey of studies dealing specifically with overcrowding; and Stanislav V. Kasl, "Effects of Housing on Mental and Physical Health," in *Housing in the Seventies: Working Ppaers,* vol. 1, pp. 286–304, for a survey of studies on health effects. Both papers include extensive bibliographies.

indirect benefits of housing and insert them into a benefit-cost study to determine whether they were sufficient to justify the program's cost. As Jerome Rothenberg showed in his detailed analysis of urban renewal, this task of quantification has proved very difficult to carry out.[39]

The demand for public intervention in the urban housing market has not proved very sensitive to the validity, or lack of it, of arguments concerning the existence of specific, measurable indirect housing benefits. Beyond the reach of these arguments there remains a widespread conviction that in some fundamental sense housing *does* matter more than other consumer goods. Housing is, after all, the immediate physical environment of one's life. Apparently we do not want people to live—or, worse, to grow up—in a squalid environment. Whether this is because we find physical squalor morally shocking in an affluent society or because we believe such squalor is ultimately a threat to the society itself is perhaps open to question. What cannot be doubted is that housing has long been, and will probably continue to be, an object of special social concern.

---

39. See Jerome Rothenberg, *Economic Evaluation of Urban Renewal* (Washington, D.C.: Brookings Institution, 1967), chs. 10 and 11, for a review of the conceptual and practical difficulties of measuring the social costs of slum housing.

THIRTEEN

Urban Housing Policy

Public concern with urban housing standards has produced, over the years, a wide range of housing policies and programs. As suggested in Chapter 12, most of these can be classified as either subsidy programs or regulatory policies. Examining them now in greater detail, we will see that subsidy programs can be further subdivided. Historically, the major programs—including such a diverse list as public housing, urban renewal, housing rehabilitation, and interest-rate subsidies—formed a single class in one important respect. In all of these programs, payment of a subsidy was linked either to the construction of specific new dwelling units or to the rehabilitation of specific buildings. The basic purpose of this kind of "new construction," or "supply side," subsidy was to increase the stock of new or high-quality dwelling units as directly as possible, in the hope of thus raising urban housing standards for the whole population. In direct contrast to this are some more recent policies that provide cash subsidies in the form of rent assistance to low-income families. Such policies operate directly on the demand side, raising the rent-paying capacity of the poor in the belief that the market will then provide them with an adequate supply of decent, standard, older housing. As the chapter proceeds, we will evaluate these alternative subsidy strategies.

We will also discuss regulatory policies that are intended to overcome specific imperfections in the urban housing and land markets, including the enforcement of housing code standards and antidiscrimination laws and the guidance of land use by means of zoning ordinances. Policies aimed directly at neighborhood revitalization will also be analyzed, as will the implications for neighborhood viability of some of the housing programs. The chapter will conclude with a discussion of proposals to "open up" the suburbs to low-income housing—proposals that generally call for combining a variety of the forms of public intervention.

Although urban housing policy in the United States has changed frequently over the years, the changes have clearly been evolutionary. Each new program arose, so to speak, from the ashes of its predecessor as government responded to criticism of previous policies or to altered circumstances. Housing programs are taken up chronologically in this chapter in the belief that the logic of each can best be understood in the context of the policies and circumstances from which it evolved.

PUBLIC HOUSING

Public housing is the oldest of all subsidized housing programs in the United States. The term *public housing* refers not to all forms of government-assisted housing but only to units that are owned and operated (or in some cases, leased) by a public housing authority. The program as we know it today dates from the Great Depression. Regarded as a radical new departure in the 1930s, it was initiated as an emergency measure to create employment by spending on new construction. In 1933 the Public Works Administration was authorized to include slum clearance projects and the construction or repair of low-cost housing among the works that it undertook, and it was neither required nor expected that such housing projects would be self-liquidating. Two and a half years of legislative battling were required, however, before Senator Wagner's United States Housing Act was passed in 1937, putting the public housing program on a permanent basis. Under the new law, site selection, ownership, and operation were decentralized to the local level, though under federal guidelines, and have remained so ever since. Initiation of projects is therefore restricted to local housing authorities. In a sense, the United States has no "national" public housing policy; it has local public housing programs that are federally subsidized and regulated. The role of the federal authorities is limited to setting standards and making loans, contributions, or grants to the appropriate local body. The choice of whether to build or not remains a local one.

As the program has operated ever since 1937, the federal government, in effect, contributes 100 percent of the capital cost of a project as a subsidy to keep rents low. Local governments also contribute substantial subsidies by forgoing ordinary property taxes in favor of much lower payments "in lieu of taxes." Since it is a matter of public policy to restrict these large subsidy benefits to the poor, tenants are not accepted for admission unless their incomes fall below a specified limit. Such limits vary locally, but they have been effective in restricting access largely to the poor. In 1983 average household income in public housing projects was only $6,191; poverty-line income in that year was $10,098 for a family of four (see Table 13.3).

Until the late 1960s public housing rents were expected to cover operating and maintenance costs plus payments in lieu of property taxes made by the local authority to the municipal government. However, in 1969 Congress limited the rent that could be charged any tenant to 25 percent of income. Since that would hold down housing authority revenue, Congress also for the first time authorized operating subsidies for public housing. During the 1970s operating costs soared as a result of inflation. Tenant incomes did not keep pace. Federal operating subsidies therefore increased rapidly, rising to almost half of operating costs by 1982. To slow the growth of operating subsidies, Congress in 1981 voted to increase rents to 30 percent of tenant income over a five-year period.[1] Even with substantial federal operating assistance, many local authorities were unable to keep up with necessary maintenance. Physical and financial conditions in some projects deteriorated, often dramatically. Raymond Struyk's 1980 study of public housing authorities in the twenty-nine largest U.S. cities found that five were in the equivalent of bankruptcy and a number of others were in decidedly difficult straits.[2]

From 1950 through 1984, as Table 13.1 shows, the inventory of low-rent public housing units under management rose from 201,700 to 1,288,000. Yet at the end of that period public housing still accounted for only 1.4 percent of the nation's total housing stock. The ratio is much higher, however, in many of the larger cities, reaching (for example) 4.1 percent of the stock in New York City, 5.6 percent in Baltimore, and 8.7 percent in Atlanta.[3]

Political support for public housing probably reached a high point with the passage of the Housing Act of 1949, which authorized construction of 810,000 additional units over a six-year period. During the 1950s, however, congressional appropriations never made possible any such massive program. In the 1960s funds were more plentiful, but by that time the program was running into trouble in the big cities, and available monies were not used to the limit. Local housing authorities were finding it increasingly difficult to obtain politically acceptable project sites. At the same time, earlier enthusiasm by public housing's traditional supporters was giving way to a rising wave of criticism. During the 1970s many public housing authorities were reluctant to expand even when federal appropriations were available because of the financial difficulty they were having managing their existing projects. Because housing for the elderly encountered relatively little neighborhood opposition, it became an increasingly important category. In the early 1980s it accounted for more than 40 percent of the units under construction, although still only about a quarter of the total inventory. (See Table 13.1.)

1. Congressional Budget Office, *Federal Subsidies for Public Housing: Issues and Options*, June 1983, p. 3.

2. Raymond J. Struyk, *A New System for Public Housing* (Washington, D.C.: Urban Institute, 1980), pp. 8, 70–73.

3. Ibid., table 2.

TABLE 13.1
Growth and Composition of the Public Housing Inventory

| | PUBLIC HOUSING INVENTORY (THOUSANDS) | | TOTAL U.S. HOUSING STOCK (THOUSANDS) | PUBLIC HOUSING AS PERCENTAGE OF TOTAL |
	Under Management	*Under Construction*		
1950	201.7	31.5	45,983	0.4
1960	478.2	36.4	58,326	0.8
1970	893.5	126.8	68,672	1.3
1980	1,195.6	20.6	88,411	1.4
1984	1,287.8	102.9	93,519[d]	1.4[d]
Composition of Public Housing Inventory, 1984				
Constructed as public housing[a]	1,154.1	93.4		
Acquired[b]	31.4	4.2		
Leased[c]	102.3	5.3		
Housing for the elderly	347.7	41.7		

[a]Includes conventionally developed public housing and units built for local authorities under "turnkey" contracts.
[b]Existing housing acquired by local housing authorities. "Under construction" indicates units undergoing rehabilitation.
[c]Existing housing leased by local housing authorities.
[d]1983
Sources: *Statistical Abstract of the United States, 1986*, tables 1308 and 1319, and *1972*, table 1153.

How Good or Bad Is Public Housing?

Public housing has come in for increasingly severe criticism on a number of grounds. Public housing in central cities has typically been built in large-scale, multibuilding projects, often covering dozens of acres. These vast "developments" have been criticized widely for their impersonality, institutional atmosphere, uninspired architecture, and inhuman scale. Moreover, their interior amenities suffer from the deliberate imposition of a "no frills" policy. Consequently, it has long been argued that public housing projects, though built at great expense, are destined to be the slums of the future. In some respects they have already taken on the characteristics of slum neighborhoods. There are frequent complaints of juvenile delinquency and violent crime within projects.

The social design of public housing policy has been criticized as severely as the physical. Income limits imposed on tenants both for admission and for continued occupancy raise seemingly insoluble problems. On the one hand, such limits seem necessary in order to confine the substantial benefits of public housing to those most in need. On the other hand, they produce a public housing population in which the proportion of tenants "on welfare" is substantial. The high concentration of poverty and distress within the projects may well have destructive effects on individual behavior.[4]

The classic case of public housing failure, resulting apparently from the overconcentration of poverty in a vast development, is the notorious Pruitt-Igoe project in St. Louis. Completed in the mid-1950s, it consisted of forty-three buildings on fifty-seven acres near the city's central business district. By 1970 the project was so ridden by crime and vandalism and so physically deteriorated as a result of the inability of the St. Louis Housing Authority to keep up with maintenance and repairs that it was virtually untenantable. At first the authority responded by closing down more than half the buildings. Eventually the entire project was vacated and demolished.

Yet it would be a mistake to take the extreme Pruitt-Igoe case as representative. Struyk's 1980 study found an enormous range of variation in such measures of service quality as vacancy rates, tenant turnover rates, and management handling of routine maintenance.[5] The fact that most public housing authorities have long waiting lists for admission suggests that whatever the critics may say about the program and however far it may fall short of the expectations with which it was launched in the 1930s, it does provide a considerable degree of tenant satisfaction. Nevertheless, no one who has studied public housing would deny that management performance is often seriously deficient and that better management could simultaneously lower costs and increase service quality.[6]

The design of public housing policy has often been criticized for creating inequities among the very people it is intended to help, the low-income population itself. Since the stock of public housing is relatively small (see Table 13.1), only a very few of those who meet the income qualifications are actually admitted. Instead of providing uniform benefits to all who qualify, the program provides costly benefits to a few and nothing for the rest.[7] (By way of analogy, imagine that free public elementary education were available only to a small proportion of families and that pupils were selected from long waiting lists.) The sums involved per family are not trivial: it has been estimated that over the future life of a public housing project initiated in 1980, the full subsidy cost to the government, in 1980 dollars, would range from $2,200 to $2,530 per dwelling unit per year.[8] (Note, however, that when consumption of

4. See evidence cited in William Julius Wilson, "The Urban Underclass in Advanced Industrial Society," in Paul E. Peterson, ed. *The New Urban Reality* (Washington, D.C.: Brookings Institution, 1985), pp. 129–160.

5. Struyk, tables 3 and 4.

6. Robert Sadacca et al., *Management Performance in Public Housing*, doc. no. 209-5-2 (Washington, D. C.: Urban Institute, January 1974), pp. 37–38, 75.

7. Richard F. Muth, *Public Housing*, Evaluative Studies no. 5 (Washington, D.C.: American Enterprise Institute, 1973), pp. 2–3.

8. Congressional Budget Office, *The Long-Term Costs of Lower Income Housing Assistance Programs*, March 1979, table 12.

a particular good is stimulated by a subsidy, it must be presumed that consumers of the good get less than a dollar's worth of benefit for each dollar spent by the government. That is why economists, in principle, prefer cash transfer to subsidies on particular commodities.[9])

A final criticism leveled at the conventional public housing program is that it fosters racial and economic segregation within neighborhoods of central cities. Minorities made up three-fourths of public housing tenantry in 1983, a proportion far higher than their share of the central city poverty population in the same year. More important is the possibility that public housing helps to maintain segregation at the macrogeographic scale. Because construction depends on local initiative, a good deal of public housing has been built in central cities, very little in the surrounding suburbs. In effect, the public housing program offers a subsidy to minorities on condition that they remain in the central city. Later in this chapter we will discuss several housing policy reforms that propose to undo this link between housing subsidies and intrametropolitan segregation.

URBAN RENEWAL

The Housing Act of 1949, which, it was pointed out, authorized a most ambitious public housing program, also gave birth to a new form of government intervention in the housing market that later came to be known as "urban renewal." The unemployment of the 1930s had been succeeded by postwar inflation. Instead of searching for socially acceptable ways to spend money, the government found itself under pressure to cut expenditures in order to check rising prices. Congress sought some means of drawing private investment into the business of improving the nation's housing standards. Urban "renewal," at that time called "redevelopment," was the agreed-upon new program.

Title I of the 1949 act provided that the federal government would give financial assistance, through local agencies, to make private redevelopment of blighted areas economically feasible. A local redevelopment authority was to select, assemble, and clear a qualified site. It would then resell the site at a loss to a private redeveloper, who presumably could not pay the full cost of acquisition and clearance and still earn any profit. The federal government would make its contribution by paying to the local authority a grant equal to two-thirds of that loss—that is to say, two-thirds of the difference between the sum of site acquisition and clearance cost and the resale price of the land in its new use.

9. See John C. Weicher, "Urban Housing Policy," in Peter Mieszkowski and Mahlon Straszheim, eds., *Current Issues in Urban Economics* (Baltimore: Johns Hopkins University Press, 1979), pp. 494–496.

It was not required that the new use be residential, and, in practice, far more sites were residential before than after redevelopment.[10] Moreover, the new housing built on redevelopment and renewal sites was predominantly for the middle- and upper-income classes, rather than for the poor. It may have been assumed, however, that although the ill-housed would gain little from redevelopment directly, they would eventually benefit when the filtering process worked itself out. We return to this question below.

The Housing Act of 1954 significantly modified the urban redevelopment program. There had been increasing opposition to the "bulldozer method" used in Title I projects. The method took its name from the fact that whole blocks, and often whole neighborhoods, were leveled to provide sites for Title I housing. The earliest opponents were tenants threatened with dislocation, who could not understand why the power of eminent domain should be employed to destroy their neighborhood and their homes in order to build anew for someone else, at private profit. The 1954 act—which changed the name of the program to "urban renewal"—sought to reduce reliance on the bulldozer by encouraging a combination of selective rehabilitation and conservation, reserving clearance for those structures or blocks that were beyond a reasonable hope of salvation.

However, the difference between renewal under the 1954 act and redevelopment under the act of 1949 was not sufficient to quiet the opposition, for the logic of the programs remained essentially unchanged. The poor continued to be displaced by application of the majestic powers of the state to make way for the middle class. The use of rehabilitation improved matters very little. Like new construction, housing rehabilitated to federal standards was too costly for low-income families. Criticism mounted.[11] Sociologists and city planners began to realize that many stable and useful social institutions were going down before the unseeing bulldozer. It became apparent that uprooting the poor in order to clear vast sites for renewal was likely to increase the social disorders associated with poverty while achieving not the elimination of slums but simply their removal from one neighborhood to another. Moreover, critics continued to point out that the link between urban renewal and slum clearance had the perverse effect of actually reducing the total housing supply, especially the supply of low-cost housing, a result that was bound to be disadvantageous to the poor.

By the late 1960s urban renewal had lost much of its political support. In 1974 it was replaced by the Community Development Block Grant program, to be discussed later in this chapter.

---

10. William Grigsby, *Housing Markets and Public Policy* (Philadelphia: University of Pennsylvania Press, 1963), p. 324.

11. The intense debate about the virtues and defects of renewal has been conveniently anthologized by James Q. Wilson in *Urban Renewal: The Record and the Controversy* (Cambridge, Mass.: M.I.T. Press, 1966).

What is the logic of urban renewal as a form of public intervention in the land market? Although the program no longer exists, analysis of it throws light on several crucial aspects of the economics of urban land use, including externalities in the housing market and the process of land use succession. An understanding of these matters is likely to be as important in judging future publicly sponsored redevelopment policies as it is to comprehending those of the past.

MARKET IMPERFECTIONS AND THE CASE FOR URBAN RENEWAL

Because it was so controversial, the urban renewal program stimulated a good deal of inquiry by economists, political scientists, sociologists, and city planners. One of the most influential economic analyses was provided by Otto A. Davis and Andrew B. Whinston in 1961.[12] Their analysis remains a very useful starting point for looking at possible imperfections in the urban land and housing markets and tracing out their implications for redevelopment policy.

Davis and Whinston suggest a number of reasons for believing that the urban housing market may not function "properly"—in the sense of providing the optimum amount and quality of housing to satisfy consumer wants, given the constraints of cost and of limited incomes. These arguments do not establish the existence of any sort of "exploitation" of tenants by landlords, but, if valid, they do make a case for government intervention.

Two kinds of imperfection may be (though not necessarily are) present. The first would result from the strong external effects of one property on the tenants and owner of another. A prospective tenant who thinks about renting an apartment takes into account the attractiveness of the neighborhood, which depends in part on the characteristics of nearby properties. Thus the rent obtainable by one landlord may be affected by the condition in which neighboring landlords keep their properties.

Consider four possible cases that involve this sort of interdependency between two adjacent owners, Smith and Jones.

1. If both owners invest in redeveloping their properties, both can earn a rate of return that makes the additional investment worthwhile. Each benefits from the fact that the other has made improvements, because tenants are willing to pay higher rents for an apartment in an improved neighborhood than in an unimproved one.

2. Owner Smith can obtain higher rents without redeveloping, provided that neighbor Jones does redevelop. Smith's rate of return may

12. Otto A. Davis and Andrew B. Whinston, "The Economics of Urban Renewal," reprinted in Wilson, pp. 50–67.

even be higher in this case because she can obtain higher rents without investing any additional capital.

3. If neither of the owners redevelops, both will continue to earn a rate of return lower than they could obtain if both had redeveloped, as in the first case.

4. Finally, if Smith were to redevelop her property while Jones did not, Smith's rate of return might actually drop below what it would be if neither she nor Jones undertook redevelopment, as in the third case.

For the sake of illustration, Davis and Whinston assign hypothetical rates of return to the four cases as follows:

	RATE OF RETURN EARNED (%)	
ALTERNATIVE CASES	*Smith*	*Jones*
1. Both invest in redevelopment	7	7
2. Jones invests, Smith does not	10	3
3. Neither invests in redevelopment	4	4
4. Smith invests, Jones does not	3	10

It is clear that society benefits most in the first case, where both owners invest in redevelopment. But Davis and Whinston use arguments from game theory (the logic of the "prisoner's dilemma" situation) to show that the actual outcome may well be case 3, where neither property is redeveloped. The argument runs as follows. First examine Smith's situation. When deciding whether to invest in redevelopment, she has to consider two possibilities— first, that Jones also redevelops and, second, that Jones does not. Looking at these two possibilities, she sees that in either case she is best off *not* investing. In the first situation, she can earn 10 percent by not investing (case 2) but only 7 percent by investing (case 1). In the second situation she can earn 4 percent by not investing (case 3) but only 3 percent by investing (case 4). Her rational decision is not to invest. Moreover, since Jones as an individual owner is logically in the same position as Smith, he, too, decides not to invest, and no redevelopment occurs, even though such redevelopment would be socially optimal. Here, then, is a case of "market failure" attributable to interdependencies.

Davis and Whinston take as their definition of urban "blight" any case in which the market fails to yield optimum development of the housing stock. They do not equate slums and blight, however, since they recognize that slum neighborhoods may be run down precisely because slum tenants cannot afford anything better. Likewise, "blight" may exist in relatively "nice" neighborhoods if interdependencies have prevented them from being improved to the optimum extent.

The researchers recognize that a suboptimal outcome is due to their assumption of interdependencies that are "sufficiently strong."[13] One can show

13. Ibid., p. 57, n. 7.

easily that with interdependencies of a weaker sort, the socially correct out-come will occur. Return to the table and suppose, for example, that we leave cases 1 and 3 as they are but change the outcome of case 2 so that Smith earns 6 percent and Jones earns 5 percent; and change case 4 so that Smith earns 5 percent and Jones earns 6 percent. We still have interdependency, since one investor's rate of return depends on what the other does. But in this situation it will be rational for Smith individually, and hence for Jones also, to undertake redevelopment.

Interdependencies of the sort described probably exist, but the important question to decide is how strong they may be. The belief that they are strong enough to block redevelopment implies that tenants have substantial demands for housing and neighborhood amenities that go perpetually unful-filled. The interdependency argument views the tenant as a prisoner of a par-ticular neighborhood, willing and able to pay for a better environment with higher rent but unable to do so because the system fails to produce the de-sired amenities. However, if the competitive, adaptive model of the housing market that was described in Chapter 12 is accepted as even roughly valid, the market produces a sufficient variety of housing and neighborhood types and qualities to suit the tastes and rent-paying capacities of a wide variety of consumers. Tenants would consequently be able to select the neighborhood and home in which they wish to live from a variety of existing neighborhoods and homes. We would not then expect tenants in a given neighborhood to nurse latent, unfulfilled demands (which they are able to back with higher rent offers) for something substantially better if only something better were offered. And if tenants do not have such unfulfilled demands, it is unlikely that interdependencies would have the powerful effects on the rate of return hypothesized by Davis and Whinston. High rates of return from redevelop-ment would occur only if higher-income households were attracted from other neighborhoods, but that outcome violates the implicit assumption of their example that it refers to housing for a given population in a given neigh-borhood.

What little direct evidence we have about tenants in deteriorating neighborhoods supports the notion that they are usually *unwilling* to pay for even moderately costly housing improvements. A survey of families in transi-tional neighborhoods of New York City in 1969 asked respondents whether they were satisfied with specific features of their housing. Those who said no were then asked whether they would be willing to pay $30 a month additional rent to correct the unsatisfactory feature. Of tenants living in units not under rent control, 78 percent were definitely unwilling to pay the additional rent for the features that would remedy the dissatisfactions they had themselves expressed.[14] Although this survey involved too small a sample to be conclu-

14. See Ira S. Lowry, Joseph S. De Salvo, and Barbara M. Woodfill, *The Demand for Shel-ter*, vol. 2 of *Rental Housing in New York City* (New York: Rand Institute, June 1971), pp. 102–104.

sive, its findings are consistent with reports in the daily press of tenants in slum areas who object to proposals to rehabilitate their buildings because they do not wish to pay the higher rent that would be required to finance the job. Given that sort of response, the strong interdependencies hypothesized by Davis and Whinston seem unlikely. The point to be stressed is not that tenants are unaffected by their neighborhoods but only that they are not able or willing to pay very much to alter the effects.

The rise of housing abandonment, with its destructive external effects on neighborhood properties, might seem to strengthen the case for the strong interdependencies of the Davis and Whinston example. Can it be that building owners in a neighborhood that is on the verge of slipping into abandonment are caught in the sort of "prisoner's dilemma" situation they described? If all owners could agree not to abandon, is it possible that none would choose or be forced to? Housing analysts who claim that abandonment is a "contagious, self-fulfilling prophecy" appear to think so.[15] Yet this argument seems to overlook the force of the most frequently mentioned micro-causes of abandonment, which are inadequate rent-paying capacity, rent delinquency, and high rates of neighborhood crime and vandalism. It may well be doubted whether any agreement by owners to stand fast would succeed in neighborhoods where these forces are at their worst. (See the discussion of abandonment in Chapter 12.)

The Problem of Site Assembly

The second market imperfection cited by Davis and Whinston has to do with "site assembly." They point out that if interdependencies between properties prevent individual owners from undertaking economically desirable redevelopment, an incentive exists for a single owner to buy out all the others and make improvements over the entire neighborhood. The single developer could thus realize the high rate of return hypothesized for the case in which all properties are improved. But now the problem of site assembly arises. In the typical American city, property is held in very small parcels. The entrepreneur wishing to assemble a large site for redevelopment not only must be willing to tie up capital during the years required to negotiate purchases but must also face the prospect that the last few parcel owners will be able to demand extraordinarily high sums as the price of not blocking the project. The outcome of negotiations is theoretically, as well as practically, unpredictable, since the case is essentially one of bilateral monopoly. Obviously this problem becomes more acute if, on account of economies of scale in redevelopment, the optimum size for a new project far exceeds the average size of existing land parcels. Real estate developers have long recognized site assembly as a

15. See the statements cited by Henry B. Schechter and Marion K. Schlefer in "Housing Needs and National Goals," Paper submitted to the Subcommittee on Housing, part I, House Committee on Banking and Currency, 1971, p. 35.

major obstacle that raises the cost of development and presumably prevents some otherwise desirable projects from going ahead.

The site assembly problem is an important market imperfection with direct implications for public policy. The implication drawn by Davis and Whinston is that when properties in a given neighborhood remain underdeveloped either because of interdependencies that the "atomistic" private market cannot cope with or because the difficulty of site assembly prevents development at an optimal scale, public intervention is clearly called for. The government is then justified in using its power of eminent domain to assemble a site by purchasing properties at their fair market value. If interdependencies and site assembly problems were the only obstacles to an otherwise profitable renewal, all obstacles that prevented private development from moving ahead would have been removed by the government's action. Consequently, the local renewal authority would be able to resell the consolidated site at cost to a private redeveloper who would then complete the project and earn a satisfactory rate of return without benefit of a land-cost write-down or other special subsidy. Market imperfections thus justify public intervention, but not public subsidy, to make renewal feasible.

Behind this piece of analysis lies the traditional argument that a freely competitive market in land tends, by an orderly process of "succession," to bring about the "highest and best use" of each parcel. The concept of highest and best use was introduced in Chapter 6 in explaining how competition between land uses results in an efficient pattern of intraurban activity location. At that point, however, we did not examine in detail the process of succession by which the highest and best use of a parcel may change over time. If we are to understand fully the general problem of urban change and development (of which urban renewal is simply a special case), we must now supply the missing details.

LAND-USE SUCCESSION IN A COMPETITIVE MARKET

In the course of time both buildings and sites pass through a succession of uses. A building constructed originally as a town house may later be converted to commercial occupancy as the business district of the town expands. Or the reverse process may occur—buildings in declining commercial areas may be converted to residential uses. These are successions of use within given structures.

Very frequently evolutionary forces in the development of the city make it profitable to tear down existing buildings and replace them with new ones. In that case we speak of "land-use succession" rather than succession of uses within given structures. With the rapid growth of cities, two of the most obvious forms of land-use succession have been the conversion of agricultural land to residential uses and the conversion of low-density areas of single-family homes to higher-density apartment house neighborhoods. In either case, according to the traditional view, the evolutionary process of development works to bring about the "highest and best use" of land. If the land market is competitive and there are no land-use externalities, we can assume that each new building, at the time it is put up, represents the highest and best use of the plot on which it stands.

Succession via the market process can be explained as follows. First, we define "highest and best" as the use that can pay the most for a given cleared site. Second, we will refer to an existing or "old" building on a particular site as building o and a new building that might succeed it as building n. We can then define the following terms:

V_o = market value of a given site and the existing building on it. This value equals the present worth of the expected future returns (gross of depreciation) from the property in the old use.

V_n = anticipated market value of the same site and a new building. This value equals the present worth of the expected future returns from the property in the new use. V_n includes an allowance for the developer's normal profit.[16]

D_o = cost of demolishing the existing building.

C_n = cost of constructing the new building, exclusive of the cost of purchasing and clearing the site.

Assume that building o actually stands on the given site. At the time it was constructed, o was presumably the highest and best use for the site, for the developer who constructed it was able to obtain the site by outbidding all other firms for its use. We now wish to see under what conditions the new building, n, would replace o by means of ordinary market operations.

The cost of acquiring the given site in order to construct n is V_o, because the developer of n has to pay the market price for the old building even though it is to be demolished. The cost of tearing it down is D_o. Thus, for the new user, we can say that

$$V_o + D_o = \text{cost of acquisition and clearance}$$

On the other hand, the highest price the developer can afford to pay for the cleared site and still earn a normal profit by constructing n is given by

$$V_n - C_n = \text{maximum value of cleared site to new user}$$

It follows that the new user can profitably undertake development on the site only if

$$V_n - C_n \geq V_o + D_o$$

---

16. The analysis has been simplified by omitting from both V_o and V_n the present worth of any future uses that might be expected to succeed them. The omitted item is sometimes called the "reversionary value" of the site. For an analysis of succession that specifically allows for reversionary values, see Wallace F. Smith, *Housing: The Social and Economic Elements* (Berkeley and Los Angeles: University of California Press, 1970), pp. 243–250.

which is therefore a necessary condition for the new building to succeed the old through ordinary market processes. As a city evolves, this necessary condition may be fulfilled either because the old building becomes increasingly obsolete, making V_o decline, or because the demand for the new one becomes stronger, making the potential value V_n rise.

Figure 13.1 illustrates the latter case. Values and costs are measured on the vertical scale, time on the horizontal. At time T_1, building o, then the highest and best use, is constructed on a given site, at a cost of C_o. V_o is assumed to remain constant as time passes. Hence V_o and $V_o - C_o$ are represented as horizontal lines. The cost of demolishing o, should that be desirable, is shown by D_o, producing the third horizontal line, $V_o + D_o$.

At time T_2, the possibility of constructing a new use n on the site occupied by o occurs to a competing developer. The cost of constructing n is estimated to be C_n. At time T_2, V_n, the expected value of the project, is not yet great enough to justify carrying out development. As the neighborhood changes with the passage of time, however, the potential value of V_n rises. Finally, at time T_4 we observe that $V_n - C_n \geq V_o + D_o$. The necessary condition for market succession is fulfilled. The old building is torn down and replaced by the new one.

The urban renewal program, by means of its land-cost write-down, worked to speed up this process of succession. In order to encourage rebuild-

FIGURE 13.1
Timing of Land-use Succession under the Market Process

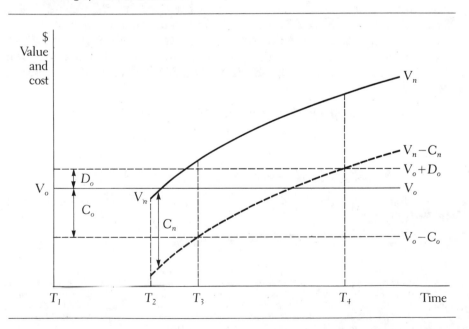

ing, the renewal authority intervened in situations in which the maximum value of the site to the new user $(V_n - C_n)$ was not yet as large as the cost of acquisition and clearance $(V_o + D_o)$. The government absorbed the excess of the latter over the former, thus enabling the new use to succeed the old one at a time when it could not have done so by market processes.

To the casual observer this speed-up, which was a principal objective of the renewal program, may seem desirable. To the economist it appears otherwise. If the market functions efficiently, speeding up the process of succession is wasteful, in the sense of unnecessarily destroying economic value. The additional value created by redevelopment of the site from use o to use n is $V_n - V_o$. But the cost of the resources used up in creating the additional value is the sum of $D_o + C_n$. Thus redevelopment adds something to society's total economic output only if

$$V_n - V_o > D_o + C_n$$

But by rearranging terms we see that this is equivalent to the market condition for succession:

$$V_n - C_n > V_o + D_o$$

Employing a subsidy to speed up succession is therefore irrational: the costs incurred for redevelopment exceed the additional economic values created. It is easy to imagine that someone who is concerned about the housing problem might find this conclusion surprising. Walking through a slum neighborhood such a person may think: "These buildings are old, run down and depressing. New housing would be a tremendous improvement. There must be something wrong with a system that allows slums such as these to stand decade after decade when we know how to build so much better." Knowing a little urban economics, our observer might even add: "Surely these slums do not represent the highest and best use of the land. If we were to start over again on this block, we certainly wouldn't put up buildings like these."

The economic analysis of succession can explain these supposed anomalies. Certainly, new housing would be a tremendous improvement. But it is very costly to build. Moreover, before a new building can be economically justified, it must be able to absorb, as its site cost, the capital value of the old structure it replaces. In other words, succession will not take place until the old property reaches the point where it is worth more as a site than it is as a building. That moment may be indefinitely delayed because old buildings often continue for a long time to have value based on their ability to render services less expensively than new structures. An old building can continue to be operated as long as rent receipts exceed operating costs, maintenance charges, and taxes, whereas a new building will not be started unless prospective rent receipts will, in addition, allow the builder to recoup the costs of demolition and new construction. Again the point is illustrated in Figure 13.1. If the site in question were vacant and the two projects o and n were competing for it, n would become the highest and best use at time T_3, when $V_n - C_n > V_o - C_o$. Yet if o already exists on the site, it is not efficient to replace it until T_4, which may be any number of years later. Thus old buildings can survive through many decades at a value less than would justify their being constructed anew but greater than would justify their demolition. During such periods they do *not* represent the highest and best use of the land in the sense employed here, since they would not be reconstructed new if the site were cleared for redevelopment. Yet it would be wasteful to tear them down.

Thus analysis of the economics of succession bears out Davis and Whinston's conclusion that if an otherwise economically desirable redevelopment is blocked only by market imperfections, the government, after intervening to overcome such obstacles, should be able to sell the cleared site to a developer at no loss. Unless additional justification can be found, the policy of subsidizing redevelopment simply to speed up succession is economically irrational.

Cost-Benefit Analysis of Subsidized Redevelopment

It is, of course, possible that the additional justification might be found in a complete cost-benefit analysis of a subsidized redevelopment project, whether under urban renewal or some other program. The market succession calculus described in the foregoing discussion takes into account only direct, or "on-site," benefits and costs. Perhaps if the indirect, or "off-site," effects were counted as well, the excess of indirect benefits over indirect costs would be sufficient to justify a subsidy. As Jerome Rothenberg's careful conceptual analysis of this problem demonstrated, the indirect effects of a large renewal scheme can be expected to ramify in complex ways through the urban housing and real estate markets.[17] For example, a possible indirect benefit from a large project would be an increase in the value of neighboring sites, a spillover effect of the improved environment within the project. Hugh Nourse reports that before-and-after studies of site values in the neighborhood of slum clearance and housing projects have found no evidence of such spillovers.[18] But even if it could be demonstrated that adjacent site values increased as a result of a project, it would remain highly uncertain how much of that increase should be counted as a net gain attributable to redevelopment. Subsidized construction may, to an undetermined extent, substitute for construction that would have occurred elsewhere in the city without subsidy, and such unsubsidized construction might also have conferred indirect benefits on adjacent sites.

If a redevelopment project demonstrably reduces the incidence of substandard housing (as urban renewal did *not*), indirect social benefits might

17. Jerome Rothenberg, *Economic Evaluation of Urban Renewal* (Washington, D.C.: Brookings Institution, 1967).
18. Hugh O. Nourse, "A Rationale for Government Intervention in Housing," in U.S. Department of Housing and Urban Development, *Housing in the Seventies: Working Papers*, vol. 1 (1976), pp. 245–248.

also occur in the form of reduced crime, delinquency, or disease. As explained at the end of Chapter 12, however, the evidence for such benefits from improved housing is not strong or consistent, and the task of measuring their value, if indeed they exist, is a formidable one.

In principle, cost-benefit analysis is the right technique to use in evaluating redevelopment projects, since it can capture indirect effects that escape the market calculus. In practice, however, it has yet to make a substantial contribution.

URBAN HOUSING POLICY: SUPPLY-SIDE STRATEGIES

Table 13.2 summarizes the history of urban housing policy from the early postwar years to the 1980s. The principal programs and their dates are listed at the left. Most of them are known by the section number of the particular housing act under which they were authorized—for example, Section 221(d)(3). The programs are grouped by type according to their general characteristics. Reading down the table, it can be seen that there was an evolution

TABLE 13.2
Urban Housing Programs: A Summary

PROGRAMS	STRATEGIES
1. Supply Side: Subsidize New Construction	
With Slum Clearance	
Public housing (1935 to date)	Demolish slums, build new housing for the poor.
Urban renewal (1949–1974)	Demolish slums, build middle-class housing, rely on filtering to help poor.
Without Slum Clearance	
Section 221(d)(3) (1961–1968) Section 235 (1968–1974) Section 236 (1968–1974) National Housing Goals (1968–1974)	New construction for the middle class and lower middle class, filtering for the poor.
Section 8, new construction (1974 to date)	New construction for the poor.
2. Demand Side: Subsidize Rent-paying Capacity of the Poor	
As an Entitlement Housing allowances (not adopted)	Private market will provide decent housing if tenants have adequate rent-paying capacity ("adaptive model" of housing market).
Not as an Entitlement Section 8, existing (1974 to date)	

of program types over time from supply-side policies, which predominated before 1974, to demand-side policies, which are dominant in the 1980s.

At the top of the table are listed the two leading programs of the 1940s and 1950s, already analyzed: public housing and urban renewal. They are described as supply-side policies in the sense that they encouraged either directly or indirectly the construction of (i.e., increased the supply of) new housing.[19] In addition, both were originally tied to the physical clearance of slums or blight, although in the case of public housing the connection was later dissolved. As urban renewal declined in favor during the 1960s, Congress enacted a widening array of other supply-side subsidy programs intended to stimulate new private construction without tying financial aid either to slum clearance or the removal of "blight." We will discuss the most important of these.[20]

Subsidies under Sections 221(d)(3), 235, and 236

Listed in Table 13.2 as supply-side policies without slum clearance are the principal programs of the 1960s and early 1970s: Sections 221(d)(3), 235, and 236.

Because they contained powerful subsidies to private developers, such programs were able to gain important political support from the real estate and construction industries. In this instance, unlike the case of public housing during the 1950s, congressional authorization was usually followed by generous appropriations rather than by financial neglect. Some of the programs, therefore, quickly reached considerable size.

Section 221(d)(3) was added to the Housing Act in 1961. Its purpose was to reduce rental costs by means of an interest-rate subsidy given to new units built for middle- and lower-middle-income families. Funds were made available at below-market interest rates to limited-profit corporations as well as to cooperatives and other nonprofit sponsors. The Department of Housing and Urban Development (HUD), which administered the program, regulated rent levels and established for admission income limits that varied geographically but generally restricted entrance to families with incomes below the local median.

The benefit to a qualifying project equaled the difference between financing costs at the 3 percent rate charged by the government and costs at whatever market rate the borrower would otherwise have had to pay for private funds. The direct subsidy cost to the government was considerably less:

19. Recall, however, that urban renewal subsidies were available also for nonhousing projects.

20. For an analysis of the major programs to subsidize private housing through 1971, see Henry J. Aaron, *Shelter and Subsidies* (Washington, D.C.: Brookings Institution, 1972), ch. 8. Later events are summarized in Congressional Budget Office, *Federal Housing Policy: Current Programs and Recurring Issues*, June 1978, ch. 3, and *Federal Housing Assistance: Alternative Approaches*, May 1982, ch. 3; and Weicher, pp. 478–483.

the difference between 3 percent and the rate at which the government borrowed. For example, if the commercial mortgage rate were 8.5 percent and the government borrowing rate 5 percent, the government was providing the project a yearly benefit equivalent to 5.5 percent (8.5 − 3) at a cost of only 2 percent (5 − 3) in its own accounts.

Opposition to 221(d)(3) eventually arose on several grounds. First, it was criticized for being a relatively "shallow" subsidy, not capable of pushing rents down far enough to reach the genuinely poor. Second, subsidies under the program could not be calibrated to the income levels of individual families but were in effect passed on as proportional rent reductions to all tenants. Finally, 221(d)(3) had what seemed to federal officials to be an unfortunate time pattern of impact on the federal budget: the full cost of each project appeared as a budget expenditure as soon as the government supplied mortgage funds. Budget makers much preferred a system—similar to the arrangement for financing public housing—in which subsidies could be paid out over the life of a project instead of being charged as a lump sum at the beginning. Most of the later subsidy programs have had just that feature.

In 1968 Congress enacted Sections 235 and 236 of the housing law, a pair of subsidy plans by which 221(d)(3) was eventually replaced. Each employed a subsidy formula designed to meet the objections that had been raised to 221(d)(3). Under the rental assistance provisions of Section 236, HUD contracted with a qualifying sponsor (who developed and operated the project) to pay a monthly rent subsidy geared to the level of each eligible tenant's income. In general, eligibility for admission was restricted to tenants whose income did not exceed the admission limit for public housing by more than 35 percent. The sponsor obtained a mortgage loan at the going market interest rate. The tenant was required to pay at least 25 percent of income in rent. The subsidy formula depended on two rent concepts: (1) "market rent," calculated to cover operating costs plus the mortgage costs actually incurred; and (2) "basic rent," equal to operating costs plus mortgage costs calculated as if the project had obtained a mortgage at a 1 percent rate of interest. The government undertook to make a monthly payment on behalf of each tenant equal to the lesser of the following:

> (1) subsidy = market rent − basic rent
> (2) subsidy = market rent − 25 percent of tenant's income

As intended, the plan did provide a deeper subsidy than had been achieved under 211(d)(3), and the program therefore reached a somewhat lower-income group. However, the double formula soon began to produce perverse effects. It had been expected that under the scheme outlined above, as incomes rose over time, the subsidies required for many tenants would gradually diminish. Instead, inflationary pressures in the early 1970s pushed operating costs up much faster than incomes. Basic rent in many instances came to exceed 25 percent of tenants' incomes. The second formula therefore became irrelevant, and tenants were forced to pay rapidly increasing rents. This was unfortunate in two respects. First, tenants of low to moderate income had been drawn into a situation they were unprepared to cope with. Second, a number of Section 236 buildings were unable to meet mortgage payments and went into default.[21]

The home ownership assistance program, enacted as Section 235, was similar in structure to the rental plan under 236. Families whose incomes fell within the qualifying limits received subsidies to help them meet the monthly carrying cost of a commercially financed mortgage on either a new or existing single-family home.

National Housing Goals

In 1968, the same year that it added Sections 235 and 236 to the housing statutes, Congress passed a Housing and Urban Development Act that included a timetable for achieving "national housing goals." For the ten-year period from 1969 through 1978, Congress set a goal of constructing or rehabilitating 26 million housing units, including 6 million subsidized units for low- and moderate-income families. Its purpose was to redeem the unfulfilled promise of "a decent home and suitable living environment for every American family" that had been set forth in the Housing Act of 1949.

The 26 million total figure was based on the assumption that

> the nation's housing problems could be substantially solved in a single decade by producing enough unsubsidized and subsidized housing units to offset expected new family formations, replace substandard housing and losses from the housing stock, increase the vacancy rate and provide income assistance in the form of housing subsidies for families who could not afford the cost of standard housing.[22]

We had, in other words, officially adopted a "new construction strategy" for solving the nation's housing problem.

Housing Subsidies and the Filtering Process

Because subsidies under Sections 235 and 236 were deep enough to reach what might be called the "upper low-income population" but not the poorest of the poor (see income and rent data in Table 13.3), the new construction strategy embodied in the national housing goals clearly implied a reliance on filtering to improve housing conditions for those at the bottom of the income distribution. In Chapter 12 we described the filtering process as

---

21. Congressional Budget Office, *Federal Housing Policy*, pp. 33–34.
22. The President of the United States, *Fourth Annual Report on National Housing Goals*, June 29, 1972, p. 27. See chart 9, p. 26, of the report for the estimate of "needs" on which the figure of 26 million was based.

TABLE 13.3
Size and Character of Federally Subsidized Housing Programs, 1983

	NUMBER OF OCCUPIED UNITS	CHARACTERISTICS OF PARTICIPATING HOUSEHOLDS		
		Mean Annual Income ($)	*Average Monthly Tenant Payment*[a] *($)*	*Average Monthly Subsidy*[a] *($)*
Public housing	1,313,816	6,191	101	108
Section 8	1,749,904	6,150	127	252
Section 236	533,469	9,456	229	55
Section 235 (original program)[b]	128,694	7,663	135	62
Section 101 (Rent Supplements)	76,919	5,289	110	168

[a]Average unit rent = (average monthly tenant payment) + (average monthly subsidy).
[b]A revised Section 235 program, initiated in 1976, accounted for an additional 101,078 occupied units by 1983.
Sources: U.S. Department of Housing and Urban Development, *Congressional Justification for Fiscal Year 1986 Estimates*, part 1, March 1985; and unpublished HUD data.

one in which housing originally built to rent at a higher price to a higher income class gradually "filters down" to a lower rent level and a poorer class of tenants. It has often been argued that subsidies to stimulate the construction of moderate- (or even upper-) income housing are justified because they encourage this filtering process, which eventually raises housing standards for lower income groups as well as for those better-off families who initially move into the subsidized housing. How credible is this argument?[23]

One problem is that subsidized new construction will to some extent displace unsubsidized activity, thus reducing the net effect of the subsidy program. Michael P. Murray found that the extent of displacement depends both on the type of financing employed and the housing sector to be served. Displacement is more likely the more the subsidized units compete with conventional new construction for mortgage funds and the higher the income level of the prospective occupants. He estimated that for government housing programs in the aggregate between 1961 and 1977, some 72 percent of subsidized activity was offset in the short run by the associated decline in unsubsidized construction.[24] It should be added that such displacement is also a strong possibility under locally operated programs that offer real estate tax abatements to stimulate new construction. Politicians favoring subsidized

23. For a more extended discussion of this issue, see William B. Brueggeman, "An Analysis of the Filtering Process with Special Reference to Housing Subsidies," *Housing in the Seventies: Working Papers*, vol. 2. pp. 842–856.
24. Michael P. Murray, "Subsidized and Unsubsidized Housing Starts, 1961–77," *Review of Economics and Statistics*, November 1983, p. 597.

new construction habitually ignore displacement effects and convey the impression that such programs produce a one-for-one addition to the housing stock. Obviously, that is far from the truth.

Granted, nevertheless, that subsidies for middle-income or lower-middle-income housing will, under the right conditions, accelerate the filtering process, the question remains, How much is that likely to improve the housing condition of the poor? The answer has already been suggested by the analysis of filtering in Chapter 12. Insofar as permanent structural characteristics of buildings are concerned—for example, room dimensions, plumbing and heating installations, access to light and air—filtered-down housing can raise standards at the lower end of the rent distribution. But the situation is quite different for other aspects of housing service, such as expenditures on cleaning, repairing, maintaining, and operating a building. In providing variable services of that sort, building owners will adapt to the rent-paying capacity of their tenants. When housing filters down to a lower income class, owners are almost certain to reduce these outlays, thus deliberately moving the building down to a lower quality level. Indeed, structural characteristics, too, may be altered in the process of adaptation: for example, large rooms or large apartments can be subdivided by remodeling. The end result is that good housing may gradually be converted to bad in the process of filtering.[25]

Moreover, the use of subsidies to stimulate new construction and accelerate filtering in the hope of raising housing standards for the poor is clearly inappropriate in local markets that are suffering substantial housing abandonment. Abandonment indicates an excess supply of housing at the lower end of the rental market. The poor would gain nothing from efforts to increase the excess further by accelerating filtering. Recognition of this fact contributed to the important changes in federal housing policy that occurred in 1973 and 1974.

Moving Away from a New Construction Strategy

Government housing policy during the early 1970s produced a record quantity of new, federally assisted low- and moderate-income dwelling units. Yet housing programs were again in trouble with their critics, and in 1973 the federal government decreed a moratorium on further subsidy commitments and moved to reexamine the whole array of housing programs. The immediate cause of the freeze may have been a desire to regain control over federal spending by reining in programs such as Sections 235 and 236 in which modest initial-year outlays led automatically to substantial, though somewhat uncertain, long-run spending commitments. In addition, there were intimations of waste, inefficiency, and scandal. Many of the new homes sold to low-

25. For empirical evidence that housing condition adapts to tenant income, see Richard F. Muth, *Cities and Housing* (Chicago: University of Chicago Press, 1969), p. 265.

income families under Section 235 were badly constructed; many of the old ones were drastically unsound and/or greatly overpriced.[26] Section 236 was criticized as providing overly generous benefits to investors.[27] (Ironically, the objections to Section 236 were reminiscent of those that had been raised against Section 608, the federal government's principal rental housing program of the immediate postwar years.[28] Congress seems to have difficulty formulating schemes that can stimulate a large flow of new, moderately priced urban rental housing without at the same time creating substantial windfalls for some investors.)

No doubt, however, the impulse to economize and to avert scandal was reinforced by widely expressed doubts about the fundamental direction taken by urban housing policy in the United States. Housing analysts both inside and outside the government began to question the wisdom of the new construction strategy on which that policy rested. They saw no good reason why benefits for specific income classes should be linked to occupancy of specific newly constructed dwelling units. It was argued that we should cut the tie between subsidies and the supply of new housing and instead pay "demand-side" subsidies to the poor, to be spent, with only a few restrictions, on old, new, or middle-aged housing at their discretion. Of all the policies discussed so far, this is the one most clearly consistent with the adaptive model of the housing market described in Chapter 12. It rests on the assumption that if subsidies bring the demand for housing up to an adequate level, the market process, largely by its own motion, will supply an adequate flow of standard-quality housing services.

HOUSING ALLOWANCES: A DEMAND-SIDE SUBSIDY

Urban housing market conditions that first developed in the 1960s and have prevailed ever since have made subsidies for housing demand rather than for supply look particularly attractive. Between 1960 and 1970 population declined in fifteen of the twenty-one cities that had a population greater than 500,000 in 1960. Of the twenty-six cities with population above 500,000 in 1970, seventeen suffered population losses by 1980. Even at the beginning of the 1970s many housing analysts had become convinced that in such cities the existing housing stock plus the new construction that would take place without subsidy would make up an ample supply of shelter. The widespread

26. See *Interim Report on HUD Investigation of Low- and Moderate-Income Housing Programs*, U.S. Congress, Hearing before the House Committee on Banking and Currency, March 31, 1971.

27. James E. Wallace, "Federal Income Tax Incentives in Low and Moderate Income Rental Housing," in U.S. Congress, Joint Economic Committee, *The Economics of Federal Subsidy Programs*, October 9, 1972, part 5, pp. 676–705.

28. Ibid., p. 692, n. 15. For a description of the 608 "scandal," see Charles Abrams, *The City Is the Frontier* (New York: Harper & Row, 1965), pp. 87–90.

incidence of abandonment provided direct evidence that there was in fact an excess supply in many cities. As they saw it, the problem was one not of insufficient quantity but of inadequate quality. To a considerable extent (as we have already argued), the inadequate quality supplied by owners of rental housing is their way of adapting to the low rent-paying capacity of tenants in relation to rapidly increasing maintenance and operating costs.

In such circumstances does it make sense to attack the housing problem by means of subsidies to accelerate the pace of costly new construction? Advocates of housing allowances thought not. Instead they proposed giving to low-income occupants subsidies that would enable them to pay the cost of adequate maintenance and operation of the existing, usable, older housing stock.

Housing allowances, as originally conceived, were to be an "entitlement" program—anyone who qualified by reason of income and family size would be eligible to participate. This would have been a radical departure from the usual federal practice of setting up housing subsidy programs in which the number of beneficiaries was strictly limited by the number of "slots" for which funds were appropriated. Partly for that reason, it seemed prudent to test a housing allowance program before deciding whether to adopt it. The federal government was sufficiently interested to carry out an extensive experiment with housing allowances during the 1970s. As we shall see, the results of the experiments were quite unexpected, confirming neither the hopes of those who advocated allowances nor the fears of those who had opposed them.

Before examining those results, however, we must explain the general structure of a housing allowance program. Although housing allowance proposals differ from one another in detail, they share an underlying logic nicely illustrated in the version developed by Ira Lowry. Although his plan called for assistance only to renters, housing allowances can in principle be made available to homeowners as well. Lowry explained the core of his proposal as follows:

> In each community a housing assistance agency would determine the rents needed to support full costs of ownership . . . for well-maintained older housing units, a standard amount varying with size of unit. Low-income families would apply to the agency for assistance, providing a Federal income tax return or other evidence of income. Applying a formula or schedule that takes into account income and size of family (and possibly other factors), the agency would determine how much the applicant could afford to contribute toward the cost of his housing. The applicant would be issued a rent certificate whose face value was equal to the difference between that amount and the standard full cost of a housing unit whose size was appropriate for the applicant's family. The certificate would consist of twelve dated coupons, covering a calendar year of rent assistance, each bearing the name of the recipient and the number of family members.

With the additional purchasing power provided by these coupons, the applicant would then seek private rental housing whose location and physical features were congenial to his needs and preferences and whose rent was within his now-augmented budget. Negotiations with the landlord over rent and conditions of occupancy would be solely the responsibility of the applicant; he could and should request evidence that the building was free of violations of the City's housing code. Once accepted as a tenant, he would present his assistance coupon in partial payment of the contracted rent, supplying the balance from his own pocket. Because each dollar of rent above the face value of the coupon would come out of the tenant's pocket he would have a clear incentive to choose housing within his means and to pay no more than the going market price for the housing he chooses.[29]

The benefit schedule described by Lowry is a version of a "housing gap formula." In its simplest form this can be written as follows:

$$P = R - bY$$

where P is the allowance payment, R is the estimated standard rent of adequate housing, Y is household income, and b is the proportion of income the tenant is required to pay in rent.

For the purpose of illustration, suppose that $b = 25$ percent. It can easily be seen that as a household's income rises, the benefit payment diminishes, finally disappearing when the family can pay for standard housing by spending 25 percent of its income.

As Lowry's statement indicates, a housing gap formula has one other important characteristic. It provides benefits based not on actual rent paid but on the estimated standard rent for adequate housing. The tenant who can find adequate housing at less the standard rent "keeps the change"; the tenant who wants housing that rents for more than the standard pays the difference out of his or her own pocket. At the margin, the tenant is paying the rent and is correspondingly drawn into the market process as an active participant. Thus housing allowances, under this formula, do not create a class of passive tenant beneficiaries, as some welfare housing assistance programs do.

Housing Allowances and Code Enforcement

It is worth examining briefly the interconnection between housing allowances and code enforcement. Most cities have housing codes that require dwelling units to be supplied with specific facilities such as plumbing, heating, and ventilation and to be kept in a state of cleanliness and good repair.[30]

29. Ira S. Lowry, "Housing Assistance for Low-Income Urban Families: A Fresh Approach," Paper submitted to the Subcommittee on Housing, part 2, U.S. Congress, House Committee on Banking and Currency, June 1971, p. 505.

30. For a detailed description of housing codes in the United States, see *Building the American City*, Report of the National Commission on Urban Problems (The Douglas Commission), 1969, part 3, ch. 4.

In rental buildings it is the responsibility of the landlord to see that essential services are maintained. Periodically it occurs to housing reformers that a "code enforcement drive" with real muscle behind it could force owners of deteriorated slum housing to bring it up to par and keep it there. Such drives are not necessarily useless, but their frequent repetition suggests at least that they do not achieve long-lasting improvement. This failure is probably explained by the inability or unwillingness of tenants in slum housing to pay rents that would cover the cost of operating a violation-free building, for if tenants were willing and able to pay such costs, there would seem to be no reason why the landlord would not wish to satisfy them by providing the necessary services. On the other hand, if tenants were not willing and able to pay, landlords would seem likely to resist incurring the extra cost of providing such services.[31]

If this explanation seems unduly simpleminded, consider the case of a well-run middle-class apartment house. No one supposes that the owner of such a building keeps it clean and in good repair only because of the threat of housing code penalties. Rather he or she does so because tenants want, and are prepared to pay for, a well-run building. Furthermore, the owner suspects that tenants will move out if they are dissatisfied. Ideally, by providing low-income tenants with enough rent-paying capacity to support well-maintained housing, an adequate rent certificate program would make code enforcement as routine and secondary a matter for low-income housing as it is today for middle-income structures. However, there would probably be a long transitional period following the introduction of housing allowances during which code enforcement would be essential to achieve rapid improvement of the housing stock and to establish a new level of expectations among both tenants and landlords. Hence the emphasis on code enforcement in every housing allowance proposal.

Lowry's plan included a provision, with teeth in it, for ensuring the maintenance of decent housing standards: rent certificates would be cashed by the housing agency only for owners of buildings that were free of all housing code violations. Thus the power of the tenant to insist on adequate maintenance (which he or she can now afford to pay for) as a condition of continued occupancy would be supported by the power of the housing agency to make the entire building ineligible for rent certificate payments. Landlords catering to a low-income clientele would find this a strong incentive to keep their buildings up to full code standards, while the public would be assured that rent subsidies were not being paid for substandard housing.

Other Arguments for Housing Allowances

Proponents of housing allowances believe they have a number of advantages, in addition to those already cited.

31. For a more extended argument of this point, see James Heilbrun, *Real Estate Taxes and Urban Housing* (New York: Columbia University Press, 1966), pp. 10–23.

1. *Equity.* A housing allowance plan is more equitable than a new construction strategy. Under the latter, a relatively small number of families receive very large benefits per household, while the majority of low-income families, equally qualified under eligibility standards, receive nothing. In 1982, according to the Congressional Budget Office, only 21.5 percent of income-eligible renter households and 5.5 percent of eligible homeowners were receiving housing assistance under federal programs.[32] (It should be noted, however, that these percentages, small though they may be, have risen substantially with the growth of housing assistance programs since the early 1970s.) By contrast, a housing allowance plan would provide less ample benefits per family but would be available to all eligible households rather than to a somewhat arbitrarily selected minority. Furthermore, the typical benefit formula provides that assistance payments are gradually reduced to zero as family income rises. Together with universal coverage for low-income families, this feature ensures the equitable result that no one receiving assistance is thereby made better off than someone else who is not. Such an outcome is *not* assured under the patchwork arrangement of present housing subsidy programs.

2. *Cost.* A housing allowance plan would be far less costly than a new construction strategy per dwelling unit brought up to standard. Lowry estimated that in New York City in 1969 the rent needed to cover the full cost of a well-maintained four-room apartment in an older building ranged from $100 to $150 per month. The equivalent full cost for either new public housing or new Section 236 units was approximately twice as high.[33] Consequently, the subsidy needed to enable a family of a given income class to occupy well-maintained older housing would be far lower than the subsidy needed to put the same family into a newly constructed unit. This conclusion is reinforced by many later studies. For example, the President's Commission on Housing reported a monthly subsidy cost of $250 per unit in the Section 8 new construction program in 1979 as compared with only $130 per month in the Section 8 program that subsidizes tenants in existing housing, much as a housing allowance plan would.[34] Thus, for a given federal outlay, about twice as many households can be assisted with housing allowances as could be served by new construction.

3. *Efficiency.* It can be argued that a considerable part of the outlay on a new construction strategy ultimately runs to waste so far as raising housing standards is concerned. Because low-income tenants cannot afford to pay its "upkeep," much of the housing that filters down as a result of subsidized new construction deteriorates into later-model slums. Thus the costly new construction program is ultimately futile, much like the efforts of a person who tries to fill up a swimming pool without first mending the leaks in the bottom.

---

32. Congressional Budget Office, *Federal Housing Assistance*, table 6.
33. Lowry, pp. 500–501.
34. *The Report of the President's Commission on Housing*, 1982, table 1.6.

Housing allowances are aimed precisely at those leaks. They are designed to prevent filtered-down housing from sinking below acceptable standards.

4. *Consumer choice.* Compared with the supply-side subsidies of a new construction strategy, housing allowances have the virtue of greatly increasing the freedom of choice for beneficiaries. If the program were set up nationwide, low-income families could obtain equivalent benefits anywhere. Within a given city they would be free to choose any building and neighborhood they could afford, instead of being constrained to live in designated subsidized projects. As between city and city, or city and suburb, they would be free to move, without losing benefits, to any place offering moderate-priced accommodation. Consequently, housing allowances might contribute to achieving a reduction in the degree of racial segregation within cities and between cities and suburbs.

5. *Reduced risk.* New construction subsidies tie government obligations to particular buildings in particular locations. A wrong decision can lead to disastrous loss to the government, as in the case of Pruitt-Igoe. Unlike new construction subsidies, housing allowances, because they are geographically mobile, cannot become permanently locked in to the wrong neighborhood or the wrong city, as new construction subsidies may. Instead, they move automatically to wherever people wish, and are able, to spend them. Although this mobility deprives local authorities of some leverage in planning, it also reduces the risk of serious public investment errors.

THE EXPERIMENTAL HOUSING ALLOWANCE PROGRAM

In 1970, Congress authorized HUD to conduct large-scale tests of the housing allowance concept. Several years were spent in planning the test, which evolved into the Experimental Housing Allowance Program.[35] EHAP consisted of three parts, a demand experiment to test the effects of allowances on the behavior of recipients, a supply experiment to test effects on entire housing markets, and an administrative agency experiment to test alternative administrative arrangements.

The demand experiment was carried out by offering housing allowances, under a variety of formulas, to samples of low-income renter households in Pittsburgh and Phoenix. The supply experiment took place in Brown County, Wisconsin (including the city of Green Bay), and St. Joseph County, Indiana (including the city of South Bend), two small but contrasting metropolitan housing markets. At these sites an allowance was made available as an

35. For a description of the background and organization of the experiments, see Joseph Friedman and Daniel H. Weinberg, eds., *The Great Housing Experiment* (Beverly Hills, Calif.: Sage Publications, 1983), ch. 1. European, Canadian and Australian versions of the housing allowance are reviewed in E. Jay Howenstine, *Housing Vouchers: A Comparative International Analysis* (New Brunswick, N.J.: Center for Urban Policy Research, Rutgers University, 1986).

entitlement to any resident, including both renters and owners, who met the income qualifications. Thus the supply experiment reproduced locally the opportunities for participation and for observing the impact of participation on the housing market that would exist nationwide under a full-scale federally financed plan. Enrollments were kept open for five years and participating households were allowed to continue in the program for ten years so that the long-run impact of the program could be observed.

A "housing gap" formula was employed for calculating benefits in most phases of the experiment. Recall that under this arrangement, the participant keeps (or pays) the difference if actual rent is below (or above) the estimated standard rent for a unit of appropriate size. Hence the tenant who moves to more expensive quarters pays the full extra cost out of his or her own pocket, just as would be the case if there were no allowance.

The results of the housing allowance experiment were surprisingly at odds with the expectations of most observers. In general, the system of allowances produced neither the large benefits its supporters had so confidently expected nor the harmful outcomes its opponents had feared. In both cases, the cause was the same: the housing market behavior of low-income families turned out to be not very responsive under the impact of a housing allowance offer.[36]

Participation Rates

The lack of response shows up in two findings (themselves interconnected) from which much else follows. First, the participation rate of the eligible population was relatively low. Second, participants showed very little inclination to spend more on housing as a result of the subsidy.

In order to receive benefits under a housing allowance plan, a household must live in a unit that meets the program's minimum standards. Some eligible families occupy units of satisfactory quality when they enroll. For them, participation is not difficult. Others, however, live in substandard units. In order to qualify for payments they must either move to a standard unit or upgrade the housing they already occupy. They might consider either of these alternatives too expensive to be worthwhile and therefore never qualify to receive benefits. At the sites of the demand experiment, between 80 and 90 percent of those in the sample to whom assistance was offered enrolled in the program, but only 40 to 45 percent satisfied the housing requirement and became recipients.[37] In the supply experiment, the participation

---

36. In addition to the sources cited in nn. 37–57, see Raymond J. Struyk and Marc Bendick, Jr., eds. *Housing Vouchers for the Poor: Lessons from a National Experiment* (Washington, D.C.: Urban Institute, 1981); Katherine L. Bradbury and Anthony Downs, eds., *Do Housing Allowances Work?* (Washington, D.C.: Brookings Institution, 1981); and Friedman and Weinberg.

37. U.S. Department of Housing and Urban Development, *A Summary Report of Current Findings from the Experimental Housing Allowance Program,* April 1978, app. I.

rate of eligible households at both sites averaged out to 44 percent in the third year of the experiment. In the aggregate, then, less than half the eligible population participated in the experiment at any one time. (Lowry points out, however, that this rate is about in line with findings for other income-transfer programs, such as AFDC.[38])

Not only were participation rates relatively low, but also the experiment provided a good deal of evidence that they fall as the required housing standard rises.[39] In other words, the more housing improvement the program requires, the fewer people will participate in it, a result that appears to frustrate the program's major purpose, the improvement of housing conditions.

Income and the Demand for Housing

The relative reluctance of households either to move or to undertake the upgrading of current quarters that would qualify them for benefit payments is connected to the second major finding: although housing allowances augment the income of beneficiaries, relatively little of the additional income is spent on housing. For example, participants in the demand experiment at Pittsburgh received an average monthly benefit of $50, but their expenditure on housing increased by an average of only $13. Comparable figures at Phoenix were $80 and $26.[40] Where did the rest of the money go? The answer is very clear. Participants used the bulk of the subsidy to reduce their own contribution to housing cost. Before participation, the median ratio of gross rent to income ranged from .34 to .53 at the twelve experimental sites. After benefit payments, the median ratio (taking the family's own payments as the numerator) declined to a range of .17 to .30, little more than half of what it had been.[41]

To put the matter in formal terms, participants in the experiment had a very low income elasticity of demand for housing. This elasticity is defined as the percentage change in housing expenditure that accompanies a 1 percent change in household income. As pointed out in Chapter 12, estimates of its value have varied widely, but there is an emerging consensus that the most reliable studies put it in the range of .3 to .5 for renters and .5 to .7 for owner-occupants. Estimates from EHAP data were at the low end of that range: .45 for owners and .19 for renters participating in the supply experiment and .33

38. Ira S. Lowry, *Housing Allowances: Lessons from the Supply Experiment*, doc. no. P-6455 (Santa Monica, Calif: Rand Corp., March 1980), table 3 and pp. 6–8.

39. Marc Bendick, Jr., and James P. Zais, *Incomes and Housing: Lessons from Experiments with Housing Allowances* (Washington, D.C.: Urban Institute, October 1978), pp. 10–15.

40. Ibid., p. 3.

41. Bernard J. Frieden, "What Have We Learned from the Housing Allowance Experiment?" *Habitat International*, 5, nos. 1 and 2 (1980), table 7. Also see John E. Mulford, George D. Weiner, and James L. McDowell, *How Allowance Recipients Adjust Housing Consumption*, doc. no. N-1456-HUD (Santa Monica, Calif.: Rand Corp., August 1980).

to .44 for renters in the demand experiment.[42] (Francis J. Cronin, however, argues that "household responses within a three-year experiment . . . may be inhibited by the normal inertia and the perception of a short time horizon created by the experiment." Using data from the demand experiment and employing a dynamic model of consumer behavior, he estimated *long-run* income elasticities in the range of .47 to .97.)[43]

As we shall see, many of the other results of the experiment appear to follow from the combination of low participation rates and low income elasticity of demand.

Effects on Mobility

Because housing allowances—unlike conventional supply-side subsidies—are not tied to specific housing projects, proponents believed that allowances would increase the intrametropolitan mobility of the poor, permitting them to escape from poverty neighborhoods and encouraging socioeconomic and racial integration. Evidence from the experiments, however, indicates that when participants are compared with control groups, the mobility of participants is only slightly higher.[44] Those who did move tended to move to less segregated or more desirable neighborhoods, but there was no indication that the program significantly increased movement to the suburbs.[45]

Marc Bendick and James P. Zais point out that "household moves are primarily associated with changes in needs and circumstances." Very large increases in income are likely to cause movement, since we know that household location choices *do* vary substantially with income. Thus the experiment might have induced more mobility had benefit levels been substantially higher. The immediate lesson for public policy, however, is that benefits offered by EHAP or other current programs influence location very little and are therefore unlikely to contribute much toward accomplishing desegregation.[46]

Improvements in Housing

Many who enrolled in the experiment were then living in dwellings that did not come up to program standards. To qualify for payments they either had to upgrade their units or move. Most of those in the supply experiment chose to stay where they were and make or obtain repairs. But these repairs

---

42. For the supply experiment, see John Mulford, *Income Elasticity of Housing Demand*, doc. no. R-2449-HUD (Santa Monica, Calif.: Rand Corp., July 1979), p. 33. For the demand experiment, see Francis J. Cronin, "Household Responsiveness to Unconstrained Housing Allowances," in Struyk and Bendick, table 7.1.

43. Cronin, p. 164 and table 7.3.

44. Bendick and Zais, pp. 16–17.

45. Frieden, pp. 245–246.

46. Bendick and Zais, pp. 18–19.

turned out to be surprisingly inexpensive. In many cases tenants themselves supplied the labor. The median cash cost of repairs was only about $10, and three-quarters of all repairs cost less than $30![47] These findings demonstrate that housing allowances *did* improve the quality of housing and did so very economically. But the small cost of the necessary improvements also suggests that they were not very substantial. For all that it increased tenants' rent-paying capacity, the program apparently did not induce massive improvements in the housing stock.

Effects on Housing Prices

Those who were skeptical about housing allowances usually feared that by subsidizing demand, allowances would cause "pure rent inflation"—an increase in the unit cost of housing not accompanied by any improvement in quality as measured by service rendered. Moreover, if rents were thus inflated in submarkets serving participants, nonparticipants in the same markets would be hurt: they would have to pay higher prices without benefit of an off-setting subsidy. At issue was the elasticity of supply of housing services. Would landlords readily respond to the increased rent-paying capacity of subsidized tenants by supplying a higher level or quality of service? Advocates of housing allowances clearly believed that they would, a view that is consistent with the adaptive model of the housing market described in Chapter 12. It was a principal purpose of the supply experiment to settle this argument by observing rent trends in two markets where a housing allowance program was in full swing.

Factually, the results of the experiment are clear-cut: no perceptible rent inflation occurred at either site.[48] As the discussion of repair costs indicated, it was possible to raise most dwelling units up to standard quality at very little cost. On this test the supply of housing services appeared to be highly elastic.[49] A skeptic might still argue, however, that this outcome depended importantly on the inertia of consumers. By rough calculation, 20 percent of households were eligible for support, but only half of those were enrolled at any one time, and only 80 percent of the enrolled qualified as participants. Thus about 8 percent of households were receiving allowances at any moment ($.20 \times .5 \times .8 = .08$).[50] If only 8 percent of households were sub-

47. Lowry, *Lessons from the Supply Experiment*, table 8.

48. C. Lance Barnett and Ira S. Lowry, *How Housing Allowances Affect Prices*, doc. no. R-2452-HUD (Santa Monica, Calif.: Rand Corp., September 1979), pp. 34–35.

49. For other studies of housing supply elasticity, see Frank de Leeuw and Nkanta F. Ekanem, "The Supply of Rental Housing," *American Economic Review*, December 1971, pp. 806–817; James R. Follain, Jr., "The Price Elasticity of the Long-Run Supply of New Housing Construction," *Land Economics*, May 1979, pp. 190–199; and John M. Mason, "The Supply Curve for Housing," *Journal of the American Real Estate and Urban Economics Association*, Fall 1979, pp. 362–377.

50. Frieden, p. 246.

sidized and those households had a very low propensity for spending additional income on housing, it is not surprising that rents were unaffected.

Cost of the Program

As expected, the unit cost of housing allowances in the experiment was low by comparison with costs under alternative policies. The average subsidy was about $800 per family per year in 1976. Administrative costs raise that to about $1,000.[51] By way of comparison, consider the cost of two "new construction" programs in 1971 and 1972, when prices were somewhat lower: the full annual subsidy cost per unit of public housing completed in 1971 was estimated at $1,980; the full subsidy cost per unit of housing under Section 236 was $1,901 in 1972.[52] Thus the data once again indicate that housing allowances cost the government only about half as much per unit as new construction does.

What about the aggregate national cost of an entitlement-based program? Cost estimates necessarily depend on the assumptions made about program housing standards, subsidy formulas, and participation rates. Using data from the experiment and varying the assumptions, Kain calculated that annual costs would have ranged from $3.3 to $8.6 billion in 1976 dollars.[53] Since the federal government in 1976 actually spent only $2.5 billion on housing assistance, it is clear that a universal housing allowance program would have required a considerable increase.

Evaluating the Results of the Experiment

After evaluating the results of the housing allowance experiment, Bernard Frieden called it "an experiment that worked." It worked in the sense of reaching those most in need to a far greater extent than other programs to subsidize private housing had done. It worked in the sense of reaching those groups without requiring, as the public housing program does, that they live in particular, and perhaps undesirable, housing projects. It worked also by allowing its beneficiaries to reduce very sharply the heavy burden of housing expenditure in their budgets.

In Frieden's view it also worked because for the first time the poor were allowed to demonstrate by their own action whether they preferred better

51. David B. Carlson and John D. Heinberg, *How Housing Allowances Work: Integrated Findings from the Experimental Housing Allowance Program*, doc. no. 249-3 (Washington, D.C.: Urban Institute, February 1978), pp. 46–47.

52. Frank de Leeuw and Sam H. Leaman, "The Section 23 Leasing Program," in U.S. Congress, Joint Economic Committee, *The Economics of Federal Subsidy Programs*, part 5, October 9, 1972, table 2, p. 655; U.S. Department of Housing and Urban Development, *Housing in the Seventies*, 1974, table 19, p. 116.

53. John F. Kain, "A Universal Housing Allowance Program," in Bradbury and Downs, table 3.

housing or more cash to spend on other goods. To a surprising degree, they preferred the cash. As Frieden put it,

> federal officials expected the typical family to move to better accommo-
> dations and to spend most of its subsidy for higher rent. The reality was
> that most families stayed put, made minor repairs if they were required to
> meet program standards, got marginally adequate housing if they did not
> have it to begin with, and used most of the payment to free their own
> funds for nonhousing expenses. As a result, the program had only limited
> impact on the quality of the housing supply and on mobility; but these
> were unavoidable consequences of respecting the wishes of families in
> the program.[54]

In the light of results from the housing allowance experiment, urban housing policy faces an as yet unresolved question. On the one hand, it is difficult to make a case for supply-side subsidies under today's circumstances. On the other hand, housing allowances, which were widely supported to replace them, have not produced the anticipated gains. Because the housing demand of low-income families responds so weakly to subsidies, housing allowances have relatively little impact on what were always thought to be the major housing problems. The strongest effect of demand-side subsidies has been to reduce the income burden of housing for the poor. But if that is to become the major policy objective, it is not clear why it would not be better served by pure income transfers than by transfers tied to the consumption of housing. (See discussion at the end of Chapter 12.)[55]

Perhaps the participants in the housing allowance experiments were trying to tell us something more. One can interpret the results as evidence that people are no longer greatly dissatisfied with the condition of their housing. That would be consistent with the data reported in Table 12.2, which suggested that citizen discontent with cities no longer arises from bad housing in the old, conventional sense of that word but rather from the necessity of living in bad neighborhoods, in environments ridden with crime, vandalism, and juvenile delinquency and pervaded by a general sense of disorder and decay. We return to the problem of deteriorating neighborhoods later in this chapter.

Section 8: Subsidies for Demand as Well as Supply

In 1973, while EHAP was still in the planning stage, President Nixon declared a moratorium on the commitment of additional federal funds for subsidized housing, and HUD began an intensive reexamination of housing policy.

---

54. Frieden, p. 250.
55. The merits of housing allowances or other housing subsidies as compared with pure income transfers are examined in William Grigsby, Morton Baratz, and Duncan Maclennan, *Shelter Subsidies for Low Income Households* (Philadelphia: University of Pennsylvania, Department of City and Regional Planning, July 1983).

As we have pointed out, criticism of the new construction strategy was already commonplace. The weight of opinion increasingly supported shifting from supply- to demand-side subsidies. The Housing and Community development Act of 1974 was, in fact, a compromise that included both subsidy types.

Section 8 of the 1974 act authorized a new program of housing assistance to lower-income families, replacing Section 236, new commitments for which were permanently frozen after the 1973 moratorium, and also superseding Section 23, which had authorized the leasing of private sector units for use as public housing. Thus Section 8 has been the principal rental housing assistance program of the federal government since 1974. It has undergone periodic revision since that date. As Table 13.4 indicates, the program grew rapidly, once under way. By 1983 it served more households than public housing did and more than the aggregate of all subsidy programs other than public housing. Its character and dimensions are indicated in Table 13.3.

Assistance under Section 8 is made available to tenants in four categories of housing. Programs for newly constructed, substantially rehabilitated, and existing units were authorized in 1974. Assistance to moderate rehabilitation was added in 1978. Eligibility is now restricted to those whose incomes do not exceed 50 percent of the area median, a level, on average, about 33 percent above the poverty line. (Under the original rules a fraction of units were also made available to those with incomes between 50 and 80 percent of

TABLE 13.4
Federal Expenditures for Housing Assistance and Community Development

	1976	1980	1986 (EST.)
Federal Outlay (millions of dollars)			
Housing assistance–total	2,479	5,331	11,235
Public housing	1,528	2,185	2,830
Section 8	42	2,104	7,480
Section 235	199	115	245
Section 236	500	656	618
Section 101			
(Rent Supplements)	210	271	62
Community development—total	2,772	4,907	4,602
Block grants[a]	983	4,126	3,575
Other	1,789	781	1,027
Percentage of Total Federal Outlay			
Housing assistance	.7	.9	1.1
Community development	.8	.8	.5

[a]Includes Community Development Block Grants and Urban Development Action Grants.
Sources: Vee Burke, *Cash and Non-cash Benefits for Persons with Limited Income,* Congressional Research Service, various years; *Budget of the United States Government, Fiscal Year* 1987.

the median.) As a result of these requirements, Section 8 units are occupied by families whose income levels are as low as those of public housing tenants and much below those of tenants in the Section 236 program, which Section 8 replaced (see Table 13.3).

As originally established, the assistance formula required the tenant to pay from 15 to 25 percent of income in rent, the fraction depending on income and family size. In 1981 President Reagan and the Congress agreed that the maximum tenant contribution should be raised to 30 percent, to be phased in over a five-year period. A subsidy from HUD makes up the difference between the tenant contribution and what HUD determines to be the unit's "fair market rent." Under this formula tenant payments are not automatically forced upward, as they were in the case of Section 236 housing, by rising operating costs. Instead, government contributions increase.

Except for changes in the assistance formula and income limits, the Section 8 programs for new construction and rehabilitation operate in much the same way as Section 236 did. HUD enters into long-term contracts with developers or rehabilitators to pay yearly subsidies on behalf of qualifying tenants in specific buildings. Like the payments under Section 236, these are supply-side subsidies in the sense that they are attached to designated projects and are intended to stimulate construction and rehabilitation.

On the other hand, the Section 8 provision for paying subsidies to tenants living in existing housing was a truly radical departure from previous policy. "Section 8–existing," as it came to be called, is a pure demand-side subsidy (see Table 13.2). It resembles a true housing allowance program except that instead of being open to all low-income households who qualify, its "slots" are strictly limited by the availability of funds. Apart from that restriction, it has most of the advantages already outlined for the housing allowance approach.

The program operates as follows. HUD contracts with a state or local housing agency to subsidize a specified number of tenants in existing privately owned rented housing. The agency enrolls qualified beneficiaries and makes payments to their landlords, under the formula described earlier. Tenants may choose where they wish to live, provided the landlord agrees to participate in the program, the premises meet minimum physical standards, and the rent does not exceed the fair market level established by HUD. The subsidy is not attached to a particular housing unit. Instead, it moves with the tenant.

Housing Policy under Reagan

The Reagan administration came into office determined to reduce federal domestic expenditures, especially those on redistributive social programs. Housing assistance was one of the most rapidly growing of those (see Table 13.4). Even a much less conservative administration would probably have in-sisted on reining it in.[56] The administration adopted a strategy of trying to reduce and ultimately eliminate commitments for additional new construction and major rehabilitation under Section 8 while concentrating new spending on the Section 8–existing program. Of the factors influencing the decision, two were especially important: First, as we have seen, the subsidy cost per household is about twice as high in the new construction/major rehabilitation program as it is in Section 8–existing. Second, the latter program was consistent with the administration's free-market orientation: if some sort of housing assistance is necessary, better to have a form of aid that maximizes consumer choice and minimizes governmental interference.

However, since most Section 8 payments are made under fifteen- to thirty-year contracts, it is impossible to reduce the size of the program in the short run. Even if no new activity is funded, outlays continue to grow as previously approved work moves to completion and/or rising rents require the government to provide larger subsidies for units already in the program. Table 13.4 shows that outlays for Section 8 assistance continued to rise sharply during the 1980s, even as efforts were under way to slow program growth.

The policy of favoring the use of the existing housing stock was reinforced by the work of the President's Commission on Housing. In its report issued in 1982, the commission concluded that substandard housing conditions had been largely eliminated in the United States and that "affordability" was now the principal housing problem facing the poor. Accordingly, rental assistance rather than subsidized new construction would now be the appropriate federal housing policy. The commission recommended the adoption of a "Housing Payments Program" as "the most efficient way to help the largest number of poor families in their quest for a decent home."[57] HPP would be a housing allowance program similar in most respects to those tested by EHAP. However, it would *not* be an entitlement but would make available a predetermined number of "slots," to be filled by those in greatest need.

In 1983 the Reagan administration sought unsuccessfully to incorporate some of the commission's recommendations in a revision of Section 8–existing. For example, in the latter program (unlike the housing allowance schemes previously described), a tenant cannot pay a rent above the fair market level established by HUD. This maximum rent rule limits tenants' freedom of choice and eliminates from the program some people, otherwise qualified, who prefer to live in apartments with higher rents and would be willing to pay the entire extra cost. Likewise, under Section 8 rules the tenant has no

56. The Reagan administration's housing policy is reviewed in detail in Raymond J. Struyk, Neil Mayer, and John A. Tuccillo, *Federal Housing Policy at President Reagan's Midterm* (Washington, D.C.: Urban Institute, 1983); and John C. Weicher, "Halfway to a Housing Allowance?" in Weicher, ed., *Maintaining the Safety Net* (Washington, D.C.: American Enterprise Institute, 1984), ch. 5.

57. *Report of the President's Commission on Housing*, p. xxiii. The Housing Payments Program is described in ch. 2.

incentive to shop around for the best bargain, since he or she cannot "keep the change" if a satisfactory apartment is found at *less* than the fair market level. The administration proposed to eliminate these economically inefficient features by basing payments on a "housing gap formula" as previously described, under which government contributions are independent of the rent actually paid. Congress, however, rejected this, as well as other proposed structural changes in Section 8, probably because the administration was also calling for drastic reductions in funding for the program.

Federal housing policy under President Reagan thus presented a curious picture: a conservative administration embraced the principles of the housing allowance, while at the same time expressing very little enthusiasm for spending money on it. Simultaneously, it succeeded in virtually eliminating the principal alternative, subsidized new construction. It is difficult not to see a powerful urge to reduce domestic spending as the rationale that bound these policies together.

THE PROBLEM OF DETERIORATING NEIGHBORHOODS

Although housing conditions for the urban poor have improved greatly in the past forty years, no one is likely to claim that low-income neighborhoods are also measurably improved. Neighborhood data of the sort shown in Table 12.2 do not go back far enough to establish clear trends, but they do show that dissatisfaction with neighborhood on some counts is now greater than dissatisfaction with the condition of housing.[58]

The federal government supports neighborhood rehabilitation through a variety of programs. Outlays under the budgetary title of "community development," most of which are "neighborhood-oriented," totaled $4.6 billion in 1986 (see Table 13.4). Community Development Block Grants accounted for almost 80 percent of that amount. These grants, established under the Housing and Community Development Act of 1974, combine into a single allotment the financial aid previously made available under separate, categorical programs for urban renewal, neighborhood development, open space, and other community development activities. Setting up the CDBG system was an important step in the process of "decategorizing" federal aid to states and localities to be discussed in Chapter 15. Under a block grant, unlike a categorical grant, there are relatively few restrictions on local use of funds within a broad range of eligible activities.

As Table 13.4 indicates, outlays increased much less rapidly during the 1970s for community development than for housing assistance. During the

---

58. For a systematic analysis of theories of neighborhood decline, see William Grigsby, Morton Baratz, and Duncan Maclennan, *The Dynamics of Neighborhood Change and Decline* (Philadelphia: University of Pennsylvania, Department of City and Regional Planning, January 1984).

1980s the former actually declined (especially if corrected for inflation) while the latter continued to climb. The difference is accounted for by the relative ease of controlling CDBG grants as compared with Section 8, under which spending is governed by long-term contracts. Thus when the Reagan administration sought cuts in the domestic budget, community development was relatively vulnerable. In addition to halting the growth of CDBG grants, the Reagan administration, consistent with its policy of reducing federal control over local activities, also relaxed some requirements introduced in the 1970s for the purpose of ensuring that a share of community development funds be spent to benefit low- and middle-income groups and neighborhoods. It remains to be seen whether this will have a significant effect on the pattern of local spending.[59]

To date, the considerable public effort to improve conditions in low-income neighborhoods appears to have had little impact. There are probably two fundamental reasons for this. First, much of the dissatisfaction with neighborhoods arises not from physical conditions but from such social problems as crime, drug abuse, and juvenile delinquency. These pathologies are not relieved by housing improvements or by neighborhood rehabilitation but, on the other hand, do make such improvements and rehabilitation more difficult to sustain. Second, the physical deterioration of neighborhoods, the problem neighborhood public policy does try to deal with directly, is essentially not controllable with the tools now at hand.[60] We can see why this is so by tracing the chain of causes and effects.

The physical deterioration of neighborhoods of the last quarter century is bound up with the problem of housing abandonment, described at length in Chapter 12. Housing abandonment has been stimulated by a filtering process set in motion by rapid population decline in the older central cities. Rapid population decline, in turn, resulted, in large measure, from the decentralization of the middle class to the suburbs. As population decreased, opportunities for movement within the city were opened up to the city's low-income residents. Since an influx of the poor was often followed some years later by abandonment as they moved on yet again, whole neighborhoods were often destroyed in the course of these internal migrations.

If the poverty population of a city is continually on the move, public policies aimed at neighborhood rehabilitation are very likely to prove fruitless. What about the possibility that effective housing and neighborhood rehabilitation would have precisely the effect of slowing down population movement and therefore stabilizing neighborhoods? The answer is that although some neighborhoods have been successfully stabilized, for the most part, the forces

59. See Struyk, Mayer, and Tuccillo, pp. 81–84; and Weicher, "Halfway to a Housing Allowance?" p. 115.
60. See Michael A. Stegman, "The Neighborhood Effects of Filtering," *Journal of the American Real Estate and Urban Economics Association*, Summer 1977, pp. 227–241; and Michael A. Stegman and David W. Rasmussen, "Neighborhood Stability in Changing Cities," *American Economic Review*, May 1980, pp. 415–419.

generating movement have simply swamped those making for stability. In areas such as the South Bronx, both public and private investment in rehabilitation have been wiped out in as little as five or six years.[61] It is scarcely an exaggeration to say that neighborhoods disappear even as plans are being made to save them.

Since population movement plays a crucial role in this sequence, it would appear that we can exercise control over neighborhood deterioration only if we can influence population movement. Two possibilities have been suggested. Michael Stegman points out that we could try to slow the population decline of central cities by deemphasizing federal programs that encourage the production of new housing in the suburbs. He argues that there is an unresolved policy conflict between federal policies to stimulate new construction and those aimed at neighborhood revitalization.[62] Alternatively, or in addition, we could try to develop local policies to guide population decline by designating certain neighborhoods for conservation and others for clearance. The purpose of such a policy would be to ensure, on the one hand, that limited funds for neighborhood revitalization are not wasted in a fruitless effort to save neighborhoods that are destined for depopulation in any case and, on the other, that neighborhoods designated for conservation retain enough population to remain viable and attractive.[63] Because there is enormous political opposition to both proposals, they cannot be treated as real possibilities. However, there are signs that population decline has now run its course in some cities (see Chapters 3 and 16). That should have the effect of slowing down intracity population movement, making policies for neighborhood rehabilitation more effective than they have been heretofore.

"OPENING UP" THE SUBURBS

A recurrent topic in this book has been the ongoing process of job and population dispersion within metropolitan areas. We have emphasized the fact that population dispersion has been highly selective rather than uniform by income and race. That fact shapes almost every policy issue raised in this book. In Chapter 10 we showed that poverty is increasingly concentrated in

61. See Frank S. Kristof, "Housing Abandonment in New York City," paper presented at the Conference on Housing, Georgia State University, Atlanta, May 8, 1978; and *The New York Times*, February 6, p. B-1, and March 9, 1978, p. B-3.
62. Stegman, pp. 234–239.
63. For a specific proposal see James Heilbrun, "On the Theory and Policy of Neighborhood Consolidation," *Journal of the American Planning Association*. October 1979, pp. 417–427. On strategies for coping with neighborhood deterioration, also see Anthony Downs, "Key Relationships between Urban Development and Neighborhood Change," ibid., pp. 462–472; and Wilbur R. Thompson, "Land Management Strategies for Central City Depopulation," in U.S. Congress, House Committee on Banking, Finance, and Urban Affairs, Subcommittee on the City, *How Cities Can Grow Old Gracefully*, December 1977, pp. 67–78.

the central cities and that racial discrimination, which restrains black movement to the suburbs, is part of the explanation. It was pointed out in Chapter 11 that job decentralization puts the central city poor at an increasing disadvantage in their struggle to improve their condition and in Chapter 12 that the concentration of the poor in the central city has led to a virtual breakdown of private housing institutions in many neighborhoods. We will argue in Chapter 15 that the unequal distribution of the poverty population between central cities and suburbs raises serious issues of both equity and efficiency in metropolitan public finance.

The disparity in racial composition and income level between central cities and suburbs is one of the most difficult, pervasive, and alarming of current urban problems. Proposals that the suburbs be somehow "opened up" to low-income and lower-middle-income families have therefore received a good deal of attention since the late 1960s. Because these proposals raise questions of housing policy first and foremost, it is appropriate to discuss them in this chapter. Because they relate housing issues to many others in urban economic policy, it is appropriate that they should make up the chapter's concluding section.

In earlier portions of the book we described the complex of forces that accounts for the present pattern of settlement of rich and poor in metropolitan areas. To recapitulate briefly, the poor are attracted to the center for several reasons. First, the central city has by far the largest concentration of old and therefore cheap housing, which is all that the poor can afford unless they are subsidized. Second, it still offers easy access to the largest single concentration of employment. On the other hand, as their incomes rise, the middle and upper classes find it increasingly desirable to pay the price of higher transportation costs in order to buy spacious housing in the suburbs. These "natural" economic forces, acting alone, would probably have sufficed to produce a pattern of richer suburbs and poorer central cities in the course of metropolitan growth. But they have not been acting alone. Rather they have been reinforced by public policy and by class and race prejudice. At the level of national policy, the provisions of the federal income tax favor home ownership over home rental. (See discussion of public policy effects in Chapter 3.) Since the incentive to ownership becomes more powerful the higher the individual's tax bracket, the middle and upper classes are far more likely than the poor to be influenced by these provisions. Because home ownership has always been much more prevalent in the suburbs than in central cities (and still is, despite the recent growth of condominium ownership of central city apartments), this bias in favor of home ownership for the well-to-do is also a bias in favor of suburban location. Equally important are the exclusionary zoning policies that suburban communities themselves can use to let the well-to-do in while barring the poor and the lower middle class. Though there seem to be a number of motives for exclusionary local policies, race and class prejudice are probably important among them.

Exclusionary Zoning

The poor and the lower middle class can be kept out of a suburban community by a few simple provisions in the local zoning ordinance. For example, a community can zone itself for single family housing only. Thus all multiple dwellings, including such relatively inexpensive forms of construction as garden apartments, are effectively banned. If that is not thought to be a sufficient barrier, the zoning ordinance can also require a large building lot for any new home—say, two acres or more—instead of the quarter-acre lots on which so much suburban housing has been built in the past. With land costs rising rapidly in the suburbs, a large lot requirement adds substantially to the cost of a home. In addition, builders are reluctant to put inexpensive homes on large lots. Thus zoning provisions can be used to raise the minimum cost of a new home high enough to exclude newcomers whose incomes are less than solidly middle class.[64]

It was pointed out in Chapter 6 that zoning originated in the United States as a means of reducing the harmful effects of externalities in land use. Negative externalities arise when one person's actions impose costs on others and the injured parties are not compensated. For example, a tall, bulky building may block the light and air of neighboring properties, or a noisy night club may disturb the quiet of a residential neighborhood. This kind of imperfection in the land market does, or could, occur frequently when people are living at typical urban densities and, when it occurs, will prevent the market from yielding optimal results. Zoning has long been accepted as a legitimate way of regulating the land market to reduce the potential damage from these imperfections.

Exclusionary zoning in the suburbs is a different matter, however. Its intent is not to correct market failure but to impose restrictions on consumer choice, thus actually restraining free market activity. There would be no objection to a plan under which a town reserved some areas exclusively for single-family homes while allowing multiple dwellings in others, since zoning can be defended as a way of preserving certain neighborhood amenities. But when we find that a town has been enacting acreage requirements and building codes far more restrictive than those that prevailed during most of its own period of development, we can hardly doubt that the intent is exclusionary.

Under the regime of local autonomy regarding land-use decisions that prevails in the United States, even public housing cannot breach the exclusionary walls of the suburbs. Although the federal government subsidizes low-income public housing, it is planned and built by local authorities. If a town does not want any, it simply does not participate in the federal program. Nor can the housing authority of one town undertake to build or operate units in another. Thus we have in the United States neither federal nor metropolitan agencies empowered to determine the location of subsidized housing.

64. See *Building the American City*, part 3, ch. 1, "Land-Use Controls: Zoning and Subdivision Regulations."

Motives for Exclusionary Practices

There are at least three important motives for exclusionary practices in the suburbs. The first is financial. Under our multilevel system, local governments are financially responsible for an important share of public services. Despite state and federal aid, a heavy local tax burden remains. As we will demonstrate in Chapter 15, the citizens of any municipality stand to gain financially by excluding in-migrants who are likely to contribute less to local tax and grant-in-aid revenue than they will add to local service costs. The property tax is the most important source of local revenue. Suburban voters therefore have a strong financial motive for trying to ensure that low- or even middle-income housing is not built in their town, because it will not "pay its way" in terms of taxes. The same financial motive that induces suburbs to keep low- or moderately low-income families out encourages them to bring clean, tax-paying industry in. An approach that combines both elements has been dubbed "fiscal zoning." It is a deliberate "beggar my neighbor" policy. The town that successfully practices it gets the industry while some other municipality is forced to bear the cost of public services for the factory's workers.[65]

A second motive for exclusionary practices is a desire to preserve neighborhood amenities. If a family was attracted to a suburb by its "rural" character, it will probably want to keep it that way by prohibiting apartment house construction and perhaps even by slowing down further intrusion of single-family homes. In the late 1960s the desire to preserve suburban amenities received support from a new source, the environmental protection movement, which gave a certain legitimacy to what otherwise might have appeared a strictly self-interested policy. One result was a wave of suburban "growth control" or "development timing" ordinances that sought, in a variety of ways, to limit the annual increase in the local housing stock.[66] These ordinances were justified as necessary to achieve "orderly development." An unfriendly observer, however, might classify them as a form of exclusionary zoning. (Also see the section on local growth control in Chapter 7.)

A final motive for exclusionary zoning is opposition to racial and/or socioeconomic integration. The distinction between feelings about race and about class is potentially significant since, if class prejudice plays an important part, we should expect opposition to integration to diminish as racial mi-

65. See Julius Margolis, "On Municipal Land Policy for Fiscal Gains," *National Tax Journal*, September 1956, pp. 247–257.

66. See Fred Bosselman, "Can the Town of Ramapo Pass a Law to Bind the Rights of the Entire World?" in David Listokin, ed., *Land Use Controls: Present Problems and Future Reform* (New Brunswick, N.J.: Center for Urban Policy Research, Rutgers University, 1974), pp. 241–272; Michelle J. White, "Self-interest in the Suburbs: The Trend Toward No-Growth Zoning," *Policy Analysis*, Spring 1978, pp. 185–203; Richard F. Babcock, "The Spatial Impact of Land-Use Controls," in Arthur P. Solomon, ed., *The Prospective City* (Cambridge, Mass.: M.I.T. Press, 1980), pp. 267–270; and Bernard J. Frieden, "The Exclusionary Effects of Growth Controls," in M. Bruce Johnson, ed., *Resolving the Housing Crisis* (San Francisco: Pacific Institute for Public Policy Research, 1982), ch. 1.

norities converge toward the majority in socioeconomic characteristics.[67] Because race and class feelings are not freely expressed, it is difficult to know how much of the opposition to integration should be attributed to these antagonisms and how much to other motives. In recent years the situation has been further complicated by the growth of crime and delinquency as a major personal and social concern. Rightly or wrongly, many residents of "safe" towns or neighborhoods are fearful that admitting low-income families, including a substantial number of minority families, will bring an increase in crime and delinquency.

What Would Be Gained by Opening Up the Suburbs?

A program that succeeded in opening up the suburbs to low- and moderate-income families might be expected to produce a variety of benefits. First of all, by encouraging the movement of blacks into the suburbs, it would obviously help to reduce the level of macrosegregation in metropolitan areas: increasingly black central cities surrounded by still largely white suburbs. If de facto integration is ever to be achieved in U.S. society, it is essential that the suburbs accept a substantially greater proportion of the metropolitan black population.

Second, it would promote freedom of choice in housing location for groups whose choices are now heavily restricted by exclusionary practices. Such freedom from imposed restrictions is a matter of right that also has practical economic consequences. The growth of suburban job opportunities was discussed in Chapter 11. It was argued that restraints on freedom of choice in housing systematically limit the access that minorities, now concentrated in the central cities, have to these attractive opportunities and also impose losses on them by limiting and distorting their consumption of housing itself. Those who do work in the new suburban plants and offices are likely to find themselves bearing unnecessarily heavy travel costs, since they cannot live near their jobs.

Finally, removing housing restrictions in the wealthier suburbs would help to even up tax costs and service levels among different local governments. The well-to-do would no longer be able to use self-segregation as a means of escaping responsibility for sharing the cost of local public services provided to those with lower incomes. (It is a curious fact that one of the important consequences of the twentieth-century revolution in transport technology has been to facilitate this self-segregation.) Low- and moderate-income families moving into wealthy communities would benefit either by receiving a higher level of service or paying lower tax rates than before.

Policies to Encourage Racial and Economic Integration

Among policies to encourage racial and economic integration within metropolitan areas, two principal types can be distinguished. "Permissive"

67. Anthony H. Pascal, "The Analysis of Residential Segregation," in John P. Crecine, ed., *Financing the Metropolis* (Beverly Hills, Calif.: Sage Publications, 1970), pp. 410–412.

policies would remove the barriers of exclusionary zoning and discriminatory practice but would not directly encourage construction of low-cost housing. "Active" policies would have the government either build such housing directly or else encourage its construction by subsidies or other means.

Civil rights laws. The most notable of "permissive" policies is the Civil Rights Act of 1968, which prohibits racial discrimination in selling or renting housing. Numerous state laws do likewise. It is not easy to know how effective these statutes have been. In Chapter 12 we described several field surveys showing that significant discrimination still occurred in market practices in the late 1970s and early 1980s. We also cited evidence provided by Kain that blacks are represented in the suburbs far less than would be predicted on the basis of their incomes and family characteristics. The clear implication is that their numbers are held down by racial discrimination, and it follows that ending such practices (even without providing active subsidies) would permit a substantial increase in black suburbanization. Moreover, Kain finds evidence in several metropolitan areas that during the 1970s there was "a movement of small but significant numbers of blacks into formerly all-white suburban communities" that were widely dispersed and distant from older black neighborhoods. He suggests that this may be the beginning of a process that "could produce significant decreases in racial segregation within a short period," and to encourage it he argues for redoubling efforts to enforce fair housing laws and provide minorities with up-to-date information about suburban housing opportunities.[68]

State zoning reform. The Civil Rights Act of 1968 and its state counterparts were designed to curb the "retail" sort of discrimination that can occur in individual housing transactions. But if the suburbs are to be fully "opened up," it is also necessary to do something about the exclusionary zoning regulations that now lend the color of legality to discrimination when it is practiced at "wholesale." Local zoning ordinances are written under authority of state law. Consequently, the states have the power to require that they conform to nonexclusionary standards or even to a statewide plan. Though local political interests have been strong enough to prevent radical revision of zoning standards by states, there have been a few instances of moderate reform.[69]

Financial reorganization. Because residents of the suburbs are genuinely concerned about the extra tax burden they would take on if they allowed an influx of low-income households, appropriate public finance reforms might

68. John F. Kain, "Black Suburbanization in the Eighties: A New Beginning or a False Hope?" in John M. Quigley and Daniel L. Rubinfeld, eds., *American Domestic Priorities* (Berkeley: University of California Press, 1985), pp. 273, 274.

69. See Robert W. Burchell and David Listokin, "The Impact of Local Government Regulations on Housing Costs and Potential Avenues for State Meliorative Measures," in George Sternlieb and James W. Hughes, *America's Housing: Prospects and Problems* (New Brunswick, N.J.: Center for Urban Policy Research, Rutgers University, 1980), pp. 313–358; Leonard S. Rubinowitz, "A Question of Choice: Access of the Poor and the Black to Suburban Housing," in Louis H. Masotti and Jeffrey K. Hadden, eds., *The Urbanization of the Suburbs* (Beverley Hills, Calif.: Sage Publications, 1973), pp. 341–343.

help to weaken support for exclusionary policies. For example, if local school outlays, which are by far the largest charge against local taxes, were to be fixed at a statewide uniform level per pupil and financed entirely by a state property tax, and if all local welfare costs were to be absorbed by either the state or the federal government, the financial motive for opposing low-income in-migration would all but disappear. More generally, any form of grant or revenue sharing, or any reassignment of functions that shifts the responsibility for financing services to a higher level of government, would help to weaken the financial motive for exclusionary policies. (These issues in public finance are analyzed in detail in Chapter 15.)

Class action suits. Unable to win support for zoning reform in state legislatures, opponents of exclusionary zoning have frequently turned to the courts for relief. Numerous law suits to halt exclusionary practices have been brought by citizen groups and by builders.[70] In state courts they have met with considerable, though not universal, success. In two landmark cases of the mid-1970s—*Oakwood at Madison* v. *Township of Madison* and *Southern Burlington County NAACP* v. *Township of Mount Laurel*—the New Jersey Supreme Court held that towns in growing regions have an obligation to accommodate a fair share of the housing needs of all income classes in the region. The Mount Laurel zoning ordinance entirely excluded multifamily dwellings, while Madison's was so restrictive that it effectively barred new housing for all but 10 percent of the general population. The court invalidated the offensive portions of both ordinances on the ground that they were contrary to the general welfare. The remedy, however, was strictly a permissive one: the towns were ordered to amend their zoning rules to allow for the construction of their "fair share" of low- and moderate-income housing, should any developers care to construct it.

As it turned out, little if any housing was built as a result of these decisions. In 1983 the court therefore handed down another decision, usually referred to as *Mount Laurel II*, in which towns were told that if the mere removal of restrictions had proved to be ineffective, they were obliged to take affirmative measures to encourage the construction of low- and moderate-income units. If other positive incentives failed, they would be expected finally to require that builders "set aside" a predetermined portion of new units for low- and moderate-income families.[71] (This sort of active policy to promote economic integration in the suburbs has been called "inclusionary

70. A thorough review of these cases can be found in Richard P. Fishman, ed., *Housing for All under Law*, Report of the American Bar Association Advisory Commission on Housing and Urban Growth (Cambridge, Mass.: Ballinger, 1978), chs. 2 and 3. Also see Jerome G. Rose, *Legal Foundations of Land Use Planning* (New Brunswick, N.J.: Center for Urban Policy Research, Rutgers University, 1979), ch. 3.

71. Allan Mallach, *Inclusionary Housing Programs* (New Brunswick, N.J.: Center for Urban Policy Research, Rutgers University, 1984), pp. 30–31. Also see Robert W. Burchell et al., *Mount Laurel II: Challenge and Delivery of Low-Cost Housing* (New Brunswick, N.J.: Center for Urban Policy Research, Rutgers University, 1983).

zoning.") Furthermore, a developer who won a suit against restrictive zoning would be entitled to a building permit issued under court order. The availability of this "builder's remedy" strengthens the hand of the developers—a major interest group opposed to exclusionary practices—and should accelerate the production of low- and moderately priced housing in the suburbs.[72]

Attempts to overturn exclusionary zoning and growth controls have proved less successful in federal than state tribunals. For example, the federal courts have long recognized a constitutional right to travel. Plaintiffs in federal cases have argued that exclusionary zoning and growth controls are unreasonable restrictions of such a right. If that position were accepted, exclusionary zoning could be readily challenged in the federal courts. However, the Supreme Court in the case of *Boraas* v. *Village of Belle Terre* in 1974 upheld a restrictive ordinance despite the plaintiff's assertion of the right to travel.[73] The Court's decisions during the 1970s have been widely interpreted as showing a reluctance to have the federal courts involved in disputes over the housing effects of zoning.

Nor have all suits opposing allegedly exclusionary zoning succeeded in the state courts. In the case of *Golden* v. *Planning Board of Ramapo* the New York State Court of Appeals in 1972 upheld the town of Ramapo's program of "planned sequential development" as not unreasonable or exclusionary.[74]

Fair share plans. Suburban towns acting independently may well resist the pressure to end exclusionary practices out of fear that "once we let down the barriers, a flood will follow." This fear can be alleviated either by a state plan binding on all jurisdictions or a regional compact under which all localities agree to accept a fair share of low-income housing so that none is asked to absorb very much. California is the only state in which an extensive fair share system has been developed through state legislation. (In New Jersey it was created by court order.) During the late 1970s and early 1980s, laws were enacted in California requiring localities to make five-year housing plans that would meet regional fair share goals by providing a variety of incentives to developers of low-cost units. Allan Mallach estimates that by 1983 a total of 17,000 low- and moderate-income units had been built or committed for construction under the California program.[75]

Among local fair share agreements, the best known is the Housing Plan for the Miami Valley Region, adopted in 1970 by the counties and municipalities centered on Dayton, Ohio. The projected need for low- and moderate-income subsidized housing was allocated among the participating jurisdictions on criteria that took into account the capacity of each to provide schools

72. Mallach, pp. 230–233. For a critical view of inclusionary zoning, see Robert C. Ellickson, "The Irony of 'Inclusionary' Zoning," in Johnson, ch. 6.
73. Kenneth Pearlman, "The Closing Door: The Supreme Court and Residential Segregation," *Journal of the American Institute of Planners*, April 1978, pp. 162–163.
74. Bosselman, pp. 248–249, 260–264.
75. Mallach, pp. 197–198, 216.

and other necessary services. These allocations were also "ceilings," a feature that helped to make the plan politically acceptable.[76] However, unless the federal or state governments provide municipalities with some incentive to take cooperative action, it seems unlikely that regional fair share plans will be widely adopted.

Active subsidy policies. Any really effective policy to move low-income households into the suburbs would probably have to include subsidies directed specifically toward those areas. One approach would be to establish metropolitan area housing authorities under state law, with the power to build or lease subsidized, low-rent public housing anywhere within the region. The authority could make plans on the basis of regional rather than purely local criteria and, if necessary, carry them out by overriding exclusionary local zoning ordinances. However, political resistance by the suburbs currently makes the creation of metropolitan housing agencies with coercive powers look highly unlikely. As a result of such resistance, New York's Urban Development Corporation, which takes the entire state as its field of operation, was deprived in 1973 of its former power to construct housing without conforming to local restrictions.[77]

On the other hand, state agencies can make it a condition of providing housing assistance to local developers that the latter adopt specified inclusionary goals. The Massachusetts Housing Finance Agency, for example, requires that "a minimum of 25 percent of the units in any development financed with tax-exempt bonds issued by the agency be rented to low-income households."[78] Similarly, the Internal Revenue Code of the federal government requires that 20 percent of the units in a rental project financed by federally tax-exempt state or local bonds be occupied by low-income households.

Nevertheless, the obstacles to active subsidy policies are, if anything, greater at the federal than the state level. The federal government does not itself build low-income housing, nor does it have the power to dictate where localities shall build it, nor does it seem likely in a nation devoted to the preservation of local autonomy that Congress would ever grant it such powers. However, a policy of rewards might be acceptable where a policy of compulsion is not. For example, special federal grants could be made to help defray the cost of municipal services in towns that accept subsidized low-income housing under a voluntary regional or state plan.[79]

76. Rubinowitz, pp. 338–341.
77. For a brief history of UDC, including its later financial difficulties, see Fishman, ed., pp. 505–508.
78. Mallach, p. 222.
79. Regarding possible federal initiatives, see Morton J. Schussheim, "National Goals and Local Practices: Joining Ends and Means in Housing," Paper submitted to the Subcommittee on Housing, part 1, U.S. Congress, House Committee on Banking and Currency, June 1971, pp. 157–158; and Herbert M. Franklin, "Land Use Controls as a Barrier to Housing Assistance," in *Housing in the Seventies: Working Papers*, vol. 1, pp. 551–560.

Many analysts had thought that housing allowances, by making it possible for the poor to move into the nearer suburbs, where relatively inexpensive older housing is available, would also actively help to promote intrametropolitan racial and economic integration. However, results of the housing allowance experiments, described earlier, indicate that the benefits offered (at least in that case) were not large enough to induce significant changes in residential location.

The Consequences of Alternative Policies

What would happen if the exclusionary practices permitted under our system of local planning autonomy were now to be replaced by policies that permit but do not subsidize low- and moderate-income housing in the suburbs? The result would probably be an increase in the quantity of new moderate-income housing built in the ring area and a more even distribution of such housing among localities of varying income levels. We have already cited the gains in the form of increased housing, job, and locality choice; reduced transportation costs; and improved public services that would accrue to those who could afford the new housing. In a society dedicated to freedom of individual choice and equality of opportunity, such gains are ample justification for the necessary policy changes. It must be emphasized, however, that putting an end to exclusionary zoning practices would, by itself, do nothing to move the poor or the lower middle class into the suburbs. Only a policy providing substantial direct subsidies would bring that about.

If an end to exclusionary zoning were to be accompanied by a decline in discriminatory housing market practices (still assuming no active subsidy policies), the results would be particularly favorable for middle-class blacks. Ironically, however, their gain would come at the cost of aggravating the divergence in socioeconomic status within the black population already noted in Chapter 10. The emerging black middle class would be increasingly attracted to the prosperous suburbs while poor and lower-middle-class blacks remained bottled up within the central city. As a result, the spatial separation of black economic classes would become more marked. This is certainly *not* an argument against opening up the suburbs. It is an argument for active policies to help move some of those with less than middle-class incomes into the suburban ring.

FOURTEEN

The Metropolitan Public Sector: Functions, Growth, Revenues

"My statistics come from the Census of Governments," announced the student describing his research to the members of a seminar in public finance. A visiting British scholar looked puzzled. "Census of Governments?" he asked, his voice rising in disbelief. "Whatever do you mean by that?" The student laughed and explained that in the United States there are so many governmental units that if the Census Bureau didn't count them every five years no one could be sure exactly how many there were or what they did.

It might be argued that in a nation devoted to competition in economics, democracy in politics, ethnicity in culture, and pluralism in social institutions, this multiplicity of governments should be counted a virtue: at once an indispensable means to, and an inevitable result of, the democratic diversity we prize. Yet we pay a price for it, too, especially in metropolitan areas, where the problems caused by an abundance of governments are frequently no laughing matter.

THE MULTILEVEL PUBLIC SECTOR

The structure of the public sector in the United States can best be described by a two-dimensional diagram, such as Figure 14.1. Along the vertical scale we mark off the three levels of government: federal, state, and local. It is conventional to treat local government as though it were a single level. In fact, the local sector in most places consists of many overlapping layers: cities, counties, school districts, water districts, and so forth. These are shown schematically in the diagram. The degree of complexity at the local level is suggested by a few statistics: there were no less than 82,290 local governmental units in the United States in

379

1982, and only 19,076 of these were "municipalities." The 305 SMSAs then recognized by the census alone contained 29,861 governmental units.[1]

The horizontal dimension of the diagram measures schematically the jurisdictional reach of the units of government in each of the layers. The pattern is clear enough at the federal and state levels. At the local level it becomes complex and unsystematic because the jurisdictions of the units vary in size both within layers and between them. A county may be larger than, equal to, or (in the sole case of New York City) smaller than a whole city. A school district may take in one or more towns as well as unincorporated rural areas. A special district may overlap cities, counties, or towns. A single citizen may thus live under a bewildering array of local governments stacked one above the other.

Metropolitan Fiscal Problems

The vertical and horizontal dimensions of Figure 14.1 are useful in describing three problems of metropolitan public finance. The first is the "assignment problem." Both the functions of government and the power to finance them by various means are distributed along the vertical scale among the federal, state, and local governments and, within the local sector, among its many overlapping units. In an optimum multilevel structure, local governments would not be required, nor would they attempt, to perform functions that could be more efficiently or equitably handled at a higher level. Arranging the most appropriate division of functions among the three levels of government as well as within the strata of the local level is the substance of the assignment problem.

Along the horizontal dimension of Figure 14.1 we can define two fiscal problems. The first is the notoriously haphazard arrangement of functions and boundaries within and across the local level. Because geographic boundaries for the provision of local services have not been drawn rationally, the local public sector is often unable to provide services at an optimum, or perhaps even acceptable, level of efficiency. A second, but related, problem in the horizontal dimension is the prevalence of geographic disparities in the distribution of needs and resources. The needs of the population for public services and the income and resources out of which to pay for them are not similarly distributed across governmental units at the local level. Serious inequities among individuals and between social classes arise from this geographic mismatch.

As we shall see, the local public sector has grown very rapidly in the United States since the 1950s. This growth, in combination with the difficulties resulting from inappropriate functional assignment, geographic dispari-

---

1. U.S. Bureau of the Census, 1982 *Census of Governments*, vol. 1, *Governmental Organization*, table P.

FIGURE 14.1
Structure of Government in the United States: A Two-dimensional View

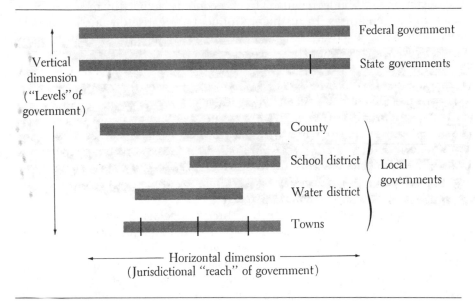

ties, and haphazard boundaries, has produced a fourth problem: a condition of severe fiscal stress in many of the older central cities that is often referred to loosely as the "urban fiscal crisis."

In the next section of this chapter we analyze the budgetary functions of government and the problem of assigning each function to the most appropriate level. That is followed by a section on the composition and growth of local public spending that concludes with an examination of the movement to limit that growth. We then study the sources and growth of local government revenue. The chapter closes with an examination of the property tax, by far the most important local levy and one about which there is a long history of debate. The three remaining problems—haphazard arrangement of functions and boundaries, geographic disparities between needs and resources, and urban fiscal distress—together with some of the major policies and reforms that have been proposed to ameliorate them, are taken up in Chapter 15.

THE ASSIGNMENT OF FUNCTIONS
TO LEVELS OF GOVERNMENT

The essence of the assignment problem is to determine the most appropriate division of functions among the federal, state, and local governments.

Let us begin by looking at broad categories of functions. Apart from regulatory action, government brings its influence to bear on the economy through the operation of its budget, which affects economic activity by means of both taxes and expenditures. In his highly influential treatise on public finance, Richard A. Musgrave usefully divides the budgetary objectives of government in a market economy into three classes.[2] The first of these he calls "allocation," the second "distribution," and the third "stabilization." The task of allocation consists of providing those goods and services that, for a variety of reasons, the private sector cannot provide at all or cannot provide at prices and in quantities that are optimal. The task of distribution might better be labeled *redistribution*, since it consists of transferring income among individuals to correct the pattern of private market rewards in order to arrive at an ethically more desirable distribution of well-being. Last, the stabilization task involves using the fiscal powers of government to smooth out fluctuations in the level of aggregate economic activity.

In a unitary political system the three budgetary functions would be performed and, ideally, coordinated by a single government. Under the multilevel system of federal, state, and local governments adopted in the United States, matters become much more complicated. Lack of coordination among governments, overlapping of jurisdictions, the mismatch between a government's objectives and its resources all contribute—not haphazardly, but systematically—to preventing the public economy as a whole from functioning efficiently. To say this is not to argue that we should abandon multilevel government, which has indispensable virtues as well as characteristic defects, but rather to explain why the search for more effective forms of federalism is apparently an unending one.

Stabilization of Economic Activity

Under a multilevel system, state and local governments perform few stabilization functions. Quite rightly, they leave stabilization largely in the hands of the federal government. In this they really have no choice. The economies of states and localities are so wide open to the influence of the national economy, through trade, that it would be hopeless for them to attempt local stabilization by means of fiscal policy, even if they were permitted by their own constitutions to do so. As economic base analysis assumes, the level of local activity is influenced significantly by the strength of outside demand for local products. That demand depends largely on the behavior of the national econ-

---

2. Richard A. Musgrave, *The Theory of Public Finance* (New York: McGraw-Hill, 1959), ch. 1. The normative approach to problems of public finance adopted in this and the following chapter is based largely on the work of Musgrave as applied to metropolitan areas by subsequent writers. See references below, and also Harvey E. Brazer, "Some Fiscal Implications of Metropolitanism," reprinted in William E. Mitchell and Ingo Walter, eds., *State and Local Finance* (New York: Ronald Press, 1979), pp. 331–345.

omy, fluctuations in which would not be perceptibly influenced by stabilization efforts financed in a single locality.

Nor would local stabilization efforts be effective in stimulating the local economy directly. Because the marginal propensity to import is high in a local area, a large proportion of any increment to local spending "leaks out" into the national economy. Instead of recirculating to stimulate local activity, it is (from the local point of view) mostly wasted on the world at large. Any stimulus or restraint that local authorities might contrive to counteract outside forces would soon dissipate its effects nationwide. Thus locally financed stabilization measures are bound to be ineffective.[3]

Redistributing Income from Rich to Poor

In Musgrave's ideal scheme the tasks of allocation and distribution are logically separated, even though both may be performed by the same government. Under the heading of allocation, the government provides public goods and services to the extent that citizens want them and are willing to pay for them with taxes. If a redistribution of income is desired, the most efficient way to carry it out is by making transfers in cash, rather than in services, from the rich to the poor. An income-maintenance scheme of the sort described in Chapter 11 would be one way to carry out such transfers. The present federal welfare program makes use of other means such as Aid to Families with Dependent Children (AFDC) and Supplemental Security Income (SSI) that are also pure transfers, unconnected with the delivery of public services. The states, too, undertake a certain amount of pure income redistribution because they are required to share the cost of AFDC and may finance other forms of cash relief as well. Even localities may become involved, since some states require them to bear part of the welfare burden.

A clear distinction between allocation and distribution is not, however, maintained in practice by any of the three levels of government in the United States. Instead, they often adopt policies that more or less deliberately combine the objectives of allocation and redistribution. One might mention, for example, programs under which the government provides services, such as medical and hospital care or education, at less than full cost or even entirely free, because a majority of citizens believe them to be particularly meritorious and therefore deserving of especially wide distribution. The redistributive effect of such policies can be seen clearly in the case of education: in a given community, benefits are received by rich and poor families in equal amounts per child, but the rich pay far higher school taxes than the poor. Even where redistribution is not an objective, however, the effect is the same: governments generally provide the poor with more service benefits than they pay for

3. For further discussion, see Wallace E. Oates, *Fiscal Federalism* (Orlando, Fla.: Harcourt Brace Jovanovich, 1972), pp. 4–6, 21–30; and Roy Bahl, *Financing State and Local Government in the 1980s* (New York: Oxford University Press, 1984), pp. 17–21.

in taxes and the rich with less. Consequently, real income is redistributed indirectly from the rich to the poor.

The extent of this redistribution cannot be observed directly. It can be approximated, however, by estimating separately the incidence of tax payments and the incidence of expenditure benefits by income class and then subtracting payments from benefits received within each class. Musgrave and Musgrave carried out such estimates for the United States, using 1979 data. They found that, on average, families with incomes in the lower half of the income distribution received more in benefits than they paid in taxes to the three levels of government combined while those in the upper half paid more in taxes than they received in benefits. The taxpayer "break-even point" was about $25,000.[4] It bears repeating that the redistributive effect of government budgets results not only from deliberate income transfers and the provision of "poverty-connected" services but also from the fact that the poor receive more in general service benefits than they pay for in taxes.

Economists usually argue that the function of redistributing income, like that of stabilization, should be left to the federal government.[5] They believe that the capacity of the lesser jurisdictions to redistribute income among their citizens is limited severely by the mobility of both taxpayers and expenditure beneficiaries. A city that taxes the rich to provide benefits for the poor to a greater extent than other cities do will tend to attract the poor and repel the rich. (See discussion in Chapter 15.) This response makes redistribution at the local level a self-defeating process. Nevertheless, as we have seen, local communities do engage in a degree of income distribution. Partly they can get away with it because not all resources are highly mobile. Partly they do not get away with it because mobile resources do often move when local fiscal pressure becomes sufficiently heavy. The self-defeating nature of locally financed income redistribution is among the strongest arguments for reexamining the assignment of fiscal responsibilities within our multilevel system of government. This difficult issue will be examined in greater detail in Chapter 15 when we analyze the problem of geographic disparities between needs and resources.

Providing Public Goods and Services

Having eliminated both stabilization and redistribution, we are left with allocation—the provision of public goods and services—as the only budgetary function that can appropriately be carried out by local government. Allocation activities are, in fact, the dominant concern of local government. Local citizens want and are willing to pay for services such as parks, sanitation, and

4. Richard A. Musgrave and Peggy B. Musgrave, *Public Finance in Theory and Practice,* 4th ed. (New York: McGraw-Hill, 1984), table 12-4.

5. For a reaffirmation of this view, see Helen F. Ladd and Fred C. Doolittle, "Which Level of Government Should Assist the Poor?" *National Tax Journal,* September 1982, pp. 323–336.

police protection. One of the principal objectives of the local public sector is to provide such services, in accordance with citizen preferences, just as the private sector provides bread and shoes and washing machines in accordance with consumer preferences.

Stimulated by the work of Samuelson, Buchanan, and Musgrave,[6] economists have devoted much thought since the 1950s to the interrelated problems of finding an optimum division of functions between the public and private sectors and then satisfying the demand for the goods and services that are properly a public-sector responsibility. One of the contributions of modern public expenditure theory has been the definition of a class of pure public goods or, as they are sometimes called, collective or joint-consumption goods. These goods and services have one or both of the following characteristics. First, they are subject to joint consumption, meaning that each consumer can enjoy such a good without diminishing the amount available to others. Examples would be national defense, the system of law and justice, public health programs, air pollution control, city planning, or police and fire services. By contrast, ordinary consumer goods are *not* subject to joint consumption: if Jones eats the loaf of bread it cannot also be consumed by Smith. Second, public goods are generally *not* subject to the exclusion process, meaning that it is not feasible to prevent anyone from consuming such a good once it is produced, whether or not he or she wishes to pay for it. Since most joint-consumption goods also have the characteristic of nonexcludability, the same examples will again serve: how can any consumer be prevented from obtaining the benefit of a defense program or of local police or public health services once they exist?

An important consequence of nonexcludability is this: if nonpurchasers cannot be prevented from benefiting, then the good cannot be sold in a market, and privately financed production is impossible. Public or joint-consumption goods thus form a core of activities for which financial responsibility *must* be assigned to the public sector. (Note that production may remain in private hands, as in the case of defense goods made under contract to the federal government or school buildings constructed by private contractors for the local school district.)

A very large question remains, however. How can society determine the optimum quantity of each public good to produce? The private sector makes use of prices to achieve an allocation of output that accords with consumer preferences. If perfect competition prevails in all markets and there are no externalities, price will equal marginal cost for every good, and the resulting allocation of resources in the market sector will be optimal. Samuelson, in his classic article "The Pure Theory of Public Expenditure," showed that a dif-

6. In addition to Musgrave's *The Theory of Public Finance*, see Paul E. Samuelson, "The Pure Theory of Public Expenditure," *Review of Economics and Statistics*, November 1954, pp. 386–389, and "Diagrammatic Exposition of a Theory of Public Expenditure," *Review of Economics and Statistics*, November 1955, pp. 350–356; and James M. Buchanan, *The Demand and Supply of Public Goods* (Chicago: Rand McNally, 1968).

ferent pricing rule would be optimal for goods subject to joint consumption. This optimal solution is unattainable, however. Price systems cannot operate in the absence of excludability. Citizens will not voluntarily pay a price for defense services when they know they cannot be prevented from benefiting even if the do not pay. (This is often referred to as the "free-rider" problem.) To finance public goods we are therefore compelled to rely upon taxes levied in a political process. One must hope that a democratic voting procedure somehow succeeds in registering citizen preferences for public goods in the same way the market does for private ones.[7]

To be sure, the public sector in the United States also supplies many goods and services that do not have the character of pure collective goods, for example, education, solid waste disposal, and hospital services. (Some of these will be analyzed further.) In many such cases the public sector could make use of prices, in the form of user charges, more often than it has done to produce services in the quantities that its citizens want.[8] Yet even after all such opportunities have been exhausted, the bulk of public activity would still have to be paid for by taxes. It is therefore important to have an assignment of functions to the various levels of government that facilitates the most rational possible budgetary decision making at each level.

An Optimum Division of Responsibility: The Principle of Fiscal Equivalence

Let us assume initially that all the services provided by the public sector are true joint-consumption goods and that each such good benefits a definable group of citizens who make up the entire population living within a perimeter that constitutes the "boundary" of that good. We want to know what division of responsibility for such goods among the levels of government will most efficiently satisfy consumer preferences. Mancur Olson's "principle of fiscal equivalence" gives us a good first approximation of the answer.[9] According to this principle, the provision of collective goods will be most efficient when the boundary of each collective good coincides with that of the government providing it. This proposition is intuitively plausible. Public goods must be provided through a budgetary rather than a market process. Supply is most likely to be optimal if the citizens who vote (or whose representatives vote) for provision are also those who will benefit. Consider two contrary cases. If the benefits of the collective good spill out beyond the boundaries of the providing government, we have the classic case of external

---

7. Roland McKean explains how the political system responds to preferences in "The Unseen Hand in Government," *American Economic Review*, June 1965, pp. 496–505.

8. See the papers in Selma J. Mushkin, ed., *Public Prices for Public Products* (Washington, D.C.: Urban Institute, 1972).

9. Mancur Olson, "The Principle of 'Fiscal Equivalence': The Division of Responsibilities among Different Levels of Government," *American Economic Review*, May 1969, pp. 479–487.

benefits. Olson adopts the standard argument that too little of the good will then be provided. (See the discussion of externalities in Chapter 15.) In the opposite case, when the boundaries of the government reach farther than those of the collective good, Olson argues that provision is again likely to be suboptimal, though he recognizes possible exceptions. In any event, it is clear that when governmental boundaries do not coincide with public good boundaries "there are systematic forces which work against allocative efficiency."[10]

As Olson points out, the analysis yields a fundamental economic argument for a federal system. "Only if there are several levels of government and a large number of governments," Olson writes, "can immense disparities between the boundaries of jurisdictions and the boundaries of collective goods be avoided."[11] A three-tiered structure—federal, state, local—can radically reduce such disparities, thus contributing greatly to the achievement of allocative efficiency. Under a federal system each public good can be assigned to the level of government that has the most nearly equivalent boundaries. To a large extent this occurs in the United States. National defense is in the hands of the federal government, because the benefits of a defense system are necessarily nationwide in scope. Fire and police services are local responsibilities because the benefits of such services are largely confined to the locality where they are produced. With local control, each town is free to choose the level of service its citizens want and are willing to pay for.

Complex Cases and Joint Responsibility

Most allocational activities in the public sector do not have the character of pure public goods. Consequently, other criteria in addition to fiscal equivalence must be brought to bear in deciding what level of government ought, ideally, to carry them out. When these more complex cases have been examined, the best solution often appears to be some sharing of responsibility either with the private sector or between levels of government. Again, it is a virtue of the federal system, in contrast with a fully centralized one, that it can accommodate intergovernmental sharing when that is desirable. In a chapter devoted primarily to the metropolitan public sector it is not feasible to examine the ideal arrangement for carrying out every allocative function. However, it is instructive to review two general cases in which shared responsibility may be indicated.

Consider first the case of merit goods. As explained in Chapter 12, a merit good is something that (the majority decides) is better for people than they realize. Society makes a judgment that, if left to themselves, consumers will buy less of such a good than would maximize their well-being within the constraint of their income. The government intervenes with a subsidy to reduce the price of the merit good in order to encourage greater consumption.

10. Ibid., p. 483.
11. Ibid. Also see Olson's elaboration of these ideas in "Toward a More General Theory of Governmental Structure," *American Economic Review*, May 1986, pp. 120–125.

This is an argument, though not the only one, that is often used to justify housing subsidies. The question is, Who should finance the subsidy? Since the merit good argument relates mainly to the consumption habits of those with low or moderately low incomes, programs justified by it are likely to be redistributive from the relatively rich to the relatively poor, and since redistribution is not an appropriate function for local governments, or perhaps even for states, it follows that subsidies to encourage the consumption of merit goods should be financed by the federal government. Expenditure for housing would thus be a private function subsidized by the federal but not the state or local governments. The same conclusion applies in the case of health service subsidies or any others that are justified by the merit good argument.

Next consider the case of a service that combines characteristics of the pure public good with those of an ordinary private good. Education is probably the most important example. It is a private good insofar as a benefit accrues directly to the person being educated, and exclusion is perfectly feasible. Yet over and above that, each individual's education also provides an external benefit that accrues to society as a whole. The nature of that externality can be explained as follows. In a democratic society we necessarily place great value on the existence of educated fellow voters. Moreover, we want the citizenry to be well educated, not only in our own town but in all localities, since those who have been poorly educated elsewhere may become a burden locally through migration or may affect events that have nationwide ramifications. The external part of the benefit of education has the character of a pure public good: each person benefits by it without diminishing the benefit available to others, nor can anyone be excluded from benefiting. Primary and secondary education have long been free, tax-supported services in the United States, not because exclusion and the collection of fees would be difficult but because the public-good aspect of schooling made it seem imperative that the whole population be sufficiently educated. Although this analysis suggests a valid national interest in the matter, public schools began and long continued as a strictly local enterprise. State school aid developed gradually in this century and is now substantial. Large-scale federal aid began with the passage of the Elementary and Secondary Education Act of 1965. Thus all three levels of government now support this function. Whether the present division among them is satisfactory, however, remains an open question to which we return in Chapter 15.

LOCAL GOVERNMENT EXPENDITURES

The functional composition of local government general expenditures is shown in Table 14.1.[12] The totals shown include spending financed by aid

12. General expenditure and general revenue are defined as all expenditure and all revenue except those of insurance trust funds and of government-owned utilities and liquor stores.

TABLE 14.1
Direct General Expenditure of Local Governments by Function, Fiscal 1983–1984

	BILLIONS OF DOLLARS	PERCENTAGE DISTRIBUTION
Total direct general expenditure[a]	302.0	100.0
Education	127.5	42.2
Health and hospitals	24.9	8.2
Police protection	16.5	5.5
Highways	16.3	5.4
Public welfare	15.6	5.2
Interest	15.6	5.2
Sewerage	11.3	3.7
General control	8.5	2.8
Housing and urban renewal	8.5	2.8
Fire protection	8.2	2.7
Parks and recreation	7.0	2.3
Financial administration	5.1	1.7
Sanitation	4.7	1.6
Other	32.3	10.7

[a]Direct general expenditure includes all outlays except payments to other levels of government and expenditures by government enterprises including public utilities, liquor stores, and insurance trust funds.
Source: U.S. Bureau of the Census, *Governmental Finances in 1983–84*, GF 84, no. 5, table 11.

from the federal and state governments. Such aid amounted to over $127 billion in 1983–1984, enough to pay for about 42 percent of expenditures. Since some intergovernmental aid is not restricted to specific functions, it is not usually possible to calculate exactly the portion of a particular function that is aid-supported. Thus while Table 14.1 accurately depicts the size of programs and functions over which local governments have *administrative* control, it cannot be used as an indicator of *fiscal* responsibility.

As column 2 of the table shows, education is by far the leading activity of local governments. Local schools account for 40 percent of their total outlays. Higher education adds 2.5 percent more. In this case, specific aid figures are available: in 1982–1983, 7 percent of the revenue needed to support local schools was contributed by the federal government and 48 percent by the states.[13] Localities thus paid a little less than half the total cost.

The next largest and currently the fastest-growing function is health and hospitals (8.2 percent). This, together with public welfare (5.2 percent) and housing and urban renewal (2.8 percent), makes up a group of "poverty-connected" services that are either wholly or partly redistributive in intent. Fortunately, federal and state aid do cover a large proportion of the costs shown here.

13. Tax Foundation, Inc., *Facts and Figures on Government Finance*, 1985.

A third group of activities, sometimes called "common municipal functions," comprises services performed by almost every general-purpose local government. A list would include police, fire, and sanitation services, sewerage, highways, parks and recreation, financial administration, and general control. These functions account for 26 percent of the outlays in Table 14.1. Here, with the recent exception of sewerage, the relative contribution of intergovernmental aid is undoubtedly lower than it is for education or the poverty-connected services. Accordingly, the common functions make a greater relative claim on local governments' resources than is suggested by the percentage distribution in the table. In that sense they remain the core responsibilities of local government. While most of these services, like police and fire protection, are in the public sector because they are true collective goods, not subject to exclusion, a few like solid waste disposal could be (and in many places are) performed by the private sector for a fee. As we shall see in the next chapter, a possible direction for reform is to pare away those functions in which the public sector enjoys no natural economic advantage.

Growth of Local Spending

The striking growth of the public sector in the United States is by now one of the familiar facts of twentieth-century history. Changes in the relative size of the public sector over time are best gauged by comparing public ex-

TABLE 14.2
Growth of Local Expenditures and of Gross National Product

FISCAL YEAR	GROSS NATIONAL PRODUCT[a] (BILLIONS OF DOLLARS)	LOCAL EXPENDITURE[b] (BILLIONS OF DOLLARS)	LOCAL EXPENDITURE AS A PERCENT OF GNP
1955–1956	411.8	24.4	5.9
1965–1966	725.5	53.7	7.4
1975–1976	1,642.7	159.7	9.7
1978–1979	2,299.3	201.5	8.8
1983–1984	3,494.1	302.2	8.6
	COMPOUND ANNUAL RATE OF GROWTH (%)		
1956 to 1966	5.8	8.2	
1966 to 1976	8.5	11.5	
1976 to 1979	11.9	8.1	
1979 to 1984	8.7	8.4	

[a]Gross national product is for fiscal years.
[b]As defined in Table 14.1.
Sources: Gross national product: U.S. Department of Commerce, *Business Conditions Digest,* various years; local expenditure: U.S. Bureau of the Census, *1977 Census of Governments,* vol. 6, no. 4, table 6, and *Governmental Finances in 1977–78,* table 10 and 1983–84, table 11.

penditures with GNP. Table 14.2 shows that local expenditures rose from less than 6 percent of GNP in fiscal year 1955–1956 to 7 percent ten years later and to 9.7 percent at their peak in 1975–1976. The severe fiscal crisis in New York City in 1975 and the subsequent nationwide movement to limit tax and expenditure growth (to be discussed later in this chapter) brought a reversal of the trend during the late 1970s. By 1983–1984 local expenditures had fallen to 8.6 percent of GNP. The mood of fiscal restraint that the American electorate has continued to display during the 1980s makes it unlikely that relative growth of the local public sector will resume in the near future. Nevertheless, it is important to investigate the causes of past growth to understand how we arrived at our present position and because some of the forces making for past growth will continue to press upon us whether we respond to them or not.

The reasons for local expenditure growth are many and complex. For analytical purposes public expenditures may be regarded as the product of two factors: the number of units of service provided and the average cost of providing a single unit. Increases in both factors have contributed to the growth of total local expenditure. Consider first the growth in quantity of services provided.

Urbanization and the Demand for Public Service

In a highly urbanized society it becomes necessary for government to provide some services such as sewage disposal, water supply, and recreation facilities that in a rural or village society individuals often provide for themselves. In addition, urban society, because of its physical density and high level of socioeconomic interdependence, intensifies the need for such functions as police and fire protection, public health services, and public transportation. It is convenient to think of individual citizens as having demands for public service just as they have demands for such private goods as bread and shoes. Using the ordinary terminology of economic analysis we can then say that we would expect the per capita demand for units of local government service to increase simply as a result of the urbanization process itself.

Yet it seems likely that quite apart from urbanization, rising living standards have also contributed to the relative growth in demand for public services. When living standards were low, as in the nineteenth century, people spent most of their incomes meeting the intense daily need for ordinary private goods such as food, clothing, and shelter. They held government spending to a bare minimum. As living standards rose, however, they chose to spend an increasing proportion of their income on the whole range of local government services, many of which were complementary to private spending. The increase can be viewed as a demand partly for a greater quantity of existing services, partly for better quality, and partly for the introduction of entirely new government functions. In formal terms this amounts to arguing that the income elasticity of demand for government services—defined as the percentage change in demand for government services divided by the percentage change in income—has probably been greater than one.

Rising Costs per Unit of Service

An increase in the per capita quantity of public services supplied undoubtedly accounts for much of the relative growth in local public expenditures during the twentieth century. However, in recent years the rising average cost of supplying each unit of service has also been a significant factor. Unit costs have been rising in the local public sector because public employees' wages and fringe benefits have gone up rapidly in recent years while output per employee has apparently risen little, if at all. Table 14.3 shows earnings in the municipal and private sectors, together with the consumer price index, at four dates. From 1965 to 1974 monthly earnings of city employees rose much faster than those of the average worker in manufacturing and also far outstripped the increase in the cost of living. During this period municipal-sector earnings, which had long lagged behind, caught up with those in the private sector and in the largest cities, such as the four shown in the table, far surpassed them. After 1974 the increase in municipal earnings moderated. City governments were forced to become more tightfisted both by the desire to avoid outright fiscal crisis and by the increasingly conservative fiscal attitudes of the electorate. From 1974 through 1979 municipal earnings rose less than earnings in manufacturing and less than the cost of living. In the early 1980s, however, self-restraint apparently eased once more. As Table 14.3 indicates, from 1979 through 1986 municipal wage increases again surpassed both the rate of inflation and the rise in manufacturing earnings. The Bureau of Labor Statistics' recently developed employment cost index for state and local government workers confirms the latter point.[14]

As any employer knows, the total cost of compensation includes not only wages but also fringe benefits such as pensions, health plans, paid holidays, and the like. A comparative study of fringe benefits in U.S. municipalities and in private industry shows that in 1979 benefits for police and fire personnel were considerably higher than the private sector average, while those for other municipal workers matched the level in private industry.[15]

City officials have been particularly inclined to offer generous retirement benefits to municipal workers because financial arrangements allow them to take current credit for generosity while avoiding some of its cost by not funding accruing obligations in full. Part of the cost of today's promises can thus be passed forward to future administrations. Although public aware-

---

14. *Monthly Labor Review*, May 1982, pp. 9–14, and August 1984, pp. 82–84.
15. See Edward H. Friend and Lorraine A. Lufkin, *Fifth National Survey of Employee Benefits for Full-Time Personnel of U.S. Municipalities* (Washington, D.C.: Labor-Management Relations Service of the United States Conference of Mayors, 1982), pp. 3–8.

TABLE 14.3
Comparison of Monthly Earnings in Municipal Employment and in Manufacturing

| | AVERAGE MONTHLY EARNINGS[a] ($) | | | | INCREASE (%) | | |
	1965	1974	1979	1985	1965–1974	1974–1979	1979–1985
Municipal wages, all cities	480	898	1,219	1,977	87.1	35.7	62.2
Cities of 50,000 or more	527[b]	964[b]	1,315	2,091	82.9	36.4	59.0
New York City	585	1,064	1,313	2,329	81.9	23.4	77.4
Chicago	588	1,107	1,408	2,039[c]	88.3	27.2	44.8[c]
Los Angeles	712	1,261	1,814	2,798	77.1	43.9	54.2
Philadelphia	479	1,064	1,577	2,213	122.1	48.2	40.3
Average monthly earnings in U.S. manufacturing	547	904	1,355	2,033	65.2	49.9	50.0
Consumer price index (1967 = 100)	94.5	147.7	217.4	322.2	56.3	47.2	48.2

[a]All full-time municipal workers, excluding education.
[b]Common municipal functions, rather than all noneducational functions.
[c]1982 rather than 1984.
Sources: Earnings in municipal employment: U.S. Bureau of the Census, *City Employment,* various years; earnings in manufacturing: U.S. Department of Commerce, *Survey of Current Business,* National Income issue (July), various years; consumer price index: *Economic Report of the President,* January 1986.

393

ness and state oversight may now have curbed this practice, the bills for past generosity are contractural obligations that will continue to mount rapidly in the future.[16]

The Effect of Productivity Lag

The impact of compensation expense on the cost of production is measured by unit labor cost, which is defined as compensation per labor hour divided by output per labor hour. For example, if a baker is paid $8 an hour and she produces sixteen loaves of bread per hour, the unit labor cost of each loaf is 50 cents. Increased output per worker allows wages to be increased without increasing unit labor cost: if the baker's output per hour rises 25 percent (to twenty loaves), wages can also be increased 25 percent (to $10 an hour) without increasing unit labor costs at all ($10 ÷ 20 loaves = 50 cents per loaf). But if output per labor hour remains constant, unit labor cost rises proportionately with wages.

How does this analysis help to explain the relative growth of local public expenditures? Except perhaps during the fiscal crisis of the 1970s, compensation costs have been rising faster in the local public sector than in private industry. Output per employee, on the other hand, is evidently rising faster in the latter. The result is that unit labor costs have probably gone up much faster in the public than in the private sector. This relative rise in the unit labor cost of public services may help to explain why local public expenditures have increased so much faster than the aggregate of public and private expenditures, as measured by GNP. To complete the argument, however, we must take account of demand as well as cost or supply conditions.

The Effect of Inelastic Demand

How a rise in the unit cost (or price) of a local public service will affect the amount spent on it depends entirely on the price elasticity of the public's demand. If demand is *in*elastic (elasticity < 1), the percentage decline in quantity is *less* than the percentage increase in unit cost, and expenditure on the service in question increases. On the other hand, if demand is elastic (elasticity > 1), quantity declines relatively *more* than price increases, and expenditure falls. The outcome thus hinges on the value of the elasticity of demand. What, in fact, is that likely to be?

Elasticity of demand depends on the availability of substitutes. If close substitutes are available, demand will be elastic: as price rises, consumers switch to the substitutes. If close substitutes are not available, demand will be inelastic: as price rises, consumers may to some extent "do without," but they

---

16. See Roy Bahl, Bernard Jump, Jr., and Larry Schroeder, "The Outlook for City Fiscal Performance in Declining Regions," in Roy Bahl, ed., *The Fiscal Outlook for Cities* (Syracuse, N.Y.: Syracuse University Press, 1978), p. 27 and table 15, p. 28.

cannot obtain nearly equivalent benefits by purchasing something else. If an activity is in the public sector because it is a true collective-consumption good with the property of nonexcludability, we know that there cannot be a commercially marketed substitute. The demand for the public good is therefore likely to be highly price-inelastic. In such cases, when the unit cost of output rises, total expenditure is certain to increase.

Admittedly, broad statements about cost per unit of output in the local public sector are difficult to substantiate because in many cases we lack the measures of physical output needed to carry out precise unit cost calculations. Nevertheless, most analysts would agree with the conclusion reached by Bradford, Malt, and Oates, after a careful study of the available data, that "rising unit costs have been a major . . . source of recent increases in local public budgets."[17]

Local government activity is much more labor-intensive than is the output of the federal and state governments. Consequently, localities feel much more budgetary pressure when civil service wages rise than do the higher levels of government. Wage pressure in recent years has been greatly increased by the advent of municipal civil service unions. Wage demands by these unions are difficult to resist for two reasons. First, the unions typically control output of public services for which there are no ready substitutes and which cannot be stockpiled by consumers in anticipation of strikes. Second, they represent sizable blocs of local voters whom mayors are not eager to antagonize by taking a hard line against wage increases.

Yet it is important to remember that the cost pressure on local governments is the result not just of wage increases but of wage increases combined with productivity lag. If municipal wages do no more than keep up with wages in private firms while output per worker-hour fails to increase as fast in municipal employment, unit costs will continue to rise faster in the public than in the private sector.[18] Unfortunately, there is no easy solution to this problem. The very nature of public services such as education, the police, or hospitals and health care makes it difficult to economize on the use of labor. Realistically, therefore, we must expect costs of local public services to continue to increase.

The Movement to Limit Spending and Taxing

We have seen in Table 14.2 that local government expenditures in the United States for many years grew faster than the economy as a whole, reaching a peak of 9.7 percent of GNP in 1975–1976. Since then the proportion has fallen slightly. The change in public attitudes toward spending and taxing—

17. D. F. Bradford, R. A. Malt, and W. E. Oates, "The Rising Cost of Local Public Services: Some Evidence and Reflections," *National Tax Journal,* June 1969, p. 201.
18. See William J. Baumol, "Macroeconomics of Unbalanced Growth: The Anatomy of Urban Crisis," *American Economic Review,* June 1967, pp. 415–426.

sometimes called the "taxpayers' revolt"—that became evident in the mid-1970s probably means that growth relative to GNP will not resume in the near future.

The fiscal limitation movement captured headline attention when California voters in June 1978 overwhelmingly approved an amendment to the state constitution known as Proposition 13. By its provisions, property tax payments to local governments were cut back 57 percent, future increases in property tax revenue were severely constrained, a two-thirds vote of qualified electors was required to adopt new local taxes or increase rates of existing nonproperty levies, and a two-thirds vote in each house of the state legislature was required to increase state tax rates. California thus combined a massive local tax cut with restraint of future tax-rate increases at both the state and local levels.

Although passage of Proposition 13 dramatized an apparent change in the public's attitude toward government, its provisions are not typical of other recently enacted fiscal limitations. These have taken a variety of forms.[19] Unlike Proposition 13, most of them involve limiting future growth rather than cutting back current magnitudes. Consider first the restraints placed on local governments. By October 1985, thirty-one states had adopted specific limits on local property tax *rates*. Twenty-one had enacted limits on the *revenue* that a local jurisdiction can raise from the property tax, and six had adopted limits on revenue to be collected from all local taxes in the aggregate. Both kinds of limitation typically operate by restricting the allowable annual increase in revenue. In addition, six states enacted analogous limits on local general expenditures. These should be regarded as an alternative to general revenue limitations, since only one state adopted both.

From 1977 through October 1985, eighteen states adopted limitations on their own fiscal activity. Most of these (unlike limits applied to localities) affect expenditures rather than revenues. Thirteen states tied the growth of expenditure or revenue to the growth rate of state personal income. Three others limited revenue or expenditure growth to the combined rates of population increase plus inflation, and two set specific ceilings on the annual rate of increase of general fund appropriations. In most but not all cases, states that limited their own activity also enacted limits of some sort on localities.

Many of its supporters believe that tax and expenditure limitation is the only way to ensure that a democratic political system will not result in "overspending." Public officials, they argue, accede too readily to the pressure of

19. See Advisory Commission on Intergovernmental Relations, *Significant Features of Fiscal Federalism, 1985–1986 Edition* (Washington, D.C.: U.S. Government Printing Office, February 1986), tables 90–92; and Anthony H. Pascal et al., *Fiscal Containment of Local and State Government*, doc. no. R–2494–FF/RC (Santa Monica, Calif.: Rand Corp., September 1979). A history of the events leading up to the passage of Proposition 13 is contained in Frank Levy, "On Understanding Proposition 13," *Public Interest*, Summer 1979, pp. 66–89. A wide-ranging set of papers on fiscal limitation is presented in "Proceedings of a Conference on Tax and Expenditure Limitations," *National Tax Journal* suppl., June 1979.

concentrated interest groups who favor expanding particular programs at the expense of the general taxpayer. Supporters of fiscal restraints are convinced that only a binding legal limit on taxing or spending can prevent such behavior.[20]

Opinion surveys in all parts of the country, however, indicate that the "taxpayers' revolt" reflects not only dissatisfaction with rising tax payments but also a strong conviction among voters that government is wasteful and inefficient. Many of those questioned express a willingness to forgo tax relief if waste can be eliminated.[21] Thus a vote for legal restraints can be interpreted as a way of trying to compel local government to operate more efficiently.[22] (We return to the issue of local government productivity at the end of Chapter 15.)

Like much other social legislation, fiscal restraint is likely to have unintended consequences at least as important as its intended results. In California, Proposition 13 immediately reduced local revenue by $7 billion. The amendment was adopted in the knowledge that a huge state surplus could be used to offset much of that loss, and so it was. The state provided $4.1 billion of emergency aid to localities. As the state "bailout" was institutionalized, Californians found that a major transfer of fiscal responsibility from local to state government had taken place. Liberals who had long sought such a transfer, in order to reduce inequalities in spending between rich and poor municipalities and school districts, found their program suddenly adopted as the result of a victory by their long-time opponents. Conservatives, who generally support tax limitation out of a preference for "less government," may eventually regret the loss of local autonomy that will probably result as financial responsibility shifts toward the state capital.[23]

Finally, the combined long-run effect of fiscal limitation and productivity lag should not be overlooked. If local spending is allowed to rise only as fast as GNP, while the unit cost of local public services is pushed upward by productivity lag, the value of local government output in real terms will be dropping relative to GNP rather than keeping pace with economic growth.

Recent changes in federal policy reinforce the effects of state and local tax and expenditure limitations. In its drive to cut domestic spending, the Reagan administration reduced the real level of aid both to cities and states. Since states are the principal source of intergovernmental assistance to cities (see Table 14.4), the combined effect of these reductions adds greatly to the pressure to hold down spending at the local level. Reductions in the absolute

---

20. See Barry N. Siegel, *Thoughts on the Tax Revolt* (Los Angeles: International Institute for Economic Research, 1979), pp. 4–5.
    21. Pascal et al., pp. 3–5.
    22. Siegel, pp. 12–13; and Helen F. Ladd and Julie Boatwright Wilson, "Why Voters Support Tax Limitations: Evidence from Massachusetts' Proposition 2½," *National Tax Journal*, June 1982, pp. 137–140.
    23. Levy, p. 88.

TABLE 14.4
Local Government Revenues by Source (fiscal years)

	1951–1952 (MILLIONS OF DOLLARS)	1983–1984 (MILLIONS OF DOLLARS)	DISTRIBUTION BY SOURCE			
			1951–1952		1983–1984	
			Total General Revenue (%)	*Tax Revenue (%)*	*Total General Revenue (%)*	*Tax Revenue (%)*
Total general revenue[a]	16,952	323,236	100.0	—	100.0	—
Tax revenue	9,466	123,399	55.8	100.0	38.2	100.0
Property tax	8,282	92,595	48.9	87.5	28.6	75.0
Sales and gross receipts taxes	627	18,296	3.7	6.6	5.1	14.8
Income taxes	93	7,215	0.6	1.0	2.0	5.8
Licenses and other taxes	465	5,293	2.7	4.9	1.6	4.3
Charges and miscellaneous general revenue	2,205	73,105	13.0	—	22.6	—
Intergovernmental revenue	5,281	126,732	31.2	—	39.2	—
From federal government	237	20,912	1.4	—	6.5	—
From state governments	5,044	105,820	29.8	—	32.7	—

[a]General revenue includes all receipts except those of government enterprises including public utilities, liquor stores, and insurance trust funds.
Sources: U.S. Bureau of the Census, *Governmental Finances in 1983–84,* table 4, and *1977 Census of Governments,* vol. 6, no. 4, table 6.

amount of local spending are not to be expected, given our expanding population and economy, but it does seem likely that local spending will not be permitted to grow faster than GNP. (See further discussion of intergovernmental assistance in Chapter 15.)

LOCAL GOVERNMENT REVENUE

The composition and growth of local government general revenue are displayed in Tables 14.4 and 14.5. Since local governments are normally required by state law to balance their current operating budgets, the rapid expenditure growth shown in Table 14.2 is matched by the steep rise in revenues indicated in Table 14.5. In 1952 local general revenue amounted to only 5.0 percent of gross national product. By 1984 it had increased to 9.3 percent.

The three major revenue categories of local government are taxes, aid from the state and federal governments, and charges plus miscellaneous general revenue. The property tax has always been by far the most important local levy. In 1983–1984 it accounted for 75 percent of tax revenues. However, Table 14.4 shows that its share is slowly declining while sales and income taxes gradually assume greater importance.

The enormous increase in local government expenditures since the early 1950s has been financed by growth in all three major revenue categories. They did not all grow equally fast, however, so the composition of revenue changed over time. Especially significant is the growing importance of federal and state aid. In 1952 it accounted for only 31 percent of general revenue, compared with 56 percent derived from local taxes. By 1984 aid was the source of 39 percent of local revenue, while taxes supplied only 38 percent. In fact, intergovernmental aid had accounted for a peak of almost 45 percent of local general revenue in 1979, before fiscal cutbacks at the state and federal levels reduced its rate of growth. The various forms of intergovernmental aid will be analyzed in Chapter 15. At this point we take a closer look at the relationship between local tax revenues and economic growth, as measured by GNP.

Tax Revenue and Economic Growth:
The Concept of Tax Base Elasticity

Each local tax has its own tax base, the financial aggregate to which the tax rate is applied. In the case of the property tax, the base is the assessed value of taxable local property. For a retail sales tax, the base is the annual value of taxable retail sales. The yield of any tax is the product of the base times the rate.

To facilitate analysis of the growth of local tax revenue, it is useful to define a GNP elasticity for each local tax. This measure, E_{LT}, indicates the rela-

TABLE 14.5
Growth of Local Government Revenues and of Gross National Product

FISCAL YEAR	GROSS NATIONAL PRODUCT[a] (BILLIONS OF DOLLARS)	TAX REVENUE (BILLIONS OF DOLLARS)	OTHER GENERAL REVENUE[b] (BILLIONS OF DOLLARS)	INTERGOVERNMENTAL REVENUE[c] (BILLIONS OF DOLLARS)	TAX REVENUE AS PERCENTAGE OF GNP
1951–1952	339.6	9.5	2.2	5.3	2.8
1961–1962	546.9	21.0	5.7	11.6	3.8
1971–1972	1,126.6	49.7	15.8	39.7	4.4
1978–1979	2,299.3	80.6	36.6	94.8	3.5
1983–1984	3,494.1	123.4	73.1	126.7	3.5
COMPOUND ANNUAL RATE OF GROWTH (%)					
1952 to 1962	4.9	8.3	10.0	8.2	
1962 to 1972	7.5	9.0	10.7	13.1	
1972 to 1979	10.7	7.1	12.7	13.2	
1979 to 1984	8.7	8.9	14.8	6.0	

[a]Gross national product is for fiscal years.
[b]Includes a variety of user charges and miscellaneous revenue.
[c]Includes all grants, shared taxes, and other payments from federal and state governments.
Sources: Gross national product: U.S. Department of Commerce, *Business Conditions Digest*, various years; local revenues: U.S. Bureau of the Census, *Governmental Finances in 1978–79*, and *1983–84*, table 4; and *1977 Census of Governments*, vol. 6, no. 4, table 6.

tionship between changes in the revenue from a tax and changes in GNP, on the assumption that tax *rates* and the definition of the base are held constant. Thus

$$E_{LT} = \frac{\text{percentage change in local tax revenue}}{\text{percentage change in GNP}}$$

The reason revenue from a particular tax changes when GNP changes, even though tax rates and definitions are held constant, is that economic growth usually causes growth in the tax base. The E_{LT} can be thought of as a measure of tax base elasticity as well as a measure of revenue elasticity with rates held constant. If a tax base has an elasticity greater than one, then as GNP increases, either through real growth or because of inflation, the revenue from that tax will increase faster than GNP, even if tax rates do not rise. On the other hand, if tax base elasticity is less than one, revenue will increase less rapidly than GNP when tax rates are held constant. Tax rates will have to be increased more or less regularly if revenue is to keep pace with the growth of GNP.

The value of E_{LT} for any tax is difficult to calculate because the objective is to measure changes over time not in tax revenue, which are easily observable, but rather in the size of the tax base, which may not be. Since the property tax accounts for three-quarters of local tax revenue, its elasticity obviously dominates the outcome for the local system as a whole. Unfortunately, estimates of its elasticity are particularly difficult to work out. First of all, the tax base of interest to the economist is the full market value of taxable property. The legal base for the property tax, however, is the assessed value of local property. This is intended to reflect market value, but, whatever the law may require, assessors do not usually assess property at its full market worth. In fact, the relationship between assessed value and market value varies widely between places and over time. A second difficulty arises because there is reason to believe that the relation between changes in the market value of property and changes in a measure of aggregate income, such as GNP, is by no means constant.

Estimates of the GNP elasticity of the property tax in the 1960s varied from a low of .8 to a high of 1.3, with the majority of estimates falling between .8 and 1.0.[24] This supported the conventional wisdom that the tax was inelastic: its yield would grow less rapidly than GNP if tax rates remained constant.

Sales and gross receipts taxes rank second in importance among local levies, accounting for 15 percent of tax revenues. The majority of statistical estimates put the GNP elasticity of this group at about 1.0.[25] The local in-

24. See estimates compiled from a variety of sources by the Advisory Commission on Intergovernmental Relations in Report M–74, *State-Local Finances: Significant Features and Suggested Legislation, 1972 Edition*, table 134, p. 301; and discussion in Dick Netzer, *Economics of the Property Tax* (Washington, D.C.: Brookings Institution, 1966), pp. 184–190.

25. Advisory Commission, 1972, table 134, p. 301.

come tax probably has an elasticity somewhat above unity but accounts for only 6 percent of tax receipts. License fees and minor taxes, which account for the remaining 4 percent of local tax revenue, probably have an elasticity well below unity.

Putting these revenue sources together, we could fairly estimate that the local tax system as a whole had a GNP elasticity of about 1.0 in the twenty years from 1952 to 1972. Using this elasticity figure, we can then estimate the extent to which changes in tax rates apparently contributed to the growth of local revenues during that period. If the system as a whole had an elasticity of 1.0, tax rates had remained constant, and no new taxes had been adopted by local governments, local tax revenues would have increased at the same rate as GNP between 1952 and 1972. The latter increased by 232 percent. If local tax revenues had increased by the same percentage, they would have amounted to $31.4 billion in 1972. In fact, they rose to $49.7 billion. This implies rate increases (plus new taxes adopted) of 58 percent, since $49.7 ÷ $31.4 = 1.58.

There is some direct evidence on property tax rates to support this estimate. Since every locality levies property taxes at a rate of its own choosing and since the ratio of assessed value to market value also varies from place to place, it is difficult to calculate a meaningful national average rate. However, a compilation of data by the Advisory Commission on Intergovernmental Relations shows that the nationwide average rate of tax, adjusted to full market value, on single-family homes with FHA-insured mortgages rose from 1.34 percent in 1958 to 1.98 percent in 1971. (See Table 14.7.) That amounts to a 48 percent increase and is roughly consistent with the 58 percent increase in *all* tax rates estimated above for a somewhat longer period.

Local tax rates would surely have risen even faster had it not been for the very rapid increase in aid from the state and federal governments indicated in Tables 14.4 and 14.5. This increase was in turn made possible by the fact that the tax systems of those governments have higher GNP elasticities than does the local tax system.

Because Washington relies so heavily on a progressive income tax for revenue, the GNP elasticity of the federal tax base as a whole is very high. As incomes rise through real economic growth, families move into higher tax brackets and automatically pay a larger percentage of their incomes in tax. The same effect occurs as a result of inflation, unless tax brackets are indexed to adjust for rising prices. Consequently, federal income tax receipts, at constant tax rates, increase much more rapidly than family incomes do as the economy grows or prices rise, and a 1 percent increase in nominal GNP leads to much more than a 1 percent rise in total federal revenues. Historically, the federal government has therefore been able to take care of its own needs, increase its grants to state and local governments, and at the same time gradually reduce federal income and excise tax rates.

The tax base of the state governments is moderately elastic since they can and do make use of income taxes at mildly progressive rates. (In 1983–

1984 individual income taxes provided 30 percent of their tax revenue.) Nevertheless, the states have had to increase their tax rates markedly in order to finance their rapidly growing expenditures. These expenditures, of course, include the sharply increased state aid to localities shown in Table 14.4.

Local tax revenues as a percentage of GNP reached a peak in 1972. Since that date they have grown more slowly than GNP as local governments responded to the gathering strength of the "taxpayers' revolt." If we continue to assume that the local tax system has a GNP elasticity of unity, the decline in tax revenue relative to GNP from 1971–1972 through 1983–1984 implies that tax rates were reduced about 20 percent in twelve years. However, it is likely that the size of the local tax base increased faster than GNP during that period because taxable property values rose so rapidly. Purchasers were vigorously bidding up property prices apparently because they viewed real property as an excellent investment during a period of rapid inflation. If we assume that the local tax system as a whole had a GNP elasticity greater than unity, the reduction in effective tax rates implied by the decline in local tax revenue relative to GNP after 1972 might be considerably greater than 20 percent.

Again, Table 14.7 provides some direct evidence: the average effective rate of tax on FHA-insured single-family homes fell from 1.98 percent in 1971 to 1.23 percent in 1984, a rapid and substantial decline. Tax payments, of course, were increasing, not declining, during those years, but the market value of property was going up much faster than tax payments, so the effective rate of tax did fall substantially. The property market, however, has always been highly cyclic. The strong performance of property values during the 1970s and early 1980s should not be taken to indicate that they will continue to outstrip GNP in the long run. If their growth rate should again fall below that of GNP, upward pressure on property tax rates is likely to resume.

THE PROPERTY TAX

The property tax deserves special attention in a book on urban economics, not only because it is by far the most important tax levied by city governments but also because its specific impact on building development and land use helps to shape the very structure of the city. For the same reasons, the tax has traditionally been the subject of much debate, as economists have argued about its effects and about the probable consequences of proposed reforms.

The most important economic questions to be answered about any tax are, first, who pays it? and, second, what effects does it have on economic activity? The first question is essentially one of income distribution, and therefore of equity, while the second is one of resource allocation, and therefore of efficiency. Although the answers to these questions are interconnected, it is convenient to separate them for purposes of analysis.

The question Who pays the tax? is the subject of tax incidence theory: the "incidence" of the tax is said to be on the persons who bear its burden. It is important to distinguish between legal incidence and economic incidence. For example, the Congress may enact a tax of so many dollars a pair on the production of leather shoes and command shoe manufacturers to pay it. The legal incidence is then on shoe manufacturers. But if, after the tax is imposed, these producers can raise their selling price sufficiently to cover the tax (or some part of it), they will have succeeded in shifting the tax (or a part of it) forward to retailers. Retailers in turn may succeed in raising prices enough to shift the tax forward to consumers. The incidence, or some part of it, then rests with consumers (who presumably can shift it no further).

When analyzing incidence, the economist tries first to establish which functional classes bear the burden of the tax and then what that implies about the distribution of the burden among income classes. A tax is said to be progressive if it takes an increasing proportion of income from an individual as income increases. It is called regressive if the proportion paid in taxes drops as income increases. If the proportion is constant over all income classes, the tax is termed proportional. In the case of the property tax, the functional classes to be considered would include such groups as landowners, building owners, tenants, owners of non–real estate capital, and consumers. The distribution of the burden among income classes will obviously depend on its functional distribution, since functional classes differ systematically in the level and distribution of income among their members.

The question of how a tax affects economic activity concerns specifically its impact on the allocation of resources. Whenever a tax is imposed, those who are affected try to adjust their economic behavior to minimize its harmful effects. Such adjustment distorts prices in the marketplace away from what they would have been in the absence of a tax. These distortions cause a welfare loss as compared with the outcome if prices had been established under perfect competition with no taxes. This welfare loss is usually referred to as the "excess burden" of the tax because it is a loss in addition to the direct burden of paying the money cost of the levy. In the example of a tax on the production of leather shoes, suppose that manufacturers and retailers raise the price of leather shoes in an attempt to shift the tax. Some consumers will pay the higher price. Others will respond by purchasing canvas, rubber, or plastic shoes as substitutes. But the same consumers considered these to be inferior alternatives when untaxed leather shoes were available. Therefore, those who switch to avoid the tax are necessarily suffering a welfare loss. This is an example of "excess burden."

Upon reflection, it is clear that a tax cannot be shifted unless some participant in the system adjusts behavior to bring about the shift. But such adjustments distort prices and create excess burden. Therefore tax shifting always implies the creation of excess burden. Conversely, a tax that cannot be shifted distorts no prices and creates no excess burden.

The property tax in the United States is almost exclusively a local levy. In each city and town all property in the form of land, buildings, or other improvements is listed in a public record and assigned a value in an appraisal process known as assessment. A local tax rate is established each year, and every owner of taxable property pays a tax equal to the product of that rate times the property's assessed value. Property used for religious, charitable, or other not-for-profit purposes is usually exempt from the tax.

Site Value Taxation

The property tax is usually levied on the assessed value of land and improvements combined. It is conventional, however, to analyze the tax in two parts, since the portion that falls on land (or site) value has quite different effects than the part that is levied on improvements. Economists dream of taxes that cannot be shifted and therefore impose no excess burden. There are not many of them, but a tax on site value is generally acknowledged to be one. Consequently, site value—the value of unimproved land—has long been regarded by economists as a particularly fit object for taxation.

A tax on site value cannot be shifted by the landowner to any other party for one very simple reason: land is in fixed supply.[26] It is perpetually durable and not reproducible, movable, or transformable. Consequently, if a city levies a tax on land value, there is no response by which the owner can reduce the burden. He or she simply pays the tax and goes on using the land in whatever way was most profitable before a tax was levied, for that will still be the most profitable use, net of tax.

This outcome is illustrated in Figure 14.2 which represents the supply and demand for sites in a hypothetical city. It is convenient to use annual rent rather than capital value as the measure of price (see discussion at the beginning of Chapter 6). Site rent per acre is measured on the vertical axis, the number of acres supplied and demanded on the horizontal. In the interest of simplicity, the dimension of distance and the effect of accessibility on site rent are suppressed. All sites are therefore equally desirable to users. On the supply side, landowners are assumed to be perfect competitors.

The area of the city is Q_1 acres, no more, no less. Consequently, the supply of sites is represented as perfectly inelastic, a vertical straight line at Q_1. The demand curve DD is assumed to have the usual downward slope: if sites were cheaper, demanders would use more land in relation to other inputs. Since the supply is fixed, however, demanders in fact use Q_1 acres and pay P_1 rent per acre. Landowners accept P_1 as the highest obtainable rent. Their only alternative is inferior: withdraw land from the market and earn nothing.

Now suppose the city were to levy a tax of 50 percent on annual site

---

26. We here ignore the possibility of adding to the supply extending landfill into waters adjacent to a city.

FIGURE 14.2
Supply and Demand for Urban Land

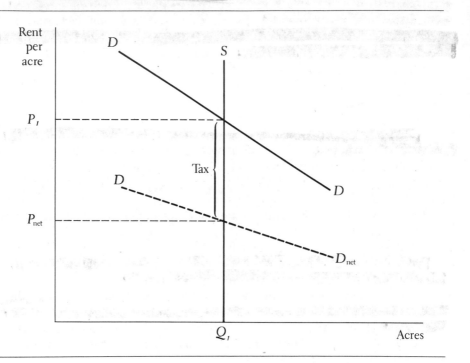

rent. The amounts payable are shown in Figure 14.2 by the distance between *DD* and *DD*net, which is 50 percent of the height of *DD* at every point. The price of land does not rise in response to the tax because it cannot pay any individual landowner to withdraw his or her supply. Consequently, users continue to pay P_1 per acre for the use of sites, and landowners retain a net rent equal to P_{net} and return to the city a tax equal to $P_1 - P_{net}$ per acre. The tax is not shifted.

Because the supply of sites is not reduced by the tax, rent does not rise, and market prices are in no way distorted. Site value taxation thus has the virtue of being perfectly neutral in the sense of not disturbing an otherwise desirable allocation of resources. No tax better satisfies the criterion of economic efficiency.

It is sometimes argued that this tax also deserves unusually high marks on grounds of equity. Site value taxation taps what has been described as an "unearned increment" in wealth. The value of land is not created by the efforts of the landowner. Rather, it is the social and economic development of the entire community that gives particular sites their value. It follows that society would be perfectly justified in recapturing through taxation the unearned increment in value that would otherwise go to the landowner. Henry

George and his followers have therefore advocated the imposition of very heavy taxes on land value. This argument, however, overlooks a pervasive complication. Since land frequently changes hands, there can be no presumption that present owners received any unearned increment. They may have paid anything up to the full current value for their parcels. Thus the unearned increment argument supports the imposition of a heavy tax on *future* gains in land value but cannot justify a tax that is levied *ex post.*[27]

The incidence of a tax on land value is clearly on those who own land at the time the tax is imposed or its rate is increased. Nor can owners escape the tax by selling their holdings, since the expected future tax burden is immediately capitalized into the present value of the land. Any subsequent buyer pays a price that takes the tax into account and thus, in effect, buys "free of tax." Since most land in the United States is owned in common with improvements, we can assume as an approximation that the tax on land is distributed among income classes in proportion to their ownership of real property. On that basis its burden would probably be distributed progressively in relation to income.

The Tax on Improvements: The Old View

The more important and analytically more controversial part of the property tax is the portion levied on improvements, including rental and owner-occupied housing and commercial and industrial property. While there has always been some disagreement about the incidence of this tax, most economists until recently concluded that in the long run the portion of the tax falling on improvements would, with some exceptions, be shifted forward from owners to users.[28] Thus the tax on department store buildings would be passed forward to customers, the tax on factories to consumers of their products, and the tax on rental housing to tenants. This traditional conclusion we shall refer to as the "old" view. In recent years it has been powerfully challenged by a "new" view, which holds that a substantial share of the tax on improvements is borne by owners of capital in general instead of being shifted to customers or tenants. In its current version the new view was first propounded by Peter Mieszkowski in 1972, building on Arnold Harberger's earlier analysis of the corporation income tax.[29]

---

27. In this discussion it is assumed that gains in land value are "real" rather than the result of general price inflation.

28. See Herbert A. Simon, "The Incidence of a Tax on Urban Real Property," reprinted in Richard A. Musgrave and Carl S. Shoup, eds., *Readings in the Economics of Taxation* (Homewood, Ill.: Richard D. Irwin, 1959), pp. 416–435 and references cited therein; and Netzer, ch. 3.

29. See Peter Mieszkowski, "The Property Tax: An Excise or a Profits Tax?" *Journal of Public Economics,* April 1972, pp. 73–96; Dick Netzer, "The Incidence of the Property Tax Revisited," *National Tax Journal,* December 1973, pp. 515–535; Henry J. Aaron, *Who Pays the Property Tax?* (Washington, D.C.: Brookings Institution, 1975). Harry Gunnison Brown is now recognized as an early (1924) proponent of the new view whose work "has been generally neglected although known to many economists." (Netzer, p. 516. Also see references to Brown in Aaron and Simon.)

The two views have radically different implications for the distribution of the property tax burden among income classes. Adherents of the old view usually found the tax to be regressive, a serious deficiency in the opinion of many observers. The new view reverses that verdict: the tax turns out to be quite progressive, an important virtue in many eyes. In the following sections we explain both views in simplified form in order to capture the essence of each—but certainly without pretending to do full justice to the sophistication of the arguments on either side. To facilitate exposition we limit the analysis initially to the example of rental housing.

The old view is most easily explained by considering the impact of the property tax within a single locality. Assume initially that property taxes are levied at a rate t in all jurisdictions. Assume also that factors of production are geographically perfectly mobile, so developers of rental housing pay prices for their inputs, including capital, that are established competitively in national markets. If the locality under consideration is a very small part of the national whole, we can assume that the supply of each input, including capital, to local developers is perfectly elastic at the going market price.

In Figure 14.3 the rental housing market is portrayed by means of a stock adjustment model. Quantity of housing available for rent is measured in square feet on the horizontal axis, rent and building cost per square foot on the vertical. As explained in Chapter 12, the housing market in the short run is dominated by the standing stock, since supply expansion is at best a very slow process. In Figure 14.3 supply in the short run is SS_1, the quantity of space in the standing stock. Consumer demand is given by DD_1, which can be thought of as showing the desired stock of housing at each price. The rent level per square foot that will yield investors in new construction the going rate of return on capital after paying property taxes at rate t is C_1. New construction leading to expansion of the standing stock will take place whenever rent exceeds C_1, which can therefore be called the "new construction rent level." Given the perfectly elastic supply of inputs, the horizontal straight line LS_1 at rent level C_1 is the long-run supply curve of housing stock. As long as tax rates remain geographically uniform, the new construction rent level is the same everywhere. In the locality depicted, SS_1 and DD_1 intersect at point e on the long-run supply curve. Hence the market is initially in long-run equilibrium with rent equal to long-run cost, C_1.

Now suppose that the local government decides to raise the rate of property tax to t'. The new construction rent level rises to C_2, the rent that developers of additional buildings must obtain to pay the higher tax rate and still earn the going rate of return on investment. The actual rent, however, remains at C_1. Thus in the short run, according to the old view, the burden of increased property taxes remains with the owner.

In the long run, however, the tax can be shifted by owners to tenants if market rent rises above C_1. This could occur because either demand in-

FIGURE 14.3
Stock Adjustment Model of the Housing Market

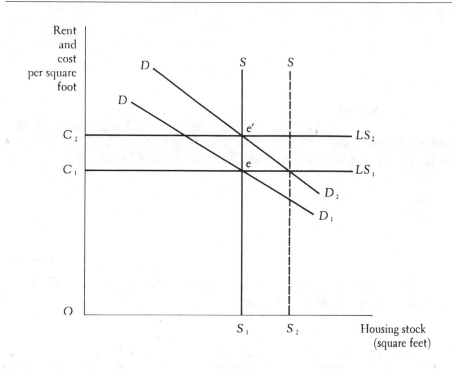

creased or supply diminished. Demand would be expected to increase as a result of growing population or rising living standards. Supply could decrease because of demolition, fire, or conversion to nonresidential use. The case of increased demand is illustrated in Figure 14.3. As the population of the city grows, more housing space is required. The demand curve shifts to the right. As it does so, the market level of rent moves up along SS_1 because investors do not expand the housing stock while rent remains below C_2. When demand has increased to DD_2, rent reaches C_2, the new construction rent level that incorporates tax rate t'. The market is now in equilibrium at point e'. The tax increase has been fully shifted to tenants. Rents are now higher in this locality than elsewhere by the amount necessary to pay the higher rate of local tax, as indicated by long-run supply curve LS_2. If the tax rate had not risen, the stock of housing would have increased to SS_2 when demand increased. Instead, the stock remained at SS_1, and rents rose. (If demand should continue to increase, new construction would begin again, expanding the housing stock, and rents would rise no farther.) Thus the general conclusion under the old view is that except in declining cities where the necessary market conditions may not occur, the burden of property taxes on rental housing is, in the long run, shifted by landlords to tenants.

The New View

The new view of the property tax reaches a quite different conclusion. According to this view, much of the burden of the tax on improvements remains with owners of capital in the form of a lower net return instead of being shifted to users of property in the form of higher rents or prices. The error of the old view arose from trying to generalize about the effects of the tax from an argument that examined only one jurisdiction at a time. If only one jurisdiction is assumed to levy the tax, it is plausible to argue, as the old view did, that the tax will not affect the nationwide going rate of return on capital. But if—as we know to be the case—all jurisdictions levy the tax, it cannot be assumed that the going rate of return will be unaffected. Indeed, to generalize from the case of the single jurisdiction is an example of the fallacy of composition. Proponents of the new view point out that the tax on improvements is essentially a nationwide tax on capital. When the tax is examined in that perspective, its incidence will depend on the characteristics of supply and demand for capital nationally rather than in a single market.

It was argued that a tax on land value cannot be shifted by landowners to tenants or consumers of the services of land because the tax does not affect the amount of land supplied and therefore cannot affect its price. Proponents of the new view have reached a similar conclusion with respect to the tax on improvements. In their view, the historical evidence indicates that the rate of saving in the United States is insensitive to variations in the net return to capital. But if the rate of saving is not affected by the rate of return to capital, the stock (or supply) of capital will not be reduced by a general tax on capital. The price charged for the use of capital will not increase to cover the cost of the tax, and the tax will not be shifted.

That the rate of saving should not vary directly with the rate of return to capital may seem counterintuitive. Nevertheless, that is what both Harberger and Mieszkowski concluded from the evidence available to them.[30] As Mieszkowski showed, it follows, more or less directly, that a uniform nationwide property tax on improvements cannot be shifted by the owners to tenants or users of property. Thus if the property tax were levied at the same rate

---

30. Arnold C. Harberger, "The Incidence of the Corporation Income Tax," *Journal of Political Economy*, June 1962, p. 216.

everywhere, the principal result according to the new view would be a reduction in the real rate of return to capital. For example, if the rate of return had been 6 percent before the tax was levied and a tax rate of 2 percent were imposed, the net return to capital would fall to 4 percent, while the gross cost of using capital (that is, its price) would remain unchanged at 6 percent, of which 4 percent would remain with owners and 2 percent would go to the tax collector. This is just the opposite of the old view, according to which the gross price of capital would eventually rise to 8 percent, so that the burden of tax would be passed on to users of capital, leaving the net return to capital owners unimpaired.

"Global" Effects and "Excise" Effects

Mieszkowski recognized, of course, that the property tax in the United States is not a uniform nationwide levy but rather a system of local taxes levied at geographically varying rates. He dealt with this complication by distinguishing between "global" effects, which result from the impact of the system as a whole, and "excise" effects, which result from the variation among local rates.[31]

Because capital is highly mobile within a national economy, it is reasonable to assume that differences in the rate of the property tax among jurisdictions will cause capital to flow from high- to low-tax areas. A hypothetical example is illustrated in Figure 14.4.

Assume that before any property tax is imposed the rate of return to capital in all localities is 6 percent, as shown in the left-hand column of the figure. Property taxes are then imposed at three different local rates: 3 percent in high-tax towns, 2 percent in towns taxing at the national average rate, and 1 percent in low-tax areas. The immediate effect in all areas is to reduce the rate of return to owners of local property by the amount of the tax. This result is shown in column 2. It follows necessarily from the fact that the supply of improvements in each locality does not change in the short run, and owners therefore cannot raise the price charged for the use of property or for its products in order to shift the tax.

Capital markets, however, are not in equilibrium in the situation depicted in column 2, since net rates of return are higher where tax rates are lower. Owners of capital, seeking the highest available returns, now move their resources from high- to low-tax towns. This reduces the supply of capital in high-tax areas, causing the net return in those areas to rise, and increases its supply in low-tax areas, causing the net return there to fall. Presumably, migration of capital continues until net returns in all areas are equal. This long-run equilibrium is shown in column 3. However, although net returns are now equal everywhere, the gross cost of capital services, which equals the

---

31. Mieszkowski, pp. 74–81.

FIGURE 14.4
"Global" and "Excise" Effects of the Property Tax

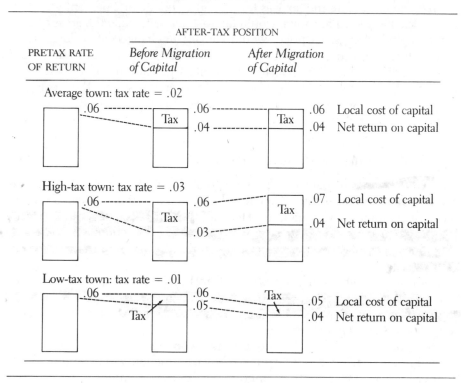

AFTER-TAX POSITION

PRETAX RATE OF RETURN	Before Migration of Capital	After Migration of Capital	

Average town: tax rate = .02

.06 ---------- Tax   .06 ----------- Tax   .06 Local cost of capital
                     .04 -----------   .04 Net return on capital

High-tax town: tax rate = .03

.06 ---------- Tax   .06 ----------- Tax   .07 Local cost of capital
                     .03 -----------   .04 Net return on capital

Low-tax town: tax rate = .01

.06 ---------- Tax   .06 ----------- Tax   .05 Local cost of capital
                     .05 -----------   .04 Net return on capital

net return plus the tax, is now higher where taxes are higher. The tax can be thought of as a wedge between the net return to owners, which is everywhere equal, and the gross cost of capital, equivalent to the price paid for capital services by local users, which is higher, the higher the local tax rate.

Figure 14.4 illustrates both the "global" and "excise" effects of the property tax. The global effect is the long-run decline in the net return to capital that occurs as a result of imposing property taxes at varying local rates. It is the difference between the net return of 6 percent in column 1 and 4 percent in column 3. This 2 percent decline, it should be noted, is equal to the average rate of tax in the nation as a whole.

If all towns levied the tax at the same rate, or if the tax were a uniform national levy, there would be only a global effect. However, since local tax rates are not equal, there are also excise effects. These are shown by the differences in the local gross cost of capital, after the capital market has fully adjusted to local taxes, as shown in column 3.

According to the old view, the property tax on improvements was, in the long run, passed forward to tenants or users of property, leaving the rate of return to capital unimpaired. The new view comes to a radically different conclusion: the rate of return to capital is reduced by approximately the nationwide average rate of property tax. That is the substance of the global effect. It is only the excise effect that can be shifted by capital owners to other agents in the economy— for example, to tenants in rental housing units or to customers of department stores.

Remember that because excise effects are measured as the difference between the local property tax rate and the national average, they impose positive burdens in some places and negative burdens (i.e., positive advantages) in others. Where excise effects are positive, taxpayers will attempt to shift the burden to others in a process that will be discussed shortly. However, where the excise burden is negative, taxpayers will be forced by competition to share the benefits of below-average tax rates with customers or suppliers, or both, in a process that is the mirror image of the one to be discussed here.

With some exceptions, adherents of the old view had emphasized forward shifting of the property tax. The new view differs in stressing that the excise effects of the tax are likely to cause "backward" shifting to land and labor (if labor is not fully mobile) as well as, or instead of, forward shifting to tenants or customers. Some of these possibilities will be discussed briefly.

Owner-occupied housing. The owner-occupant stands in a double relation to housing. He or she is both the owner who produces housing services and the tenant who consumes them. According to the new view, the global effect of the tax does not raise the cost of housing but, rather, reduces the return to capital. In the role of owner, the owner-occupant cannot escape that part of the burden. If the local tax rate exceeds the national average, however, there is also a positive excise effect. This will increase the local cost of capital and, therefore, of housing services. As the tenant consuming such services, the owner-occupant would also bear that burden. If that were the whole story, it would be clear that the owner-occupant cannot shift any part of the tax. However, the possibility that higher taxes will be capitalized into lower land values must be taken into account. Higher taxes on improvements will reduce the demand for building sites and will therefore lead to lower prices for land that will, in part, offset the higher cost of local capital. This will not help owner-occupants in possession of sites at the time the tax is raised, since it is their land that falls in value, but subsequent home buyers will benefit.

Industrial and commercial property. Again, the global effect of the tax is not shiftable: businesses that own property bear the burden of the global effect in their capacity as owners of capital. Excise effects, however, may be shifted both forward and backward. But since the tax is a local one, it is important to distinguish carefully between firms that sell only in the local market and those that export products or services to other communities. The former typically have little competition from outside the jurisdiction and consequently would be able, in the long run, to pass at least part of the excise effect of high taxes forward to local customers in the form of higher prices.

Firms that export to the national market face a different situation. They must compete with producers who may pay lower taxes in other towns. In that case they could not shift the excise effect forward to customers. One would expect such firms, in the long run, to locate away from high-tax jurisdictions. There is one exception, however: if the high-tax town has locational advantages for a given firm's production, the firm could, so to speak, pay the higher taxes out of its locational advantages without becoming either noncompetitive or less than normally profitable.[32] (This explains why cities may be tempted to assess very heavily the property of established local industries for which they believe they have special locational advantages.) Finally, backward shifting to landowners may help to offset the excise effect of high local taxes for both local-market and national-market firms, but with the same caveat regarding current owners that pertains for owner-occupied housing.

Is the Property Tax Regressive or Progressive?

What does the foregoing analysis imply about the incidence of the property tax by income class? Let us dispose of the tax on land first, since it is the least controversial element. It is almost universally agreed among economists that a tax on unimproved land value is borne by landowners in proportion to the value of their holdings. Since land ownership is on average distributed progressively with respect of income, that portion of the tax is a progressive one.

Concerning the tax on improvements, there are many more complications and much less agreement. No tax is beloved, but the levy on property for many years had a poor reputation, even among taxes, because generations of economists, relying on the old view of its incidence, pronounced it seriously regressive. As already explained, proponents of the old view usually concluded that the tax on rental housing would, in the long run, be passed forward to tenants in the form of higher rent; the tax on owner-occupied housing would be borne by owners in their capacity as consumers of housing service; the tax on business property would be largely passed forward to customers in the form of higher prices. Housing expenditures were thought to be highly regressive to income and other consumption outlays moderately so. Hence a tax that impinged on households in proportion to such outlays would be distinctly regressive.

Proponents of the new view, on the other hand, have concluded that the tax on improvements is highly progressive. The global effect falls unambiguously on owners of capital. Income from capital is distributed progressively with respect to total income; ergo, that part of the tax is highly progressive. But what about excise effects? From a national perspective these conveniently cancel out: it is plausible to argue that the burdens borne by

32. See Netzer, *Economics of the Property Tax*, p. 115.

those in high-tax towns are offset by the gains of those in low-tax communities, so that the net impact of excise effects by income class can be ignored.[33]

Table 14.6 illustrates these conclusions with Joseph A. Pechman's estimates of the actual incidence of the tax in 1980, employing alternately the assumptions of the new view in the first column and the old view in the second. The difference between the two estimates is striking: according to the old view, those in the lowest income class pay 7.9 percent of their income in property tax, while those in the highest pay only 2.3 percent; according to the new view, the burden on the lowest class is only 1.0 percent, while the highest income group pays 5.8 percent.

It should be pointed out that the version of the new view presented here, in which the global effect is completely unshiftable by owners of capital, depends on the strong assumption that saving, and hence the supply of capital, is completely unresponsive to changes in the rate of return. The relation between saving and the rate of return is best summarized by a measure known as the interest elasticity of saving, defined as the ratio of a percentage change in saving to the percentage change in the rate of return that brings it about. If saving is completely unresponsive to changes in the rate of return, as assumed by Mieszkowski in first presenting the new view, the value of the interest elasticity is zero.

The actual value of this elasticity, however, must be settled by empirical investigation. The question has received far less attention than it deserves, and for many years the available evidence has been regarded as inconclusive. In 1978 a study by Michael J. Boskin concluded that the interest elasticity of saving is substantial; he offered a series of estimates ranging from .2 to .6.[34] Should other studies confirm a value in that range, the conclusion that no part of the global effect of the property tax can be shifted is incorrect. If the interest elasticity is positive, the property tax discourages capital formation, reduces the stock of improvements, and raises their price. Consumers of the services produced by real property would, in the long run, share the tax burden with owners of capital.

Since the empirical question, What is the true value of the interest elasticity of saving? has not been resolved, a large element of uncertainty remains in the analysis of property tax incidence. Unfortunately, it is not helpful to say that its incidence probably falls somewhere between the two extremes shown in Table 14.6.

Local versus National Perspective

It is important to recognize that answers to questions about the property tax will vary radically, depending on the point of view from which they

33. Mieszkowski, pp. 79–80.

34. Michael Boskin, "Taxation, Savings, and the Rate of Interest," *Journal of Political Economy*, April 1978, pt. 2, pp. S3–S27.

TABLE 14.6
Estimates of Property Tax Incidence by Income Class, 1980ᵃ

ADJUSTED FAMILY INCOME ($)	PROPERTY TAX AS PERCENT OF INCOME	
	New View	*Old View*
0–5,000	1.0	7.9
5,000–10,000	.6	3.0
10,000–15,000	.9	2.4
15,000–20,000	.9	2.1
20,000–25,000	1.0	2.1
25,000–30,000	1.2	2.1
30,000–50,000	1.4	2.2
50,000–100,000	2.2	2.3
100,000–500,000	3.9	2.2
500,000–1,000,000	5.2	2.2
1,000,000 +	5.8	2.3

ᵃIncidence assumptions: Old view: tax on land borne by landowners, tax on housing borne by occupants, tax on business property borne by consumers; new view: tax on land and all improvements borne by property owners in general.
Source: Joseph A. Pechman, *Who Paid the Taxes, 1966–85?* (Washington, D.C.: Brookings Institution, 1985), tables 3–1 and 4–9.

are asked. For example, the most frequently heard question may be, Is the property tax regressive or progressive? From the national point of view the answer depends on the global effect of the tax, since positive and negative excise effects probably cancel out at the national scale. If one believes that the global effect cannot be shifted, its burden clearly rests on owners of capital and the tax is markedly progressive with respect to income. Many will think that desirable.

From the local point of view the situation is entirely different. For any decision that will be made locally, the global effect is of no consequence. It would be a mistake for local voters to support an increase in property tax rates because they had heard that the tax was progressive. Increasing the local tax rate will have no perceptible impact on the (progressive) global effect. Instead it will increase the excise effect, which depends on the difference between the local tax rate and the national average. By raising the cost of local capital relative to the national average, higher local property taxes have three effects that are likely to be considered undesirable. First, they raise the cost of housing, thus impeding progress toward improved housing standards. As we have already seen in Chapter 12, the elimination of substandard housing has long been a major objective of both local and national policy. Second, part of the burden of excise effects is also likely to be passed forward to consumers of other local goods in a pattern that may well be regressive to income. Third, higher local property taxes increase local business costs, rendering the locality economically less attractive, especially to firms that must compete in outside markets with companies that may be located in lower tax jurisdictions. Business firms frequently enjoy a degree of freedom in the choice of location—not that one place is as good as another, but rather that there may be many almost as good as the best. Even businesses that serve a local market may be able to move within the metropolitan area to reduce tax costs. Consequently, if local governments impose tax burdens on business much above those prevailing in other places, they may find some firms moving away and the tax base shrinking.

Thus the new view propounds a paradox. From a national perspective the property tax is made to look quite attractive—at any rate, not regressive and not a burden on housing consumption. Yet the tax is a local, not a national, one, and any locality that raises its property tax rates above the average is likely to bring on itself all the old evils.

In the United States variation in property tax rates—the source of excise effects—is, in fact, very large. Table 14.7 shows the average rate of tax, adjusted to full market value, on single-family homes with FHA-insured mortgages. The nationwide average rate can be taken as an approximate measure of the "global effect." It stood at 1.23 percent in 1984. In that year taxes in the five states with the highest rates averaged 2.5 percent, or double the national average, while those in the five states with the lowest rates averaged .49 percent, or 60 percent below the national mean. Indeed, the figures in Table 14.7 suggest that inter-state variation in property tax rates has increased considerably since 1958. Moreover, since the table is based on statewide averages of local rates, the variation in local rates themselves must be considerably greater than these figures suggest. In the face of such data one cannot dismiss excise effects, and the burdens and distortions they imply, as unimportant.

Further Complications: Variation in Assessment Practices and Tax Rates

The incidence estimates in Table 14.6 are based on aggregate data for households in the United States. They have been constructed by taking the observed total of property tax payments for the United States and distributing it across income classes in proportion to whatever allocator economic theory suggests is appropriate. Under the old view the tax burden is distributed in proportion to housing expenditures and general consumption, under the new view in proportion to income from capital. Unfortunately, this method of estimating incidence systematically conceals effects that might show up in a study of individual taxpayers or jurisdictions. Some of these will now be developed for the case of owner-occupied housing.

The relationship between tax payments on housing and the income of an owner-occupant taxpayer can be analyzed into two components by means of the following equation (an analogous argument applies to renters):

$$T/Y = T/MV \cdot MV/Y$$

TABLE 14.7
*Property Tax Rates on Single-Family Homes with FHA-insured Mortgages,
Adjusted to Full Market Value*

	1958	1971	1984
U.S. average	1.34%	1.98%	1.23%
Five states with highest rates	2.07	3.09	2.51
Five states with lowest rates	.55	.79	.49

Source: Advisory Commission on Intergovernmental Relations, *Significant Features of Fiscal Federalism, 1985–86 Edition* (Washington, D.C.: U.S. Government Printing Office,) February 1986, table 69.

On the left-hand side is the ratio of property tax payments *(T)* to household income *(Y)*. The tax is progressive if this ratio rises, regressive if it falls as income rises, and proportional if it is constant over all income classes.

Algebraically, *T/Y* equals the product of the two ratios on the right-hand side. The first of these is the ratio of tax payments to the market value of the owner-occupant's house *(MV)*. This ratio is a measure of the "effective property tax rate." Two sources of variation in this ratio are of interest because they may systematically affect the value of *T/Y*. First of all, state law usually requires that within a given jurisdiction all properties be assessed at the same ratio to full market value, that is, that the "assessment ratio" be constant for all properties. If that were done, the value of *T/MV* would also be the same for all local taxpayers. However, numerous studies have turned up systematical local variation in the assessment ratio, so one cannot assume that *T/MV* will be uniform within any jurisdiction. Second, the ratio *T/MV* may vary systematically across jurisdictions, because the effective property tax rate, which it measures, is higher in some types of communities than in others. These two sources of variation in *T/MV* will now be analyzed.

First, consider tax incidence within the single jurisdiction. Assume for simplicity that the ratio *MV/Y* is constant across all income groups. If the locality applies a single assessment ratio to all properties, *T/MV* will also be equal for all owners. In that case *T/Y* will also be constant: the tax will be proportional to income. Starting from this case one can easily see the potential impact of variation in the assessment ratio. For example, if the ratio is higher for low-income than for high-income families, *T/Y* will also be higher for low-income families, and the tax will be regressive instead of proportional.

In separate studies of data for the city of Boston, both Robert F. Engle and David E. Black found a strongly inverse relationship between the assessment ratio for a residential property and its market value.[35] This intrajurisdic-

35. Robert F. Engle, "De Facto Discrimination in Residential Assessments: Boston," *National Tax Journal*, December 1975, pp. 445–451; David E. Black, "Property Tax Incidence: The Excise-Tax Effect and Assessment Practices," *National Tax Journal*, December 1977, pp. 429–434.

tional bias in assessment practice means that the property tax could be quite regressive in practice even when it would be proportional or progressive if assessment ratios were uniform. Engle showed that the bias resulted from the failure to adjust assessments as market values changed: in neighborhoods where market value was rising rapidly the ratio fell relative to its level in neighborhoods where values rose more slowly. Since the latter were primarily poor neighborhoods, the result was a tax system biased against the poor. Keith R. Ihlanfeldt's 1982 study of Atlanta and Philadelphia confirmed the presence of assessment bias in those two central cities.[36] Ihlanfeldt stratified each housing market into low-, middle-, and upper-income segments and found that regressive assessment occurred mostly within the first two groups.

The three studies cited here, and many others, show that assessments in the United States are subject both to large random error and to important systematic bias. Both lead to intrajurisdictional inequities that better administration could substantially reduce.

Of course, the expression "better administration" makes the problem of assessment bias sound apolitical, as if it were simply an accident of sloppy practice when in fact it usually has deep political roots. For example, a study of the property tax in New York City directed by Dick Netzer found that in 1979 the assessment ratio for one- and two-family houses was only 24.6 percent, whereas it was 59.3 percent for all other residential property.[37] One- and two-family units in New York are occupied by the substantial middle class, while the poor are concentrated largely in the "other," or rental, sector. Thus assessment bias clearly works against the poor. Yet when the state legislature, under court order, was forced to deal with the problem of unequal assessments, the political power of New York City's minority of homeowners was so great that instead of requiring equalized assessment of housing in the city, the legislators adopted a law that virtually legalized the existing unequal pattern.

The ratio of property tax payment to house value varies between as well as within jurisdictions in ways that may be correlated with household income and so affect the nationwide incidence of the property tax. For example, Henry J. Aaron noted that for the 356 United States cities with a population above 50,000 in 1971, there is a significant positive correlation between the effective property tax rate and average per capita income: tax rates are higher in cities where incomes are higher.[38] Such a finding suggests that the property tax is less regressive, or more progressive, than is indicated by estimates of the type presented in Table 14.6, which do not reflect the influence of local variations in tax rates.

36. Keith R. Ihlanfeldt, "Property Tax Incidence on Owner-occupied Housing: Evidence from the Annual Housing Survey," *National Tax Journal*, March 1982, pp. 89–97.

37. New York University Graduate School of Public Administration, *Real Property Tax Policy for New York City*, 1980, p. I-11.

38. Aaron, p. 46.

This line of reasoning, however, raises serious problems. If property tax rates differ between jurisdictions, local expenditures, which confer benefits on local taxpayers, may also differ in the same direction. Higher tax rates may be deliberately employed in some localities to provide the citizenry with a richer mixture of public services. In that case the equity implications of a higher ratio of tax payments to income become unclear. No such problem arises in connection with intrajurisdictional studies, such as the studies of assessment ratios just cited, since it is a tenable assumption that expenditure benefits do not vary systematically with tax payments within a single jurisdiction. For that reason, some analysts would argue that the local tax jurisdiction is the most appropriate area in which to measure the incidence of the property tax.

Permanent Income versus Current Income

A final question to be discussed is the appropriate concept of income for use in estimating the incidence of the property tax. The relationship between house value or rent and household income is best summarized by the income elasticity of demand for housing, which can be defined as the percentage change in the value of housing per family divided by the percentage change in family income with which it is associated. If the value of this elasticity is unity, the ratio MV/Y in the equation in the previous section will remain constant as income increases, because its numerator and denominator will change by the same percentage. If the elasticity has a value less than one, the ratio will fall, and if the elasticity is greater than one, it will rise as income rises. It is well established that the value obtained for this elasticity in empirical estimates depends on the income concept employed. If current annual income is the measure used, the income elasticity of housing demand always has a value well below one, and the ratio MV/Y falls as income rises. In that case, and if T/MV were independent of income, as would be the case in the absence of assessment bias, the left-hand term, T/Y, would also fall as income rises, and the tax on owner-occupants would be regressive to income.

In recent years, however, a number of economists have argued that the appropriate concept to use is "permanent income"—measured by a household's average income over a number of years—rather than current income.[39] Using permanent income, the income elasticity of housing demand is usually found to have a higher value. (The incidence estimates in Table 14.6 were calculated with respect to current income, which undoubtedly contributes to the regressivity of the pattern shown for the old view.) In the 1960s some studies using the permanent income concept placed the income elasticity at or above one. In that case the ratio MV/Y would be constant or even increasing as income rises, and the tax on owner-occupied housing would therefore

39. The argument is developed in Aaron, pp. 27–32.

be either proportional or progressive. More recent estimates, however, put the income elasticity for owner-occupants somewhat below unity, even when measured against permanent income, thus indicating a moderately regressive burden.[40] However, the range of estimated values remains wide enough to introduce considerable uncertainty into the resulting conclusions on incidence.

Ihlanfeldt's 1982 study adds yet another dimension. He found, for Philadelphia and Atlanta, that the elasticity of house value with respect to permanent income is very low for low-income owners but close to or above unity for middle- and upper-income groups.[41] This finding would indicate that the incidence of the property tax on homeowners approaches a U shape: highly regressive over a range of low incomes but becoming much less regressive or even mildly progressive over a middle and upper range. The pattern of demand for housing that underlies these results might be explained as follows. There is a minimum quantity of housing that even those at the lowest income levels require. As income rises, housing demand at first increases only slightly but, further up the scale, rises more rapidly. "Better-quality" housing then has almost the character of a luxury good.

The Unique Role of the Property Tax in Local Finance

When Benjamin Franklin wrote that "in this world nothing is certain but death and taxes," he was thinking, surely, of the property tax, which then, as now, was the fiscal mainstay of American local government. Especially since the late nineteenth century the tax has been subject to periodic storms of criticism. Not only have its incidence and effects been debated, but the adequacy of its administration has often been seriously questioned. There have been abundant proposals for both administrative and structural reform.[42] Reliance of local school districts on property tax revenues has been successfully challenged in state courts. Dissatisfaction with property taxes was crucial in making possible the passage in 1978 of Proposition 13 to limit local government levies in California. Yet despite the long history of such outcries, the property tax has survived as a major fiscal institution.

Its persistence is best explained by the unique function it performs in the local tax-expenditure system. The property tax has been designed, and is administered, to serve as the automatic balancer of the local budget. Sche-

---

40. See discussion in Chapter 12 and references cited in Chapter 12, n. 10, and Chapter 13, nn. 42 and 43.

41. Ihlanfeldt, p. 94.

42. On the problem of administration see Netzer, *Economics of the Property Tax*, pp. 173–183; and Arthur D. Lynn, Jr., ed., *The Property Tax and Its Administration* (Madison: University of Wisconsin Press, 1969). Proposals for administrative reform are examined critically in Aaron, ch. 4. Broad structural reforms are discussed in Aaron, ch. 5; Netzer, ch. 8; James Heilbrun, *Real Estate Taxes and Urban Housing* (New York: Columbia University Press, 1966); and George E. Peterson, ed., *Property Tax Reform* (Washington, D.C.: Urban Institute, 1973).

matically, this is how the system works. At the beginning of the budget year the local government decides what its total expenditures are going to be. Next, all revenues, except those from the property tax, are estimated. These are then subtracted from total expenditures. The difference, called the "levy," is then raised by a charge on the assessed value of all taxable property. The levy divided by the aggregate value of taxable property yields a tax rate that will necessarily provide enough revenue to balance the proposed budget. The process can be summarized in three equations:

$$\text{Proposed expenditures} - \text{other revenue} = \text{amount of levy}$$
$$\text{Amount of levy} \div \text{aggregate assessed value of taxable property} = \text{tax rate}$$
$$\text{Tax rate} \times \text{assessed value of owner's property} = \text{owner's tax bill}$$

With this arrangement, the local government can vary the tax rate each year (within possible state constitutional tax limits) to raise automatically whatever revenue is needed to cover expenditures. Other local taxes, where they exist, generally cannot be varied except by some sort of (probably difficult) legislative act.

This system is not only convenient but also facilitates a rational approach to making allocation decisions in the public sector. As Netzer points out,

> Assessments and expenditure budgets are independently determined, and the tax rate is the result. Thus, the fiscal issue in local finance is apt to be joined on the question of expenditures rather than tax rates, which seems an appropriate arrangement. To the extent that expenditures and tax rates are simultaneously determined in the local political process, citizens are consciously relating the value of additional expenditures to their tax costs, which surely approaches the ideal prescription for the budget process with respect to the resource allocation "branch" of the public sector.[43]

By contrast, in the typical state budget process (and in the U.S. Congress until budgetary reform went into effect in 1976–1977), proposals for additional expenditure are made with no reference at all to their tax implications, an approach that certainly doesn't encourage participants to make their decisions on the rational basis of willingness to pay for expected benefits.

Because it is so important in local budgets, the property tax becomes an issue in numerous questions of local public policy. In the next chapter we shall examine several of these, including the connection between the size of the property tax base and urban fiscal distress, the possibility of property tax base sharing between central cities and their suburbs, and the problem of attaining equity among school districts when school outlays depend heavily on the value of local taxable property.

---

43. Netzer, *Economics of the Property Tax*, pp. 170–171.

FIFTEEN

Problems of the Metropolitan Public Sector: Inefficiency Inequity, Insolvency

Governmental organization and finance occupy a special place in the catalog of urban and metropolitan problems. On the one hand, unless the metropolitan public sector is efficiently organized and adequately financed, we cannot expect local government to contribute optimally to the solution of the urban problems we have analyzed in the areas of housing, poverty, transportation, and land use. On the other hand, the same changes in technology, population, and income that have generated those other problems have also, in many cases, undermined the ability of local governmental institutions to cope with them. What can be done to strengthen and improve the local public sector?

The problem of arranging the most appropriate division of budgetary functions among the three levels of government was discussed at the beginning of Chapter 14. It was concluded that local governments should not undertake either economic stabilization or the redistribution of income but should confine themselves to allocative functions—the provision of goods and services that for a variety of reasons are best paid for out of the public budget. Yet it must be recognized that serious problems arise for the metropolitan public sector even in carrying out the appropriate allocative functions. These problems can be summarized as "inefficiency," "inequity," and "insolvency." In this chapter we will analyze all three in detail and examine some of the major policies and reforms that have been proposed to ameliorate them.

HAPHAZARD BOUNDARIES: THE PROBLEM OF INEFFICIENCY

Within metropolitan areas the local public sector is notoriously fragmented. A single metropolis may contain hundreds of governmental units. Their boundaries and the division of functions among them are usually the result of long-gone historical forces and are rarely altered to reflect later circumstances. Because boundaries have not been drawn rationally in relation to current needs, it is often difficult for local governments to provide services efficiently.

The extent to which present arrangements interfere with efficient public sector operation can best be understood if we review the various goals of local government and see what criteria for drawing boundaries and assigning functions must be met in order to achieve each of them. It will become clear that there may be inescapable conflicts between the patterns that would maximize the fulfillment of each of the objectives taken separately. Any comprehensive "solution" is therefore likely to be a compromise involving only partial achievement of many desirable ends.

Providing the Optimum Level and Combination of Public Services

Producing the optimum level and combination of public services is the task of "allocation," described at the beginning of Chapter 14. For most public services there is not (nor could there be) a market through which individual demand would be more or less automatically registered and satisfied, as happens in the private sector. A political voting process must therefore be relied on to shape the provision of public goods and services in accordance with citizen preferences.

The "Tiebout solution." It is tempting to argue that satisfaction of voters' preferences for public goods proceeds best when political jurisdictions are small and their populations are homogeneous in taste. As jurisdictions grow smaller, sensitivity of government to individual preferences is likely to increase because government and citizen are "closer." The possibility of homogeneity of tastes also increases as area size decreases, and the more homogeneous the desires of the population, the more likely it is that citizens who fit the local norm will find all their wants nicely fulfilled. In fact, as Charles M. Tiebout argued, if there are enough minor jurisdictions within a metropolitan area and if individuals are not denied the choice of locality through discrimination, zoning, or lack of income, one might expect people with similar preferences to flock together in order to create communities congenial to their particular set of tastes.[1] Clearly the "Tiebout solution" to the problem of preference satisfaction could work only if governmental units within metropolitan areas remained small and very numerous.

Economists have by now offered a variety of criticisms of the Tiebout solution. One of these goes directly to the question of preference satisfaction. From the high degree of daily mobility in the metropolitan way of life—the fact that many people work, live, and shop in three or more different

1. Charles M. Tiebout, "A Pure Theory of Local Expenditures," reprinted in William E. Mitchell and Ingo Walter, eds., *State and Local Finance* (New York: Ronald Press, 1970), pp. 21–29.

jurisdictions—it follows that metropolitan residents regularly consume public services in several places while expressing their preferences through voting in only one. In these circumstances it is not clear that small homogeneous communities maximize the possibility of preference satisfaction for their resident citizens.

One might go further, however, and question just how much importance we should concede to the objective of satisfying local differences in the "taste" for public services. A community containing many retired couples may prefer to spend very little on schools, but if the state sets a standard, the community cannot be allowed to express its preferences by violating the standard. An upper-middle-class family may move from the central city to the suburbs because it finds public services there more suited to its "wants." But one suspects that a good deal of the improvement consists of being able to receive back as service benefit most of what it pays out to the local tax collector instead of seeing a substantial part of its tax payments go to provide services for the poorer families that do not "pay their way" in the tax-expenditure calculus and who are found mostly in the central city. This is not an improvement that we can properly label as "better preference satisfaction," except to the extent that many people have a preference for not paying other people's bills.

Other things being equal, a maximum opportunity for satisfying individually different preferences for public services is, of course, desirable. But other things are not unaffected if we maintain small jurisdictions for that purpose, for small jurisdictions within metropolitan areas certainly hamper effective areawide planning, create demonstrable fiscal inequities, and may possibly prevent the realization of economies of scale in local government.

The problem of externalities. The process of satisfying local demand for public goods and services is seriously impeded by the existence of benefit and cost externalities, or spillovers. These occur when a service produced by one town for itself also yields benefits for or imposes costs on neighboring towns whose interests have not been taken systematically into account. Metropolitan areas are, by definition, densely settled, and the localities within them are systematically interdependent. In such a setting externalities are probably more the rule than the exception.

Consider a very simple case. Suppose that a town engages in mosquito abatement by means of chemical spraying within its own boundaries. The rational course of action for the single town would be to expand the program to the point where the marginal cost to the town of additional spraying just equals the marginal benefit to the town of the resulting additional abatement. The situation is depicted in Figure 15.1. The horizontal scale measures gallons of spray applied per year. The vertical scale shows marginal cost and marginal benefit (in dollars) for each additional gallon used. We assume that the cost of buying and spraying the chemical is constant per gallon. Hence the marginal cost curve is a horizontal straight line. The marginal local benefit from incremental gallons of spray, however, declines over the relevant range because there are diminishing returns in mosquito abatement as more gallons are used. From the town's point of view optimum program size is OG gallons per year. To the left of G, marginal town benefit exceeds marginal town cost: it pays to continue expanding the program. To the right of G, marginal town benefit is less than marginal town cost: the program has been overexpanded. The optimum from the town's point of view is therefore at the point where the two curves intersect and marginal town benefit and cost are just equal.

If we consider the welfare of the society, however, rather than of the single town, the optimum program is larger. Because mosquitoes have wings, abatement in one town confers external benefits on neighboring localities, as indicated by the marginal external benefit curve. Regional benefit equals the sum of town benefit plus external benefit. Hence the regional benefit curve lies above that for town benefits only, and from the point of view of society as a whole it would be desirable for the town to expand the program to point H, where marginal cost just equals marginal regional benefit. This case illustrates the general rule that when externalities exist, ordinary decision-making processes usually lead to socially suboptimal outcomes.[2]

Benefit or cost spillovers probably exist for many urban public services. The subject of externalities has received a good deal of attention in recent years and will not be treated in detail here.[3] Suffice it to say that local education is now thought to produce nationwide external benefits, local pollution control clearly yields external benefits over a wide region, and even the activity of the local police force in suppressing crime probably confers benefits far outside the local jurisdiction.

There are two responses to the problem of externalities in the public sector, either of which would help to overcome distortions due to geographic spillovers and bring us closer to the optimum level of output for a given service. (1) Enlarge the jurisdiction providing the service until it takes in most of the area over which significant cost or benefit spillovers occur. In this way externalities are "internalized," and the interests of the jurisdiction become identical with those of society. Therefore the enlarged jurisdiction could be expected to make socially optimal output decisions. (2) In the case of external benefits, arrange for a higher level of government to subsidize the local agency providing the service by means of open-ended, matching, functional grants. In the case illustrated in Figure 15.1 it would be necessary to contrive a subsidy that would increase program size from OG to OH. (Intergovernmental grants for such purposes will be analyzed in detail later.)

2. Undersupply when external benefits exist, as in the example, was once thought to be the general case. More recently it has been shown that with reciprocal externalities among suppliers, oversupply is also a possible outcome. See J. M. Buchanan and M. Z. Kafoglis, "A Note on Public Goods Supply," *American Economic Review*, June 1963, pp. 403–414; and Alan Williams, "The Optimal Provision of Public Goods in a System of Local Government," *Journal of Political Economy*, February 1966, pp. 18–33.

3. See, for example, the discussion in Werner Z. Hirsch, *Urban Economic Analysis* (New York: McGraw-Hill, 1973), pp. 22–26, 412–417, and the sources cited therein.

FIGURE 15.1
Optimal Provision of a Local Service with External Benefits

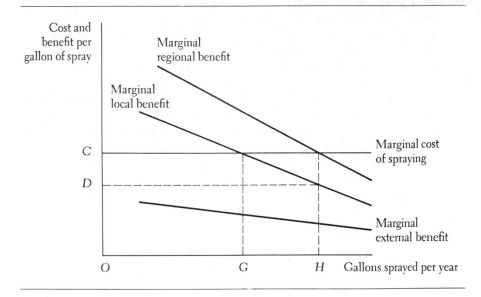

Supplying Public Services at Minimum Unit Cost

Whatever services are to be supplied to satisfy citizens' preferences ought to be produced at the lowest possible unit costs. It is therefore important to discover how unit cost varies with the size of the jurisdiction in the output of particular local services. Although it is difficult to measure the output of a public-service-producing agency, economists have published some useful studies of unit costs.[4] If the technical conditions of production are such that a range of decreasing unit costs is followed by a range of increasing unit costs as the size of the jurisdiction increases, the average-cost curve is U-shaped, and unit cost is lowest for a jurisdiction whose size corresponds to the bottom of the U. Thus if the average unit cost curve for a particular public service is U-shaped, the minimum unit cost criterion can indicate the best jurisdictional size for that service. Of course, if average unit cost curves are approximately horizontal, indicating that unit costs do not vary with the scale of output, this criterion becomes irrelevant.

The situation is made more complicated if we allow for the fact that *producing unit* need not be synonymous with *jurisdiction.* It is sometimes possible for smaller jurisdictions to purchase services from larger ones or from large private contractors. In that way governmental units can remain small

4. See ibid., pp. 326–334 and studies cited therein, and William F. Fox, *Size Economies in Local Government Services: A Review,* U.S. Department of Agriculture, Rural Development Research Report No. 22, 1980 (NTIS No. PB80-219355).

without sacrificing the possible advantages of economies of scale in the production of local services. This sort of arrangement, sometimes called the Lakewood plan, has been used successfully in Southern California.[5] (Also see discussion of "contracting out" in this chapter.)

It is important to note that the minimum unit cost criterion can indicate when jurisdictions are too large to be efficient as well as when they are too small. Further study of public service costs may reveal, for example, that very large cities are now encountering diseconomies of scale in public output and that unit costs could be reduced by the decentralization of production, at least for some public services. This is only speculation, however, and the strong interest in the decentralization of urban services that began in the 1960s took its impetus less from considerations of economic cost than from a desire to increase democratic participation and to make government more accessible to the governed. These political objectives are the next category to be discussed.

Political Participation and Accessibility

Political as well as economic objectives must, of course, be taken into account in discussing the arrangement of metropolitan functions and boundaries. It is in the American tradition to favor small local governments on the ground that they encourage voter participation, are accessible to citizens in the conduct of their daily business, and are sensitive to local needs. The influence of this very old tradition has been reinforced since the early 1960s by new demands within the larger cities for neighborhood government, community control, and administrative decentralization.[6] While there may be an element of romanticism in the notion that decentralization necessarily returns power to the people or the community, no one who has lived in a large city is likely to dismiss the charge of excessive centralization or unresponsive bureaucracy as unfounded. As George F. Break has written:

> Among the major challenges to the U.S. federal system in the next few
> years, it now seems clear, will be the formation of more rational and effec-
> tive systems of local government. . . . What seems to be needed is some
> magic blend of centralizing and decentralizing changes that will create
> simultaneously both larger and smaller units of local government than
> any that now exist.[7]

5. See Robert Warren, "A Municipal Services Market Model of Metropolitan Organiza-
tion," *Journal of the American Institute of Planners*, August 1964, pp. 193–204.
6. See, for example, Milton Kotler, *Neighborhood Government* (Indianapolis: Bobbs-
Merrill, 1969); and Howard W. Hallman, *Neighborhood Government in a Metropolitan Setting*
(Beverly Hills, Calif.: Sage Publications, 1974).
7. George F. Break, "Changing Roles of Different Levels of Government," in
Universities-National Bureau Committee for Economic Research, *The Analysis of Public Output*
(New York: Columbia University Press, 1970), p. 182.

It should be borne in mind, however, that public services differ greatly in the extent to which they involve politically sensitive issues. Voters by and large are not much interested in having access to the officials who operate the fire department, inspect meat markets, or distribute the water supply. On the other hand, they are most certainly concerned about access to the school board and the police department. The criterion of political accessibility does not apply with equal force to all services.

Planning and Coordination

The metropolitan area is in its very nature an interconnected, organic whole. Consequently, many of its governmental functions ought to be planned on an areawide scale. Transportation, recreation, and environmental protection are only the the most obvious of these. A more ambitious reckoning would certainly include areawide planning of land-use densities and housing policy.

The typically fragmented pattern of metropolitan jurisdictions makes such planning very difficult. Local units, sanctioned by the strong tradition favoring the right to local self-government, can often prevent effective action from being taken on a metropolitan scale. Nevertheless, areawide planning *is* on the increase. Partly this results from a growing recognition that in the long run, planning and coordination can be in everyone's interest; partly it results from pressure applied by the federal government. Since the mid-1960s many federal grant programs have carried the stipulation that recipient local projects must be part of a comprehensive regional plan, and special grants have been made available to help finance new metropolitan planning agencies.

Meanwhile, within the larger cities, the neighborhood activism that has accompanied the movement for decentralization further complicates the process of planning and coordination. The neighborhood movement had its origins in opposition to the incursions of highway and urban renewal schemes. Its success in halting many of these projects has made both planners and politicians highly sensitive to the need for reconciling conflicting interests as part of the planning process. Of course, there is no technically "correct" way of doing that, if it can be done at all. This nicely illustrates the conflict between the various objectives of local government: if we increase the number of minor jurisdictions in order to maximize the formal representation of neighborhood interests, we run the risk of seriously impeding large-scale urban planning.

GEOGRAPHIC DISPARITIES: THE PROBLEM OF INEQUITY

The problem of geographic disparities is easily summarized: the needs of the population for public services and the taxable resources out of which to pay for them are not similarly distributed across the map of local areas. Because local government plays such an important role in American life, geographic inequality in the distribution of local needs and resources is a serious issue. Rich towns can provide a higher level of service than poor ones. It may not matter *who* you are, but it does matter *where* you are. From the point of view of the individuals and social classes involved this appears to be an inequity, a denial of social justice. From the point of view of society it is more than that: the maldistribution of local resources impedes progress toward achieving major social goals such as better education, improved health, and reduced poverty.

Disparities in taxable resources give rise to differences between localities in the "tax price" of a given bundle of services. For example, residents in a poor school district might have to pay a property tax rate of 3 percent to supply themselves with school services identical to those that a richer district could supply with a 2 percent tax. Such differences in tax price are used by some analysts as an indicator of "fiscal disparity."[8] The term *geographic disparities*, employed here, is broader, since it allows for interarea differences in the cost of services as well as in the resources out of which to pay for them. We turn first to differences in resources.

Disparities in the Distribution of Taxable Resources

Within metropolitan areas the distribution of resources and population between central cities and suburban rings has been shifting rapidly. As we pointed out in Chapter 10, the influx of the poor to the central cities, combined with the outward migration of middle- and upper-income families to the suburbs, has reversed the earlier pattern in which income was higher in central cities than in the ring. Today income levels are distinctly higher in the suburbs, and the gap is widening steadily. At the same time, under the influence of forces described in earlier chapters, business as well as personal wealth has been dispersing to the suburbs.

Tables 15.1 and 15.2 measure disparities between central cities and suburban areas in the level of two taxable resources, income and property value. As Table 15.1 shows, in 1959 median family income in central cities was already 11 percent below the suburban level. By 1983 the gap had widened to 24 percent. When income is measured per capita rather than per household, the disparity is somewhat reduced because suburban households are larger, and household income is therefore spread a little thinner. Even on this basis, however, central city income in 1980 was 16 percent below the level in the suburbs. Moreover, the trend toward increased disparity is clear under both income measures.

8. See, for example, William H. Oakland, "Central Cities: Fiscal Plight and Prospects for Reform," in Peter Mieszkowski and Mahlon Straszheim, eds., *Current Issues in Urban Economics* (Baltimore: Johns Hopkins University Press, 1979), p. 330.

TABLE 15.1
Disparities in Income between Central Cities and Suburban Areas

		CENTRAL CITIES	OUTSIDE CENTRAL CITIES	RATIO: cc/occ
Median family income (current dollars)				
	1959	5,897	6,639	.89
	1983	22,311	29,314	.76
Income per capita (current dollars), 37 largest SMSAs[a]				
All regions[a]	1960	2,054	2,170	.95
	1976	4,947	5,603	.88
	1980	7,086	8,543	.84
Northeast	1960	1,999	2,309	.87
	1976	4,716	5,856	.81
	1980	6,483	8,753	.74
North Central	1960	2,035	2,277	.89
	1976	4,773	5,584	.85
	1980	6,711	8,594	.78
South	1960	1,848	1,868	.99
	1976	4,832	5,352	.90
	1980	6,907	8,246	.84
West	1960	2,404	2,129	1.13
	1976	5,713	5,521	1.03
	1980	8,241	8,577	.96

[a]These are the 37 SMSAs for which systematic fiscal data are available back to 1957. See list in app. table A-9 of Advisory Commission, 1984, cited in the *Sources.*
[b]Regions are similar to Census Bureau definitions except that Washington and Baltimore are included in the Northeast rather than the South.
Sources: Median family income: U.S. Bureau of the Census, *Current Population Reports,* series P-23, no. 37, June 1971, table 7, and series P-60, no. 146, April 1985, table 21; income per capita: from three publications of the Advisory Commission on Intergovernmental Relations: 1960 data from *Trends in Metropolitan America,* February 1977, table 10; 1976 data from *Central City–Suburban Fiscal Disparity & City Distress, 1977,* December 1980, app. table A-7; 1980 data from *Fiscal Disparities: Central Cities & Suburbs, 1981,* August 1984, app. table A-7.

The per capita income measures in Table 15.1 are for the thirty-seven largest SMSAs. When these are grouped geographically the table shows a marked difference in income disparity by region. The gap is widest in the large SMSAs of the Northeast, slightly narrower in the North Central (i.e., Midwest) region, still narrower in the South, and smallest of all in the West where as late as 1976 per capita income was actually slightly higher in central cities than in suburban areas. In all regions, however, central city income declined markedly relative to suburban income between 1960 and 1980. The regional pattern of income disparities shown in Table 15.1 is strongly associated with differences in the average age of central cities in the four regions. As explained in Chapter 10, the older the central city, the lower its socioeconomic status is likely to be in comparison to its own suburbs.

TABLE 15.2
Disparities in Property Value Per Capita Between Central Cities and Suburban Areas

		AVERAGE PROPERTY VALUE PER CAPITA (CURRENT DOLLARS)		
		Central Cities	Outside Central Cities	Ratio: CC/OCC
17 large older cities[a]	1961	6,223	6,074	1.02
	1971	9,419	11,282	.83
	1981	22,273	30,897	.72
26 largest cities[b]	1971	8,088	9,585	.84
	1981	25,740	33,984	.76
Northeast	1971	6,844	8,732	.78
	1981	17,278	27,370	.63
North Central	1971	6,947	9,652	.72
	1981	15,631	27,416	.57
South	1971	7,534	8,692	.87
	1981	32,955	44,046	.75
West	1971	11,504	11,083	1.04
	1981	43,353	42,064	1.03

[a]A sample of large older U.S. cities chosen to illustrate central city fiscal problems. See William H. Oakland, "Central Cities: Fiscal Plight and Prospects for Reform," in Peter Mieszkowski and Mahlon Straszheim, eds., *Current Issues in Urban Economics* (Baltimore: Johns Hopkins University Press, 1979), pp. 325, 327. Data for 1961 and 1971 from Oakland; for 1981 estimated from *1982 Census of Governments.*
[b]All U.S. cities that had a population greater than 500,000 in either 1960 or 1970, except Washington, D.C. (omitted as not comparable) and Honolulu and Jacksonville (in which the city covered the entire SMSA in 1970). See George E. Peterson, "Finance," in William Gorham and Nathan Glazer, eds., *The Urban Predicament* (Washington, D.C.: Urban Institute, 1976), pp. 47, 76–77. Data for 1971 from Peterson; for 1981 estimated from *1982 Census of Governments.*
Sources: Oakland, table 10.3; Peterson, table 13; and U.S. Bureau of the Census, *1982 Census of Governments*, vol. 2, tables 20 and 21.

Although income taxes account for only 6 percent of local tax revenues (see Table 14.4), it is indisputable that personal income underlies much of the local tax base. First of all, retail sales are heavily dependent on personal income, and sales and gross receipts taxes account for nearly 15 percent of local tax revenue. More important, there is a direct relationship between personal income and wealth in the form of residential property. Towns with wealthier families can therefore be expected to have more taxable residential property per capita than towns where the average income level is lower. Since the property tax produces 75 percent of local tax revenues, perhaps as much as half of it from residential property, wealth in that form obviously makes up an important part of the local tax base.

Nevertheless, the casual observer may suppose that despite the dispersal of industry and middle-and upper-income population to the suburbs, the typical central city, with its towering CBD and dense development, must still have a larger property tax base per capita than the suburbs. In fact, such is not the case. Table 15.2 presents some evidence on this point. Data for a sample of seventeen SMSAs containing large, older central cities show that per capita property value in 1961 averaged 2 percent higher in the central cities than in the suburbs. In 1971 the level in the same central cities averaged 17 percent below that in ring areas. By 1981 the disparity had widened to 28 percent. A larger sample that includes both older and newer cities shows almost the same level of disparity in both 1971 and 1981. When this larger sample is subdivided geographically, a pattern of regional differences emerges that (not surprisingly) resembles the regional pattern of income differentials. The property tax base of central cities was lowest relative to that of suburbs in the Northeast and North Central regions. It was relatively higher, though still below the suburban average, in the South, while in the West it slightly exceeded the outside central city level.

The present situation of the older central cities contrasts strongly with their position forty or fifty years ago. Then as now, the data suggested that residential property value per capita was higher in the suburbs than in the central cities. But this disparity was offset by the overwhelming central city concentration of commercial and industrial property. Although the core cities then contained large populations of the immigrant poor, they were also centers of wealth that could be taxed for the support of local services. In recent decades, however, the evolving pattern of metropolitan settlement has inexorably turned the tables against them: the older central cities house an increasing proportion of the nation's poor, whom they must service out of taxes on a decreasing proportion of the nation's wealth.

Disparities in the Cost of Services

The increasing concentration of the poor into the nation's inner cities has already been documented in Chapter 10. The rate of poverty in central cities as a whole is more than twice the rate in suburban areas. Fiscally, this puts the central cities at a double disadvantage. The concentration of poverty not only reduces their tax base but also adds to their service costs.

Poverty affects the cost of public services in several ways. First, the higher the incidence of poverty the more a locality is likely to spend for poverty-connected services such as welfare, medical programs, housing assistance, and social services. Although most of these functions are heavily subsidized by the state and federal governments, they are also likely to involve direct costs to the localities themselves.

Second, the presence of a poverty population raises the cost of providing services that are not ordinarily thought of as poverty-connected. As

George E. Peterson puts it, "Population traits ... help to determine how much it will cost to reach any given level of service quality."[9] Children from culturally and educationally deprived homes are more difficult to educate than are the daughters and sons of the middle class; crime rates are higher in poverty areas; street cleanliness is more difficult to maintain in slum neighborhoods because poor residents use the streets so heavily for recreation and social life.

In addition to paying the higher public service costs that result from the concentration of poverty, large inner cities also bear the burden of higher costs associated with their role as the center of a metropolitan economy. They must provide police and fire protection, traffic regulation, transportation facilities, and so on for a daytime work population much of which lives and pays the bulk of its taxes outside the city limits. These extra costs have sometimes been referred to as "municipal overburden."

To indicate the combined effect of population characteristics and "overburden" in raising the cost of providing common municipal services in central cities, Peterson calculated expenditure per capita on police protection in 1972–1973 in the central cities and suburbs for a sample of twenty-six SMSAs. On the average, central cities spent $49 per capita, almost exactly double the $24 per capita spent by suburbs. In the older SMSAs of the Northeast and North Central regions, central cities spent 135 percent more per capita than did the suburbs.[10]

Fiscal disparities within SMSAs are summarized in Table 15.3 using data developed by Seymour Sacks for the Advisory Commission on Intergovernmental Relations. The table refers to the thirty-seven largest SMSAs, a group for which systematic data are available back to 1957, which permits an examination of the trend in disparities over time. Reflecting the greater cost of providing public services, per capita expenditures in core cities were 29 percent higher than in the suburbs in 1957 and 39 percent higher in 1981. The per capita cost of noneducational expenditures was double the suburban level in 1957 and 84 percent above it in 1981. Expenditures per capita on education are slightly lower in central cities than in suburbs, though they have gradually been catching up.

Disparities in Tax Burden

Table 15.3 shows that to finance their higher level of expenditures, central cities collect substantially more tax dollars per capita than do the suburbs:

9. George E. Peterson, "Finance," in William Gorham and Nathan Glazer, eds., *The Urban Predicament* (Washington, D.C.: Urban Institute, 1976), p. 47. The effect of environmental factors, including population traits, on the cost of local public service outputs was first systematically analyzed by D. F. Bradford, R. A. Malt, and W. E. Oates in "The Rising Cost of Local Public Services: Some Evidence and Reflections," *National Tax Journal*, June 1969, pp. 185–202.

10. Peterson, table 13, pp. 76–77.

TABLE 15.3
Local Government Tax and Expenditure Disparities between Central Cities and Suburban Areas in the 37 Largest SMSAs[a]

	1957			1981		
	Central Cities	Outside Central Cities	Ratio CC/OCC	Central Cities	Outside Central Cities	Ratio CC/OCC
Expenditures per capita ($)	196	154	1.29	1,453	1,058	1.39
Education	61	80	.80	420	471	.91
Noneducation	135	74	2.02	1,023	586	1.84
Federal and state aid per capita ($)	40	40	1.01	705	451	1.63
Tax receipts per capita ($)	117	80	1.57	556	449	1.29
Taxes as percentage of income[b]						
All regions	5.7	3.7	1.54	7.8	5.3	1.47
Northeast	6.8	4.4	1.54	11.0	6.6	1.67
North Central	5.7	3.5	1.63	7.5	5.0	1.50
South	4.8	2.8	1.71	6.9	4.3	1.60
West	5.2	3.7	1.41	5.8	4.5	1.29

[a]See Table 15.1, note a.
[b]Average tax receipts per capita (1957 and 1981) divided by average income per capita (1960 and 1980). No allowance is made for possible tax exporting.
Sources: Fiscal data: Advisory Commission on Intergovernmental Relations, *Fiscal Disparities: Central Cities & Suburbs, 1981*, August 1984, table 4; income data: Table 15.1 in this chapter.

57 percent more in 1957, diminishing to a margin of 29 percent more by 1981. The disparity in tax receipts could decline while the difference in expenditures was growing because federal and state aid per capita to central cities increased more than did aid to suburban areas. In 1957 aid per capita was equal in the two parts of SMSAs. By 1981 central cities were receiving 63 percent more per capita.

Despite the sharp increase in federal and state aid and the decline in the intrametropolitan disparity in tax receipts, central cities continue to tax their citizens more heavily in relation to income than do the suburbs. A rough measure of tax effort can be obtained by dividing tax receipts per capita by income per capita. On that basis, the rate of tax in 1957 was 5.7 percent of income in central cities but 3.7 percent in suburbs, a relative difference in excess of 50 percent (see Table 15.3). This difference resulted from the combination of higher tax receipts and lower income in central cities. By 1981 the rate had increased to 7.8 percent in central cities and 5.3 percent in the suburbs. In absolute terms the disparity rose moderately. In relative terms it showed a slight decline.

When SMSAs are grouped by region, the old central cities of the Northeast stand out as having by far the highest taxes in relation to income and the largest absolute margin above the suburban level. Relative disparities between central cities and suburbs, however, are not very different in the Northeast, North Central, and Southern regions. In the West, intrametropolitan disparities are substantially smaller, again suggesting that the socioeconomic contrast between central cities and suburbs is less pronounced in the newer SMSAs of that region.

To be sure, these calculations do not allow for the possibility of "tax exporting" by local jurisdictions. This may occur, for example, when a tax is levied on local business property. If the taxed firm sells some of its output outside the local community it may, in effect, "export" some of the tax burden in the form of higher prices. Or if the tax reduces profits and the firm is owned by nonresidents, some of the burden may be exported through lower dividends to outsiders. Netzer points out that the export percentage tends to be higher for central cities than for suburbs because a higher proportion of central city taxable property is commercial. In general, however, this difference in the capacity to export taxes is not large enough to eliminate the difference between local tax burdens in central cities and suburbs.[11]

Effects of Redistributive Local Budgets

Up to this point the discussion of geographic disparities has concentrated on differences in the average level of taxes or the average level of expenditures between central cities and their suburbs. Average tax levels and

11. Dick Netzer, "Impact of the Property Tax: Its Economic Implications for Urban Problems," in Mitchell and Walter, pp. 166–168.

average benefit levels within localities do not tell the whole story, however. It was pointed out in Chapter 14 that local budgets tend to redistribute income from rich to poor by giving the poor more benefits than they pay for and the rich less. We now wish to examine the process of income redistribution in greater detail and to show, in particular, how differences between communities in the average level of income interact with redistributive policies within localities both to create horizontal inequities—that is, violations of the ethical rule requiring equal treatment of equals—and to speed up the counterproductive process of tax base erosion.

Redistribution occurs at the local level for two reasons. First, local governments *do* contribute funds to redistributive programs in the fields of health, welfare, and housing, even though (as shown in Chapter 14) an ideal division of budgetary functions would leave all such activities to the federal government. Second, and probably more important, even if local governments confined themselves entirely to allocative functions such as the provision of school, police, fire, and sanitation services, the manner in which these are typically financed would necessarily redistribute income from rich to poor. Let us see why this is so.

Following the argument of James M. Buchanan, we define fiscal pressure on the taxpayer as the difference between the sum paid in taxes and the value of benefits received.[12] Buchanan labels this difference the "fiscal residuum" of the individual. It is defined as positive if tax payments exceed benefits, negative if benefits exceed taxes, and zero if they are equal.

Table 15.4 presents a hypothetical comparison of the fiscal residuals received by taxpayers in two towns that differ in average level of income. Each town has three citizens. Wealthy taxpayers, each of whom owns residential property worth $100,000, are denoted W1, W2, W3. Poor taxpayers, whose residential property is worth only $10,000, are denoted P1, P2, P3. The wealthy town consists of two wealthy taxpayers and one poor one; the poor town reverses these proportions. Each town raises all its revenue by a 2 percent tax on residential property.

In each of the hypothetical towns benefits are distributed on an equal per capita basis, as might well be the case with purely allocative functions. Since tax payments are proportional to wealth, while expenditure distribution is regressive to wealth, the rich in both towns pay more in taxes than they receive in benefits, while the poor receive more benefits than they pay for in taxes. Thus both towns redistribute real income from rich to poor. The right-hand column, labeled "Fiscal Residual or Net Gain," shows the extent of the redistribution. It indicates that both rich and poor are better off in the wealthy town. Each individual pays the same amount of tax no matter where he or she lives, but the benefit level is higher in the rich town because the tax

12. James M. Buchanan, "Federalism and Fiscal Equity," in R. A. Musgrave and C. S. Shoup, eds., *Readings in the Economics of Taxation* (Homewood, Ill.: Richard D. Irwin, 1959), p. 99.

TABLE 15.4

Taxes and Expenditure Benefits as a Function of Local Per Capita Wealth: A Hypothetical Example

	VALUE OF RESIDENTIAL PROPERTY	TAX PAYMENTS AT 2% OF PROPERTY VALUE	BENEFITS RECEIVED	FISCAL RESIDUAL OR NET GAIN
Wealthy Town				
Citizen W1	$100,000	$2,000	$1,400	− $ 600
W2	100,000	2,000	1,400	− 600
P1	10,000	200	1,400	+ 1,200
Total	$210,000	$4,200	$4,200	0
Poor Town				
Citizen P2	$ 10,000	$ 200	$ 800	+ $ 600
P3	10,000	200	800	+ 600
W3	100,000	2,000	800	− 1,200
Total	$120,000	$2,400	$2,400	0

base is larger. In the wealthy town the poor person enjoys a net gain of $1,200 via the public budget. In the poor town he or she would gain only $600. In the wealthy town the rich lose $600 on account of budgetary transactions. Their counterpart in the poor town loses $1,200.

Thus differences in the fiscal resources of local communities, when coupled with redistributive tax-expenditure systems, create inequities: people of like income or wealth status are treated differently by the local government depending on whether they happen to live in a rich or a poor community. This is the equity problem in local public finance.

True, if localities were willing and able to charge for services on the benefit principle, that part of the local budget devoted to allocative functions would not be redistributive. Each resident would make payments equal in amount to the value of benefits individually received. There would be no fiscal residuum and, consequently, no redistribution of real income. Payment in proportion to benefit is, in fact, the theoretically preferred means of financing allocative functions. It was pointed out in Chapter 14, however, that citizens will not voluntarily pay prices based on benefits received when services are not subject to exclusion.[13] Nor can involuntary payments do the job, for there exists no general method of benefit taxation under which a government could collect compulsory payments that bear any close relation to individual benefits received.[14] As a practical matter, therefore, local budgets are likely to

13. The point is developed in full in R. A. Musgrave, *The Theory of Public Finance* (New York: McGraw-Hill, 1959), ch. 4.

14. For a discussion of the rather limited possibilities that do exist for benefit taxation, see Richard A. Musgrave and Peggy B. Musgrave, *Public Finance in Theory and Practice*, 4th ed. (New York: McGraw-Hill, 1984), pp. 228–232. A more optimistic view is presented in George F. Break, *Financing Government in a Federal System* (Washington, D.C.: Brookings Institution, 1980), pp. 226–242.

remain redistributive from rich to poor, even if localities perform only allocative functions.[15]

Selective Migration and the Erosion of the Central City Tax Base

The fact that taxpayers of equal income are treated differently depending on where they live contributes to the problem of central city tax base erosion. Both rich and poor could improve their situation by moving from poorer to richer communities. The rich are able to do so at their own option. The poor can do so also, if the move involves migrating from relatively low-income rural or nonmetropolitan areas or from outside the United States to the relatively more affluent U. S. central cities. But within a given metropolitan area the situation is different. The rich are able to improve their fiscal lot by moving from the central city to the suburbs, where the average income level is still higher.[16] But the poor are effectively prevented from following them, not just by racial discrimination and large-lot zoning but by the absence in the suburbs of a plentiful supply of the old low-rent housing on which they typically rely and by the high transportation cost required for suburban living. Selective migration consequently speeds the erosion of the central city tax base.

Table 15.4 illustrates the effect on taxpayer welfare of differences in the average wealth level of local jurisdictions. It is obvious that differences in the "redistributiveness" of local budgets have analogous effects. Whatever its average wealth level, the more a community makes use of the local budget to redistribute income to the poor, the more attractive it will become to the poor and the more repellent to the rich. Since the 1960s the older central cities, with their concentration of the impoverished and of ethnic minorities, have been under great pressure to direct public resources to the benefit of the lowest income classes. Thus they face a painful dilemma: if they spend more on the poor, they increase the fiscal pressure that encourages the rich to move out, thus eroding the tax base and undermining future prospects for those who remain; if they attempt to defend the tax base by choosing policies that are less redistributive, they can be accused of turning their backs on their poorest citizens.

Geographic Disparities, Tax Competition, and the Level of Public Expenditure

The existence of large geographic disparities in needs and resources between central cities and suburbs provides a powerful argument for both state

15. For a statistical estimate of the net redistributive effect of school taxes and benefits in a suburban Philadelphia school district, see M. Brian McDonald, "Educational Equity and the Fiscal Incidence of Public Education," *National Tax Journal*, March 1980, pp. 45–54. McDonald finds a significant inverse relationship between net benefits (benefits – taxes) and family income for this purely "allocative" function.

16. For recent evidence that fiscal incentives do affect location decisions of the well-to-do, see references in Ch. 6, n.17.

and federal aid to localities. As Table 14.4 shows, such aid did increase substantially during the 1960s and 1970s. There were probably two motives at work. First, it was recognized that heavy reliance on local finance was inequitable, given the extent of geographic disparities. Moreover, as we have seen, these disparities were not simply the result of natural economic development but were reinforced by local policy. The tax-benefit calculus in Table 15.4 shows that it is strongly in the interest of residents in a wealthy town to keep out those whose wealth level is below the town average, since such people will not "pay their way" vis-à-vis the local fisc. The exclusionary housing and land-use policies by which the suburbs have tried to prevent lower-middle-class and lower-class families from moving in were described in Chapter 13. This deliberate self-segregation by the suburban middle and upper classes reduced their own burdens at the expense of those remaining in the core cities. Self-interested local policy thus reinforced the development of geographic disparities in wealth. Second, there is more at stake than who pays the bills: the disparity between needs and taxpaying capacity at the local level also reduces the commitment of resources that is made toward meeting the national problems of poverty and inequality, because the phenomenon known as "tax competition" comes into play. Localities are reluctant to raise taxes much above those prevailing in other places for fear of driving away taxpaying businesses and individuals.[17] These fears are inversely related to the size of the taxing jurisdiction. The federal government can ignore the remote possibility that higher taxes will drive resources out of the country. States are sensitive to the potential mobility of taxpayers but less so than localities, which fear that businesses serving local markets and wealthy taxpayers holding local jobs might easily be tempted to move across municipal boundaries in response to tax differentials. It is probable that fears associated with tax competition keep the provision of services, especially those for the poor, below the level they would otherwise attain.

What can be done to overcome fiscal disparities within metropolitan areas? Possible solutions to the major problems of metropolitan public finance will be taken up at length later in this chapter. In addition, recall that in Chapter 13 we analyzed a variety of policies designed to open up the suburbs to poor and lower-middle-income families. One purpose of these policies is to give racial minorities the opportunity to exercise wider choice of residential location within metropolitan areas. There are sufficient arguments in favor of this as a matter of right, but, in addition, a relatively uniform geographic distribution of the poor (if one may speak in such crude terms) would also make it possible to use the entire metropolitan tax base in financing local services for that part of the population that does not "pay its own way." However,

---

17. Dick Netzer, "Federal, State and Local Finance in a Metropolitan Context," in Harvey S. Perloff and Lowdon Wingo, Jr., eds., *Issues in Urban Economics* (Baltimore: Johns Hopkins University Press, 1968), p. 444. Concerning the effects of tax differentials on business location, see Netzer's extensive citations on the same page.

even the most active policies to open up the suburbs could hardly work fast enough to count as a solution to present metropolitan fiscal inequities.

To be sure, evolutionary forces, such as the aging of housing in the older suburbs, are already helping to bring about some movement of poor and lower-middle-income minority families into the suburbs and will continue to do so. But the dispersion of poverty that takes place as a result of natural evolutionary forces is already having its own unfortunate fiscal results. As low-income families concentrate in a relatively small number of older suburban towns, those areas are beginning to face the same sort of fiscal squeeze already endured by the central cities. The natural processes of metropolitan development are not likely to eliminate intrametropolitan fiscal disparities in the foreseeable future.

URBAN FISCAL DISTRESS

Although there had been earlier signs of trouble, the nation suddenly became conscious of an "urban fiscal crisis" when New York City teetered on the brink of bankruptcy in 1975. New York averted bankruptcy by means of sweeping budgetary reforms combined with emergency regulation and support by the state and federal governments. In the years following that financial cataclysm, other large cities have moved in and out of "crisis," as evidenced by temporary inability to meet payrolls, school years radically shortened to cut expenses, and even failure to meet debt obligations on time.[18] Such events are the most dramatic signs of urban fiscal distress, but that problem itself is both more pervasive and less highly charged than these occasional symptoms would suggest.

Because the problem is many-sided, it is difficult to frame a concise definition of "urban fiscal distress." Perhaps an acceptable general statement would be that it involves an acutely painful imbalance between needs and resources.[19] Since localities are usually required by state law to balance their operating budgets, there cannot be an imbalance between expenditures and revenues. Fiscal distress is therefore measured not by budget deficits but by the pain generated in trying to avoid them.

18. For a colorful description of New York's financial crisis and the events leading to it, see Ken Auletta, *The Streets Were Paved with Gold* (New York: Random House, 1979). A scholarly analysis of its causes is contained in *The City in Transition: Prospects and Policies for New York*, Final Report of the Temporary Commission on City Finances, Raymond D. Horton, Staff Director, June 1977 (New York: Arno Press, 1978). Other municipal fiscal crises from 1972 through 1983 are reviewed in Advisory Commission on Intergovernmental Relations, *Bankruptcies, Defaults, and Other Local Government Financial Emergencies* (Washington, D.C.: U.S. Government Printing Office, March 1985).

19. This definition is borrowed from the title of ch. 9, "Fiscal Distress: An Imbalance between Resources and Needs," in U.S. Department of Housing and Urban Development, *Occasional Papers*, vol. 4, July 1979, ed. by Robert Paul Boynton. Stephen M. Barro draws an interesting distinction among fiscal disadvantage, fiscal decline, and acute fiscal crisis in *The Urban Impacts of Federal Policies*, doc. no. R2114-KF/HEW vol. 3, *Fiscal Conditions* (Santa Monica, Calif.: Rand Corp., 1978), pp. 11–17.

We have already shown that central cities are under pressure to spend more per capita on public services than do the suburbs but have fewer resources per capita out of which to pay for them. If they are to meet the demand for services while balancing their budgets, they must tax themselves at higher rates than do the suburbs. Many of them have been doing so for some time. That kind of fiscal pain becomes fiscal distress when a gradually deteriorating central city tax base makes substantial cuts in service necessary while tax rates remain high or even increase.

Difficulty of Intercity Comparisons

Fiscal comparisons among U.S. cities are notoriously difficult to carry out. First of all, the division of functions between states and their localities varies widely from state to state. At one extreme lies the state of Hawaii, where local governments account for only 20 percent of combined state and local direct general expenditure. At the other is Florida, where localities are responsible for 68 percent of combined expenditure. In the United States as a whole, the local share averages 69 percent.[20] In states where localities bear a higher than average share of expenditure responsibilities, local taxes are also likely to be higher than elsewhere.

Second, functional arrangements at the local level vary widely.[21] For example, county governments carry out significant functions in most states, including functions within the boundaries of the cities they contain. However, a number of cities, including Baltimore, Denver, New York, Philadelphia, St. Louis, and San Francisco are either completely or substantially consolidated with their county governments. In general, these cities will be found to carry out a wider and more costly range of functions than such places as Chicago, Cleveland, Detroit, or Los Angeles, or indeed most smaller cities, which are serviced by a functioning county government.

At the height of the fiscal crisis it was pointed out that the City of New York annually spent about $1,500 per resident for public services, while Chicago managed quite nicely on only $300 per head. No wonder New York City was going broke! Such a bald comparison, however, was pointless, since New York supported many functions, including public schools, a public university, welfare, and a health and hospital system, services that in Chicago are left almost entirely in the hands of the state or of an independent (and noncoterminous) county government. When such differences are overlooked, comparisons become meaningless. Yet the range of variation across the nation is so great that standardized comparisons are difficult to carry out.

20. U.S. Bureau of the Census, *Governmental Finances in 1983–84*, series GF-84 no. 5, October 1985, table 13.
21. For a concise description of the variation in local functional responsibilities, see U.S. Bureau of the Census, *City Employment in 1984*, series GE-84, no. 2, July 1985, pp. vii–viii.

Causes of Urban Fiscal Distress

The underlying causes of urban fiscal distress can be quickly summarized. Fiscally distressed cities are likely to have experienced the following:

1. *Population exchange.* Massive out-migration of the middle class accompanied by a heavy influx of low-income population weakens the city's tax base while simultaneously increasing the cost of providing public services.
2. *Population and job decline.* Decentralization of jobs and population into the suburbs leaves the central city with a smaller population and a shrinking economy.

We have already analyzed the effect of population exchange on central city budgets. The budgetary squeeze it produces can obviously cause fiscal distress. That analysis need not be repeated here.

What does require a further explanation is why job and population decline *per se* should also be troublesome. To be sure, such declines could be expected to reduce a city's tax base, thus generating pressure for higher tax rates if service levels were to be maintained.[22] On the other hand, would not a smaller population also reduce the need for services, thus matching on the expenditure side the decline taking place in revenues? The cost of providing services, however, may not diminish in step with falling population. In that case population and job decline would indeed add to the fiscal distress of central cities. There are two very different reasons why population loss may not lead to a proportionate reduction in public service costs. The first is structural, the second political.

Structural Problems of Declining Cities

The structural problem of decline is essentially one of excess capacity. As a city grows, its public infrastructure—streets, sewers, schools, transit systems, and so on—is expanded to serve the larger population. If the population then falls, the city is left with excess physical capacity. The per capita cost of running the infrastructure increases as the number of users declines.

To illustrate the effect of excess capacity, consider two kinds of public service. The first is provided over the whole area of the city through a network of physical structures: functions such as streets and highways, sewers, water supply, and rail mass transit. Once these systems are in place, there is little possibility of closing down portions of them to economize, should the population of the city begin to decline. Instead, each system must be operated and maintained more or less in full. To the extent that part or all of these

22. Tax revenue per job (New York City, 1970) by industrial sector and type of tax is estimated in Roy Bahl, Alan Campbell, and David Greytak, *Taxes, Expenditures and the Economic Base: Case Study of New York City* (New York: Praeger, 1974) table 2.45, p. 142.

costs remain fixed, cost per person will increase as population falls. For example, as we pointed out in Chapter 9, the cost per passenger of operating a rail mass transit system rises markedly as the number of riders drops.

Next consider services such as education, police and fire protection, and hospital care that are provided on a district-by-district basis. As population declines, schools and hospitals become underutilized, which increases the cost per unit of service delivered. Likewise, the cost per resident of maintaining and operating a given number of fire and police facilities increases as population shrinks.

Some saving in operating costs might be achieved by closing schools, hospitals, and perhaps even police stations and firehouses. But there is typically strong neighborhood resistance to such moves. Moreover, if the population thins out haphazardly, it may be difficult to find neighborhoods where facilities could plausibly be shut down.[23]

It must be noted, too, that closing down facilities does not reduce capital costs. Unless buildings can be sold back to the private sector (unlikely in a declining city), the capital embodied in them is a sunk cost and cannot be recovered. Debt service continues whether or not facilities are used. Indeed, the cost per taxpayer of servicing debt previously issued to finance the development of infrastructure increases as population declines.

Political Problems of Budget Making in Declining Cities

The second reason why service costs may not decline as rapidly as population can be labeled political. Although the normative theory of public expenditure tells us that the economic objective of local government should be to supply goods and services that cannot be provided efficiently by the private sector, it must be acknowledged that city governments, to use Peterson's phrase, also act as "suppliers of jobs."[24] There is, of course, a long tradition of city government "patronage" dating back to the nineteenth century, but it was only with the rapid growth of local spending after World War II that city governments became relatively substantial employers.

During the 1960s and early 1970s, when private-sector employment in most of the older cities was dropping, the number of local government jobs frequently continued to expand.[25] These jobs were especially important to racial minorities, for whom they often provided initial entry to white-collar occupations. Public employee unions, potent for the first time during the 1960s, also exerted pressure to expand the number of jobs, and increased intergovernmental aid often made such expansion seem relatively inexpensive to local

23. For a proposal to deal with the problem of population distribution and land use in declining cities, see James Heilbrun, "On the Theory and Policy of Neighborhood Consolidation," *Journal of the American Planning Association*, October 1979, pp. 417–427.

24. See discussion in Peterson, pp. 112–115.

25. See ibid., table 23, p. 112.

taxpayers. Under these circumstances it is not surprising that local politicians responded by "supplying" more jobs.

Once jobs were built into the local budget, the same political forces that helped put them there resisted their removal. Consequently, even after it became clear that massive economic and population decline was under way, the older central cities did not immediately move to reduce public employment and expenditure. Public employment per capita therefore rose rapidly until the mid-1970s. Although some cities began "belt tightening" earlier, it took the near bankruptcy of New York City in 1975 and the ensuing disruption of the municipal bond market to bring the era of municipal government expansion decisively to an end.

For the purpose of studying urban fiscal problems, Peterson and Muller constructed a sample of large cities grouped into three classes: growing throughout the study period; growing to 1970, declining thereafter; and declining all the way.[26] Peterson found that in 1964 there was relatively little difference in the level of local government employment per thousand residents in the three classes. By 1973 the "declining cities" and the "growing, then declining" group had reached per capita levels, respectively, 49 and 28 percent above the level of "growing" cities.[27] In the mid-1970s, however, a turning point occurred. Employment per capita in growing cities leveled off, while in the two other groups it began to decrease. (See Table 15.5, in which we have carried Peterson's analysis forward to 1984.) Writing around 1975, Peterson hypothesized that the period during which public employment and spending levels per capita were far higher in declining than in growing cities may have been "little more than an aberrant interval, during which the old cities temporarily refused to accept the fiscal implications of their economic decline."[28] By 1984 employment per capita in the "growing, then declining" group had, indeed, fallen 12 percent below its 1977 level, but it had dropped only 5 percent in the "declining" group, where it appeared to be stabilizing at a level substantially above the number for growing cities. Peterson's hypothesis implied that the structural and political problems of declining cities would not permanently encumber their budgets. The evidence to date does not clearly support that analysis. Apparently the fiscal problems of decline are deeprooted and will not soon be overcome.

Measuring Urban Distress

In analyzing geographic disparities in the distribution of resources between cities and suburbs (see Tables 15.1 and 15.2) we pointed out the influence of city age and showed that the old cities of the North and East are much worse off in relation to their suburbs than are the relatively newer cities

---

26. See Thomas Muller, *Growing and Declining Urban Areas: A Fiscal Comparison* (Washington, D.C.: Urban Institute, 1975); and Peterson, pp. 47–64, 75–78. In both studies New York City is treated separately as a fourth category.

27. Peterson, table 6, p. 50.

28. Ibid., p. 51.

TABLE 15.5
Local Public Employees, Growing versus Declining Cities[a]

	GROWING	GROWING TO 1970, THEN DECLINING	DECLINING
Number of cities in sample	7	6	14
Public employees per 1000 residents			
1964	22.2	22.5	25.4
1973	24.0	30.6	35.8
1977	26.7	32.6	35.1
1981	26.4	30.7	33.8
1982	27.0	30.0	32.3
1983	26.7	29.7	32.3
1984	25.8	28.8	33.3
Change (%)			
1964–1977	20.3	44.9	38.2
1977–1984	– 3.4	– 11.7	– 5.1

[a]Full-time equivalent employment, including education.
Sources: Values for 1964 and 1973 from George E. Peterson, "Finance," in William Gorham and Nathan Glazer, eds., *The Urban Predicament* (Washington, D.C.: Urban Institute, 1976), table 6. Values for 1977 and later calculated using data from U.S. Bureau of the Census, *Local Government Employment in Selected Metropolitan Areas and Large Counties* and *City Employment*, various years; *Census of Governments*, 1977 and 1982; and unpublished Census Bureau tabulations.

of the South and West. In the discussion of fiscal distress, building on the work of Peterson and Muller, we have emphasized the effects of growth and decline rather than age. In fact, however, declining cities are mostly "old" and growing cities mostly "new," so the fiscal effects of age are difficult to disentangle from those of decline. In recent years a number of analysts have constructed indices intended to measure relative urban distress, and these indices usually include statistical factors measuring both age and growth. For example, the index developed by James W. Fossett and Richard P. Nathan is the product of three components. The value of the index is larger—and the level of distress presumably higher—the lower the city's income, the greater its age, and the less its rate of population growth, each measured in relation to the mean of all cities in the sample.[29] Such indices can throw light on the

29. James W. Fossett and Richard P. Nathan, "The Prospects for Urban Revival," in Roy Bahl, ed., *Urban Government Finance* (Beverly Hills, Calif.: Sage Publications, 1981), pp. 65–67. The index is calculated from the following formula:

$$\frac{\dfrac{\text{Mean per capita income}}{\text{City per capita income}} \times \dfrac{\text{city percent pre-1940 housing}}{\text{mean percent pre-1940 housing}}}{\dfrac{100 + \text{city rate of population change}}{100 + \text{median rate of population change}}}$$

The percentage of housing built before 1940 serves as a proxy for city age.

question of whether disparities between distressed and healthy cities are growing or diminishing. However, their power to reveal the "true condition" of cities must not be exaggerated. They cannot do more than combine the ingredients put into them. Distressed cities are then simply those that rank high on the particular measures chosen for the index. The Fossett and Nathan index, for example, measures "urban conditions" but does not focus on *fiscal* conditions, since it contains no explicitly fiscal variables. With these caveats in mind, let us see what an urban conditions index can tell us about trends in distress over time.

Two hypotheses suggest themselves.[30] It might be argued on the one hand that in an economy where labor and capital are mobile we should expect disparities between cities eventually to be corrected by those equilibrating mechanisms that connect markets across the nation. For example, we explained in Chapter 3 how the migration of labor from poor to rich regions and of capital in the opposite direction could be expected to reduce interregional differences in wages and incomes.[31] On the other hand, one could argue that because of our fragmented system of local government, fiscal disparities will tend to be self-reinforcing. Cities with a growing poverty population will exhibit rising tax rates, probably combined with deteriorating public service quality. Middle- and upper-income families, including many of the more highly skilled members of the labor force, will move away, causing further fiscal deterioration. High tax rates, low service quality, and a decline in the average skill level of the population will render such cities increasingly unattractive to business. Economic decline will cause further fiscal distress in a cycle of self-reinforcing deterioration.

Trends in the Fossett and Nathan index lend support to the hypothesis that disparities in urban conditions are currently self-reinforcing: from 1960 to 1980 the most distressed cities tended to deteriorate further, while those better off remained relatively unchanged or improved slightly. Fossett and Nathan calculated the index for fifty-three of the fifty-seven largest U.S. cities for 1960 and 1970; in Table 15.6 the index has been carried forward to 1980. Scores in each year were standardized to an average of 100. The table shows results for the central cities of the six largest SMSAs in the North and East and in the South and West.[32] These scores confirm earlier analyses, which stressed the difference between the older cities of the former region and the predominantly newer cities of the latter. All the cities in the North and East group rank well above average on the index of distress. In the South and West category only San Francisco—by far the "oldest" in that class—is above the

---

30. See U. S. Department of Housing and Urban Development, *Occasional Papers*, vol. 4, pp. 86–88.
31. For an interesting critique of this view, see ibid.
32. The cities were chosen to correspond as closely as possible with the two groups analyzed in Chapter. 3. Since Washington and Anaheim were not included in Fossett and Nathan's study, the central cities of the next biggest SMSAs, St. Louis in the North and East and San Diego in the South and West, were substituted.

mean, and even San Francisco scores better than any city in the North and East category. As in Fossett and Nathan's larger sample, the disparity between the better- and worse-off groups widened between 1960 and 1970 and again between 1970 and 1980. In the latter period the average score of the six North and East cities deteriorated from 169 to 192, while the average for the six South and West cities improved slightly.

It must not be assumed that distressed cities are inevitably fated to suffer continuing decline. Among the 25 cities in Fossett and Nathan's sample that ranked above the average in hardship in 1960, such major centers as Boston and Cincinnati showed little or no further deterioration by 1980. Five of the twenty-five—Oakland, Kansas City, Toledo, New Orleans, and Birmingham—actually improved their scores substantially. These five, however, were in the second rather than the first (i.e., most distressed) quintile of distressed cities in 1960.

TABLE 15.6
Urban Conditions in Large Central Cities

| | URBAN CONDITIONS INDEX | | | CHANGE |
	1960	1970	1980	1960–1980 (%)
North and East				
St. Louis	207.6	232.6	266.2	28.2
Philadelphia	166.2	168.5	208.8	25.6
Boston	201.0	193.2	205.7	2.3
Detroit	154.0	151.9	173.2	12.5
Chicago	138.6	146.9	157.1	13.3
New York City	127.6	117.8	141.8	11.1
Average of these six	165.8	168.5	192.1	15.9
South and West				
San Francisco	115.0	116.4	135.9	18.2
Atlanta	70.7	67.0	70.2	− .7
Los Angeles	57.9	51.1	48.0	− 17.1
San Diego	33.8	36.1	24.3	− 28.1
Dallas	38.9	28.1	19.9	− 48.8
Houston	40.2	27.7	13.8	− 65.7
Average of these six	59.4	54.4	52.0	− 12.5
Average of 53 cities	100.0	100.0	100.0	—

Sources: Values for 1960 and 1970 from James W. Fossett and Richard P. Nathan, "The Prospects for Urban Revival," in Roy Bahl, ed., *Urban Government Finance: Emerging Trends* (Beverly Hills, Calif.: Sage Publications, 1981), table 3.1. Values for 1980 calculated using Fossett and Nathan's index formula, given in note 29.

SUMMARY OF PROBLEMS AND PROPOSALS

In this and the preceding chapter we have discussed four major problems of the metropolitan public sector: the inappropriate assignment of functions to levels of government, the haphazard arrangement of local functions and boundaries, the existence of geographic disparities between local needs and resources, and the pressure of urban fiscal distress. What can or should be done about these problems? A number of programs already exist, and various additional reforms have been proposed. To discuss them, we will group them into four categories:

1. *Reassignment of functions:* proposals to transfer fiscal responsibility for specific functions between the levels of government
2. *Reorganization of the local public sector:* proposals to rationalize the arrangement of functions and boundaries at the local level
3. *Intergovernmental grants:* programs that transfer funds from higher to lower levels of government
4. *Economic self-help:* policies that cities themselves can adopt to improve their fiscal and economic performance

As we shall see, some of these reforms promise to mitigate several problems at once. There is no simple one-to-one correspondence between problems and proposed reforms. We have more than one stone to kill each bird, as well as some that may bring down more than one bird at a time.

REASSIGNMENT OF FUNCTIONS: PROPOSALS TO TRANSFER FISCAL RESPONSIBILITY

In the 1960s there occurred an extended debate on the nature of American fiscal federalism between reformers who favored increased fiscal assistance from higher to lower levels of government by such means as revenue sharing and others who argued instead for structural reorganization. Revenue sharing, which we take up later in this chapter, is a form of fiscal assistance given by the federal government to states and localities with virtually no strings attached. An important argument in its favor was that it would counteract "fiscal imbalance" in the American federal system. During the 1960s tax revenues from the federal government's highly elastic personal and corporate income taxes tended to increase faster than the need for federal expenditures. During the recovery phase of the business cycle, the federal government was in danger of running a budget surplus even before the economy reached full employment. Such a surplus would constitute a "fiscal drag," impeding the movement toward full employment and creating an argument for a federal tax cut.

The situation was just the opposite at the state and local levels. Needs for expenditure—generated to a large extent by the population explosion of the 1950s and 1960s—were increasing faster than tax receipts from the relatively inelastic property and sales taxes. Consequently, as shown in Chapter 14, these governments found themselves under continuous pressure to raise tax rates. Proponents of revenue sharing believed that transfering funds from the federal government, with its vast revenue-raising powers, to state and local governments, whose tax resources were far more limited, could not only prevent fiscal drag but improve the performance of the American federal system in other ways as well.[33]

Advocates of structural reform maintained that the major defects in the American system arose not from deficient revenue-raising powers at the lower levels but from an inappropriate division of functions among the federal, state, and local governments, which revenue sharing would paper over rather than correct. They took the position that instead of moving funds downward from higher to lower levels of government, the preferable reform would be to transfer fiscal responsibility for certain major functions from lower to higher levels. Both approaches, it might be noted, called for an increase in federal taxing and spending that would probably be offset only in part by a decline in the tax effort of states and localities.

Proposals to Increase the Functional Role of the Federal Government

Richard Ruggles made the case for radically altering the assignment of fiscal responsibilities by reviewing the strengths and weaknesses of each level of government. As he pointed out, "The federal government should be the instrument for developing national policy."[34] It is also an efficient instrument for collecting taxes and disbursing funds. It is not well suited, however, to administering the details of complex public service programs at the point of delivery. If the public decides that as a matter of national policy every citizen is entitled to a first-rate education, good health care, and relief from poverty, then, according to this line of argument, it is the duty of the federal government to guarantee that this takes place by providing sufficient funds so that despite geographic differences in wealth, every locality will be well served at equitable tax rates. In the language of economic theory, such services as health and education have nationwide externalities. Therefore decisions about the proper level of "output" must be reached nationally and made ef-

---

33. For a thorough statement of the case for revenue sharing, see Walter W. Heller, *New Dimensions of Political Economy* (New York: W. W. Norton, by arrangement with the Harvard University Press, 1967), ch. 3.

34. Richard Ruggles, "The Federal Government and Federalism," in Harvey S. Perloff and Richard P. Nathan, eds., *Revenue Sharing and the City* (Baltimore: The Johns Hopkins University Press, 1968), p. 70.

fective everywhere. Ruggles proposed that the federal government take over the costs not only of welfare but also of providing a minimum standard level of education and health care.[35]

The strength of state and local government lies in the production, coordination, and delivery of public services at the regional and local levels. Therefore these governments should be entrusted with the administration even of those programs for which the federal government sets minimum standards and provides basic funds. If state and local governments wished to exceed the national standards, they could do so by adding revenue from their own sources. For services not charged with a national interest, such as police and fire protection, sanitation, and correctional institutions, state and local governments should have both financial and administrative responsibility. With some or most of the burden for "national" services lifted from their shoulders, they would have no difficulty financing the rest of their needs.

Much the same conclusions can be reached by applying to a multilevel system of government Musgrave's normative theory of budgetary functions. As explained in Chapter 14, the functions of stabilization and income redistribution are best left to the federal government. The only budgetary function appropriate to local governments is allocation—the provision of goods and services that cannot be supplied efficiently by the private sector. The allocative function should in turn be divided among the three levels of government according to the "reach" of the goods in question, so that Olson's "principle of fiscal equivalence" is as nearly as possible fulfilled. Each level of government should attempt to provide just the quantity of every public service that its citizens want and are willing to pay for. If the federal government has indeed done its job of bringing about a desirable distribution of personal income, there will be no problem of individuals too poor to pay for their share.[36]

A variety of specific plans have been offered for altering the assignment of functional responsibilities. The least sweeping calls only for the federal takeover of all welfare costs up to some acceptable national standard. Considerably more ambitious is the recommendation by the Advisory Commission on Intergovernmental Relations that the federal government assume all welfare costs and the state governments, thereby relieved of a heavy burden, in turn relieve localities of the major responsibility for the cost of elementary and secondary education.[37]

35. Ibid., pp. 62–68.
36. See Charles E. McClure, Jr., "Revenue Sharing: Alternative to Rational Fiscal Federalism?" reprinted in R. C. Amacher, R. D. Tollison, and T. D. Willett, eds., *The Economic Approach to Public Policy* (Ithaca, N.Y.: Cornell University Press, 1976), pp. 225–243.
37. Advisory Commission on Intergovernmental Relations, *Improving Urban America: A Challenge to Federalism* (Washington, D.C.: U.S. Government Printing Office, September 1976), pp. 16, 45–46, 70–76, and *The Future of Federalism in the 1980s* (Washington, D.C.: U.S. Government Printing Office, July 1981), pp. 129–130.

Proposals to Decrease the Federal Role: Reagan's New Federalism

Among proponents of reform in the 1960s and 1970s, the dominant view was that the federal government, for reasons already discussed, should assume additional fiscal responsibilities, especially for income-support and poverty-connected services. Ronald Reagan had been a notable dissenter, and as president he proposed just the opposite course. In his 1982 State of the Union address he outlined a new federalism under which Washington would have returned major responsibilities to the states. Specifically, he proposed that the federal government accept full responsibility for Medicaid, in exchange for which the states would take over the entire burden of financing the AFDC and food stamp programs. In addition, sixty-one smaller federal grant programs were to be terminated. After a period of transition, the federal government would relinquish the use of excise taxes of an amount sufficient to cover the sixty-one programs, leaving it up to the individual states to continue the programs and levy the necessary taxes if they wished. This would have been reform on a grand scale, but it soon died for lack of support. As we shall see, however, President Reagan did introduce other important changes in the scope and structure of the federal grant system.

According to Peterson, "If consummated in full, the New Federalism would have severed intergovernmental ties to such an extent that, by 1991, the grant-in-aid share of state and local budgets would have fallen to 3 to 4 percent, the lowest level since the first year of the New Deal." (In the late 1970s it had climbed as high as 21 percent.)[38] What was the rationale for such a striking reversal of direction?

First of all, by 1980 many observers believed that the federal grant system had become too broad, complex, and cumbersome to operate efficiently.[39] President Reagan's New Federalism reflected a desire to simplify the system and clarify lines of responsibility by ending federal-state sharing in two major programs and sharply reducing the number of smaller federal grants. A second motive was the desire to return decision making to lower levels of government, which, it was argued, were "closer to the people." Next, and perhaps most important, the proposal was consistent with a conservative emphasis on expenditure reduction. Although the plan itself did not address the question of spending levels, it undoubtedly reflected a conviction that federal grants, through their matching provisions, had encouraged an undesirable increase in expenditures by state and local governments, and that contracting the grant system would therefore induce them to cut back. (The economic effects of intergovernmental grants will be examined in detail later in

---

38. George E. Peterson, "Federalism and the States: an Experiment in Decentralization," in John L. Palmer and Isabel V. Sawhill, eds., *The Reagan Record* (Washington, D.C.: Urban Institute, 1984), p. 220 and table 7.2. On the predicted effects of the new federalism, see also Robert P. Inman "Fiscal Allocations in a Federalist Economy: Understanding the 'New' Federalism," in John M. Quigley and Daniel L. Rubinfeld, eds., *American Domestic Priorities: An Economic Appraisal* (Berkeley: University of California Press, 1985), ch. 1.

39. See, for example, Advisory Commission, *The Future of Federalism in the 1980s*, pp. 128–130.

this chapter.) Furthermore, when fiscal responsibility for services, especially for redistributive functions like AFDC and food stamps, is shifted to lower levels of government, one can count on tax competition among jurisdictions to hold down the level of spending. Thus, although a policy of shifting responsibility to lower levels of government has been popular with conservatives because it can be defended on grounds of promoting local autonomy, it is difficult to avoid the suspicion that its unstated purpose is to guarantee shrinkage of the public sector.[40] Moreover, here as elsewhere, policies that increase local control also tend to increase inequality in the level of public services among local areas, a subject to which we now turn.

Effects of Reassignment on Geographic Disparities and Fiscal Distress

In general, reorganizational proposals that shift fiscal responsibilities upward to the federal government would help to offset the effects of geographic disparities in taxable resources, while those that, like Reagan's, shift them downward tend to accentuate such effects. The reason is that if functions were reassigned upward, the level of public services, including the redistribution of income, delivered to any citizen would depend *less* than it now does, and if downward, *more* than it now does, on local income and wealth. Perhaps the effect can best be understood by considering the "polar case." If all public services were taken over by the federal government, distributed equally across the nation, and paid for out of federal taxes, geographic disparities in income and wealth would continue to exist but would have no effect on the level of public services or income redistribution in any locality. Reassigning functions to higher levels of government would move us ever so slightly in that direction; reassigning them downward would move us the other way.

What effect would reassignment of functions have on urban fiscal distress? The answer would depend on details of the plans. For example, if the federal government were to take over the burden of paying for welfare programs, it would be unlikely to do so at anything like the level of suport now provided in high-benefit states such as California, Massachusetts, Michigan, or New York. Instead, benefits might be leveled up to, say, the 65th percentile of prevailing state levels. Taxpayers in distressed cities in high-benefit states would probably find themselves paying additional federal income tax to support higher welfare payments in the formerly low-benefit states. These added taxes might well outweigh the benefit of slightly higher federal contributions in their own states.[41] In any case reorganizational proposals that require the outright assumption of additional responsibilities by the federal government have never been easy to bring about and seem especially unlikely during a period of fiscal restraint.

---

40. See Henry J. Aaron, "Commentary," in Quigley and Rubinfeld, pp. 73–74.

41. For a more extended discussion see Peterson, "Finance," pp. 93–96; and Alan Fechter, "The Fiscal Implications of Social Welfare Programs: Can They Help the Cities?" in L. Kenneth Hubbell, ed., *Fiscal Crisis in American Cities: The Federal Response* (Cambridge, Mass.: Ballinger, 1979), esp. pp. 139–147.

Increasing the Responsibilities of the States: The Case of Education

Regardless of whether the federal government eventually increases or decreases its own functional responsibilities, there exists the possibility of important structural reorganization at the state level. If states were to take over fiscal responsibility for some functions now financed by local governments, they could greatly reduce the importance of income and wealth disparities at the local level. This issue came to the fore in the 1970s in connection with education.[42]

In a series of lawsuits, residents of relatively poor school districts alleged that the typical system of local public school finance deprives them of the right to an equal education. In the case of *Serrano v. Priest*, the California Supreme Court in August 1971 held that to finance education by a local property tax violated the "equal protection" clauses of both the federal and the California constitutions. The court based this finding on the fact that local property tax financing of education leads inevitably to great disparities among districts in the level of spending on education. Thereafter, similar suits were brought by aggrieved families in federal or state courts in a majority of states. The first federal case to reach the United States Supreme Court came from the state of Texas. In March 1973 that tribunal overturned the lower court decision in the case of *Rodriguez v. San Antonio School District* and held that the Texas school finance system, though based on the local property tax and fraught with inequalities, was not in violation of the federal Constitution.

While the decision in *Rodriguez* effectively closed the federal courts to this issue, it certainly did not halt the drive for equalization at the state level. Suits brought under state law have been successful and cannot be appealed to the federal courts. For example, the New Jersey Supreme Court in *Robinson v. Cahill* (April 1973) held that the state's system of educational finance failed to fulfill a mandate for equal educational opportunity in the state constitution. Furthermore, many states were already studying the possibility of full state assumption of all educational costs or of strengthening the equalizing effect of their existing school support payments even before the flood of suits began. Under the pressure of court action, all are now pushed in that direction.

Aggregate data do indicate that the relative contribution of states to local public school revenue increased sharply after *Serrano*. For two decades prior to that decision, the state share was virtually stable at a level just under 40 percent. In 1971–1972 it was 38.3 percent. Thereafter it rose steadily, reaching 48.3 percent by 1982–1983.[43]

42. For a thoroughgoing analysis of this complex question, see Robert D. Reischauer and Robert W. Hartman, with the assistance of Daniel J. Sullivan, *Reforming School Finance* (Washington, D.C.: Brookings Institution, 1973).

43. Tax Foundation, Inc., *Facts and Figures on Government Finance*, 1986, table F-26.

It is uncertain what effect the movement for tax and expenditure limitation will have on this trend. In California, where passage of Proposition 13 sharply cut back local tax revenue, the existence of a large state surplus made possible an immediate, massive increase in state funding of education. Elsewhere, as indicated in Chapter 14, tax and expenditure limitations tend only to restrict *future* fiscal growth. To the extent that these limitations are more numerous at the local than the state level, they are likely to put pressure on the states to assume a gradually increasing share of the financial responsibility for education.

In the conservative 1980s political support for policies to promote equality has surely weakened. But as Robert Berne and Leanna Stiefel point out in their comprehensive study of ways of measuring school equity, when "the public-education pie fails to grow as quickly as in the past, or possibly even begins to shrink, equity may become more of an issue than ever before."[44]

REORGANIZING THE LOCAL PUBLIC SECTOR

The local level of government in the United States contains a bewildering set of overlapping layers of cities, counties, school districts, special-purpose districts, and regional authorities. The geographic boundaries built into this system are often of ancient origin and may therefore not reflect current economic realities. Many of the problems of the metropolitan public sector could be ameliorated by reorganizing this governmental hodgepodge. Reform might involve altering the assignment of functions within the local sector, rationalizing local government boundaries, or a combination of both.[45]

Analysis of the problem of haphazard boundaries at the beginning of this chapter suggested that for each public service they should ideally be drawn so as to (1) eliminate significant externalities, (2) minimize the unit cost of production, (3) provide political accessibility for services where that is important, and (4) facilitate areawide planning and coordination. Even for a single service these criteria may well conflict. For example, political accessibility is important in the case of public housing, indicating the desirability of small jurisdictions. Yet housing policies ought to be planned on a regional basis, which suggests the need for a single metropolitan jurisdiction. For each service, therefore, even in an ideal system, it might be necessary to compromise among objectives in drawing boundaries. A second round of compromise is necessary in combining many functions under the jurisdiction of one or a few local governments. The alternative of setting up a separate "government" for

44. Robert Berne and Leanna Stiefel, *The Measurement of Equity in School Finance* (Baltimore: Johns Hopkins University Press, 1984), p.2. Also see their extensive bibliography, pp. 112–116.

45. For an institutionally detailed discussion of these issues, see Advisory Commission, *Improving Urban America*, chs. 3 and 4.

each function in order to enjoy the optimum-size jurisdiction for each one is obviously absurd, since it would make planning and coordination of services at the local level virtually impossible and, by dividing power among a multitude of elected officials, would seriously weaken political accountability.

Metropolitan Federation

In recent years, most advocates of metropolitan reorganization have rejected the notion of a monolithic, single-level regional government (even if that were possible), since such an arrangement would sacrifice too many values that are best realized under smaller local units. Instead they have tended to favor establishing a less centralized form, such as metropolitan "federation." This is a two-tiered system in which some functions are assigned to the metropolitan government to be conducted uniformly throughout the region while others are left to be performed within the discretion of the constituent local governments. Ideally, functions would be divided between the two levels by applying the sort of criteria just enumerated. Functions with important externalities or economies of scale or requirements for areawide planning would be assigned to the "central government" of the federation. Functions that lacked those characteristics or in which political access was an overriding consideration would be left in the hands of the traditional, smaller local units. Reorganization could thus overcome many of the inefficiencies that arise under our present haphazard arrangements.

A two-tiered system could also go a long way toward eliminating the fiscal effects of intrametropolitan disparities in taxable resources. The higher-tier government would finance whatever services it was designated to provide by means of uniform metropolitanwide taxes. In addition, the services left for purposes of administration in the hands of the local governments could be financed in whole or in part by uniform federationwide taxes. As a result, the weight of services dependent for financing on the taxable resources of the lower-tier governments would diminish. The fiscal impact of intercommunity differences in wealth and income within the metropolitan area would be reduced.

The best-known example of federation is the Municipality of Metropolitan Toronto. It was established in 1954 as a federation comprising the central city of Toronto and twelve suburbs. A reorganization in 1967 consolidated the twelve suburban municipalities into five boroughs and increased the powers and responsibilities of the metropolitan government.[46] The success of Metropolitan Toronto has undoubtedly stimulated interest in federation in the United States.

46. The Toronto experience, as well as other versions of the "two-level" approach, are described in John C. Bollens and Henry J. Schmandt, *The Metropolis*, 4th ed. (New York: Harper & Row, 1982), ch. 11.

Counties as Metropolitan Governments

In more than a third of all SMSAs, the entire metropolitan area lies within a single county. This coincidence can facilitate the creation of a metropolitan-wide government because it allows an already existing unit, the county, to be used as the major building block. In Florida, the Miami SMSA lies entirely within Dade County. A two-tiered metropolitan structure—the only example in the United States—was created in 1957, giving the county government greatly expanded powers to perform region-oriented services over the whole SMSA while allowing the local governments within the county to retain control of other services such as police, fire, and education. A less tidy arrangement results from "city-county consolidation." In this scheme the central city government consolidates with that of the overlying county to form a new unit that provides one set of services over the entire county and an additional set within the smaller central city area. City-county consolidation along these lines took place during the 1960s in three cases: Nashville consolidated with Davidson County in 1962; Jacksonville, Florida, with Duval County in 1967; and Indianapolis with Marion County in 1969.[47]

The creation of a two-tiered structure of metropolitan government would mitigate the effects of geographic fiscal disparities by partially "regionalizing" both the metropolitan tax base and the provision of local services. A less ambitious plan, known as tax base sharing, calls for regionalizing a part of the tax base only. Supporters of this approach are attracted by the fact that it can produce some equalization without interfering with local control over the provision of services. An arrangement for tax base sharing has operated in the Minneapolis–St. Paul metropolitan area since 1974.[48]

Netzer has written that "the income and wealth of the country is centralized within metropolitan areas and . . . despite regional differences in economic growth rates, whole metropolitan areas are viable fiscal entities for nearly all non-income-redistributing public services."[49] Yet however attractive schemes for regionalizing the metropolitan public sector through federation, city-county consolidation, or tax base sharing may appear to civic reformers and to students of economics and public administration, they have not yet impressed American voters sufficiently to be adopted in more than a few places. Residents of the suburbs, given a choice, have understandably re-

47. For further detail see ibid; Demetrios Caraley, *City Government and Urban Problems* (Englewood Cliffs, N.J.: Prentice-Hall, 1977), ch. 5; and Melvin B. Mogulof, *Five Metropolitan Governments* (Washington, D.C.: Urban Institute, 1972).

48. Regarding the Twin Cities plan, see Andrew Reschovsky, "An Evaluation of Metropolitan Area Tax Base Sharing," *National Tax Journal*, March 1980, pp. 55–66. For a critical discussion of tax base sharing, see Roy Bahl and David Puryear, "Regional Tax Base Sharing: Possibilities and Implications," *National Tax Journal*, September 1976, pp. 328–335.

49. Dick Netzer, "Public Sector Investment Strategies in the Mature Metropolis," in Charles L. Leven, ed., *The Mature Metropolis* (Lexington, Mass.: Heath, Lexington Books, 1978), p. 244.

sisted sharing the fiscal burdens of the central cities, and they, together with nonmetropolitan interests, ususally dominate the state legislatures that would have to authorize any form of local governmental reorganization. Except for instances in which the courts have been able to intervene on constitutional grounds, changes in the structure and performance of American local government occur more readily through gradual adaptation to new conditions than through sweeping reform. A less polite way of putting it would be that we are strongly committed to a policy of "muddling through."

Policies for "Muddling Through"

In practice, response to the problem of governmental fragmentation in metropolitan areas has taken three forms in recent years: the creation of metropolitanwide special districts for selected functions, the formation of regional planning and coordinating councils of local governments, and the increasing reliance on the states as effective regional authorities. Let us consider these responses in order.

Most special district governments are set up to perform a single function, such as water supply, transportation, fire protection, sewerage, or housing and urban renewal. A few are empowered to perform multiple functions. To finance themselves special districts are given the power to levy taxes, charge fees, receive grants, and incur debt. The 305 SMSAs surveyed in the 1982 Census of Governments contained no less than 11,725 such units, which averages out to 38 per SMSA and provides ample evidence that most special districts are not metropolitan areawide jurisdictions.[50] However, a small number of important multicounty special districts dealt with such large-area functions as air pollution, airports, and mass transportation. A well-known example is the Port Authority of New York and New Jersey, which owns and operates bridges, tunnels, bus terminals, part of the rail transit system, and numerous port facilities as well as the major airports in the New York–New Jersey port region.

Along such lines, special districts can and do perform functions across entire metropolitan regions that at the level of general-purpose local government are almost hopelessly fragmented. But the horizontal coordination and planning that the special district may (but does not always) achieve for a single function is bought at the price of making coordination among functions more difficult than ever in the vertical direction, of fragmenting responsibility and accountability, and of weakening citizen influence in decision making. Special districts continue to proliferate, but they are a far from satisfactory response to the problem of metropolitan jurisdictional fragmentation.

The vacuum left by the inability of metropolitan areas to cope with their own problems has to some extent been filled by state governmental

50. U.S. Bureau of the Census, *1982 Census of Governments*, vol. 5, *Local Government in Metropolitan Areas*, table 2.

action. As Netzer points out, "State governments under our constitutional system have very broad powers. . . . The states are the best regional governments we have, and they may be the best we are likely to get."[51] Since the 1960s state governments have played an increasingly active role in developing transportation, housing, open space, and other programs that require large-scale planning for metropolitan regions within their boundaries. There is every reason to believe this role will continue to grow.

INTERGOVERNMENTAL GRANTS

Grants are transfers of money from higher to lower levels of government. There would be a role for such transfers in even the most rationally organized federal society. In the less than perfectly rational American federal system, grants must do the additional job of compensating for the deficiencies in fiscal organization.

It was pointed out in Chapter 14 that intergovernmental transfers were a rapidly rising source of local government revenue through the late 1970s. Such aid accounted for a peak of 45 percent of local revenue in 1978–1979 before its growth was curtailed by fiscal cutbacks at the federal and state levels. Its growth and subsequent decline have been accompanied by an extensive literature on the economics of intergovernmental grants, including both theoretical analyses of their likely effects on the spending and taxing decisions of recipient governments and attempts to measure empirically what those effects have actually been.

Table 15.7 presents in matrix form a useful classification of grants according to two important characteristics. If the grantor stipulates that the funds must be used for a specific purpose, such as housing rehabilitation, sewage treatment, or public schooling, the grant is said to be "conditional." If use of the funds is not restricted, it is called "unconditional." If the recipient government is required to put up some of its own funds as a condition of obtaining the grant—whether dollar for dollar or one dollar for ten—the grant is called "matching"; if not, it is "nonmatching."

Three of the four spaces in the matrix correspond to existing grant types. At the upper left the category of conditional matching grants encompasses a wide variety of actual programs. Because these grants usually apply to carefully defined categories of activity, they are often referred to as "categorical grants." They can be further subdivided. They are open-ended if the grantor is willing to provide funds without limit as long as the recipient government wishes to match them (e.g., federal aid to the states to support the AFDC and Medicaid programs). They are non-open-ended if the grantor limits the amount of available aid (e.g., when Congress authorizes a limited sum

51. Dick Netzer, *Economics and Urban Problems*, 2nd ed., (New York: Basic Books, 1974), p. 237.

TABLE 15.7
Classification of Grants

	CONDITIONAL	UNCONDITIONAL
MATCHING	Categorical Open-ended AFDC Medicaid Non-open-ended (numerous)	(none)
NONMATCHING	Categorical (numerous) Block grants Community Development Elementary and Secondary Education	General Revenue Sharing

to be distributed to states or localities on a matching basis to support, say, mass transit improvement).

At the lower left are conditional grants for which there are no matching requirements. Some of these are "categoricals" for which the federal government pays the whole bill. Others are "block grants," providing funds that can be spent within much broader functional categories and without matching requirements. Examples are the federal government's Community Development Block Grant and its Elementary and Secondary Education Block Grant.

At the beginning of 1984 there were, by one count, 392 separate federal categorical grant programs, of which 55 percent required state or local matching. As we shall see, the number of categorical grant programs has been considerably reduced from the 534 counted in 1981 by consolidating them into additional block grants.[52]

At the lower right of Table 15.7 are grants to which no conditions are attached: the funds can be spent on any object and have no matching requirements. General Revenue Sharing was such a program. At the upper right is an empty space: there exists no program in which funds are granted unconditionally but subject to a matching requirement.

Effects of Grants on Fiscal Behavior

The expected effects of grants on the taxing and spending behavior of local governments can be explained with the help of Figure 15.2. This diagram shows how a community chooses the optimum combination of public

52. Advisory Commission on Intergovernmental Relations, *A Catalog of Federal Grant-in-Aid Programs to State and Local Governments: Grants Funded FY 1984* (Washington, D.C.: U.S. Government Printing Office, December 1984), pp. 1–3.

and private spending, given its level of income. The horizontal axis of Figure 15.2 measures dollars spent by members of the community on private goods (P); its vertical axis, dollars spent on the public good (G), which is assumed to be the only output of the local government. The curves I_1, I_2, I_3 are members of a set of "community indifference curves."[53] Points on any one curve show combinations of public and private goods that yield equal satisfaction or utility to the community as a whole. For example, on indifference curve I_1 the community considers itself as well off with the combination at E_1 as with the combination at E_4. Well-being increases with the movement to indifference curves farther from the origin. Thus the community is better off at E_2 than at E_1 and at E_3 than at E_2.

In the absence of grants from a higher level of government, the community's income is OA dollars and its budget constraint is the line AB. It can purchase OA of public goods, or OB of private goods, or any combination of the two along AB. Since the quantities of both goods are measured in dollar units, the distance $OA = OB$ and the budget line has a 45° slope. Given the income OA, the community would choose the combination P_1 of private goods and G_1 of public goods as indicated by point E_1, since that point lies on the highest indifference curve attainable along budget line AB. Since E_1 is the position in the absence of outside aid, it becomes the reference point as we examine the effects of various types of grants on fiscal behavior.

Conditional Matching Grants

It was shown earlier in this chapter that when the benefit of a public service spills over local boundaries, the producing jurisdiction will generally provide less than the socially optimal quantity of the service. We can now show that an open-ended matching grant is an efficient instrument for correcting this misallocation of resources. Thus fiscal transfers can be used to overcome a problem that arises either because a function has been wrongly assigned to a lower level of government or because, within the local level, boundaries do not correspond closely to benefit areas.

As illustrated in Figure 15.1, a local government, left to its own devices, will ignore the external portion of a service benefit and produce up to the point where the internal benefit—the marginal local benefit in Figure 15.1— equals the marginal cost of production. In the presence of an externality, the local government will produce the socially optimal quantity only if the cost of providing the service is reduced by means of a subsidy to the level of the mar-

---

53. In *The Economics of State and Local Government* (New York: McGraw-Hill, 1970), p. 129, Werner Z. Hirsch assumes that I_1, I_2, etc., represent "the preference function of the local government" rather than that of the community. The assumption that they are community indifference curves ("subject to all their acknowledged shortcomings") follows the treatment in Wallace E. Oates, *Fiscal Federalism* (Orlando, Fla.: Harcourt Brace Jovanovich, 1972), p. 75. Students unfamiliar with the use of indifference curves can consult any textbook on microeconomic theory—for example, Jack Hirshleifer, *Price Theory and Applications*, 3rd ed. (Englewood Cliffs, N.J.: Prentice-Hall, 1984), chs. 3 and 4.

FIGURE 15.2
Effect of Grants on Public and Private Spending

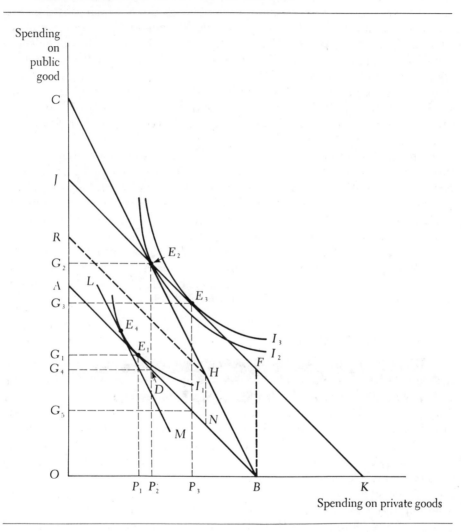

ginal local benefit at the socially optimal level of output. In Figure 15.1 the optimal output is H gallons per year, and the subsidy needed to induce it would be $C - D$ dollars per unit of output.

Using Figure 15.2, we can show how an open-ended matching grant serves as the instrument for paying such a subsidy and how it will affect fiscal behavior. Let us assume that the conditions of production and distribution of the service are such that the external benefit per unit is equal in value to the local benefit. In that case a grant that matches local expenditure on the public good dollar for dollar would cover the cost of producing the external portion of the benefit and induce the local government to produce the socially optimal quantity. Such a grant is indicated by the budget line CB in Figure 15.2. The one-for-one matching basis of the grant is indicated by the fact that from any point on AB the distance to the horizontal axis (which measures the community's contribution to paying for the public good) equals the vertical distance to CB (which measures the amount of grant support received). In the absence of a grant, the community consumes G_1 of the public good, as indicated by point E_1. The grant induces movement to E_2, on a higher indifference curve. Consumption of the public good rises to G_2, the socially optimal amount.

When indifference curves are used to analyze the behavior of individual consumers, the response to a change in price can be resolved into a substitution (or price) effect and an income effect. The same logic applies in this case. The matching grant has a substitution effect because it cuts the price of the public good, to the local community, in half. It has an income effect because the grant payment adds directly to the spendable income of the community. The substitution effect by itself induces the community to buy more of the public good and fewer private goods. The income effect by itself induces it to buy more of both goods, assuming that neither is an inferior good.

The income effect of the grant depicted by budget line CB, measured in real terms, is shown by movement of the community from indifference curve I_1 to the higher curve I_2. In order to show the pure price effect of the grant, we have to remove this income effect while leaving intact the price change induced by the grant. We can do so by reducing the community's money income to the level indicated by budget line segment LM. Since LM is parallel to CB, it preserves the postgrant price ratio between public and private goods. Since it has a point of tangency with indifference curve I_1, it allows the community to enjoy the same real income as at E_1. Given the budget line LM, the community would choose to be at E_4. The pure price effect of the grant with no change in real income is then the movement from E_1 to E_4. The movement from E_4 to E_2 measures the pure income effect of the grant, after its price effect has been removed. The sum of the two movements is an increase in the consumption of the public good from G_1 to G_2 and of private goods from P_1 to P_2. Private goods consumption increases because the positive income effect $(E_4$ to $E_2)$ more than offsets the negative substitution effect $(E_1$ to $E_4)$. Since the two effects work in opposite directions for private goods, one cannot say a priori what the net outcome will be. With a different preference configuration, private goods consumption could have fallen instead of rising.

To pay for the increase in private goods consumption the local community has diverted funds that were formerly spent on the public good. In the absence of grants, the community spent OG_1 on the public good and the remainder of its income (G_1A) on private consumption. When the grant program is in effect, total spending on the public good rises to OG_2, but half of that is paid for by grant funds. As indicated by point D along budget line AB, the community now spends only OG_4 of its own funds on the public good. The difference, $G_1 - G_4$, is diverted to private consumption. Since the community's own spending on the public good is financed by local taxes, it follows that local tax payments are therefore reduced. When a grant program thus leads to a reduction in a community's own spending on public services, the effect of the grant is said to be "substitutive." When the community spends more of its own funds after receiving the grant, the effect is called "stimulative."[54]

Although the theoretical case is strong for using open-ended matching grants to subsidize the production of services that provide external benefits, they are not, in fact, widely used for that purpose. In the United States they serve a wholly different purpose—to reimburse state and local governments for a portion of their welfare and Medicaid expenditures. With a few exceptions, the very numerous matching-grant programs in the United States are closed rather than open-ended.[55] If they are intended to stimulate spending on particular services, the fact that they are not open-ended deprives them of much of their stimulative power. To illustrate, suppose that the matching grant depicted by budget line BC were subject to the limitation that aid activity cannot total more than $HN(= AR)$ per year in any locality. In that case the postgrant budget line becomes BHR. To the left of the kink at H, matching ceases, and the grant no longer provides the stimulus of a substitution effect favorable to the consumption of the public good. Instead it takes on the attributes of the conditional nonmatching grants to be discussed shortly.

The Debate over Categorical Grants

Table 15.8 shows federal outlays for grants to state and local governments, classified by type of grant. The fourth row, "Categorical grants," includes the matching conditional grants just discussed as well as categorical grants for which there is no matching requirement. Categorical grants now provide about $89 billion a year to state and local governments, or more than four-fifths of the $109 billion total. Even if we subtract Medicaid and public assistance grants, which are essentially reimbursement for welfare expenditures rather than typical categorical grant programs, we are left with about $55 billion of other categorical aid.

---

54. See George A. Bishop. "Stimulative versus Substitutive Effects of State School Aid in New England," *National Tax Journal*, June 1964, pp. 133–143.

55. For a description of the various ways in which categorical grants are allocated, see George F. Break, "Intergovernmental Fiscal Relations," in Joseph A. Pechman, ed., *Setting National Priorities: Agenda for the 1980s* (Washington, D.C.: Brookings Insitution, 1980), pp. 251–256; and the Advisory Commission, *Catalog.*

The proliferation of categorical grants has been much debated in the past twenty-five years. Advocates of this form of aid believe that it is the appropriate choice when there are national purposes to be served using state and local governments as the administering agents and that the federal government has both a duty and a right to set national standards in such cases. Consequently, they argue that a considerable degree of federal oversight is desirable.[56]

Critics, on the other hand, have long claimed that categorical grants, each with its own narrowly defined objectives, its detailed federal performance standards, and its own matching formula, waste time and money at all levels of government by generating an almost impenetrable web of red tape. To meet this line of criticism a system of broad-based "block grants" has been gradually developed since the late 1960s. Within major functional areas such as community development, health, employment and training, social services, and criminal justice, grant programs have been combined, matching provisions dropped, requirements simplified, and objectives broadened. The federal government thus retains the power of directing its funds toward nationally defined and ordered objectives while leaving more responsibility in the detailed choice of means to state and local officials. The economics of these "conditional, nonmatching grants," including some questions about their effectiveness, will be taken up later in this chapter.

The Reagan administration, although it failed to enact its proposed New Federalism, did legislate an increase in the number and scope of broad-based grants. In 1981 nine new block grants were approved by Congress, combining seventy-six categorical grants.[57] The dollar value of block grants for selected years is indicated in Table 15.8, line 3. Evidently the Reagan initiative did not greatly alter the overall pattern: after 1982, spending again increased more rapidly on categorical than on broad-based grants.

Unconditional, Nonmatching Grants

As we have seen, open-ended matching grants derive much of their power to influence the behavior of recipient governments from the fact that they have a substitution effect as well as an income effect. The substitution effect is produced by the matching provision, which lowers the price of the subsidized activity relative to all other goods. As Wallace E. Oates aptly puts it, this alters "the terms of choice" facing the community and thus stimulates consumption of the subsidized good.[58]

---

56. For a discussion of these issues, see Helen F. Ladd, "Federal Aid to State and Local Governments," in Gregory B. Mills and John L. Palmer, eds., *Federal Budget Policy in the 1980s* (Washington, D.C.: Urban Institute, 1984), pp. 186–189.
57. See Peterson, in "Federalism and the States," p. 229.
58. Oates, p. 77.

TABLE 15.8
Federal Grants to State and Local Governments

	GRANTS (FISCAL YEARS, MILLIONS OF DOLLARS)				CHANGE (%)	
	1972	1978	1982	1986 (est.)	1978–1982	1982–1986
General Revenue Sharing	0	6,823	4,569	4,433	–33	–3
Other general-purpose grants	516	2,780	1,941	2,026	–30	4
Broad-based grants[a]	2,855	11,533	11,482	13,799	0	20
Categorical grants[b]	31,001	56,753	70,202	88,544	24	26
Public assistance and Medicaid	13,220	17,296	25,338	33,362	47	30
Other categorical	17,781	39,457	44,864	55,182	14	23
Total	34,372	77,889	88,194	108,897	13	23
Total as percent of state-local expenditure	22.0	26.8	21.9	—		

[a]Primarily nonmatching within broadly defined categories.
[b]Both matching and nonmatching, within highly specific categories.
Source: *Special Analyses, Budget of the United States Government,* various years.

Unconditional, nonmatching grants, such as those provided by General Revenue Sharing, stand in complete contrast to this. They are virtually free gifts of income, which the community can spend as it wishes. The "terms of choice" are not altered by the grant. The contrast between the two types is illustrated in Figure 15.2. The matching conditional grant moved the community from E_1 to E_2. The amount of aid received at E_2 is $E_2 - D \, (= K - B)$. If the higher level of government were to offer the same amount of aid in the form of un unconditional, nonmatching grant, the postgrant budget line would be JK. Since this line passes through E_2, we know that it offers aid equal in amount to the matching grant; since it is parallel to AB, we know that it augments the community's income by that amount no matter how the community arranges its spending.

Offered such a grant, the community would choose the combination of goods indicated by E_3, since that point lies on the highest attainable indifference curve. Since E_3 is on a higher curve than E_2, we see that the community is better off with an unrestricted grant than with a matching conditional grant yielding the same revenue. The reason, of course, is that the latter does not allow the community to select the combination of goods it would most prefer, given a free choice. This "distortion" of behavior, while not in the interest of the community itself, is the price that is paid to achieve the particular national objective implied in the conditional grant.

At E_3 the community buys more of both the public good and private goods than it would at E_1 (the "no-grant" position). However, payment for the public good out of its own resources drops from G_1 to G_5, and those funds are devoted to increasing private consumption from P_1 to P_3. Thus total spending for the public good rises by less than the amount of the grant. In this case, unlike the matching conditional grant, there is no substitution effect to introduce ambiguity about the effect on private consumption. Unambiguously, local private consumption rises, and local tax payments fall.

General Revenue Sharing

General Revenue Sharing, a system of unconditional, nonmatching federal grants to state and local governments, was adopted in 1972 and remained in effect until 1986. The concept was first developed by Walter W. Heller and Joseph A. Pechman in the mid-1960s as a way of using expected surplus federal tax revenues to relieve financial pressure on state and local units.[59] When the war in Vietnam eliminated the expected federal surplus, the proposal was temporarily shelved. It was revived later in a somewhat different form by President Nixon. The State and Local Fiscal Assistance Act of 1972 authorized $30.6 billion of federal funds for General Revenue Sharing to be paid out in a series of five yearly installments. Thus the act provided an average of

59. See Heller, ch. 3.

just over $6 billion per year in grant money to the states and localities, a significant increase in the level of assistance being provided at that time (see Table 15.8). When General Revenue Sharing was renewed in 1980 Congress, reflecting the national mood of fiscal restraint, cut the states out of the program and reduced the allocation to $4.6 billion per year, directed exclusively to localities. Then, in fiscal year 1986, under pressure to reduce the federal deficit, they allowed the program to expire.

In the legislation adopted in 1972, General Revenue Sharing funds were granted to the states and through them to all "general-purpose" local governments. School districts and other special districts were thus not eligible for any of the funds. The allotment to each state was calculated on the basis of the more favorable of two formulas reflecting such factors as population, tax effort, per capita income, urbanized population, and state income tax collections. Within each state two-thirds of the allotment was required to be distributed to localities by means of an additional formula. There were virtually no restrictions on the use of funds.

It was expected (and intended) that revenue sharing would redistribute income from rich states to poor. This would occur in part because allotments were weighted inversely to per capita state income. But some redistribution would have occurred even if each state's share had been strictly in proportion to population, with no special adjustment for income levels, since poor states contribute a much smaller amount per capita to federal tax revenues than do rich ones. However, the redistributive effect of revenue sharing at the local level was weakened by two limitations built into the allocation rules: first, every locality was guaranteed at least 20 percent of the average per capita distribution made to localities within its state, and, second, none could receive more than 145 percent of the average.

Redistributive Effects

Certainly, from the perspective of the theory of public finance, redistribution is the principal justification for revenue sharing. In a multilevel system of government, no matter how rational the assignment of functions and arrangement of boundaries, there will still be geographic disparities in the distribution of taxable resources among communities. As we have shown earlier, citizens in poor jurisdictions will have to pay higher tax rates to finance a standard bundle of public services than citizens in a well-to-do locality. To many observers this will appear inequitable. On grounds of equity they might wish, as Oates puts it, "to ensure that every individual has access to a sound program of public works within his chosen locality at a cost in line with what he would pay elsewhere."[60] If that is the objective, then unconditional, nonmatching grants are the logical instrument to employ. In principle, then, reve-

60. Oates, p. 88.

nue sharing provides a way of overcoming the geographic disparities in fiscal resources that we have cited as one of the major problems of the metropolitan public sector.

In practice, General Revenue Sharing proved to be redistributive, but on a very modest scale. The Congressional Budget Office estimated that in 1982 "the effect of GRS payments was to reduce interstate disparities in fiscal capacity by less than 2 percent, on average."[61] Redistributive effects among localities were also quite modest.[62] Since the fund to be shared was not large by national standards and the rules of the game ensured that every player would take home a prize, that outcome was not unexpected.

Effects on Tax Effort

What effect did revenue sharing have on expenditure levels and tax effort in the receiving juridictions? According to the theory developed for Figure 15.2, nonmatching, unconditional grants should be expected to finance less than a dollar-for-dollar increase in total spending by the recipient jurisdiction. Grant funds would be expected to substitute in part for public expenditure previously paid for out of a locality's own pocket. This, in turn, would allow taxes to be reduced. Indeed, one of the purposes of General Revenue Sharing was to allow hard-pressed jurisdictions some tax relief, if that was the alternative they preferred.

Revenue sharing did, in fact, lead to tax reduction, but not very much of it. A Brookings research team estimated the effects of revenue sharing on fiscal behavior by closely observing a sample of sixty-five jurisdictions, including eight states, fifty-six localities, and one Indian tribe. They found that localities, on the average, used about 50 percent of their first two revenue sharing allotments for various forms of new spending. An average of only 4.4 percent of allotments went for tax reduction. In addition, however, localities on average used 15.3 percent of their allotments to forestall tax increases that would otherwise have occurred. If these estimates are accurate, a total of about one-fifth of local allotments was substituted for tax effort.[63]

Economists have found these results puzzling. According to the standard theory presented here, nonmatching grants have only an income effect. The impact on local government spending should be the same as that of an ordinary change in private income. The marginal propensity to spend out of income on local public goods has been estimated to be 5 to 10 percent. Yet the Brookings study, among others, found that a dollar of unmatched aid raises local spending by something between 40 and 50 percent. A general ex-

61. Congressional Budget Office, *The Federal Government in a Federal System: Current Intergovernmental Programs and Options for Change,* August 1983, p. 104.

62. See Peterson, "Finance," pp. 87–88 and table 15.

63. See Richard P. Nathan et al., *Revenue Sharing: The Second Round* (Washington, D.C.: Brookings Institution, 1977), table 2.1.

planation would be that "bureaucrats and politicians find it easier to avoid cutting taxes when the government receives revenue sharing monies than they do to raise taxes when some exogenous event raises the income of the community."[64] This has been called the "flypaper effect" because money seems to "stick where it hits". Some more recent work, however, fails to indicate a flypaper effect, so the question of its existence, as well as how the theory of grants could be modified to account for it if indeed it does exist, remains open.[65]

Conditional, Nonmatching Aid: Block Grants

In a sense, conditional, nonmatching grants stand halfway between the first two types we have discussed. They resemble categorical matching grants in stipulating what purposes the funds can be used for, but they resemble General Revenue Sharing in having no matching provisions.

Again, Figure 15.2 can illustrate the case. Suppose that the higher level of government wishes to encourage the production of the public good G, but without requiring that the recipient government match its contributions. Assume that the subsidy is to be equal in amount to the revenue sharing grant of BK ($= FB$) analyzed earlier. Since the grant "must" be spent on the public good, the postgrant budget line of the community becomes BFJ. The highest indifference curve that is attainable along this budget line is again I_3 at point E_3. But that is the same point that was chosen under revenue sharing. The conditional, nonmatching grant has precisely the same effect on local fiscal behavior as the unconditional grant had. The reason is this: as long as the community would *voluntarily* spend at least BF on the subsidized good out of its postgrant income, the formal *requirement* that it do so is without effect. This is obviously the case in Figure 15.2. In the region of E_3 the community freely chooses to spend far more on the public good than the amount BF. In practice, the fact that the grant is awarded for expenditure on G is defeated by the fungibility of money. In a budgetary context, no one can tell when a particular dollar of income is being spent on a particular object. Upon receiving the grant of BF, the community can reduce its own contribution toward the purchase of the public good from G_1 to G_5 and divert the difference to private spending. Yet the community *does* spend at least BF on the required object: fungibility does the rest.

As we pointed out, block grants, a form of nonmatching conditional aid, have been introduced in recent years as a way of consolidating selected cate-

64. Paul N. Courant, Edward M. Gramlich, and Daniel L. Rubinfeld, "The Stimulative Effects of Intergovernmental Grants, or Why Money Sticks Where It Hits," in Peter Mieszkowski and William H. Oakland, eds., *Fiscal Federalism and Grants-in-Aid* (Washington, D.C.: Urban Institute, 1979), p. 6.

65. See other papers in Mieszkowski and Oakland. Gramlich's later paper, "An Econometric Examination of the New Federalism," in *Brookings Papers on Economic Activity*, vol. 2 (1982), pp. 327–360, does not find a "flypaper effect."

gorical grant programs into a simpler, more flexible system. However, if fungibility renders ineffective the requirement that block grants be spent on a particular activity, some troublesome questions arise. First, as Helen F. Ladd suggests, if the effects of block grants are no different from those of unconditional aid, equalization of fiscal resources among jurisdictions is their only rationale, and in that case, "cost-effective use of federal grants requires that they be much more targeted to needy jurisdictions than they currently are."[66] Second, if block grant spending requirements are ineffective, why should anyone wish to retain them? Why not go all the way to a system of unconditional aid instead of stopping at this halfway point? In part the answer is political. First, as Break points out, "grantors . . . may find it politically easier to justify appropriations of money presumably directed toward specific problems than those offered on an unrestricted basis."[67] Second, each block grant is distributed by means of a legislated formula that determines how much of the available fund goes to each state or locality. Participants in the political process readily become enthusiastic about a block grant program if its allocation formula is notably generous to their constituents. For these reasons an economist might endorse conditional nonmatching grants as a practical way of achieving the fiscal objectives that pure theory ascribes to General Revenue Sharing. Finally, there is a minimum standards argument: block grants do ensure that recipients spend at least the amount of the grant on a specific objective of national policy. For this last reason they might have a place in even the most rationally organized federal system.

The Rise and Decline of Federal Aid

Table 15.9 documents the rise and decline of federal grants to state and local governments. In 1963, the last year of the Kennedy administration, such aid amounted to only 8 percent of all federal outlays and only 1.5 percent of GNP. President Johnson's Great Society programs of the 1960s and the revenue sharing initiative of President Nixon in the early 1970s greatly expanded federal aid: by 1975 it totaled 15 percent of the federal budget and 3.4 percent of GNP. In terms of constant dollars (last column of Table 15.9), the peak was reached in 1978, when President Carter's antirecessionary Economic Stimulus Program provided $13.2 billion of aid, lifting federal intergovernmental grants to 17 percent of federal outlays and 3.7 percent of GNP. Federal aid measured in constant dollars began to decrease in the later Carter years when the antirecessionary programs automatically expired. President Reagan was elected with a commitment to cut domestic expenditures sharply, and in his first budget (fiscal year 1982) he did substantially reduce the real level of aid to state and local governments. Thereafter the real value of grants leveled off.

66. Ladd, p. 189.
67. Break, "Intergovernmental Fiscal Relations," p. 258.

TABLE 15.9
Rise and Decline of Federal Grants to States and Localities

	FEDERAL GRANTS-IN-AID (FISCAL YEARS, CURRENT DOLLARS)			FEDERAL GRANTS
	Amount (billions)	As a Percentage of Total Federal Outlays	As a Percentage of Gross National Product	IN CONSTANT 1982 DOLLARS (BILLIONS)
1963	8.6	7.7	1.5	31.7
1975	49.8	15.0	3.4	89.3
1978	77.9	17.0	3.7	111.7
1979	82.9	16.5	3.5	109.1
1980	91.5	15.5	3.6	108,9
1981	94.8	14.0	3.3	103.3
1982	88.2	11.8	2.9	89.5
1983	92.5	11.4	2.9	89.2
1984	97.6	11.5	2.7	89.3
1985	106.0	11.2	2.7	92.2
1986 (est.)	108.8	11.1	2.6	91.4

Sources: Advisory Commission on Intergovernmental Relations, *Significant Features of Fiscal Federalism, 1985–86 Edition*, February, 1986, table 8, and *Special Analyses, Budget of the United States Government*, 1987, table H-9. (Figures are consistent with Table 15.8, but differ slightly from U.S. Bureau of Census data in Tables 14.4. and 14.5. For reconciliation see *Special Analyses*, table H-10.)

The share of grants in the expanding federal budget, however, steadily declined, and by 1986 was the lowest it had been since the late 1960s.

An important political event during the years of growing federal aid was the development of a direct federal-local fiscal connection. President Johnson's Great Society programs, responding to the racial unrest of the 1960s, consisted almost entirely of categorical grants that were strongly oriented toward large cities. Most of these programs were continued by subsequent administrations. In addition, in the 1970s, two-thirds of General Revenue Sharing monies went directly to localities. (However, these funds were spread more widely among small jurisdictions than the earlier programs had been.) Finally, aid to localities received an additional boost in the mid-1970s when the Carter administration chose cities as the agents through which to provide antirecessionary fiscal stimulation. For all these reasons, during the period when federal aid to states and localities was growing most rapidly, the proportion going directly to local governments was also growing: they were getting a larger slice of a larger pie. In 1965 the local share was less than one-eighth the size of that going to the states. By 1978 it had grown to about 39 percent of the size of the state share.[68] (These ratios are for direct federal aid only. They

68. Ratios calculated from data in table 43 in Advisory Commission on Intergovernmental Relations, *Significant Features of Fiscal Federalism, 1985–1986 Edition* (Washington, D.C.: U.S. Government Printing Office, February 1986).

do not reflect the fact that more than a quarter of federal aid to the states is "passed through" indirectly to local governments.)

When the real level of federal aid to states and localities declined after 1978, the relative size of the local share began to shrink as well. In 1984 localities received only 27 percent as much direct aid as went to the states. With the termination of General Revenue Sharing, which in its last years went only to localities, the downtrend continued. Thus localities are now getting a smaller slice of a smaller pie.

Because the political power of the older urban areas is waning, there seems little chance that they will be able to recover the share of federal support they had in the 1970s. Population decline has steadily eroded their representation in Congress. The national parties are increasingly oriented toward seeking the support of the suburban rather than the central city voter. The Reagan administration, although unsuccessful in its larger attempts to construct a new federalism, did succeed in diverting aid from the localities back toward the states, which were its preferred instruments when intergovernmental aid seemed unavoidable.[69]

State governments were the designated recipients for the nine new block grants set up in 1981. Ladd has pointed out that of the seventy-seven categorical grant programs consolidated into those block grants, forty-seven had formerly "delivered federal funds directly to localities."[70] Increasingly, the cities will have to rely on the state governments to help them meet their legitimate needs. But, of course, the same forces that have eroded the cities' political power at the federal level have also weakened it in state capitals.

Effects on City Budgets

We have already pointed out that in the 1960s and 1970s, when the federal-local connection was growing, federal social policy was strongly oriented toward solving "big city" urban problems. During those years the per capita amount of combined federal and state aid was much higher in central cities than in their suburbs. Yet despite the high level of outside aid, central cities continued to tax their citizens at a much higher rate in relation to income than did suburban jurisdictions (see Table 15.3). This suggests that while outside aid provided important fiscal relief in the cities, it was not enough to offset the fiscally destructive effects of a continuing decline in the central city economic base accompanied by a continuing rise in the incidence of urban poverty. High local tax rates are strong evidence that the older, declining cities remain under great fiscal pressure. With the real level of federal aid to states and localities now declining and the local share in the total declining too, these pressures are likely to grow even more intense.

69. See discussion in David R. Beam, "New Federalism, Old Realities: The Reagan Administration and Intergovernmental Reform," in Lester M. Salamon and Michael S. Lund, eds., *The Reagan Presidency and the Governing of America* (Washington, D.C.: Urban Institute, 1984), p. 424.

70. Ladd, p. 190.

How have state and local governments responded to cutbacks in the real level of federal categorical assistance? Consider some of the possible cases suggested by the theory of grants. (The reader may wish to work these out in greater detail by returning to Figure 15.2 and reversing the case of a conditional matching grant developed there.) On the one hand, lower-level governments could use revenues from their own sources to replace the amount by which federal funds for a particular program were reduced. In that case total spending on the program would be maintained despite the smaller federal contribution. Alternatively, lower-level governments could hold their own contribution constant, replacing none of the lost federal aid. Total spending on the activity would then fall by the amount of the decline in the federal contribution. Of course, lower-level units might also choose an intermediate course, undertaking partial replacement.

To ascertain what actually happened as a result of cutbacks during the first Reagan administration, Richard P. Nathan and Fred C. Doolittle monitored state and local behavior with the help of a network of field observers.[71] They found that the state-local response varied by type of program. As one might have anticipated, there was little or no replacement of reduced federal aid in categories such as housing assistance, AFDC, community antipoverty services, and training for the unemployed, all of which are thought of as highly redistributive, with benefits concentrated among the urban poor. On the other hand, they found more replacement (though not always a great deal) in categories such as education, health, and capital infrastructure, where there is a long tradition of state-local responsibility and where much of the benefit flows to middle-income taxpayers. In addition, in cases where states acquired control (through new block grants) over funds that had formerly been distributed from the federal government directly to localities or school districts, Nathan and Doolittle found a tendency for large cities to suffer greater cutbacks than other parts of the state: under state control, aid is less highly focused than it had been on problem areas and populations.

With support weakening at both the federal and state levels, it thus appears that a trend of some twenty years' duration has been reversed. In dealing with social and economic problems, the cities of America are now required to rely increasingly on their own resources.

WHAT CITIES CAN DO FOR THEMSELVES: IMPROVING ECONOMIC AND FISCAL PERFORMANCE

In this chapter we have described the causes of urban fiscal distress and examined three kinds of policies that could help to mitigate it: transfering

---

71. Richard P. Nathan and Fred C. Doolittle, "Federal Grants: Giving and Taking Away," in *Political Science Quarterly*, Spring 1985, pp. 53–74. Also see Nathan and Doolittle, *The Consequences of Cuts* (Princeton, N.J.: Princeton Urban and Regional Research Center, 1983).

functional responsibilities to higher levels of government, reorganizing the structure of the metropolitan public sector, and providing grants-in-aid. We come now to a fourth category, the things that cities can do for themselves to improve their economic and fiscal performance.

A Strategy of Private Development and Public Frugality

There is not much disagreement among economists about the appropriate strategy for cities in fiscal distress. Most would agree on two policies. First, fiscally distressed cities must work hard to slow or reverse the economic decline made evident in their loss of jobs. Second, they must not only hold down or reduce real aggregate spending but must also manage the programs they do undertake more efficiently. (In discussing aggregate spending, the effect of general inflation must be borne in mind. The real value of expenditures will be falling as long as their money value does not rise as fast as the general price level.)

To hold on to their job base, declining cities must make themselves more attractive as places to do business. In the context of budget making, that means choosing tax and expenditure policies with an eye to their effect on the business sector. Policies that hold or attract jobs will in turn generate tax revenue that can help to relieve fiscal distress. Needless to say, they will also generate much-needed private income.

A policy of budget restraint is obviously necessary in cities under fiscal stress simply to balance the current budget. In addition, it would be expected to help make the city more attractive as a business location, since lower expenditures allow lower tax rates.[72] Because the property tax is the residual balancer of the local budget, spending cuts translate into lower property tax rates, which, as was explained in Chapter 14, would be expected to stimulate local business investment (or at least discourage disinvestment).

Some expenditures, however, provide benefits of direct interest to business—police, fire, transit, street, and highway outlays, to name only the most obvious. Consequently, the reduction of spending does risk taking away benefits to business, the loss of which would at least partially offset the gain from lower tax rates. This risk can be reduced to the extent that budget cuts are biased in the direction of human services rather than services of direct interest to business, but such a policy would be greatly to the disadvantage of the urban poor. Even budget cuts that affect all services equally will disproportionately hurt the low-income population, since local budgets are redistributive in nature. Thus fiscally distressed cities are truly on the horns of a dilemma. The rate of poverty in central cities continues its alarming increase

---

72. Empirical studies, however, do not show conclusively that differences in tax rates affect industrial location decisions. See William H. Oakland, "Local Taxes and Intraurban Industrial Location: A Survey," in George F. Break, ed., *Metropolitan Financing and Growth Management Policies* (Madison: University of Wisconsin Press, 1978), pp. 13–30.

(see Chapter 10). At the same time, it is acknowledged that distressed cities thwart their own economic recovery (which is to no one's advantage) if they maintain highly redistributive budgets. Yet society has been unable to agree on an alternative way of providing local services for the poor. The list of rejected alternatives need not be repeated here. During the 1970s increased federal aid rescued most cities from the necessity of deep expenditure cuts. Now that such aid is decreasing, cities have no choice but to reduce the output of public service, with all that implies for welfare, especially the welfare of their low-income populations.

To this proposition the reader may quite properly respond that there is more than one way to reduce expenditures and that some may be less painful than others. We have already pointed out that central cities during the 1960s and early 1970s were to some extent acting as "suppliers of jobs." That implies a component of waste in city budgets. More than one politician has been elected on the promise of cutting out only the waste.

Economizing

Arranged systematically, the possible methods of budget-cutting are these:

Reduce the output of government services[73]
  Across the board
  Selectively
Reduce the unit cost of output
  By reducing municipal wages
  By increasing municipal labor productivity
  By "contracting out" to private suppliers

Let us examine these possibilities in turn.

When budget cuts are to be achieved by reducing the quantity of service offered, the question to be answered is whether the cuts should be selective or across-the-board. Cutting across the board by a uniform fraction implies that all programs are equally beneficial at the margin. This is a proposition economists and public policy analysts find highly implausible. They would argue, instead, for selective or differential cuts that go deepest into programs offering the lowest marginal benefits. An optimum set of selective cuts could be worked out, for example, through "zero-base budgeting," a technique in which every program is systematically reviewed under the possibility of being cut back even to zero.[74]

Political realities, however, do not usually allow mayors to be very selective about reductions in spending. Every program has its constituency and,

---

73. "Reduce" should be understood to mean "reduce or restrain increase in."
74. See David W. Singleton, Bruce A. Smith, and James R. Cleaveland, "Zero-Based Budgeting in Wilmington, Delaware," reprinted in Charles H. Levine, ed., *Managing Fiscal Stress* (Chatham, N.J.: Chatham House, 1980), pp. 179–193.

very likely, its organized body of municipal workers who resist energetically the prospect of becoming unemployed. Budget cutting is never easy, but a plan to cut all departments or programs by about the same fraction, on the principle of sharing the misery, is likely to meet the least resistance. Consequently, the urban fiscal crisis has not been seized upon as an opportunity to rationalize the local public sector by selective pruning.

From the viewpoint of the public it is obviously preferable to economize by reducing the unit cost of public output rather than by simple budget trimming, since lower unit cost allows expenditures to be reduced without cutting the level of public service. One way of lowering unit costs would be to reduce public-sector wages. The wage factor in local budget costs was analyzed in Chapter 14. From 1965 through 1974 public employees' earnings rose much faster than either earnings in manufacturing or the cost of living (see Table 14.3). However, these relationships reversed after the onset of the urban fiscal crisis. From 1974 through 1979 municipal wages rose less than either private-sector wages or the cost of living. Thus "real" public-sector wages were temporarily reduced. Municipal employee unions have become less militant since their position was weakened first by the urban fiscal crisis, then by the success of the tax limitation movement, and more recently by the example of concessions made by unions in the private sector. Nevertheless, it would be unrealistic to expect further real wage cuts. Indeed, Table 14.3 shows that since 1979 municipal employees' earnings have risen slightly faster than both manufacturing wages and the cost of living.

Improving Productivity and/or Contracting Out Services

Unit cost can also be reduced either by increasing public-sector productivity, as measured by output per worker, or by purchasing services from private suppliers when their costs are lower. Interest in both approaches has developed rapidly since the 1970s in response to the soaring cost of municipal services.[75] Research often links the two approaches because one way of assessing productivity in municipal departments is to compare the unit cost of public and private production for functions such as street paving and refuse collection that are performed in both sectors. If private production turns out to be significantly cheaper, a case can be made either for contracting the service out to private providers or for adopting in municipal departments the more cost-efficient methods of private firms.

A study carried out in the Los Angeles metropolitan area for the U.S. Department of Housing and Urban Development in 1983 compared the unit

75. See Harry P. Hatry, *A Review of Private Approaches for Delivery of Public Services* (Washington, D.C.: Urban Institute, 1983); Carl F. Valente and Lydia D. Manchester, *Rethinking Local Services: Examining Alternative Delivery Approaches* (Washington, D.C.: International City Management Association, 1984); *Measuring Productivity in State and Local Government*, U.S. Bureau of Labor Statistics, Bulletin 2166, December 1983; E.S. Savas, *Privatizing the Public Sector* (Chatham, N.J.: Chatham House, 1982); and Willis D. Hawley and David Rogers, eds., *Improving the Quality of Urban Management* (Beverly Hills, Calif.: Sage Publications, 1974).

cost of services in ten cities that produced them using municipal employees and ten that contracted them out. Using multiple-regression analysis to hold quality and frequency of service and scale of output constant, it was found that for seven out of eight services, unit cost was significantly higher for public production. Listed below are the eight services and the percentages by which public costs were higher:[76]

Street cleaning	43%
Janitorial services	73%
Refuse collection	42%
Traffic signal maintenance	56%
Laying asphalt	95%
Lawn mowing	40%
Tree trimming along streets	37%
Payroll preparation	not significant

What explains these cost differences? Interestingly, the study found that wage differences were not, on the average, an explanation for lower unit costs in the private sector. On the other hand, the longer vacations and larger number of holidays in the public sector did significantly increase costs. More important, however, were a number of differences in management. For example, private contractors were less likely to use "overqualified" (and hence overpaid) workers and were more likely to use part-time labor, to allow supervisors the right to fire workers, and to require that managers be responsible for equipment maintenance as well as for the organization of the work force.[77] The study found a surprisingly wide variation in unit costs for each of the services, which suggests that the less efficient municipalities could greatly improve their performance by learning from the more efficient.[78]

Private provision of services is not always less costly than public. Studies have turned up contrary cases as well. In addition, contracting brings its own set of problems—for example, a potential for corruption and a need for regular monitoring of performance by a public agency. At the very least, however, municipal governments should periodically compare their costs with the yardstick provided by the private sector to see where and how they could improve their own performance.

Given the tremendous inertia of established institutions, it is not easy to be optimistic about the prospects for increasing the productivity of local government. Changing public attitudes, however, may gradually force an improvement. The rapid growth of intergovernmental aid during the 1960s and early 1970s led to a certain weakening of moral fiber at the lower levels of gov-

76. Barbara J. Stevens, ed., *Delivering Municipal Services Efficiently: A Comparison of Municipal and Private Sector Delivery: Summary*, U.S. Department of Housing and Urban Development, June 1984 (HUD User no. RP 3744), Exhibit 8.

77. Ibid., pp. 15–17.

78. Ibid., p. 6.

ernment. The more such aid became an accepted fact of life, the more local public officials were tempted to attribute all their troubles to its inadequacy. Blaming Washington or the state capital for insufficient aid became the all-purpose response to criticism. Urban voters tended to accept the explanation and failed to hold local officials responsible for keeping their own house in order. Now public sentiment has changed. Voters have grown wary of solutions that require spending more money. In the long run, the same mood of restraint that created budgetary problems for distressed cities by limiting the availability of intergovernmental aid may also cause citizens to demand more efficient performance by local government and encourage public officials to risk trying to give it to them.[79]

79. See Barry N. Siegel, *Thoughts on the Tax Revolt* (Los Angeles: International Institute for Economic Research, 1979), pp. 11–14.

SIXTEEN

Postscript: The Future of Central Cities

Few things are more hazardous to predict than the future pattern of metropolitan settlement. The "City of the Future"—when we arrive at it—rarely resembles the drawings of the visionary artist or designer of an earlier age, and the projections of economists and sociologists are not likely to be much more reliable. Yet the developmental approach taken throughout this book, which has consistently focused attention on the process and direction of change, naturally raises the question of where current trends are carrying us.

OUTLOOK FOR THE OLDER CITIES

Discussion in early chapters emphasized the contrast between the central cities of the South and West and those of the North and East. The former are, for the most part, relatively young and prosperous. They are located in regions of rapid economic and population growth, which provides great buoyancy to their economies, even when their own populations are no longer increasing. In the near term at least, their continued prosperity is scarcely in doubt. For the older cities of the North and East, the story is quite different. Located in regions suffering relative economic decline, most of them endured substantial population and job loss, housing abandonment, neighborhood deterioration, and fiscal distress during the 1960s and 1970s. In the early 1980s some of these cities experienced population and job stability or even a modest revival. Others continued to decline. It would be fair to say that in either case a good deal of anxiety remains about their economic prospects.

Heretofore we have stressed the self-reinforcing nature of central city decline. Several self-reinforcing processes were described in earlier chapters. First, the outward movement of the middle class and their replacement by the (until recently) in-migrating poor contributed to a cycle of deterioration that is linked to the spatially fragmented structure of metropolitan government. Middle-class families leave the city in part to avoid paying taxes to support governmental services for its low-income residents. But their exit further reduces the tax base, rendering the central city still more unpalatable for the well-to-do who remain behind. At the same time, the rising tax rates that accompany this process make the city less attractive as a business location, hasten the decline in jobs and economic activity, and thus further aggravate the city's fiscal situation. Second, it was pointed out in Chapter 15 that declining population may cause the unit cost of local public services to increase. This increase, in turn, would be expected to encourage further population and job loss in a self-reinforcing cycle. Third, population and job loss can lead to an additional self-reinforcing process of decline by reducing the positive economies of agglomeration offered by a city. Economies of agglomeration in the form of specialized services of production and consumption accrue as a city grows, attracting further growth. They are likely to diminish as it shrinks, encouraging further decline.[1]

That is not the end of the story, however. In general, economists expect processes of change in a market economy to generate counterforces that prevent either explosive growth or continuous decline and move the system instead toward a new equilibrium. Other things remaining the same, it is possible that such forces, operating naturally within the market system, would eventually slow down or even halt the decline of a central city. The equilibrating factor in this case would probably be a relative decline in central city costs. As population and business activity fall off, we would expect the prices (or rents) of housing, commercial and industrial space, and land all to decline relative to their levels elsewhere, including the surrounding suburbs. A reduction in relative costs would in turn make the city more competitive with other locations, thus slowing its rate of decline. For example, it is probable that the low price of old inner city housing relative to accommodation in the suburbs was an important factor in initiating the wave of housing renovation that has improved many old inner city neighborhoods since the late 1960s. (We will return to the topic of housing renovation shortly.)

Of course, other things need not remain the same. Instead, fundamental forces may change in ways that are favorable to the prosperity of the inner city. Two factors that merit discussion are the growing importance of services

1. Concerning self-reinforcing versus self-correcting processes, see Katharine L. Bradbury, Anthony Downs, and Kenneth A. Small, *Urban Decline and the Future of American Cities* (Washington, D.C.: Brookings Institution, 1982), ch. 9; Daniel Garnick and Vernon Renshaw, "Competing Hypotheses on the Outlook for Cities and Regions," *Papers of the Regional Science Association*, 45 (1980), 105–124; and John W. Pickering and Harold Bunce, "The Dynamics of Urban Distress," in U.S. Department of Housing and Urban Development, *Occasional Papers in Housing and Community Affairs*, vol. 4 (Washington, D.C.: U.S. Government Printing Office, July 1979), ch. 4, esp. pp. 86–88.

in the U.S. economy and the radical shift in American lifestyle reflected in demographic changes such as falling marriage and birth rates and the increased labor force participation of women.

The Service Sector and Central City Revival

It was pointed out in Chapter 3 that business and financial services have in the past been strongly attracted to the central city. Indeed, in the early 1980s the rapid growth of service jobs more than offset losses in manufacturing in some older cities and (at least temporarily) halted their economic contraction. However, in cities like Detroit, St. Louis, and Cleveland where the economic base is particularly dependent on manufacturing, the growth of service jobs has not yet been sufficient to stem decline. No one can doubt that services will continue to be the leading growth sector in the U.S. economy. But will they remain locationally oriented toward the central city? The suburbs already support a large and growing service sector. Some analysts suggest that innovations in the technology of transportation and communications will eventually make it possible for business and financial service jobs to decentralize into the suburbs or even into nonmetropolitan areas to a much greater extent than they have done so far.[2] That is speculation, not prediction, but it serves to emphasize the fact that growth of the service sector at the national level does not necessarily mean either stability or revival for the older central cities.

We next examine the possibility that recent changes in the lifestyle of the U.S. population will have a favorable impact on central cities.

Demographic Change and the Future of the Inner City

William Alonso coined the expression "population factor" to describe the way people "arrange and rearrange themselves into families and households . . . their participation in the labor force, how they run their households and how they raise their children, if they have them."[3] Following World War II the population factor strongly reinforced the growth of the suburbs. The postwar baby boom gave rise to a child-centered, family-oriented lifestyle that for two decades became the American norm. Almost everyone got married and had children, and young families with kids to raise and send to school were strongly attracted to the suburbs.

With the end of the baby boom in the 1960s, however, the population factor began to change in a direction more favorable to the inner cities. Family size decreased as the birth rate fell from 23.7 per thousand of population in

2. See sources cited in Chapter 4, n. 17.
3. William Alonso, "The Population Factor and Urban Structure," in Arthur P. Solomon, ed., *The Prospective City* (Cambridge, Mass.: M.I.T. Press, 1980), p. 32.

1960 to 15.6 in 1984. The proportion of young married couples without children rose dramatically. An increasing number of women postponed marriage or chose not to marry, and the divorce rate reached record levels.[4]

These changes produced a marked shift in the composition of households. Those made up of married couples increased only 13 percent from 1970 to 1985, while the number of nonfamily households—consisting of single persons living alone or with nonrelatives—more than doubled.[5] When the number of married couples without children is combined with the number of nonfamily households, it is clear that there has been a rapidly growing population segment that is likely to be more favorably disposed toward living in the inner city than were the predominantly child-centered families of the baby boom decades.

Linked to these changes in attitudes toward marriage and childbearing, both as cause and as effect, has been the rise of the working woman. In recent decades women have joined the labor force in unprecedented numbers: their overall labor force participation rate rose from 38 percent in 1960 to 55 percent in 1985. The increase was even sharper among younger women: for those aged 25 to 34, the rate went from 36 percent in 1960 to 71 percent in 1985. More than half of all wives are now in the labor force.[6]

It is uncertain how the increase in the proportion of women who work outside the home will affect residential location choice and therefore the pattern of metropolitan settlement. On the one hand, a higher rate of labor force participation probably makes for later marriage and smaller families, and single women and married women without children tend to choose more centrally located housing than do married women with children. On the other hand, we know that households with higher incomes tend to live farther from their workplaces. Thus the additional income provided by working wives encourages families to choose a more suburban residential location. (For theoretical analysis on this point, see Chapter 6.) The net effect of increased labor force participation by women on the pattern of metropolitan settlement will therefore depend on whether its impact on the "population factor" outweighs its income effects.[7]

RENOVATION AND REVIVAL?

Theories of urban form descended from Burgess's concentric zone model (see Chapter 6) have always implied that the passage of time might

4. U.S. Bureau of the Census, *Current Population Reports*, series P–23, no. 145, September 1985, table A–1; and *Statistical Abstract of the United States*, 1986, table 7.

5. U.S. Bureau of the Census, Current Population Reports, series P-20, no. 402, October 1985, table 7.

6. U.S. Bureau of Labor Statistics, *Employment and Earnings*, January 1986, tables 2, 3, and 8.

7. Janice F. Madden, "Urban Land Use and the Growth in Two-Earner Households," *American Economic Review*, May 1980, pp. 191–197. Also see Madden's "Why Women Work Closer to Home," *Urban Studies*, June 1981, pp. 181–194.

bring a cycle of revival at the center of the oldest cities. In Burgess's original version, formulated in the 1920s, the middle and upper classes were driven from the urban center toward the suburbs by the combined forces of an expanding central business district that encroached on old inner city neighborhoods and their own desire to live in new and better housing. Fifty or more years later the city has evolved to a very different stage. Central business districts have long since ceased to expand. Transportation improvements have moved heavy industry and blue-collar jobs out of the inner city. The remaining employment is increasingly concentrated in the service sector, in professional, managerial, and white-collar occupations that might be expected to attract the middle class. Finally, the decline in population in the older central cities has opened up a substantial amount of vacant land for potential reuse.

One might argue that these evolutionary changes, taken together, have prepared the way for a new era in metropolitan development. By building new or renovated housing near the center, cities could begin to attract the middle class back from the suburbs, sparking a self-sustaining revival that would carry them into a new era of prosperity. Such, at least, has been the perennial dream of inner city optimists. For many years there was little evidence of the projected revival. Then in the late 1960s came some good news, a wave of housing renovation that moved a select number of inner city neighborhoods from the "run-down" to the "reviving" category. Does this interesting development mark the beginning of an inner-city Renaissance? What is its potential and what are its limitations?

Studies of housing renovation conducted in a number of cities reveal a common set of characteristics of neighborhoods, of structures, and of the renovators themselves.[8] The neighborhoods are usually close to the center of the city and have well-defined boundaries. Some are historic districts. Most were run-down or shabby before renovation began but were not considered slums. The renovated units are usually owner-occupied, single-family structures, often row houses, generally dating from the nineteenth century (which lends a certain "period" charm to their architectural style) and often built originally for middle- or upper-class families. The renovators are predominantly young, highly educated, well-to-do households, often with two wage earners, frequently childless, and rarely with more than two children. It is a consistent finding that the great majority of renovators were residents of the same city before undertaking renovation. Few came from the suburbs. Hence the new wave of renovation is not evidence of a back-to-the-city movement. It does, however, indicate that cities are now holding on to some middle-class households that might formerly have moved to the ring area.

8. See J. Thomas Black, Allan Borut, and Robert Dubinsky, *Private Market Housing Renovation in Older Urban Areas* (Washington, D.C.: Urban Land Institute, 1977); Franklin J. James, "The Revitalization of Older Urban Housing and Neighborhoods," in Solomon, pp. 130–160; and "Symposium on Neighborhood Revitalization," *Journal of the American Planning Association*, October 1979, esp. papers by Shirley B. Laska and Daphne Spain and by Neil Smith. Much of this literature is reviewed in Dennis E. Gale, *Neighborhood Revitalization and the Postindustrial City* (Lexington, Mass.: Heath, Lexington Books, 1984), chs. 2 and 3.

Changes in the "population factor" certainly help to explain the growth of that category of young adults who are doing most of the current renovation. The rise in suburban housing prices relative to those in central cities in the 1960s and early 1970s also stimulated the demand for inner city accommodation by young households seeking more space.[9] Thus the renovation movement does draw strength from several fundamental economic changes. Nevertheless, it is not, and probably cannot be, of sufficient magnitude to make more than a modest contribution to central city revival. Clifford R. Kern found that in New York City during the 1960s the loss of upper-income residents in the rest of the city far exceeded the gain in the central area where revival and renovation were taking place. From 1970 through 1976, when the city's economy was weak, even the center suffered a net loss of upper-income households.[10]

If we try to gauge the potential impact of the renovation movement by looking at the housing stock and its distribution among neighborhoods, we see that the kinds of structures and of neighborhoods that are amenable to renovation as it is now being done make up only a small fraction of the whole. The most deteriorated neighborhoods, occupied predominantly by low-income families, are not being rehabilitated in this process, and if they were, their poor residents would be displaced, with the likely result of spreading deterioration elsewhere. Indeed, inner city housing renovation in old neighborhoods is now commonly called "gentrification" (a term with unpleasant connotations) precisely because it does usually displace those with low or moderately low incomes.[11]

Although the long-run significance of changes in the population factor is undeniable, we should not overestimate its aggregate impact. Income data show that the central city poverty population actually increased during the 1970s and early 1980s. Against that background, a gradual rise in the number of middle- and upper-middle-class nonfamily households is not going to keep the average income level in central cities from continuing to sink below the level in the suburbs and, indeed, below the national mean. As for population size, the growth of nonfamily and childless-couple households will help central cities to hold on to some locally employed people who would have moved to the suburbs in an earlier period, but such changes are not likely to be a major factor in reversing the decline in total central city population, since their effects are constrained by the availability of jobs. In short, growth or decline

9. James, p. 131.
10. Clifford R. Kern, "Upper Income Residential Revival in the City: Some Lessons from the 1960s and 1970s for the 1980s," in Robert B. Ebel, ed., *Research in Urban Economics*, vol. 4 (Greenwich, Conn.: JAI Press, 1984), tables 2, 3, and 4.
11. Concerning the problem of displacement, see Gale, pp. 21–36, 85–108, 163–165; Howard J. Sumka, "Neighborhood Revitalization and Displacement," *Journal of the American Planning Association*, October 1979, pp. 480–487; and "Comment . . ." by Chester Hartman and "Response to Hartman" by Sumka, ibid., 488–494.

in central city population will ultimately depend on growth or decline in the number of local jobs.

Coping with Decline

Whatever the future may bring, many Americans are now living in cities whose population has already shrunk well below its greatest size. Decline has proved to be a painful experience for local citizens and a baffling one for politicians and city planners. The United States has always been a growth-oriented society. Until very recently, city planning was understood to mean planning for growth, and growth is very much easier to cope with than decline. When a city is expanding, problems are not so much solved as they are outgrown. In the past, expanding central cities could often pay the cost of adjusting to the dictates of technological and other economic change by borrowing, so to speak, against the present value of expected future growth. If the old infrastructure of streets, water supply, schools, and housing was becoming obsolete, it could readily be replaced by the new facilities that would in any case be needed to meet the requirements of rapidly rising demand. Old errors could be buried under new construction. Someone was always willing to pay for a second chance.

Today the situation in the older cities is quite different. Even in those where population and job decline has now halted, future prospects remain in doubt, making it difficult to attract capital for the replacement of obsolete structures and unsatisfactory neighborhoods. One might think that as its population declined a city's need for capital outlays would drop substantially, because additional capacity in schools, hospitals, and other expensive facilities would not be required. Budgetary relief from that source is minimized, however, by the facts of neighborhood change and the intraurban redistribution of population. The old facilities, even if not obsolete, are often located in the wrong place to serve current demands. To make matters worse, it is now apparent that the older cities also have to catch up on an enormous backlog of neglected maintenance.[12] Bridges are corroding, sewer and water mains bursting, streets, highways, and subway systems crumbling with age. "Rehabilitation of infrastructure" is not an exciting program on which to run for reelection, but many local public officials believe it is now one of their most serious problems.

In general, adjustment to change becomes more difficult when change is accompanied by decline. For example, widespread housing abandonment would seem to provide an opportunity for the creation of attractive parks and open spaces in old, formerly crowded slum areas. But the cities do not seem to know how to go about planning such change or how to pay for it even if

12. See Advisory Commission on Intergovernmental Relations, *Financing Public Physical Infrastructure*, rep. no. A-96, June 1984.

they did.[13] It has been said, only half in jest, that our older cities now face insurmountable opportunities.[14]

If one believes that in the long run the health of a city's economy depends on the skill, productivity, and social cohesion of its people, the social problems of the older cities may be even more alarming than their abandoned neighborhoods and deteriorating infrastructure. As we have shown in Chapter 10, our central cities are increasingly divided into the well-to-do and the poor. The web of difficulties in which the urban poor find themselves includes educational failure, lack of skill, unemployment, withdrawal from the labor force, and welfare dependency. These human problems, which remain far from solution, surely deserve as much attention as the city's crumbling bricks and mortar and may be much more difficult to put right.

13. Regarding policies to cope with neighborhood decline, see "The Problem of Deteriorating Neighborhoods" in Chapter 13, references cited in Chapter 13, nn. 58 and 63, and "Symposium on Neighborhood Revitalization," cited in n. 8 above.

14. Quoted in Norman Krumholz, "The Aging Central City: Some Modest Proposals," in U.S. Congress, House Committee on Banking, Finance and Urban Affairs, Subcommittee on the City, *How Cities Can Grow Old Gracefully*, December 1977, p. 100.

ACKNOWLEDGMENTS (continued)

tion," from *Location and Land Use*, William Alonso, Harvard University Press, 1964. Reprinted with permission.

Table 7.2, "Estimates of Export Percentages Based on Surveys and on Location Quotients, 1955–56," from *The Community Economic Base Study* by Charles M. Tiebout; published by the Committee for Economic Development. Printed with permission of the Committee for Economic Development.

Table 7.3 "Ratios of Nonbasic to Basic Activity in Large and Small Metropolitan Areas, 1972," Andrew M. Isserman, "Estimating Export Activity in a Regional Economy: A Theoretical and Empirical Analysis of Alternative Methods," *International Regional Science Review*, Winter 1980, tables 2 and 3. Reprinted with permission.

Figure 8.1, "Optimal Pricing on a Congested Highway," adapted from A. A. Walters, *The Economics of Road User Charges*, The Johns Hopkins University Press, 1968. Reprinted with permission.

Figure 8.3, "Intermodal Comparison of Trip Costs as a Function of Traffic Volume," adapted from Theodore E. Keeler and Kenneth A. Small, *The Full Costs of Urban Transport*, part III, Monograph 21, Institute of Urban and Regional Development, July 1975.

Table 8.2, "Trends in Urban Transportation Use," compiled from *Highway Statistics*, various issues, Federal Highway Administration and *Transit Fact Book*, American Public Transit Association, 1985.

Table 8.5, "Elasticity of Demand for Urban Transportation," T. A. Domencich, G. Kraft, and J. P. Valette, "Estimation of Urban Passenger Travel Behavior: An Economic Demand Model," *Highway Research Record*, no. 238 (1968), Transportation Research Board, National Research Council, Washington, D.C.

Table 8.6, "Optimal Congestion Tolls, San Francisco Bay Area, 1972," Theodore E. Keeler and Kenneth A. Small, "Optimal Peak-Load Pricing, Investment and Service Levels on Urban Expressways," *Journal of Political Economy*, February 1977. The University of Chicago Press. Reprinted with permission.

Figure 9.2, "Percentage of Users in Each Income Class for Each Mode U.S. Metropolitan Areas, 1977–78," calculated from John Pucher, "Equity in Transit Finance," Reprinted by permission of the *Journal of the American Planning Association*, October 1981.

Table 9.1, "Highway Expenditures and Receipts from Users, 1975 (Pay-as-You-Go Basis)," based on data from Kiran Bhatt, Michael Beesley, and Kevin Neels, *An Analysis of Road Expenditures and Payments by Vehicle Class (1956–1975)*. Copyright: The Urban Institute, March 1977.

Table 9.2, "Transit Industry Revenues and Costs," American Public Transit Association, *Transit Fact Book*, 1985 and 1981.

Table 10.7, "Segregation Indices for Selected U.S. Cities," for 1970 and 1980, Karl Taeuber, *Racial Residential Segregation, 28 Cities, 1970–1980*, University of Wisconsin—Madison, Center for Demography and Ecology, CDE Working Paper 83–12, table 1; for 1960, Karl E. Taeuber and Alma F. Taeuber, *Negroes in Cities*, table 4, Aldine Publishing Company, 1965.

Figure 12.1, "Comparison of Trends in Construction Cost, Income and the Price level," from E. H. Boeckh and Associates (index of construction costs for small residential structures). Copyright American Appraisal Associates, Inc.

Table 14.6, "Estimates of Property Tax Incidence by Income Class, 1980," Joseph A. Pechman, *Who Paid the Taxes, 1966–85?*, Tables 3–1 and 4–9, The Brookings Institution, 1985.

Table 15.5, "Local Public Employees, Growing vs. Declining Cities," Values for 1964 and 1973 from George E. Peterson, "Finance," in William Gorham and Nathan Glazer, eds., *The Urban Predicament*. Copyright: The Urban Institute, 1976.

Table 15.6, "Urban Conditions in Large Central Cities," values for 1960 and 1970 from James W. Fossett and Richard P. Nathan, "The Prospects for Urban Revival," p. 66, table 3.1 in *Urban Government Finance: Emerging Trends*, ed. Roy Bahl. Copyright © 1981 by Sage Publications. Reprinted by permission of Sage Publications, Inc.

Index